Let Us Come Before His Presence

365 days to learn, meditate and pray from the Psalms and the Sermon on the Mount

Yann Opsitch

Keledei
PUBLICATIONS

An Imprint of Sulis International Press
Los Angeles I Dallas I London

LET US COME BEFORE HIS PRESENCE: 365 DAYS TO LEARN, MEDITATE AND PRAY FROM THE PSALMS AND THE SERMON ON THE MOUNT
Copyright ©2021 by Yann Opsitch. All rights reserved.

Except for brief quotations for reviews, no part of this book may be reproduced in any form or by any electronic or mechanical means, including information storage and retrieval systems, without written permission from the publisher. Email: info@sulisinternational.com.

All scripture quotations are from the New King James Version ©1982 by Thomas Nelson, Inc., unless otherwise noted.

Cover Photo by Sinitta Leunen

Library of Congress Control Number:
ISBN (print): 978-1-946849-94-6
ISBN (eBook): 978-1-946849-95-3

Published by Keledei Publications
An Imprint of Sulis International
Los Angeles | Dallas | London

www.sulisinternational.com

Contents

Let us Come Before His Presence in the Psalms 1
Week 1: The God of Blessing 3
Week 2: God's Anointed Son 15
Week 3: The God of Creation 23
Week 4: The God of Glory 33
Week 5: The God of the Downtrodden 45
Week 6: When we Fall 55
Week 7: Trusting God 67
Week 8: God's People 77
Week 9: Nations 89
Week 10: Parents 99
Week 11: Babies and Children 109
Week 12: The Elderly 121
Week 13: The Humble 133
Week 14: Times of Pain 143
Week 15: Kings and Rulers 153
Week 16: The Rejected 165
Week 17: God's Word 175
Week 18: Heaven 187
Week 19: Angels 199
Week 20: Waiting Upon the Lord 211
Week 21: Blessing God 225
Week 22: Prayer 237
Week 23: Praise 249
Week 24: The Tender Mercies of God 259
Week 25: God our Father 269
Week 26: The Good Shepherd 279
Week 27: Words of Grace 291
Week 28: Wisdom from Above 303
Week 29: The Heart 313
Week 30: Death 323
Week 31: Anguish 335
Week 32: Repentance 349
Week 33: Glorifying the LORD 361

Week 34: Joy 373
Week 35: Singing to the Lord 385
Week 36: The Suffering Messiah 397
Week 37: Thankfulness 409
Week 38: The God of Salvation 423
Week 39: God's House 437
Week 40: God the King 451
Week 41: The God of Hope 465
Let us Come Before his Presence in the Sermon on the Mount . 479
Week 42: Blessed by God (Matt 4.25 -5.12) 481
Week 43: Salt, Light and the Law (Matt 5.13-20) 495
Week 44: But I say to you (Matt 5.21-37) 509
Week 45: The Second Mile and Enemies (Matt 5.38-48) 523
Week 46: Doing Good Deeds 537
Week 47: Our Father (Matt 6.5-15; Luke 11.1-13) 551
Week 48: Fasting, Treasures and Worry (Matt 6.16-34; Luke
12.13-34) 567
Week 49: Do not Judge, Ask, Seek and Knock (Matt 7.1-12; Luke
7.37-40) 581
Week 50: The Narrow Way and False Prophets (Matt 7.13-20) ... 595
Week 51: Judgment Day (Matt 7.21-23; 3.7-12; 10.12-15; 11.20-24;
25.37-43) 607
Week 52: Wisdom, foolishness and Jesus' supreme authority (Matt
7.24–27; Luke 6.46–49); Matt 28.18; Rev 1.12–18) 619

*To my dear and lovely wife Rita,
who encouraged me greatly in writing this book.*

Let us Come Before His Presence in the Psalms

Week 1: The God of Blessing

Day 1

1 "Blessed is the man
Who walks not in the counsel of the ungodly,
2 Nor stands in the path of sinners,
Nor sits in the seat of the scornful;"
      (Psalm 1.1,2)

The Hebrew word used here for "blessed" (*ashrei*) begins and sets the tone for the entire book of Psalms. Sometimes translated as "happy" (as in Deuteronomy 33.29, KJV) the word *ashrei* concludes the second Psalm about the coming Messiah (God's anointed Son): "Blessed are all who take refuge in him."

Blessings from God are the result or fruit of something else. This is illustrated in the first Psalm by the picture of the tree planted by the waters and bringing its fruit in its season. Blessings and happiness are offered to the forgiven (Psalms 32.1); to a nation under God (Psalms 33.12); to the one who trusts in God (34.8). The same can be said of the Sermon on the Mount where Jesus also introduced his teachings with the word "blessed" (Matthew 5.1-12). The blessed are those who meditate — "moan" or "lament" (*hagah*) in their hearts — over the Word. "Blessed are those who mourn, for they shall be comforted" Matthew 5.4 (see James 4.9).

In Jewish literature, to bless is often connected to the bringing down of divine abundance (*aish*). As in Psalm 34.8 the blessed enjoy the goodness of God; they are partakers of His promises: "Oh, taste and see that the Lord *is* good; blessed *is* the man *who* trusts in Him!"

The blessed are known by their actions; by their difference of behavior as opposed to the ungodly, sinners or scornful who mock the things of God and deride biblical wisdom in order to involve others in their folly.

The scornful *(leitz)* mock out of pride and arrogance. They are among the incorrigible fools of the book of Proverbs. The mockers or scornful of the Bible are unteachable and refuse to listen (Proverbs 9.8; 13.1). To be seated with them is a waste of time (Proverbs 15.12). Unbelievers and Pharisees often mocked Jesus' teachings (Luke 8.53; Mark 5.40; Matthew 9.24; Luke 16.14). Both the Gentiles and chief priests, along with elders and scribes, mocked Jesus at his trial and crucifixion (Matthew 27.31, 41; Mark 10.34; 15.20; Luke 22.63). The apostle Paul was mocked for his preaching of the resurrection (Acts 17.32).

The "blessed" can also be a group of people, a family or even an entire nation: "Blessed *is* the nation whose God *is* the Lord, the people He has chosen as His own inheritance." (Psalms 33.12)

The words of Psalms 1 are echoed by the prophet Jeremiah:

> "But blessed is the one who trusts in the Lord,
> whose confidence is in him.
> They will be like a tree planted by the water
> that sends out its roots by the stream.
> It does not fear when heat comes;
> its leaves are always green.
> It has no worries in a year of drought
> and never fails to bear fruit." (Jeremiah 17.17,18)

The blessed are like trees planted or rather "replanted" (*ke'etz shatul*) in the divine soil watered by God's Word. In its season or at the proper time, these trees bring fruit. The leaves of these trees don't wither or "dry up" because they are "replanted" in eternity (see Isaiah 41.19.20; 44.4; Proverbs 11.30; Matthew 7.17-19; Galatians 5.22-26).

The blessed are fruitful throughout their lives in everything they do: "That you may walk worthy of the Lord, fully pleasing him, being fruitful in every good work and increasing in the knowledge of God" (Colossians 2.10).

The counsel of the ungodly or wicked lead to death and destruction. They are like chaff, not good or useful for anything. Their end is opposite to the end of the blessed. They shall not be able to stand on the day of judgment. The way or path of the wicked leads to destruction, ruin.

Prayer

Lord, we want to delight every day in your Word. We thank you for speaking to us through the prophets and your Son. Give us today a heart to avoid evil and do what is good. We pray that we can produce good fruits to your glory through your Holy Spirit. Amen.

Day 2

> 1 "Blessed *are* the undefiled in the way,
> Who walk in the law of the Lord!
> 2 Blessed *are* those who keep His testimonies,
> Who seek Him with the whole heart!
> 3 They also do no iniquity;
> They walk in His ways.
> 4 You have commanded *us*
> To keep Your precepts diligently.
> 5 Oh, that my ways were directed
> To keep Your statutes!
> 6 Then I would not be ashamed,
> When I look into all Your commandments.
> 7 I will praise You with uprightness of heart,
> When I learn Your righteous judgments.
> 8 I will keep Your statutes;
> Oh, do not forsake me utterly!"
> (Psalms 119.1-3)

Psalm 119 is written as an acrostic poem. The Psalm has twenty-two strophes (paragraphs), corresponding to the twenty-two letters of the Hebrew alphabet. Each of the strophes has eight lines (verses). Each line in each strophe begins with the appropriate Hebrew letter marking that stanza. The first eight lines begin with *aleph*, the first letter of the Hebrew alphabet.

The first word of Psalm 119 is "blessed" from the Hebrew word *asrei*. The word and its cognates are used 45 times in the OT. This word translated "blessed" is close to the idea of "happiness". The word is very close to the Hebrew *ashar* meaning "to go straight, to go on, to advance, to go forward" used for example in Genesis 30.13; Psalms 41.2. The word connects the idea of "blessing" to the concept of one being guided and walking in a straight way. The word "blessed" used in Psalm 1 also connects God's blessings to how one walks in life.

The word "blessed" describes those who walk undefiled in the way of God, who walk in the law of the Lord (an idea repeated in verses 3 and 5). Happiness is the fruit or result of how we walk, how we direct our steps in life. Happiness is not the goal or the purpose, but the result of those who walk in the ways of the Lord.

In order to walk in the ways of the Lord, one needs to trust and obey the "law" of the Lord. The Psalm uses ten different words that refer to the law (law, word, saying, commandment, statute, precept, ordinance, testimony, way, path).

In the sermon on the mount, Jesus connects "blessings" from God to how one lives and walks. He teaches that "broad is the way" that leads to destruction, and "there are many who go in by it". Difficult is the way that leads to life, and "there are few who find it" (Matthew 7.13,14).

Prayer

Lord, our God and Savior, we want to serve you today. We pray that you will keep our hearts close to your will. Lord, we thank you for your constant help and support. Give us renewed strength today, so we will know how to walk in your ways, in your will. We pray this in the name of Jesus. Amen.

Day 3

7 "Oh, taste and see that the Lord is good;
Blessed is the man who trusts in Him!
9 Oh, fear the Lord, you His saints!
There is no want to those who fear Him.
10 The young lions lack and suffer hunger;
But those who seek the Lord shall not lack any good thing."
    (Psalm 34.8-10)

To taste that the Lord is good, one needs to trust, and trust is foremost trust in God's Word. Those who have received salvation and have been reconciled to God through Jesus the Christ have tasted "the good word of God and the powers of the age to come" (Hebrews 6.5); they have "tasted that the Lord is gracious" (1 Peter 2.3). Happiness and the joy one can find in the Lord, is the result of tasting that the Lord is good, tasting that He is gracious. The "good news" is a message that brings joy and goodness to our lives.

At the time of the writing of this Psalm, David was being persecuted by Saul and his life was in danger. David was "tasting" trials and obstacles, but he did not cease from trusting the Lord and "tasting" his goodness. Trials and obstacles are temporary, are connected to the world of sin and rebellion we live in. But the Lord remains good, whatever happens on this earth.

David did not fear his enemies. He did not fear those who wanted to destroy him. But he "feared" the Lord. The fear of men leads to death and disappointment. But the fear of the Lord leads to wisdom and satisfaction in life:

"How great is Your goodness
Which You have stored up for those who fear You,
Which You have wrought for those who take refuge in You,
Before the sons of men!" (Psalm 31.19)

"Praise the Lord!
How blessed is the man who fears the Lord
Who greatly delights in His commandments." (Psalms 112.1)

"The fear of the Lord leads to life,
So that one may sleep satisfied, untouched by evil." (Psalms 19.23)

"Behold, the eye of the Lord is on those who fear Him,
On those who hope for His lovingkindness,
To deliver their soul from death
And to keep them alive in famine." (Psalms 33.18,19)

Prayer

Our Father in heaven, we thank you for giving us a new day. We thank you for all the opportunities you will show us to serve you and do good in this world. Help us to open our eyes and hearts to all that you want to show us. With the trials and the difficulties of the day, help us to remain steadfast in our love and trust for you. We pray this in the name of Jesus. Amen.

Day 4

1 "The Lord *is* my shepherd;
I shall not want.
2 He makes me to lie down in green pastures;
He leads me beside the still waters.
3 He restores my soul;
He leads me in the paths of righteousness
For His name's sake.
    4 Yea, though I walk through the valley of the shadow of death,
I will fear no evil;
For You *are* with me;
Your rod and Your staff, they comfort me.

5 You prepare a table before me in the presence of my enemies;
You anoint my head with oil;
My cup runs over.
6 Surely goodness and mercy shall follow me
All the days of my life;
And I will dwell in the house of the Lord
Forever."
(Psalms 23)

Throughout the Old Testament, we find the theme of God as the shepherd (or pastor) of his people. For example, Genesis 49.24; Psalms 78.70-72; 80.1; 95.7; 79.13; 100.3; Jeremiah 50.7; Isaiah 40.11; Micah 5.4; 7.14; Jeremiah 31.10; Isaiah 53.6; Zechariah 11.16.

The image of the "shepherd" illustrates perfectly the idea of God as one who blesses His people. The prophet Ezekiel prophesied of the time when God himself would come among his people to be their shepherd, "**11** 'For thus says the Lord God: "Indeed I Myself will search for My sheep and seek them out. **12** As a shepherd seeks out his flock on the day he is among his scattered sheep, so will I seek out My sheep and deliver them from all the places where they were scattered on a cloudy and dark day." (Ezekiel 34).

Jesus proclaimed himself as the "good shepherd" of God's people. Jesus the good shepherd would lay down his life for his sheep, "**14** I am the good shepherd; and I know My *sheep* and am known by My own. **15** As the Father knows Me, even so I know the Father; and I lay down My life for the sheep. **16** And other sheep I have which are not of this fold; them also I must bring, and they will hear My voice; and there will be one flock *and* one shepherd. **17** "Therefore My Father loves Me because I lay down My life that I may take it again. **18** No one takes it from Me, but I lay it down of Myself. I have power to lay it down, and I have power to take it again. This command I have received from My Father." (John 10.14-18)

The Hebrew word for pasture is from the root word *naah*, which has the broad meaning of habitation, pasture, pleasant place. In such a place, the sheep lie at ease and can rest. It can refer to a dwelling place one finds as he or she travels, in particular an oasis or verdant spot in the desert (Psalms 65.12; 74.20; 83.12; Jeremiah 9.10; Amos 1.2). Those who respond to the voice of Jesus find "pasture" in him, where they receive life abundantly (John 10.9,10). In this abundance of life, one does not lack or need anything (compare Deuteronomy 2.7; 8.9; Colossians 2.6-23).

Prayer

Our Father in heaven, we thank you for giving us a new day. We know you are the good shepherd and came to us in this world of lack and sin. We thank you for your forgiveness through the death of our Lord Jesus on the cross. We thank you for his resurrection and all of his teachings. We pray that today we will live with the promise of his return rooted in our hearts. Bless us through Jesus today! In His name, we pray. Amen.

Day 5

> **18** "Their soul abhorred all manner of food,
> And they drew near to the gates of death.
> **19** Then they cried out to the Lord in their trouble,
> *And* He saved them out of their distresses.
> **20** He sent His word and healed them,
> And delivered *them* from their destructions.
> **21** Oh, that *men* would give thanks to the Lord *for* His goodness,
> And *for* His wonderful works to the children of men!
> **22** Let them sacrifice the sacrifices of thanksgiving,
> And declare His works with rejoicing."
> (Psalms 107.18-22)

This Psalm describes God's deliverance and blessings by using several metaphors: protection through the perils of traveling (vs.4-9); release from prison (vs.10-16); recovering from sickness (vs.17-22); deliverance from a perilous voyage on the sea (vs.23-32).

God's deliverance or healing should be followed by thankfulness, gratefulness and produce praise towards God. This is the theme of this Psalm. It reminds us of the ten lepers healed by Jesus and who did not return with thankfulness and to glorify God:

> **15** And one of them, when he saw that he was healed, returned, and with a loud voice glorified God, **16** and fell down on *his* face at His feet, giving Him thanks. And he was a Samaritan. **17** So Jesus answered and said, "Were there not ten cleansed? But where *are* the nine? **18** Were there not any found who returned to give glory to God except this foreigner?" **19** And He said to him, "Arise, go your way. Your faith has made you well." (Luke 17.15-19)

Psalm 107 begins with praise (other translations have "thankfulness" to God), "I will praise you with my whole heart". There is no valid praise of God without thankfulness. As the apostles write to the early Christians, they encourage them to be grateful, to express thankfulness to God:

> **17** "Therefore, do not be unwise, but understand what the will of the Lord *is*. **18** And do not be drunk with wine, in which is dissipation; but be filled with the Spirit, **19** speaking to one another in psalms and hymns and spiritual songs, singing and making melody in your heart to the Lord, **20** giving thanks always for all things to God the Father in the name of our Lord Jesus Christ, **21** submitting to one another in the fear of God." (Ephesians 5.17-20)

> **6** "Be anxious for nothing, but in everything by prayer and supplication, with thanksgiving, let your requests be made known to God; **7** and the peace of God, which surpasses all understanding, will guard your hearts and minds through Christ Jesus." (Philippians 4.6,7)

> **6** "As you therefore have received Christ Jesus the Lord, so walk in Him, **7** rooted and built up in Him and established in the faith, as you have been taught, abounding in it with thanksgiving." (Colossians 2.6,7)

> "And whatever you do in word or deed, *do* all in the name of the Lord Jesus, giving thanks to God the Father through Him" (Colossians 3.17)

> "Continue earnestly in prayer, being vigilant in it with thanksgiving." (Colossians 4.2)

> **16** "Rejoice always, **17** pray without ceasing, **18** in everything give thanks; for this is the will of God in Christ Jesus for you." (1 Thessalonians 5.16-18)

Prayer

Our Father, give us the strength and wisdom to be thankful to you this day. Preserve our souls from discouragement or hopelessness when we go through trials and pains. May we be a source of encouragement and hope to our brothers and sisters who deal with suffering. May our words reflect gratefulness to you. We pray this in the name of Jesus our Lord, Amen.

Day 6

> **7** "Though I walk in the midst of trouble You will revive me;
> You will stretch out Your hand
> Against the wrath of my enemies,
> And Your right hand will save me.
> **8** The Lord will perfect *that which* concerns me;
> Your mercy, O Lord, *endures* forever;
> Do not forsake the works of Your hands."
>   (Psalms 138.7,8)

Verse 7 of this Psalm reminds us of Psalm 23.4, "Yea, though I walk through the valley of the shadow of death, I will fear no evil; for You *are* with me; your rod and Your staff, they comfort me." Even though the faithful walk "in the midst of trouble" they still praise the Lord with their whole heart (verse 1); they still praise God for his lovingkindness (verse 2). The faithful do not forget the goodness of God in the past (verse 3). The Lord watches the lowly and "the proud he knows from afar" (verse 6).

As with David, the faithful must exhibit a profound trust in God and full confidence in his promises. Ungratefulness and complaining against God exhibit pride and mistrust rather than humility and faith.

The sin of David is often preached about. But the story is there as a contrast to his repentance. The important thing in David's life is not his sin, but his turning back to God and his change of heart. Our sins are forgiven in Christ. We are now to live a new resurrected life and seek holiness through the Holy Spirit (Romans 8). The important thing is our new relationship with God through Jesus, our High priest.

The Lord is watching and aware of what the faithful are going through. He is also the Lord of our enemies. Wrath against them belongs to him (Romans 12.19). There is not the thought of personal revenge in the words of David, but simply trust that God will deal with those who wish him harm, will protect him from their evil intents. Verses 7 and 8 of this Psalm remind us of Jesus, who walked in the midst of trouble and was threatened by enemies. He went to the cross, but God delivered him,

> **7** "who, in the days of His flesh, when He had offered up
> prayers and supplications, with vehement cries and tears to

Him who was able to save Him from death, and was heard because of His godly fear, **8** though He was a Son, *yet* He learned obedience by the things which He suffered. **9** And having been perfected, He became the author of eternal salvation to all who obey Him, **10** called by God as High Priest according to the order of Melchizedek," (Hebrews 5.7-10)

Prayer

Father in heaven, we thank you for a new day. We want to hear your word today and ask that it will transform our hearts. We pray for true repentance when we have sinned. Change our hearts by the power of your Gospel and the power of your Holy Spirit. Father, we know you will protect us from those who wish us harm. We also pray for them, that they might open their hearts to your word and received your salvation through faith. We pray this in the name of Jesus. Amen.

Day 7

> **4** "I sought the Lord, and He heard me,
> And delivered me from all my fears.
> **5** They looked to Him and were radiant,
> And their faces were not ashamed.
> **6** This poor man cried out, and the Lord heard *him*,
> And saved him out of all his troubles.
> **7** The angel of the Lord encamps all around those who fear Him,
> And delivers them."
> (Psalms 34.4-7)

One of the greatest blessings from God — from trust in Him — is to be delivered from all fears. This trust which helps us face all our fears and find assurance and hope is expressed in numerous ways in the Bible and especially in the Psalms:

> **3** "Whenever I am afraid,
> I will trust in You.
> **4** In God (I will praise His word),
> In God I have put my trust;
> I will not fear.
> What can flesh do to me?" (Psalms 56.3,4)

> **1** "Truly my soul silently *waits* for God;
> From Him *comes* my salvation.
> **2** He only *is* my rock and my salvation;
> *He is* my defense;
> I shall not be greatly moved.
> "Some *trust* in chariots, and some in horses;
> But we will remember the name of the Lord our God.
> **8** They have bowed down and fallen;
> But we have risen and stand upright." (Psalms 62.6,7)
>
> **20** "Our soul waits for the Lord;
> He *is* our help and our shield.
> **21** For our heart shall rejoice in Him,
> Because we have trusted in His holy name.
> **22** Let Your mercy, O Lord, be upon us,
> Just as we hope in You." (Psalms 33.20-22)

But what about those who have trusted the Lord and have had to face death or rejection? Can it be said that God has delivered them? Jesus teaches us that it is not what happens to the body that is to be feared, but what happens to our soul,

> **24** "A disciple is not above *his* teacher, nor a servant above his master. **25** It is enough for a disciple that he be like his teacher, and a servant like his master. If they have called the master of the house Beelzebub, how much more *will they call* those of his household! **26** Therefore do not fear them. For there is nothing covered that will not be revealed and hidden that will not be known. **27** Whatever I tell you in the dark, speak in the light; and what you hear in the ear, preach on the housetops. **28** And do not fear those who kill the body but cannot kill the soul. (Matthew 10.24-28)

Prayer

Father in heaven, we thank you for a new day. We pray that today we can be strengthened in our trust in you. That we can know in our hearts that you love us and will always take care of us. We believe in your Word, and we believe in your promises. We come to you today with a desire to grow in our faith, hope and love. We pray this in the name of Jesus. Amen.

Week 2: God's Anointed Son

Day 1

"Why do the nations rage, and the people plot vain things?"'
(Psalm 2.1)

"Why" is a question we often ask. And here the Psalm does not provide an answer to this "why" question. It only provides God's way of looking at it. God wants us to learn how he views the nations and their plots. The Psalm also provides an encouragement to "kings": "Now therefore, be wise, O Kings. Be instructed you judges of the earth. Serve the Lord with fear. And rejoice with trembling." (vv.10,11).

"Who being the brightness of His glory and the express image of His person and upholding all things by the word of His power, when He had by himself purged our sins, sat down at the right hand of the Majesty on high, having become so much better than the angels, as He has by inheritance obtained a more excellent name than they. For to which of the angels did He ever say 'You are my Son, today I have begotten You'" Hebrews 1.3-5

God's word also consistently points out the God who "sits in heaven", who carries out his plans, his "decree": "Yet I have set my King on My holy hill of Zion." (v.6). "I will declare the decree: the LORD has said to me, 'you are My Son. Today I have begotten you. Ask of Me, and I will give you the nations for your inheritance, and the ends of the earth for Your possession." (v.7,8). Acts 13.33; Hebrews 5.5

"For God so loved the world that he gave His only-begotten Son, that whoever believes in Him should not perish but have everlasting life." (John 3.16)

"I have glorified You on the earth. I have finished the work which You have given Me to do. And now, O Father, glorify Me together with Yourself, with the glory which I had with You before the world was." (John 17.4,5).

Prayer

Thank you, O Lord, for your Son. Thank you for the glory he had before the creation of the world. Thank you that he has the finished the work you gave him to do and that in him we can know you and have eternal life. Amen.

Day 2

> **8** "I have set the Lord always before me;
> Because *He is* at my right hand I shall not be moved.
> **9** Therefore my heart is glad, and my glory rejoices;
> My flesh also will rest in hope.
> **10** For You will not leave my soul in Sheol,
> Nor will You allow Your Holy One to see corruption."
> (Psalm 16.8-10)

"Men and brethren let me speak freely to you of the patriarch David, that he is both dead and buried, and his tomb is with us to this day. Therefore, being a prophet, and knowing that God had sworn with an oath to him that of the fruit of his body, according to the flesh, He would raise up the Christ to sit on his throne, he foreseeing this spoke concerning the resurrection of the Christ, that His soul was not left in Hades, not did his flesh see corruption. This Jesus God has raised up, of which we are all witnesses." (Acts 2.29-32). See Acts 2.35.

Death is not what it appears to be. Death is not the end of our story, is not the end of what God has planned for us. Because we have been joined to Him in His death, we have also been raised with Him in his life, "For if we have been united together in the likeness of His death, certainly we also shall be in the likeness of his resurrection, knowing this that our old man was crucified with him, that the body of sin might be done away with, that we should no longer be slaves of sin." (Romans 6.5,6; see Colossians 2.9-14).

Prayer

Thank you, Father in heaven, for having given us a new life through Jesus the Christ. Thank you for having raised us from death. Thank you for our new birth and new life. We also thank you for giving us a new day to live in the light of His resurrection, waiting for his return. Amen.

Day 3

> **1** "The Lord said to my Lord,
> 'Sit at My right hand,
> Till I make Your enemies Your footstool.'
> **2** The Lord shall send the rod of Your strength out of Zion.
> Rule in the midst of Your enemies!"
> (Psalm 110.1,2).

In Psalm 2 the LORD had said: "I have set My King on My holy hill of Zion." (Psalms 2.6). In Psalms 110 God's word provides us with a vision of the Priest-King, Messiah (vv. 1-4), as well as his warfare and victory (vv.5-7). The LORD declares his King to be also a priest "according to order of Melchizedek".

In the book of Genesis (Gen 14:18-20), after defeating a coalition of Mesopotamian kings to rescue his kidnapped nephew Lot, Abraham is greeted by Melchizedek king of Salem, who gives him bread and wine (Genesis 14.18-20). The book of Hebrews sees Melchizedek as foreshadowing Christ, the definitive true king of righteousness (*zedek*) and peace (*salem*), Hebrews 7.11-28. Psalm 110 is also quoted in Matthew 22.43-45; Acts 2.33-36; Hebrews 1.13.

The Messiah sits at the right hand of God — a place of supreme honor and authority. This is alluded to throughout Scripture: Matthew 26.63,64; Mark 16.19; Acts 5.30,31; Acts 7.55,56; Romans 8.34; 1 Corinthians 15.24,25. To this may be added New Testament teaching on the position of authority now belonging to Christ (as in Hebrews 1.3 and Ephesians 1.20-22). The book of Revelation repeats the biblical teaching of Christ's authority at the right hand of God (Revelation 5.13; 7.9,10; 12.10; 22.1,3).

The warfare and victories of the Christ (vv.5-7) are of a spiritual nature; see Ephesians 6.10-20. In verse 5 the kings of the earth and of nations bear a greater burden of responsibility in the evil of the world and their opposition to the Messiah (as in Psalms 2) — See Acts 2.25-31.

Prayer

Father in heaven, we thank you for the King Jesus, who has received all authority and power in heaven and on earth. We thank you for Him who is seated in heavenly places. Angels, powers and authorities having been subjected to him we have no fear of these, and we live with confident hope knowing that nothing shall be able to separate us from your love which is in Christ Jesus our Lord. Amen.

Day 4

> **6** "Your throne, O God, *is* forever and ever;
> A scepter of righteousness *is* the scepter of Your kingdom.
> **7** You love righteousness and hate wickedness;
> Therefore God, Your God, has anointed You
> With the oil of gladness more than Your companions."
>   (Psalm 45.6,7)

See Hebrews 1.8,9. In this Psalm and in Hebrews 1 the Messiah is among the "sons of men" and is called God. His perfect divinity and perfect humanity are laid out clearly in Scripture (see John 1.1-5, 14).

The majesty of the Christ flows from his love of truth, humility and righteousness (vv.4,7).

The Messiah is a teacher. The grace of his teachings is "poured" on his lips. "Then the officers came to the chief priests and Pharisees, who said to them, 'Why have you not brought Him?' The officers answered them, 'No man ever spoke like this Man'" John 7.45,46. "And so it was, when Jesus had ended these sayings, that the people were astonished at His teaching, for He taught them as one having authority, and not as the scribes." Matthew 7.28,29.

Prayer

Holy God, we want to be attentive to your teachings given to us in your Word. Help us, God that we might understand your will and practice it today. Give us the desire to grow in knowledge, wisdom and holiness. Amen.

Day 5

> **21** "I will praise You,
> For You have answered me,
> And have become my salvation.
> **22** The stone *which* the builders rejected
> Has become the chief cornerstone.
> **23** This was the Lord's doing;
> It *is* marvelous in our eyes.
> **24** This *is* the day the Lord has made;
> We will rejoice and be glad in it."
>   (Psalm 118.21-24).

Even today Psalms 113 to 118 are called the *Hallel* and are recited on the festivals of *Pesach*, *Shavu'ot*, and *Sukkot* (Passover, Pentecost and Tabernacles).

Jesus is the stone rejected by the builders but who has become the "chief cornerstone" of God's temple, God's assembly or church (Matthew 21.41-43; Mark 12.10,11; Acts 4.11; Ephesians 2.19-22). Matthew writes that "when the chief priests and the Pharisees heard Jesus' parables, they knew he was talking about them."

Peter quotes Psalm 118 in Acts 4.11 when speaking to the rulers and elders of Israel and adds, in keeping with the salvation theme of the Psalm: "Nor is there salvation in any other, for there is no other name under heaven given among men by which we must be saved."

Prayer

We praise you, O Lord for your salvation. We praise you for Jesus, the foundation of this salvation, and of your redemptive work. May we glorify you in everything we will be doing and saying today. Amen,

Day 6

> **7** "Because for Your sake I have borne reproach;
> Shame has covered my face.
> **8** I have become a stranger to my brothers,
> And an alien to my mother's children;
> **9** Because zeal for Your house has eaten me up,
> And the reproaches of those who reproach You have fallen on me."
> (Psalm 69.7-9).

Jesus spoke the words of verse 9 when he cleared the temple of the money changers (John 2.17). This psalm and Psalms 22:1-31 are the psalms most of all applied to Christ in the New Testament (John 15:25, cf. Psalms 69:4; John 2:17, cf. Psalms 69:9; also, Romans 15:3).

The one who speaks in this Psalm is described as having "zeal" for God's house. In Jesus' ministry, the "house" of God is the temple where God's people gathered to worship and learn.

He is pleading for God to be saved from "deep waters", to be delivered from those who hate him without a cause.

Those who reproach the righteous are also those who reproach God (v.9). Love for God goes hand in hand with love for our neighbor. But hatred for God will also lead to hatred for human beings. "If the world hates you, you know that it hated Me before it hated you. If you were of the world, the world would love its own. Yet because you are not of the world, but I chose you out of the world, therefore the world hates you." (John 15.18,19).

We must be very careful and repent when we "reproach God". If we express any bitterness towards God and persist in doing so, the time is coming when that bitterness will spill over into all our relationships.

In this Psalm there is never any doubt that the LORD is full of lovingkindness, full of "tender mercies" (v.16).

Prayer

God in heaven, give us a heart that will know to always praise you for your love and holiness. Give us a heart that will never grow bitter towards you or towards any human being. As we meet people today, give us the wisdom to trust your word and promises even when those around us do not acknowledge you or even reject you. Amen.

Day 7

> **11** "By this I know that You are well pleased with me,
> Because my enemy does not triumph over me.
> **12** As for me, You uphold me in my integrity,
> And set me before Your face forever."
>   (Psalm 41.11,12).

This Psalm starts by blessings on the one who considers the poor (v.1). The integrity of this one lies in the fact that he "considers the poor". A consideration for the poor shows a consideration for the creator of the poor, "He who oppresses the poor reproaches his Maker, but he who honors Him has mercy on the needy." (Proverbs 14.31).

The Psalm teaches us how integrity before the LORD does not mean sinlessness: "As for me, You uphold me in my integrity and set me before Your face forever." (v.12). "LORD, be merciful to me; heal my soul, for I have sinned against You." (v.4). Integrity consists in being honest before the LORD, in recognizing our failures and sins. Integrity is foundational to repentance and spiritual growth.

This Psalm is also a prophecy of the betrayal of Judas, "Even my familiar friend in whom I trusted, who ate my bread, has lifted up his heel against me." (v.9). John 13.18.

Prayer

Father in heaven, we praise you for your willingness to forgive and strengthen us. Help us to grow in integrity, in recognizing our shortcomings and sins. Help us LORD today to show true compassion and love towards the poor. Amen.

Week 3: The God of Creation

Day 1

> **1** "The heavens declare the glory of God;
> And the firmament shows His handiwork.
> **2** Day unto day utters speech,
> And night unto night reveals knowledge.
> **3** *There is* no speech nor language
> *Where* their voice is not heard.
> **4** Their line has gone out through all the earth,
> And their words to the end of the world."
> (Psalm 19.1-4)

In Psalm 18 God is celebrated for His Messiah — the son of David. In Psalm 19 God is celebrated for His creation and for His law. In both Psalms, the LORD deserves to be called "rock and fortress" (Psalms 18.1), "strength and redeemer" (Psalms 19.14).

There are two parts in Psalm 19: the heavens tell of the glory of God, while the law tells of His will. The revelation of God in the law does what the glory of creation is not able to do. The law "converts the soul", "makes wise the simple", "rejoice the heart", "enlightens the eyes" (vv.7,8).

In the law are found the "judgments" of the LORD (his will and revelation) which are true and righteous altogether (v.9).

The judgments of the LORD are to be desired more than gold; they are sweeter than honey; they bring great reward (vv.10, 11). The judgments of the LORD will help us understand our errors, cleanse us from secret faults and presumptuous sins — those sins we ourselves are not always able to discern. They will direct the words of our mouth and the meditation of our hearts.

Those who acknowledge only the greatness of creation are missing out on God's revelation about his will. The Psalm — itself a revelation from God — attributes the glory of creation to God the creator. Thus, even in that sense we need God's revelation, his Word, to fully appreciate His creation.

Prayer

We thank you God for the beauty of your creation which brings joy to our hearts. We also thank you Father for your will. May we always pray, saying, "Your will be done on earth as it is in heaven." May we today seek your will more than we seek worldly success or riches.

Day 2

> **1** "Give unto the Lord, O you mighty ones,
> Give unto the Lord glory and strength.
> **2** Give unto the Lord the glory due to His name;
> Worship the Lord in the beauty of holiness.
> **3** The voice of the Lord *is* over the waters;
> The God of glory thunders;
> The Lord *is* over many waters.
> **4** The voice of the Lord *is* powerful;
> The voice of the Lord *is* full of majesty."
>   (Psalm 29.1-4)

The word "thunder" is repeated seven times in Psalm 29. Note the "seven thunders" in Revelation 10.3,4. The "mighty ones" are angels, invisible to the human eye. The invisible world is the source of the visible world (see Hebrews 11.1,2). The angelic world praises the LORD and worships Him for "the beauty of His holiness". The glory and holiness of the LORD was manifest during the flood: "The LORD sat enthroned at the Flood, and the LORD sits as King forever" (v.10; Genesis 6-11). Yes, he is the "God of many waters" who is in control of nature. In Psalms 29:3 the first sounds of thunder are heard; in Psalms 29:4 the storm is coming nearer, and the sounds become stronger, and comes in full force, breaking and splintering the great cedar trees of Lebanon.

The power of the LORD is also seen in the power of fire (v.7). "For our God is a consuming fire" (Hebrews 12.29). It is by the power of the LORD that the deer — and every other creature — gives birth (v.9). "Shall I bring to the time of birth, and not cause delivery?" says the Lord. Shall I who cause delivery shut up *the womb?*' says your God (Isaiah 66.9). The majesty of Jesus was seen in the calming of the storm (Mark 4.35-41).

The power of the LORD is made available to His people to give them strength and to bless them with peace (v.11). Psalm 29 shows the heavens opened and the throne of God in the midst of the angelic songs of praise. It closes with a vision of his people on earth, victorious and blessed with peace. Thus, His power is not manifested to produce fear, but guarantees peace and strength to those who glorify Him through their lives.

Prayer

Father in heaven, we praise your holiness, your beauty and power. In your Son we are blessed with peace and victory. We pray for faith in all your promises; faith in your words of comfort and words of hope given to us by Jesus and His apostles. Amen.

Day 3

> **24** "O Lord, how manifold are Your works!
> In wisdom You have made them all.
> The earth is full of Your possessions—
> **25** This great and wide sea,
> In which *are* innumerable teeming things,
> Living things both small and great.
> **26** There the ships sail about;
> *There is* that Leviathan
> Which You have made to play there."
>   (Psalm 104.24-26)

Psalm 104 is a song of praise to God the creator of all things, "O LORD my God, You are very great: You are clothed with honor and majesty" (v.1). The Psalm begins with "light" and ends with praises and worship, the purpose of God's seventh day of rest.

Wisdom is at the source of and is reflected in God's creation (Proverbs 8.22-36). The design of every living thing reveals supreme intelligence and science.

The LORD is also the sustainer of His creation: "These all wait for you, that You may give them their food in due season." (v.27). We must never forget how much we depend on the LORD for every need, for our very breath (vv.28-30). A sense of autonomy and pride will lead us far away from God and from praising Him (v.35).

This assurance of God's provision for all our needs should not, however, lead us to take for granted God's care and provision. The Lord taught us to pray, "Give us this day our daily bread." (Matthew 6.11). The Word of God judges severely an ungrateful attitude towards God and taking Him for granted. Such ungratefulness reflects a sense of autonomy and pride which the Lord will not tolerate.

"**1** But know this, that in the last days perilous times will come: **2** For men will be lovers of themselves, lovers of money, boasters, proud, blasphemers, disobedient to parents, unthankful, unholy, **3** unloving, unforgiving, slanderers, without self-control, brutal, despisers of good, **4** traitors, headstrong, haughty, lovers of pleasure rather than lovers of God, **5** having a form of godliness but denying its power. And from such people turn away!" (2 Timothy 3.1-5).

Prayer

"Our Father in heaven. Hallowed be Your name. Your kingdom come. Your will be done on earth as it is in heaven. Give us this day our daily bread. And forgive us our debts as we forgive our debtors. And do not lead us into temptation, but deliver us from the evil one. For Yours is the kingdom and the power and the glory forever. Amen."

Day 4

5 *"By* awesome deeds in righteousness You will answer us,
O God of our salvation,
You who are the confidence of all the ends of the earth,
And of the far-off seas;
6 Who established the mountains by His strength,
Being clothed with power;
7 You who still the noise of the seas,
The noise of their waves,
And the tumult of the peoples."
　(Psalm 65.5-7)

In this Psalm God rules out of Zion, out of Jerusalem where David was king (v.1). This is a reminder of God's covenant with David, which was accomplished in the son of David, Jesus of Nazareth (Acts 15.14-17; 2 Samuel 7). See Luke 24.47.

Our God who has power over the ocean and the mountains has also power over the "tumult of the peoples". The will of man and especially of entire nations can never prevail over the will of the LORD.

God who is in control of the natural world is also in control of human history (as in Psalms 8:1-9; Psalms 19:1-14; Psalms 29:1-11). Observation of the natural world should teach us our dependence on God and about his sustaining power.

However, blessed is the one whom God chooses and who may dwell in God's presence (v.4). Entire nations may turn away from God, but He still sees one who is righteous.

God who provides for his creatures also provides forgiveness to human beings (v.3). The provision of God is not only towards Israel but towards "all flesh" which includes all nations of the earth, as the promise to Abraham indicates (v.2, Genesis 121.1-3; Acts 3.25).

Prayer

We praise you, O LORD for the Word you have given us in this Psalm. As in the Psalm, we want to begin and end our day with praises to you. We want to begin and end our day with gratefulness and "shouts of joy".

Day 5

> **3** "When I consider Your heavens, the work of Your fingers,
> The moon and the stars, which You have ordained,
> **4** What is man that You are mindful of him,
> And the son of man that You visit him?
> **5** For You have made him a little lower than the angels,
> And You have crowned him with glory and honor."
> (Psalm 8.3-5)

When we consider the universe — infinite when we try to understand its size; bewildering in the complexity, greatness and power it manifests — we may feel insignificant. How can we then believe the words of Jesus:

> "**29** Are not two sparrows sold for a copper coin? And not one of them falls to the ground apart from your Father's will. **30** But the very hairs of your head are all numbered." (Matthew 10. 29,30).

And how strange that the majesty and glory of God would be declared from the "mouth of babes and nursing infants" (v.2). "**15** But when the chief priests and scribes saw the wonderful things that He did, and the children crying out in the temple and saying, 'Hosanna to the Son of David!' they were indignant. **16** and said to Him, 'Do You hear what these are saying?' And Jesus said to them, "Yes. Have you never read, 'Out of the mouth of babes and nursing infants You have perfected praise'?" (Matthew 21.15,16).

The greatness of God and the overwhelming nature of His creation should not lead us to think that we are insignificant: "What is man that You are mindful of him, and the son of man that You visit him?" (v.4).

As God intended from the time of creation man was "made a little lower than the angels" and has been crowned "with glory and honor" (v.5) — "Then God said, 'Let Us make man in Our image, according to Our likeness; let them have dominion over the fish of the sea, over the birds of the air, and over the cattle, over all the earth and over every creeping thing that creeps on the earth. So God created man in His own image; in the image of God He created him; male and female He created them." (Genesis 1.26, 27).

However, "human beings suppressed the truth (…) They did not glorify Him as God, nor were thankful, but became futile in their thoughts, and their foolish hearts were darkened. Professing to be wise, they became fools, and changed the glory of the incorruptible God into an image made like corruptible man — and birds and four-footed animals and creeping things." (Romans 1.18-23).

We learn that there is a truth about human beings which needs to be known and understood. If that truth is "suppressed" human beings fall into foolishness and start worshipping, admiring, corruptible man and even animals.

Prayer

Lord, as we contemplate the grandeur and the overwhelming size of your creation and universe, help us to remember your words of comfort and encouragement towards us. Help us understand how much you care for each one of us. We pray for this world Lord, for our neighbors who may not know you, for the families, youth and elderly of our communities that need teaching from your Word.

Day 6

7 "Where can I go from Your Spirit?
Or where can I flee from Your presence?
8 If I ascend into heaven, You *are* there;

> If I make my bed in hell, behold, You *are there.*
> **9** *If* I take the wings of the morning,
> *And* dwell in the uttermost parts of the sea,
> **10** Even there Your hand shall lead me,
> And Your right hand shall hold me."
> (Psalm 139.7-10)

Is it possible to hide somewhere and not be seen by God? Should we feel distressed by the thought of his constant gaze upon us? Is it a burden for us to know that he knows are very thoughts, even before we have them?

Even darkness and the night cannot hide us from the LORD. The darkness and the light appear only to us as dark and light, not to God. Thus, our senses should not lead us to think God perceives reality — whether space or time — like we do.

It can be tempting for us to choose flight from God over trust and love. But such a choice will be disastrous because we can never run away from reality. Those who persist in wanting to run away from God's presence will be tempted to rush into all the "virtual" worlds promised to us by technology and the world of drugs. It can even be tempting for them to flee this life by taking their own lives. But even death cannot change the reality of God's presence.

The Psalm sees the gaze of God on us, his eyes watching over us, as beneficial: "Even there Your hand shall lead me, and Your right hand shall hold me." (v.10). The eyes of the LORD were on us even as we were being formed in the womb of our mothers. As we were being formed before our birth, God had already written in His book all the days of our lives (vv. 13-16).

No, the Psalm does not lead us to want to flee the gaze and presence of God. The words of the Psalm are reassuring and telling us the blessing of God's presence in our lives. And if there are those who want to harm us, we know that God sees them and knows they speak against Him (vv.19,20).

Instead of wanting to flee from God's presence, let us welcome Him as he searches our hearts. Let us ask him to lead us "in the way everlasting" (vv. 23,24).

Prayer

Lord, help us not to be anxious. Help us to come to you with supplication and thanksgiving in order to find the peace which surpasses all understanding, which will guard our hearts and minds through Christ Jesus. Amen. (Philippians 4.6).

Day 7

> **17** "How precious also are Your thoughts to me, O God!
> How great is the sum of them!
> **18** *If* I should count them, they would be more in number than the sand;
> When I awake, I am still with You."
>   (Psalm 139.17,18)

Do we enjoy meditating upon the Word of God? Do we spend time in His presence? Does our imagination struggle to seek deeper understanding of God's purposes?

Do we understand the limitless science and power of God? Do we realize how little we know and how much we can still learn?

Psalm 139 extols the omnipresence of the LORD, His divine presence encompasses the entire visible universe as well as the invisible creation (vv. 1-12, Colossians 1.16); the power of the LORD, especially as seen in the forming of the baby in the mother's womb (vv. 13-16); the omniscience of the LORD, which is His infinite knowledge (vv. 17,18).

> **14** "For this reason I bow my knees to the Father of our Lord Jesus Christ, **15** from whom the whole family in heaven and earth is named, **16** that He would grant you, according to the riches of His glory, to be strengthened with might through His Spirit in the inner man, **17** that Christ may dwell in your hearts through faith; that you, being rooted and grounded in love, **18** may be able to comprehend with all the saints what *is* the width and length and depth and height— **19** to know the love of Christ which passes knowledge; that you may be filled with all the fullness of God.
> **20** Now to Him who is able to do exceedingly abundantly above all that we ask or think, according to the power that works in us, **21** to Him *be* glory in the church by Christ Jesus to all generations, forever and ever. Amen." (Ephesians 3.15-20).

This knowledge of God's presence, power and knowledge should lead us to seek him with a sincere heart. It should also calm our anxieties (v.23).

Prayer

Lord we rejoice in You always. Thank you for being close to us. Please Father in heaven give us peace in the midst of the battles of this world; give us gentleness even as we face aggressivity. We want to be grateful as we make our requests known to you. Grant us your peace. We pray in the name of our Lord Jesus.

Week 4: The God of Glory

Day 1

> **4** "My soul *is* among lions;
> I lie *among* the sons of men
> Who are set on fire,
> Whose teeth *are* spears and arrows,
> And their tongue a sharp sword.
> **5** Be exalted, O God, above the heavens;
> *Let* Your glory *be* above all the earth."
>   (Psalms 57.4,5)

Verse 5 describes "the glory of God above all the earth" and is part of a refrain repeated twice in and which divides Psalm 57 in two equal parts (each part falls into two stanzas of six lines). David has adversaries who want to destroy him. The men who are set on fire are those who "breathe forth fire" or set and kindle destructive fires (Deuteronomy 32.22; Psalms 83.14).

Despite these murderous behaviors, the Psalm expresses trust in the God who is exalted above the heavens, whose glory is above all the earth. The word "glory" (*kabowd*) first describes the idea of "heaviness" or "weight". But in everyday speech it meant a person of worth, of importance, greatness, fulness, abundance, wealth, splendor or power — used mostly about God.

We see here the contrast between the enemies of David who are murderers and the glory of God. The Psalm praises God for his glory,

> **7** "My heart is steadfast, O God, my heart is steadfast;
> I will sing and give praise. **8** Awake, my glory!"

The Gospel of John describes Jesus as "the word that was with God" and "became flesh and dwelt among us". He also says, "And we beheld his glory, the glory as of the only-begotten of the Father, full of grace and truth" (John 1.1,14). When Jesus performed his first sign at Cana of Galilee (water changed into wine) "he manifested his glory and his disciples believed in him" (John 2.11).

Jesus begins his prayer before the cross with these words, "Father, the hour has come. Glorify Your Son that Your Son also may glorify You." (John 17.1).

God reserves "eternal life to those who by patience continuance in doing good seek for glory, honor and immortality" (Romans 2.7). Those who are called to salvation through the Gospel and respond to that call with faith are "justified" and even "glorified" with Christ.

Prayer

Father in heaven, it is our prayer that this day will be one dedicated fully to you. We want to honor you and proclaim your glory through our lives. We pray for our loved ones that they too will seek you and honor you. May you give us wisdom and strength for the day. In Jesus we pray, Amen.

Day 2

> **13** "You will arise *and* have mercy on Zion;
> For the time to favor her,
> Yes, the set time, has come.
> **14** For Your servants take pleasure in her stones,
> And show favor to her dust.
> **15** So the nations shall fear the name of the Lord,
> And all the kings of the earth Your glory.
> **16** For the Lord shall build up Zion;
> He shall appear in His glory.
> **17** He shall regard the prayer of the destitute,
> And shall not despise their prayer."
> (Psalms 102.13-17)

The superscription to this Psalm states that this is "a prayer of the afflicted, when he is overwhelmed and pours out his complaint before the Lord". The writer says in verse 11, "My days are like a shadow that lengthens, and I wither away like grass". This is contrasted to the Lord, who "shall endure forever, and the remembrance of your name to all generations" (verse 12).

The writer knows he is destitute and without hope outside of our heavenly Father. He remembers that what is important for him as for all other servants of God is to take pleasure in what God wants, what God is building (v.14). He believes with all true believers that all peoples, all nations, all rulers shall have to recognize the glory of the Lord.

The hope of the destitute one — which describes the condition of all human beings — is in the Lord who at some point, when He decides to, will "appear in His glory", will "regard the prayer of the destitute and shall not despise their prayer". God's glory is not changed by our circumstances or what happens in this sinful world.

As prophesied by Jeremiah, there was a set time for Zion to be rebuilt after 70 years of captivity (Jeremiah 25.11; 29.10). This was also the prayer of Daniel in chapter 9. The temple of Solomon was destroyed by Babylon in 587 BC. The Second temple was completed and dedicated in 517 B.C., which is exactly 70 years. Daniel prayed, saying 'Lord, look with favor on your desolate sanctuary".

The promises of God always come true, which is also part of His glory. As human beings, our life span is very short, and it can be difficult for us to see God's perspective of human history taken as a whole. This is why Peter writes these words,

> **8** "But, beloved, do not forget this one thing, that with the Lord one day *is* as a thousand years, and a thousand years as one day. **9** The Lord is not slack concerning *His* promise, as some count slackness, but is long-suffering toward us, not willing that any should perish but that all should come to repentance." (2 Peter 3.8,9)

Prayer

Our Father in heaven, we commit to you this day. We want to live every moment of the day as true disciples of Jesus, listening to him and being faithful to him. So we pray that our thoughts, our words and actions may be directed by your Holy Spirit. And when we are troubled or sad, we pray that we come to you in prayer and with trust in your word. We pray this in the name of our Lord Jesus. Amen.

Day 3

> **1** "Bless the Lord, O my soul!
> O Lord my God, You are very great:
> You are clothed with honor and majesty,
> **2** Who cover *Yourself* with light as *with* a garment,
> Who stretch out the heavens like a curtain.
> **3** He lays the beams of His upper chambers in the waters,
> Who makes the clouds His chariot,
> Who walks on the wings of the wind,
> **4** Who makes His angels spirits,
> His ministers a flame of fire."
>   (Psalms 104.1-4)

The creation extols and demonstrates God's glory. This Psalm mentions for example light, the heavens, water, clouds, wind and even angels as all part of this evidence of God's glory. The beauty and complexity of the creation is endless. God knows every star, every flower and every bird he has created. Everything God had created in the beginning was declared to be "very good" (Genesis 1.31). The first man and woman were created to live in a beautiful garden abounding with beautiful vegetation and all kinds of trees and animals.

God's creation is still "very good". Problems on this earth are always linked to man's sinfulness or the fall, as described in Genesis chapter 3. The fact is that "all have sinned and fall short of the glory of God" (Romans 3.23). Human beings live in a good world, a beautiful creation, but their lives are characterized by so much that is not good because of this separation from God's glory. The message of the Gospel is a call to reconciliation with God and with His glory. To trust in Jesus, in his death and resurrection, to turn away from sin and to become united with Jesus' death and resurrection (Romans 6.1-4) is how we come to a new life, a resurrected life. This is the way to be reconciled to God and to His glory.

The beauty of the creation is not what can reconcile us to God or what can bring us hope. We are warned in the Scriptures not to make creation an idol or the source of our hope (or anything else !). This is what Paul discusses in Romans chapter 1 when he writes,

> **18** "For the wrath of God is revealed from heaven against all ungodliness and unrighteousness of men, who suppress the truth in unrighteousness, **19** because what may be known of God is manifest in them, for God has shown *it* to them. **20** For since the creation of the world His invisible *attributes* are clearly seen, being understood by the things that are made, *even* His eternal power and Godhead, so that they are without excuse, **21** because, although they knew God, they did not glorify *Him* as God, nor were thankful, but became futile in their thoughts, and their foolish hearts were darkened. **22** Professing to be wise, they became fools, **23** and changed the glory of the incorruptible God into an image made like corruptible man —and birds and four-footed animals and creeping things." (Romans 3.18-22)

The creation endures the pain of death and suffering, just as we do ever since the fall (Romans 8.18). The creation itself is to be renewed by God at the appearing of Christ and the resurrection (Romans 8.18-25). This is also confirmed in Hebrews:

10 "You, Lord, in the beginning laid the foundation of the earth,
And the heavens are the work of Your hands.
11 They will perish, but You remain;
And they will all grow old like a garment;
12 Like a cloak You will fold them up,
And they will be changed.
But You are the same,
And Your years will not fail." (Hebrews 1.10-12)

Prayer

Our Father in heaven, we praise you for your beautiful creation. We see in it your glory, power and wisdom. We want to be faithful stewards of the creation. Help us also to be faithful as Jesus' disciples, committed to live a holy life, a life of purity. May your Holy Spirit purify our hearts today, and may all our actions reflect your love. We pray this in the name of Jesus. Amen.

Day 4

1 "O God, You *are* my God;
Early will I seek You;
My soul thirsts for You;
My flesh longs for You
In a dry and thirsty land
Where there is no water.
2 So I have looked for You in the sanctuary,
To see Your power and Your glory.
3 Because Your lovingkindness *is* better than life,
My lips shall praise You.
4 Thus I will bless You while I live;
I will lift up my hands in Your name.
5 My soul shall be satisfied as with marrow and fatness,
And my mouth shall praise *You* with joyful lips."
(Psalms 63.1-5)

Even though the writer of this Psalm, David is living in a dry and thirsty land, he does not forget the Lord but seeks Him from the bottom of his soul and praises Him with "joyful lips". This Psalm comes from the heart and lips of David, who is already a king (verse 11) but who is temporarily denied access to the tabernacle during the rebellion of his son Absalom. He is now in the deserted region west of the Dead Sea.

David knows that God's glory is not restricted to the tabernacle or even the city of Jerusalem. He understands that God's power and glory are in the heavenly sanctuary, and it is from this sanctuary that he seeks comfort and help. God's love and lovingkindness can be found even in the deserted areas of Judea. And his love and lovingkindness are still available to us in the deserted times of our lives, when our souls need comfort and strength.

Will we continue to praise God in the midst of our deserted areas? This is an important question to ask and to answer. Will we find satisfaction in our intimate connection with God through Jesus, despite what we are going through? This is also an important question to ask and to answer.

We can follow the example of Jesus in the highs and lows of our lives. He who was king, who was "in the form of God" made himself of no reputation and came in the likeness of men. He humbled himself and became obedient to the point of death, even the death of the cross. (Philippians 2.6-8). If we have obeyed the call of the Gospel and have died with Christ, we have been made kings and queens,

> **5** "To Him who loved us and washed us from our sins in His own blood, **6** and has made us kings and priests to His God and Father, to Him *be* glory and dominion forever and ever. Amen." (Revelation 1.5,6)
>
> **22** "For to this you were called, because Christ also suffered for us, leaving us an example, that you should follow His steps: "Who committed no sin, nor was deceit found in His mouth"; **23** who, when He was reviled, did not revile in return; when He suffered, He did not threaten, but committed *Himself* to Him who judges righteously;" (1 Peter 2.22-23)

Prayer

Our Father in heaven, we praise you for your goodness and faithfulness. We see in Jesus your glory, power and wisdom. We give to your service this new day. We pray you can continually help us grow in our faith and that today our actions and our words will reflect that faith.
Keep us from temptation, from evil or any lying. Purify our hearts, Lord. We pray this in the name of Jesus. Amen.

Day 5

> **5** "I will meditate on the glorious splendor of Your majesty,
> And on Your wondrous works.
> **6** *Men* shall speak of the might of Your awesome acts,
> And I will declare Your greatness.
> **7** They shall utter the memory of Your great goodness,
> And shall sing of Your righteousness."
> (Psalms 145.5-7)

God's wondrous works include his creation and also his works of salvation and redemption. Psalm 145 describes the righteousness and goodness of God. While all of creation was very good (Genesis 1.31), this is only a reflection of God's perfect goodness as extolled in this Psalm and in the Bible as a whole. It is a great mistake to see God in the New Testament as good as opposed to the Old Testament, where he would not be good or righteous. The actions of God, including his work of creation, are a reflection of the goodness of his character.

The miracles and signs performed by Jesus demonstrated power from God and Jesus as the Messiah, but also the goodness of God. Thus, the signs described in John's Gospel are chosen among many that Jesus performed, and each sign shows an aspect of God's goodness, from the changing of water into wine to the resurrection of Lazarus.

God is also the one who provides for the needs of those who depend on him. This parallels the teachings of Jesus (Matthew 6.25-34).

> **15** "The eyes of all look expectantly to You,
> And You give them their food in due season.
> **16** You open Your hand
> And satisfy the desire of every living thing." (verses 15,16)

The God who is almighty and has made us as well as all of creation is neither cruel nor indifferent. He is also gracious and full of compassion. And this is not just God in the Old Testament, this is God throughout the Bible and human history.

> **8** "The Lord *is* gracious and full of compassion,
> Slow to anger and great in mercy.
> **9** The Lord *is* good to all,
> And His tender mercies *are* over all His works." (vs 8,9)

Job and his friends struggled with the question of suffering. Their statements and discussions show this struggle. Thus, the first 40 chapters of

Job show a deep lack of comprehension concerning the nature of God. Is God himself to be blamed for Job's afflictions is one of the questions raised. Job confesses at the end of the book that he did not know or understand the nature of God. God demonstrates compassion and forgiveness to Job not because he understood everything but because of his faithfulness (see James 5.10,11) despite his sufferings and also because he repented.

> **3** "Then Job answered the Lord and said: **4** 'Behold, I am vile;
> What shall I answer You?
> I lay my hand over my mouth.
> **5** Once I have spoken, but I will not answer;
> Yes, twice, but I will proceed no further.'" (Job 40.3-5)
> "Then Job answered the Lord and said: **2** 'I know that You can do everything,
> And that no purpose *of Yours* can be withheld from You.
> **3** *You asked,* 'Who *is* this who hides counsel without knowledge?'
> Therefore I have uttered what I did not understand,
> Things too wonderful for me, which I did not know.
> **4** Listen, please, and let me speak;
> *You said,* 'I will question you, and you shall answer Me.'
> **5** "I have heard of You by the hearing of the ear,
> But now my eye sees You.
> **6** Therefore I abhor *myself,*
> And repent in dust and ashes." (Job 43.1-6)

Prayer

Our God and Father, we want to learn perseverance. We want to learn the patience of Job who came to realize that he understood very little about God, but who loved God and remained faithful to him in his heart. We too Father want to be faithful and persevere in what is right and just before you, whatever our circumstances. So today with the help of your Holy Spirit we ask you to keep our hearts faithful to you. We pray this in the name of Jesus. Amen.

Day 6

> **1** "The heavens declare the glory of God;
> And the firmament shows His handiwork.
> **2** Day unto day utters speech,
> And night unto night reveals knowledge.

3 *There is* no speech nor language
Where their voice is not heard.
4 Their line has gone out through all the earth,
And their words to the end of the world."
(Psalms 19.1-4)

This Psalm can be divided into two parts. Verses 1-6 are about the glory and power of God shown in the sun, stars and celestial bodies. In Job 38.7 we read that at creation "the morning stars sang together, and all the sons of God shouted for joy?" In Revelation 4.11 we read, "You created all things and by your will they exist and were created".

Verses 7-14 describe the excellence and wisdom of God shown in his is law. Thus, God reveals himself in nature and in the law. The one who recognizes God's glory in the creation and in his word is then in a position to be made wise, to be enlightened and cleansed from his sins (verses 7-14). It is then that this one can truly say, "O LORD, my strength and my redeemer" (v.14).

Wherever there are human beings living and speaking, in whatever language they use, the glory of God in creation can be seen by them; the "words" or speech spoken by God through creation extend to all human beings whatever their language — this is a universal language as the apostle Paul confirms in his quote of this Psalm in Romans 10.18 and his argumentation about God's making himself known through creation in Romans 1.18-32. We note that in Romans 10.18 Paul uses the Greek word for "sound" to render the Hebrew translated "line" (NKJV) in verse 4.

We learn in this Psalm as in all of Scripture that the heavens tell of the glory of God but not of his will. Creation alone is insufficient to bring us closer to God, to convert our souls. The worship of creation in fact is a sin and contrary to God's revealed will in his Word:

21 "…although they knew God, they did not glorify *Him* as
God, nor were thankful, but became futile in their thoughts, and
their foolish hearts were darkened. **22** Professing to be wise,
they became fools, **23** and changed the glory
ofthe incorruptible God into an image made like corruptible
man—and birds and four-footed animals and creeping things."
(Romans 1.21-23).

"…who exchanged the truth of God for the lie and worshiped
and served the creature rather than the Creator, who is blessed
forever. Amen." (Romans 1.24).

When human beings admire or worship what God was created — for example talent, intelligence, beauty, accomplishments — and do not honor and worship God, they are prone to idolizing other human beings and fall into jealousy, immorality, pride, and being ungrateful.

John wanted to worship the angel who revealed himself to him, but the angel did not let him:

> **8** "Now I, John, saw and heard these things. And when I heard and saw, I fell down to worship before the feet of the angel who showed me these things. **9** Then he said to me, 'See *that you do* not *do that*. For I am your fellow servant, and of your brethren the prophets, and of those who keep the words of this book. Worship God.'" (Revelation 22.8,9)

Prayer

Our God and Father, we want to worship you today. We want to learn how to honor you above everyone and everything else. Help us be worshipful towards you today, even in our daily tasks. Help us speak and act as worshippers and servants of yours. We love you, Father and want to do your will today and every day. Thank you for every blessing you have poured on us. We pray this in the name of Jesus our Lord, Amen.

Day 7

> **1** "Praise the Lord!
> Praise, O servants of the Lord,
> Praise the name of the Lord!
> **2** Blessed be the name of the Lord
> From this time forth and forevermore!
> **3** From the rising of the sun to its going down
> The Lord's name *is* to be praised.
> **4** The Lord *is* high above all nations,
> His glory above the heavens.
> **5** Who *is* like the Lord our God,
> Who dwells on high,
> **6** Who humbles Himself to behold
> *The things that are* in the heavens and in the earth?"
> (Psalms 113.1-6)

This Psalm of begins and ends with the words "Praise the Lord" (in Hebrew, *hallelujah*). Psalms 115 to 118 were often used as closing songs for times of praise or of assembly (feast of Tabernacles, Pentecost, Passover) and may have been sung by Jesus and his apostles following the last supper (Matthew 26.30; Mark 14.26).

We need to keep a humble heart when considering the LORD. The remaining verses of this Psalm tell us that we praise the God who is infinitely exalted himself but turns towards the lowly ones, the poor and humble.

> **7** "He raises the poor out of the dust,
> *And* lifts the needy out of the ash heap,
> **8** That He may seat *him* with princes—
> With the princes of His people.
> **9** He grants the barren woman a home,
> Like a joyful mother of children.
> Praise the Lord!"

God's work of redemption and sanctification are accomplished in the most humble ways, as we see in the life of Christ,

> **5** "Let this mind be in you which was also in Christ Jesus, **6** who, being in the form of God, did not consider it robbery to be equal with God, **7** but made Himself of no reputation, taking the form of a bondservant, *and* coming in the likeness of men. **8** And being found in appearance as a man, He humbled Himself and became obedient to *the point of* death, even the death of the cross." (Philippians 2.5-8)

Prayer

We thank you, Father, for your constant love towards us. We thank you for the example and life of Jesus. We know that you are a loving God, a perfectly holy God, and we praise you for that. Give us today strength and holiness through your Holy Spirit. May we live today in a way that honors you and your Son, Jesus. We pray in His name. Amen.

Week 5: The God of the Downtrodden

Day 1

> **1** "Give the king Your judgments, O God,
> And Your righteousness to the king's Son.
> **2** He will judge Your people with righteousness,
> And Your poor with justice.
> **3** The mountains will bring peace to the people,
> And the little hills, by righteousness.
> **4** He will bring justice to the poor of the people;
> He will save the children of the needy,
> And will break in pieces the oppressor."
> (Psalm 72.1-4)

According to the Targum ("O God, give thy regulations of right to the King Messiah") the subject of this Psalm is the Messiah. the king's son is the anointed one, the Messiah. He will be characterized by care and compassion towards the poor and downtrodden.

The kingships of David and Salomon were in the final analysis disappointing if one considers the breadth of this and other Psalms about the Anointed one. The kingships of these two great kings could only be a vague shadow of the greater King to come who would not disappoint and would finally establish perfect righteousness and also forgiveness for God's people (Daniel 7.13,14; 9.24). This is even more so as we follow the lives and work of all the other kings that followed in Israel and Juda. The reign of king Hezekiah and some of the better kings were like sudden blazes, quickly fading away.

But we still have the poor among us. How is it then that the future King will deliver the needy when they cry? How is it that he will spare the needy? He does it today through the power of His Good News and the power of His Holy Spirit, given to all those who will open their hearts to Him and receive Him through trust and obedience. "Therefore, if anyone is in Christ, he is a new creation; old things have passed away; behold all things have become new." (2 Corinthians 5.17).

Until he returns to bring eternal peace and joy, His true followers have a heart for the downtrodden. They do not exploit or despise those who carry heavy burdens and have lost hope. They are generous to the poor and caring for every human being they know to be in pain and grief.

"Come, you blessed of My Father, inherit the kingdom prepared for you from the foundation of the world. For I was hungry, and you gave Me food. I was thirsty and you gave Me drink; I was a stranger, and you took me in…" (Matthew 25.34,35).

Prayer

LORD God, give us today a heart for all the downtrodden of the earth. Help us see them as you saw them. Help us to be generous in our ways, in our deeds and words. May we today understand what you expect of us as we meet the stranger.

Day 2

12 "For He will deliver the needy when he cries,
The poor also, and *him* who has no helper.
13 He will spare the poor and needy,
And will save the souls of the needy.
14 He will redeem their life from oppression and violence;
And precious shall be their blood in His sight."
   (Psalm 72.12-14)

How precious was the blood of the poor and weak for the ancient nations surrounding Israel, and later for the Greek and Roman conquerors? How significant were for these ancient peoples the multitude of slaves, which lived short and miserable lives? How caring were the shepherds of Israel towards the sick sheep and starving even in the times of Ezekiel?

4 "The weak you have not strengthened, nor have you healed those who were sick, nor bound up the broken, nor brought back what was driven away, nor sought what was lost; but with force and cruelty you have ruled them. **5** So they were scattered because *there was* no shepherd; and they became food for all the beasts of the field when they were scattered. **6** My sheep wandered through all the mountains, and on every high hill; yes, my flock was scattered over the whole face of the earth, and no one was seeking or searching *for them*." (Ezekiel 4.4-6).

Thus, the LORD himself would come down to show His people how to be true shepherds.

> **11** "For thus says the Lord God: 'Indeed I Myself will search for My sheep and seek them out. **12** As a shepherd seeks out his flock on the day he is among his scattered sheep, so will I seek out My sheep and deliver them from all the places where they were scattered on a cloudy and dark day. **13** And I will bring them out from the peoples and gather them from the countries, and will bring them to their own land; I will feed them on the mountains of Israel, [a]in the valleys and in all the inhabited places of the country. **14** I will feed them in good pasture, and their fold shall be on the high mountains of Israel. There they shall lie down in a good fold and feed in rich pasture on the mountains of Israel. **15** I will feed My flock, and I will make them lie down,' says the Lord God." (Ezekiel 34.11-15).

> **11** "I am the good shepherd. The good shepherd gives His life for the sheep. **12** But a hireling, *he who is* not the shepherd, one who does not own the sheep, sees the wolf coming and leaves the sheep and flees; and the wolf catches the sheep and scatters them. **13** The hireling flees because he is a hireling and does not care about the sheep. **14** I am the good shepherd; and I know My *sheep* and am known by My own. **15** As the Father knows Me, even so I know the Father; and I lay down My life for the sheep. **16** And other sheep I have which are not of this fold; them also I must bring, and they will hear My voice; and there will be one flock *and* one shepherd. **17** "Therefore My Father loves Me, because I lay down My life that I may take it again. **18** No one takes it from Me, but I lay it down of Myself. I have power to lay it down, and I have power to take it again. This command I have received from My Father." (John 10.11-18).

Prayer

Dear God in heaven, this day may we open our hearts to those around us who struggle daily for survival. May we open our hearts even to those whose own choices have brought them so low they have no one to call for help. This day may we have the kind of love which is more than feeding the poor. The love that is kind, does not envy and is not puffed up.

Day 3

> **1** "Do you indeed speak righteousness, you silent ones?
> Do you judge uprightly, you sons of men?
> **2** No, in heart you work wickedness;
> You weigh out the violence of your hands in the earth.
> **3** The wicked are estranged from the womb;
> They go astray as soon as they are born, speaking lies.
> **4** Their poison *is* like the poison of a serpent;
> *They are* like the deaf cobra *that* stops its ear,
> **5** Which will not heed the voice of charmers,
> Charming ever so skillfully."
> (Psalm 58.1-5)

This Psalm is primarily about those who "judge", those who are in a position of power and authority. The circumstance of this Psalm of David is the treason of his son Absalom, who turned against his father David. Absalom and those who followed him used the administration of justice to steal from David the heart of his people. Absalom feigned to be the more impartial judge,

> **12** "And the conspiracy grew strong, for the people with Absalom continually increased in number. **13** Now a messenger came to David, saying, 'The hearts of the men of Israel are with Absalom.' (2 Samuel 15.12,13).

Unjust "judges" are often mentioned in the Psalms and the history of Israel (Psalm 82.1-8). Corrupt judicial or political leadership is one of the central issues of the Old Testament prophets. This is an issue still today. The Psalm gives an answer as to how God views corrupt leaders. They are compared to deadly snakes that bring death: "Their poison is like the poison of a serpent..." (vv. 4,5).

The Psalm assures us that the day is coming for divine judgment or revenge on those who abuse the weak, who trample those who have no power: "He shall take them away as with a whirlwind, as in His living and burning wrath." (v.9).

God's judgment is inevitable in its own time because He is himself a righteous judge (and not because there is any hatred in God's heart even towards those evil judges).

Prayer

Righteous God, be with our spirit this day. We believe in your perfect justice. When we face the wickedness of evil and deceiving leaders, let us not grow hateful or bitter. Let us remember your perfect righteousness and your unfailing judgment. Let us remember the words of this Psalm, "Surely there is a reward for the righteous; surely He is God who judges in the earth."

Day 4

> **22** "Oh, do not let the oppressed return ashamed!
> Let the poor and needy praise Your name.
> **22** Arise, O God, plead Your own cause;
> Remember how the foolish man reproaches You daily.
> **23** Do not forget the voice of Your enemies;
> The tumult of those who rise up against You increases continually."
> (Psalm 74.21-23)

In this Psalm, the enemies of God are those nations and rulers given to greed for power and conquest. They are also those individuals who through greed don't mind crushing and destroying the lives of the needy.

The poor are like "turtledove" exposed to the wild beast (v.19). In other passages and the New Testament, God's faithful are like "sheep among wolves" (Luke 10.1-12). "For your sake we are killed all day long; we are accounted as sheep for the slaughter." (Psalm 44.22 and Romans 8.36).

We are reminded of Psalms 74 in Lamentations 2:2 (cf. Psalms 74:7), Psalms 2:7 (cf. Psalms 74:4), and other passages.

In this Psalm, we are confronted with God's patience, which can be mistaken for some kind of forgetfulness on the part of God (v.22). See 1 Peter 3.20 and 2 Peter 3.9.

To accept and understand God's "patience", which is not forgetfulness or naivety, may be one of the most difficult areas of faithfulness. The best is for us to realize how patient God is being towards us and our slowness to grow in holiness (1 Timothy 1. 13,16).

Prayer

Dear Lord, help us today to grow, to come closer to your righteousness and holiness. Help us to exercise patience towards all, just as you do. Help us remember the words of the apostle, "Love suffers long and is kind; love does not envy; love does not parade itself, is not puffed up; does not behave rudely, does not seek its own, is not provoked, thinks no evil; does not rejoice in iniquity but rejoices in the truth; bears all things, believes all things, hopes all things; endures all things". Amen.

Day 5

> **1** "God stands in the congregation of the mighty;
> He judges among the gods.
> **2** How long will you judge unjustly,
> And show partiality to the wicked? *Selah*
> **3** Defend the poor and fatherless;
> Do justice to the afflicted and needy.
> **4** Deliver the poor and needy;
> Free *them* from the hand of the wicked."
>   (Psalm 82.1-4)

God is introduced in this Psalm as the direct speaker to his people. We see this also in Psalm 58.1-11 or 94 as well as Isaiah 3.13-15. God is speaking specifically against the leaders of Israel who have perverted God's truth and have acted as tyrants without any heart or concern.

The word "gods" (*elohim*) can mean "mighty ones" and refers especially to the judges and rulers of Israel. The Psalm reminds us that God knows when men judge unjustly and show partiality to the wicked. It has always been a question for some people why God would tolerate wicked judges. But that question opens up a larger question which is "Why does God tolerate any sin, even from us?" Thus, if we want God to act swiftly and punish, this would necessarily apply to all of us. Is that what we want? Do we not understand that God's patience towards all sinners is also his patience towards us?

God is a judge who does not show partiality to the wicked because he is no "respecter of persons" (2 Chronicles 19.7; Job 34.19; Romans 2.10,11; Galatians 5.6; 1 Peter 1.17). See Acts 10.34 "God is no respecter of persons". God does not offer salvation only to the Jew just because he is a Jew, or to the Gentile because he is a Gentile. The word translated "respecter" of persons in the KJV describes a judge who looks at a man's face instead of the facts of the case and makes a decision based on whether or not he likes the man.

God is not a mere human judge. He will judge impartially the earth and even all the nations (v.8).

Prayer

We pray Father in heaven that today we will learn to be righteous in our judgments and decisions and like you will not be "respecter of persons". We are grateful for your righteousness and holiness, on which we can always depend. May we glorify your name. May your will be done in our lives today. Amen.

Day 6

> **4** "He counts the number of the stars;
> He calls them all by name.
> **5** Great *is* our Lord, and mighty in power;
> His understanding *is* infinite.
> **6** The Lord lifts up the humble;
> He casts the wicked down to the ground."
>   (Psalm 147.4-6)

Can we measure the universe or really understand its size? Can we really count the number of stars? Of course, not. Can we even explain everything there is to be known about an ant or an elephant? So, it is not surprising that the creator's power and understanding are infinite. It is upon this that the humble rely, and not upon their own strength or wisdom.

> **10** "Behold, the Lord God shall come with a strong *hand,*
> And His arm shall rule for Him;
> Behold, His reward *is* with Him,
> And His work before Him.
> **11** He will feed His flock like a shepherd;
> He will gather the lambs with His arm,
> And carry *them* in His bosom,
> *And* gently lead those who are with young.
> **12** Who has measured the waters in the hollow of His hand,
> Measured heaven with a span
> And calculated the dust of the earth in a measure?
> Weighed the mountains in scales
> And the hills in a balance?
> **13** Who has directed the Spirit of the Lord,
> Or *as* His counselor has taught Him?
> **14** With whom did He take counsel, and *who* instructed Him,
> And taught Him in the path of justice?

Who taught Him knowledge,
And showed Him the way of understanding?" (Isaiah 40.10-14)

"Now to Him who is able to do exceedingly abundantly above all that we ask or think, according to the power that works in us, **21** to Him *be* glory in the church by Christ Jesus to all generations, forever and ever. Amen." (Ephesians 3.20,21)

> **4** "Rejoice in the Lord always. Again, I will say, rejoice! **5** Let your gentleness be known to all men. The Lord *is* at hand.**6** Be anxious for nothing, but in everything by prayer and supplication, with thanksgiving, let your requests be made known to God; **7** and the peace of God, which surpasses all understanding, will guard your hearts and minds through Christ Jesus." (Philippians 4.4-6)

Prayer

Lord of heaven and earth, we come before you with all our limitations and anxieties. We come before you with grateful hearts because we know that our standing before you and our future do not depend on our own strength or vision, but depend on your goodness and faithfulness. For this new day you are giving us, we ask for faithfulness in prayer and trust, faithfulness in our actions and speech.

Day 7

> **1** "Praise the Lord from the heavens;
> Praise Him in the heights!
> **2** Praise Him, all His angels;
> Praise Him, all His hosts!
> **3** Praise Him, sun and moon;
> Praise Him, all you stars of light!
> **4** Praise Him, you heavens of heavens,
> And you waters above the heavens!"
>   (Psalm 148.1-4)

There is a powerful but invisible reality out there in the world created by God. However, in all things He the Lord Jesus has preeminence.

Angels in heaven and "all his hosts" are the part of creation that is invisible to our eyes, even though at times they appear and can be seen. All things created include more than meets the eye, "whether thrones or dominions or principalities or powers" as Paul writes in Colossians.

13 "He has delivered us from the power of darkness and conveyed *us* into the kingdom of the Son of His love, **14** in whom we have redemption through His blood, the forgiveness of sins. **15** He is the image of the invisible God, the firstborn over all creation. **16** For by Him all things were created that are in heaven and that are on earth, visible and invisible, whether thrones or dominions or principalities or powers. All things were created through Him and for Him. **17** And He is before all things, and in Him all things consist. **18** And He is the head of the body, the church, who is the beginning, the firstborn from the dead, that in all things He may have the preeminence." (Colossians 1.13-18).

The Church is also part of God's creation. It was built by Jesus Christ on the foundation of the faith that Jesus is the Son of the living God (Matthew 16.13-20; 1 Corinthians 3.9-11; Ephesians 2.19-22).

The word "church" also describes Israel in the Old Testament (The Hebrew uses the word *qahal*). In English translations of the Old Testament, (*qahal*) is translated as *multitude, company, congregation or assembly*. The Greek translation of the Old Testament (Septuagint) used the Greek *ekklesia* to translate *qahal*. Thus, the word church is not new when we read the New Testament. It simply describes God's people. We should not be as concerned with using the word "church", "assembly" or "congregation" but understand what those words mean in describing God's people as a special group with a unique relationship to God and to each other characterized by love for God and one another.

Prayer

Father in heaven, we thank you for your amazing creation. We recognize and praise your power displayed in heaven and earth. We also pray that we can trust in the power of the Lord Jesus who has received all power in heaven and on earth and submit to him. We pray today for the "church", for God's people worldwide. We pray for the brothers and sisters with whom we assemble and worship. May you bring each one closer to you and change each brother and each sister so that each one might be more like our Lord. Help us never to neglect loving our brothers and sisters as you commanded us to do. Amen.

Week 6: When we Fall

Day 1

> **1** "To the Chief Musician. With stringed instruments. On an eight-stringed harp. A Psalm of David.
> O Lord, do not rebuke me in Your anger,
> Nor chasten me in Your hot displeasure.
> **2** Have mercy on me, O Lord, for I *am* weak;
> O Lord, heal me, for my bones are troubled.
> **3** My soul also is greatly troubled;
> But You, O Lord—how long?"
> (Psalm 6.1-3)

The chief musician was a Levite who directed the music in the temple. It was David who introduced and structured the music performed in the temple (1 Chronicles 25). In the Old Testament, music was also used as a means of securing victory, as part of Israel's warfare. Praising the LORD was an essential strategy of warfare for Israel. We see this from the time of the Exodus (Exodus 18). See also the worship song of David in Psalm 18 echoed in 2 Samuel 22, written "when the LORD delivered him from the hand of all his enemies, and from the hand of Saul." These songs were part of Israel's life confronted with fierce enemies and having to depend on the Lord for deliverance.

The praises of the Church today are also part of the spiritual battle "against principalities, powers and the rulers of darkness of this age" (Ephesians 6.10-12; 5.18-20).

It is significant that in confessing his weakness, this Psalm of David starts with praise and music. Some Christians are so burdened by their sins or their past that they dare not come before the Lord or praise him. What they do not understand is that this praise is in itself one of the best ways to confess their weakness to God and seek his forgiveness and strength. They feel unworthy of praising the Lord. But really there is only one "who is worthy" to come close to God (Revelation 4.10,11; 5.8-

14). We do not come before the Lord or worship him out of a sense of worthiness, but out of a sense of weakness and need.

The "mercies" of God are the source of our coming to God and seeking his forgiveness, strength or wisdom (v.4). The Psalm also expresses the need to come close to God as we are confronted by evil people who want to harm us (vv.8-10).

Prayer

Father in heaven, we come before you full of weakness. We pray that you will forgive our sins. Have mercy on us as we seek you in praise. Deliver us also from those who want to harm us. We pray for them that you would enlighten their hearts and forgive them. We also pray that you would give us the wisdom to know how to help them return to you. Amen.

Day 2

> **6** "Remember, O Lord, Your tender mercies and Your lovingkindness,
> For they *are* from of old.
> **7** Do not remember the sins of my youth, nor my transgressions;
> According to Your mercy remember me,
> For Your goodness' sake, O Lord."
> (Psalm 25.6,7)

Does God listen to our prayers when we know we have turned away from Him? Does God really forget our sins? The writer does remember the sins of his youth. He does not come to God as one who is blameless, but as seeking God's mercy. He understands that God's mercy and love are "from of old" — they were already blessing the writer's life before he sinned.

The blessings of the Father are even present in the life of the sinner. How could that be? This is part of God's goodness and patience, while not being an excuse to sin. "He makes His sun rise on the evil and on the good, and sends rain on the just and the unjust" (Matthew 5. 45). "Or do you despise the riches of His goodness, forbearance, and longsuffering, not knowing that the goodness of God leads you to repentance?" (Romans 2.4). "The Lord is not slack concerning *His* promise, as some count slackness, but is longsuffering toward us, not willing that any should perish but that all should come to repentance." (2 Peter 3.9).

The Psalm teaches us that it is a consideration of God's mercy and goodness which should lead us to repentance and a changed life. The prodigal son of the parable remembered the love and kindness of his Father which stood in stark contrast to the "citizen" who had hired him and did not even provide him with food while his father had even enough food for his hired servants (Luke 15.15-17).

Prayer

Our Father in heaven, we praise you for your love and mercy. We thank you for your patience towards us and your forgiveness. Help us live with such gratitude towards you that we will always choose obedience and trust. Deliver us from evil. Amen.

Day 3

> **1** "Blessed *is he whose* transgression *is* forgiven,
> *Whose* sin *is* covered.
> **2** Blessed *is* the man to whom the Lord does not impute iniquity,
> And in whose spirit *there is* no deceit.
> **3** When I kept silent, my bones grew old
> Through my groaning all the day long.
> **4** For day and night Your hand was heavy upon me;
> My vitality was turned into the drought of summer. *Selah*
> **5** I acknowledged my sin to You,
> And my iniquity I have not hidden.
> I said, "I will confess my transgressions to the Lord,"
> And You forgave the iniquity of my sin. *Selah"*
> (Psalm 32.1-5)

The writer begins with a declaration of "blessing". As in Psalms 1 blessings and happiness are the fruit or result of something else. In this Psalm the blessed or "happy" are the forgiven, those whose "sin is covered".

A characteristic of the ungodly is that they, not only live in sin, but they are not ashamed of their sinful lives. They refuse to repent and come back to God.

> **28** "And even as they did not like to retain God in *their* knowledge, God gave them over to a debased mind, to do those things which are not fitting; **29** being filled with all unrighteous-

ness, sexual immorality, wickedness, covetousness, maliciousness; full of envy, murder, strife, deceit, evil-mindedness; *they are* whisperers, **30** backbiters, haters of God, violent, proud, boasters, inventors of evil things, disobedient to parents, **31** undiscerning, untrustworthy, unloving, unforgiving, unmerciful; **32** who, knowing the righteous judgment of God, that those who practice such things are deserving of death, not only do the same but also approve of those who practice them." (Romans 1.28-32).

These sinners "know the righteous judgment of God" but that does not deter them from persisting in their evil ways. They are also those who despise the riches of God's goodness and longsuffering and thus refuse to repent: "Or do you despise the riches of His goodness, forbearance, and longsuffering, not knowing that the goodness of God leads you to repentance?

> "But in accordance with your hardness and your impenitent heart you are treasuring up for yourself wrath in the day of wrath and revelation of the righteous judgment of God" (Romans 2.5).

The forgiveness of the Lord requires acknowledgment of sin or "confession of sin" on the part of the sinner:

> **8** "If we say that we have no sin, we deceive ourselves, and the truth is not in us. **9** If we confess our sins, He is faithful and just to forgive us *our* sins and to cleanse us from all unrighteousness. **10** If we say that we have not sinned, we make Him a liar, and His word is not in us. My little children, these things I write to you, so that you may not sin. And if anyone sins, we have an Advocate with the Father, Jesus Christ the righteous. **2** And He Himself is the propitiation for our sins, and not for ours only but also for the whole world." (1 John 1.9 – 2.2).

Prayer

Father in heaven, forgive us our sins. Help us to live as the Holy Spirit would have us to live. May we produce the fruit of the Spirit in our lives such as love, joy and peace. Give us wisdom Father that we may know how to help and en-

courage those who have fallen into sin and how to do this in a spirit of gentleness. Amen.

Day 4

> **1** "O Lord do not rebuke me in Your wrath,
> Nor chasten me in Your hot displeasure!
> **2** For Your arrows pierce me deeply,
> And Your hand presses me down.
> **3** *There is* no soundness in my flesh
> Because of Your anger,
> Nor *any* health in my bones
> Because of my sin.
> **4** For my iniquities have gone over my head;
> Like a heavy burden they are too heavy for me.
> **5** My wounds are foul *and* festering
> Because of my foolishness."
> (Psalm 38.1-5)

In a number of his Psalms, David confesses his sin with Bathsheba or his sin of having ordered a census not required by God. In confessing his sin, David describes himself as full of wounds and having no health in his bones. By these words, David is describing the pain he has endured because of his sin. Even in good health, a person who indulges in sin is spiritually ill and doomed to death.

The writer mentions the fact that his body is full of pains and wounds because of his sin. Is this teaching us that physical illness and pains are always and necessarily the consequences of sin?

Sin can sometimes bring about disease. However, we should not understand this language of David as teaching that illness and physical pain are always a direct result of a person's sins (see John 9.1-3). The book of Job teaches us the opposite. He was a righteous man who became very ill, but had not sinned against God (see also Ecclesiastes 8.14). His friends made the mistake to judge his spiritual condition based on his sickness. God condemned Job's friends for their accusations against Job (Job 42. 7-9).

Neither should we think that sickness is a proof of lack of faith when we pray to God for healing and do not receive this healing. Job did not receive healing, which he surely desired and asked of God:

20 "Only two *things* do not do to me,
Then I will not hide myself from You:
21 Withdraw Your hand far from me,
And let not the dread of You make me afraid." (Job 13.20,21)

Paul had a "thorn in the flesh" for which he prayed and from which he was not delivered (2 Corinthians 12.7-10). Trophimus, Epaphroditus and even Timothy had to endure illness or physical pain and were men of faith (2 Timothy 4.20; Philippians 2.25-27; 1 Timothy 5.23).

The prophet Isaiah described the saving work of Christ as "by His stripes we were healed" (Isaiah 53.5). The salvation that the Messiah would bring about is described as a "healing" and even a "resurrection" of God's people Israel and even Gentiles. We also see the healing power of Jesus during his ministry. Thus, some have taught that if we believe in Christ, we can be assured not to be sick or if sick, we can be assured to be healed by God. They have made of the Gospel a "Good News" of physical healing or even a "Good News" of financial and material blessings, not understanding that the language of the Bible concerning God's healing, resurrection from the dead or finding a pearl of great price are ways to describe the spiritual blessing and healing of the heart and soul, the spiritual resurrection of those dead through sin (See Ezekiel 37.1-14; Daniel 12.1-3); not understanding that this language of Scripture points to the "restoration of all things" when the Lord returns and brings about "the glory which shall be revealed in us".

> "For I consider that the sufferings of this present time are not worthy *to be compared* with the glory which shall be revealed in us." (Romans 8.18)

> **10** "But I rejoiced in the Lord greatly that now at last your care for me has flourished again; though you surely did care, but you lacked opportunity. **11** Not that I speak in regard to need, for I have learned in whatever state I am, to be content: **12** I know how to be abased, and I know how to abound. Everywhere and in all things, I have learned both to be full and to be hungry, both to abound and to suffer need. **13** I can do all things through Christ who strengthens me." (Philippians 4.10-13).

Prayer

We come to you, Father, for healing. We know you have the power to heal our bodies, as well as our souls, so we come with faith to you. We pray you will give us patience and perseverance, whatever our circumstances. We pray Lord that we can learn to be content in all things while believing in your care and love towards us, and while continuing to come to you for all our needs. Amen.

Day 5

> **10** "Create in me a clean heart, O God,
> And renew a steadfast spirit within me.
> **11** Do not cast me away from Your presence,
> And do not take Your Holy Spirit from me.
> **12** Restore to me the joy of Your salvation,
> And uphold me *by Your* generous Spirit.
> **13** *Then* I will teach transgressors Your ways,
> And sinners shall be converted to You."
> (Psalm 51.10-13)

How can we overcome our sinful nature? How does God answer our prayers when we have fallen into greed, lust or pride? This Psalm encourages us to never give up seeking God's help and forgiveness, since God does not give up on us. Our Father is an understanding teacher and mentor. We do not come to him in vain. But as we come to Him for help, we should also be willing to listen to Him and learn from Him.

God's Holy Spirit is a promise and given to those who have come in faith and repentance to the salvation which is in Christ.

> **37** "Now when they heard *this*, they were cut to the heart, and said to Peter and the rest of the apostles, 'Men *and* brethren, what shall we do?' **38** Then Peter said to them, "Repent, and let every one of you be baptized in the name of Jesus Christ for the remission of sins; and you shall receive the gift of the Holy Spirit. **39** For the promise is to you and to your children, and to all who are afar off, as many as the Lord our God will call."
> (Acts 2.37-39)

The work of transformation in the human heart is the work of God's Spirit, which "convinces the world of sin, and of righteousness and of judgment" (John 16.8). Faith and repentance are gifts granted by God (Ephesians 2.8; 2 Timothy 2.24-26). The Gospel is the power that changes the human heart and brings us to saving faith (Romans 1.16).

If we have received the wonderful gift of the Spirit, we must be careful not to "grieve the Spirit by whom we were sealed for the day of redemption" (Ephesians 4.30). We must "redeem the time because the days are evil" and "be filled with the Spirit, speaking to one another in psalms and hymns and spiritual songs" (Ephesians 5.16-18).

"Restore to me the joy of Your salvation and uphold me *by Your* generous Spirit. *Then* I will teach transgressors Your ways and sinners shall be converted to You." The Lord calls his people to speak and teach on his behalf out of joy and a renewing of the heart.

Prayer

Our Father in heaven, we are grateful for your Word, which gives us assurance to be transformed day by day. We pray especially for a purifying of our hearts and a renewing of our love towards you. We pray also that you be with us and guide us as we reach out and speak to those who don't know you or have known you and need to return to you. Amen.

Day 6

    1 "Out of the depths I have cried to You, O Lord;
    2 Lord, hear my voice!
    Let Your ears be attentive
    To the voice of my supplications.
    3 If You, Lord, should mark iniquities,
    O Lord, who could stand?
    4 But *there is* forgiveness with You,
    That You may be feared.
    5 I wait for the Lord, my soul waits,
    And in His word I do hope.
    6 My soul *waits* for the Lord
    More than those who watch for the morning—
    Yes, more than those who watch for the morning.
    7 O Israel, hope in the Lord;
    For with the Lord *there is* mercy,
    And with Him *is* abundant redemption.
    8 And He shall redeem Israel
    From all his iniquities."
        (Psalm 130)

In verse 1 the writer appeals to the LORD (Yahweh) — the God of the covenant with Israel — "out of the depths" which is the lowest point where one can be. It is often when we are at our lowest point in life that we appeal to the Lord for help. In verse 2 the writer appeals to God as Adonai, the Master of the universe. The "voice of my supplications" is a groaning — a crying to God — out of inner pain. This reminds us of the words of Paul: "Likewise the Spirit also helps in our weaknesses. For we do not know what we should pray for as we ought, but the Spirit Himself makes intercession for us with groanings which cannot be uttered.

> **27** Now He who searches the hearts knows what the mind of the Spirit *is*, because He makes intercession for the saints according to *the will of* God." (Romans 8.26,27).

In verse 3 of Psalm 130 the Lord does not "mark" (*tishmor*), guard or keep watch over) our iniquities. The writer's hope is founded on God's goodness and grace, and not on his own righteousness. In verse 4 the "forgiveness" of the Lord should lead one to fearing the Lord. In verse 5, the verb to wait (*kiviti*) is from the same root word as "hope" (*tikvah*). Hope implies waiting for the word of God to be accomplished. The "waiting" in verses 5 and 6 is a waiting for the Lord himself, and not for something from the Lord. This "waiting" for the Lord is not wishful thinking; it is like the waiting of those who "watch for the morning", for the sunrise of a new day.

> "But those who wait on the Lord
> Shall renew *their* strength;
> They shall mount up with wings like eagles,
> They shall run and not be weary,
> They shall walk and not faint." (Isaiah 40.31)

In verses 7 and 8 the writer's supplication and "waiting" is also for the entire community or congregation of God's people. This community enjoys the "redemption" (a ransom paid for deliverance) from all iniquity:

> "For even the Son of Man did not come to be served, but to serve, and to give His life a ransom for many." (Mark 10.45).

> "In Him we have redemption through His blood, the forgiveness of sins, according to the riches of His grace." (Ephesians 1.7).

"*There is* therefore now no condemnation to those who are in Christ Jesus, who do not walk according to the flesh, but according to the Spirit." (Romans 8.1).

Prayer

We come to you, Lord, with a heart full of hope. We thank you for your Son Jesus, who gave his life as a ransom, who came to redeem us from our sins. In the midst of dark hours or dark days be with us Father, help us to wait patiently and with hope for the accomplishing of your Word. Amen.

Day 7

> **1** "Hear my prayer, O Lord,
> Give ear to my supplications!
> In Your faithfulness answer me,
> *And* in Your righteousness.
> **2** Do not enter into judgment with Your servant,
> For in Your sight no one living is righteous.
> **3** For the enemy has persecuted my soul;
> He has crushed my life to the ground;
> He has made me dwell in [a]darkness,
> Like those who have long been dead.
> **4** Therefore my spirit is overwhelmed within me;
> My heart within me is distressed."
> (Psalm 143.1-4)

God's faithfulness and righteousness guarantees that He listens to the pleas of the repentant believer. His faithfulness lies in the fact that he is always true to His Word and promises. His righteousness describes him as the righteous but also gracious judge, since "no one is righteous" in His sight. God's grace and forgiveness is not merely a New Testament teaching; it is found throughout the Old Testament and in His relationship with those who lived under the old covenant. Were it not for God's grace, we would stand condemned under the judgment of God (see Job 9.32; 14.3; 22.4).

> **1** "Therefore, having been justified by faith, we have peace with God through our Lord Jesus Christ, **2** through whom also we have access by faith into this grace in which we stand, and rejoice in hope of the glory of God." (Romans 5.1)

6 "For when we were still without strength, in due time Christ died for the ungodly. **7** For scarcely for a righteous man will one die; yet perhaps for a good man someone would even dare to die. **8** But God demonstrates His own love toward us, in that while we were still sinners, Christ died for us. **9** Much more then, having now been justified by His blood, we shall be saved from wrath through Him." (Romans 5.6-9)

Despite the fact that the writer has to endure persecution from enemies, his first thought is to his own sin and need of forgiveness. Could it be that sometimes opposition can lead us to a reflex of superiority and smugness? Is that one of the reasons we are to pray for our enemies and bless them? (Matthew 5.43-45).

Prayer

Our Father in heaven, we come to you seeking your forgiveness. Give us a heart of humility as we seek you. We pray for growing understanding of your forgiveness and grace. Give us also a heart that does not lose hope in you when there is opposition or persecution. We pray that you will bless any enemy we may have and draw them to you through the power of your Holy Spirit. Amen.

Week 7: Trusting God

Day 1

> **10** "Now therefore, be wise, O kings;
> Be instructed you judges of the earth.
> **11** Serve the Lord with fear,
> And rejoice with trembling.
> **12** Kiss the Son, lest He be angry,
> And you perish *in* the way,
> When His wrath is kindled but a little.
> Blessed *are* all those who put their trust in Him."
>   (Psalm 2.10-12)

This warning to receive instruction, to serve and to trust God concerns everyone, but the writer begins with kings and judges. As people are endowed with some kind of authority or power, they can easily forget that God is the LORD and exercises authority over them. In this Psalm, the kings and rulers even set themselves against the LORD and his anointed (v.2).

In verse 10 the kings are advised to be wise or to obtain "understanding" (*sekhel*). The judges are advised to become wise, instructed, to obtain discipline (from *yasar*, to instruct, to chasten). They are to serve with fear, which is "awe" (*b'yirah*) — to serve with high respect for the holiness and righteousness of the LORD and his anointed.

> **25** "See that you do not refuse Him who speaks. For if they did not escape who refused Him who spoke on earth, much more *shall we not escape* if we turn away from Him who *speaks* from heaven, **26** whose voice then shook the earth; but now He has promised, saying, "Yet once more I shake not only the earth, but also heaven." **27** Now this, "Yet once more," indicates the removal of those things that are being shaken, as of things that are made, that the things which cannot be shaken may remain. **28** Therefore, since we are receiving a

kingdom which cannot be shaken, let us have grace, by which we may serve God acceptably with reverence and godly fear. **29** For our God *is* a consuming fire." (Hebrews 12.25-28).

The Psalm reminds us of Jesus, in the book of Revelation, described as supreme Lord and Judge over nations and rulers.

> **5** "To Him who loved us and washed us from our sins in His own blood, **6** and has made us kings and priests to His God and Father, to Him *be* glory and dominion forever and ever. Amen. **7** Behold, He is coming with clouds, and every eye will see Him, even they who pierced Him. And all the tribes of the earth will mourn because of Him. Even so, Amen." (Revelation 1.5-7)
>
> **11** "Now I saw heaven opened, and behold, a white horse. And He who sat on him *was* called Faithful and True, and in righteousness He judges and makes war. **12** His eyes *were* like a flame of fire, and on His head *were* many crowns. He had a name written that no one knew except Himself. **13** He *was* clothed with a robe dipped in blood, and His name is called The Word of God. **14** And the armies in heaven, clothed in fine linen, white and clean, followed Him on white horses. **15** Now out of His mouth goes a sharp sword, that with it He should strike the nations. And He Himself will rule them with a rod of iron. He Himself treads the winepress of the fierceness and wrath of Almighty God. **16** And He has on *His* robe and on His thigh a name written: KING OF KINGS AND LORD OF LORDS." (Revelation 19.11-16)

Prayer

Our God and Savior, we pray that this day we can learn from you and accept your discipline. We ask for wisdom as we deal with temptation and as we meet men and women around us. Give us understanding in the workplace and in every relationship. Help us to keep our hearts close to you and to your Word. May your Holy Spirit comfort us this day. Amen.

Day 2

> **1** "To the choirmaster. With stringed instruments. A Psalm of David.
> Answer me when I call, O God of my righteousness!
>   You have given me relief when I was in distress.

> Be gracious to me and hear my prayer!
> **2** O men, how long shall my honor be turned into shame?
> How long will you love vain words and seek after lies? *Selah*
> **3** But know that the Lord has set apart the godly for himself;
> the Lord hears when I call to him.
> **4** Be angry, and do not sin;
> ponder in your own hearts on your beds and be silent. *Selah*
> **5** Offer right sacrifices,
> and put your trust in the Lord."
> (Psalm 4.1-5)

Music and praise always accompanied the offerings and sacrifices. The God to whom we pray is a righteous God who exercises justice righteously. He is also a God who knows who is acting with righteousness and who is not.

The "distress" describes in Hebrew (*tzar*) a tight, a restricted space. This is contrasted to the "relief" provided by God; a word which in Hebrew describes a large and spacious space. God is gracious: His grace or favor means receiving from God a gift, something one does not deserve or cannot purchase. Verses 3 to 5 describe righteous behavior; however, the faithful must always come to God as people who are not deserving (Psalm 13.5; 52.8; Ephesians 2.8).

Those "who seek after lies" or "falsehood" have fallen into deliberate misrepresentation of the truth. They are also those who make promises which they do not keep. "But now you must put them all away: anger, wrath, malice, slander, and obscene talk from your mouth.

> **9** Do not lie to one another, seeing that you have put off the old self with its practices **10** and have put on the new self, which is being renewed in knowledge after the image of its creator.
> (Colossians 3.8-10).

"Be angry and do not sin" is a principle mentioned by Paul in Ephesians 4.26. It is mentioned here in the context of men who are not honoring God by their behavior. Faced with anger, we must "ponder in our own hearts" and also learn the virtue of silence before God. "Be silent, all flesh, before the Lord, for he has roused himself from his holy dwelling." (Zechariah 2.13).

Offerings and sacrifices to God mean nothing when there is no knowledge of God or steadfast love towards Him. "For I desire steadfast love and not sacrifice, the knowledge of God rather than burnt offerings." (Hosea 6.6)

Let Us Come Before His Presence

Prayer

Father in heaven, we come before your throne with all our pains and disappointments. We trust in your goodness and grace. We know that you can see our very thoughts. Give us today and in the future a heart given to you, a heart full of love for you. Lead us into a better understanding of your grace. May we offer sacrifices that are pleasing to you. Amen.

Day 3

> **1** "Give ear to my words, O Lord,
> Consider my meditation.
> **2** Give heed to the voice of my cry,
> My King and my God,
> For to You I will pray.
> **3** My voice You shall hear in the morning, O Lord;
> In the morning I will direct *it* to You,
> And I will look up."
>   (Psalm 5.1-3)

> **11** "But let all those rejoice who put their trust in You;
> Let them ever shout for joy, because You defend them;
> Let those also who love Your name
> Be joyful in You.
> **12** For You, O Lord, will bless the righteous;
> With favor You will surround him as *with* a shield."
>   (Psalm 5.11,12)

Foundational to authentic "trust in the Lord" is what we nourish our thoughts with, is a disposition to think in a way that is harmonious with God's will.

"Consider my meditation" (*binah hagigi*, or the thoughts of the heart). The writer wants to be open to God discerning his very thoughts. He is aware that this part of his life is also under God's rule.

> **8** "Finally, brethren, whatever things are true, whatever
> things *are* noble, whatever things *are* just, whatever
> things *are* pure, whatever things *are* lovely, whatever things *are* of
> good report, if *there is* any virtue and if *there is* anything praise-
> worthy—meditate on these things. **9** The things which you
> learned and received and heard and saw in me, these do, and the
> God of peace will be with you." (Philippians 4.8,9)

The writer prays with hopeful anticipation (*atzapeh*, I will look up); he waits with anticipation of the Lord's intervention.

As in the letter to the Philippians, the thoughts of the one who prays need to be in harmony with the prayer uttered from the mouth.

> **6** "Be anxious for nothing, but in everything by prayer and supplication, with thanksgiving, let your requests be made known to God; **7** and the peace of God, which surpasses all understanding, will guard your hearts and minds through Christ Jesus." (Philippians 4.5).

Prayer

Our Lord in heaven, may we always look into our hearts and meditate upon our very thoughts. May we come to you for a pure heart for meditations that bring us close to you. Amen.

Day 4

> **4** "Be angry, and do not sin.
> Meditate within your heart on your bed and be still. *Selah*
> **5** Offer the sacrifices of righteousness,
> And put your trust in the Lord."
>   (Psalm 4.5)

> **11** "To what purpose *is* the multitude of your sacrifices to Me?"
> Says the Lord.
> "I have had enough of burnt offerings of rams
> And the fat of fed cattle.
> I do not delight in the blood of bulls,
> Or of lambs or goats.
> **12** "When you come to appear before Me,
> Who has required this from your hand,
> To trample My courts?
> **13** Bring no more futile sacrifices;
> Incense is an abomination to Me.
> The New Moons, the Sabbaths, and the calling of assemblies—
> I cannot endure iniquity and the sacred meeting.
> **14** Your New Moons and your appointed feasts
> My soul hates;
> They are a trouble to Me,

I am weary of bearing them.
15 When you spread out your hands,
I will hide My eyes from you;
Even though you make many prayers,
I will not hear.
Your hands are full of blood."
   (Isaiah 1.11-15)

In verse Psalms 4.5 the NKJV translation "be angry" is the verb *ragaz*, which means "to tremble". This refers to the fear of the Lord which brings "trembling", fear and awe. The very thought of sinning ("and do not sin") can be dealt with by fear of the Lord. The writer is dealing with those who practice "falsehood" against him (v.2). In order to avoid sin and especially falsehood, the believer needs to "meditate" within his heart and be still, even silent (v. 4).

We should never abandon the fear of the Lord and take sin lightly.

> **28** "Therefore, since we are receiving a kingdom which cannot be shaken, let us have grace, by which we may serve God acceptably with reverence and godly fear. **29** For our God *is* a consuming fire." (Hebrews 12.28–29).

> **13** "Their throat *is* an open tomb;
> With their tongues they have practiced deceit";
> "The poison of asps *is* under their lips";
> **14** "Whose mouth *is* full of cursing and bitterness."
> **15** "Their feet *are* swift to shed blood;
> **16** Destruction and misery *are* in their ways;
> **17** And the way of peace they have not known."
> **18** "There is no fear of God before their eyes." (Romans 3.13-18; Psalm 36.1-4)

It is possible for someone to lose the fear of God. The penitent thief told his fellow thief on the cross, "Do you not even fear God, seeing you are under the same condemnation?" (Luke 23:40).

A believer can come to the point of forgetting about God in his or her life. To the extent to which a believer refuses to respect God, he becomes more distant from the moral compass that God wants him to have.

Prayer

Our Lord you taught us to pray saying "do not lead us into temptation, but deliver us from the evil one". From the depth of our hearts, we today say these words of our Lord so that we may not sin and harden our hearts. Amen.

Day 5

> **5** "Your mercy, O Lord, *is* in the heavens;
> Your faithfulness *reaches* to the clouds.
> **6** Your righteousness *is* like the great mountains;
> Your judgments *are* a great deep;
> O Lord, you preserve man and beast.
> **7** How precious *is* Your lovingkindness, O God!
> Therefore the children of men put their trust under the shadow of Your wings.
> **8** They are abundantly satisfied with the fullness of Your house,
> And You give them drink from the river of Your pleasures.
> **9** For with You *is* the fountain of life;
> In Your light we see light."
> (Psalm 36.5-9)

In this Psalm, David addresses the moral corruption of those ("the wicked") who have "no fear of God" (v.1). This corruption contrasts with the God whose "faithfulness reaches to the clouds", whose "righteousness is like the great mountains" (vv. 5-12). The contrast is also between the "wicked" and those "who put their trust under the shadow of Your wings" (v. 7).

> **1** "An oracle within my heart concerning the transgression of the wicked:
> *There is* no fear of God before his eyes.
> **2** For he flatters himself in his own eyes,
> When he finds out his iniquity *and* when he hates.
> **3** The words of his mouth *are* wickedness and deceit;
> He has ceased to be wise *and* to do good.
> **4** He devises wickedness on his bed;
> He sets himself in a way *that is* not good;
> He does not abhor evil." (verses 1-4)

> **1** "Therefore, laying aside all malice, all deceit, hypocrisy, envy, and all evil speaking, **2** as newborn babes, desire the pure milk

of the word, that you may grow thereby, **3** if indeed you have tasted that the Lord *is* gracious." (1 Peter 2.1-3)

11 "Beloved, I beg *you* as sojourners and pilgrims, abstain from fleshly lusts which war against the soul, **12** having your conduct honorable among the Gentiles, that when they speak against you as evildoers, they may, by *your* good works which they observe, glorify God in the day of visitation." (1 Peter 2.11–12).

Prayer

Father in heaven, we look to you, who is perfectly holy and good. We know that by coming to you for wisdom and holiness, you will respond and shower upon us what we ask for. May we grow in holiness before your eyes and before the eyes of men. Amen.

Day 6

1 "I cried out to God with my voice—
To God with my voice;
And He gave ear to me.
2 In the day of my trouble I sought the Lord;
My hand was stretched out in the night without ceasing;
My soul refused to be comforted.
3 I remembered God, and was troubled;
I complained, and my spirit was overwhelmed. *Selah*
You hold my eyelids *open*;
I am so troubled that I cannot speak.
5 I have considered the days of old,
The years of ancient times.
6 I call to remembrance my song in the night;
I meditate within my heart,
And my spirit makes diligent search.
7 Will the Lord cast off forever?
And will He be favorable no more?
8 Has His mercy ceased forever?
Has *His* promise failed forevermore?
9 Has God forgotten to be gracious?
Has He in anger shut up His tender mercies? *Selah*"
    (Psalm 77.1-9).

The writer has cried out to God and testifies that God has heard him (v.1). However, the entire Psalm describes the anxiety of the writer as so troubled that he cannot speak; filled with questions about God's mercy and graciousness for which he finds no answers (vv. 7-9).

May we cry to God with all of our anxiety, our feelings of confusion? Certainly, we can — just as Job did and was not reproached for it by God. His friends gave the wrong answers. They often suggested that his hardship was the result of sin, and that it was meant for discipline and reproof. However, God declared that Job was "blameless and upright."

So, in this Psalm, a believer cries out to God for help and asks God difficult questions. This man is a true believer, not a skeptic or one who has no consideration for God's will. He has not forgotten the story of God and His people. He has not forgotten what God has done in his own life. But his heart aches for this closeness with God, which seems lost and so difficult to find.

Having said all of this, the writer first asserts that God gave ear to him (v.1). Thus, we learn that God will bless those who go through so much and have no answers to their questions. We have also a perfect example of this in the person of Jesus: "who, in the days of His flesh, when He had offered up prayers and supplications, with vehement cries and tears to Him who was able to save Him from death, and was heard because of His godly fear:

> **7** "…who, in the days of His flesh, when He had offered up prayers and supplications, with vehement cries and tears to Him who was able to save Him from death, and was heard because of His godly fear: **8** though He was a Son, *yet* He learned obedience by the things which He suffered." (Hebrews 5.7-9).

Prayer

Lord we know that you are full of mercy and grace, that you hear our please as we go through grief, through pain or loneliness. We thank you for your Word, which reminds us of how you have been faithful to those who are faithful to you. Strengthen our faith even as we are going through so much hardship, and forgive us of any sin we may have committed. Amen.

Day 7

1 "Why do you boast in evil, O mighty man?
The goodness of God *endures* continually.

> **2** Your tongue devises destruction,
> Like a sharp razor, working deceitfully.
> **3** You love evil more than good,
> Lying rather than speaking righteousness. *Selah*
> **4** You love all devouring words,
> *You* deceitful tongue."
> (Psalm 52.1-4)

What should we do when we have been betrayed by corrupt or wicked people? When their words have hurt our ruined our reputation? When they have brought shame on our community or family?

The Word of God reveals to us clearly that evil people exist. These are not just regular sinners (since all have sinned!). They are the kind of people mentioned in the Bible who actually enjoy hurting others, who crave for deceit. They are those who have forsaken all fear of God and have forgotten God's coming judgment. In this category is a warning to those who have accumulated wealth and trust in the abundance of their riches (v.7).

The wicked man is like an uprooted tree which will be burned up (see also Psalm 1). The one faithful to God and who suffers at the hands of the wicked is like a green-foliage olive tree (Jeremiah 11.16). He is planted in the "house of Elohim", thus in a place that is sacred and inaccessible to the wicked (see Isaiah 60.13).

As we are mistreated by some, we should never forget that we are "in God's house" and thus in a special way protected from the evil around us. The Church should be to us the "presence of the saints" which brings comfort to our souls.

> **34** "A new commandment I give to you, that you love one another; as I have loved you, that you also love one another. **35** By this all will know that you are My disciples, if you have love for one another." (John 13.34–35)

Prayer

Our Father in heaven, we know that evil exists in this world. We pray for discernment and for wisdom. May we better understand what it means to be in your house, in the assembly of the saints. May we not lose sight of your protection as we remain faithful to you. Amen.

Week 8: God's People

Day 1

> 1 "Make a joyful shout to the Lord, all you lands!
> 2 Serve the Lord with gladness;
> Come before His presence with singing.
> 3 Know that the Lord, He *is* God;
> *It is* He *who* has made us, and not we ourselves;
> *We are* His people and the sheep of His pasture.
> 4 Enter into His gates with thanksgiving,
> *And* into His courts with praise.
> Be thankful to Him *and* bless His name.
> 5 For the Lord *is* good;
> His mercy *is* everlasting,
> And His truth *endures* to all generations."
> (Psalm 100.1-5)

The Lord who is in covenant with His people is also the Lord of all lands, of all peoples. The writer is not praising a local "god" limited by time and space, as are the false gods. He is praising the God "who made us", whose mercy is "everlasting" and whose truth "endures to all generations".

God's people are his "sheep". He is the good shepherd who comes to lead His people since human beings have failed Him in regard to this. **11** 'For thus says the Lord God: "Indeed I Myself will search for My sheep and seek them out." (Ezekiel 34.11). Jesus' reference to the "good shepherd" points to the prophecy of Ezekiel chapter 34 (see John 10).

Thankfulness should be the essence of who we are as God's people: "Be thankful to Him and bless His name". "Thanks be to God, who always leads us in triumphal procession in Christ and through us spreads everywhere the fragrance of the knowledge of him." (2 Corinthians 2.14). "Therefore, since we are receiving a kingdom that cannot be shaken, let us be thankful, and so worship God acceptably with reverence and awe." (Hebrews 12.28). Peter encourages Christians to remain thankful even in "grief and all kinds of trials," saying that, through the hardships, our faith "may be proved genuine and may result in praise, glory and honor when Jesus Christ is revealed" 1 Peter 1.6,7).

Prayer

Our Father in heaven, we want to thank you for a new day. Renew our faith, hope, and love, which are all gifts from you. We want to listen to your voice as the sheep listen to the Good Shepherd. We pray that your Word of comfort will fill our hearts with gratitude this day. Amen.

Day 2

> **1** "When Israel went out of Egypt,
> The house of Jacob from a people of strange language,
> **2** Judah became His sanctuary,
> *And* Israel His dominion."
>   (Psalm 114.1,2)

Through God's miraculous deliverance and guidance of His people, the Lord demonstrated his power and called the earth to fear His name:

> **7** "Tremble, O earth, at the presence of the Lord, at the presence of the God of Jacob,**8** Who turned the rock *into* a pool of water, the flint into a fountain of waters." (vv. 7,8).

God called His people out of Egypt so that they would become "His sanctuary" — the place where He would be worshipped. More important even than the "tabernacle" and later the "temple" was the people themselves who were called to be God's sanctuary.

This is also the case for the Church. The language of "temple" is used in the New Testament, but as in this Psalm, the concern is with the people and not a building. Paul wrote to the Corinthians, saying:

> **18** "Flee sexual immorality. Every sin that a man does is outside the body, but he who commits sexual immorality sins against his own body. **19** Or do you not know that your body is the temple of the Holy Spirit *who is* in you, whom you have from God, and you are not your own? **20** For you were bought at a price; therefore, glorify God in your body and in your spirit, which are God's." (1 Corinthians 6.18-20).

The Greek pronoun translated "you" in English is a plural in Greek, meaning "you all": the Church in Corinth as a community should see herself as the "temple" of God.

This "temple of God" is alive and moving about. It is built with living stones and reaches all over the earth:

4 "Coming to Him *as to* a living stone, rejected indeed by men, but chosen by God *and* precious, **5** you also, as living stones, are being built up a spiritual house, a holy priesthood, to offer up spiritual sacrifices acceptable to God through Jesus Christ." (1 Peter 2.4,5).

Prayer

Father in heaven, we pray for wisdom as we live a new day of service to you. We pray that we will be faithful to you as part of your people, your Church. Keep us pure in our thoughts and in our ways, and deliver us from all evil. We pray in the name of our Lord Jesus. Amen.

Day 3

1 "O God, the nations have come into Your inheritance;
Your holy temple they have defiled;
They have laid Jerusalem in heaps.
2 The dead bodies of Your servants
They have given *as* food for the birds of the heavens,
The flesh of Your saints to the beasts of the earth.
3 Their blood they have shed like water all around Jerusalem,
And *there was* no one to bury *them.*
4 We have become a reproach to our neighbors,
A scorn and derision to those who are around us."
   (Psalms 79)

This Psalm is a prayer to God at a time when Jerusalem is a destroyed city. The temple has been trampled by enemies from other nations who are worshipping false gods and idols. These enemies scorn God's people ; they think Israel has come to her end and will never recover from her pains.

These enemies also scorn the God of Israel, saying, "Where is their God?" (v.10). When calamities fall on God's people the question is immediately about God who apparently has not intervened, has not acted on behalf of His people.

The words of this Psalm remind us of the words quoted by Jesus on the cross from Psalm 22:

1 "My God, My God, why have You forsaken Me?
Why are You so far from helping Me,
And from the words of My groaning?

2 O My God, I cry in the daytime, but You do not hear;
And in the night season I am not silent." (Psalm 22.1,2).

These are strong words and might give the impression that the Lord is now doubting his God. Of course, the remaining words of Psalm 22 teach exactly the opposite, that the Lord on the cross is fully trusting His God.

The question "why?" is expressed in this Psalm as it is in so many other places in the Bible, "Why should the nations say, 'Where is their God?' (v.10). As in the question quoted by Jesus on the cross, this "why?" question does not receive a clear response.

The "why" question of suffering is found throughout Job. One could answer that Satan was the main culprit (Job chapter 1). But one could respond with another question starting with "why?" like for example "Why would Satan even exist in a universe created and governed by a loving and all-powerful God?"

All these "why?" questions if they do not provide immediately clear and satisfying answers teach us at least two things: 1. God understands our questions and does not condemn us for asking and seeking answers. 2. Our answers may not be at all the right answers (as in the case of Job's friends).

So, when our friends or neighbors are going through horrendous pain, when they ask us the question "why?" it is not our duty to give clear-cut answers despite the fact that it is tempting to try and do so. And we are reminded in the story of Job that his friends did more damage trying to answer questions God had not given them answers to.

In this Psalm, we find the writer invoking the greatness of God's power, which can free the prisoner and preserve those who are appointed to die (vv. 11). Biblical faith is not a faith that depends on having all the answers to our questions. However, it is a faith that is maintained through our best and worst days,

> **11** "Not that I speak in regard to need, for I have learned in whatever state I am, to be content: **12** I know how to be abased, and I know how to abound. Everywhere, and in all things, I have learned both to be full and to be hungry, both to abound and to suffer need. **13** I can do all things through Christ who strengthens me." (Philippians 4.11-13).

"I can do all things" does not mean "I can do all things I want or wish". It means I am even able to go through hardship or lack of it and still maintain my trust in God while remaining grateful and obedient. It is the trust we find in Psalm 79, the book of Job and so many other Scriptures. It is the trust of martyrs throughout the ages, even to this day.

Prayer

Our Father, we pray for your people worldwide. We pray that your Spirit may be poured out in abundance on all of your people and even on this world. A Spirit of joy, love and peace. Give us wisdom, Lord, as we meet today those who are in great pain and are asking us many questions. May we respond with the compassionate response of love. May we respond with the deeds of love. Amen.

Day 4

1 "Oh, give thanks to the Lord, for *He is* good!
For His mercy *endures* forever.
2 Who can utter the mighty acts of the Lord?
Who can declare all His praise?
3 Blessed *are* those who keep justice,
And he who does righteousness at all times!
4 Remember me, O Lord, with the favor *You have toward* Your people.
Oh, visit me with Your salvation,
5 That I may see the benefit of Your chosen ones,
That I may rejoice in the gladness of Your nation,
That I may glory with Your inheritance."
  (Psalm 106.1-5)

47 Save us, O Lord our God,
And gather us from among the Gentiles,
To give thanks to Your holy name,
To triumph in Your praise.
48 Blessed *be* the Lord God of Israel
From everlasting to everlasting!
And let all the people say, "Amen!"
Praise the Lord!"
  (Psalm 106.47,48).

This Psalm pronounces blessings on those who keep justice and who do righteousness all the time (v.3). This is an amazing promise, which contrasts with the parts of the Psalm describing the unfaithfulness of God's people in so many instances: "They soon forgot His works; they did not wait for his counsel." (v.13).

In relationship to the past, they forgot; in relationship to the present and future, "they did not wait for his counsel". The expression "not waiting for his counsel" is directly linked to the sin of "lust": "But lusted exceedingly in the desert". This "lust" had to do with food and drink; it also had to do with envy for Moses' position and with falling into idol worship (vv. 14-20).

If they had not forgotten what God had done, they would not have fallen into "lust". Why did they forget? When God has provided temporal and material success or even prosperity, that is a time when believers need to persevere in the worship of God and the meditation and study of His Word.

In prosperity as in great need, we need to remain steadfast in our worship and obedience to God. We need to remind ourselves of these words:

"Blessed *are* those who keep justice,
And he who does righteousness at all times!" (v.3).

31 "Therefore, do not worry, saying, 'What shall we eat?' or 'What shall we drink?' or 'What shall we wear?' **32** For after all these things the Gentiles seek. For your heavenly Father knows that you need all these things. **33** But seek first the kingdom of God and His righteousness, and all these things shall be added to you. **34** Therefore do not worry about tomorrow, for tomorrow will worry about its own things. Sufficient for the day *is* its own trouble." (Matthew 6.32-34).

Prayer

Father in heaven, we give thanks to you for your goodness and mercy. Today, we will seek your kingdom and righteousness in everything we do. Today, we will remember your faithfulness to those who are faithful to you. We will wait upon you as we find ourselves in difficult situations. Give us today our daily bread. Deliver us from evil and lead us not into temptation. Amen.

Day 5

1 "Bow down Your ear, O Lord, hear me;
For I *am* poor and needy.
2 Preserve my life, for I *am* holy;
You are my God;

Save Your servant who trusts in You!
3 Be merciful to me, O Lord,
For I cry to You all day long.
4 Rejoice the soul of Your servant,
For to You, O Lord, I lift up my soul.
5 For You, Lord, *are* good, and ready to forgive,
And abundant in mercy to all those who call upon You.
6 Give ear, O Lord, to my prayer;
And attend to the voice of my supplications.
7 In the day of my trouble I will call upon You,
For You will answer me."
   (Psalm 86.1-5)

Psalm 86 is the prayer of the poor and needy, but also the prayer of the righteous one.

To say that "all have sinned and fallen short of the glory of God" (Romans 3.23) does not mean righteous people cannot be found. The universal condition of sin which has fallen on every human being does not mean we should not recognize and thank God for manifestations of goodness and righteousness we can see around us or even in our own lives. The utter moral corruption of every single human being, the absence of any goodness or righteousness, is not what God wants to teach us in His Word. Zacharias and Elizabeth, the parents of John the Baptist were "both righteous before the Lord" (Luke 1.6). Paul the apostle even recognized righteous behavior in some of the Gentiles who did not have the law, but:

> **14** "for when Gentiles, who do not have the law, by nature do the things in the law, these, although not having the law, are a law to themselves, **15** who show the work of the law written in their hearts, their conscience also bearing witness, and between themselves *their* thoughts accusing or else excusing *them* **16** in the day when God will judge the secrets of men by Jesus Christ, according to my gospel." (Romans 2.14-16).

> Cornelius the centurion was known as "a devout man, one who feared God with all his household, who gave alms generously to the people, and prayed to God always." (Acts 10.2).

This goodness and righteousness found in countless individuals is not something anybody can boast about. As in every blessing enjoyed by human beings — whether spiritual or material in nature — that blessing comes from the same source, which is God himself. There is no good deed done by anyone — believer or non-believer— that is merely the product of the human heart. It is the gift of God to humanity.

So, as we encounter goodness and righteousness in our neighbors or anybody else — believer or non-believer— let us be grateful for this gift from God and let us not discourage anyone from persisting in doing what is right. And if we feel that would undermine their understanding of their need of salvation, we need to review our understanding of what Scripture means by the statement that "all have sinned and fallen short of the glory of God".

This righteous one who prays is not so righteous that he cannot ask God to teach him His ways (v.11). He is not so righteous that he cannot ask for mercy (v.16).

As we walk in trust and righteousness, let us thank God for His good work in our lives. In order to do this, we don't need to be like the Pharisee of the parable who compared himself to others:

> **11** "The Pharisee stood and prayed thus with himself, 'God, I thank You that I am not like other men—extortioners, unjust, adulterers, or even as this tax collector. **12** I fast twice a week; I give tithes of all that I possess.'" (Luke 18.11,12).

Prayer

We thank you, God, for the work you accomplish daily in our lives. We thank you for sanctifying us, comforting us, correcting us, teaching us and sanctifying us. We are open Lord to your teachings. Change our hearts today and every day through your Holy Spirit. Our prayer is in the name of Jesus. Amen.

Day 6

> **8** "Among the gods *there is* none like You, O Lord;
> Nor *are there any works* like Your works.
> **9** All nations whom You have made
> Shall come and worship before You, O Lord,
> And shall glorify Your name.
> **10** For You *are* great, and do wondrous things;
> You alone *are* God."
>   (Psalms 86.8-10)

In the Scriptures, there is a deep connection between God's plans for Israel and His plans for all the nations. God wants to bring all nations to a knowledge of himself. He promised Abraham that through his posterity all peoples of the earth would be blessed (Genesis 12.1-13). Jesus reminded the Samaritan woman that "You worship what you do not know; we know what we worship, for salvation is of the Jews." He promised her that "whoever drinks of the water that I shall give him shall never thirst" (John 4.22, 14).

The water that Jesus gives freely to all is the gift of the Holy Spirit and is to be received by faith:

> "**37** On the last day, that great *day* of the feast, Jesus stood and cried out, saying, "If anyone thirsts, let him come to Me and drink. **38** He who believes in Me, as the Scripture has said, out of his heart will flow rivers of living water." **39** But this He spoke concerning the Spirit, whom those believing in Him would receive; for the Holy Spirit was not yet *given,* because Jesus was not yet glorified." (John 7.37-39)

> **37** "Now when they heard *this,* they were cut to the heart, and said to Peter and the rest of the apostles, "Men *and* brethren, what shall we do?" **38** Then Peter said to them, "Repent, and let every one of you be baptized in the name of Jesus Christ for the remission of sins; and you shall receive the gift of the Holy Spirit. **39** For the promise is to you and to your children, and to all who are afar off, as many as the Lord our God will call." (Acts 2.37, 38).

> **8** "Now, when He had taken the scroll, the four living creatures and the twenty-four elders fell down before the Lamb, each having a harp, and golden bowls full of incense, which are the prayers of the saints. **9** And they sang a new song, saying:
> "You are worthy to take the scroll,
> And to open its seals;
> For You were slain,
> And have redeemed us to God by Your blood
> Out of every tribe and tongue and people and nation,
> **10** And have made us kings and priests to our God;
> And we shall reign on the earth." (Revelation 5.8-10)

Prayer

Father in heaven, we pray for all the nations, for men and women of all races and nationalities. We pray that the Good News may reach every corner of the earth and that your Holy Spirit might be given to all who trust in the work of Jesus on the cross, repent and come to you with a grateful heart. Amen.

Day 7

> **6** "Oh come, let us worship and bow down;
> Let us kneel before the Lord our Maker.
> **7** For He *is* our God,
> And we *are* the people of His pasture,
> And the sheep of His hand.
> Today, if you will hear His voice:
> **8** 'Do not harden your hearts, as in the rebellion,
> As *in* the day of trial in the wilderness,
> **9** When your fathers tested Me;
> They tried Me, though they saw My work.'"
>   (Psalms 95. 6-8)

The "bowing down" and "kneeling" before our Maker describe humility and reverence in the face of God's greatness and holiness. There is a connection between worship and preserving our hearts, so they do not become hardened through sin.

There is no true worship of the Lord without humility before him. Humble worship leads and transforms the heart and mind into greater holiness (Romans 12.1-3). The worship mentioned here is not solitary and individual; it is the worship of the community: "Let us worship and bow down". The warning not to be hardened of heart is given to the entire community, just as in Hebrews 3 where this Psalm is quoted. This is why the writer to the Hebrews encourages the disciples to "exhort one another daily" (Hebrews 3.13).

> **40** "And with many other words he testified and exhorted them, saying, "Be saved from this perverse generation." **41** Then those who gladly received his word were baptized; and that day about three thousand souls were added *to them*. **42** And they continued steadfastly in the apostles' doctrine and fellowship, in the breaking of bread, and in prayers." (Acts 2.37,38).

> **23** "Let us hold fast the confession of *our* hope without wavering, for He who promised *is* faithful. **24** And let us consider one

another in order to stir up love and good works, **25** not forsaking the assembling of ourselves together, as *is* the manner of some, but exhorting *one another*, and so much the more as you see the Day approaching. **26** For if we sin willfully after we have received the knowledge of the truth, there no longer remains a sacrifice for sins, **27** but a certain fearful expectation of judgment, and fiery indignation which will devour the adversaries." (Hebrews 10.24-27)

Prayer

Father, we thank you for your people, for the faithful throughout the ages. We thank you for brothers and sisters, for evangelist, elders and teachers. We pray you will give strength to those who minister by teaching and preaching your Word. Bless them, Lord, and sanctify their hearts as well as our hearts. Amen.

Week 9: Nations

Day 1

> **27** "All the ends of the world
> Shall remember and turn to the Lord,
> And all the families of the nations
> Shall worship before You.
> **28** For the kingdom *is* the Lord's,
> And He rules over the nations."
> (Psalms 22.27,28)

In an extraordinary way, this Psalm of David describes in great detail the passion of the Christ introduced by the famous words "My God, My God, why have You forsaken Me?" (v.1 and Matthew 27.46). This first verse of the Psalm introduces the description of His sufferings as they actually occurred. Those who blasphemed and those who shook their head at Him as they passed by His cross (Matthew 27:39; Psalms 22:8). Scoffers cried out to Him, "Let the God in whom He trusts help Him" (Matthew 27:43; Psalms 22:9). His garments were divided, and lots were cast for His coat (John 19:23; Psalms 22:19).

In His sufferings, the Christ remains steadfast in His trust in the LORD. The Psalm looks forward to the blessings brought about through His sufferings and concludes with these words of blessing:

> "**30** A posterity shall serve Him. It will be recounted of the Lord to the *next* generation, **31** They will come and declare His righteousness to a people who will be born, that He has done *this*."
> (vv. 30, 31).

Jesus announced that "When I am lifted up from the earth, I will draw all men to myself." (John 12.32). Today, His name is glorified all over the earth by people of all nations and tongues.

Prayer

Father in heaven, we pray that you will bless the nations with your Good News. We pray that you will send your Spirit of love into the hearts of all peoples. May we proclaim to all nations your message of salvation with truth, compassion and love. Amen.

Day 2

> **9** "I will praise You, O Lord, among the peoples;
> I will sing to You among the nations.
> **10** For Your mercy reaches unto the heavens,
> And Your truth unto the clouds.
> **11** Be exalted, O God, above the heavens;
> *Let* Your glory *be* above all the earth."
> (Psalms 57. 9-11)

This Psalm runs from "great calamities" (v.1), "They have prepared a net for my soul; they have dug a pit before me" (v.6) to "My heart is steadfast, I will sing and give praise" (v.7) and reaches its climax in verses 9-11 which describe mercy poured on all the nations and reaching even "unto the heavens". Thus, it is similar to the theme of Psalm 22.

The universality of God's mercy offered to "all nations" is clear here, as in so many other passages of the Old Testament and especially the Psalms.

God is the creator of all peoples and every single human being (Psalms 24.1,2). God's good news is to be proclaimed to all nations (Matthew 28.16-20). Followers of Jesus must be prepared to give an answer to "everyone who asks about their hope" (1 Peter 3.15,16).

This universality of God's plan of redemption is not a way for "Gentiles" to boast over Israel or worse to mistreat the descendants of Abraham, Isaac and Jacob. Israel still has a special place in God's heart:

> **11** "I say then, have they stumbled that they should fall? Certainly not! But through their fall, to provoke them to jealousy, salvation *has come* to the Gentiles. **12** Now if their fall *is* riches for the world, and their failure riches for the Gentiles, how much more their fullness!" (Romans 11.11).

The change of heart and repentance of Gentiles would bring the people of Israel to the "fullness" of God's plan for them, which is salvation in the Lord Jesus Christ.

Romans chapter 11 emphasizes God's good plan for the people of Israel so that His mercy may be applied to them. Gentiles are not to "boast" or be "haughty" in their new standing before God. They are like the "wild olive tree" which has been grafted to the "the cultivated olive tree" (Israel). Thus, the apostle continues by saying:

> **25** "For I do not desire, brethren, that you should be ignorant of this mystery, lest you should be wise in your own opinion, that blindness in part has happened to Israel until the fullness of the Gentiles has come in. **26** And so all Israel will be saved, as it is written: 'The Deliverer will come out of Zion, and He will turn away ungodliness from Jacob; **27** For this *is* My covenant with them, when I take away their sins.'" (quote from Isaiah 59.20, 21).

This has been interpreted in a "historical way" as meaning that there will come a time when all the Israelites, descendants of Abraham, will come to repentance and salvation. But this could also mean that God's blessings for Israel are always available through the Gospel and through repentance (as for example in Acts 3.18-26).

> "**18** But those things which God foretold by the mouth of all His prophets, that the Christ would suffer, He has thus fulfilled. **19** Repent therefore and be converted, that your sins may be blotted out, so that times of refreshing may come from the presence of the Lord, **20** and that He may send Jesus Christ, who was preached to you before, **21** whom heaven must receive until the times of restoration of all things, which God has spoken by the mouth of all His holy prophets since the world began." (Acts 3.18-21)

> **25** "You are sons of the prophets, and of the covenant which God made with our fathers, saying to Abraham, 'And in your seed all the families of the earth shall be blessed.' **26** To you first, God, having raised up His Servant Jesus, sent Him to bless you, in turning away every one *of you* from your iniquities." (Acts 3.25,26)

Prayer

Lord in heaven, we pray for Israel, for the descendants of Abraham. We pray that we might understand your loving plan of redemption for all peoples, all nations. We pray that you will give us wisdom to know how to proclaim your Good News to the world. Amen.

Day 3

> **6** "Your throne, O God, *is* forever and ever;
> A scepter of righteousness *is* the scepter of Your kingdom.
> **7** You love righteousness and hate wickedness;
> Therefore God, Your God, has anointed You
> With the oil of gladness more than Your companions."
>   (Psalms 45.6,7)

These verses are quoted in Hebrew 1 as applied to Jesus the Christ. This Psalm also refers to the Messiah (Christ) as one "fairer than the sons of men" (v. 2). A tradition of the ancient synagogue, in accordance with the Targumist, renders Psalms 45:2, *"Thy beauty, O King Messiah, is greater than that of the children of men."* The glory, majesty and power of the "anointed" is the central message of this Psalm.

In Psalm 44.4 the king who is full of majesty is God (Elohim): "You are my king, O God". In Judaism, identifying the person addressed in Psalm 45 has been a matter of controversy. Thus, Psalm 44 exalts Elohim as the glorious king and Psalm 45 exalts in similar terms the glorious king who is the coming Messiah.

The manifestation of God in the flesh is at the heart of the Gospel message,

> "God was manifested in the flesh,
> Justified in the Spirit,
> Seen by angels,
> Preached among the Gentiles,
> Believed on in the world,
> Received up in glory." (1 Timothy 3.16)

The anointed one of Psalm 45 is not only "fairer than the sons of men" and majestic, he loves righteousness and hates wickedness. Love of righteousness and hatred of wickedness is also an attribute of God in Psalms 5.5 and 61.8.

Prayer

We thank you, Lord of heaven and earth, for your anointed Son, for the savior of the world. We thank you for the perfect life of Jesus, who is now at your right hand and will return as He promised. We pray that you will teach us today to love righteousness. Amen.

Day 4

> **6** "Sing praises to God, sing praises!
> Sing praises to our King, sing praises!
> **7** For God *is* the King of all the earth;
> Sing praises with understanding.
> **8** God reigns over the nations;
> God sits on His holy throne.
> **9** The princes of the people have gathered together,
> The people of the God of Abraham.
> For the shields of the earth *belong* to God;
> He is greatly exalted."
> (Psalms 47.6-9)

This Psalm reminds us that the LORD (Yahweh) is king over all the nations. God's rule is not determined by race, nationality or borders. The biblical vision is that all nations without exception are under God's rule. Thus, the message of the Gospel is also about the reign and authority of the one who said, "All authority has been given to me in heaven and on earth" (Matthew 28.18). This authority of the anointed one is also announced in the first Gospel sermon preached by Peter, "Therefore let all the house of Israel know assuredly that God has made this Jesus, whom you crucified, both Lord and Christ." (Acts 2.36).

This Psalm describes a battle between God and the nations:

> **3** "He will subdue the peoples under us, And the nations under our feet.
> **4** He will choose our inheritance for us,
> The excellence of Jacob whom He loves. *Selah*" (vv. 3,4)

The great opposition Israel experienced in her history from surrounding nations provides the background for the past, present and especially future of God's reign. God's reign is the foundation of our hope as we battle spiritual dominions and powers (Ephesians 6.12).

"Then the seventh angel sounded: And there were loud voices in heaven, saying, 'The kingdoms of this world have become *the kingdoms* of our Lord and of His Christ, and He shall reign forever and ever!'" (Revelation 11.15).

Prayer

Father in heaven, on this new day you have given us to live on this earth, we shout with the voice of triumph and declare your reign of love and righteousness over us and over all nations. We pray for deliverance from evil and for renewal of our hearts and minds through your Holy Spirit. Amen.

Day 5

> **4** "Oh, let the nations be glad and sing for joy!
> For You shall judge the people righteously,
> And govern the nations on earth. *Selah*
> **5** Let the peoples praise You, O God;
> Let all the peoples praise You."
>   (Psalms 67.4,5)

This Psalm and a good part of the Old Testament look forward to a time when all nations will turn to God and worship Him. The promises made to Abraham included blessings for all the nations through Abraham's seed (Genesis 12.1-3). Isaiah's prophecies often describe Israel as a source of blessing for all nations. Jesus is the faithful servant of Isaiah, whose sufferings bring healing and hope to all nations (see also Acts 8.30-40).

The Psalm reminds us that the proper praise and worship of God is always an incalculable benefit, even to people's temporal needs. Under such a state, nations enjoy true fertility and productiveness, which they sought through their pagan gods,

> **6** "*Then* the earth shall yield her increase; God, our own God,
> shall bless us. **7** God shall bless us, and all the ends of the earth
> shall fear Him." (vv. 6,7).

God's rule is a rule of perfect righteousness, "You shall judge the people righteously and govern the nations on earth." The perfectly righteous God has revealed to us how we should live and treat each other so that we would imitate him.

43 "You have heard that it was said, 'You shall love your neighbor and hate your enemy.' 44 But I say to you, love your enemies, bless those who curse you, do good to those who hate you, and pray for those who spitefully use you and persecute you, 45 that you may be sons of your Father in heaven; for He makes His sun rise on the evil and on the good, and sends rain on the just and on the unjust. 46 For if you love those who love you, what reward have you? Do not even the tax collectors do the same? 47 And if you greet your brethren only, what do you do more *than others*? Do not even the tax collectors do so? 48 Therefore you shall be perfect, just as your Father in heaven is perfect." (Matthew 5.43-48)

Prayer

Father, we ask for wisdom as we read and study your Word. Today we want to learn from your righteousness, your goodness and holiness. We want to change our ways and grow up in the knowledge of your righteousness. Thank you for your Holy Spirit, who helps us in our daily walk. Amen.

Day 6

4 "I will make mention of Rahab and Babylon to those who know Me;
Behold, O Philistia and Tyre, with Ethiopia:
'This *one* was born there.'"
5 And of Zion it will be said,
"This *one* and that *one* were born in her;
And the Most High Himself shall establish her."
6 The Lord will record,
When He registers the peoples:
"This *one* was born there." *Selah*
7 Both the singers and the players on instruments *say*,
"All my springs *are* in you."
 (Psalms 87.4,5)

This Psalm is in line with the repeated promises of God first made to Abraham that He would bless all the nations of the earth. God wants all peoples to be saved.

1 "Therefore, I exhort first of all that supplications, prayers, intercessions, *and* giving of thanks be made for all men, 2 for kings

and all who are in authority, that we may lead a quiet and peaceable life in all godliness and reverence. **3** For this *is* good and acceptable in the sight of God our Savior, **4** who desires all men to be saved and to come to the knowledge of the truth. **5** For *there is* one God and one Mediator between God and men, *the* Man Christ Jesus, **6** who gave Himself a ransom for all, to be testified in due time, **7** for which I was appointed a preacher and an apostle—I am speaking the truth in Christ *and* not lying—a teacher of the Gentiles in faith and truth." (1 Timothy 2.1-7; see Romans 9.24-26).

The Psalm also underscores the benefits of having been born in a land where true faith prevails; of having been taught biblical truth even from birth. This idea is brought out when the Psalm mentions places like Babylon, Philistia or Tyr as now places where it would be a privilege to be born: "This one was born there… This one and that one were born in her…This one was born there" (vv. 4.5.6).

No matter where one is born, no matter one's race or nationality, our God loves all mankind and wants all men to come to a knowledge of the truth (1 Timothy 2.4).

> **19** "Go therefore and make disciples of all the nations, baptizing them in the name of the Father and of the Son and of the Holy Spirit, **20** teaching them to observe all things that I have commanded you; and lo, I am with you always, *even* to the end of the age." Amen. (Matthew 28.19,20).

Prayer

Lord, we thank you for loving us in our weaknesses and ignorance. We thank you that your blessings are offered freely and graciously. Today we ask for grateful hearts expressed in grateful living through your Holy Spirit. Amen.

Day 7

> **1** "The Lord reigns;
> Let the peoples tremble!
> He dwells *between* the cherubim;
> Let the earth be moved!
> **2** The Lord *is* great in Zion,
> And He *is* high above all the peoples.

3 Let them praise Your great and awesome name—
He *is* holy."
(Psalms 99.1-3)

"Let the people tremble!" Fear ("tremble" in Hebrews or awe, reverence) is essential when we approach God and even to gain any kind of wisdom for this life: "The fear of the Lord *is* the beginning of wisdom and the knowledge of the Holy One *is* understanding. (Proverbs 9.10)

Through the history of Israel, God has demonstrated to all peoples that he should be feared. He has shown himself great "in Zion" — in his manifestations toward his own people. He has exercised power on behalf of His people. He has been there for them in times of danger and has vanquished Israel's enemies.

God was with his servants such as Moses, Aaron and Samuel who "called upon His name'"; "They called upon the LORD and he answered them." (vv. 6). These men kept God's testimonies revealed in His Word, but He also at times "took vengeance on their deeds" (vv.7,8).

The history of Israel and men and women of faith is undergirded by the LORD'S love of justice and equity (v.4). It is not a history of "favoritism" towards one as opposed to another, towards one nation (Israel) as opposed to other nations. God's choice of Israel is a choice which underscores his graciousness, but it does not mean "favoritism" on God's part in how He judges individuals and nations.

Prayer

We thank you, Father in heaven, for your perfect righteousness. We pray that today we can grow in righteous behavior towards everyone we encounter. We know that we always have to keep learning and growing up, and we thank you for your patience towards us. Amen.

Week 10: Parents

Day 1

> **3** "Behold, children *are* a heritage from the Lord,
> The fruit of the womb *is* a reward.
> **4** Like arrows in the hand of a warrior,
> So *are* the children of one's youth.
> **5** Happy *is* the man who has his quiver full of them;
> They shall not be ashamed,
> But shall speak with their enemies in the gate."
> (Psalms 127.3-5)

In Israel to have children was considered one of the greatest blessings from God : **12** "Then it shall come to pass, because you listen to these judgments, and keep and do them, that the Lord your God will keep with you the covenant and the mercy which He swore to your fathers. **13** And He will love you and bless you and multiply you; He will also bless the fruit of your womb and the fruit of your land, your grain and your new wine and your oil, the increase of your cattle and the offspring of your flock, in the land of which He swore to your fathers to give you." (Deuteronomy 7.12,13).

Rachel was greatly upset not to be able to have children and said to Jacob: "Give me children, or else I die!" (Genesis 30.2).

Children are a "heritage" (v.3) — an inheritance not according to hereditary right, but in accordance with the free-will of the giver; parents are "given" children as a free and undeserved gift from God.

In the days when Israel was threatened by neighboring peoples, the sword was carried side by side with the trowel. It was not sufficient then to have arrows in the quiver; one was obligated to have them not merely at hand, but in the hand in order to be able to defend one's self.

In the battles we face in life ("like arrows in the hand of a warrior") children are a source of strength for parents as they might face evil enemies.

Parents who have raised children strong in their faith and ready for the "spiritual battle" they encounter daily are truly blessed by God: "Finally, my brethren, be strong in the Lord and in the power of His might.

11 Put on the whole armor of God, that you may be able to stand against the wiles of the devil. **12** For we do not wrestle against flesh and blood, but against principalities, against powers, against the rulers of the darkness of this age, against spiritual *hosts* of wickedness in the heavenly *places*." (Ephesians 6.10-12).

Prayer

Father in heaven, we thank you for children who are a great gift from you. We pray for our friends and neighbors who miss having their own children. We pray that you will bless them with this precious gift. We thank you that we ourselves are "adopted" into your family by your grace. May we look upon children we encounter as precious gifts you have given to all of us and treat them as highly precious in your sight. Amen.

Day 2

1 "Give ear, O my people, *to* my law;
Incline your ears to the words of my mouth.
2 I will open my mouth in a parable;
I will utter dark sayings of old,
3 Which we have heard and known,
And our fathers have told us.
4 We will not hide *them* from their children,
Telling to the generation to come the praises of the Lord,
And His strength and His wonderful works that He has done."
   (Psalms 78.1-4)

God wants people to hear His teachings. He wants people to know about His past deeds and His present will. We are blessed when we have had parents who have taught us the ways of the LORD.

God has given to parents the solemn responsibility to tell their children "the praises of the LORD, His strength and His wonderful works."

It is only when parents have taught their children that they are in a position to "set their hope in God":

5 "For He established a testimony in Jacob,
And appointed a law in Israel,
Which He commanded our fathers,
That they should make them known to their children;
6 That the generation to come might know *them*,

The children *who* would be born,
That they may arise and declare *them* to their children,
7 That they may set their hope in God,
And not forget the works of God,
But keep His commandments;" (Psalms 78.5-7)

This Psalm also mentions an entire generation that turned away from God in unbelief, and the consequences of their unfaithfulness:

17 "But they sinned even more against Him
By rebelling against the Most High in the wilderness.
18 And they tested God in their heart
By asking for the food of their fancy.
19 Yes, they spoke against God:
They said, 'Can God prepare a table in the wilderness?'" (Psalms 78.17-19)

Prayer

Father in heaven, we pray for wisdom and perseverance as we do our best to teach our children your will. Inspire us with the right words. May we be faithful day by day to your will and confess to you our sins. Give us the ability to teach our children in a way that will touch their hearts and strengthen their faith. This is our prayer in the name of our Lord Jesus. Amen.

Day 3

56 "Yet they tested and provoked the Most High God,
And did not keep His testimonies,
57 But turned back and acted unfaithfully like their fathers;
They were turned aside like a deceitful bow.
58 For they provoked Him to anger with their high places,
And moved Him to jealousy with their carved images.
59 When God heard *this*, He was furious,
And greatly abhorred Israel,
60 So that He forsook the tabernacle of Shiloh,
The tent He had placed among men,
61 And delivered His strength into captivity,
And His glory into the enemy's hand."
   (Psalms 78.56-61)

Psalm 78 mentions a generation that "acted unfaithfully like their fathers". What makes an entire generation rebellious towards the LORD? Psalm 78 tells the story of two generations. First, the Psalm mentions the generation that came out of Egypt. This generation murmured against God. They had been delivered from Egypt, but were never satisfied (vv. 40-42). When a generation is blessed by the LORD, it should be careful not to become complacent because of these blessings. The second generation mentioned in this Psalm is the generation which entered into the land and also became complacent because of God's blessings in the land. Like their fathers, the tribes of Joseph and Ephraim became disloyal and fell into idolatry (vv. 67). However, God chose Judah and David His servant to be the "shepherd of His people" (vv. 68-72). David is also a figure of the Messiah who will be the "good shepherd" for God's people (see Ezekiel chapter 34 and John 10).

In the case of unfaithfulness on the part of parents, the LORD continues to be the "father" of all his creation, of every single human being; God is "the Father of our Lord Jesus Christ, from whom the whole family in heaven and on earth is named" (Ephesians 3.14,15). God is father to Israel, and calls Ephraim his firstborn (Jer. 31:9). God is also the father of the fatherless, and a judge of the widows (Ps. 68:5); He is a father to those oppressed and who need a father. God is the defender of those unable to defend themselves.

Disciples of Jesus pray to God as their father in heaven, who has a will for their lives:

> **5** "And when you pray, you shall not be like the hypocrites. For they love to pray standing in the synagogues and on the corners of the streets, that they may be seen by men. Assuredly, I say to you, they have their reward. **6** But you, when you pray, go into your room, and when you have shut your door, pray to your Father who *is* in the secret *place;* and your Father who sees in secret will reward you openly. **7** And when you pray, do not use vain repetitions as the heathen *do.* For they think that they will be heard for their many words. **8** Therefore do not be like them. For your Father knows the things you have need of before you ask Him. **9** In this manner, therefore, pray:
> Our Father in heaven,
> Hallowed be Your name.
> **10** Your kingdom come.
> Your will be done
> On earth as *it is* in heaven." (Matthew 6.5-10).

Prayer

Our Lord and Father in heaven, we pray for wisdom today. We pray that our hearts will overflow with goodness and compassion as we encounter the fatherless, the widow and those who have been abused and mistreated by others. Thank you for Jesus, who has brought to us the light of your grace and truth. We pray in His name, Amen.

Day 4

> **4** "Sing to God, sing praises to His name;
> Extol Him who rides on the clouds,
> By His name Yah,
> And rejoice before Him.
> **5** A father of the fatherless, a defender of widows,
> *Is* God in His holy habitation.
> **6** God sets the solitary in families;
> He brings out those who are bound into prosperity;
> But the rebellious dwell in a dry *land.*"
> (Psalms 68.4-6)

The God who is fierce towards his enemies, who "rides in the clouds" is not the tyrant type who crushes the weak. It is "the wicked" who perish in the presence of God (v.2), not the righteous or the weak. The God who rules over nations takes interest in the lowliest, especially the fatherless and widows.

God is just and all powerful. We cannot "mock him". But his heart is full of compassion for those who have no father or mother. The God of Israel is also "He who gives strength and power to His people" (vv.35). He is the God who "loads us with benefits, the God of our salvation!" (vv.19).

The Lord is gentle and humble of heart and offers rest to the souls of those who will receive instruction from Him:

> **28** "Come to Me, all *you* who labor and are heavy laden, and I will give you rest. **29** Take My yoke upon you and learn from Me, for I am gentle and lowly in heart, and you will find rest for your souls. **30** For My yoke *is* easy, and My burden is light."
> (Matthew 11.28-30).

The goodness and humility of God which he also manifested in Jesus do not cancel his righteous judgment, do not make him a "weak God" in the face of unrighteousness. He remains the one to whom we ascribe "strength" and "excellence" (v.34).

> "He rules by His power forever;
> His eyes observe the nations; do not let the rebellious exalt themselves. *Selah*" (Psalms 66.7).

> "Or do you despise the riches of His goodness, forbearance, and longsuffering, not knowing that the goodness of God leads you to repentance?" (Romans 2.4)

Prayer

Father in heaven, we thank you for your perfect goodness and your patience towards us. Our prayer today is that we will be led to repentance, to a heart willing to confess our sins and to turn to you. Help us through your Holy Spirit grow in goodness and compassion for those who struggle through life and need our care. Amen.

Day 5

> **7** "Hear, O Lord, *when* I cry with my voice!
> Have mercy also upon me, and answer me.
> **8** *When You said,* "Seek My face,"
> My heart said to You, "Your face, Lord, I will seek."
> **9** Do not hide Your face from me;
> Do not turn Your servant away in anger;
> You have been my help;
> Do not leave me nor forsake me,
> O God of my salvation.
> **10** When my father and my mother forsake me,
> Then the Lord will take care of me."
>   (Psalms 27.7-10)

This Psalm describes the strength and protection we receive from the LORD when we put our trust in Him. When the righteous meet with opposition, they are not afraid (v.1,2). Strength comes to those who "wait upon the LORD" (v. 14).

Even those who have lost mother or father or have been forsaken by them will find refuge in God. There is however a condition found in the Psalm, that those who have been forsaken by parents are willing to listen to God who teaches them in His word: "Teach me Your way, O Lord and lead me in a smooth path, because of my enemies." (v,11).

As the writer of the Psalm faces "enemies" and "adversaries" as well as those who "breathe violence" (vv.12) his first concern is for his own ways. It can be tempting when facing those who are opposed to God or His truth to focus on them and on their opposition. However, the focus of our lives should always be on maintaining ourselves faithful to God and to His will.

> **1** "Brethren, if a man is overtaken in any trespass, you who *are* spiritual restore such a one in a spirit of gentleness, considering yourself lest you also be tempted. **2** Bear one another's burdens, and so fulfill the law of Christ. **3** For if anyone thinks himself to be something, when he is nothing, he deceives himself. **4** But let each one examine his own work, and then he will have rejoicing in himself alone, and not in another. **5** For each one shall bear his own load." (Galatians 6.1-5).

David is not praying for an easy (smooth) path. The translation "smooth" path can also be translated "plain" path and describes a "straight" or "right" path. "In all your ways, acknowledge Him, And He will make your paths straight." (Proverbs 3,6). Watch the path of your feet, and all your ways will be established. Do not turn to the right nor to the left; Turn your foot from evil. (Proverbs 4.26-27). "Make straight paths for your feet, so that the limb which is lame may not be put out of joint, but rather be healed." (Hebrews 12.13).

Prayer

Lord, we thank you for this day. Like David, we pray that you will teach us today and lead us into the path of righteousness. We also pray that we will examine our own works and that we will always restore others in a spirit of gentleness. Amen.

Day 6

> **15** "*As for* man, his days *are* like grass;
> As a flower of the field, so he flourishes.
> **16** For the wind passes over it, and it is [b]gone,
> And its place remembers it no more.
> **17** But the mercy of the Lord *is* from everlasting to everlasting
> On those who fear Him,

And His righteousness to children's children,
18 To such as keep His covenant,
And to those who remember His commandments to do them."
   (Psalms 103.15-18)

"As for man" includes all men and all women. The Genesis chapter 2 creation account uses the word *anish* for man and *anishah* for woman (Genesis 2.23). This Psalm shows a contrast between the LORD (with a number of wonderful statements in vv.1-14) and "man" in verses 15-18.

We were born on this earth and called to live in covenant with the LORD. This life lived in covenant with God is described throughout Psalms 103. Our days are like grass or like a flower of the field.

Our mortal condition is not all that can be said about who we are, since "the mercy of the LORD is from everlasting to everlasting on those who fear Him" (v.17). Our destiny is dependent on our relationship with God, who does not want death to be our final destination.

In Psalm 103 The LORD is calling us to live under His care, to benefit from His mercy and righteousness, to remember his commandments. His care, mercy and righteousness are everlasting blessings we are called to receive by trusting and loving God. God's promises should also be understood in the perspective of "hope" and eternity. Living as faithful Christians can even be the cause of poverty or persecution, as it still is in many places in the world, but God's mercy extends into His eternal promises and should be part of our hope:

> **35** Who shall separate us from the love of Christ? *Shall* tribulation, or distress, or persecution, or famine, or nakedness, or peril, or sword? **36** As it is written:
> "For Your sake we are killed all day long;
> We are accounted as sheep for the slaughter."
> **37** Yet in all these things we are more than conquerors through Him who loved us. **38** For I am persuaded that neither death nor life, nor angels nor principalities nor powers, nor things present nor things to come, **39** nor height nor depth, nor any other created thing, shall be able to separate us from the love of God which is in Christ Jesus our Lord." (Romans 8.35-39)

These everlasting blessings should encourage us to see each day as a unique opportunity to walk in the path of an everlasting life full of glory and joy.

24 "All flesh *is* as grass,
And all the glory of man as the flower of the grass.
The grass withers,
And its flower falls away,
25 But the word of the Lord endures forever."
"Now this is the word which by the gospel was preached to you. Therefore, laying aside all malice, all deceit, hypocrisy, envy, and all evil speaking, **2** as newborn babes, desire the pure milk of the word, that you may grow thereby, **3** if indeed you have tasted that the Lord *is* gracious." (1 Peter 1.24-2.3)

Prayer

Father in heaven, as we look today on our children or grandchildren, may we bless you by the way we live, speak and think. We have words of blessings towards you that come from our soul. Today, we want to remember your calling and your promised blessings. We are grateful for your Word and for Jesus, our Lord and Savior. Amen.

Day 7

12 "That our sons *may be* as plants grown up in their youth;
That our daughters *may be* as pillars,
Sculptured in palace style;
13 *That* our barns *may be* full,
Supplying all kinds of produce;
That our sheep may bring forth thousands
And ten thousands in our fields;
14 *That* our oxen *may be* well laden;
That there be no breaking in or going out;
That there be no outcry in our streets.
15 Happy *are* the people who are in such a state;
Happy *are* the people whose God *is* the Lord!"
   (Psalms 144.12-15)

All parents desire the best for their children, for their sons and daughters. All parents desire for barns to be full! But if this is the priority of parents is seeking God's blessings, this is the wrong priority. The LORD is the one we need to seek out of love and trust — not what we can receive from the LORD. Material blessings or even happiness without love for

God in the heart is "vapor" as we are taught in the book of Ecclesiastes and throughout the Bible.

Why is it sometimes so difficult for parents to raise their children in the ways of the Lord? One answer is that parents oftentimes need help. They need to be surrounded by other godly parents. Their children and youth need other children or youth touched by God's Word; people, a nation, whose God is the LORD is truly happy!

It is also difficult for godly parents to raise their children in an ungodly culture. Father and mothers need the support of those who lead the nation, instead of opposition from those leaders. The Church is God's people and should also be a source of inspiration for parents and children. Caring for families should be of the utmost importance to every member of the Church. In fact, if an "overseer" (also called pastor or elder) does not know how to manage his own family, he is not qualified to take care of or shepherd God's Church (1 Timothy 3.5).

> **1** "Therefore I exhort first of all that supplications, prayers, intercessions, *and* giving of thanks be made for all men, **2** for kings and all who are in authority, that we may lead a quiet and peaceable life in all godliness and [c]reverence. **3** For this *is* good and acceptable in the sight of God our Savior, **4** who desires all men to be saved and to come to the knowledge of the truth. **5** For *there is* one God and one Mediator between God and men, *the* Man Christ Jesus, **6** who gave Himself a ransom for all, to be testified in due time, **7** for which I was appointed a preacher and an apostle—I am speaking the truth in Christ *and* not lying—a teacher of the Gentiles in faith and truth." (1 Timothy 2.1-7).

Prayer

Lord in heaven, we pray today for families, for mothers and fathers. We pray for children and young people. We want you to be at the heart of all of our thinking and all of our actions. We pray that political leaders will not be a stumbling block for your people, for the Church. In Jesus' name, we pray that you will bless our leaders. Amen.

Week 11: Babies and Children

Day 1

> **13** "For You formed my inward parts;
> You covered me in my mother's womb.
> **14** I will praise You, for I am fearfully *and* wonderfully made;
> Marvelous are Your works,
> And *that* my soul knows very well.
> **15** My frame was not hidden from You,
> When I was made in secret,
> *And* skillfully wrought in the lowest parts of the earth.
> **16** Your eyes saw my substance, being yet unformed.
> And in Your book they all were written,
> The days fashioned for me,
> When *as yet there were* none of them."
>   (Psalms 139.13-16)

In this Psalm, the LORD is the all-knowing God (vv. 6–11,17,18). He is the God whose works are marvelous (vv. 13-16). He is the God who is ever present everywhere (vv. 7-10). He is the righteous God who punishes the wicked and whom we should seek (vv. 19-24).

Among the "marvelous works" of the LORD the formation of the baby in the mother's womb stands out. The development of the child in the womb is one of the greatest mysteries reflecting God's power:

> "As you do not know what *is* the way of the wind
> *Or* how the bones *grow* in the womb of her who is with child,
> So you do not know the works of God who makes everything."
>   (Ecclesiastes 11.5)

God "forms" (*quanita*) the baby in the mother's womb. The Hebrew verb used here implies that the one formed in the mother's womb belongs to the LORD. The meaning is that the one who "forms" is the one who is the rightful owner. In several passages, the verb is even translated "to purchase"; thus, in Psalms 74.2 God's people have been formed or "purchased" by God: "Remember Your congregation, *which* You have purchased [*quanita*] of old". The one who forms a human being is his or her rightful owner (cf. Psalm 24).

God "covers" (from the verb *cakak*) the baby in the mother's womb as in Psalm 140.8 and Job 40.22. The verb is sometimes translated by the verb "to weave" (NAS) since the covering implies a weaving for protection or safety (here with bones, sinews and veins as in Job 10.11). Thus, the baby in the mother's womb is under the LORD'S protection.

The baby in the mother's womb is presented as the epitome of God's works manifested in creation. This goes back to the original idea of creation, where God made man and woman in His image and gave them authority over His creation (Genesis 1.26,27).

The baby in the mother's womb is "fearfully" (*nowraoth*) and "wonderfully" (*nipleti*) made. We should be fearful or in "awe" when considering God's work of forming the baby. The first verb is used of the midwives in Egypt, who feared God and refused to put to death the babies (Exodus 1.17). The LORD "the great and awesome God" brings us to awe — Nehemiah 1.5 (Deuteronomy 7.21; 10.17; Nehemiah 9.32; Daniel 9.4). The word *nipleti*, "wonderfully" is from the Hebrew *palah*, to be distinct, separated. The baby in the mother's womb is distinct, unique in all of God's creation, and to be treated with great respect. This is similar to the idea that God's people are distinct among all peoples as in Exodus 33.16, "So we shall be *separate*, your people and I, from all the people who *are* upon the face of the earth."

The formation of the baby "in the lowest parts of the earth" reminds us how God created Adam from the earth (Genesis 2.7; 3.19). The lowest parts of the earth (also Psalms 63.10) describes the ultimate place of origin for human beings:

> "Naked I came from my mother's womb, and naked shall I return there. The Lord gave, and the Lord has taken away; Blessed be the name of the Lord." (Job 1.21)

Prayer

Lord in heaven, we pray for our times when every day babies are put to death before they can enjoy their life. We pray that you touch a culture that does not recognize you as the Creator and ultimate source of all blessings, including babies and children. May you lead many to a better understanding of your will through the Gospel of Christ and your Holy Spirit. We pray in Jesus' name. Amen.

Day 2

> **1** "O Lord, our Lord,
> How excellent *is* Your name in all the earth,
> Who have set Your glory above the heavens!
> **2** Out of the mouth of babes and nursing infants
> You have ordained strength,
> Because of Your enemies,
> That You may silence the enemy and the avenger."
> (Psalms 8.1,2)

> **14** "*The* blind and *the* lame came to Him in the temple, and He healed them. **15** But when the chief priests and scribes saw the wonderful things that He did, and the children crying out in the temple and saying, 'Hosanna to the Son of David!' they were indignant **16** and said to Him, 'Do You hear what these are saying?' And Jesus said to them, 'Yes. Have you never read, 'Out of the mouth of babes and nursing infants you have perfected praise'?'" (Matthew 21.13-16)

This Psalm begins and ends with the same statement: "O Lord, our Lord, how excellent *is* Your name in all the earth" (v.9). Thus, the emphasis and the cause for worship is not the stars and heavens, human beings or angels but the Creator, the LORD.

When the Psalm says that his "name" is excellent, the point is not about pronouncing or understanding the name revealed to Moses in Exodus 3.15 (of which there are several possible spellings in English, such as Yahweh or Jehovah). The "name" is equivalent to the personhood of God — who He is as the LORD. To do everything "in the name" of the Lord does not mean his name needs to be uttered in every action we do (such as eating or drinking! 1 Corinthians 10.31) but that we do all that we do to honor and glorify who He is and honor His will : "And whatever you do in word or deed, *do* all in the name of the Lord Jesus, giving thanks to God the Father through Him." (Colossians 3.17; 3.27).

God delivered Israel from Egyptian slavery though a baby (Moses). Through this "baby" God "avenged" his enemies. The baby of Bethlehem was the one who destroyed Satan, "the great enemy" (see Revelation 12.1-6). God displayed his glory and power through the lowly and humble (1 Corinthians 1.27-29).

Jesus also taught that the Kingdom of God is for those who are like little children. They had no difficulty in recognizing Jesus as Lord and

Savior. They are pure and not tainted by evil. Thus, we are encouraged to resemble them in behavior and innocence (Matthew 19.4).

The example of "babies" or "little children" given to Christians should not be misunderstood. There is a sense in which we need to be like little children, but we also need to become adults. Thus, Christians are encouraged to become adults in understanding:

> "**20** Brethren, do not be children in understanding; however, in malice be babes, but in understanding be mature." (1 Corinthians 14.20). In "malice" don't act like "adults" who often have "malice" but be like babies who are innocent and do not hurt others. In "understanding" believers need to grow up: "And I, brethren, could not speak to you as to spiritual *people* but as to carnal, as to babes in Christ. **2** I fed you with milk and not with solid food; for until now you were not able *to receive it,* and even now you are still not able; **3** for you are still carnal." (1 Corinthians 3.1).

> **11** "When I was a child, I spoke as a child, I understood as a child, I thought as a child; but when I became a man, I put away childish things. **12** For now we see in a mirror, dimly, but then face to face. Now I know in part, but then I shall know just as I also am known." (1 Corinthians 13.11).

> **12** "For though by this time you ought to be teachers, you need *someone* to teach you again the first principles of the oracles of God; and you have come to need milk and not solid food. **13** For everyone who partakes *only* of milk *is* unskilled in the word of righteousness, for he is a babe. **14** But solid food belongs to those who are of full age, *that is,* those who by reason of use have their senses exercised to discern both good and evil." (Hebrews 5.12,13)

Prayer

Our Father in heaven, we thank you for babies and little children. We thank you that through them, you teach us an example of purity and innocence. We pray that we can be pure of heart and also grow up in understanding your will. We pray that you will help us walk in ways that will honor you. Amen.

Day 3

> **6** "But I *am* a worm, and no man;
> A reproach of men, and despised by the people.
> **7** All those who see Me ridicule Me;
> They shoot out the lip, they shake the head, *saying,*
> **8** "He trusted in the Lord, let Him rescue Him;
> Let Him deliver Him, since He delights in Him!"
> **9** But You *are* He who took Me out of the womb;
> You made Me trust *while* on My mother's breasts.
> **10** I was cast upon You from birth.
> From My mother's womb
> You *have been* My God.
> **11** Be not far from Me,
> For trouble *is* near;
> For *there is* none to help."
>   (Psalms 22.8-11)

Psalm 22 is a prophecy of the sufferings of the Messiah (vv. 1-18) followed by his victory and glory (vv.19-31). The first verse of this Psalm is quoted by Jesus as he suffers torture on the cross: "My God, My God, why have you forsaken me" (v.1 and Matthew 27.46,47).

The Messiah's garments are divided among those who crucify him as they cast lots (v.18 and Mark 15.24; Luke 23,34; John 19.24). The words of verse 8 are pronounced by those who watch him being crucified (Matthew 27.43). His thirst is prophesied in verse 15 (Matthew 27.48). The Psalm also prophecies the piercing of his hands and feet (v. 16 and John 20.25).

In the midst of this prophetical text is the reference to his mother and his birth (vv.9-11). The child Jesus was born of Mary, a faithful young woman, a virgin of Israel honored by God by being chosen as His mother (Luke 1.26-38 and 39-56). There is no mention in prophecy or the Gospels of a human father to Jesus conceived of the Holy Spirit, "The Holy Spirit will come upon you and the power of the Highest will overshadow you; therefore, also, that Holy One who is to be born will be called the Son of God." (Luke 1.35)

The song of Mary describes the mercy of the Lord, who has "scattered the proud" and has "put down the mighty" but has "exalted the lowly". The savior of the world, God's anointed King, was born of a humble virgin who calls herself the "maidservant" of God (Luke 1.48). His humble mother, his humble birth and humble life as a small child are powerful testimonies to the workings of God through the humble of the earth.

Since childhood, the Messiah was full of trust in God (v.9). Since his early childhood, the Messiah grew in wisdom and "the grace of God was upon him" (Luke 2.40; 2.49,52). The child still in the womb of his mother has known of God's closeness and presence (v.10; see also Luke 2.42,43). Now He cries to His God and says, "Be not far from me, for trouble is near, for there is none to help" (v.11, 19).

Prayer

Father in heaven, as we read of the sufferings of your servant, we pray that you will continue to strengthen our faith and our hope. We pray that we can face the difficulties and challenges of the day with trust in your promises. We pray for mothers and their children who go through pain and loneliness. May we be touched deeply by these pains and be willing to provide affection and encouragement to mothers and children in need. Amen.

Day 4

> **73** "Your hands have made me and fashioned me;
> Give me understanding, that I may learn Your commandments.
> **74** Those who fear You will be glad when they see me,
> Because I have hoped in Your word.
> **75** I know, O Lord, that Your judgments *are* right,
> And *that* in faithfulness You have afflicted me.
> **76** Let, I pray, Your merciful kindness be for my comfort,
> According to Your word to Your servant.
> **77** Let Your tender mercies come to me, that I may live;
> For Your law *is* my delight."
> (Psalm 119.73-77)

What are some essential or fundamental truths believers need to teach their children? An essential truth which needs to be taught is that God is our creator. The creative work of God starts the biblical account because from this truth flow all other truths. In fact, numerous biblical texts refer to creation all the way from Genesis to the book of Revelation (Psalms 24; Jeremiah 32,17; Psalms 121; Isaiah 40.28; Psalms 90,2; 33.6; Hebrews 3.4; Romans 1.20; 11.36).

The "fear" of the Lord is awe and reverence, respect for Him as our creator and legislator. The fear of the Lord is the beginning of true wisdom (Proverbs 9.10). It is only through His revelation, His Word, that we can know the difference between good and evil, right and wrong (see Romans 7.7; Hebrews 5.12-14; James 1.21-24).

God is not only our Creator and legislator, he is also our deliverer who shows "lovingkindness" even when we sin and have turned away from Him. Without this lovingkindness of God, we would have not hope (v.74).

> **11** "For I know the thoughts that I think toward you, says the Lord, thoughts of peace and not of evil, to give you a future and a hope. **12** Then you will call upon Me and go and pray to Me, and I will listen to you. **13** And you will seek Me and find *Me*, when you search for Me with all your heart." (Jeremiah 29.11-13)

> **17** "That the God of our Lord Jesus Christ, the Father of glory, may give to you the spirit of wisdom and revelation in the knowledge of Him, **18** the eyes of your understanding being enlightened; that you may know what is the hope of His calling, what are the riches of the glory of His inheritance in the saints, **19** and what *is* the exceeding greatness of His power toward us who believe" (Ephesians 1.17,18)

Prayer

Father in heaven, we pray for our children and for all the children we meet and see. We pray that we can be good to them and wise in our words and actions so that these children can find in us the care and righteousness you have taught us in your Word and through Jesus. Amen.

Day 5

> **25** "I have been young, and *now* am old;
> Yet I have not seen the righteous forsaken,
> Nor his descendants begging bread.
> **26** *He is* ever merciful and lends;
> And his descendants *are* blessed.
> **27** Depart from evil and do good;
> And dwell forevermore.
> **28** For the Lord loves justice,
> And does not forsake His saints;

> They are preserved forever,
> But the descendants of the wicked shall be cut off."
> (Psalm 37.25-28)

This Psalm answers the question of how we should deal with evildoers, how we should react to those who do wrong. There is a paradox in this Psalm due to the fact that evildoers do exist, and they do evil; they "draw the sword" to slay those who are upright (v.14); they "plot against the just" (v.12). If this is the case, how can it be said that "the Lord upholds the righteous" and that "he knows the days of the upright"? How can the writer say that he has not seen the righteous forsaken nor his descendants begging bread (v.25) while at the same time saying that the wicked "have cast down the poor and needy" (v.14)?

We learn from this Psalm of the pain and suffering that come from evildoers, from wicked people. At the same time, God remains the one who promises justice and blessings to the meek and those who fear his name. This teaches us that we should not blame God for the injustice and violence of human beings.

The Psalm also teaches us of the brevity of life and brevity of success of the wicked, who are like grass that "shall soon be cut down" (v.2). There is a contrast here between the wicked and the righteous, whose "inheritance shall be forever". God looks at the righteous through their eternal destiny; despite the pains of the righteous, God "delights in his ways" (v.23).

The future of the righteous turns out to be good. The future of the wicked is destruction (v.38):

> **37** "Mark the blameless *man* and observe the upright;
> For the future of *that* man *is* peace.
> **38** But the transgressors shall be destroyed together;
> The future of the wicked shall be cut off.
> **39** But the salvation of the righteous *is* from the Lord;
> *He is* their strength in the time of trouble.
> **40** And the Lord shall help them and deliver them;
> He shall deliver them from the wicked,
> And save them,
> Because they trust in Him." (Psalms 37.37-40)

Prayer

Father in heaven, we pray that we can be upright and humble in our ways. We pray that you will give us strength and wisdom to avoid wicked ways. Today, we want to seek first your kingdom and righteousness. We do not want to be discouraged by evildoers and the wickedness we see in the world. We know you will protect us and uphold us all the days of our life. For this, we are grateful to you. Amen.

Day 6

> **5** "For He established a testimony in Jacob,
> And appointed a law in Israel,
> Which He commanded our fathers,
> That they should make them known to their children;
> **6** That the generation to come might know *them,*
> The children *who* would be born,
> *That* they may arise and declare *them* to their children,
> **7** That they may set their hope in God,
> And not forget the works of God,
> But keep His commandments;
> **8** And may not be like their fathers,
> A stubborn and rebellious generation,
> A generation *that* did not set its heart aright,
> And whose spirit was not faithful to God."
> (Psalm 78.5-8)

God's people should always keep in mind the generations yet to be born. A generation can be a blessing not only to their children, but to their grand-children and great-grand-children. We should realize that the good we do today, the teachings we share today, will continue to have an impact on future generations.

The danger for human beings is always to set their hope on something or someone besides God. The Word of God is a word of hope, a word about the good future God has for those who trust in Him. The loss of hope will always produce the loss of obedience and righteous behavior: "That they may set their hope in God and not forget the works of God, but keep His commandments" (v. 7).

God alone knows the extent of our work for him, whether towards our families, the Church or the world. But God will give increase to the small seeds we have planted. The seed of His Word will produce fruit and like the rain will not return without having produced good on this earth:

10 "For as the rain comes down, and the snow from heaven,
And do not return there,
But water the earth,
And make it bring forth and bud,
That it may give seed to the sower
And bread to the eater,
11 So shall My word be that goes forth from My mouth;
It shall not return to Me void,
But it shall accomplish what I please,
And it shall prosper *in the thing* for which I sent it." (Isaiah 55.10,11)

Prayer

Father in heaven, we pray that today we will seize the opportunities you give us to help our children learn from your Word. We pray that our lives can demonstrate how you want people to live. We pray that you will protect our children from those who would lead them astray, whether adults or friends. Lord, keep our family in your will. We pray this in the name of our Lord Jesus. Amen.

Day 7

11 "Come, you children, listen to me;
I will teach you the fear of the Lord.
12 Who *is* the man *who* desires life,
And loves *many* days, that he may see good?
13 Keep your tongue from evil,
And your lips from speaking deceit.
14 Depart from evil and do good;
Seek peace and pursue it."
   (Psalms 34.11-14)

The children mentioned here can be the youth or a tender way for the writer to address adults, as in Proverbs 1.8. Jesus often addressed his disciples as "children" as in John 13.33. They were "children" in their need of being taught and having to grow in maturity. The apostle John also addresses Christians as "children" (1 John 2.12-17).

There is also a sense in which all believers are "children" because they all have God as their Father showing a care and closeness of God towards those who trust in Him, both in the Old and New Testaments.

Deuteronomy 32.6; Isaiah 63.16; 64.8; Psalms 89.26; Matthew 5.45; 6.9; 10.32,33; 18.19.

These verses of Psalms are quoted by Peter (1 Peter 3.10-12). Both in Psalm 34 and in 1 Peter, we read that it is not a bad thing to "desire" or "love" life or to want to see "good days". It is clear from the Bible that there is a sense in which trust in God and obedience to Him lead to a better life. This is a general principle, of which we find examples in the book of Proverbs and other parts of the Old Testament (11.1-21; Deuteronomy 28).

The "tongue" is the most difficult thing for human beings to control.

> **1** "My brethren, let not many of you become teachers, knowing that we shall receive a stricter judgment. **2** For we all stumble in many things. If anyone does not stumble in word, he *is* a perfect man, able also to bridle the whole body. **3** Indeed, we put bits in horses' mouths that they may obey us, and we turn their whole body. **4** Look also at ships: although they are so large and are driven by fierce winds, they are turned by a very small rudder wherever the pilot desires. **5** Even, so the tongue is a little member and boasts great things." (James 3.1-5).

When people live in harmony with God's moral and natural law, they open themselves up to a good life. However, those who go against God's moral and natural law bring on "themselves the penalty of their error" (Romans 1.26,27). This principle has sometimes been used to teach that only good things and abundance follow those who live according to God's will — forgetting the fact that there is a spiritual battle going on and that those who want to follow Christ will be reviled and persecuted (Matthew 5.11,12).

So, which is true? Well, both! In this area, we trust God's Word to be true for different reasons. One being the goodness of God's moral and natural order. The other being the reality of evil and the battle against Satan (Ephesians 6. 10-12).

Prayer

Our Father in heaven, we believe in your perfect holiness and goodness. We believe in the perfection of your moral and natural law. We come to you today as children in order to learn from you and to obey your will. We thank you for the blessings of life. In Jesus' name, we pray, Amen.

Week 12: The Elderly

Day 1

> **4** "Sing to God, sing praises to His name;
> Extol Him who rides on the clouds,
> By His name Yah,
> And rejoice before Him.
> **5** A father of the fatherless, a defender of widows,
> *Is* God in His holy habitation.
> **6** God sets the solitary in families;
> He brings out those who are bound into prosperity;
> But the rebellious dwell in a dry *land*."
> (Psalms 68.4-6)

Widows can be young or older women. However, widows who are older suffer both the loss of their beloved husband and the pains associated with old age. In both the old and new covenants God has given younger generations the responsibility to care of the older people and especially of the widows (Deuteronomy 15.7-11; 24.17-21; Exodus 22.22,23; Psalms 82.3; James 1.27; Acts 6.1; 1 Timothy 5.3-8).

Believers are not to merely believe in God's love towards the widows, they are called to exercise that love towards those widows, to show the goodness and care of God through their actions.

There are those who ask the question about God's concern for the fatherless and widows. They wonder why God allows for the fatherless or widows to be in that situation in the first place. This question shows a misunderstanding about the human condition in the world as taught in the Bible. Because we are in a fallen world, we all endure the effects of sin and death (Ephesians 2.1-3). To rebel against the reality of death and its disastrous effects is to refuse to accept the reality we live in, which is that we were born and live in a fallen and dying world.

There are those who think that faith in God's revelation about death and pain means we should not do anything to better people's lives, to improve their health. Nothing in God's Word teaches this. In fact, we are taught to take care to comfort and do our best towards those who go through pain, face death or suffer the loss of a loved one. It was Christians who were the first in history to create hospitals to take care of the sick.

There are those who reject God because of the kind of world we live in, and especially because death and suffering are part of this world. But unbelief and rejection of the truth of God's revelation in this area do not bring about a better world. Death and sin are still there.

There are those who believe that our purpose on earth as human beings is to get rid of death, of all pain and that somehow, we will be able to achieve this through science and technology. Those people often rely on ideologies or political systems to improve the world to the point that these ideologies will be able to create some kind of "paradise" on earth. But improvements in health and longevity of life will not change the intrinsic nature of the dying world we live in. Human beings do not have the power to create "paradise" on earth.

Prayer

Our Father in heaven, we believe that you are a father to the fatherless and a defender of the widows. We pray that we can understand your goodness towards those in pain and learn from that goodness. We pray that today you will give us the wisdom and love to show compassion and kindness to the fatherless and widows. Amen.

Day 2

> **9**"Do not cast me off in the time of old age;
> Do not forsake me when my strength fails.
> **10** For my enemies speak against me;
> And those who lie in wait for my life take counsel together,
> **11** Saying, 'God has forsaken him;
> Pursue and take him, for *there is* none to deliver *him*.'"
> (Psalms 71.9-11)

The Septuagint (Greek translation of the Old Testament) mentions in a superscription that David is the author of this Psalm. In his old age, king David underwent a lot of trials, especially the betrayal of his sons Absalom and Adonijah (2 Samuel 15 and 1 King 1).

There is a striking contrast in this Psalm how David was "taught from his youth" (v.17) and what we learn from the book of kings about Adonijah: "His father had never rebuked him by asking, "Why do you behave as you do?" He was also very handsome and was born next after Absalom."

If we consider that the betrayals and enemies mentioned are some of David's own sons and close relatives, the Psalm is even more moving. The betrayal of one's own children or family members would certainly cause a greater grief than betrayal from anyone else.

We are reminded of the betrayal of Jesus and the words of Jesus who called Judas "friend",

> **47** "And while He was still speaking, behold, Judas, one of the twelve, with a great multitude with swords and clubs, came from the chief priests and elders of the people. **48** Now His betrayer had given them a sign, saying, 'Whomever I kiss, He is the One; seize Him.' **49** Immediately he went up to Jesus and said, 'Greetings, Rabbi!' and kissed Him. **50** But Jesus said to him, 'Friend, why have you come?' Now His betrayer had given them a sign, saying, 'Whomever I kiss, He is the One; seize Him.' **49** Immediately he went up to Jesus and said, 'Greetings, Rabbi!' and kissed Him. **50** But Jesus said to him, 'Friend, why have you come?'" (Matthew 26.47-50)

Judas had walked with Jesus, had seen his miracles and had heard his teachings. For at least three years, Judas and Jesus had been close to one another daily. As the other apostles, Judas had been sent on preaching missions. But Judas' love of money was stronger than his love for Jesus: "But one of His disciples, Judas Iscariot, Simon's *son*, who would betray Him, said,

> **5** 'Why was this fragrant oil not sold for three hundred denarii and given to the poor?' **6** This he said, not that he cared for the poor, but because he was a thief, and had the money box; and he used to take what was put in it." (John 12.4,5).

The betrayal of Judas proves the truth of Jesus' words: "No one can serve two masters; for either he will hate the one and love the other, or else he will be loyal to the one and despise the other. You cannot serve God and mammon." (Matthew 6.24)

Through their love of power, David's sons and others who joined them in their betrayal became "unrighteous and cruel" men (v.4).

The writer of this Psalm knows from experience that in the midst of fierce trials he can trust and serve the LORD — his "strong refuge", his "rock" and "fortress" (vv.1-3). He knows that the LORD is the only one who can deliver him from the most difficult circumstances in his life (vv.4).

Prayer

Father in heaven, we come to you today for patience and trust. We know that this world presents to us times that can be so painful that we are at loss for words and to know what to do. We believe that in those times you remain our rock, our refuge. We pray in the name of Jesus for deliverance and strength as we go through these trials. Amen.

Day 3

> **17** "O God, You have taught me from my youth;
> And to this *day* I declare Your wondrous works.
> **18** Now also when *I am* old and gray headed,
> O God, do not forsake me,
> Until I declare Your strength to *this* generation,
> Your power to everyone *who* is to come."
> (Psalms 71.18,19)

In these verses, David recalls that he has been instructed and had walked in God's ways since his youth. However, we know from the life of David that he also had sins in his life. Thus, this language in Scripture never means one is without sin or completely flawless. David's right standing with God is also the result of his repentant heart and God's forgiveness (see Psalms 51 and 52).

David mentions the fact that now he is old and gray headed. The infirmities and pains of old age are encroaching upon his strength, and he has special needs; he seeks help from God, which is expressed by the words "O God, do not forsake me" (v.18 and v.9).

This appeal not to be forsaken at an older age is also a lesson for us human beings, that we should never forsake the elders, especially those who are part of our family. This is what is meant and applied to widows by the words of the apostle Paul: "Honor widows who are really widows.

> **4** But if any widow has children or grandchildren, let them first learn to show piety at home and to repay their parents; for this is good and acceptable before God. **5** Now she who is really a widow, and left alone, trusts in God and continues in supplications and prayers night and day. **6** But she who lives in pleasure

is dead while she lives. **7** And these things command, that they may be blameless. **8** But if anyone does not provide for his own, and especially for those of his household, he has denied the faith and is worse than an unbeliever." (1 Timothy 5.3-7).

David even in his old age is mindful of the "next generation". He must continue to declare God's "strength" to the youth. The words translated "strength" is also the word for arm in Hebrew. The "arm" of the Lord describes his action in human history and the impossibility of opposing his purposes and plans. These words remind us of another Psalm:

29 "A posterity shall serve Him.
30 It will be recounted of the Lord to the *next* generation,
31 They will come and declare His righteousness to a people who will be born that He has done *this.*" (Psalm 22.29–31).

The most important work of the elderly is to teach the younger generations:

1 "But as for you, speak the things which are proper for sound doctrine: **2** that the older men be sober, reverent, temperate, sound in faith, in love, in patience; **3** the older women likewise, that they be reverent in behavior, not slanderers, not given to much wine, teachers of good things— **4** that they admonish the young women to love their husbands, to love their children, **5** *to be* discreet, chaste, homemakers, good, obedient to their own husbands, that the word of God may not be blasphemed.
6 Likewise, exhort the young men to be sober-minded, **7** in all things showing yourself *to be* a pattern of good works; in doctrine *showing* integrity, reverence, incorruptibility, **8** sound speech that cannot be condemned, that one who is an opponent may be ashamed, having nothing evil to say of you." (Titus 2.3-6)

Prayer

Father in heaven, we pray for care and love towards the elderly, especially for our parents and those who are members of our families. We pray that today, as we meet elderly men or women, we might be respectful of them and willing to be a source of comfort to them. Amen

Day 4

> **24** "You will guide me with Your counsel,
> And afterward receive me *to* glory.
> **25** Whom have I in heaven *but You?*
> And *there is* none upon earth *that* I desire besides You.
> **26** My flesh and my heart fail;
> *But* God *is* the strength of my heart and my portion forever.
> **27** For indeed, those who are far from You shall perish;
> You have destroyed all those who desert You for harlotry.
> **28** But *it is* good for me to draw near to God;
> I have put my trust in the Lord God,
> That I may declare all Your works."
> (Psalms 73.24-28)

This Psalm of Asaph is a confession by the author that his "feet had almost stumbled" (v.2) when considering the prosperity of the boastful and wicked (v.3). The thought of the happiness and success of wicked people was "too painful" for him. However, he was able to overcome this pain when he focused his thoughts on God and came into his presence: "It was too painful for me — until I went into the sanctuary of God; then I understood their end." (vv. 16,17).

Asaph is also well aware that his "flesh and heart" will fail. He may be speaking still of his carnal self, which struggles with the injustices he sees around. His heart may always be in danger of being hardened or of bitterness, and thus he says:

> My flesh and my heart fail;
> *But* God *is* the strength of my heart and my portion forever."

As we face difficult questions such as the one brought up by Asaph, we must "draw near to God"; we must focus on God and his goodness. We must also not forget that there is a coming judgment on the wicked (vv.27).

In the New Testament this truth is also taught as we are encouraged to:

> **1** "let us lay aside every weight, and the sin which so easily ensnares *us*, and let us run with endurance the race that is set before us, **2** looking unto Jesus, the author and finisher
> of *our* faith, who for the joy that was set before Him endured the cross, despising the shame, and has sat down at the right hand of the throne of God." (Hebrews 12.1,2).

Being aware of our temptation to become bitter or even angry at what we see in this world, we must not forsake prayer, worship or meditating on God's word. We must not forsake the assembly of believers:

> **23** "Let us hold fast the confession of *our* hope without wavering, for He who promised *is* faithful. **24** And let us consider one another in order to stir up love and good works, **25** not forsaking the assembling of ourselves together, as *is* the manner of some, but exhorting *one another,* and so much the more as you see the Day approaching." (Hebrews 10.23-25).

Prayer

Father in heaven, we thank you for this day. We pray for strength as we face the pains of life or as we meet those who are in pain. We want to set aside the time and place to meditate upon your wonderful qualities and upon your word. We want to look at Jesus, the author and finisher of our faith and who will be coming back for judgment. It is in his name that we pray. Amen.

Day 5

> **9** "We finish our years like a sigh.
> **10** The days of our lives *are* seventy years;
> And if by reason of strength *they are* eighty years,
> Yet their boast *is* only labor and sorrow;
> For it is soon cut off, and we fly away.
> **11** Who knows the power of Your anger?
> For as the fear of You, *so is* Your wrath.
> **12** So teach *us* to number our days,
> That we may gain a heart of wisdom."
> (Psalms 90.9,10).

This Psalm is the first of book 4 of the Psalms, which contains 17 Psalms. Rabbinic tradition assigns Psalms 91-100, to Moses. Moses lived to be 120 years old (Deuteronomy 34.7). The shortness of man's life is contrasted with the eternity of God: "Before the mountains were brought forth, or ever You had formed the earth and the world, even from everlasting to everlasting, you *are* God." (v.2).

The shortness of man's life should not drive us to despair or despondence. This Psalm is full of anticipation for what God will do for us if we remain faithful to him. We have good reason to "rejoice and be glad all our days":

> **13** "Return, O Lord!
> How long?
> And have compassion on Your servants.
> **14** Oh, satisfy us early with Your mercy,
> That we may rejoice and be glad all our days!
> **15** Make us glad according to the days *in which* You have afflicted us,
> The years *in which* we have seen evil.
> **16** Let Your work appear to Your servants,
> And Your glory to their children.
> **17** And let the beauty of the Lord our God be upon us,
> And establish the work of our hands for us;
> Yes, establish the work of our hands." (vv.13-17).

God's "beauty" (*noam*) is his "favor" or "graciousness" as in Psalms 27.4:

> "One *thing* I have desired of the Lord,
> That will I seek:
> That I may dwell in the house of the Lord
> All the days of my life,
> To behold the beauty of the Lord,
> And to inquire in His temple."

Those who live by God's will during their earthly pilgrimage are blessed: "Blessed are the dead who die in the Lord, assuredly, for they shall rest from their labors, and their work's follow with them" (Revelation 14:13). The works of the righteous will survive them and follow them even to the day of judgment.

Prayer

Our Lord and Father, we thank you for a new day. We begin this day with words to you and to learn from your word. We pray that this day we can glorify you and live according to your will. We desire to see you, Father, and know that you will never disappoint us in any way. We depend on your graciousness to come to you, and we do this through our High Priest, Jesus. We pray in His name, Amen.

Day 6

> **14** "Because he has set his love upon Me, therefore I will deliver him;

I will set him on high, because he has known My name.
15 He shall call upon Me, and I will answer him;
I *will be* with him in trouble;
I will deliver him and honor him.
16 With long life I will satisfy him,
And show him My salvation."
   (Psalm 91.14-16)

This is mostly a Psalm about the Messiah who is coming. Verses 11 and 12 are quoted by Satan when he tempts Jesus:

5 "Then the devil took Him up into the holy city, set Him on the pinnacle of the temple, **6** and said to Him, "If You are the Son of God, throw Yourself down. For it is written: 'He shall give His angels charge over you,' and, 'In *their* hands they shall bear you up, lest you dash your foot against a stone.'" (Matthew 4.5,6).

The Messiah who has set his love upon the LORD will be set up on high and will be delivered and honored by God. As in other Scriptures, the Messiah's life endures even into eternity:

"Yet it pleased the Lord to bruise Him;
He has put *Him* to grief.
When You make His soul an offering for sin,
He shall see *His* seed, He shall prolong *His* days,
And the pleasure of the Lord shall prosper in His hand." (Isaiah 53.16)

9 "Therefore, my heart is glad, and my glory rejoices;
My flesh also will rest in hope.
10 For You will not leave my soul in Sheol,
Nor will You allow Your Holy One to see corruption.
11 You will show me the path of life;
In Your presence *is* fullness of joy;
At Your right hand *are* pleasures forevermore." (Psalms 16.9-11)

Sometimes we see a clear link between a long life and faithfulness to God:

"Honor your father and your mother, so that you may live long in the land the Lord your God is giving you." (Exodus 20.12).

"Gray hair is a crown of glory; it is gained in a righteous life." (Proverbs 16.31)

"Long life is in her right hand; in her left hand are riches and honor." (Proverbs 3.16)

"The fear of the Lord prolongs life, but the years of the wicked will be short." (Proverbs 10.27)

"Children obey your parents in the Lord, for this is right. 'Honor your father and mother' (this is the first commandment with a promise), 'that it may go well with you and that you may live long in the land.' Fathers, do not provoke your children to anger, but bring them up in the discipline and instruction of the Lord." (Ephesians 6.1-4)

But we must also remember that this is not necessarily the case for every faithful believer. Jesus died at a young age and so did many of the prophets of God or the martyrs.

This helps us understand that we often live "in tension" between God's ideal and eternal plan for us and the earthly and temporary nature of our life in the body:

16 "Therefore, we do not lose heart. Though outwardly we are wasting away, yet inwardly we are being renewed day by day. **17** For our light and momentary troubles are achieving for us an eternal glory that far outweighs them all. **18** So we fix our eyes not on what is seen, but on what is unseen, since what is seen is temporary, but what is unseen is eternal." (2 Corinthians 4.16-18)

Prayer

Father in heaven, these words of the Psalm remind us of Jesus on whom you set your love, your affection. But he went through great pains because of his faithfulness. So we pray that you will give us today the strength to serve you with a humble heart and continue to listen to your word as it resonates in our hearts. We pray this in the name of our Lord Jesus. Amen.

Day 7

34 "Hope in the Lord
and keep his way.
He will exalt you to inherit the land;
when the wicked are destroyed, you will see it.

35 I have seen a wicked and ruthless man
   flourishing like a luxuriant native tree,
36 but he soon passed away and was no more;
   though I looked for him, he could not be found." (Psalm 37.34-36)

These verses address the question often asked in the Psalms of why the wicked appear prosperous and happy.

Here the wicked and ruthless are "flourishing". The Ecclesiast makes a similar remark:

14 "There is something else meaningless that occurs on earth: the righteous who get what the wicked deserve, and the wicked who get what the righteous deserve. This too, I say, is meaningless. **15** So I commend the enjoyment of life, because there is nothing better for a person under the sun than to eat and drink and be glad. Then joy will accompany them in their toil all the days of the life God has given them under the sun." (Ecclesiastes 8.15)

This is an important lesson from the Bible: there is no necessary correlation between one's prosperity or health and one's righteousness. Often the righteous endures pain. Often the unrighteous enjoys a good life. This is illustrated by Jesus in the story of Lazarus and the rich man:

19 "There was a rich man who was dressed in purple and fine linen and who lived in luxury every day. **20** At his gate was laid a beggar named Lazarus, covered with sours **21** and longing to eat what fell from the rich man's table. Even the dogs came and licked his sores." (Luke 16.19-21)

There is no law of "karma" in the Bible (the law of "karma" teaches that the good people have a good and prosperous life, and the bad people have a bad and painful life.)

Ecclesiastes acknowledges this to be part of the world we live in:

12 "Although a wicked person who commits a hundred crimes may live a long time, I know that it will go better with those who fear God, who are reverent before him. **13** Yet because the wicked do not fear God, it will not go well with them, and their days will not lengthen like a shadow.**14** There is something else meaningless that occurs on earth: the righteous who get what the wicked deserve, and the wicked who get what the righteous deserve. This too, I say, is meaningless. **15** So I commend the enjoyment of life, because there is nothing better for a person under the sun than to eat and drink and be glad. Then joy will accompany them in their toil all the days of the life God has given them under the sun." (Ecclesiastes 8.12-15)

The message of the Gospel, the message of salvation, is not that in following Christ we will have a prosperous, easy or healthy life on this earth. This is a distortion of biblical truth. This is, in fact, another kind of "good news" (Galatians 1.6-9); this is preaching another "Jesus" (2 Corinthians 11.2-4).

Prayer

Father in heaven, we want to glorify you today. We pray for wisdom in our words and actions. We also pray for understanding of your will, of your Word. We ask for your Spirit to produce in us his fruit of love, peace and righteousness. Amen.

Week 13: The Humble

Day 1

> "**25** With the merciful You will show Yourself merciful;
> With a blameless man You will show Yourself blameless;
> **26** With the pure You will show Yourself pure;
> And with the devious You will show Yourself shrewd.
> **27** For You will save the humble people,
> But will bring down haughty looks."
>   (Psalm 18.25-27)

This Psalm refers to the way of the LORD as "perfect"; He is a shield to all who trust in Him (v.30). The wicked and proud individual is mistaken if he thinks God is indifferent to his behavior: "Do not be deceived, God is not mocked; for whatever a man sows, that he will also reap." (Galatians 6.7).

The idea of "recompense" or "reward" should never be forgotten when it comes to our faith in God (Hebrews 11.6):

> **21**"For I have kept the ways of the Lord,
> And have not wickedly departed from my God.
> **22** For all His judgments *were* before me,
> And I did not put away His statutes from me.
> **23** I was also blameless [f]before Him,
> And I kept myself from my iniquity.
> **24** Therefore the Lord has recompensed me according to my righteousness,
> According to the cleanness of my hands in His sight." (Psalm 18.21-24)

This idea of "reward" from God should not be understood as merit based or as a payment due for doing good. It is rather the idea of God's grace being available to those who trust Him, who consider His will in their lives and are willing to confess their sins. The "reward" is still based on God's graciousness, since all have sinned and fallen short of the glory of God (Romans 3.23).

God offers his grace to those who live humbly before Him. But the "payment" for those who reject Him and who live in wickedness is "death": "For the wages of sin is death, but the gift of God is eternal life in Christ Jesus our Lord." (Romans 6.23).

God's conduct towards the wicked is a reflection of the choice the wicked have made in placing himself against God (as in 1 Samuel 2.30; 15.23). The individual must choose to be enlightened by God in his darkness (v.28). God hates proud and lofty eyes (Proverbs 6.17). The proud must humble themselves with shame (Isaiah 2.11).

Prayer

Father in heaven, we pray that today you will create in us a growing sense of your graciousness towards us. We believe in your Word, which promises reward for those who trust in you. We believe the greatest reward is to be in communion with you and to be part of your heavenly Kingdom. Amen.

Day 2

> **8** "Good and upright *is* the Lord;
> Therefore He teaches sinners in the way.
> **9** The humble He guides in justice,
> And the humble He teaches His way.
> **10** All the paths of the Lord *are* mercy and truth,
> To such as keep His covenant and His testimonies.
> **11** For Your name's sake, O Lord,
> Pardon my iniquity, for it *is* great."
> (Psalms 25.8-10)

The writer of this Psalm does not shy away from recognizing his sinfulness: "Pardon my iniquity, for it is great." (v.11). This is the mark of the truly humble individual:

> **6** "Remember, O Lord, your tender mercies and Your lovingkindnesses,
> For they *are* from of old.
> **7** Do not remember the sins of my youth, nor my transgressions;
> According to Your mercy remember me,
> For Your goodness' sake, O Lord."
> (Psalms 25.6,7)

Only the humble (or meek) will let God instruct them and guide them. That is the reason God only teaches the humble. The humble (*anawim*) are also the lowly, the poor and afflicted (Proverbs 14,21). They are those who are often afflicted by the rich and powerful (Amos 2.7; Isaiah 29.19; 32.7). The Bible says about Moses that he "*was* very humble, more than all men who *were* on the face of the earth." (Numbers 12.3).

Those who choose to walk in the "paths of the Lord" are following the paths of mercy and truth. This describes also the covenant and testimonies of God (Deuteronomy 7.9; Psalms 103.17,18).

> **28** "Come to Me, all *you* who labor and are heavy laden, and I will give you rest. **29** Take My yoke upon you and learn from Me, for I am gentle and lowly in heart, and you will find rest for your souls. **30** For My yoke *is* easy and My burden is light." (Matthew 11.28-30)

Prayer

Father in heaven, you are perfectly good and righteous in all your ways. Teach us every day to recognize our errors and sins. Forgive us of all our sins as we confess them to you. Teach us also to be humble in our ways, to be lowly in heart as Jesus was. In His name we pray, Amen.

Day 3

> **1** "I will bless the Lord at all times;
> His praise *shall* continually *be* in my mouth.
> **2** My soul shall make its boast in the Lord;
> The humble shall hear *of it* and be glad.
> **3** Oh, magnify the Lord with me,
> And let us exalt His name together."
>   (Psalms 34.1-3)

As in all of his Psalms, David wants to bring us to consider the greatness and faithfulness of God. Although he is a repentant man, he does not dwell forever on his sin or parade his sins before others, as if that was the heart of the message God is conveying. It is not a sign of humility to constantly mention one's sins privately or in public as if they were great battles one had undertaken and won. Confessing one's sins should mostly be done to God, while confessing Christ should be what is done publicly (1 John 1.8,9; Romans 10.9).

David praises the LORD in all circumstances. Christians are taught to pray and continually be grateful to God: "Giving thanks always for all things in the name of our Lord Jesus" (Ephesians 5:20)." Pray without ceasing; in everything give thanks, for this is the will of God" (1 Thessalonians 5:17-18).

The "humble" (*anawim*) are the lowly, poor, or afflicted (as in Psalms 25). In this Psalm, the humble are touched by the praises given to God and rejoice in these praises. The afflicted are encouraged and strengthened by praises given to God. In prayer as in praise, the point is to exalt the LORD and not ourselves or anyone else. To "exalt his name" is to exalt his person and character. It does not mean that it is necessary to use Yahweh (or Jehovah) in our praises of God.

The name "Jesus" (Joshua) was common in Judaism. Merely pronouncing that name does not save us. But if we understand who Jesus is and the meaning of his life and death, we can truly say that we are saved through His name,

> **10** "…let it be known to you all, and to all the people of Israel, that by the name of Jesus Christ of Nazareth, whom you crucified, whom God raised from the dead, by Him this man stands here before you whole. **11** This is the 'stone which was rejected by you builders, which has become the chief cornerstone.' **12** Nor is there salvation in any other, for there is no other name under heaven given among men by which we must be saved." (Acts 4.10-12)

Prayer

Father in heaven, we glorify your name. We thank you for your salvation in Jesus your Son. We pray that today our lives will reflect your goodness and holiness. We pray that our behavior and our praises will touch those who are seeking you and your kingdom with all their hearts. Amen.

Day 4

> **16** "Let all those who seek You rejoice and be glad in You;
> Let such as love Your salvation say continually,
> "The Lord be magnified!"
> **17** But I *am* poor and needy;
> *Yet* the Lord thinks upon me.

You *are* my help and my deliverer;
Do not delay, O my God."
   (Psalms 40.16,17)

King David describes himself as "poor and needy". When we look at ourselves, we cannot think that we are so rich and without the need for God. We cannot forget that whatever we have is an undeserved gift from God. We cannot be boastful of our status without displeasing God. This is not only about our "spiritual" condition, but touches everything we "own" or accomplish: it all belongs to the LORD and has been given to us.

The word translated poor (*ani*) which also means afflicted and the word humble (*anawim*) are very close in meaning. God is concerned for the afflicted, the poor and lowly. One's "prosperity" should never lead to pride or ungratefulness (Psalm 35.27). God wants us to know that "poverty" (we are lowly and needy) is our condition, even if others think of us as rich or successful.

> **14** "And to the angel of the church of the Laodiceans write, 'These things says the Amen, the Faithful and True Witness, the Beginning of the creation of God: **15** "I know your works, that you are neither cold nor hot. I could wish you were cold or hot. **16** So then, because you are lukewarm, and neither cold nor hot, I will vomit you out of My mouth. **17** Because you say, 'I am rich, have become wealthy, and have need of nothing'—and do not know that you are wretched, miserable, poor, blind, and naked— **18** I counsel you to buy from Me gold refined in the fire, that you may be rich; and white garments, that you may be clothed, *that* the shame of your nakedness may not be revealed; and anoint your eyes with eye salve, that you may see." (Revelation 3.14-18).

Prayer

Father in heaven, we pray today for an understanding of our poverty and need of you. We pray that we will not take for granted any blessing received from you. We pray that we will never be proud of any achievement, but instead give you praises for what you have done for us. Amen.

Day 5

> **1** "Why do You stand afar off, O Lord?
> *Why* do You hide in times of trouble?
> **2** The wicked in *his* pride persecutes the poor;
> Let them be caught in the plots which they have devised.
> **3** For the wicked boasts of his heart's desire; He blesses the greedy *and* renounces the Lord.
> **4** The wicked in his proud countenance does not seek *God;*
> God *is* in none of his thoughts.
> His ways are always prospering;
> Your judgments *are* far above, out of his sight;
> *As for* all his enemies, he sneers at them.
> **6** He has said in his heart, "I shall not be moved;
> I shall never be in adversity."
> **7** His mouth is full of cursing and deceit and oppression;
> Under his tongue *is* trouble and iniquity."
> (Psalms 10.1-7)

The wicked in his pride persecutes the poor (v.2). The wicked boasts in his heart's desires (v.3). The wicked in his proud countenance does not seek God (v.4). The wicked is characterized by his pride. It is his pride that drives him to persecute the poor. The prosperity of the wicked leads him to turn away from the LORD and bless the greedy.

The wicked and proud individual cannot see the judgments of God. He is blind to his true condition, as he must face God's judgment. He believes that he will never be in adversity, that his condition is secure. His words are full of deceit and oppression, trouble and iniquity.

Jesus opposes the proud throughout his teachings: "Beware of the scribes who like to walk around in long robes, and like respectful greetings in the marketplace and chief seats in the synagogues, and places of honor at banquets, who devour widows' houses, and for appearance's sake offer long prayers; these will receive greater condemnation." (Mark 12:38-40)

"Woe to you Pharisees! For you love the front seats in the synagogues, and the respectful greetings in the marketplace. "Woe to you! For you are like concealed tombs, and the people who walk over them are unaware of it." (Luke 11:43-44)

"The greatest among you will be your servant. For those who exalt themselves will be humbled, and those who humble themselves will be exalted." (Matt 23:2-12)

In the book of Revelation, the "beast" that opposes disciples of Jesus is characterized by a proud mouth: "And he was given a mouth speaking great things and blasphemies, and he was given authority to continue for forty-two months.

> **6** Then he opened his mouth in blasphemy against God, to blaspheme His name, His tabernacle, and those who dwell in heaven. **7** It was granted to him to make war with the saints and to overcome them. And authority was given him over every tribe, tongue, and nation." (Revelation 13.5-7)

Prayer

Father in heaven, we come to you to ask for faithfulness and humility, whatever our circumstances. We pray for gratefulness when we receive health and abundance. We are thankful for everything we have in this life. We pray that we will never take for granted anything we have. Amen.

Day 6

> **18** "Do not let me be ashamed, O Lord, for I have called upon You;
> Let the wicked be ashamed;
> Let them be silent in the grave.
> Let the lying lips be put to silence,
> Which speak insolent things proudly and contemptuously against the righteous.
> **19** Oh, how great *is* Your goodness,
> Which You have laid up for those who fear You,
> *Which* You have prepared for those who trust in You
> In the presence of the sons of men!"
>   (Psalms 31.17-19)

There are those who deplore what they call the "imprecatory psalms" where prayers are offered in view of the destructive ways of the wicked. The book of Revelation reports the same kind of prayer for God's judgment on the wicked (Revelation 6.10).

The Lord Jesus is not some kind of "do-gooder" who will tolerate every evil behavior and wickedness, no matter how evil. Did not our Lord himself say, "But these mine enemies that would not that I should reign over them, bring hither, and slay them before me" (Luke 19:27)?

There is a tone of severity throughout the Scriptures concerning evil and wickedness not repented of:

"And that no man transgress and defraud his brother in the matter because the Lord is the avenger in all these things, just as we also told you before and solemnly warned you." (1 Thessalonians 4.6)

"For all who have sinned without the Law will also perish without the Law, and all who have sinned under the Law will be judged by the Law." (Romans 2.12)

"But transgressors will be altogether destroyed; The posterity of the wicked will be cut off." (Psalms 37,38)

"Assuredly, the evil man will not go unpunished, but the descendants of the righteous will be delivered." (Proverbs 11.21)

"And inasmuch as it is appointed for men to die once and after this comes judgment." (Hebrews 9,27)

"And that slave who knew his master's will and did not get ready or act in accord with his will, will receive many lashes, but the one who did not know it, and committed deeds worthy of a flogging, will receive but few from everyone who has been given much, much will be required; and to whom they entrusted much, of him they will ask all the more." (Luke 12.47,48)

"But because of your stubbornness and unrepentant heart you are storing up wrath for yourself in the day of wrath and revelation of the righteous judgment of God, who will render to each person according to his deeds." (Romans 2.5,6)

"Every tree that does not bear good fruit is cut down and thrown into the fire. (Matthew 7.19)

"But I tell you that every careless word that people speak, they shall give an accounting for it in the day of judgment. "For by your words you will be justified, and by your words you will be condemned." (Matthew 12.36-39)

"Whoever causes one of these little ones who believe to stumble, it would be better for him if, with a heavy millstone hung around his neck, he had been cast into the sea. If your hand causes you to stumble, cut it off; it is better for you to enter life crippled, than having your two hands, to go into hell, into the unquenchable fire…" (Mark 9.42-49)

Prayer

Our Lord, we pray for grateful hearts. We pray that we can overcome any evil or wickedness in our own hearts. We ask for forgiveness. Thank you for Jesus and the cross. Thank you for his resurrection and his coming back. May our hearts be transformed today and every day. Amen.

Day 7

> **4** "Blessed *is* that man who makes the Lord his trust,
> And does not respect the proud, nor such as turn aside to lies.
> **5** Many, O Lord my God, *are* Your wonderful works
> *Which* You have done;
> And Your thoughts toward us
> Cannot be recounted to You in order;
> *If* I would declare and speak *of them*,
> They are more than can be numbered."
> (Psalms 40.4,5)

The man (*ish*, the human being) who makes the Lord his trust is blessed, happy. This is the theme of the very first Psalm and a central theme in the book of Psalms.

Putting one's trust in the Lord requires humility. Pride goes along with trusting oneself or something else besides God. In verse 5 the reason is given for trusting God instead of the proud: His wonderful works and his thoughts towards us which cannot be recounted.

The Messiah is the one who "delights" to do God's will. He is the one who proclaims the "good news" of righteousness in the great assembly (vv. 6-9 and Hebrews 10.8).

> **13** "Be pleased, O Lord, to deliver me;
> O Lord, make haste to help me!
> **14** Let them be ashamed and brought to mutual confusion
> Who seek to destroy my life;
> Let them be driven backward and brought to dishonor
> Who wish me evil.
> **15** Let them be confounded because of their shame,
> Who say to me, 'Aha, aha!'" (Psalms 40.13-15)

As Psalm 31, this Psalm has been called "imprecatory" by some who look critically at these words concerning the wicked. As already mentioned, there are those who deplore what they call the "imprecatory psalms" where prayers are offered in view of the destructive ways of the wicked. They forget the biblical truth that the Lord will judge all nations (Acts 17.31; Matthew 25).

Prayer

Our Father and Lord in heaven, we thank you today for giving us life. We thank you for every blessing. We pray for faithfulness and perseverance whether we are living at peace and in prosperous times or we are led into trials. May we always come close to you for help and wisdom through your Holy Spirit. Amen.

Week 14: Times of Pain

Day 1

> **9** "The Lord also will be a refuge for the oppressed,
> A refuge in times of trouble.
> **10** And those who know Your name will put their trust in You;
> For You, Lord, have not forsaken those who seek You."
> (Psalms 9.9,10)

The LORD will be or is a refuge for the oppressed. The tense of the verb can be understood both as a present and a future. God's promise is not constrained by time. Every promise He has ever made is already accomplished for the faithful.

The LORD is a refuge (*misgab*) for the oppressed. A *misgab* is a secured height, a retreat or stronghold; a high, steep place, where one is removed from danger. It conveys the idea for the oppressed of being out of reach from the wicked. A refuge is a safe place. God is our safe place when we need protection from something.

> "God *is* our refuge and strength,
> A very present help in trouble." (Psalm 46.1)

One of the ways we should pray is to declare that God is our refuge, is to pour out our hearts to Him about what is going on in our lives. Thus, we can always turn to God for help and protection, for all our needs and concerns:

> **6** "Be anxious for nothing, but in everything by prayer and supplication, with thanksgiving, let your requests be made known to God; **7** and the peace of God, which surpasses all understanding, will guard your hearts and minds through Christ Jesus."
> (Philippians 4.6-7)

> **13** "Have mercy on me, O Lord!
> Consider my trouble from those who hate me,

You who lift me up from the gates of death,
14 That I may tell of all Your praise
In the gates of the daughter of Zion.
I will rejoice in Your salvation." (Psalms 9.13,14)

The righteous one is hated and has enemies, as stated also in Psalm 69:

"Those who hate me without a cause
Are more than the hairs of my head;
They are mighty who would destroy me,
Being my enemies wrongfully;
Though I have stolen nothing,
I *still* must restore *it*." (Psalms 69.4)

This is applied to Jesus in John's Gospel:

22 "If I had not come and spoken to them, they would have no sin, but now they have no excuse for their sin. **23** He who hates Me hates My Father also. **24** If I had not done among them the works which no one else did, they would have no sin; but now they have seen and also hated both Me and My Father. **25** But *this happened* that the word might be fulfilled which is written in their law, 'They hated Me without a cause.'" (John 15.25)

Prayer

Father in heaven, we thank you for a new day. We come to you with all our concerns and worries because we believe you peace will be granted to us. We also believe that you are the only true and lasting refuge for whatever we need to face. If we face enemies or hatred, we pray for trust in you and peace in our hearts. In Jesus' name, Amen.

Day 2

6 "But I *am* a worm, and no man;
A reproach of men, and despised by the people.
7 All those who see Me ridicule Me;
They shoot out the lip, they shake the head, *saying,*
8 'He trusted in the Lord, let Him rescue Him;
Let Him deliver Him, since He delights in Him!'"
  (Psalm 22.6-8)

This Psalm of David begins with the words "My God, My God, why have You forsaken Me?" quoted by Jesus on the cross (Matthew 27.46). This Psalm written a thousand years before Christ also describes the sneers of his enemies (vv.7,8), the piercing of the hands and feet (v.16), the casting of lots for his garments (v.18). None of these statements are applicable to David, or to any other known event or person in the history of mankind except Jesus.

One of the important teachings of the Bible is that the good and righteous do not necessarily have a good and prosperous life. Quite often we read of the wicked and evil who are prosperous and enjoy their lives (Psalm 10; Ecclesiastes 8). The righteous do not escape pain, rejection or death. And as they live through these they may be mocked by unbelievers for their faith, "He trusted in the LORD, let Him rescue Him".

In the midst of his sufferings, Job spoke to his wife:

> **9** "His wife said to him, 'Are you still maintaining your integrity? Curse God and die!' **10** He replied, 'You are talking like a foolish woman. Shall we accept good from God, and not trouble?' In all this, Job did not sin in what he said." (Job 2.9,10)

> "I will maintain my innocence and never let go of it; my conscience will not reproach me as long as I live." (Job 27.6)

Prayer

Lord in heaven, we thank you for a new day. We pray that as we face difficulties or pain, we will find inspiration in your word, in your promises. We believe that the cross of Jesus is the way you have chosen to one day heal all pain and wipe away all tears. In Jesus' name, Amen.

Day 3

1 "The Lord is my shepherd, I lack nothing.
2   He makes me lie down in green pastures,
he leads me beside quiet waters,
3 He refreshes my soul.
He guides me along the right paths
   for his name's sake.
4 Even though I walk
   through the darkest valley,
I will fear no evil,

> for you are with me;
> your rod and your staff,
> they comfort me."
> (Psalm 23.1-4)

The word "shepherd" is derived from the Hebrew *re'a* meaning friend. The good shepherd Jesus acts like a friend and never an enemy. The good shepherd is our friend; he is still by our side even when we walk in a death-like valley completely filled with darkness. The LORD is "Adonai Shammah": the God always present, the "God who is there" (Ezekiel 48.35).

In our fallen world we too, at some point, will make the long, slow and painful walk through the "valley of the shadow of death". The Hebrew describes the most fearful darkness as of Hades in Job 10.21. The word was used of a shaft of a mine (Job 28.3) or the darkness felt in a wild and uninhabited desert (Jeremiah 2.6). Thus, there is also an impression of loneliness, of having nobody to lean on in this darkness.

This could be true right now for you. It could mean that a doctor has just given you a bad report. Maybe your spouse has left you or your child has left the faith. The picture of the "death-like valley" filled with darkness also teaches us that is there is such a valley and if there is such darkness this means that there is also light.

Jesus is the light of the world despite all of its darkness. We are not alone when we are with Him: "When Jesus spoke again to the people, he said, 'I am the light of the world. Whoever follows me will never walk in darkness, but will have the light of life.'" (John 8.12)

Even in the midst of the darkness that surrounds us, we are not fearful of evil hurting us or overcoming us because of the presence of the Lord in our lives and in our hearts.

> **5** "You prepare a table before me
> in the presence of my enemies.
> You anoint my head with oil;
> my cup overflows.
> **6** Surely your goodness and love will follow me
> all the days of my life,
> and I will dwell in the house of the Lord
> forever." (Psalms 23. 5,6)

> **14** "I am the good shepherd; I know my sheep and my sheep know me— **15** just as the Father knows me and I know the Father—and I lay down my life for the sheep. **16** I have other

sheep that are not of this sheep pen. I must bring them also. They too will listen to my voice, and there shall be one flock and one shepherd. **17** The reason my Father loves me is that I lay down my life—only to take it up again. **18** No one takes it from me, but I lay it down of my own accord. I have authority to lay it down and authority to take it up again. This command I received from my Father." (John 10. 14-18)

Prayer

Father in heaven, we thank you for a new day. We come to you as we walk in this present darkness of our lives. We believe you are the light of the world and there is no darkness in you. We believe in Jesus and his death for us. Give us your peace and comfort for another day. Amen.

Day 4

11 "Do not withhold your mercy from me, Lord;
     may your love and faithfulness always protect me.
12 For troubles without number surround me;
     my sins have overtaken me, and I cannot see.
They are more than the hairs of my head,
     and my heart fails within me.
13 Be pleased to save me, Lord;
     come quickly, Lord, to help me." (Psalm 40.11-13)

This Psalm is also an encouragement to wait patiently for the LORD and to continue to do His will despite the troubles we go through.

There are times when "troubles without number" surround us. There are also times when our sins ("iniquities" in other translations) have "overtaken us" and we cannot see. In both cases, we can come with assurance to the LORD for mercy and protection.

The word for "sins" or "iniquities" in verse 12 is the Hebrew *raowt* found numerous times in the Old Testament and which comes from *ra* meaning evil, adversity or calamity. The word is used for example of the tree of the knowledge of good and evil (*ra*). Thus, the text may be understood as referring to the evil and adversity the author is enduring.

Part of this Psalm (vv. 6-8) is about Jesus the Messiah, of whom it is said:

6 "Sacrifice and offering you did not desire—
     but my ears you have opened —

burnt offerings and sin offerings you did not require.
7 Then I said, 'Here I am, I have come—
it is written about me in the scroll.
8 I desire to do your will, my God;
your law is within my heart.'" (Psalms 40.6-8 and Hebrews 10.8).

Jesus said to his disciples: "My food is to do the will of Him who sent Me, and to finish His work." (John 4.34).

When it says that God does not delight in sacrifices (see Jeremiah 7:22; Amos 5:21.) it does not mean that the sacrifices instituted in the Tora were not from God. This is saying what also the prophets say that the true, essential will of God is not directed to such sacrifices but to a heart of trust and obedience.

Prayer

Father in heaven, we thank you for this day. We ask for your wisdom and strength through your Holy Spirit, especially when we face difficult people or decisions to be made. We believe that what you want from us today is to seek first your kingdom and righteousness. In Jesus' name, we pray. Amen.

Day 5

1 "Hear my cry, O God;
Attend to my prayer.
2 From the end of the earth I will cry to You,
When my heart is overwhelmed;
Lead me to the rock that is higher than I.
3 For You have been a shelter for me,
A strong tower from the enemy.
4 I will abide in Your tabernacle forever;
I will trust in the shelter of Your wings. *Selah*"
'(Psalm 61.1-4)

"When my heart is overwhelmed" is a statement that many can identify with. This statement comes as results of one being away from his land or abode. The Psalm expresses the feeling of being homeless and separated from loved ones and from a familiar land.

It can be difficult for those who have never been exiled from their land to understand the "overwhelming" feelings of those who are far from their country or relatives.

For the exile or the one far from his home, God remains "the rock that is higher than I". This one cannot find shelter in himself or herself. Only the LORD can lead this one to the rock, shelter and strong tower he needs. This rock, shelter and strong tower is God himself. The "rock" (*tsur*) is here the "clift of the rock": a rock under which one finds protection, as in Exodus 33.22,

> "**20** But He said, 'You cannot see My face; for no man shall see Me, and live.' **21** And the Lord said, 'Here is a place by Me, and you shall stand on the rock. **22** So it shall be, while My glory passes by, that I will put you in the cleft of the rock (*tsur*) and will cover you with My hand while I pass by. **23** Then I will take away My hand, and you shall see My back; but My face shall not be seen.' The image is similar to that of the wings of the bird under which one finds shelter."

The dwelling place for the exiled one is God's tabernacle (v.4) which describes the presence of God. This place of safety is one "forever" (*olam*, used numerous times throughout the Old Testament, as in Genesis 3.22; Exodus 3.15).

> **5** "You prepare a table before me in the presence of my enemies;
> You anoint my head with oil;
> My cup runs over.
> **6** Surely goodness and mercy shall follow me
> All the days of my life;
> And I will dwell in the house of the Lord
> Forever." (Psalms 23.5,6).

Prayer

Lord God, we pray for all who are exiled from their land and relatives. We pray that as we meet with the exiles, we can bring them your love and care, we can show them kindness and friendship. We thank you for our families and loved ones, and for our land. We thank you if we enjoy peace and daily food. May our hearts be grateful today for all your blessings. Amen.

Day 6

> **49** "Remember the word to Your servant,
> Upon which You have caused me to hope.

50 This *is* my comfort in my affliction,
For Your word has given me life.
51 The proud have me in great derision,
Yet I do not turn aside from Your law.
52 I remembered Your judgments of old, O Lord,
And have comforted myself."
   (Psalms 119.49-52)

These verses from Psalm 119 start with the word "remember" (*zakar*) form the section called *zayin,* the seventh letter of the Hebrew alphabet. The word *zakar* occurs over two thousand times in the Old Testament, as in Genesis 8,1; 9.15; 19.29; Exodus 2,24. It is mostly used of God, who "remembers". The word used in such a way does not mean God could have "forgotten" anything. It means God was "mindful" to express His intervention at that particular moment of history.

The writer prays that God will act on his behalf as promised in His word and upon which he has built his hope. The hope of God acting upon His word comforts the one who is afflicted. This word in fact is that word of God that has given us life. This is a key concept linked to faith in Christ the savior,

> **1** "Therefore, having been justified by faith, we have peace with God through our Lord Jesus Christ, **2** through whom also we have access by faith into this grace in which we stand, and rejoice in hope of the glory of God. **3** And not only *that,* but we also glory in tribulations, knowing that tribulation produces perseverance; **4** and perseverance, character; and character, hope. **5** Now hope does not disappoint, because the love of God has been poured out in our hearts by the Holy Spirit who was given to us." (Romans 5.1-4)

The "proud" are also the mockers, the scornful (*luts*) as in Job 16.20; Psalms 1.1; Proverbs 1.22; 9.7; 9.8): "A proud *and* haughty *man* —'Scoffer' *is* his name; he acts with arrogant pride" (Proverbs 21.24).

Prayer

Father in heaven, we thank you for Jesus, for his life and teachings. We thank you for the Scriptures given to us through the centuries. We believe in all your promises, the ones that are clear to us and the ones we still do not grasp fully. We pray for humility through your Holy Spirit. Amen.

Day 7

> **9** "If I ascend into heaven, you *are* there;
> If I make my bed in hell, behold, You *are there.*
> *If* I take the wings of the morning,
> *And* dwell in the uttermost parts of the sea,
> **10** Even there Your hand shall lead me,
> And Your right hand shall hold me.
> **11** If I say, 'Surely the darkness shall fall on me,'
> Even the night shall be light about me;
> **12** Indeed, the darkness shall not hide from You,
> But the night shines as the day;
> The darkness and the light *are* both alike *to You.*"
> (Psalms 139.9-12)

Psalm 139 reminds us that the knowledge of God is perfect and is not limited by time or space: "Such knowledge is too wonderful for me; it is high, I cannot attain it." (v.6).

Verses 9 to 12 are comforting words for those who find themselves far away in the heavens or in *hades* (the realm of the dead), on the sea or in the middle of a dark night. The key statement in these verses is that "even there your hand shall guide me".

This repeats the statement "You have hedged me behind and before and laid your hand upon me." In verse 5, the faithful are "hedged" or enclosed *(sartani)* all around by the LORD. This is the only time in the Old Testament that the verb *tsuwr*, to confine, to wrap or to besiege (for example Deuteronomy 20.12; 1 Samuel 23.8) is used in this form of the verb and in this way. The use of this verb may also indicate the impossibility for the sinner, who may want to do so, to flee from God's presence and judgment.

What is a comfort to the faithful (God's hedging, enclosing) is a warning to the unfaithful, who are mentioned later in this Psalm (vv.19-22). It is also a reminder that God can see if there is any wicked way in the believer and can lead him in the way everlasting (vv.23,24).

"But the Lord is faithful, and he will strengthen you and protect you from the evil one. 4 We have confidence in the Lord that you are doing and will continue to do the things we command. 5 May the Lord direct your hearts into God's love and Christ's perseverance." (2 Thessalonians 3.3-5)

"The Lord will rescue me from every evil attack and will bring me safely to his heavenly kingdom. To him be glory for ever and ever. Amen." (2 Timothy 4.18)

Prayer

Father in heaven, we are thankful to you for this day. We thank you for your care and protection. Even when we find ourselves in difficulties or in pain, you are there and you remain faithful to your word of promise. Give us wisdom through your Holy Spirit as we face temptations or trials. Amen.

Week 15: Kings and Rulers

Day 1

> "Why do the nations rage,
> And the people plot a vain thing?
> **2** The kings of the earth set themselves,
> And the rulers take counsel together,
> Against the Lord and against His Anointed, *saying,*
> **3** 'Let us break Their bonds in pieces
> And cast away Their cords from us.'"
> (Psalms 2.1-3)

Psalms 1 and 2 are often considered as introductory Psalms to the entire book of Psalms. Psalm 2 is about God's Son who is chosen by God to rule over the nations (also Hebrews 5.5; Acts 13.33 applied to Jesus).

> "I will declare the decree:
> The Lord has said to Me,
> 'You *are* My Son,
> Today I have begotten You.
> **8** Ask of Me, and I will give *You*
> The nations *for* Your inheritance,
> And the ends of the earth *for* Your possession.'" (vv.6-8)

> "But God raised Him from the dead. **31** He was seen for many days by those who came up with Him from Galilee to Jerusalem, who are His witnesses to the people. **32** And we declare to you glad tidings — that promise which was made to the fathers **33** God has fulfilled this for us their children, in that He has raised up Jesus. As it is also written in the second Psalm: 'You are My Son, today I have begotten You.'" (Acts 13.30-33)

By his resurrection, Jesus was declared the anointed Son and king promised in the Old Testament:

> "Paul, a bondservant of Jesus Christ, called *to be* an apostle, separated to the gospel of God **2** which He promised
> before through His prophets in the Holy Scriptures, **3** concerning His Son Jesus Christ our Lord, who was born of the seed of David according to the flesh, **4** *and* declared *to be* the Son of
> God with power according to the Spirit of holiness, by the resurrection from the dead." (Romans 1.1-4)

In Acts 4 the rulers who "rage against the Son" are Herod and Pontius Pilate,

> **27** "For truly against Your holy Servant Jesus, whom You anointed, both Herod and Pontius Pilate, with the Gentiles and the people of Israel, were gathered together **28** to do whatever Your hand and Your purpose determined before to be done." (Acts 4.27,28).

Through the hands of these rulers, whether Gentile (Romans) or from Israel (the High priest and Sanhedrin) the prophecy of Psalm 2 was accomplished.

This Psalm warns "kings and judges of the earth" that they should be wise and serve the Lord with fear (v.10). No political system can justify the actions of evil or foolish leaders, even today. Even for leaders of nations, the statement of verse 12 is true: "Blessed are all those who put their trust in Him".

> **1** "Therefore, I exhort first of all that supplications, prayers, intercessions, *and* giving of thanks be made for all men, **2** for kings and all who are in authority, that we may lead a quiet and peaceable life in all godliness and reverence. **3** For this *is* good and acceptable in the sight of God our Savior, **4** who desires all men to be saved and to come to the knowledge of the truth." (1 Timothy 2.1-4)

Prayer

Father in heaven, we thank you for a new day. We pray for all of our leaders. We pray for men and women in position of authority. We pray for peace in our land and peace in the world, and for the preaching of the Gospel in our land and throughout the world. In Jesus' name. Amen.

Day 2

> "He *is* the Lord our God;
> His judgments *are* in all the earth.
> **8** He remembers His covenant forever,
> The word *which* He commanded, for a thousand generations,
> **9** *The covenant* which He made with Abraham,
> And His oath to Isaac,
> **10** And confirmed it to Jacob for a statute,
> To Israel *as* an everlasting covenant,
> **11** Saying, 'To you I will give the land of Canaan
> As the allotment of your inheritance,'
> **12** When they were few in number,
> Indeed very few, and strangers in it.
> **13** When they went from one nation to another,
> From *one* kingdom to another people,
> **14** He permitted no one to do them wrong;
> Yes, He rebuked kings for their sakes,
> **15** *Saying*, 'Do not touch My anointed ones,
> And do My prophets no harm.'"
> (Psalms 105.7-15)

This Psalm is a chronological survey of the history of Israel from the days of the patriarchs to the Promised land. The first fifteen verses of this Psalm are quoted in 1 Chronicles 16.8-22.

In verse 7 the God of Israel is also the judge of all the earth. God rebuked kings for the sake of Israel (v.14). When Joseph was in prison, the pharaoh at the time released him and made him lord of his house (vs 20,21). God demonstrated his power to Pharaoh in the plagues (vv.26-36). The fear of Israel fell on Egypt (v.38). God gave to his people the lands of the Gentiles; they inherited the labors of the nations (v.44).

Thus, this Psalm does not only recall the history of Israel from the times of the patriarchs, it underlines God's rule over the nations in favor of his people and for the realization of his plans.

God's plans cannot be thwarted by human rulers or kings. God is on the side of the faithful and of the Church. God is still the judge of the earth today.

> "The king's heart *is* in the hand of the LORD,
> *Like* the rivers of water;
> He turns it wherever He wishes." (Proverbs 21.1)

"And He has made from one blood every nation of men to dwell on all the face of the earth and has determined their pre-appointed times and the boundaries of their dwellings." (Acts 17.26)

"Then Pilate said to Him, 'Are You not speaking to me? Do You not know that I have power to crucify You, and power to release You?' Jesus answered, 'You could have no power at all against Me unless it had been given you from above. Therefore, the one who delivered Me to you has the greater sin.'" (John 19.10,11)

"And Jesus came and spoke to them, saying, "All authority has been given to Me in heaven and on earth." (Matthew 28.18)

Prayer

Father in heaven, we thank you for this day. We are grateful for Jesus, who has received all authority in heaven and on earth. We pray for the leaders of our land. We pray for your people, for Christians in our land and in the world. May you bless them with peace and wisdom. In Jesus's name, we pray.

Day 3

16 "Moreover He called for a famine in the land;
He destroyed all the provision of bread.
17 He sent a man before them—
Joseph—*who* was sold as a slave.
18 They hurt his feet with fetters,
He was laid in irons.
19 Until the time that his word came to pass,
The word of the Lord tested him.
20 The king sent and released him,
The ruler of the people let him go free.
21 He made him lord of his house,
And ruler of all his possessions,
22 To bind his princes at his pleasure,
And teach his elders wisdom."
   (Psalms 105.16-22)

Through the famine and story of Joseph, God was accomplishing his plans declared to Abraham and through his descendants. The famine in the land was no accident, but was part of God's plan.

The sufferings of Joseph are described in verse 18: "They hurt his feet with fetters, he was laid in irons." This describes his years in prison until "the king sent and released him" (v.19). When we see leaders acting in rebellion against God, we need to remember that God is still their judge and can use who he wants to accomplish his plans.

Physical pain is often considered the worst thing that can fall on human beings. And although physical pain is dreadful, God looks at sin and rebellion as a worse condition since it destroys the soul and brings spiritual death (Ephesians 2.1-4). The "deeds" and "works" of the Lord we need to remember (vv.1,2) are those that bring human beings to trust and repentance, to reconciliation with God.

> **1** "And you *He made alive,* who were dead in trespasses and sins, **2** in which you once walked according to the course of this world, according to the prince of the power of the air, the spirit who now works in the sons of disobedience, **3** among whom also we all once conducted ourselves in the lusts of our flesh, fulfilling the desires of the flesh and of the mind, and were by nature children of wrath, just as the others. **4** But God, who is rich in mercy, because of His great love with which He loved us, **5** even when we were dead in trespasses, made us alive together with Christ (by grace you have been saved), **6** and raised *us* up together, and made *us* sit together in the heavenly *places* in Christ Jesus, **7** that in the ages to come He might show the exceeding riches of His grace in *His* kindness toward us in Christ Jesus. **8** For by grace you have been saved through faith, and that not of yourselves; *it is* the gift of God, **9** not of works, lest anyone should boast. **10** For we are His workmanship, created in Christ Jesus for good works, which God prepared beforehand that we should walk in them." (Ephesians 2.1-10)

Prayer

Father in heaven, we thank you for the salvation you have brought about through Jesus and your plan of redemption. We thank you for your grace and gift of salvation through faith. We pray that today we can accomplish faithfully the good works you have prepared for us to do. Amen.

Day 4

> **7** "Praise the Lord from the earth,
> You great sea creatures and all the depths;
> **8** Fire and hail, snow and clouds;
> Stormy wind, fulfilling His word;
> **9** Mountains and all hills;
> Fruitful trees and all cedars;
> **10** Beasts and all cattle;
> Creeping things and flying fowl;
> **11** Kings of the earth and all peoples;
> Princes and all judges of the earth;
> **12** Both young men and maidens;
> Old men and children.
> **13** Let them praise the name of the Lord,
> For His name alone is exalted;
> His glory *is* above the earth and heaven.
> **14** And He has exalted the horn of His people,
> The praise of all His saints—
> Of the children of Israel,
> A people near to Him.
> Praise the Lord!"
> (Psalms 148.7-14)

In this Psalm, the whole of creation is to praise the LORD. All peoples, princes and judges are part of that creation and are called by God to praise Him. Princes and judges, kings and rulers need to remember that the LORD'S name is alone exalted and that His glory is above the earth (v.13). Exalting the LORD'S name (LORD is Yahweh) does not mean that believers or God's people are required to pronounce that name. To praise "the name" of someone is to praise all that this person is. God is called by a number of different names in the Bible (like Father) which can be rightly used when addressing Him. But, as we address God, we should do so with an understanding of who He is and of His will.

> **5** "Let this mind be in you, which was also in Christ
> Jesus, **6** who, being in the form of God, did not consider it robbery to be equal with God, **7** but made Himself of no reputation, taking the form of a bondservant, *and* coming in the likeness of men. **8** And being found in appearance as a man, He humbled Himself and became obedient to *the point of* death, even

the death of the cross. **9** Therefore God also has highly exalted Him and given Him the name, which is above every name, **10** that at the name of Jesus every knee should bow, of those in heaven, and of those on earth, and of those under the earth, **11** and *that* every tongue should confess that Jesus Christ *is* Lord, to the glory of God the Father." (Philippians 2. 5-11)

We are called to give glory to Christ as we give glory to the Father in heaven.

22 "For the Father judges no one, but has committed all judgment to the Son, **23** that all should honor the Son just as they honor the Father. He who does not honor the Son does not honor the Father who sent Him." (John 5.22,23)

"And He is the radiance of His glory and the exact representation of His nature, and upholds all things by the word of His power When He had made purification of sins, He sat down at the right hand of the Majesty on high." (Hebrews 1.3)

28 "Him we preach, warning every man and teaching every man in all wisdom, that we may present every man perfect in Christ Jesus. **29** To this *end* I also labor, striving according to His working which works in me mightily." (Colossians 1.28,29)

"But we all, with unveiled face, beholding as in a mirror the glory of the Lord, are being transformed into the same image from glory to glory, just as from the Lord, the Spirit." (2 Corinthians 3.8)

"For God, who said, 'Light shall shine out of darkness,' is the One who has shone in our hearts to give the Light of the knowledge of the glory of God in the face of Christ." (2 Corinthians 4.6)

"When Christ, who is our life, is revealed, then you also will be revealed with Him in glory." (Colossians 3.4)

Let Us Come Before His Presence

Prayer

Lord our God and Father, we praise you today. We give praise to Jesus, our Lord and savior. We thank you for the forgiveness and hope of glory we find in Christ. We come to you with confidence that all your promises will be fulfilled in Jesus. May we today praise you and be faithful to you. Our prayer is in the name of Jesus, our Lord. Amen.

Day 5

> **1** "Do you indeed speak righteousness, you silent ones?
> Do you judge uprightly, you sons of men?
> **2** No, in heart you work wickedness;
> You weigh out the violence of your hands in the earth.'"
> (Psalms 58.1,2)

This Psalm starts with a question about unjust and wicked judges and rulers. Literally, the Psalm says: "You silent ones, do you speak righteousness uprightly?" The Hebrew uses two words to emphasize that this is about judges sitting in courts: do you speak righteousness (*tsedek*) uprightly (*mesarim*). The word *tsedek* often describes just balances or weights in business dealings (Leviticus 19.36). The word *mesarim* describes uprightness, equity, evenness or fairness (1 Chronicles 29.17).

The answer to the question in verse 2 is "No". These judges work wickedness out of their wicked hearts. The evil done by wicked judges is compared to the poison of serpents or the teeth of young lions ready to devour their prey. This Psalm has often been criticized for its emphasis on God avenging himself on these wicked judges. Such a criticism only shows little understanding of the harm done by bad judges and the certainty of God's justice when dealing with wicked rulers.

There is also a reward for those who rule righteously: "Surely *there is* a reward for the righteous; surely He is God who judges in the earth." (v.11) This verse reminds human judges and rulers that there is a judge over all the earth — God — to whom they must give account.

Jesus is the supreme judge in the New Testament and also a perfect judge. All nations will stand in judgment before Him:

> "And Jesus said to them, 'Truly I say to you, that you who have followed Me, in the regeneration when the Son of Man will sit on His glorious throne, you also shall sit upon twelve thrones, judging the twelve tribes of Israel.'" (Matthew 19.28)

"He gave Him authority to execute judgment, because He is the Son of Man." (John 5.27)

"He has fixed a day in which He will judge the world in righteousness through a Man whom He has appointed, having furnished proof to all men by raising Him from the dead." (Acts 17.31)

"For we must all appear before the judgment seat of Christ, so that each one may be recompensed for his deeds in the body, according to what he has done, whether good or bad." (2 Corinthians 5.10)

31 "When the Son of Man comes in His glory, and all the holy angels with Him, then He will sit on the throne of His glory. **32** All the nations will be gathered before Him, and He will separate them one from another, as a shepherd divides *his* sheep from the goats." (Matthew 25.31,32)

Prayer
Father in heaven, we thank you for this day. We believe you are the perfect judge of all and have given Jesus all authority to judge the world because he is your Son from eternity. We pray for wisdom and righteousness when we lead others or have authority over them. We pray for forgiveness when we have failed in our responsibilities. In Jesus' name, we pray, Amen.

Day 6

1 "God stands in the congregation of the mighty;
He judges among the gods.
2 How long will you judge unjustly,
And show partiality to the wicked? *Selah*
3 Defend the poor and fatherless;
Do justice to the afflicted and needy.
4 Deliver the poor and needy;
Free *them* from the hand of the wicked."
   (Psalm 82.1-4)

God is present among his people. God is aware of the evil and unjust judgments made by men in authority — some even having divine authority, and why they are called "gods" in verse 1 and "sons of god" (or the Most-High) in verse 6. Jesus himself reveals to us that "sons of god" in this Psalm is a reference to human beings when he spoke to the Pharisees, saying:

> **34** "Is it not written ... I said, Ye are gods? **35** If he called them gods unto whom the Word of God came (and the scripture cannot be broken), how say ye of him ... **36** whom the Father sent into the world, thou blasphemest, because I said, I am the Son of God?" (John 10:34-36).

The Scriptures contain a number of judgments against wicked judges in Israel. Zephaniah 3:3 refers to those judges as "evening wolves"; and Amos repeatedly stated that they would sell the poor "for a pair of shoes" (Amos 2:6; 8:6). Note: "You shall not oppress a hired servant who is poor and needy, whether he is one of your countrymen or one of your aliens who is in your land in your towns." (Deuteronomy 24.14)

The temptation is great for those who are in a position of power to abuse their power and to forget that God will ask them to account for what they have done.

> **42** "Calling them to Himself, Jesus said to them, 'You know that those who are recognized as rulers of the Gentiles lord it over them; and their great men exercise authority over them.' **43** But it is not this way among you, but whoever wishes to become great among you shall be your servant; **44** and whoever wishes to be first among you shall be slave of all." (Mark 10.42-44)

Even leaders in the Church must be careful not to abuse their authority,

> **2** "Shepherd the flock of God among you, exercising oversight not under compulsion, but voluntarily, according to the will of God; and not for sordid gain, but with eagerness; **3** nor yet as lording it over those allotted to your charge, but proving to be examples to the flock." (1 Peter 5.2,3)

Men who hold positions of power have a responsibility towards those who are most vulnerable: the poor and fatherless. God asks them to do justice to the afflicted and needy, to deliver the poor and needy. When rulers and people in authority are unjust and uncaring, the very foundations of the earth (or land) are unstable. This describes the unstable nature of a society that is not led by righteous rulers.

Prayer

Lord, we pray for our rulers and all those who have authority. May you guide them and lead them to your righteous ways. We pray for the poor and needy. May we be willing to help out those we meet today and need our help. Thank you for your blessings, lord. Amen.

Day 7

> **70** "He also chose David His servant,
> And took him from the sheepfolds;
> **71** From following the ewes that had young He brought him,
> To shepherd Jacob His people,
> And Israel His inheritance.
> **72** So he shepherded them according to the integrity of his heart,
> And guided them by the skillfulness of his hands."
> (Psalms 78.70-72)

Psalm 78 recalls the history of Israel from the time of the Exodus out of Egypt to the kingship of David. These are the last verses of this Psalm. David was a king and is here described as a shepherd. God wanted the rulers to act as shepherds, to take good care of His people. The good shepherd needed to have integrity of heart and to be a skillful leader.

The qualities of the shepherd are what God wanted from kings and rulers. These qualities are well described in Ezekiel chapter 34 when contrasted with the evil and irresponsible shepherds condemned by the prophet:

> **4** "The weak you have not strengthened, nor have you healed those who were sick, nor bound up the broken, nor brought back what was driven away, nor sought what was lost; but with force and cruelty you have ruled them. **5** So they were scattered because *there was* no shepherd; and they became food for all the beasts of the field when they were scattered. **6** My sheep wandered through all the mountains, and on every high hill; yes, my flock was scattered over the whole face of the earth, and no one was seeking or searching *for them*." (Ezekiel 34.4-6)

God himself will come and shepherd his people:

11 "For thus says the Lord God: 'Indeed I Myself will search for My sheep and seek them out. **12** As a shepherd seeks out his flock on the day he is among his scattered sheep, so will I seek out My sheep and deliver them from all the places where they were scattered on a cloudy and dark day. **13** And I will bring them out from the peoples and gather them from the countries, and will bring them to their own land; I will feed them on the mountains of Israel, [b]in the valleys and in all the inhabited places of the country. **14** I will feed them in good pasture, and their fold shall be on the high mountains of Israel. There they shall lie down in a good fold and feed in rich pasture on the mountains of Israel. **15** I will feed My flock, and I will make them lie down,' says the Lord God. **16** 'I will seek what was lost and bring back what was driven away, bind up the broken and strengthen what was sick; but I will destroy the fat and the strong, and feed them in judgment.'" (Ezekiel 34.11-16)

This prophecy was fulfilled in Jesus, who is the good shepherd:

14 I am the good shepherd; and I know My *sheep* and am known by My own. **15** As the Father knows Me, even so I know the Father; and I lay down My life for the sheep. **16** And other sheep I have which are not of this fold; them also I must bring, and they will hear My voice; and there will be one flock *and* one shepherd. **17** Therefore My Father loves Me, because I lay down My life that I may take it again. **18** No one takes it from Me, but I lay it down of Myself. I have power to lay it down, and I have power to take it again. This command I have received from My Father." (John 10.14-18)

Prayer

We thank you, Father, for your Son Jesus. We thank you for his sacrifice on the cross and the salvation that you offer through him. We thank you for his resurrection and his coming back one day. We pray that we can fully understand the meaning of this sacrifice and of this salvation. We pray in Jesus' name.

Week 16: The Rejected

Day 1

> **7** "Hear, O Lord, *when* I cry with my voice!
> Have mercy also upon me, and answer me.
> **8** *When You said,* 'Seek My face,'
> My heart said to You, 'Your face, Lord, I will seek.'
> **9** Do not hide Your face from me;
> Do not turn Your servant away in anger;
> You have been my help;
> Do not leave me nor forsake me,
> O God of my salvation.
> **10** When my father and my mother forsake me,
> Then the Lord will take care of me."
> (Psalm 27.7-10)

This Psalm starts with God described as our light and strength (or stronghold). God is also our salvation, the one who delivers us from evil. Without God, no salvation is possible. In his Son Jesus Christ, God's salvation is offered to all men if they will accept it. The apostle John sums up the offer of salvation in these words, "God gave unto us eternal life; and this life is in his Son" (1 John 5:11).

David was not abandoned by his mother or father, but the Psalm teaches us that even those who have been abandoned by their mother or father will find in God one who will take care of them. God is himself described as our heavenly Father to whom we can pray with assurance (Matthew 6.9). He is the Father of glory, who can give us a "spirit of wisdom and revelation in the knowledge of him" (Ephesians 1.17).

One who has no mother or father can be described as someone who is lost and wandering and needs guidance. As a Father does with his children, God also wants to teach us and lead us (v.11). Those who take refuge in Him and listen to His teachings will find assurance and will be "strengthened" in their heart. In Romans 8:31, we have the New Testament elaboration of what is taught here: "If God be for us, who can be against us?"

"Wait on the Lord;
Be of good courage,
And He shall strengthen your heart;
Wait, I say, on the Lord!" (v.14)

Prayer

We thank you, Father, for being our father. We thank you for your perfect goodness and for your Words of comfort and guidance. You are the light of our salvation and our source of strength. With you, we know that we are not abandoned or rejected. We pray that you will guide our steps today and strengthen our hearts. Amen.

Day 2

12 "Blessed *is* the man whom You instruct, O Lord,
And teach out of Your law,
13 That You may give him rest from the days of adversity,
Until the pit is dug for the wicked.
14 For the Lord will not cast off His people,
Nor will He forsake His inheritance.
15 But judgment will return to righteousness,
And all the upright in heart will follow it."
   (Psalms 94.12-15)

Those who are instructed by the LORD and listen to His instruction are blessed. Even in the days of adversity, God provides them rest. God will not abandon or forsake those who listen to Him.

The connection between instructions from the LORD and rest despite adversity is clearly made by Jesus:

28 "Come to Me, all *you* who labor and are heavy laden, and I will give you rest. **29** Take My yoke upon you and learn from Me, for I am gentle and lowly in heart, and you will find rest for your souls. **30** For My yoke *is* easy and My burden is light." (Matthew 11.28-30). God's Word provides the answers and the encouragement we need in order to go through adversity.

The adversity of the righteous comes in this Psalm through the actions of the wicked who "break" God's people in pieces, who afflict His heritage, who slay the widow and strangers and murder the fatherless and who say, "The LORD does not see".

A clear teaching from the LORD is that divine judgment is inevitable and will fall on the unrighteous. This is stated at the start of this Psalm:

> **1** "O LORD God, to whom vengeance belongs — O God, to whom vengeance belongs, shine forth! **2** Rise up, O Judge of the earth; render punishment to the proud. Lord, how long will the wicked, how long will the wicked triumph?" (vv.1,2).

There is no spirit of revenge in God. He is good, gracious and merciful. But he is also a righteous judge. Evil will not win in the battle of good over evil, of truth over lies. Jesus himself mentioned God's judgment in a great part of His teachings and made it clear that God's justice will not be frustrated. In fact, all will be judged on the basis of his teachings:

> **46** "I have come *as* a light into the world, that whoever believes in Me should not abide in darkness. **47** And if anyone hears My words and does not believe, I do not judge him; for I did not come to judge the world but to save the world. **48** He who rejects Me, and does not receive My words, has that which judges him—the word that I have spoken will judge him in the last day. **49** For I have not spoken on My own *authority;* but the Father who sent Me gave Me a command, what I should say and what I should speak. **50** And I know that His command is everlasting life. Therefore, whatever I speak, just as the Father has told Me, so I speak." (John 12.46-50)

Prayer

Father in heaven, we thank you for your Word. We thank you for the teachings of Jesus. We pray that on this day we can be good listeners of those teachings. Give us the wisdom and strength to know how to put into practice these teachings. Help us to live with the guidance and help of your Holy Spirit. We pray in Jesus' name. Amen.

Day 3

> **21** "I will praise You,
> For You have answered me,
> And have become my salvation.
> **22** The stone *which* the builders rejected
> Has become the chief cornerstone.
> **23** This was the Lord's doing;

It *is* marvelous in our eyes.
24 This *is* the day the Lord has made;
We will rejoice and be glad in it."
(Psalm 118.21-24)

The language of this Psalm is that of a king who speaks in his personal name: "I called on the LORD in distress" (v.5) and "All nations surrounded me, but in the name of the LORD I will destroy them" (v.10). This is about God's king who has been rejected but continues to trust the LORD.

Jesus quotes this Psalm as being about himself, the Messiah. He does this to confirm the meaning of the parable of the wicked vinedressers who killed the servants and son of the landowner (Matthew 21.33-39).

> **42** "Jesus said to them, "Have you never read in the Scriptures:
> 'The stone which the builders rejected
> Has become the chief cornerstone.
> This was the Lord's doing,
> And it is marvelous in our eyes'?
> **43** "Therefore I say to you, the kingdom of God will be taken from you and given to a nation bearing the fruits of it. **44** And whoever falls on this stone will be broken; but on whomever it falls, it will grind him to powder."
> **45** Now when the chief priests and Pharisees heard His parables, they perceived that He was speaking of them. **46** But when they sought to lay hands on Him, they feared the multitudes, because they took Him for a prophet." (Matthew 21.42-46).

This Psalm is about the king chosen by God, rejected by the leaders of his own people and also the rulers of the nations. Just as it was the case in the history of Israel, it was never all the people of God who rejected God's messengers but mainly the leaders (kings and priests); see Ezekiel 9.1-4 or Isaiah 10.21).

This is identical to the message of Psalm 2 where the kings of the earth "plot against the LORD and His anointed, His Son" (Psalm 2.1-12).

Prayer

Father in heaven, we thank you for the precious gift of eternal life. We believe in your Son, whom you sent to this earth for our salvation. We thank you for the forgiveness we have in Him. We pray that we can be faithful to you today in what we do and how we speak. Through the work of the Holy Spirit in our hearts, may we be a blessing from you to every person we meet today. Amen.

Day 4

> "Yea, though I walk through the valley of the shadow of death,
> I will fear no evil;
> For You *are* with me;
> Your rod and Your staff, they comfort me."
>   (Psalm 23.4)

The metaphor of the shepherd leading the sheep describes a time when the shepherd must lead the sheep through some dangerous areas where wild beasts are lying in wait. The safety of the sheep was assured by the presence of the shepherd.

The shepherd is present with His sheep even when they pass through a valley dark and gloomy as the shadow of death, where difficulties and calamities threaten them. The faithful also go through such dark valleys which can be loss of a loved one, loss of freedom or loss of health. In these "valleys" the good shepherd is there who made this promise to his disciples: "I am with you always, *even* to the end of the age" (Matthew 28.20)

God's sheep are those faithful to Him and who listen to His voice. They are the sheep Jesus talks about in John 10 who hear his voice and follow Him. They are safe in His hands:

> **27** "My sheep hear My voice and I know them and they follow Me. **28** And I give them eternal life, and they shall never perish; neither shall anyone snatch them out of My hand. **29** My Father, who has given *them* to Me, is greater than all; and no one is able to snatch *them* out of My Father's hand. **30** I and *My* Father are one." (John 10.27-30)

Even in death the living God is there, for He is not the God of the dead but of the living (Mark 12.27). Jesus on the cross promises the thief that that very day he would be with Him in paradise. The resurrected Jesus is alive and watches over those who follow him.

Death is said to be the "last enemy" that will be defeated by Christ:

> **20** "But now Christ is risen from the dead *and* has become the first fruits of those who have fallen asleep. **21** For since by man *came* death, by Man also *came* the resurrection of the

dead. **22** For as in Adam all die, even so in Christ all shall be made alive. **23** But each one in his own order: Christ the first fruits, afterward those *who are* Christ's at His coming. **24** Then *comes* the end, when He delivers the kingdom to God the Father, when He puts an end to all rule and all authority and power. **25** For He must reign till He has put all enemies under His feet. **26** The last enemy *that* will be destroyed *is* death." (1 Corinthians 15.21-25)

Nothing can separate the sheep from the love of God:

37 "Yet in all these things we are more than conquerors through Him who loved us. **38** For I am persuaded that neither death nor life, nor angels nor principalities nor powers, nor things present nor things to come, **39** nor height nor depth, nor any other created thing, shall be able to separate us from the love of God which is in Christ Jesus our Lord." (Romans 8.37-39)

Prayer
Father in heaven, we thank you for the precious gift of eternal life we have in Jesus. We thank you for the hope we have, which is firmly grounded in your Word. We pray that today we can listen to the voice of your Son as he speaks to us in the Scriptures. We pray that we can live in harmony with your Holy Spirit given to us as our guide and comforter. In Jesus' name, we pray. Amen.

Day 5

15 "The eyes of the Lord *are* on the righteous,
And His ears *are open* to their cry.
16 The face of the Lord *is* against those who do evil,
To cut off the remembrance of them from the earth.
17 *The righteous* cry out, and the Lord hears,
And delivers them out of all their troubles.
18 The Lord *is* near to those who have a broken heart,
And saves such as have a contrite spirit."
    (Psalms 34.15-18)

Troubles can pile up on those who have been abandoned or rejected. This was the case with Jesus, mostly abandoned by those who had followed him. Verse 20 of this Psalm is quoted in the Gospel of John about

Jesus, whose bones were not broken as was the custom with those crucified (John 19.36).

In this Psalm, those who are faced with pain or adversity are called to seek Him and look to Him:

> **4** "I sought the Lord, and He heard me,
> And delivered me from all my fears.
> **5** They looked to Him and were radiant,
> And their faces were not ashamed.
> **6** This poor man cried out, and the Lord heard *him,*
> And saved him out of all his troubles." (vv. 4-6)

For those who feel abandoned or rejected, God's Word teaches that "The Lord is near to those who have a broken heart and saves such as have a contrite spirit".

Coming to the Lord with the right spirit and a contrite heart is the answer to all our troubles.

The "contrite" spirit is part of the text and should not be forgotten. It is not enough to have troubles and a broken heart in order to be under God's protection. The LORD asks for trust and a contrite spirit: "None of those who trust in Him shall be condemned" (v.22).

Prayer

Lord in heaven, we pray today for faith and a contrite heart. We want to bless you and praise you at all times. Lead us today in the way of love and humility. When we come to you with a broken heart, help us to keep a contrite heart, a trusting spirit. We pray for the Holy Spirit to fill our hearts with love for you. In Jesus' name we pray. Amen.

Day 6

> **11** "Give us help from trouble,
> For the help of man *is* useless.
> **12** Through God we will do valiantly,
> For *it is* He *who* shall tread down our enemies."
>   (Psalms 60.11,12)

Those who are praying in this Psalm have gone through hardship. They have been broken (v.1). They are even asking themselves if it is the LORD who has "cast them off" (v.10). This Psalm expresses the feelings of those who have gone through humiliation, through a reversal of their way of life. Additionally, this was due to those who sinned and rebelled against God.

The Psalm is a prayer for God to restore His people. Complete dependence on God requires us to realize the limitations of human beings.

Verses 11 and 12 express a truth often conveyed in the Bible, which is that "the help of man is useless":

> "Don't put your confidence in powerful people; there is no help for you there" (Psalms 146.3)

> "It is better to take refuge in the LORD than to trust in princes" (Psalms 118.9)

> "Don't put your trust in mere humans. They are as frail as breath. What good are they?" (Isaiah 2.22)

This Psalm ends with a declaration of complete victory for God's people. We understand that complete victory can never be the result of what human rulers do or what human power does. The victory that we receive in Christ is such that it is complete and total over everything that hurts us as human beings, even death.

> "These things I have spoken to you, that in Me you may have peace. In the world you will have tribulation; but be of good cheer, I have overcome the world." (John 16.33)

> "Therefore, take up the whole armor of God, that you may be able to withstand in the evil day, and having done all, to stand." (Ephesians 6.13)

> "For whatever is born of God overcomes the world. And this is the victory that has overcome the world—our faith." (1 John 5.4)

> **31** "What then shall we say to these things? If God *is* for us, who *can be* against us? **32** He who did not spare His own Son, but delivered Him up for us all, how shall He not with Him also freely give us all things? **33** Who shall bring a charge against God's elect? *It is* God who justifies." (Romans 8.31,32)

Prayer

Father in heaven, we thank you for Jesus who died for us and who is alive today. We thank you that we have been raised with Him to a new life. We pray that we can understand today the great victory we have in Him. Keep today our loved ones and friends. Give them comfort and a heart of contrition and trust. In Jesus' name we pray, Amen.

Day 7

> **1** "How long, O Lord? Will You forget me forever?
> How long will You hide Your face from me?
> **2** How long shall I take counsel in my soul,
> *Having* sorrow in my heart daily?
> How long will my enemy be exalted over me?
> **3** Consider *and* hear me, O Lord my God;
> Enlighten my eyes,
> Lest I sleep the *sleep of* death;
> **4** Lest my enemy say,
> "I have prevailed against him";
> *Lest* those who trouble me rejoice when I am moved.
> **5** But I have trusted in Your mercy;
> My heart shall rejoice in Your salvation.
> **6** I will sing to the Lord,
> Because He has dealt bountifully with me."
>   (Psalm 13.1-6)

This Psalm begins with the question of someone who wonders if he has been forgotten by God. This is someone who feels God to be far away.

This feeling of "abandonment" however is not a declaration of unbelief. In the same Psalm, the writer says that he has trusted in the Lord and His mercy. Despite his present pain, he declares that the Lord has dealt bountifully with him.

This reminds us of Job, who in the midst of his misery continues to trust God. He loses everything God has given to him, but he remains attached to God who gave him everything:

> **20** "Then Job arose, tore his robe, and shaved his head; and
> he fell to the ground and worshiped. **21** And he said:
> 'Naked I came from my mother's womb,
> And naked shall I return there.

The Lord gave, and the Lord has taken away;
Blessed be the name of the Lord.'
22 In all this Job did not sin nor charge God with wrong. (Job 1.20-22)

"These things I have spoken to you, that in Me you may have peace. In the world you will have tribulation; but be of good cheer, I have overcome the world." (John 16.33)

1 "Therefore, having been justified by faith, we have peace with God through our Lord Jesus Christ, **2** through whom also we have access by faith into this grace in which we stand, and rejoice in hope of the glory of God. **3** And not only *that,* but we also glory in tribulations, knowing that tribulation produces perseverance; **4** and perseverance, character; and character, hope. **5** Now hope does not disappoint, because the love of God has been poured out in our hearts by the Holy Spirit who was given to us." (Romans 5.1-5)

Prayer

Our Lord, we worship you and praise you for your perfect love. We thank you for teaching us in your Word. We thank you for the salvation we have in Jesus. We know that you are by our side and continually watch over us even when we go through difficult times. Give us peace and give us joy through your Holy Spirit. Amen.

Week 17: God's Word

Day 1

> **1** "Blessed *is* the man
> Who walks not in the counsel of the ungodly,
> Nor stands in the path of sinners,
> Nor sits in the seat of the scornful;
> **2** But his delight *is* in the law of the Lord,
> And in His law he meditates day and night."
> (Psalm 1.1,2)

God's word is food for the nourishment of the soul:

> **1** "And you shall remember that the Lord your God led you all the way these forty years in the wilderness, to humble you *and* test you, to know what *was* in your heart, whether you would keep His commandments or not. **3** So He humbled you, allowed you to hunger, and fed you with manna which you did not know nor did your fathers know, that He might make you know that man shall not live by bread alone; but man lives by every *word* that proceeds from the mouth of the Lord."
> (Deuteronomy 8.1-3; Matthew 4.4)

God does not ask us to "empty our minds". Instead, He asks us to fill our minds with His Word. And we can do this "day and night". "Oh, how I love Your law! It *is* my meditation all day." (Psalm 119.97)

We are to pray God for an open heart and a desire to practice the teachings of His word:

> **17** "Deal bountifully with Your servant, *that* I may live and keep Your word. **18** Open my eyes, that I may see wondrous things from Your law." (Psalms 119.17,18)

As we meditate upon God's Word, we flourish and produce fruit like a well-watered tree (v.3). The Word of God is indispensable for spiritual growth, for sanctification,

> **1** "Therefore, laying aside all malice, all deceit, hypocrisy, envy, and all evil speaking, **2** as newborn babes, desire the pure milk of the word, that you may grow thereby, **3** if indeed you have tasted that the Lord *is* gracious." (1 Peter 2.1)

We cannot separate the reading or study of the Scriptures from progress in holiness. We will grow through the Word only if we are willing to practice what we learn:

> **21** "Therefore, lay aside all filthiness and overflow of wickedness, and receive with meekness the implanted word, which is able to save your souls. **22** But be doers of the word, and not hearers only, deceiving yourselves. **23** For if anyone is a hearer of the word and not a doer, he is like a man observing his natural face in a mirror; **24** for he observes himself, goes away, and immediately forgets what kind of man he was. **25** But he who looks into the perfect law of liberty and continues *in it* and is not a forgetful hearer but a doer of the work, this one will be blessed in what he does." (James 1.21-25)

Prayer

We thank you, Father, for the Scriptures, your Word revealed to us. We pray today that we will meditate your work, that we will seek to better understand it. Through the Holy Spirit, help us Father to put into practice the teachings of Jesus and his apostles. In Jesus' name we pray. Amen.

Day 2

> **6** "By the word of the Lord the heavens were made,
> And all the host of them by the breath of His mouth.
> **7** He gathers the waters of the sea together as a heap;
> He lays up the deep in storehouses."
>   (Psalms 33.6)

We see the truth of this Psalm in the first chapter of Genesis. God spoke and this universe as well as life on earth were created.

1 "Now faith is the substance of things hoped for,
the evidence of things not seen. **2** For by it the elders obtained
a *good* testimony.**3** By faith we understand that the worlds were
framed by the word of God, so that the things which are seen
were not made of things which are visible." (Hebrews 11.1-3)

8 "Let all the earth fear the Lord;
Let all the inhabitants of the world stand in awe of Him.
9 For He spoke, and it was *done;*
He commanded, and it stood fast." (Psalm 33.8,9)

God's creation manifests His wisdom, his supreme intelligence in ordering the universe and life on earth. The book of Proverbs also describes this as God's wisdom at work in the creation of the world.

22 "The Lord possessed me [wisdom] at the beginning of His way,
Before His works of old.
23 I have been established from everlasting,
From the beginning, before there was ever an earth." (Proverbs 8.22,23)

26 "While as yet He had not made the earth or the fields,
Or the primal dust of the world.
27 When He prepared the heavens, I *was* there,
When He drew a circle on the face of the deep,
28 When He established the clouds above,
When He strengthened the fountains of the deep,
29 When He assigned to the sea its limit,
So that the waters would not transgress His command,
When He marked out the foundations of the earth,
30 Then I was beside Him *as* a master craftsman;
And I was daily *His* delight,
Rejoicing always before Him,
31 Rejoicing in His inhabited world,
And my delight *was* with the sons of men." (Proverbs 8.26-31)

Prayer

'Father in heaven, we thank you for your creation. We see your wisdom in how you created everything. We also see your power in the creation. We believe that

you have the power over death and will raise the dead at the coming of the Lord Jesus. We pray that today we will glorify you in everything we do or say. Amen.

Day 3

> **6** "For the oppression of the poor, for the sighing of the needy,
> Now I will arise," says the Lord;
> I will set *him* in the safety for which he yearns.
> The words of the Lord *are* pure words,
> *Like* silver tried in a furnace of earth,
> Purified seven times.
> **7** You shall keep them, O Lord,
> You shall preserve them from this generation forever."
>   '(Psalms 12.6,7)

The pure words from God stand in contrast to the words of the wicked:

> **2** "They speak idly everyone with his neighbor;
> *With* flattering lips *and* a double heart they speak.
> **3** May the Lord cut off all flattering lips,
> *And* the tongue that speaks proud things,
> **4** Who have said,
> 'With our tongue we will prevail;
> Our lips *are* our own;
> Who *is* lord over us?'" (Psalms 12.2-4)

The contrast between words coming from men and words from God can be striking. The apostle Paul writes that the Gospel he preaches did not originate with men and human ideas or words, but was given by God through his Spirit:

> **7** "But we speak the wisdom of God in a mystery, the hidden *wisdom* which God ordained before the ages for our glory, **8** which none of the rulers of this age knew; for had they known, they would not have crucified the Lord of glory.
> **9** But as it is written:
> 'Eye has not seen, nor ear heard,
> Nor have entered into the heart of man
> The things which God has prepared for those who love Him.'
> **10** But God has revealed *them* to us through His Spirit. For the Spirit searches all things, yes, the deep things of God. **11** For what man knows the things of a man except the spirit of the

man which is in him? Even so no one knows the things of God except the Spirit of God. **12** Now we have received, not the spirit of the world, but the Spirit who is from God, that we might know the things that have been freely given to us by God." (1 Corinthians 2.7-12)

Thus, we are not to preach another Gospel or pervert the Gospel (Galatians 1.6-9)

The Scriptures warn us not to add to God's Word or take away from His Word (Deuteronomy 4.2; Proverbs 30.5,6; Revelation 22.18,19).

"The entirety of Your word *is* truth,
And every one of Your righteous judgments *endures* forever."
(Psalms 119.160)

Prayer

Lord in heaven, we thank you for your word. We thank you for the Gospel of salvation in Jesus Christ. We pray that we will be faithful today when we share this Gospel with others. We pray that we can be faithful to the truth of the Gospel in how we live today. In Jesus' name we pray, Amen.

Day 4

"How can a young man cleanse his way?
By taking heed according to Your word.
10 With my whole heart I have sought You;
Oh, let me not wander from Your commandments!
11 Your word I have hidden in my heart,
That I might not sin against You."
   (Psalm 119.9-11)

The truths of God's word always need to be in the heart of the believer, even under the old covenant. God promised that in the new covenant believers will have His Word written in their hearts through His own working (Jeremiah 31.33; Ezekiel 36.26; Psalms 37.31; Hebrews 8.10). The reason for this is that the new covenant brings a new heart in the believer through the forgiveness offered in Christ and through the working of the Holy Spirit which convinces sinners through the power of the Gospel and is offered to those who enter the new covenant (Romans 1.16; Acts 2.37-41).

Those who have believed in the Gospel and have repented, who have been risen with Christ, are taught to live a life worthy of their calling:

> **1** "I, therefore, the prisoner of the Lord, beseech you to walk worthy of the calling with which you were called, **2** with all lowliness and gentleness, with longsuffering, bearing with one another in love, **3** endeavoring to keep the unity of the Spirit in the bond of peace. **4** *There is* one body and one Spirit, just as you were called in one hope of your calling; **5** one Lord, one faith, one baptism; **6** one God and Father of all, who *is* above all, and through all, and in you all." (Ephesians 4.1-6)

Christians are encouraged to "desire the pure milk of the word" (1 Peter 2.1,2). They are taught to grow in their knowledge and understanding of the Word of God (Hebrews 5.12-14).

Not all Christians are apostles, prophets or speak in tongues (1 Corinthians 12.29,30). In fact, God will not continually reveal new truths and provide new knowledge through revelation (1 Corinthians 13.8-10). New revelations were given to the Church in its infancy and are not needed when the Church reaches maturity:

> **11** "When I was a child, I spoke as a child, I understood as a child, I thought as a child; but when I became a man, I put away childish things. **12** For now we see in a mirror, dimly, but then face to face. Now I know in part, but then I shall know just as I also am known. **13** And now abide faith, hope, love, these three; but the greatest of these *is* love." (1 Corinthians 13.11-13).

Maturity in these verses is outlined by three words which are faith, hope and love. By having faith, hope, and love, Christians can see the Lord face to face and know the Lord as they are known by Him. Love is the greatest work produced by God's revelation, and it is also "a more excellent way" (1 Corinthians 13.31). "But if anyone loves God, this one is known by him" (1 Corinthians 8.3).

Prayer

Father in heaven, we thank you for our salvation in Christ our Lord. We thank you for a life under your grace and forgiveness. We pray that today we can grow in the knowledge of your love and holiness. We pray our loved ones, our family members, will also grow today in their knowledge of you. Strengthen our hearts in doing your will. Amen.

Day 5

> **7** "The law of the Lord *is* perfect, converting the soul;
> The testimony of the Lord *is* sure, making wise the simple;
> **8** The statutes of the Lord *are* right, rejoicing the heart;
> The commandment of the Lord *is* pure, enlightening the eyes;
> **9** The fear of the Lord *is* clean, enduring forever;
> The judgments of the Lord *are* true *and* righteous altogether.
> **10** More to be desired *are they* than gold,
> Yea, than much fine gold;
> Sweeter also than honey and the honeycomb.
> **11** Moreover by them Your servant is warned,
> *And* in keeping them *there is* great reward."
>   (Psalms 19.7-11).

The heavens declare the glory and power of God (v.1) but His law is perfect and declares his will, testimony and statutes.

Six words describe God's revelation to His people: law, testimony, statutes, commandment, fear, judgments. Through these six words, we learn six ways that God speaks to His people through His word.

The law is perfect as a means to convert the soul. Faith, repentance and turning back to God are an effect of God's word:

> **12** "For the word of God *is* living and powerful, and sharper
> than any two-edged sword, piercing even to the division of soul
> and spirit, and of joints and marrow, and is a discerner of the
> thoughts and intents of the heart. **13** And there is no creature
> hidden from His sight, but all things *are* naked and open to the
> eyes of Him to whom we *must give* account." (Hebrews 4. 12.13).

The testimony of the Lord is sure and makes wise the simple. God's Word is "sure" means it is firm, solid, dependable. Every word, every phrase spoken by God contains wisdom. There cannot be true wisdom without a knowledge of God's revelation. Without this, human beings remain "simple", have no real understanding of the world they live in, of the reality that surrounds them. "So, keep and do them, for that is your wisdom and your understanding in the sight of the peoples who will hear all these statutes and say, 'Surely this great nation is a wise and understanding people.'" (Deuteronomy 4.6).

> **24** "Therefore, whoever hears these sayings of Mine, and does
> them, I will liken him to a wise man who built his house on the

rock: **25** and the rain descended, the floods came, and the winds blew and beat on that house; and it did not fall, for it was founded on the rock." (Matthew 7.24,25)

The statutes (or precepts) of the LORD are true (or right). The word "true" has to do with uprightness, justice — as in "You came down also on Mount Sinai, and spoke with them from heaven, and gave them just ordinances and true laws, good statutes and commandments." (Nehemiah 9.13). The statutes of the LORD reflect God's own uprightness. This uprightness of God's statutes rejoices, cheers or makes glad the heart. Joy is clearly connected to our abiding by God's word.

The fear of the Lord is also closely linked to the revealed will of God. The "fear" mentioned here describes honor or respect given to God's commandments. It is this respect for the will of God which purifies the heart and life of the faithful. God's word reveals how and why the LORD should be feared (Psalms 34.12; see Proverbs 15.33; Deuteronomy 17.19).

The judgments (or ordinances) of the LORD are true and righteous. The word true (*emet*) is close to the idea of faithful or firm. The judgments of the LORD are like himself, an unchangeable moral and spiritual foundation.

> **16** "Do not be deceived, my beloved brethren. **17** Every good gift and every perfect gift is from above, and comes down from the Father of lights, with whom there is no variation or shadow of turning. **18** Of His own will He brought us forth by the word of truth, that we might be a kind of first fruits of His creatures." (James 1.16-18)

Those who hold to God's revelation given to His people are "wealthy" and enjoy all its benefits as they would honey. In keeping God's command, the faithful will receive great reward (see Hebrews 11.6).

Prayer

Our Father in heaven, we thank you today for the Word you gave to your people. We are grateful that you have spoken truth to us through the Scriptures and through the teachings of Jesus and your Holy Spirit as he guided your apostles into all truth. Help us to walk in your commandments and trust your promises. We pray this in Jesus' name, Amen.

Day 6

> **105** "Your word *is* a lamp to my feet
> And a light to my path.
> **106** I have sworn and confirmed
> That I will keep Your righteous judgments.
> **107** I am afflicted very much;
> Revive me, O Lord, according to Your word.
> **108** Accept, I pray, the freewill offerings of my mouth, O Lord,
> And teach me Your judgments."
> (Psalms 119.105-108)

God's revelation to His people is called His "word". At the creation, God spoke the words "let there be light" and there was light (Genesis 1.3). At God's word, the world that was "without form and void" and "dark" (Genesis 1.2) was filled with light.

The different terms used in the Psalms and the Scriptures that refer to God's revelation to His people can be called "His word":

> "For the word of God is alive and active. Sharper than any double-edged sword, it penetrates even to dividing soul and spirit, joints and marrow; it judges the thoughts and attitudes of the heart." (Hebrews 4.12 NIV).
>
> "Do not merely listen to the word, and so deceive yourselves. Do what it says." (James 1.22 NIV).
>
> "He replied, 'Blessed rather are those who hear the word of God and obey it.'" (Luke 11.28).
>
> "Therefore, get rid of all moral filth and the evil that is so prevalent and humbly accept the word planted in you, which can save you." (James 1.21 NIV).

Those who are faithful to God's Word can also be going through affliction, grief or pain: "My soul clings to the dust; revive me according to Your word." (Psalms 119.25).

"I am afflicted" (*anah*): he is brought low, put down, oppressed as under a tyrant or oppressor, as in Exodus 1.11: "Therefore they set taskmasters over them to afflict them with their burdens. And they built for Pharaoh supply cities, Pithom and Ramses."

Though the life of the faithful is threatened (Psalms 119.87) he does not waver or depart from God's word. He will be faithful forever (Psalms 119.98).

14 "Do all things without complaining and disputing, **15** that you may become blameless and harmless, children of God without fault in the midst of a crooked and perverse generation, among whom you shine as lights in the world, **16** holding fast the word of life, so that I may rejoice in the day of Christ that I have not run in vain or labored in vain." (Philippians 2.14-16)

12 "Here is the patience of the saints; here *are* those who keep the commandments of God and the faith of Jesus. **13** Then I heard a voice from heaven saying to me, 'Write: Blessed *are* the dead who die in the Lord from now on.' "Yes," says the Spirit, 'that they may rest from their labors, and their works follow them.'" (Revelation 14.12,13)

Prayer

We thank you Father for the life you have given us. Today, we come to you and pray for those we love and are in pain at the present time. Give them strength and wisdom to remain in your will. Give them hope and endurance. We also pray for all our neighbors who need to come to you in faith and repentance. May you touch their hearts with your Gospel. We pray in Jesus' name, Amen.

Day 7

89 "Forever, O Lord,
Your word is settled in heaven.
90 Your faithfulness *endures* to all generations;
You established the earth, and it abides.
91 They continue this day according to Your ordinances,
For all *are* Your servants.
92 Unless Your law *had been* my delight,
I would then have perished in my affliction.
93 I will never forget Your precepts,
For by them You have given me life."
   (Psalms 119.89-93)

As in other Scriptures, God's revelation is described as his "word" (v.89). The unchanging nature of God's word is affirmed. The word of God is unchanging, as God himself does not change:

16 "Do not be deceived, my beloved brethren. **17** Every good gift and every perfect gift is from above, and comes down from the Father of lights, with whom there is no variation or shadow of turning. **18** Of His own will He brought us forth by the word of truth, that we might be a kind of first fruits of His creatures." (James 1.16-18)

The word of God gives life only if we trust the Christ, of whom the Scriptures bear witness.

Jesus says to the Pharisees,

> **39** "You search the Scriptures, for in them you think you have eternal life; and these are they which testify of Me. **40** But you are not willing to come to Me that you may have life." (John 5.39,40).

Jesus says in Luke 24:

> **25** "O foolish ones, and slow of heart to believe in all that the prophets have spoken! **26** Ought not the Christ to have suffered these things and to enter into His glory?" **27** And beginning at Moses and all the Prophets, He expounded to them in all the Scriptures the things concerning Himself." (Luke 24.25-27)

The inspired and enduring nature of God's Word does not mean we have no responsibility in how we teach or preach that word. The apostle Paul warns Timothy concerning his work as an evangelist and teacher, saying:

> **14** "Remind them of these things, charging them before the Lord not to strive about words to no profit, to the ruin of the hearers. **15** Be diligent to present yourself approved to God, a worker who does not need to be ashamed, rightly dividing the word of truth. **16** But shun profane and idle babblings, for they will increase to more ungodliness. **17** And their message will spread like cancer." (2 Timothy 2.14-17)

James warns Christians, saying:

> **1** "My brethren, let not many of you become teachers, knowing that we shall receive a stricter judgment. **2** For we all stumble in many things. If anyone does not stumble in word, he *is* a perfect man, able also to bridle the whole body. **3** Indeed, we put bits in horses' mouths that they may obey us, and we turn their whole body." (James 3.1-3)

Peter also warns Christians concerning the teachings of Paul, which are part of "Scriptures" and should be heeded to :

> **15** "and consider *that* the longsuffering of our Lord *is* salvation—as also our beloved brother Paul, according to the wisdom given to him, has written to you, **16** as also in all his epistles, speaking in them of these things, in which are some things hard to understand, which untaught and unstable *people* twist to their own destruction, as *they do* also the rest of the Scriptures. (2 Peter 3.15,16)

Prayer

We thank you today for your word, which we find in the Scriptures. We thank you for the testimony to the Christ given in Scriptures. We pray that we will grow in our faith, hope and love as we continue to read and study your Word. Help us, Lord, in how we talk about your Word and how we teach it. Amen.

Week 18: Heaven

Day 1

> **21** "Thus, my heart was grieved,
> And I was vexed in my mind.
> **22** I *was* so foolish and ignorant;
> I was *like* a beast before You.
> **23** Nevertheless I *am* continually with You;
> You hold *me* by my right hand.
> **24** You will guide me with Your counsel,
> And afterward receive me *to* glory.
> **25** Whom have I in heaven *but You?*
> And *there is* none upon earth *that* I desire besides You.
> **26** My flesh and my heart fail;
> *But* God *is* the strength of my heart and my portion forever."
> (Psalms 73.21-26)

This Psalm expresses the hope of the believer to be received in glory. The hope that despite the failings of the flesh which ends in death, there is a portion provided to the believer by his relationship with God.

God himself is our "portion" and promise of glory. With God and with a right relationship with God, the faithful are guaranteed life and fulfillment:

> "But without faith *it is* impossible to please *Him*, for he who comes to God must believe that He is, and *that* He is a rewarder of those who diligently seek Him." (Hebrews 11.6)

> "Therefore, my dear brothers and sisters, stand firm. Let nothing move you. Always give yourselves fully to the work of the Lord, because you know that your labor in the Lord is not in vain." (1 Corinthians 15.58)

"Let us not become weary in doing good, for at the proper time we will reap a harvest if we do not give up." (Galatians 6.9)

"His master replied, 'Well done, good and faithful servant! You have been faithful with a few things; I will put you in charge of many things. Come and share your master's happiness!'" (Matthew 25.21)

"Blessed is the one who perseveres under trial because, having stood the test, that person will receive the crown of life that the Lord has promised to those who love him." (James 1.12)

Note in verses 24 and 25 the assurance of the Psalmist concerning his future. There is no idea here that life ends with the physical death of the body. There is no idea here that there is neither heaven nor paradise.

In this Psalm the contrast is obvious between the difficulties of life, the pains inflicted by mockers and arrogant people and the glory that awaits the faithful. This "glory" and "heaven" come from the very presence of God:

2 O *my soul,* you have said to the Lord,
"You *are* my Lord,
My goodness is nothing apart from You."
3 As for the saints who *are* on the earth,
"They are the excellent ones, in whom is all my delight." (Psalms 16.1-3)

Prayer

Father in heaven, we pray that the words of this Psalm can be written in our hearts. We believe you have given us these words for comfort and strength. We thank you for Jesus, who gave his life but is alive today. We pray that our loved ones and brothers and sisters can receive comfort and strength as they go through difficult times. In Jesus' name we pray. Amen.

Day 2

1 "Praise God in His sanctuary;
Praise Him in His mighty firmament!
2 Praise Him for His mighty acts;
Praise Him according to His excellent greatness!"
(Psalms 150.1,2)

This Psalm describes the different musical instruments used in tabernacle and temple worship. The history of tabernacle and temple worship in Israel in the Old Testament is an interesting one. King David introduced a number of musical instruments in the tabernacle worship when the ark of the covenant was brought back from the land of the Philistines, after they were defeated by Israel (1 Chronicles 15). Levites were chosen to lead the musical worship in the tabernacle (1 Chronicles 16).

When Salomon dedicated the temple, the Levites worshiped "with instruments of music of the Lord, which king David made to praise the LORD" (2 Chronicles 7.6). The music was quite regulated in the temple. God himself commanded David to use specific instruments to be used in the temple to worship God (2 Chronicles 7.6; 29.25-27 and 8.14). The instruments were the harp, lute, lyre, cymbal, tambourine and horn mentioned in Psalms 150.

About five hundred years after David, the priests who returned from captivity restored David's instruments for temple worship (Ezra 3.9,10; Nehemiah 12.27,36).

The statement to "praise the LORD" is repeated twelve times in the Psalm. Twelve is the number that represents the totality of God's people. The heavenly Jerusalem which comes from heaven in the Revelation given to John has twelve gates and twelve names written on them, which are "the names of the twelve tribes of Israel". The wall of the city has twelve foundations and on them the names of the twelve apostles of the lamb (Revelation 21.12-14).

The first verse of this Psalm mentions the praise to the LORD which is given in his sanctuary, in heaven. The last verse exhorts "everything that has breath" to praise the LORD and ends with the words "Praise the LORD!" The true tabernacle of God is heaven, not the tabernacle of temple we read about in the Old Testament. In fact, there is no need even of a temple in heaven, "for the Lord God almighty and the lamb are its temple" (Revelation 21.22).

In verse 6, "everything that has breath" is ordered to praise the LORD. The Hebrew verb to praise is in the imperative (*tehallel*) and concerns all of humanity, all of those to whom God has given "*nephesh*" (soul, breath). All human beings are called upon to praise the LORD. All will at some point worship the one whom God has appointed to as savior and Lord:

> **9** "Therefore God also has highly exalted Him and given Him the name which is above every name, **10** that at the name of Jesus every knee should bow, of those in heaven, and of those on

earth, and of those under the earth, **11** and *that* every tongue should confess that Jesus Christ *is* Lord, to the glory of God the Father." (Philippians 2.9-11).

Prayer

Father in heaven, we thank you for these words of Psalm 150. We thank you for all who have worshipped you throughout the ages and worship you today. We praise your name today. We praise you not only in songs or words, but through every action and through every word that comes out of our mouth. Amen.

Day 3

> "The Lord *is* in His holy temple,
> The Lord's throne *is* in heaven;
> His eyes behold,
> His eyelids test the sons of men."
>   (Psalms 11.4)

The LORD, unlike the idols made by human hands, can see everything done by "the sons of men". He is not restricted by space or time, as human beings are. He remains righteous and even loves righteousness: "For the LORD is righteous, he loves righteousness; his countenance beholds the upright." (v.7).

God was in his heavenly and holy temple not made with human hands, even when there was a tabernacle as in David's time or a temple as with Salomon. These are the words of Stephen about to be stoned and who quotes the prophet Isaiah as he preaches to those who are about to kill him:

> **47** "But Solomon built Him a house. **48** However, the Most
> High does not dwell in temples made with hands, as the prophet says:
> **49** 'Heaven *is* My throne,
> And earth *is* My footstool.
> What house will you build for Me?' says the Lord,
> 'Or what *is* the place of My rest?
> **50** Has My hand not made all these things?'" (Acts 7.47-50 and Isaiah 66.1).

In Psalm 11 the decrees and judgments of God do not originate from the tabernacle. And later on, they did not originate from the temple which, in fact, will be desecrated by idolatry (Ezekiel chapters 1-9).

The decrees and judgments of God originate from His "holy temple", from his throne, which is in heaven. It is from there that all divine and final decision in earthly matters come (Habakkuk 2:20; Micah 1:2.)

God's eyelids test the sons of men. The mention of the eyelids is an intentional image. In order to observe something closely, we draw the eyelids together in order for our vision to be more precise and direct and become like a ray piercing what we are looking at. Nothing and nobody can escape God's gaze, decrees and judgments.

Prayer

Lord in heaven, we pray today for our loved ones, for our parents and children. We pray that their hearts will always seek you and will find you. We pray for more faith and more courage as we face the evils of this world. We thank you for your goodness and mercies. In Jesus' name we pray. Amen.

Day 4

> **1** "The Lord reigns, He is clothed with majesty;
> The Lord is clothed,
> He has girded Himself with strength.
> Surely the world is established, so that it cannot be moved.
> **2** Your throne *is* established from of old;
> You *are* from everlasting."
> (Psalms 93.1,2)

The language of this Psalm is about kingship and military might. It is military in the sense that the LORD is described as in other Psalms as waging war against the unjust and unrepentant sinners.

"He has girded himself", is the Hebrew *hitazzar* which means 'to gird, to encompass, to equip.' It is always used in the sense of gaining strength, of readiness for combat as in Isaiah 45.5; 50.11; Jeremiah 1.17 as in Psalms 29:1-1 which points to God's battle against His enemies.

God is triumphant through his strength, even his omnipotence. He has put on his strength (Isaiah 51:9); with His power He has girded Himself — a military word (Isaiah 8:9). Thus, the LORD makes war against everything in antagonism to Himself, and casts it to the ground with the weapons of His wrathful judgments. We find other descriptions of this in Isaiah 59:17; Isaiah 63:1; cf. Daniel 7:9.

The God who reigns is here the God who battles for righteousness and justice. His power in exercising justice is greater than the power of waters in a flood:

> **3** "The floods have lifted up, O Lord,
> The floods have lifted up their voice;
> The floods lift up their waves.
> **4** The Lord on high *is* mightier
> Than the noise of many waters,
> *Than* the mighty waves of the sea." (vv. 3,4)

This battle of God and the power he uses is not a physical or fleshly battle. It is the battle for His holiness and his testimonies which is an eternal battle, even today (see Ephesians 6.10-20; 2 Corinthians 10.4).

> "Your testimonies are very sure;
> Holiness adorns Your house,
> O Lord, forever." (verse 5)

Prayer

Our Lord and Father, we thank you for a new day. We thank you for our families and friends. We pray for our loved ones and also for our neighbors and this world. Forgive our sins and refresh our hearts and souls so that we will be able to engage in the spiritual battle for truth and righteousness. In Jesus' name we pray. Amen.

Day 5

> **19** "The Lord has established His throne in heaven,
> And His kingdom rules over all.
> **20** Bless the Lord, you His angels,
> Who excel in strength, who do His word,
> Heeding the voice of His word.
> **21** Bless the Lord, all *you* His hosts,
> *You* ministers of His, who do His pleasure.
> **22** Bless the Lord, all His works,
> In all places of His dominion.
> Bless the Lord, O my soul!"
>   (Psalms 103.19-22)

The LORD has not simply created the world and abandoned it, as a watchmaker would do with a watch. The entire Psalms describes the LORD who is active in the world:

> **2** "Bless the Lord, O my soul,
> And forget not all His benefits:
> **3** Who forgives all your iniquities,
> Who heals all your diseases,
> **4** Who redeems your life from destruction,
> Who crowns you with lovingkindness and tender mercies,
> **5** Who satisfies your mouth with good *things*,
> *So that* your youth is renewed like the eagle's." (vv. 2-5)

Nebuchadnezzar the king of Babylon was humiliated under the hand of God and compelled to eat grass for seven years. He learned that "The Most-High rules in the kingdom of men and giveth it to whomever he chooses" (Daniel 4:25). The LORD is the supreme king over the visible and invisible creation, over human beings and over angels.

His angels "excel in strength, who do His word, heed the voice of His word." The angels are God's "host", a word that describes an organized army ready for battle. They are also described as "ministers" or servants who do His will (Hebrews 1.7).

The book of Hebrews shows the contrast between the Son of God, "the firstborn", and the angels worship the "firstborn" and they are merely servants, ministers of God: "But when He again brings the firstborn into the world, He says 'Let all the angels of God worship Him.' **7** And of the angels He says: 'Who makes His angels spirits and His ministers a flame of fire.'" (Hebrews 1.5-7)

This Psalm is also a reminder that the will of God is accomplished in heaven, and that we need to pray for his will to be accomplished on this earth as well.

> **9** "Our Father in heaven,
> Hallowed be Your name.
> **10** Your kingdom come.
> Your will be done
> On earth as *it is* in heaven." (Matthew 6.9,10)

Prayer

Father in heaven, we come to you as the only source of life and blessings. We come to you as the only perfect and Holy one. We pray, Father, that your will be done on earth as it is in heaven. We pray for the coming of your kingdom as people open their hearts to you and obey your Word. In Jesus' name we pray. Amen.

Day 6

> **4** "The Lord *is* high above all nations,
> His glory above the heavens.
> **5** Who *is* like the Lord our God,
> Who dwells on high,
> **6** Who humbles Himself to behold
> The *things that are* in the heavens and in the earth?"
>   (Psalms 113.4-6)

In Judaism and Jesus' time, Psalms 113 and 114 were sung in fragments before the Passover meal and 115 to 118 at the closing of the Passover meal. These songs were the ones the Lord and his disciples sang at the last supper (Matthew 26.30).

The LORD is high above the heavens, higher than anything human beings can perceive from their earthly position. But at the same time, nothing on the earth escapes his sight; nothing is so low that it is unnoticed by Him. In fact, he is especially caring and watchful of that which is lowly and humble:

> **7** "He raises the poor out of the dust,
> *And* lifts the needy out of the ash heap,
> **8** That He may seat *him* with princes—
> With the princes of His people."
> **9** He grants the barren woman a home,
> Like a joyful mother of children.
> Praise the Lord!" (vv. 7-9)

After his resurrection, the Lord Jesus declared that all authority had been given to him in heaven and on earth (Matthew 28. 18). We see this rule of Christ throughout the New Testament and especially in the book of Revelation:

> **7** "Behold, He is coming with clouds, and every eye will see
> Him, even they who pierced Him. And all the tribes of the earth
> will mourn because of Him. Even so, Amen."
> **8** "I am the Alpha and the Omega, *the* Beginning

and *the* End," says the Lord, "who is and who was and who is to come, the Almighty." (Revelation 1.7,8)

"…To him who sits on the throne [God] and to the Lamb be praise and honor and glory and power, for ever and ever!" (Revelation 5.13)

"And they cried out in a loud voice: 'Salvation belongs to our God, who sits on the throne, and to the Lamb.'" (Revelation 7.10)

"The seventh angel sounded his trumpet, and there were loud voices in heaven, which said: "The kingdom of the world has become the kingdom of our Lord [God] and of his Christ [Jesus], and he will reign for ever and ever." (Revelation 11.15)

"Then I heard a loud voice in heaven say: 'Now have come the salvation and the power and the kingdom of our God, and the authority of his Christ….'" (Revelation 12.10)

22 "I did not see a temple in the city, because the Lord God Almighty and the Lamb are its temple. **23** The city does not need the sun or the moon to shine on it, for the glory of God gives it light, and the Lamb is its lamp." (Revelation 21.22,23)

"Then the angel showed me the river of the water of life, as clear as crystal, flowing from the throne of God and of the Lamb." (Revelation 22.1)

Prayer

Lord and Father in heaven, we come to you and worship you. We come to you, who is holy and just. We pray that today we can serve you and love you with all our heart. We pray for wisdom as we serve our fellow human beings today. We thank you for your precious Son, Jesus. In His name we pray, Amen.

Day 7

1 "The Lord reigns;
Let the earth rejoice;
Let the multitude of isles be glad!

> **2** Clouds and darkness surround Him;
> Righteousness and justice *are* the foundation of His throne.
> **3** A fire goes before Him,
> And burns up His enemies round about.
> **4** His lightnings light the world;
> The earth sees and trembles.
> **5** The mountains melt like wax at the presence of the Lord,
> At the presence of the Lord of the whole earth.
> **6** The heavens declare His righteousness,
> And all the peoples see His glory."
> '(Psalms 97.1-6)

Even while nations and peoples are in turmoil or have turned away from the LORD, He still reigns. Those who serve carved images and boast in idols are put to shame (v.7). When the glory of the LORD becomes manifest, everything that is opposed to the LORD will be consumed by His light. Shame and terror come then on those who have turned to idols (Isaiah 42.17; Jeremiah 10.14).

The physical manifestations of God's power should lead people to consider His justice and righteousness. Fear of the LORD is the beginning of wisdom (Proverbs 9.10).

> **28** "Therefore, since we are receiving a kingdom which cannot be shaken, let us have grace, by which we may serve God acceptably with reverence and godly fear. **29** For our God *is* a consuming fire." (Hebrews 12.28,29).

The rule of God is connected to his justice and judgment.

For those who fear the LORD and serve Him, there is continual joy and reasons to be glad. The Gospel is "Good News" or "Joyful News" because it declares God's power that saves "everyone who believes" (Romans 1.16). This salvation is not based on anyone's goodness or keeping of God's laws, but on a justification "by Jesus' blood" (Romans 5.9); a justification based on the fact that Jesus received the penalty of death in our place that we might not receive the "wages of our sins" (Romans 6.23). Those who trust God's work of salvation through the cross of Christ rejoice because they have received the abundance of God's grace in Christ:

> **20** "Moreover, the law entered that the offense might abound. But where sin abounded, grace abounded much more, **21** so that as sin reigned in death, even so grace might reign through right-

eousness to eternal life through Jesus Christ our Lord." (Romans 5.20,21)

Having been justified by faith, those who have been united with Jesus' death and resurrection in baptism have been raised to a new life which includes the promise of the resurrection:

> **4** "Therefore, we were buried with Him through baptism into death, that just as Christ was raised from the dead by the glory of the Father, even so we also should walk in newness of life. **5** For if we have been united together in the likeness of His death, certainly we also shall be *in the likeness* of *His* resurrection, **6** knowing this, that our old man was crucified with *Him,* that the body of sin might be done away with, that we should no longer be slaves of sin. **7** For he who has died has been freed from sin. **8** Now if we died with Christ, we believe that we shall also live with Him, **9** knowing that Christ, having been raised from the dead, dies no more. Death no longer has dominion over Him." (Romans 6.4-8)

Prayer

Father in heaven, we thank you for Jesus our Lord. We thank you for his death on the cross and the forgiveness we have through his death. We also thank you for Jesus' resurrection and his reign of justice. We pray that through your Holy Spirit, we will live today a life consecrated to loving and serving you with all our heart. Amen.

Week 19: Angels

Day 1

> **9** "Because you have made the Lord, *who is* my refuge,
> *Even* the Most High, your dwelling place,
> **10** No evil shall befall you,
> Nor shall any plague come near your dwelling;
> **11** For He shall give His angels charge over you,
> To keep you in all your ways.
> **12** In *their* hands they shall bear you up,
> Lest you dash your foot against a stone.
> **13** You shall tread upon the lion and the cobra,
> The young lion and the serpent you shall trample underfoot."
> (Psalms 91.9-13)

This Psalm declares the power of angels to protect the faithful from plagues, to keep the faithful in all their ways. It also teaches us that the angels are under God's orders. The devil used this Scripture in tempting Jesus (Matthew 4.5-7). The promise of God to be a refuge to the faithful became a way for the devil to tempt Jesus and make him fall. Even at the point of Jesus' arrest, we see how angels could easily have delivered Jesus. But Jesus did not allow it because for Him doing the Father's will came first:

> **50** "Then they came and laid hands on Jesus, and took Him. **51** And suddenly, one of those *who were* with Jesus stretched out *his* hand and drew his sword, struck the servant of the high priest, and cut off his ear. **52** But Jesus said to him, 'Put your sword in its place, for all who take the sword will perish by the sword. **53** Or do you think that I cannot now pray to My Father, and He will provide Me with more than twelve legions of angels? **54** How then could the Scriptures be fulfilled, that it must happen thus?'" (Matthew 26.50-54)

The Christ came to do His Father's will, and he knew all the sufferings he would need to go through in order to accomplish the salvation of mankind. Thus, beyond the promise of God to the faithful or how one understands the way God will accomplish that promise, there is a work to be done for God — a mission God has entrusted the Messiah.

What will prove that Jesus is the Son of God? Throwing himself from the top of the temple? Jesus knew otherwise. He was declared Son of God with power by his resurrection from the dead:

> **1** "Paul, a bondservant of Jesus Christ, called *to be* an apostle, separated to the gospel of God **2** which He promised before through His prophets in the Holy Scriptures, **3** concerning His Son Jesus Christ our Lord, who [a]was born of the seed of David according to the flesh, **4** *and* declared *to be* the Son of God with power according to the Spirit of holiness, by the resurrection from the dead." (Romans 1.1-4)

Prayer

Father in heaven, we believe in your power over all things. We believe in the power of the angels you created. We pray today that we can have full confidence in your power as your reign over all the universe. We look to Jesus as our example in how to live and how to serve you, even when it means pain and suffering. In Jesus' name, we pray. Amen.

Day 2

> **19** "The Lord has established His throne in heaven
> And His kingdom rules over all.
> **20** Bless the Lord, you His angels,
> Who excel in strength, who do His word,
> Heeding the voice of His word.
> **21** Bless the Lord, all *you* His hosts,
> *You* ministers of His, who do His pleasure.
> **22** Bless the Lord, all His works,
> In all places of His dominion.
> Bless the Lord, O my soul!"
>   (Psalms 103.19-22)

The LORD is the sovereign ruler over all His creation. There is an order in the universe and even in the natural world which reflects God's perfect order. The LORD has a will which is expressed in His word.

God's angels or hosts (a military term) are servants who do God's will. It can be difficult for independent modern man to take this seriously. Very often today, people around us have a sense of complete freedom to do whatever they want. The notion they are under authority and need to do God's will can be abhorrent to them. God is sovereign over all his works and over all places, but he is a God of love who wants only our good. His love is beyond anything we can measure or even understand (Ephesians 3.14-19).

People can have a hard time understanding the concept of God's will when they have placed God under human judgment, when they believe those who speak against God and pretend to judge His actions and His words, those who believe the original lie of Satan that God does not want our good and wants even to prevent us from enjoying good things (Genesis 3.1-4).

This Psalm extols God's goodness:

> **1** "Bless the Lord, O my soul;
> And all that is within me, *bless* His holy name!
> **2** Bless the Lord, O my soul,
> And forget not all His benefits:
> **3** Who forgives all your iniquities,
> Who heals all your diseases,
> **4** Who redeems your life from destruction,
> Who crowns you with lovingkindness and tender mercies,
> **5** Who satisfies your mouth with good *things,*
> *So that* your youth is renewed like the eagle's." (vv. 1-5)

Prayer

Father in heaven, we believe you are full of love and goodness. We believe you want to bless us and protect us from the evil one. We pray that today we will be attentive to your word and have a humble heart to obey it. We praise you for the salvation we enjoy in the Lord Jesus Christ. We pray in His name, Amen.

Day 3

> **1** "Praise the Lord!
> Praise the Lord from the heavens;
> Praise Him in the heights!
> **2** Praise Him, all His angels;
> Praise Him, all His hosts!

> **3** Praise Him, sun and moon;
> Praise Him, all you stars of light!
> **4** Praise Him, you heavens of heavens,
> And you waters above the heavens!"
>   (Psalms 148.1-4)

All creation worships and praises the LORD. The sun and moon and many of the stars were worshipped in most ancient civilizations. But here the sun and moon praise the LORD.

The angels and God's host are part of creation and also praise the LORD. Being God's messengers, the angels praise the LORD. The angels are with "the heavens and their host" part of creation (Psalms 33.6). God has set them when they did not previously exist (Nehemiah 6.7; Psalms 33.9; 119.91) — They remain part of creation that praises God and are not to be worshipped themselves.

Note the words of the angel to John:

> **9** "Then he said to me, "Write: 'Blessed *are* those who are called to the marriage supper of the Lamb!'" And he said to me, "These are the true sayings of God." **10** And I fell at his feet to worship him. But he said to me, "See *that you do* not *do that!* I am your fellow servant, and of your brethren who have the testimony of Jesus. Worship God! For the testimony of Jesus is the spirit of prophecy." (Revelation 19.9,10)

Since all of creation praises God, it follows that human beings, including kings and rulers, must do the same:

> **11** "Kings of the earth and all peoples;
> Princes and all judges of the earth;
> **12** Both young men and maidens;
> Old men and children.
> **13** Let them praise the name of the Lord,
> For His name alone is exalted;
> His glory *is* above the earth and heaven." (vv. 11-13)

Prayer

Father in heaven, we praise your name, we worship you. We come to you with hearts full of gratefulness and trust. We pray for our loved ones, for our friends and neighbors. Bless them, Lord, and work in their lives, so they might all turn to you. In Jesus' name, we pray. Amen.

Day 4

> **1** "Bless the Lord, O my soul!
> O Lord my God, you are very great:
> You are clothed with honor and majesty,
> **2** Who cover *Yourself* with light as *with* a garment,
> Who stretch out the heavens like a curtain.
> **3** He lays the beams of His upper chambers in the waters,
> Who makes the clouds His chariot,
> Who walks on the wings of the wind,
> **4** Who makes His angels spirits,
> His ministers a flame of fire."
>   (Psalms 104.1-4)

The entire Psalm shows God's rule over all of creation. No part of creation is to be worshipped, since all of creation points to the Creator. This Psalm which extols God's reign finishes with the prayer that evil will be expelled from this good creation.

> **33** "I will sing praise to my God while I have my being.
> **34** May my meditation be sweet to Him;
> I will be glad in the Lord.
> **35** May sinners be consumed from the earth,
> And the wicked be no more.
> Bless the Lord, O my soul!
> Praise the Lord!" (vv.33-35)

Verses 1-4 bring us back to Genesis 1.1-5, the first five days of creation. Angels are part of the original creation when God made them "spirits", "ministers", a flame of fire. It thus appears from this Psalm that we can situate the creation of angels in the first five days of creation.

Even though the Psalm refers to the original creation it is here referred to with participles of the present tense showing that the original point of creation is continued in the preservation of the world by God (see Amos 4:13; Isaiah 44:24; Isaiah 45:7; Jeremiah 10:12).

In verse 4 the Hebrew text literally says: "On the wings of the wind He makes his angels spirits, his ministers a flame of fire." This is a difficult verse to interpret. However, the reference to "wind" and "fire" can mean that God gives wind and fire to His angels, by which they act upon the world. In other words, the angels can use what God has created in order to accomplish His purposes. Thus, for example, while winds parted the sea at the Exodus, we also know that angels had a part in the events of the Exodus (Exodus 14.21). We see in the events of the Exodus the intervention of an "angel" which God sends to guide and guard His people as Moses leads them forward (Exodus 13.21,22; 23.20-26).

Hebrews 1.7 quotes this Psalm and applies it to angels who are contrasted with the Son whose name is far above angels.

Prayer

Lord in heaven, we praise your name today. We thank you for your daily blessings. We pray that today we can serve you faithfully and love you with all our heart, mind and strength. We pray for our country and its leaders, for those who are in authority. Give peace to our land, and may your Gospel be preached to many today. We pray in Jesus' name. Amen.

Day 5

> **1** "O Lord, our Lord,
> How excellent *is* Your name in all the earth,
> Who have set Your glory above the heavens!
> **2** Out of the mouth of babes and nursing infants
> You have ordained strength,
> Because of Your enemies,
> That You may silence the enemy and the avenger.
> **3** When I consider Your heavens, the work of Your fingers,
> The moon and the stars, which You have ordained,
> **4** What is man that You are mindful of him,
> And the son of man that You visit him?
> **5** For You have made him a little lower than the angels,
> And You have crowned him with glory and honor."
>   (Psalms 8.1-5)

Psalm 8 brings us back to Genesis 1.-26-28, where God's Word reveals to us that God created man to rule and subdue the world. Even in a fallen world, man continues to exercise a certain rule over creation, even though in his sinful state he is not able to fulfill his rule as he should (see Genesis 3).

Psalm 8 is quoted four times in the New Testament. In Matthew 21.16 Jesus quotes from Psalm 8.2 to teach that God uses babies to speak the truth and confound the wise. Psalms 8.6 is quoted to teach that mankind is destined in Christ to reign upon the earth (which will be a renewed earth). Hebrews 2.5-8 teaches that Psalms 8 is yet to be fulfilled "in the world to come" thus at the return of Christ. Paul in 1 Corinthians 15.27 and Ephesians 1.22 shows how Psalms 8 is and will be fulfilled in the glorification of Christ. Because of sin and the fall, man cannot fulfill the Psalm 8 expectations. But mankind's rule over creation will occur because of the ultimate man, the Last Adam, who is Jesus.

In all of this however, we see that it is the LORD who is to be glorified. What is said about babies who express God's power or human beings who are "crowned with glory and honor" points to God himself, the source of all these blessings.

Prayer

Father in heaven, we thank you for a new day. We praise you for your wonderful works in creation and your redemption through Christ. Give us today a spirit of love for everyone we encounter. Give us the words that will uplift each person we meet and bring them to an understanding of your salvation through Jesus. We pray in His name. Amen.

Day 6

> **1** "Give ear, O Shepherd of Israel,
> You who lead Joseph like a flock;
> You who dwell *between* the cherubim, shine forth!
> **2** Before Ephraim, Benjamin, and Manasseh,
> Stir up Your strength,
> And come *and* save us!
> **3** Restore us, O God;
> Cause Your face to shine,
> And we shall be saved!"
>   (Psalms 80.1-3)

God is the shepherd of Israel, to whom His people cry for help. He is the God who shines forth and dwells between the cherubim. The cherubim (plural of cherub) are mentioned about 40 times in the Old Testament. They were placed by God as the guardians of paradise in Genesis 3.24 after the expulsion of Adam and Eve from the garden of Eden. They protect the way with "flaming sword" to the tree of life.

Just like the cherubim protected the access to God's presence in the garden of Eden, we see that the cherubim placed on the ark of the covenant on top of the mercy-seat protected God's access to the Holy of holies in the tabernacle (Exodus 25.19-22). With this in mind, God is then said to be sitting enthroned above the cherubim:

> **1** "Again David gathered all *the* choice *men* of Israel, thirty thousand. **2** And David arose and went with all the people who *were* with him from Baal Judah to bring up from there the ark of God, whose name is called by the Name, the Lord of Hosts, who dwells *between* the cherubim." (2 Samuel 6.2)

The cherubim are described as attendants of the Deity — beautiful angels, of whom one fell from glory and was hurled from the sanctuary which he had polluted. In Ezekiel 28.12-19, the king of Tyre is compared in his glory and power to the *cherub* that God had put in His garden and who is compared to a beautiful precious stone. The king of Tyre fell like the original Cherub of God's garden because of pride.

The function of the cherubim as bearers and movers of the divine throne is seen in the vision given to Ezekiel (chapters 1 and 10). In chapter 1 they are described as "living creatures" (*chayyoth*) and cherubim (Ezekiel 10.2 and 10.20). In Ezekiel 9.3 the chariot or throne of God is spoken as a cherub. The cherubim resemble coals of fire (Ezekiel 10.2,6) burning like torches. The cherubim run and vanish as does lightning; they do not turn as they change direction but always go forward (Ezekiel 1.9,17; 10.11) as do the wheels of the chariot with a ring full of eyes round about it. The cherubim represent in Ezekiel the spirit or the will within the wheels.

Ezekiel's cherubim are clearly related to the seraphim in Isaiah's vision (Isaiah 6). Like the cherubim, the seraphim are the attendants of God as He is seated upon a throne high and exalted; they are also winged creatures.

The "four living creatures" of Revelation 4.6 are modeled upon Ezekiel, with elements from Isaiah. Full of eyes before and behind, they are in the midst of the throne, and round about it. "They have no rest day and night, saying, Holy, holy, holy, is the Lord God, the Almighty, who was and who is and who is to come."

Prayer

We pray to you, O Lord who is full of glory and majesty. We see in Jesus your glory, and we are grateful for His life and sacrifice. We believe through our Lord Jesus we have access to your glorious kingdom. Forgive us our sins and keep us faithful to you this day. Amen.

Day 7

> **4** "I sought the Lord, and He heard me,
> And delivered me from all my fears.
> **5** They looked to Him and were radiant,
> And their faces were not ashamed.
> **6** This poor man cried out, and the Lord heard *him*,
> And saved him out of all his troubles.
> **7** The angel of the Lord encamps all around those who fear Him,
> And delivers them.
> **8** Oh, taste and see that the Lord *is* good;
> Blessed *is* the man *who* trusts in Him!
> **9** Oh, fear the Lord, you His saints!"
> (Psalm 34.4–9)

David praises the LORD for the deliverance he enjoyed. The deliverance from "fears" is the most significant aspect of the LORD'S deliverance.

The fear of the LORD is the beginning of wisdom (Proverbs 9.10). But this fear leads to loving the Lord, which casts away all fears:

> **17** "Love has been perfected among us in this: that we may have boldness in the day of judgment; because as He is, so are we in this world. **18** There is no fear in love; but perfect love casts out fear, because fear involves torment. But he who fears has not been made perfect in love. **19** We love Him because He first loved us." (1 John 4.17-19)

It is in this context of praise for God's deliverance that the Psalm mentions the angel of the LORD, who encamps all around those who fear Him and delivers them. We see a reference to this when Jacob leaves Laban, who had dealt treacherously with him. Jacob offered a sacrifice and Laban left without harming Jacob (Genesis 31.51-55). After this...

> **1** "Jacob went on his way, and the angels of God met him. **2** When Jacob saw them, he said, 'This *is* God's camp.' And he called the name of that place Mahanaim." (Genesis 32.2)

The "angel of the LORD" encamped around Israel from the time of their deliverance from Egypt and during the entering of the promised land (Joshua 5.14). This angel appeared to Joshua in the form of a man and stated that he was "the commander of the army of the LORD". Being an angel not limited by space, this being can protect God's people on every side (see Zechariah 9.8). Some have speculated that this was Jesus, but the Scriptures teach clearly that Jesus is not an angel (see Hebrews chapter 1).

The Scriptures teach that those who look unto the LORD find deliverance and an access to His grace. The "bronze serpent" of Numbers (21.9), by which the Israelites who had sinned found deliverance from death, is a prophetical picture of the work of the Messiah who will be lifted up (on the cross) from the earth and will bring salvation to those who look upon Him for salvation:

> **14** "And as Moses lifted up the serpent in the wilderness, even so must the Son of Man be lifted up, **15** that whoever believes in Him should not perish but have eternal life. **16** For God so loved the world that He gave His only-begotten Son, that whoever believes in Him should not perish but have everlasting life. **17** For God did not send His Son into the world to condemn the world, but that the world through Him might be saved." (John 3.14-17; see John 12.32).

Those of Israel who look upon the Messiah who was pierced and who mourn, who repent, will find access to God's grace: "And I will pour on the house of David and on the inhabitants of Jerusalem the Spirit of grace and supplication; then they will look on Me whom they pierced. Yes, they will mourn for Him as one mourns for *his* only *son* and grieve for Him as one grieves for a firstborn." (Zechariah 12.10)

This promise is also proclaimed by Peter for those who repent when he preaches the Gospel to the Israelites in Acts:

> **17** "Yet now, brethren, I know that you did *it* in ignorance, as *did* also your rulers. **18** But those things which God foretold by the mouth of all His prophets, that the Christ would suffer, He has thus fulfilled. **19** Repent therefore and be converted, that your sins may be blotted out, so that times of refreshing may come from the presence of the Lord, **20** and that He may send Jesus Christ, who was preached to you before, **21** whom heaven must receive until the times of restoration of all things, which God has spoken by the mouth of all His holy prophets since the world began." (Acts 3.17-21)

Yann Opsitch

Prayer

Father in heaven, we thank you today for your work of deliverance, of forgiveness. We thank you for how you have worked through your angels to protect those who belong to you. We ask for forgiveness of our sins and for deliverance from our fears. We pray in Jesus' name. Amen.

Week 20: Waiting Upon the Lord

Day 1

> **13** *"I would have lost heart,* unless I had believed
> That I would see the goodness of the Lord
> In the land of the living.
> **14** Wait on the Lord;
> Be of good courage,
> And He shall strengthen your heart;
> Wait, I say, on the Lord!"
>   (Psalms 27.13,14)

This Psalm is from one who has to endure opposition from many evil individuals:

> "When the wicked came against me
> To eat up my flesh,
> My enemies and foes,
> They stumbled and fell." (v.2)

> "And now my head shall be lifted up above my enemies all around me…" (v.6)

> "Do not deliver me to the will of my adversaries;
> For false witnesses have risen against me,
> And such as breathe out violence." (v.12)

These verses are prophetical statements about the coming Messiah, who would encounter great opposition and would even be put to death (See Psalms 22; Isaiah 53; Matthew 16.21).
  Verse 6 mentions the victory and glorification of the Christ:

> "He will glorify Me, for He will take of Mine and will disclose it to you. All things that the Father has are Mine; therefore, I said

that He takes of Mine and will disclose it to you." (John 16.14,15).

"Then I looked, and behold, a white cloud, and sitting on the cloud was one like a son of man, having a golden crown on His head and a sharp sickle in His hand." (Revelation 14.14)

In Psalms 27.14 the Hebrew verb to wait (*qavah*) comes from a root word meaning to stretch or twist. When strings or ropes were twisted or knit together, they became much stronger. The idea is confirmed by the statement "He shall strengthen your heart". As the faithful are closely knit with God, as they live in harmony with the LORD, they receive courage and strength. The strength is from "waiting" upon the LORD, from being in this close-knit relationship with Him.

4 "Abide in Me, and I in you. As the branch cannot bear fruit of itself, unless it abides in the vine, neither can you, unless you abide in Me. **5** I am the vine, you *are* the branches. He who abides in Me, and I in him, bears much fruit; for without Me you can do nothing." (John 15.4,5)

6 "As you therefore have received Christ Jesus the Lord, so walk in Him, **7** rooted and built up in Him and established in the faith, as you have been taught, abounding in it with thanksgiving." (Colossians 2.7)

Prayer

Father in heaven, we are thankful for your Son Jesus. We are thankful for his life and earth and the glory He now has at your right hand. We pray, Lord, for strength as we come close to you today and daily. We pray this also for our loved ones, for our brothers and sisters in Christ. In Jesus' name, we pray. Amen.

Day 2

5 "Commit your way to the Lord,
Trust also in Him,
And He shall bring *it* to pass.
6 He shall bring forth your righteousness as the light,
And your justice as the noonday.
7 Rest in the Lord and wait patiently for Him;
Do not fret because of him who prospers in his way,

Because of the man who brings wicked schemes to pass.
8 Cease from anger and forsake wrath;
Do not fret—*it* only *causes* harm.
9 For evildoers shall be cut off;
But those who wait on the Lord,
They shall inherit the earth."
   (Psalms 37.5-9)

As in Psalm 27 the writer expresses his anguish concerning evil doers who not only harm others but who seem to enjoy life and apparently face no pains:

"Do not fret because of evildoers,
Nor be envious of the workers of iniquity." (v.1)

"The wicked plots against the just,
And gnashes at him with his teeth." (v.12)

"The wicked have drawn the sword
And have bent their bow,
To cast down the poor and needy,
To slay those who are of upright conduct." (v.14)

Waiting for the Lord is an exercise in patience, also called "longsuffering". And patience comes from humility and love:

1 "I, therefore, the prisoner of the Lord, beseech you to walk worthy of the calling with which you were called, **2** with all lowliness and gentleness, with longsuffering, bearing with one another in love" (Ephesians 4.2). "Love suffers long *and* is kind; love does not envy; love does not parade itself, is not puffed up;" (1 Corinthians 13.4).

The waiting is not just being patient as a virtue: it is waiting patiently for Him. In the Greco-Roman world, "patience" was one of the personal virtues to which every citizen needed to aspire. It was called *firmitas*, which meant tenacity, strength of mind, the ability to stick to one's purpose. These virtues were called the *via romana* (the Roman Way) which were considered qualities which gave the Roman Republic the moral superiority which allowed them to conquer and civilize the world. Before Rome, the Old Testament Scriptures recognized the importance of patience but connected this patience to people's relationship with God, their real source of strength.

Christian virtues do not stand on their own. They are not like the virtues of the *via romana*, produced simply by the will and learning of men. Willingness and learning are important, but the source of this willingness and learning must be God, who is the source of all wisdom and strength and offers them graciously to those who seek Him. This was something foreign to the Greco-Roman mind, and it is still foreign to many in today's world.

There is a promise for those who "wait upon the Lord": "They shall inherit the earth" and they "shall delight themselves in the abundance of peace" (vv. 9,11). Jesus refers back to this Psalm and similar Old Testament Scriptures in his sermon on the Mount (see Exodus 19.5; Genesis 15.18; Isaiah 11.4):

> **3** "Blessed *are* the poor in spirit,
> For theirs is the kingdom of heaven.
> **4** Blessed *are* those who mourn,
> For they shall be comforted.
> **5** Blessed *are* the meek,
> For they shall inherit the earth." (Matthew 5.3-5)

Prayer

Our LORD and Father, we come to you with grateful hearts. We entrust this day to you and everything we will be doing and saying. Thank you for watching over us, for guiding us, for protecting us. Keep our loved ones safely close to you. We pray this in Jesus' name. Amen.

Day 3

> **5** "I wait for the Lord, my soul waits,
> And in His word I do hope.
> **6** My soul *waits* for the Lord
> More than those who watch for the morning—
> *Yes, more than* those who watch for the morning.
> **7** O Israel, hope in the Lord;
> For with the Lord *there is* mercy,
> And with Him *is* abundant redemption.
> **8** And He shall redeem Israel
> From all his iniquities."
>   (Psalms 130.5-8)

The Psalmist repeats three times that he "waits for the Lord". And as he repeats this thought, he states that it is his soul that waits. He also lets us know that his waiting for the Lord is directly connected to the hope that comes from the LORD'S word. His waiting for the LORD is compared to the watchman who watches for the morning. For the spiritual watchman, God's mercy and forgiveness are the "morning" that he eagerly waits for and which follows the dark night of sin and guilt.

This Psalm is a prayer to God for forgiveness. In the first verse, the author cries to the LORD "out of the depths". The repeated mention of the soul indicates that this is about "the depths" of the soul, which includes one's realization of sinfulness and coming to God for forgiveness:

> **3** "If You, Lord, should mark iniquities,
> O Lord, who could stand?
> **4** But *there is* forgiveness with You,
> That You may be feared." (vv. 3,4)

The soul and the heart are the "inward man" mentioned by Paul. We are commanded to love God with all our heart, souls and mind. The soul will perish in hell when there is no repentance.

> **37** "Jesus said to him, 'You shall love the Lord your God with all your heart, with all your soul, and with all your mind.' **38** This is *the* first and great commandment. **39** And *the* second *is* like it: 'You shall love your neighbor as yourself.' **40** On these two commandments hang all the Law and the Prophets." (Matthew 22.37-40)

> "Beloved, I pray that you may prosper in all things and be in health, just as your soul prospers." (3 John 1.2)

> **16** "Therefore, we do not lose heart. Even though our outward man is perishing, yet the inward *man* is being renewed day by day. **17** For our light affliction, which is but for a moment, is working for us a far more exceeding *and* eternal weight of glory, **18** while we do not look at the things which are seen, but at the things which are not seen. For the things which are seen *are* temporary, but the things which are not seen *are* eternal." (2 Corinthians 4.16,17)

> **26** "For what profit is it to a man if he gains the whole world, and loses his own soul? Or what will a man give in exchange for

his soul? **27** For the Son of Man will come in the glory of His Father with His angels, and then He will reward each according to his works." (Matthew 16.26,27)

27 "Whatever I tell you in the dark, speak in the light; and what you hear in the ear, preach on the housetops. **28** And do not fear those who kill the body but cannot kill the soul. But rather fear Him who is able to destroy both soul and body in hell." (Matthew 10.27,28)

29 "But from there you will seek the Lord your God, and you will find *Him* if you seek Him with all your heart and with all your soul. **30** When you are in [i]distress, and all these things come upon you in the latter days, when you turn to the Lord your God and obey His voice **31** (for the Lord your God *is* a merciful God), He will not forsake you nor destroy you, nor forget the covenant of your fathers which He swore to them." (Deuteronomy 4.29-31)

"Now set your heart and your soul to seek the Lord your God." (2 Chronicles 22.19)

12 "Then you will call upon Me and go and pray to Me, and I will listen to you. **13** And you will seek Me and find *Me,* when you search for Me with all your heart." (Jeremiah 29.12,13)

Prayer

Our Father in heaven, we confess our sins and failings. We confess to you our lack of love and our need to grow in our faith, hope and love. Lord, give us strength and perseverance in the midst of trials and temptations. And give also strength to our loved ones, to our brothers and sisters in Christ. In His name, we pray. Amen.

Day 4

1 "To You, O Lord, I lift up my soul.
2 O my God, I trust in You;
Let me not be ashamed;
Let not my enemies triumph over me.
3 Indeed, let no one who waits on You be ashamed;

Let those be ashamed who deal treacherously without cause.
4 Show me Your ways, O Lord;
Teach me Your paths.
5 Lead me in Your truth and teach me,
For You *are* the God of my salvation;
On You I wait all the day."
  (Psalms 25.1-5)

No one who "waits" on the LORD will be ashamed. This "waiting" upon the LORD is from a Hebrew word that means "tied, twisted together" like strings or ropes tied together and thus become stronger. "O my God, I trust in You": to wait upon the LORD is to be intimately connected to Him through faith and an unwavering hope.

This close connection to God is the result of seeking understanding from God and receiving this understanding. This means one needs to be constantly learning from God's word, and this can only be done with God's help, God's strength (Colossians 1.11).

This close connection to God through faith is a reality that endures all day long for the true believer. It is a connection of every moment which springs from fully trusting God and not merely a ritual that one performs from time to time or on a regular basis as if closeness to God would depend on the calendar, the day or the hour.

The Christian has been provided a "helper" the Holy Spirit in order to stay closely connected to God (sometimes translated "comforter"). The word "helper" (*parakletos*) describes "one called at the side". It is used broadly in Greek for a legal advocate or counsel for defense ; for an intercessor or a helper. Thus, the Holy Spirit comes to the help of the faithful in a number of different ways. A good way to understand how the Holy Spirit is a "helper" to the faithful is to read the references to the Holy Spirit in their specific contexts. As we do this, we realize that there are a number of ways God's Spirit (or the Spirit of Christ) comes to our help.

Here are some of these ways:

He gives us hope and peace during difficult times (Rom. 14:17, 15:13, 1 Thess. 1:6). "Now may the God of hope fill you with all joy and peace in believing, that you may abound in hope by the power of the Holy Spirit." (Rom. 15:13)

He helps us pray (Rom. 8:26-27, Eph. 6:18, Jude 20).

> **26** "Likewise the Spirit also helps in our weaknesses. For we do not know what we should pray for as we ought, but the Spirit Himself makes intercession for us with groanings which cannot

be uttered. **27** Now He who searches the hearts knows what the mind of the Spirit *is*, because He makes intercession for the saints according to *the will of* God." (Romans 8.26,27)

He grows within us the fruit of the Spirit (Galatians 5:22-23).

> **22** "But the fruit of the Spirit is love, joy, peace, longsuffering, kindness, goodness, faithfulness, **23** gentleness, self-control." (Gal 5:22-23)

He gives wisdom for decision making (Eph. 1:17)

> "That the God of our Lord Jesus Christ, the Father of glory, may give to you the spirit of wisdom and revelation in the knowledge of Him," (Eph. 1:17)

He provides confidence over fear (2 Timothy 1:7).

> "For God has not given us a spirit of fear, but of power and of love and of a sound mind." (2 Tim. 1:7)

He provides power over temptation (Galatians 5:16).

> "I say then: Walk in the Spirit, and you shall not fulfill the lust of the flesh." (Gal. 5:16)

Prayer

Father in heaven, we thank you for all your precious promises and the salvation you have given us through Jesus your Son. We thank you for the Spirit which you give to those who trust in you and your salvation. We pray LORD that we will walk in the Spirit and not follow the lusts of the flesh. In Jesus' name, we pray. Amen.

Day 5

> **1** "I waited patiently for the Lord;
> And He inclined to me,
> And heard my cry.
> **2** He also brought me up out of a horrible pit,
> Out of the miry clay,
> And set my feet upon a rock,
> *And* established my steps.

3 He has put a new song in my mouth—
Praise to our God;
Many will see *it* and fear,
And will trust in the Lord."
   (Psalms 40.1-3)

It is difficult not to see in this Psalm, as in so many others, a reference to the coming Messiah. And the New Testament confirms this prophetical picture of a suffering Messiah who remains faithful to the end, who is brought out of a horrible pit and is finally established by the LORD — his death, resurrection and exaltation at the right hand of God.

This is especially the case since verses 6-8 are quoted and applied to Jesus in the book of Hebrews:

6 "Sacrifice and offering You did not desire;
My ears You have opened.
Burnt offering and sin offering You did not require.
7 Then I said, 'Behold, I come;
In the scroll of the book *it is* written of me.
8 I delight to do Your will, O my God,
And Your law *is* within my heart.'" (vv. 6-8; see also Hebrews 10.5-10)

It is true that the Psalm also refers to the "sins" of the author, in this case David. However, the Psalm also refers to the sacrificial offering of the righteous Messiah who died for the sins of humanity, who was the lamb "that carries the sin of the world" (John 1.29). God "laid upon him the iniquity of us all" (Isaiah 53.6) and "made him to be sin on our behalf" despite the fact that he committed no sin (2 Corinthians 5.21; 1 Peter 2.22; Hebrews 4.15; 1 John 3.5).

The Messiah "waited patiently" to be delivered from the darkness and evil that surrounded him. In this way he was an example for all of his disciples:

20 "For what credit *is it* if, when you are beaten for your faults, you take it patiently? But when you do good and suffer, if you take it patiently, this *is* commendable before God. **21** For to this you were called, because Christ also suffered for us, leaving us an example, that you should follow His steps: **22** "Who committed no sin, nor was deceit found in His mouth" (1 Peter 2.20-22)

Prayer

We thank you LORD for your Son who came and offered his life as a sacrifice for our sins, for the sin of the world. We thank you for His teachings and comforting words. Give us today a trusting and repentance heart. Give us today the wisdom we need to live in this dark world. We pray in Jesus' name. Amen.

Day 6

> **1** "Truly my soul silently *waits* for God;
> From Him *comes* my salvation.
> **2** He only *is* my rock and my salvation;
> *He is* my defense;
> I shall not be greatly moved."
> **5** "My soul, wait silently for God alone,
> For my expectation *is* from Him.
> **6** He only *is* my rock and my salvation;
> *He is* my defense;
> I shall not be moved.
> **7** In God *is* my salvation and my glory;
> The rock of my strength,
> *And* my refuge, *is* in God."
> (Psalms 62.1-2, 5-7)

In 1Chronicles 25.1-4 we read about Jeduthun and five of his sons who were among the singers of Israel and had charge of the music. Psalm 62 is a Psalm of David dedicated to Jeduthun.

We can take note of the constant thought in this Psalm of God as a rock, a refuge for the faithful:

Note the expressions "my rock," "my salvation," "my high tower" (v.2); and again, "my rock," "my salvation," and "my high tower" (v.6); "my strength," "my refuge" (v.7); "God is a refuge for us" (v.8).

It is this truth about God our refuge that leads the faithful to wait patiently even in silence for God alone. In this Psalm the Messiah is depicted as he is attacked and mocked but endures the pain and rejection in silence as is often noted even in the Old Testament Scriptures:

> "He was oppressed, and He was afflicted,
> Yet He opened not His mouth;
> He was led as a lamb to the slaughter,

And as a sheep before its shearers is silent,
So He opened not His mouth." (Isaiah 53.7)

11 "Now Jesus stood before the governor. And the governor asked Him, saying, "Are You the King of the Jews?" Jesus said to him, "*It is as* you say." **12** And while He was being accused by the chief priests and elders, He answered nothing. **13** Then Pilate said to Him, "Do You not hear how many things they testify against You?" **14** But He answered him not one word, so that the governor marveled greatly." (Matthew 27.11-14)

10 "Then Pilate said to Him, 'Are You not speaking to me? Do You not know that I have power to crucify You, and power to release You?' **11** Jesus answered, 'You could have no power at all against Me unless it had been given you from above. Therefore, the one who delivered Me to you has the greater sin.'" (John 19.10,11)

Prayer

Our LORD, we thank you for Jesus and the salvation you offer in Him. We pray that we can follow Jesus as an example who trusted in You in the midst of pain and rejection. We pray that we can learn in silence and be willing to be silent when it is wise to do so. Help us LORD! Give us the wisdom through the Holy Spirit to know when to speak and when to be in silence. We pray in Jesus' name. Amen.

Day 7

1 "Save me, O God!
For the waters have come up to *my* neck.
2 I sink in deep mire,
Where *there is* no standing;
I have come into deep waters,
Where the floods overflow me.
3 I am weary with my crying;
My throat is dry;
My eyes fail while I wait for my God."

6 "Let not those who wait for You, O Lord God of hosts, be ashamed because of me;

Let not those who seek You be confounded because of me, O
God of Israel.
7 Because for Your sake I have borne reproach;
Shame has covered my face.
8 I have become a stranger to my brothers,
And an alien to my mother's children;
9 Because zeal for Your house has eaten me up,
And the reproaches of those who reproach You have fallen on
me."
(Psalm 69.1-3, 6-9)

The Lord Jesus offered cries to the Father as he went through the torments of being offered as a lamb sacrificed for the sin of the world:

6 "As *He* also says in another *place:* 'You *are* a priest forever according to the order of Melchizedek'; **7** who, in the days of His flesh, when He had offered up prayers and supplications, with vehement cries and tears to Him who was able to save Him from death, and was heard because of His godly fear, **8** though He was a Son, *yet* He learned obedience by the things which He suffered. **9** And having been perfected, He became the author of eternal salvation to all who obey Him, **10** called by God as High Priest "according to the order of Melchizedek,' **11** of whom we have much to say, and hard to explain, since you have become dull of hearing." (Hebrews 5.7-9)

As he preached and taught, Jesus was even at one point a stranger to his own family (Matthew 12.46-50; John 7.1-5). Those who "wait upon the LORD" can also be these believers who for their faith have been forsaken by loved ones, by close friends.

The words "Because zeal for Your house has eaten me up" are quoted when Jesus cleansed the temple (John 2.1-17). The Messiah waited upon the LORD, which does not mean He was passive and did not act strongly for the sake of the LORD.

The words "And the reproaches of those who reproach You have fallen on me" are quoted about Jesus in Romans 15.3 to teach Christians how to treat each other and live together in peace, starting from the example of Christ:

1 "We then who are strong ought to bear with the scruples of
the weak, and not to please ourselves. **2** Let each of us
please *his* neighbor for *his* good, leading to edification. **3** For

even Christ did not please Himself; but as it is written, 'The reproaches of those who reproached You fell on Me.' **4** For whatever things were written before were written for our learning, that we through the patience and comfort of the Scriptures might have hope." (Romans 15.1-4)

This Psalm shows us that the Messiah gives us the best example of what it means to "wait upon the LORD".

Prayer

Father in heaven, we come to today fully trusting in your word, in hour commands and promises. Help us to live today in a manner that is worthy of you. Be with us in how we love and serve people we meet. Give us patience and understanding through your Holy Spirit. In Jesus' name, we pray. Amen.

Week 21: Blessing God

Day 1

> **4** "Enter into His gates with thanksgiving,
> *And* into His courts with praise.
> Be thankful to Him *and* bless His name.
> **5** For the Lord *is* good;
> His mercy *is* everlasting,
> And His truth *endures* to all generations."
> (Psalms 100.4,5)

Jesus spoke to the Samaritan woman and taught her about true worship, saying:

> **21** "Woman, believe Me, the hour is coming when you will neither on this mountain, nor in Jerusalem, worship the Father. **22** You worship what you do not know; we know what we worship, for salvation is of the Jews. **23** But the hour is coming, and now is, when the true worshipers will worship the Father in spirit and truth; for the Father is seeking such to worship Him. **24** God *is* Spirit, and those who worship Him must worship in spirit and truth." (John 4.21-24)

Psalm 100 describes true worship, or worship "in spirit and truth". After entering the gates, the true worshipper expresses thanksgiving, praise, prayer and a recognition of God's goodness, mercy and truth which endure for generations.

In the Psalms and throughout the Scriptures, "blessing" God describes thankfulness and praise. When addressed to God, "blessings" do not enhance His condition or strength but are a recognition of His blessings upon us, an exclamation of gratitude. In the same way, when we say "I magnify the LORD" or "Let us exalt His name" we are not enhancing anything in God's character or condition but are recognizing his magnificence and exalted status.

In this Psalm, "bless His name" reinforces the statement "be thankful to Him". Blessings from God are the expression of His goodness, His everlasting mercy and His enduring truth. Blessing God is a recognition of these blessings, which flow from His perfect character and nature.

It is important to note that God's mercy (sometimes translated lovingkindness) and His truth (sometimes translated faithfulness) endure forever, to all generations. God is not just the God of a past history, even a biblical history; He is the God of the present, the "I am" who does not change:

> **16** "Do not be deceived, my beloved brethren. **17** Every good gift and every perfect gift is from above, and comes down from the Father of lights, with whom there is no variation or shadow of turning." (James 1.16,17)

> **10** "Thus, says the Lord: 'Again there shall be heard in this place —of which you say, "It *is* desolate, without man and without beast"—in the cities of Judah, in the streets of Jerusalem that are desolate, without man and without inhabitant and without beast, **11** the voice of joy and the voice of gladness, the voice of the bridegroom and the voice of the bride, the voice of those who will say: 'Praise the Lord of hosts, for the Lord *is* good, for His mercy *endures* forever'— *and* of those *who will* bring the sacrifice of praise into the house of the Lord. For I will cause the captives of the land to return as at the first,' says the Lord." (Jeremiah 33.10-13)

Prayer

Our LORD, we praise you for your mercy and goodness, which are everlasting. We praise you for your faithfulness to Israel and to all who will believe in you. We thank you for your word of promise to your people and to all the families of the earth, all who will come to you through Jesus the Christ. We pray in His name, Amen.

Day 2

> **1** "I will bless the Lord at all times;
> His praise *shall* continually *be* in my mouth.
> **2** My soul shall make its boast in the Lord;
> The humble shall hear *of it* and be glad.
> **3** Oh, magnify the Lord with me,
> And let us exalt His name together."
> (Psalms 34.1-3)

"I will bless the LORD at all times" is an expression of true worship which cannot be restricted to a day of the week or an hour of the day. The writer adds: "His praise shall continually be on my mouth" which confirms the first statement.

Worship expresses what is deep in the heart, in the soul: "My soul shall make its boast in the LORD". Blessing the LORD is expressing thankfulness to Him for His blessings and this is primarily a matter of the heart and the soul not the matter of time and space, position of the body, words used, or music performed.

The Hebrew word often used for "worship" (*histahawa*) indicates prostration and humility, respect and awe before the LORD. It refers primarily to the idea of respect and homage to the LORD, which spring from humility: "The humble shall hear of it and be glad":

> **6** "Oh come, let us worship and bow down;
> Let us kneel before the Lord our Maker.
> **7** For He *is* our God,
> And we *are* the people of His pasture,
> And the sheep of His hand." (Psalms 95.6,7)

The main Greek word for "worship" in the New Testament is *proskuneo*, which has the same meaning as the Hebrew *histahawa*. The wise men prostrated themselves (*proskuneo*) before the baby (see Revelation 5.14; 7.11 and Hebrews 1.6).

Every knee of every creature in heaven and on earth will bend at the name Jesus (Philippians 2.10).

Prayer

We praise your name, LORD. We thank you for saving us, for your forgiveness. We praise you for Jesus, who came and gave His life for us. We thank you for His resurrection and His work in the hearts of all peoples throughout the world.

Let Us Come Before His Presence

We thank you for having brought us together into your family, into your fold. In Jesus' name, we pray.

Day 3

> **1** "Praise, O servants of the Lord,
> Praise the name of the Lord!
> **2** Blessed be the name of the Lord
> From this time forth and forevermore!
> **3** From the rising of the sun to its going down
> The Lord's name *is* to be praised."
>   (Psalms 113.1-3)

In this Psalm, it is the "name of the LORD" (Yahweh) which is to be blessed and praised. The idea is repeated three times in these verses. The same thought is found in other Psalms, as in 115.1: "Not unto us, O Lord, not unto us, but to Your name give glory, because of Your mercy, because of Your truth."

Having said this, the same Psalms adds these words:

> **2** "Why should the Gentiles say,
> "So where *is* their God?"
> **3** But our God *is* in heaven;
> He does whatever He pleases." (Psalms 115. 2,3)

In Psalm 115.1 the name LORD (Yahweh) stands for God's glory, mercy and truth. It is because of these characteristics of God that the LORD (Yahweh) is to be praised. In verse 3 the Psalmist adds "But our God is in heaven" using *Elohim* the Hebrew word for God, which we find from the first verse of the Bible (Genesis 1.1).

Yahweh stands also as the name of the God who made a covenant with Israel. It is the "covenant" name between God and the people of Israel. This begins with Genesis chapter 2. When the creative aspect of God is mentioned, the name Elohim is used (Genesis chapter 1). But when a relationship is involved between God and human beings, the Scripture uses the name Yahweh (Genesis chapter 2).

Often, both names come together as Yahweh-Elohim (the LORD God) to describe the God who is the creator of His people and their redeemer and Lord. When Adam and Eve sinned, Yahweh-Elohim made them garments of skin (Genesis chapter 3).

When the Israelites are about to be liberated from Egypt and to enter into Covenant with Yahweh, Moses is told by God to use the name "I am" (Yahweh) when he goes to Egypt:

> **13** "Then Moses said to God, 'Indeed, *when* I come to the children of Israel and say to them, 'The God of your fathers has sent me to you,' and they say to me, 'What *is* His name?' what shall I say to them?' **14** And God said to Moses, 'I AM WHO I AM.' And He said, 'Thus you shall say to the children of Israel, 'I AM has sent me to you.'" **15** Moreover God said to Moses, 'Thus you shall say to the children of Israel:
> 'The Lord God of your fathers, the God of Abraham, the God of Isaac, and the God of Jacob, has sent me to you. This *is* My name forever, and this *is* My memorial to all generations.'" (Exodus 3.13-15)

The name Yahweh was not revealed to Moses in Exodus 3 as if the name had never been used before, especially by the patriarchs (see for example Genesis 15.7; 22.14; 26.22). But it is given to Moses as the name by which they will "know" God as the one who liberated them, who called them out of Egypt and made a covenant with them.

When the Scriptures mention those who "know" God or His name, the verb "to know" must be understood in its Hebrew sense of "to know by experience" (*yada*) or by an intimate relationship. Thus, Adam "knew" Eve means they had an intimate relationship (Genesis 4.1). When Samuel was growing up, the Bible mentions that "he did not yet know Jehovah" does not mean he was unaware of that name; it means he did not know God in an intimate, personal way. In Egypt, God says to the people, "I will take you as My people, and I will be your God. Then you shall know that I *am* the Lord your God who brings you out from under the burdens of the Egyptians." (Exodus 6.7)

In the days of Isaiah, the people of God are told that they would get "to know" God's name through what they would learn by experience in the captivity of Assyria:

> "Therefore, my people shall know My name;
> Therefore *they shall know* in that day
> That I *am* He who speaks:
> 'Behold, *it is* I.'" (Isaiah 52.5,6)

Knowing God or "knowing His name" is not merely being aware of the name Yahweh or using it in prayer; it is "to know" God, "to know" His name, through a saving relationship in Christ:

> **1** "Jesus spoke these words, lifted up His eyes to heaven, and said: "Father, the hour has come. Glorify Your Son, that Your Son also may glorify You, **2** as You have given Him authority over all flesh, that He should give eternal life to as many as You have given Him. **3** And this is eternal life, that they may know You, the only true God, and Jesus Christ whom You have sent." (John 17.1-3)

Prayer

Father in heaven, we thank you for Jesus, your Son. We thank you for delivering us from sin, from condemnation, and for giving us eternal life in Jesus. Forgive our sins. Forgive our shortcomings. Through your Holy Spirit help us grow in faith, hope and love. We pray this in Jesus' name. Amen.

Day 4

> **1** "I will extol You, my God, O King;
> And I will bless Your name forever and ever.
> **2** Every day I will bless You,
> And I will praise Your name forever and ever.
> **3** Great *is* the Lord, and greatly to be praised;
> And His greatness *is* unsearchable."
> (Psalms 145.1-3)

Psalm 145 goes over many of the reasons human beings should "extol" the LORD, bless His name forever and ever and praise His name (verses 1-13):

- His great goodness.
- His righteousness.
- The splendor of His majesty.
- His wondrous works.
- His awesome acts.
- His compassion.
- His mercy.
- The majesty of His everlasting kingdom.

Psalms 145 describes the relationship God desires to have with human beings (verses 14-21):

- He upholds those who fall.
- He raises up those who are bowed down.
- He preserves those who love Him.
- He will destroy the wicked.
- He is near to those who call upon Him.
- He fulfills the desire of those who fear Him.

Prayer

Lord in heaven we praise your name today. May this new day be entirely given to you, to your service. May we meditate on all the reasons to bless your name and to praise you. May we remain humble in our ways, call upon you and fear you. In the name of our Lord Jesus, we pray. Amen.

Day 5

> **1** "Bless the Lord, O my soul;
> And all that is within me, *bless* His holy name!
> **2** Bless the Lord, O my soul,
> And forget not all His benefits:
> **3** Who forgives all your iniquities,
> Who heals all your diseases,
> **4** Who redeems your life from destruction,
> Who crowns you with lovingkindness and tender mercies,
> **5** Who satisfies your mouth with good *things,*
> *So that* your youth is renewed like the eagle's."
> (Psalms 103.1-5)

This Psalm begins with blessing the LORD from the depth of one's soul. This is a personal matter between each one and God.

At the end of the Psalm "blessing" the Lord is also an activity of angels and all His works:

> "**20** Bless the Lord, you His angels,
> Who excel in strength, who do His word,
> Heeding the voice of His word.
> **21** Bless the Lord, all *you* His hosts,
> *You* ministers of His, who do His pleasure.
> **22** Bless the Lord, all His works,

In all places of His dominion.
Bless the Lord, O my soul!" (vv.20-22)

Blessing the LORD is the outcome of trusting in who He is. It is a recognition of His kingdom or kingship by which He rules over all (v.19). At the return of Jesus, all will confess that He is Lord:

5 "Let this mind be in you which was also in Christ Jesus, **6** who, being in the form of God, did not consider it robbery to be equal with God, **7** but [c]made Himself of no reputation, taking the form of a bondservant, *and* coming in the likeness of men. **8** And being found in appearance as a man, He humbled Himself and became obedient to *the point of* death, even the death of the cross. **9** Therefore God also has highly exalted Him and given Him the name which is above every name, **10** that at the name of Jesus every knee should bow, of those in heaven, and of those on earth, and of those under the earth, **11** and *that* every tongue should confess that Jesus Christ *is* Lord, to the glory of God the Father." (Philippians 2.5-11)

Prayer

Father in heaven, we praise your name for all your good works, for your healings, for your forgiveness and tender mercies. We thank you for our daily food, for strength to work. May we be grateful to you this day. May we learn to trust you daily for all our needs. In Jesus' name, we pray. Amen.

Day 6

1 "I will bless the Lord at all times;
His praise *shall* continually *be* in my mouth.
2 My soul shall make its boast in the Lord;
The humble shall hear *of it* and be glad.
3 Oh, magnify the Lord with me,
And let us exalt His name together."
   (Psalm 34.1-3)

This Psalm contains this superscription (not an inspired part of the Psalm): "*A Psalm* of David when he pretended madness before Abimelech, who drove him away, and he departed." Abimelech was a title given to Philistine kings (similar to the word pharaoh in Egypt). The title

Abimelech was already known when Moses wrote Genesis 20 and Genesis 26.

The account of this event in David's life is found in 1 Samuel 21.11-15. David's action has been sometimes the subject of criticism. However, this is the account of a war situation between Israel and the Philistines. The shrewdness of David that allowed him to escape the hands of this cruel and pagan king should be understood in this context.

This Psalm is messianic in referring to the bones of the righteous one:

> **19** "Many *are* the afflictions of the righteous, but the Lord delivers him out of them all. **20** He guards all his bones; not one of them is broken." (vv.19,20; see John 19.33)

Blessing the Lord is not restricted to a day of the week or an hour of the day: "I will bless the Lord at all times". And he adds: "His praise shall continually be in my mouth". This is the attitude of the true worshipper.

Coming together as a congregation to "praise" and "bless the Lord" is an important part of worship. But the true believer also blesses the LORD in his "soul" (Psalm 103.1). His blessing the LORD is a disposition of the mind and heart, not an activity set by the clock or the calendar.

> "I will praise You, O Lord my God, with all my heart,
> And I will glorify Your name forevermore." (Psalms 86.12)

> "Behold, you desire truth in the inward parts,
> And in the hidden *part* You will make me to know wisdom."
> (Psalms 51.6)

> "Therefore, the Lord said: 'Inasmuch as these people draw near with their mouths
> And honor Me with their lips,
> But have removed their hearts far from Me,
> And their fear toward Me is taught by the commandment of men'" (Isaiah 29.13)

Prayer

Lord in heaven, we come to you today to praise your name. We pray that you will give us wisdom that me might understand true humility and true obedience to you. Forgive all our sins. We also want to forgive those who have sinned against us.

Bless them, Lord, lead them to you if they have gone astray. We pray this in the name of Jesus. Amen.

Day 7

> **1** "Oh, sing to the Lord a new song!
> Sing to the Lord, all the earth.
> **2** Sing to the Lord, bless His name;
> Proclaim the good news of His salvation from day to day.
> **3** Declare His glory among the nations,
> His wonders among all peoples.
> **4** For the Lord *is* great and greatly to be praised;
> He *is* to be feared above all gods.
> **5** For all the gods of the peoples *are* idols,
> But the Lord made the heavens.
> **6** Honor and majesty *are* before Him;
> Strength and beauty *are* in His sanctuary."
> (Psalms 96.1-6)

A number of different words describe the worship by which we extol the LORD: to sing, bless, proclaim, declare. All these words are not only about something done privately or in secret. They describe a personal but also public action of worship.

Worship is not restricted to Israel but is done among "all nations", "all the peoples". This aspect of the Psalm is messianic and reminds the readers of God's purpose to save and bless all the nations of the earth (Genesis 12.1-3; 22.18; 27.29; Jonah 1.16; 3.1-42; Numbers 24.9; Acts 17.26; Revelation 11.15):

> "Say among the nations, 'The Lord reigns;
> The world also is firmly established,
> It shall not be moved;
> He shall judge the peoples righteously.'" (v.10)

> **16** "Then I remembered the word of the Lord, how He
> said, 'John indeed baptized with water, but you shall be baptized
> with the Holy Spirit.' **17** If therefore God gave them the same
> gift as *He gave* us when we believed on the Lord Jesus
> Christ, who was I that I could withstand God? **18** When they
> heard these things, they became silent; and they glorified God,

saying, 'Then God has also granted to the Gentiles repentance to life.'" (Acts 11.16-18)

God is the "God of Abraham, Isaac and Jacob" who made promises to the patriarchs. God would bless all the families of the earth, all the nations, through Abraham's seed (Galatians 3.10-29).

Through the Messiah, God has grafted the gentiles (the wild olive tree) into the olive tree (Israel) planted by God since the call of the patriarchs (the roots of the olive tree). The God of Abraham, Isaac and Jacob has become the God of the gentiles who come to the Messiah:

13 "For I speak to you Gentiles; inasmuch as I am an apostle to the Gentiles, I magnify my ministry, **14** if by any means I may provoke to jealousy *those who are* my flesh and save some of them. **15** For if their being cast away *is* the reconciling of the world, what *will* their acceptance *be* but life from the dead? **16** For if the first fruit *is* holy, the lump *is* also *holy;* and if the root *is* holy, so *are* the branches. **17** And if some of the branches were broken off, and you, being a wild olive tree, were grafted in among them, and with them became a partaker of the root and fatness of the olive tree, **18** do not boast against the branches. But if you do boast, *remember that* you do not support the root, but the root *supports* you." (Romans 11.13-18)

Prayer

Father in heaven, we thank you for the promises you made to the patriarchs. We thank you for your plan of salvation of all nations and peoples through Jesus the Messiah. We pray that you will lead many from Israel to faith in the Lord Jesus. We pray for their salvation. May we always recognize the wisdom of your ways. In Jesus' name, we pray. Amen.

Week 22: Prayer

Day 1

> **2** "Lord, how they have increased who trouble me!
> Many *are* they who rise up against me.
> Many *are* they who say of me,
> '*There is* no help for him in God.' *Selah*
> **3** But You, O Lord, *are* a shield for me,
> My glory and the One who lifts up my head.
> **4** I cried to the Lord with my voice,
> And He heard me from His holy hill. *Selah*
> **5** I lay down and slept;
> I awoke, for the Lord sustained me.
> **6** I will not be afraid of ten thousands of people
> Who have set *themselves* against me all around."
>   (Psalms 3.1-6)

The circumstances of this Psalm of David are distressful, since the superscription informs us that the Psalm was written by David when he fled after the betrayal of his son Absalom (see 2 Samuel 15 to 19).

During these events and battles, we see those like Shimei who curse David during his affliction:

> **11** "And David said to Abishai and all his servants, 'See how my son who came from my own body seeks my life. How much more now *may this* Benjamite? Let him alone and let him curse; for so the Lord has ordered him. **12** It may be that the Lord will look on my affliction, and that the Lord will repay me with good for his cursing this day.' **13** And as David and his men went along the road, Shimei went along the hillside opposite him and cursed as he went, threw stones at him and kicked up dust. **14** Now the king and all the people who *were* with him became weary; so, they refreshed themselves there." (2 Samuel 16.11-14)

It is difficult to imagine the feelings of David being betrayed by his own son, who wanted to be on the throne of his father.

This betrayal of David the king is in keeping with the messianic prophecies about Judas' betrayal (Zechariah 11.12,13):

> **47** :And while He was still speaking, behold, a multitude; and he who was called Judas, one of the twelve, went before them and drew near to Jesus to kiss Him. **48** But Jesus said to him, 'Judas, are you betraying the Son of Man with a kiss?'" (Luke 22.47,48)

Betrayal for position of power happen all the time, and even among siblings or "friends". Thus, this Psalm is more touching when one considers the context.

Those who come against the king say: "There is no help for him in God" These words remind us of the words pronounced by those who condemned Jesus while he was on the cross:

> **41** "Likewise, the chief priests also, mocking with the scribes and elders, said, **42** 'He saved others; Himself He cannot save. If He is the King of Israel, let Him now come down from the cross, and we will believe Him. **43** He trusted in God; let Him deliver Him now if He will have Him; for He said, 'I am the Son of God.'" (Matthew 27.41-44)

Prayer

Father in heaven, we pray to you for deliverance and strength. You know all our troubles and griefs. You know the sadness of our hearts when we are betrayed. We bring to you those who have betrayed us or grieved us with their words. May you Lord touch their hearts by the truth of your Word and through your Holy Spirit. We pray this in the name of Jesus. Amen.

Day 2

> **1** "Have mercy upon me, O God,
> According to Your lovingkindness;
> According to the multitude of Your tender mercies,
> Blot out my transgressions.
> **2** Wash me thoroughly from my iniquity,
> And cleanse me from my sin.
> **3** For I acknowledge my transgressions,
> And my sin *is* always before me.

4 Against You, You only, have I sinned,
And done *this* evil in Your sight—
That You may be found just when You speak,
And blameless when You judge."
   (Psalms 51.1-4)

In this Psalm, the name Elohim — the "creator God" (Genesis 1.1) — is used five times by David, starting in verse 1. God's promise in forgiving goes beyond forgiveness: it is the promise that through His power God will create anew and transform the heart and life of the sinner: "Create in me a clean heart, O God, and renew a steadfast spirit within me." (v. 10). Beyond the personal forgiveness granted to David, this prayer looks to the future of the people and the holy city to be rebuilt by God: "Do good in Your good pleasure to Zion; build the walls of Jerusalem." (v.18)

God's work in the life of the sinner is a work of recreating, of rebuilding, of transformation:

> "Therefore, if anyone *is* in Christ, *he is* a new creation; old things have passed away; behold, all things have become new." (2 Corinthians 5.17).

> **1** "I beseech you therefore, brethren, by the mercies of God, that you present your bodies a living sacrifice, holy, acceptable to God, *which is* your reasonable service. **2** And do not be conformed to this world, but be transformed by the renewing of your mind, that you may prove what *is* that good and acceptable and perfect will of God." (Romans 12.1,2).

The work of God in the life of the repentant sinner is one of "restoration" through the Holy Spirit:

> **11** "Do not cast me away from Your presence, and do not take Your Holy Spirit from me. **12** Restore to me the joy of Your salvation and uphold me *by Your* generous Spirit." (vv.11,12)

God is calling the repentant and forgiven sinner to witness and teach:

> "*Then* I will teach transgressors Your ways, and sinners shall be converted to You." (v.13)

Prayer

Our Father in heaven, we thank you for forgiveness. We thank you for offering freely to forgive us through your Son Jesus. You are full of mercy despite our sins. Lord, renew our spirits, our minds. Create in us a greater desire to please you and serve you. We pray this in Jesus' name. Amen.

Day 3

> **1** "O God, You *are* my God;
> Early will I seek You;
> My soul thirsts for You;
> My flesh longs for You
> In a dry and thirsty land
> Where there is no water.
> **2** So I have looked for You in the sanctuary,
> To see Your power and Your glory.
> **3** Because Your lovingkindness *is* better than life,
> My lips shall praise You.
> **4** Thus I will bless You while I live;
> I will lift up my hands in Your name.
> **5** My soul shall be satisfied as with marrow and fatness,
> And my mouth shall praise *You* with joyful lips."
> (Psalms 63.1-5)

The writer seeks God in a personal and intimate way. He is thirsty and longing for God. These truths are important in the teachings of Jesus:

> **31** "Therefore, do not worry, saying, 'What shall we eat?' or 'What shall we drink?' or 'What shall we wear?' **32** For after all these things the Gentiles seek. For your heavenly Father knows that you need all these things. **33** But seek first the kingdom of God and His righteousness, and all these things shall be added to you." (Matthew 6. 31-34)

> "Blessed *are* those who hunger and thirst for righteousness,
> For they shall be filled." (Matthew 5.6)

The joy experienced by David comes from his hunger and thirst for God, his seeking God from the depths of his soul. Joy is not the goal for the believer, but the fruit. This joy comes from the knowledge of God's presence and protection:

"Because You have been my help,
Therefore in the shadow of Your wings I will rejoice." (v.7)

The king is not too high or important in his own mind to find joy in God:

"But the king shall rejoice in God; everyone who swears by Him shall glory; but the mouth of those who speak lies shall be stopped." (v.11)

Joy is a fruit that accompanies the walk "in the Spirit": "I say then: Walk in the Spirit, and you shall not fulfill the lust of the flesh." (Galatians 5.16).

22 "But the fruit of the Spirit is love, joy, peace, longsuffering, kindness, goodness, faithfulness, **23** gentleness, self-control. Against such there is no law." (Galatians 5.22,23).

Prayer

Dear Father in heaven, we are grateful to you today. We come to you for our joy and our comfort. We seek in you all the treasures of your goodness and care. May we walk today by your Holy Spirit and listen to His teachings. May we find our joy in you. We pray in Jesus' name, Amen.

Day 4

1 "I will extol You, O Lord, for You have lifted me up,
And have not let my foes rejoice over me.
2 O Lord my God, I cried out to You,
And You healed me.
3 O Lord, You brought my soul up from the grave;
You have kept me alive, that I should not go down to the pit.
4 Sing praise to the Lord, you saints of His,
And give thanks at the remembrance of His holy name.
5 For His anger *is but for* a moment,
His favor *is for* life;
Weeping may endure for a night,
But joy *comes* in the morning."
  (Psalms 30.1-5)

This Psalm expresses rejoicing after God answered prayers. It is believed that this Psalm was written on the occasion of the dedication of the

Threshing Floor of Araunah that followed the plague that came as a consequence of David's numbering of the people (2 Samuel 24.25 and 1 Chronicles 21.26). A number of statements in the Psalm correspond to this historical occasion.

Verses 1-3 are messianic and remind us of the victory of the Messiah over death announced in so many places (Isaiah 53; Psalms 16 and 22): "O Lord, you brought my soul up from the grave. You have kept me alive, that I should not go down to the pit." In this verse, the verb "brought up" is the Hebrew *alah* which means to arise, raise, ascend, bring back. The writer talks about arising, ascending from the grave. The language is clearly messianic and refers to the Messiah's resurrection when He would be brought back to life.

The Messiah cried out to the LORD, who answered his prayer:

> **7** "who, in the days of His flesh, when He had offered up prayers and supplications, with vehement cries and tears to Him who was able to save Him from death, and was heard because of His godly fear, **8** though He was a Son, *yet* He learned obedience by the things which He suffered." (Hebrews 5. 7,8).

The "joy" of the Messiah came up on the morning of His resurrection on the first day of the week: "looking unto Jesus, the author and finisher of *our* faith, who for the joy that was set before Him endured the cross, despising the shame, and has sat down at the right hand of the throne of God." (Hebrews 12.2)

Prayer

Father in heaven, we look to the morning when the night is there. We know that you came to us to wipe all tears away by carrying our burdens and dying for our sins. You rose from the dead and conquered death for us. We pray that this day we will live in the light of Jesus' resurrection and joy. In His holy name, we pray, Amen.

Day 5

> 8 "I cried out to You, O Lord;
> And to the Lord I made supplication:
> 9 'What profit *is there* in my blood,
> When I go down to the pit?
> Will the dust praise You?

Will it declare Your truth?
10 Hear, O Lord, and have mercy on me;
Lord, be my helper!'
11 You have turned for me my mourning into dancing;
You have put off my sackcloth and clothed me with gladness,
12 To the end that *my* glory may sing praise to You and not be silent.
O Lord my God, I will give thanks to You forever."
   (Psalms 30.8-12)

This is the prayer of supplication of the faithful one whose life is threatened by evil people: "I will extol You, O Lord, for You have lifted me up, and have not let my foes rejoice over me." (v.1)

The writer of this Psalm has no "self-confidence". All of his hope is in the God who can help him. The change of emotions of the writer is the result of God's work and not anything in the writer: "You have turned my mourning into dancing". "You have clothed me with gladness".

We often hear the world telling us "believe in yourself" when the truth is, we have no good reason to believe in ourselves. We don't have the power to bring ourselves back from the grave. We are dust and will return to dust. But the Lord is the Lord of death and has the power to bring us back to life.

Some situations in life are like a "resurrection". When everything seems lost and there is little hope, the LORD still has the power to change everything. From verse 10 to verse 11 the change is sudden when God turns mourning into dancing.

Abraham obeyed God:

> **17** "By faith Abraham, when he was tested, offered up Isaac, and he who had received the promises offered up his only-begotten *son,* **18** of whom it was said, 'In Isaac your seed shall be called,' **19** concluding that God *was* able to raise *him* up, even from the dead, from which he also received him in a figurative sense." (Hebrews 11.17-19).

Many of the Old Testament faithful ones suffered hardship "that they might obtain a better resurrection" (Hebrews 11.35). Even Job trusted God his redeemer who would be able to keep him alive and whom he would see:

> **25**"For I know *that* my Redeemer lives,
> And He shall stand at last on the earth;

26 And after my skin is destroyed, this *I know*,
That in my flesh I shall see God,
27 Whom I shall see for myself,
And my eyes shall behold, and not another." (Job 19.25-27)

Prayer

Father in heaven, we come to you today for help, for strength and wisdom. We trust you to fully take care of us and protect us through the day. We pray for our loved ones and for every person we meet today. Give us the right words for each one. We pray that we can share truth with everyone through our words and through our actions. In Jesus' name, we pray. Amen.

Day 6

1 "I will extol You, my God, O King;
And I will bless Your name forever and ever.
2 Every day I will bless You,
And I will praise Your name forever and ever.
3 Great *is* the Lord, and greatly to be praised;
And His greatness *is* unsearchable.
4 One generation shall praise Your works to another,
And shall declare Your mighty acts.
5 I will meditate on the glorious splendor of Your majesty,
And on Your wondrous works."
   (Psalms 145.1-5)

The theme of this Psalm is the righteousness and goodness of God, expressed through the praises of David.

The Psalm shows a very high and noble view of God. It stands in contrast with the modern tendency of putting God under human judgment, especially when it comes to God as He is revealed in the Old Testament.

Reading the Old Testament, people can be under the impression that God is in favor or conflict and war, even bloodshed. But in fact, an attentive reading especially of the prophets shows that God's nature is revulsed by the bloodshed and wars among individuals or nations. As the prophet Ezekiel says on a number of occasions, "I do not desire the death...."

God brings judgment on Israel and also other nations around Israel because of all the bloodshed found among those nations. See Ezekiel 18.23; 33.11

The words of God against *Seir* (Edom) show clearly how God views national hatred against other peoples. The idea that God in the Old Testament is favorable to hatred and bloodshed comes from basic misunderstandings of the biblical account. It also comes from misconstrued understandings of Jesus' teachings about the Christian life. Sometimes biblical interpreters feel compelled to explain these difficulties by denying the divine inspiration of the biblical texts. However, the denial of the inerrancy and inspiration of the biblical text is an explanation that is unnecessary and hurts the faith. Also, when this happens, it reduces our ability to praise God with full confidence in His divine qualities.

The teachings of Jesus should be remembered when we face difficulties in understanding the biblical account. The Son of God expresses complete confidence in the goodness and love of the Father, who is not a different God from the God of Abraham, Isaac and Jacob. This confidence forms the basis of Jesus' exhortation to "be perfect as the Father in heaven is perfect" (Matthew 5.48).

Prayer

Father in heaven, we pray for wisdom as we read your Word. We pray that you will enlighten our hearts and minds in understanding your goodness and love. We believe in the teachings of your beloved Son. We pray to you as our Father in heaven, who is the source of life and all goodness. This we pray in Jesus' name. Amen.

Day 7

17 "The Lord *is* righteous in all His ways,
Gracious in all His works.
18 The Lord *is* near to all who call upon Him,
To all who call upon Him in truth.
19 He will fulfill the desire of those who fear Him;
He also will hear their cry and save them.
20 The Lord preserves all who love Him,
But all the wicked He will destroy.
21 My mouth shall speak the praise of the Lord,
And all flesh shall bless His holy name
Forever and ever."
  (Psalms 145.17-21)

Psalms 145 extols the goodness and mercy of God and ends with a judgment on the wicked in verse 20. This is an example of how someone could read this and pit God's mercy against His justice. However, both the mercy and justice of God are part of his nature and character. And this is not different from Jesus. Some who extol the compassion and love of Jesus seem to balk when Jesus talks about justice and God's judgment (as in Matthew 25).

Verses 8 and 9 of this Psalm show how the patience and goodness of God weigh more than His justice.

> **8** "The Lord *is* gracious and full of compassion,
> Slow to anger and great in mercy.
> **9** The Lord *is* good to all,
> And His tender mercies *are* over all His works." (vv.8,9)

The LORD is full of compassion, slow to anger and great in mercy. Does this mean there is no justice, no righteous indignation and even anger in God? Of course not. The judgments of God in the Old Testament as in the flood or even towards the people of Israel or other nations come after long periods of pleading and waiting.

This was the work of the prophets, who pleaded for repentance and change of heart on behalf of God. This was the work of Jesus, who preached repentance:

> **1** "There were present at that season some who told Him about the Galileans whose blood Pilate had [a]mingled with their sacrifices. **2** And Jesus answered and said to them, 'Do you suppose that these Galileans were worse sinners than all *other* Galileans, because they suffered such things? **3** I tell you, no; but unless you repent you will all likewise perish. **4** Or those eighteen on whom the tower in Siloam fell and killed them, do you think that they were worse sinners than all *other* men who dwelt in Jerusalem? **5** I tell you, no; but unless you repent you will all likewise perish.'" (Luke 13.1-5)

This pleading of God for repentance is still fundamental today in understanding God's relationship to human beings and to sin:

> **31** "Truly, these times of ignorance God overlooked, but now commands all men everywhere to repent, **31** because He has appointed a day on which He will judge the world in righteousness

by the Man whom He has ordained. He has given assurance of this to all by raising Him from the dead." (Acts 17.30,31)

Prayer

Our Father in heaven, open our hearts to a better understanding of your mercy and justice. May we count on your mercy and goodness and seek your justice. May we today exercise mercy towards all. We pray for your Holy Spirit to produce in our hearts and lives the fruit you desire to see in us. This we pray in the name of Jesus. Amen.

Week 23: Praise

Day 1

> **10** "All Your works shall praise You, O Lord,
> And Your saints shall bless You.
> **11** They shall speak of the glory of Your kingdom,
> And talk of Your power,
> **12** To make known to the sons of men His mighty acts,
> And the glorious majesty of His kingdom.
> **13** Your kingdom *is* an everlasting kingdom,
> And Your dominion *endures* throughout all generations."
> (Psalms 145.10-13)

The LORD is slow to anger and great in mercy (v.8). His tender mercies are all over His works (v.9).

Thus, all His works praise Him. His saints bless Him:

> **9** "But you *are* a chosen generation, a royal priesthood, a holy nation, His own special people, that you may proclaim the praises of Him who called you out of darkness into His marvelous light; **10** who once *were* not a people but *are* now the people of God, who had not obtained mercy but now have obtained mercy." (1 Peter 2.9,10).

> **15** "Therefore, by Him let us continually offer the sacrifice of praise to God, that is, the fruit of *our* lips, giving thanks to His name. **16** But do not forget to do good and to share, for with such sacrifices God is well pleased." (Hebrews 13.15,16)

The praises given to God are to reach "the sons of men" (v.12). They are to be known by all nations and people speaking all different kinds of languages:

> **1** "Praise the Lord, all you Gentiles!
> Laud Him, all you peoples!

2 For His merciful kindness is great toward us,
And the truth of the Lord *endures* forever.
Praise the Lord!" (Psalms 117.1,2)

3 "Great and marvelous *are* Your works,
Lord God Almighty!
Just and true *are* Your ways,
O King of the saints!
4 Who shall not fear You, O Lord, and glorify Your name?
For *You* alone *are* holy.
For all nations shall come and worship before You,
For Your judgments have been manifested." (Revelation 15.3,4)

Prayer

We praise you Lord for your love and mercy. We praise you today for your message of salvation offered to all peoples. Give us the right and true words to share your love and goodness with everyone we meet. May we show today a sincere love for our neighbors and a desire to do good to them. We pray this in Jesus's name. Amen.

Day 2

7 "Give to the Lord, O families of the peoples,
Give to the Lord glory and strength.
8 Give to the Lord the glory *due* His name;
Bring an offering, and come into His courts.
9 Oh, worship the Lord in the beauty of holiness!
Tremble before Him, all the earth.
10 Say among the nations, 'The Lord reigns;
The world also is firmly established,
It shall not be moved;
He shall judge the peoples righteously.'"
   (Psalms 96.7-10)

The "families of the peoples" are called to give glory to the LORD. The nations need to hear that "the LORD reigns". God is the judge of all the peoples, and the entire world is firmly established and shall not be moved. The promise of God to Abraham was that through him He would bless all the families of the earth (Genesis 12.3; Galatians 3.26-29).

These statements are an echo of the first verse of this Psalm: "Oh, sing to the LORD a new song! Sing to the LORD all the earth."

The LORD is not only the God of Israel or the God of Abraham, Isaac and Jacob. He is the God of all peoples. The lamb of God came to take away "the sin of the world" (John 1.29).

The reign of God is universal and is eternal. The kings of Babylon and Persia were brought to a point where they confessed this truth (Daniel 3.26-30; 6.25-27).

The reign of God's Son is also the reign of God. All peoples and nations are invited to be part of this reign:

> **12** "Giving thanks to the Father who has qualified us to be partakers of the inheritance of the saints in the light. **13** He has delivered us from the power of darkness and conveyed *us* into the kingdom of the Son of His love, 14 in whom we have redemption through His blood, the forgiveness of sins." (Colossians 1.12-14).

> **1** "If then you were raised with Christ, seek those things which are above, where Christ is, sitting at the right hand of God. **2** Set your mind on things above, not on things on the earth. **3** For you died, and your life is hidden with Christ in God. **4** When Christ *who is* our life appears, then you also will appear with Him in glory." (Colossians 3.1-4)

Prayer

Father in heaven, we thank you for giving us a new day to serve you and know you. We pray for an open heart, an open mind to the truths of your Word. We also pray that we will today walk in the Spirit and let your Holy Spirit produce good fruit in our lives. We pray this in the name of Jesus. Amen.

Day 3

> **1** "Praise the Lord, O my soul!
> **2** While I live, I will praise the Lord;
> I will sing praises to my God while I have my being.
> **3** Do not put your trust in princes,
> *Nor* in a son of man, in whom *there is* no help.
> **4** His spirit departs, he returns to his earth;
> In that very day his plans perish."
> (Psalms 146.1-4)

It is a mistake to put our faith in people, even powerful people. But one might reply, "Have not human beings done good to you, have they not helped you?" The answer to this is that the help provided by human beings would not have existed without God's work in their heart, in the conscience of those who do good (Romans 2.4, 25-29). Even for those of us who are good need to praise the LORD and not put our faith in human beings.

It is significant that the plans of people are limited by the reality of death. This reminds us of the words of wisdom from James:

> **3** "Come now, you who say, 'Today or tomorrow we will go to such and such a city, spend a year there, buy and sell, and make a profit'; **14** whereas you do not know what *will happen* tomorrow. For what *is* your life? It is even a vapor that appears for a little time and then vanishes away. **15** Instead you *ought* to say, 'If the Lord wills, we shall live and do this or that.' **16** But now you boast in your arrogance. All such boasting is evil." (James 4.13-16)

Neglecting to praise God often is the result of putting our faith in human beings, in their plans and their ideas. Believers need to make sure their faith rests on the unchanging Word of God.

In verses 7 to 10 the LORD does what "sons of men" cannot do on their own: he executes justice for the oppressed; he gives freedom to the prisoners; he opens the eyes of the blind; he raises those who are bowed down... He reigns forever.

The words of this Psalm remind us of the response of Jesus to John the Baptist who was inquiring about Jesus:

> **22** "Jesus answered and said to them, 'Go and tell John the things you have seen and
> heard: that *the* blind see, *the* lame walk, *the* lepers
> are cleansed, *the* deaf hear, *the* dead are raised, *the* poor have the gospel preached to them. **23** And blessed is *he* who is not offended because of Me.'" (Luke 7.22,23).

Prayer

Lord, we praise you for the Word you have given us. We praise you for Jesus your Son and the salvation you have provided through His sacrifice, through the cross and His resurrection. We thank you for a new day and pray that we can love and serve you from the bottom of our hearts. We pray in the name of Jesus. Amen.

Day 4

> **4** "One generation shall praise Your works to another,
> And shall declare Your mighty acts.
> **5** I will meditate on the glorious splendor of Your majesty,
> And on Your wondrous works.
> **6** *Men* shall speak of the might of Your awesome acts,
> And I will declare Your greatness.
> **7** They shall utter the memory of Your great goodness,
> And shall sing of Your righteousness."
> (Psalms 145.4-7)

The knowledge of God is passed from one generation to another. The Scriptures teach that it is the responsibility of one generation to teach a younger generation (Deuteronomy 6.6,7 Psalms 78.1-8).

However, here it is affirmed that the memory of God will not be lost; that the knowledge of His might and goodness will be preserved. The fact is that it is God who took the initiative to provide a revelation of his will to mankind and to provide a way for His people to keep records of His actions (Hebrews 1.1-4). The LORD makes sure that His will is known to mankind. That is the purpose of the Scriptures, first preserved through Israel (Romans 9.1-5).

> **19** "O Lord, for Your servant's sake, and according to Your own heart, You have done all this greatness, in making known all these great things. **20** O Lord, *there is* none like You, nor *is there any* God besides You, according to all that we have heard with our ears. **21** And who *is* like Your people Israel, the one nation on the earth whom God went to redeem for Himself *as* a people—to make for Yourself a name by great and awesome deeds, by driving out nations from before Your people whom You redeemed from Egypt? **22** For You have made Your people Israel Your very own people forever; and You, Lord, have become their God." (1 Chronicles 17.19-22)

This Psalm is stating what God will do, but also how "I" — each individual — can meditate on His wondrous works and declare His greatness.

God himself has made it possible for mankind to know His mighty works. His people have been given the responsibility to teach the coming generations. The individual believer contributes to the spreading of the knowledge of God.

> **16** "For we did not follow cunningly devised fables when we made known to you the power and coming of our Lord Jesus Christ but were eyewitnesses of His majesty. **17** For He received from God the Father honor and glory when such a voice came to Him from the Excellent Glory: "This is My beloved Son, in whom I am well pleased." **18** And we heard this voice which came from heaven when we were with Him on the holy mountain. **19** And so we have the prophetic word confirmed, which you do well to heed as a light that shines in a dark place, until the day dawns and the morning star rises in your hearts; **20** knowing this first, that no prophecy of Scripture is of any private interpretation, **21** for prophecy never came by the will of man, but holy men of God spoke *as they were* moved by the Holy Spirit." (2 Peter 1.16-20)

Prayer

Father in heaven, we praise you for the Word you have given us through your Son and through prophets and apostles. We thank you for your work in our hearts and lives that allows us to be faithful and grow in your sight. Give us today the wisdom to know how to teach and encourage others. We pray this in Jesus' name. Amen.

Day 5

> **1** "Praise the Lord, all you Gentiles!
> Laud Him, all you peoples!
> **2** For His merciful kindness is great toward us,
> And the truth of the Lord *endures* forever.
> Praise the Lord!"
>   (Psalms 117.1,2)

This is the shortest of all the Psalms. However, it is a witness to God's plan to save and bless the Gentiles, as He had promised Abraham.

This Psalm is quoted by the Paul in Romans 15.11 where the apostle makes clear God's plan of salvation towards the Gentiles (with quotes from Psalms 18.49; Deuteronomy 32.43; Psalms 117; Isaiah 11.10):

7 "Therefore receive one another, just as Christ also received us, to the glory of God. **8** Now I say that Jesus Christ has become a servant to the circumcision for the truth of God, to confirm the promises *made* to the fathers, **9** and that the Gentiles might glorify God for *His* mercy, as it is written:
'For this reason, I will confess to You among the Gentiles,
And sing to Your name.'
10 And again he says:
'Rejoice, O Gentiles, with His people!'
11 And again:
'Praise the Lord, all you Gentiles!
Laud Him, all you peoples!'
12 And again, Isaiah says:
'There shall be a root of Jesse;
And He who shall rise to reign over the Gentiles,
In Him the Gentiles shall hope.'" (Romans 15.7–12)

Prayer

Lord in heaven, we are grateful to you Father for your mercy and salvation. We thank you for forgiveness of sins through Jesus, our High Priest. We confess to you our sins and pray for strength and wisdom as we face a new day. We pray this in the name of our Lord Jesus. Amen.

Day 6

1 "Be merciful to me, O God, for man would swallow me up;
Fighting all day he oppresses me.
2 My enemies would hound *me* all day,
For *there are* many who fight against me, O Most High.
3 Whenever I am afraid,
I will trust in You.
4 In God (I will praise His word),
In God I have put my trust;
I will not fear.
What can flesh do to me?"
 (Psalms 56.1-4)

This Psalm was written by David when he was captured by the Philistines (1 Samuel 21) ; it echoes and repeats "I will praise His word" (vv.

4,10,11). In the midst of strong opposition and threats to his life, the king of Israel says, "Il will trust in you" and "I will praise His word".

The Philistines where enemies of David because of His faith and devotion to God. The Philistines depended on their worship of Dagon for harvests and success in wars. The Philistine god is already mentioned in passages such as Judges 16.23,24, 1 Samuel 5 and 1 Chronicles 10.10.

David as a type of the Messiah endured a lot of opposition, and his life was often threatened. A mistaken and common notion is that the "reign of the Messiah" would be a time of universal peace and acceptance among human beings. However, the fact is that the coming of the reign of Christ and even his introduction as king all happened in the midst of conflict and strong opposition. This enmity against the reign of the Messiah continues until death itself, "the last enemy" is destroyed (1 Corinthians 15.26). The kingdom of the Son, the kingdom of heaven (Matthew 28.18-20) is a time of great tribulations and persecutions; a time of hatred first against the apostles and beyond against all who "live a godly life" (2 Timothy 3.12).

> **10** "Blessed *are* those who are persecuted for righteousness' sake,
> For theirs is the kingdom of heaven.
> **11** Blessed are you when they revile and persecute you and say all kinds of evil against you falsely for My sake. **12** Rejoice and be exceedingly glad, for great *is* your reward in heaven, for so they persecuted the prophets who were before you." (Matthew 5.10-12)

Prayer

Lord in heaven and our Father, today we want to rely on your mercy and grow in our love for you. Help us Father to grow in this way and also to learn how to be merciful to others. We pray this in the name of Jesus, our Lord. Amen.

Day 7

> **5** "For in the time of trouble
> He shall hide me in His pavilion;
> In the secret place of His tabernacle
> He shall hide me;
> He shall set me high upon a rock.
> **6** And now my head shall be lifted up above my enemies all around me;

> Therefore I will offer sacrifices of joy in His tabernacle;
> I will sing, yes, I will sing praises to the Lord."
> (Psalms 27.5,6)

Praises in the midst of opposition are part of true faith in God, a source of courage and strength:

> "Wait on the Lord.
> Be of good courage,
> And He shall strengthen your heart;
> Wait, I say, on the Lord!" (v.14).

As in Psalms 56 the king of Israel is a type of the Messiah who knows constant opposition but continues to put his trust in God and is finally victorious.

> "And when the scribes and Pharisees saw Him eating with the tax collectors and sinners, they said to His disciples, 'How *is it* that He eats and drinks with tax collectors and sinners?'" (Mark 2.16)

> **1** "Then all the tax collectors and the sinners drew near to Him to hear Him. **2** And the Pharisees and scribes complained, saying, 'This Man receives sinners and eats with them.'" (Luke 15.1,2)

> **53** "And as He said these things to them, the scribes and the Pharisees began to assail *Him* vehemently, and to cross-examine Him about many things, **54** lying in wait for Him, and seeking to catch Him in something He might say, that they might accuse Him." (Luke 11.53,54)

> "From that time Jesus began to show to His disciples that He must go to Jerusalem and suffer many things from the elders and chief priests and scribes, and be killed, and be raised the third day." (Matthew 16.21)

> **21** "And He strictly warned and commanded them to tell this to no one, **22** saying, 'The Son of Man must suffer many things, and be rejected by the elders and chief priests and scribes, and be killed, and be raised the third day.'" (Luke 9.21,22)

Let Us Come Before His Presence

Prayer

We pray to you Father for patience and trust. We thank you for your gift of the Holy Spirit, which produces fruit in our lives. We thank you for your patience and kindness towards us. Be with us today as we serve you in everything we say and do. Give us your wisdom and a grateful heart. In Jesus' name, we pray. Amen.

Week 24: The Tender Mercies of God

Day 1

> **6** "Remember, O Lord, Your tender mercies and Your loving kindnesses,
> For they *are* from of old.
> **7** Do not remember the sins of my youth, nor my transgressions;
> According to Your mercy remember me,
> For Your goodness' sake, O Lord."
>   (Psalms 25.6,7)

In this prayer, David is not seeking God's mercy based on his achievements or his goodness. He does not believe he has deserved anything from God. This is very different from the prayer of the Pharisee:

> **11** "The Pharisee stood and prayed thus with himself, 'God, I thank You that I am not like other men—extortioners, unjust, adulterers, or even as this tax collector. **12** I fast twice a week; I give tithes of all that I possess.'" (Luke 18.11,12).

David's disposition comes from having received the teaching of "truth" concerning the LORD : "Lead me in Your truth and teach me" (v.5); "Therefore he teaches sinners in the way" (v.8); "And the humble he teaches His way" (v.9).

This teaching is part of the "covenant" the faithful need to keep: "All the paths of the LORD are mercy and truth, to such as keep His covenant and His testimonies" (v.10).

The mercy and goodness of God is not an allowance to transgress God's covenant. In fact, the recognition of sin and a humble disposition are part of what is required in God's covenants:

> **8** "Draw near to God and He will draw near to
> you. Cleanse *your* hands, *you* sinners;

and purify *your* hearts, *you* double-minded. **9** Lament and mourn and weep! Let your laughter be turned to mourning and *your* joy to gloom. **10** Humble yourselves in the sight of the Lord, and He will lift you up." (James 4.8-10)

Confession of sins is to be done in prayer to God (1 John 1.8-2.2). There is room to confess sins to one another as instructed by the Lord (see Matthew 18.1-5; Luke 17.3; Galatians 6.1; James 5.16). However, the public confession of our sins for all to be heard was not practiced in the New Testament church. We see no example of such practice in the book of Acts or New Testament epistles. There is reason to believe that some sins should be brought up only with great care in the Church (Ephesians 5.11,12; Colossians 3.8,17).

Prayer

Father in heaven, we pray that you will enlighten our hearts as to the dangers of pride. Through your Holy Spirit, shape our hearts in a way that will please you. Give us confidence to confess all our sins and to believe in your forgiveness. Strengthen our resolve to grow in holiness. This we pray in Jesus' name. Amen.

Day 2

5 "But I have trusted in Your mercy;
My heart shall rejoice in Your salvation.
6 I will sing to the Lord,
Because He has dealt bountifully with me."
   (Psalms 13.5,6)

How can there be any rejoicing without a knowledge of God's salvation? How can we sing with all our heart without an understanding of His forgiveness? There needs to be an understanding and belief in revealed truth for rejoicing to occur or for singing to be meaningful.

We see this in the case of the Ethiopian eunuch following his understanding of the Gospel and his baptism:

37 "Then Philip said, 'If you believe with all your heart, you may.'
And he answered and said, 'I believe that Jesus Christ is the Son of God.'
38 So he commanded the chariot to stand still. And both Philip and the eunuch went down into the water, and he baptized

him. **39** Now when they came up out of the water, the Spirit of the Lord caught Philip away, so that the eunuch saw him no more; and he went on his way rejoicing." (Acts 8.37-39)

8 I will instruct you and teach you in the way you should go;
I will guide you with My eye.
9 Do not be like the horse *or* like the mule,
Which have no understanding,
Which must be harnessed with bit and bridle,
Else they will not come near you.
10 Many sorrows *shall be* to the wicked;
But he who trusts in the Lord, mercy shall surround him.
11 Be glad in the Lord and rejoice, you righteous;
And shout for joy, all *you* upright in heart! (Psalms 32.8-11)

Prayer

Father in heaven, we rejoice today for your salvation in the Lord Jesus. We thank you for the plan of salvation, which you carried out in history and through Jesus. We want to have an open heart to your teachings. Guide us, Lord, today in the way we should walk. We pray this in Jesus' name. Amen.

Day 3

"Surely goodness and mercy shall follow me
All the days of my life;
And I will dwell in the house of the Lord
Forever."
  (Psalms 23.6)

Goodness (*tov*) and mercy or "unfailing love" (*chesed*) follow the faithful every day. Exodus 34.6–7 lists the characteristics of God's mercy:

6 "And the Lord passed before him and proclaimed, 'The Lord, the Lord God, merciful and gracious, longsuffering, and abounding in goodness and truth, **7** keeping mercy for thousands, forgiving iniquity and transgression and sin…'"

The word translated "follow" is the Hebrew *radaf*, which means to run after, to track (like a hunter might track a prey). The LORD is the good shepherd. He will seek the sheep that has lost its way. The parable of the lost sheep brings us back to this Psalm (Luke 15).

The mercy or unfailing love of the LORD is what makes us "return" to the "house of the LORD" where we can "dwell" (from the Hebrew *shuv*, to turn or to return).

Jesus is the good shepherd who gathers the lost sheep of Israel. This is made possible because the good shepherd lays down his life for the sheep:

> **17** "Therefore My Father loves Me, because I lay down My life that I may take it again. **18** No one takes it from Me, but I lay it down of Myself. I have power to lay it down, and I have power to take it again. This command I have received from My Father." (John 10.17–18).

It is the unfailing love of the good shepherd which opens to us the way to heaven, the way to God,

> **5** "Thomas said to Him, 'Lord, we do not know where You are going, and how can we know the way?' **6** Jesus said to him, 'I am the way, the truth, and the life. No one comes to the Father except through Me.'" (John 14.5,6)

Prayer

Our God and Savior, we come to you for wisdom today. We pray that all our actions and words will give honor to you and will reflect your mercy and love. We pray today for those we will meet or work with today. May our life be a good witness to them. We pray this in Jesus' name. Amen.

Day 4

> **18** "Behold, the eye of the Lord *is* on those who fear Him,
> On those who hope in His mercy,
> **19** To deliver their soul from death,
> And to keep them alive in famine.
> **20** Our soul waits for the Lord;
> He *is* our help and our shield.
> **21** For our heart shall rejoice in Him,
> Because we have trusted in His holy name.
> **22** Let Your mercy, O Lord, be upon us,
> Just as we hope in You."
>   (Psalms 33.18-22)

God's mercy and the hope of the faithful are connected in verses 18 and 22. Mercy (*chesed*) is "unfailing love" — a love that is maintained even when we don't deserve it. There would be no true hope if our destiny and lives depended on our achievements or our goodness.

The first verses of this Psalm describe those who seek righteousness and are upright. The Psalm is dedicated to the God who "loves righteousness and mercy" (v.5). The LORD "looks from heaven and sees all the sons of men... He considers all their works" (vv.13,15).

God's mercy is not "cheap grace" by which the sinner can continue to live in sin and disobedience:

> "Rejoice in the Lord, O you righteous!
> *For* praise from the upright is beautiful." (v.1).

As God is merciful, the faithful are also to exercise mercy:

> **21** "Therefore, as *the* elect of God, holy and beloved, put on tender mercies, kindness, humility, meekness, longsuffering; **13** bearing with one another, and forgiving one another, if anyone has a complaint against another; even as Christ forgave you, so you also *must do.*" (Colossians 3.12,13)

Prayer

Our LORD and Father, we come to you for strength and faithfulness. We believe in your continued mercy towards us. We pray that we can exercise mercy towards every person we encounter today. Help us in what we see as difficult for us today. Help us to trust in your presence in our lives and in your love. This we pray in Jesus' name. Amen.

Day 5

> **17** "Unless the Lord *had been* my help,
> My soul would soon have settled in silence.
> **18** If I say, "My foot slips,"
> Your mercy, O Lord, will hold me up.
> **19** In the multitude of my anxieties within me,
> Your comforts delight my soul."
>   (Psalms 94.17-19)

The writer of this Psalm is having to deal with the prideful and the wicked, who seem to triumph (vv.1-3). These individuals speak with insolence. They boast in their iniquity and break to pieces God's people. They slay the widow, the stranger and fatherless (vv. 4-6). They say, "The LORD does not see" (v.7)

Focusing on evil individuals and their wicked actions can bring us down and discourage us. This can bring about a "multitude of anxieties" to the soul. It is in this context that the writer reminds us that the LORD held him up through his mercy and comforted his soul.

The LORD himself often repeats that he does not wish the death of the sinner. His judgments, his "vengeance" are not out of a hateful heart:

> "Do I have any pleasure at all that the wicked should die?" says the Lord God, "*and* not that he should turn from his ways and live?" (Ezekiel 18.23)

> Say to them: '*As* I live,' says the Lord God, 'I have no pleasure in the death of the wicked, but that the wicked turn from his way and live. Turn, turn from your evil ways! For why should you die, O house of Israel?' (Ezekiel 33.11)

> "For You, Lord, *are* good, and ready to forgive,
> And abundant in mercy to all those who call upon You."
> (Psalms 86.5)

The writer admits to having "a multitude of anxieties" produced by the evil and injustice that surrounds him. This is a common theme in the Scriptures:

> "For I have heard a voice as of a woman in labor,
> The anguish as of her who brings forth her first child,
> The voice of the daughter of Zion bewailing herself;
> She spreads her hands, *saying*,
> 'Woe *is* me now, for my soul is weary
> Because of murderers!'" (Jeremiah 4.31)

> "Why did I come forth from the womb to see labor and sorrow,
> That my days should be consumed with shame?" (Jeremiah 20.18)

> **16** "And now my soul is poured out because of my *plight;*
> The days of affliction take hold of me.
> **17** My bones are pierced in me at night,
> And my gnawing pains take no rest." (Job 30.16,17)

Jesus was "sorrowful and troubled" (Matthew 26:37). His soul was "overwhelmed" to the "point of death" (Matthew 26:38).

> "And being in anguish, he prayed more earnestly, and his sweat was like drops of blood falling to the ground" (Luke 22:44).

Prayer

Father in heaven, we seek comfort in you as we go through grief and pain. We ask for strength in moments of weakness and trust in moments of temptation. We need the wisdom that comes from you, Lord. May your Holy Spirit comfort our troubled hearts. We pray this in Jesus' name. Amen.

Day 6

> **8** "The Lord *is* merciful and gracious,
> Slow to anger, and abounding in mercy.
> **9** He will not always strive *with us*,
> Nor will He keep *His anger* forever.
> **10** He has not dealt with us according to our sins,
> Nor punished us according to our iniquities."
>   (Psalms 103.8-10)

Both the "justice" and "mercy" of God are intrinsic to his nature. This Psalm brings this out:

> "The Lord executes righteousness and justice for all who are oppressed." (v.6)

> "The Lord *is* merciful and gracious,
> Slow to anger, and abounding in mercy." (v.8)

> "For as the heavens are high above the earth,
> *So* great is His mercy toward those who fear Him." (v.11)

> "But the mercy of the Lord *is* from everlasting to everlasting
> On those who fear Him." (v.17)

In God there is a perfect balance between justice and mercy. Human beings on the other hand tend to forget either his justice or his mercy. They can be harsh and merciless with the sinner or themselves. Or they can forget God's justice and start believing His mercy means they are free to sin without consequences.

Prayer

Our Father who is in heaven, we come to you for forgiveness today. We need your constant help and presence for all our needs. We pray that you will give us a heart that understands your mercy and justice and is able to consider the importance of both. We pray this in the name of Jesus, our Lord. Amen.

Day 7

> 26 "Help me, O Lord my God!
> Oh, save me according to Your mercy,
> 27 That they may know that this *is* Your hand—
> *That* You, Lord, have done it!
> 28 Let them curse, but You bless;
> When they arise, let them be ashamed,
> But let Your servant rejoice.
> 29 Let my accusers be clothed with shame,
> And let them cover themselves with their own disgrace as with a mantle."
>   (Psalms 109.26-29)

This Psalm tells of the sufferings of the innocent and poor at the hands of evil individuals who render evil for good, who render cursing for blessings. This is the kind of evil person described in the book or Proverbs: "Whoever rewards evil for good, evil will not depart from his house." (Proverbs 17,13).

The list of their evil deeds against the innocent and the poor is long. They speak with a lying tongue against the righteous (v.2). They accuse and hate in return for love (v.4). They don't show mercy, but persecute the poor and needy (v.16). They slay the broken in heart (v.16). They delight in cursing instead of blessing (v.17). We can compare this to Proverbs 6.16-19, which describes "six things the Lord hates". Such behavior explains the sharpness of the condemnation that these individuals can expect from God and which is described throughout this Psalm (which is not about personal revenge but descriptive of God's righteous judgment; see also Romans 12.19).

The faithful disciple of Jesus is required to act differently:

17 "Repay no one evil for evil. Have regard for good things in the sight of all men. **18** If it is possible, as much as depends on you, live peaceably with all men." (Romans 12.17)

This Psalm is also Messianic in showing the sufferings of the innocent man at the hands of wicked people of power (Isaiah 53.7; Psalm 22). As in verse 26 the Son of God offered supplications to God in his sufferings and was delivered (Hebrews 5.7-11).

Prayer

Father, we pray today for faith in your Word of promise. We believe in your goodness and mercy, Lord. You are the judge, Lord, of every single person. May we know in our hearts that you are faithful and that you keep your Word. Give us a spirit of love and compassion for every sinner. In Christ we pray. Amen.

Week 25: God our Father

Day 1

> **13** "As a father pities *his* children,
> *So* the Lord pities those who fear Him.
> **14** For He knows our frame;
> He remembers that we *are* dust."
>   (Psalm 103.13,14)

One should be very careful not to equate the fatherhood of God with any kind of abuse or mistreatment that can occur on the part of human fathers. Note the words of Jesus:

> **11** "If a son asks for bread from any father among you, will he give him a stone? Or if *he asks* for a fish, will he give him a serpent instead of a fish? **12** Or if he asks for an egg, will he offer him a scorpion? **13** If you then, being evil, know how to give good gifts to your children, how much more will *your* heavenly Father give the Holy Spirit to those who ask Him!" (Luke 11.11-13)

It is assumed in the Scriptures that fathers are caring for their sons and daughters. However, it should not be forgotten that human beings can be sinful, even evil. Thus, there are sinful and evil fathers. The apostle Paul even warns fathers with these words:

> "Fathers, do not provoke your children, lest they become discouraged." (Colossians 3.21).
>
> "And you, fathers, do not provoke your children to wrath, but bring them up in the training and admonition of the Lord." (Ephesians 6.4).

To consider the biblical "fatherhood" of God as some kind of encouragement to tyranny shows ignorance of the Word of God and of the holy character of our Father in heaven.

In Psalm 103 God is the merciful God but also the God of justice, of righteousness. As a father, the LORD shows mercy towards his children, but also disciplines them and requires from them obedience.

> **17** "But the mercy of the Lord *is* from everlasting to everlasting
> On those who fear Him,
> And His righteousness to children's children,
> **18** To such as keep His covenant,
> And to those who remember His commandments to do them."
> (vv.17,18)

The leadership of fathers in the home and also in the Church is well established in Scripture. However, this should never be understood as God's acceptance of abuse or mistreatment on the part of male leaders.

Note the words of Peter concerning elders, the shepherds (also called bishops) over local churches:

> **1**"The elders who are among you I exhort, I who am a fellow elder and a witness of the sufferings of Christ, and also a partaker of the glory that will be revealed: **2** Shepherd the flock of God which is among you, serving as overseers, not by compulsion but willingly, not for dishonest gain but eagerly; **3** nor as being lords over those entrusted to you, but being examples to the flock; **4** and when the Chief Shepherd appears, you will receive the crown of glory that does not fade away." (1 Peter 5.1-4)

Prayer

We pray Father in heaven for fathers and their children. We pray especially for Christians who are fathers. Give them a growing understanding of what they need to do in your sight, whether in their families or in the Church. We pray that today we can be an encouragement to fathers. This we pray in Jesus' name. Amen.

Day 2

> **24** "But My faithfulness and My mercy *shall be* with him,
> And in My name his horn shall be exalted.
> **25** Also I will set his hand over the sea,
> And his right hand over the rivers.
> **26** He shall cry to Me, 'You *are* my Father,

My God, and the rock of my salvation.'
27 Also I will make him *My* firstborn,
The highest of the kings of the earth.
28 My mercy I will keep for him forever,
And My covenant shall stand firm with him.
29 His seed also I will make *to endure* forever,
And his throne as the days of heaven."
   (Psalms 89.24-29)

This Psalm of Ethan is a reminder of God's covenant with David concerning his seed (see 2 Samuel 7). The Messiah is called "God's firstborn" in the promise made to David.

> **12** "When your days are fulfilled and you rest with your fathers, I will set up your seed after you, who will come from your body, and I will establish his kingdom. **13** He shall build a house for My name, and I will establish the throne of his kingdom forever. **14** I will be his Father, and he shall be My son. If he commits iniquity, I will chasten him with the rod of men and with the blows of the sons of men. **15** But My mercy shall not depart from him, as I took *it* from Saul, whom I removed from before you. **16** And your house and your kingdom shall be established forever before you. Your throne shall be established forever." (2 Samuel 7.12-16)

The words of this covenant constitute a promise that will be fulfilled through God's anointed one, God's Messiah, "I have found my servant David; with My holy oil I have anointed him…"

This Messiah, son of David, will be called by God His "firstborn" because to him God will give all that is His, especially His power and authority (see Psalm 2; Matthew 28.18; Colossians 1.13-15). The kingdom of the Messiah, of Jesus, is an eternal kingdom, and he is the king of kings (1 Timothy 6.15; Revelation 1.5; 17.14; 19.16).

34 "My covenant I will not break,
Nor alter the word that has gone out of My lips.
35 Once I have sworn by My holiness;
I will not lie to David:
36 His seed shall endure forever,
And his throne as the sun before Me;
37 It shall be established forever like the moon,

Even *like* the faithful witness in the sky." *Selah* (Psalms 89. 34-37)

Those whose faith is in the salvation of Jesus, who have become one with him in his death and resurrection, have been "delivered from the power of darkness and conveyed into the kingdom of the Son of His love" (Colossians 1.13; 2.11-13).

Prayer

Father in heaven, we praise you for the salvation we have in your Son Jesus. We thank you for your faithfulness in accomplishing your covenants. Today we will sing of your mercies and proclaim your faithfulness. Today, we will serve you through all are words and actions. In Jesus' name, we pray. Amen.

Day 3

> **5** "A father of the fatherless, a defender of widows,
> *Is* God in His holy habitation.
> **6** God sets the solitary in families;
> He brings out those who are bound into prosperity;
> But the rebellious dwell in a dry *land.*"
>   (Psalms 68.5,6)

God cares for those who are in distress, with little or no help on this earth, such as "the fatherless and the widows". These stand in contrast to the ones mentioned in verses 1 and 2 of Psalm 68, the enemies of God, those who hate Him, the wicked.

God provides from His goodness to the poor (v.10). Only those who hunger for righteousness, who know their poverty and need of God, come to His salvation (Matthew 5.3-6; Matthew 11. 28-30).

"God sets the solitary in families": He provides a family for those who are lonely and seek Him. This is the same truth taught by Jesus,

> **31** "So Jesus answered and said, 'Assuredly, I say to you, there is no one who has left house or brothers or sisters or father or mother or wife or children or lands, for My sake and the gospel's, **30** who shall not receive a hundredfold now in this time —houses and brothers and sisters and mothers and children and lands, with persecutions—and in the age to come, eternal

life. **31** But many *who are* first will be last, and the last first.'"
(Mark 10.29-31)

Those who are solitary and are faithful to Him are, in fact, brought into His "house", His "holy habitation". This is what is meant by the "Church" in the New Testament: it is the house or family of God (1 Timothy 3.15; Ephesians 2.22; see 2 Peter 2.5). It is God and not human beings who add to the Church, to His house, those who receive salvation through their faith and repentance (Acts 2.47).

Verse 18 of this Psalm is quoted by the apostle Paul in his letter to the Ephesians, writing about the gifts of teaching and preaching provided by God to the Church (Ephesians 4.8). The Church is God's holy habitation, the temple within which dwells His Holy Spirit (Ephesians 1.13,14).

Prayer

We thank you, Father, for your goodness and care for the fatherless and widows. We pray that we can learn to be caring for those in need, for the poor, for those who are lonely. May we grow today in our love for our neighbor and for our brethren. We pray this in Jesus' name. Amen.

Day 4

> **7** "I will declare the decree:
> The Lord has said to Me,
> 'You *are* My Son,
> Today I have begotten You.
> **8** Ask of Me, and I will give *You*
> The nations *for* Your inheritance,
> And the ends of the earth *for* Your possession.
> **9** You shall break them with a rod of iron;
> You shall dash them to pieces like a potter's vessel.'"
>   (Psalms 2.7-9)

This Psalm is quoted in the New Testament. See especially:

> **32** "And we declare to you glad tidings, that promise which was made to the fathers. **33** God has fulfilled this for us their children, in that He has raised up Jesus. As it is also written in the second Psalm, 'You are My Son, today I have begotten You.'"
> (Acts 13.32,33)

26 "And he who overcomes, and keeps My works until the end, to him I will give power over the nations — **27** 'He shall rule them with a rod of iron; they shall be dashed to pieces like the potter's vessels' (Revelation 2.26, 27)

"For to which of the angels did He ever say:
'You are My Son,
Today I have begotten You'? (Hebrews 1.5)

We should not be surprised at the voice declaring Jesus as His Son at his baptism and at the mount of transfiguration (Mark 1.11; Matthew 17.5). It should not be surprising that Jesus talks about God as his "Father" or approves the confession of his disciples "You are the Christ, the Son of the living God" (Matthew 16.16).

Jesus' resurrection from the dead was a formal declaration by God of Jesus' sonship or position as the Messiah:

1 "Paul, a bondservant of Jesus Christ, called *to be* an apostle, separated to the gospel of God **2** which He promised before through His prophets in the Holy Scriptures, **3** concerning His Son Jesus Christ our Lord, who was born of the seed of David according to the flesh, **4** *and* declared *to be* the Son of God with power according to the Spirit of holiness, by the resurrection from the dead. **5** Through Him we have received grace and apostleship for obedience to the faith among all nations for His name." (Romans 1.1-5)

Prayer

Father in heaven, we believe that Jesus is your beloved Son who died for our sins and rose from the dead. We thank you for Jesus and for your salvation. We pray that we can grow today in holiness and in wisdom. We pray that today you will keep and guide our loved ones, our parents and friends. This we pray in Jesus' name. Amen.

Day 5

3 "Behold, children *are* a heritage from the Lord,
The fruit of the womb *is* a reward.
4 Like arrows in the hand of a warrior,
So *are* the children of one's youth.
5 Happy *is* the man who has his quiver full of them;

> They shall not be ashamed,
> But shall speak with their enemies in the gate."
> (Psalms 127.3-5)

God gives children to men and women as a "heritage" from Him. The children we have are also the children of God. They are precious and a reward from God.

Little children were not always valued at the time of Christ and in the Greco-Roman world. Their value only grew with time, as they came closer to adulthood. However, Jesus shows how the smallest of children are highly valued by God and are a reflection of His glory and His kingdom:

> **13** "Then they brought little children to Him, that He might touch them; but the disciples rebuked those who brought *them*. **14** But when Jesus saw *it*, He was greatly displeased and said to them, "Let the little children come to Me, and do not forbid them; for of such is the kingdom of God. **15** Assuredly, I say to you, whoever does not receive the kingdom of God as a little child will by no means enter it." **16** And He took them up in His arms, laid *His* hands on them, and blessed them." (Mark 10.13-16)

It is significant that we need to become "as little children" in order to enter the kingdom of God, in order to become children of God. Teaching the Christians in Corinth, the apostle Paul exhorts them to be innocent as "babes" or little children when it comes to "evil" or "malice" but to be adults when it comes to intelligence and maturity (1 Corinthians 14.20). These Christians who were prideful and divided needed to develop purity of life coupled with a deeper understanding of God's will.

Prayer

We thank you, Lord, for our children. We pray for them today. Bless our children so that they will grow in their spiritual walk. Give them wisdom and strength. We pray Father that we can be good fathers and mothers and able to lead our children close to you. In Jesus' name, we pray. Amen.

Day 6

> **7** "Sing to the Lord with thanksgiving;
> Sing praises on the harp to our God,
> **8** Who covers the heavens with clouds,
> Who prepares rain for the earth,

Who makes grass to grow on the mountains.
9 He gives to the beast its food,
And to the young ravens that cry."
(Psalms 147.7-9)

God is the one who provides food for his creatures. He is the "father of all" (Ephesians 4.6). God is our Father in heaven, who is the source only of goodness and light:

> **16** "Do not be deceived, my beloved brethren. **17** Every good gift and every perfect gift is from above, and comes down from the Father of lights, with whom there is no variation or shadow of turning". (James 1.16,17)

The prophet Isaiah said: "You, O Lord, *are* our Father; our Redeemer from everlasting *is* Your name." (Isaiah 63.16).

The prophet Malachi reminds God's people that they only had one Father, who is God:

> "Have we not all one Father?
> Has not one God created us?
> Why do we deal treacherously with one another
> By profaning the covenant of the fathers?" (Malachi 2.10)

We know that fathers or mothers are not always caring for their children. We know that some have even abandoned their own children. But we also know of many fathers and mothers who take good care of their children and love them.

This is the way God is a father to his children and cares for them, and the way we should see God:

> **7** "Ask, and it will be given to you; seek, and you will find; knock, and it will be opened to you. **8** For everyone who asks receives, and he who seeks finds, and to him who knocks it will be opened. **9** Or what man is there among you who, if his son asks for bread, will give him a stone? **10** Or if he asks for a fish, will he give him a serpent? **11** If you then, being evil, know how to give good gifts to your children, how much more will your Father who is in heaven give good things to those who ask Him! **12** Therefore, whatever you want men to do to you, do also to them, for this is the Law and the Prophets." (Matthew 7.8-12)

Jesus taught us to pray to our Father for our daily bread: "Give us this day our daily bread" (Matthew 6. 11).

Prayer

Our Father in heaven, we thank you for providing for us every day. We thank you for the gift of life that we might seek you and serve you. May we learn from your fatherhood how to be good parents. As you take good care of your creation, we too, Father, pray we will take good care of our children. This we pray in Jesus' name. Amen.

Day 7

> **8** "I will instruct you and teach you in the way you should go;
> I will guide you with My eye.
> **9** Do not be like the horse *or* like the mule,
> *Which* have no understanding,
> Which must be harnessed with bit and bridle,
> Else they will not come near you."
>   (Psalms 32.8,9)

Fathers are to teach and guide their children in the ways of the LORD:

> **6** "And these words which I command you today shall be in your heart. **7** You shall teach them diligently to your children and shall talk of them when you sit in your house, when you walk by the way, when you lie down, and when you rise up. **8** You shall bind them as a sign on your hand, and they shall be as frontlets between your eyes. **9** You shall write them on the doorposts of your house and on your gates." (Deuteronomy 6.6-9)

> **11** "My son, do not despise the chastening of the Lord,
> Nor detest His correction;
> **12** For whom the Lord loves He corrects,
> Just as a father the son *in whom* he delights." (Proverbs 3.12)

> "Train up a child in the way he should go,
> And when he is old, he will not depart from it." (Proverbs 22.6)

> **1** "Children obey your parents in the Lord, for this is right. **2** "Honor your father and mother," which is the first commandment with promise: **3** "that it may be well with you,

and you may live long on the earth." **4** And you, fathers, do not provoke your children to wrath, but bring them up in the training and admonition of the Lord." (Ephesians 6.1-4)

Prayer

Our God and Father, you are the source of all wisdom and knowledge. We come to you for help in being parents. Give us of your wisdom. Help us to grow in our knowledge, so we will be able to teach our children and the youth around us. May your Holy Spirit produce in us all the fruit needed to help the youth. We pray this in the name of Jesus. Amen.

Week 26: The Good Shepherd

Day 1

> **1** "Give ear, O Shepherd of Israel,
> You who lead Joseph like a flock;
> You who dwell *between* the cherubim, shine forth!
> **2** Before Ephraim, Benjamin, and Manasseh,
> Stir up Your strength,
> And come *and* save us!
> **3** Restore us, O God;
> Cause Your face to shine,
> And we shall be saved!"
> (Psalms 80.1-3)

This Psalm resembles Psalms 74 and 79 and refers to a time of adversity, probably the Babylonian captivity.

God promised Israel in captivity that He will be himself come as the shepherd of His people. He will seek His sheep and gather them together:

> **11** "For thus says the Lord God: 'Indeed I Myself will search for
> My sheep and seek them out. **12** As a shepherd seeks out his
> flock on the day he is among his scattered sheep, so will I seek
> out My sheep and deliver them from all the places where they
> were scattered on a cloudy and dark day.'" (Ezekiel 34.11,12)

Jesus' teachings about being the good shepherd and seeking the lost sheep refers back to the Old Testament references to God being the shepherd of His people (John 10 and Luke 15).

This Psalm is a prayer to God the shepherd. He leads "Joseph" like a flock (a reference to God's blessings on "Joseph" in Genesis 49.22-26). At the time of the captivity the temple is no more and the presence of God's glory between the cherubim is not present in a visible way. However, God's glory was still there, even if it was not seen in the physical temple built by Salomon.

In the same way the glory of God was manifested in the presence of His Son: "And the Word became flesh and dwelt among us, and we beheld His glory, the glory as of the only-begotten of the Father, full of grace and truth." (John 1.14).

> **1** "That which was from the beginning, which we have heard, which we have seen with our eyes, which we have looked upon, and our hands have handled, concerning the Word of life — **2** the life was manifested, and we have seen, and bear witness, and declare to you that eternal life which was with the Father and was manifested to us— **3** that which we have seen and heard we declare to you, that you also may have fellowship with us; and truly our fellowship *is* with the Father and with His Son Jesus Christ. **4** And these things we write to you that your joy may be full." (1 John 1.1-4)

Despite the absence of the temple, the ark and the visible "glory" between the cherubim, the psalmist believes in God's glory and His power to shine once more in the life and history of His people : "Now faith is the substance of things hoped for, the evidence of things not seen. "For by it the elders obtained a *good* testimony." (Hebrews 11.2)

Prayer

Father in heaven, we come to you our Good shepherd, the light of our lives. We believe that you came to us in this dark world and proved to us your love and kindness. We thank you for Jesus Christ. We thank you for his life, his teachings, his death and his resurrection. We wait for his coming in glory. We pray in Jesus' name. Amen.

Day 2

> **6** "Oh come, let us worship and bow down;
> Let us kneel before the Lord our Maker.
> **7** For He *is* our God,
> And we *are* the people of His pasture,
> And the sheep of His hand."
> (Psalms 95.6,7)

God's sheep are the people of His pasture. Often it is thought or even said that "sheep" are stupid and that it is for this reason God's people are called "sheep". But we should take note that Jesus was the "lamb of God" but in Him is found the fullness of the godhead and the full wisdom of God (Colossians 1.9; 2.3).

In the biblical text, the image of "sheep" does not convey stupidity but lostness, vulnerability. The lost sheep is the one who like the prodigal son has strayed from the Father's house. And this straying away is not a matter of intelligence, but a problem of sin. All have sinned and strayed from God; even those who see themselves as smart and strong have strayed and are ignorant of God's ways (Romans 3.23; 3.11).

This is why this Psalm is also an exhortation to respond to God's call today:

> **7** "Today, if you will hear His voice: **8** 'Do not harden your
> hearts, as in the rebellion, as *in* the day of trial in the wilderness,
> **9** When your fathers tested Me.'" (vv.8,9).

This is quoted in Hebrews and applied today (Hebrews 3.7-4.13) Also, this text in Hebrews is applied to conversion and to salvation. Salvation and eternal life with God are "the rest" mentioned in this Psalm and Hebrews 4.4: "So I swore in My wrath, 'They shall not enter My rest.'" (v.11). The Sabbath rest given to Israel was an image or prefiguration of the spiritual rest enjoyed by those who put their trust in Jesus and are faithful to Him (Matthew 11.28-30).

Prayer

We thank you, our God for the promise of rest in Jesus. We pray that today you will touch our hearts and bring us to a better understanding of your salvation and will. We ask for forgiveness of our sins, and we pray for our loved ones, our friends and our brethren. May you Lord be with all of them and lead them into your rest. We pray this in Jesus' name. Amen.

Day 3

> **1** "Make a joyful shout to the Lord, all you lands !
> **2** Serve the Lord with gladness;
> Come before His presence with singing.
> **3** Know that the Lord, He *is* God;
> *It is* He *who* has made us, and not we ourselves;
> *We are* His people and the sheep of His pasture."
> (Psalms 100.1-3)

Joy and gladness are closely linked to worship, to singing. This joy comes from knowing God as our shepherd. It is the joy and gladness of an entire community and even extends to "all lands". Worship is not a solitary exercise. It is the privilege and joy of a community, a people, a congregation.

The Church has the privilege to praise God through songs. These songs are essential for teaching and exhortation:

> **16** "Let the word of Christ dwell in you richly in all wisdom, teaching and admonishing one another in psalms and hymns and spiritual songs, singing with grace in your hearts to the Lord. **17** And whatever you do in word or deed, *do* all in the name of the Lord Jesus, giving thanks to God the Father through Him." (Colossians 3.16,17).

> **14** "For here we have no continuing city, but we seek the one to come. **15** Therefore by Him let us continually offer the sacrifice of praise to God, that is, the fruit of *our* lips, giving thanks to His name." (Hebrews 13.14,15).

The LORD who is the shepherd of His people is also the creator: "It is He who made us" In the context of the Psalm 100 it is God who "created" or "made" His people. Israel as a nation is the fruit of God's initiative. The LORD did not look around to pick a nation with which He would enter into a covenant. He took Abraham and Sarah from the land of the Chaldeans and through their descendants "created" a nation with which He entered into covenant (Isaiah 43. 48,49).

God "formed" Israel from the womb, as when a child is formed in the womb of a woman:

> **1** "Yet hear now, O Jacob My servant,
> And Israel whom I have chosen.
> **2** Thus says the Lord who made you
> And formed you from the womb, *who* will help you:
> 'Fear not, O Jacob My servant;
> And you, Jeshurun, whom I have chosen.'" (Isaiah 44.1,2)

Those who believe the Gospel and put their trust in Jesus have received the right to be "children of God":

> **12** "But as many as received Him, to them He gave the right to become children of God, to those who believe in His

name: **13** who were born, not of blood, nor of the will of the flesh, nor of the will of man, but of God." (John 1.12,13)

Prayer

Our Father in heaven, we pray that this day you will keep our hearts in your will, that we will act and speak with wisdom. We pray that we will be faithful as disciples of Christ, that we will know how to speak to each one. God, our shepherd, we thank for your care. We pray this in Jesus' name. Amen.

Day 4

> **1** "The Lord *is* my shepherd;
> I shall not want.
> **2** He makes me to lie down in green pastures;
> He leads me beside the still waters.
> **3** He restores my soul;
> He leads me in the paths of righteousness
> For His name's sake.
> Yea, though I walk through the valley of the shadow of death,
> I will fear no evil;
> For You *are* with me;
> Your rod and Your staff, they comfort me."
> (Psalms 23.1-4)

This Psalm presents two metaphors: (1) The metaphor of the shepherd (23.1-4) and (2) the metaphor of the gracious host (23.5,6).

The metaphor of the shepherd is what Jesus alludes to when presenting himself as the good shepherd:

> **14** "I am the good shepherd. The good shepherd gives His life for the sheep." (John 10.11).

> "I am the good shepherd; and I know My *sheep* and am known by My own. **15** As the Father knows Me, even so I know the Father; and I lay down My life for the sheep." (John 10.14,15)

> "My Father, who has given *them* to Me, is greater than all; and no one is able to snatch *them* out of My Father's hand." (John 10.29)

The prophet Ezekiel is told by God that we would come to His people as their personal shepherd (Ezekiel 34). Throughout the Old Testament, God is the shepherd of His people.

In this Psalm, the metaphor of the shepherd is used in a very personal sense: "The Lord is my shepherd". Thus, God is the shepherd of all of his people and the shepherd of every single sheep that is part of his people. The individual relationship between the faithful believer and God is not undermined by the communal aspect of God's work. In fact, the people of Israel are warned by the prophets that despite God's insistence on being the LORD and shepherd of His people, He is still concerned with every single Israelite (Ezekiel 18).

This Psalm is most encouraging because one can understand how God is concerned about each person. This is clear in the teachings of Jesus. We note how in the Gospel of John and the other Gospels Jesus spends time and shows concern with individuals (for example Nicodemus or the woman from Samaria, John chapters 3 and 4).

This personal aspect of the metaphor of the shepherd and the sheep is clear throughout the four verses. This is also true for the metaphor of the gracious host in verses 5 and 6. The Psalm shows the constant presence and care of God the shepherd. This presence is demonstrated by the Shepherd providing for all the needs of the sheep, by the shepherd leading and protecting the sheep.

Prayer

We thank you, Father, for being the good shepherd of your people. We praise you for your tender care and for what you have done to provide salvation and forgiveness for us. You are the good shepherd, and you take care of us even when we find ourselves in the shadow of death. We are thankful to you and pray in Jesus' name. Amen.

Day 5

> 6 "Blessed *be* the Lord,
> Because He has heard the voice of my supplications!
> 7 The Lord *is* my strength and my shield;
> My heart trusted in Him, and I am helped;
> Therefore my heart greatly rejoices,
> And with my song I will praise Him.
> 8 The Lord *is* their strength,
> And He *is* the saving refuge of His anointed.

9 Save Your people,
And bless Your inheritance;
Shepherd them also,
And bear them up forever."
    (Psalms 28.6-9)

This Psalm is a prayer of David (vv.1-5) and God's answer (vv.6-9). In verse 8 God answers and saves His "anointed". However, in verse 9 God's anointed prays for the salvation and blessing of the people. We see the love and care of the anointed towards God's people.

This is a picture of the anointed (the Messiah or King) who intercedes for God's people. Throughout the Psalms and the Bible, we see the priestly work of intercession on the part of the Messiah. This is especially the case in Psalm 110:

"The Lord said to my Lord,
"Sit at My right hand, till I make Your enemies Your footstool."
(v.1)

"The Lord has sworn and will not relent, 'You *are* a priest forever according to the order of Melchizedek.'" (v.4)

Zechariah 6:13 reveals that Messiah will rule from His throne and sit as priest on His throne (see Hebrews 5.5,6).

The intercession of Jesus as high priest is a crucial part of the biblical teaching, which we find especially in the letter to the Hebrews. The work of the Messiah as a priest and intercessor brings "salvation" to God's people in response to this prayer: "Save your people" (v.9).

The death of Christ on the cross satisfies God's judgment on sin and allows sinners to have peace with God:

1 "Therefore, having been justified by faith, we have peace with God through our Lord Jesus Christ, **2** through whom also we have access by faith into this grace in which we stand, and rejoice in hope of the glory of God." (Romans 5.1,2)

"*There is* therefore now no condemnation to those who are in Christ Jesus, who do not walk according to the flesh, but according to the Spirit." (Romans 8.1)

When they sin, Christians need to confess their sins to God knowing that they have an "advocate" in Jesus the righteous who is "the propitiation for our sins" (1 John 1.9 – 2.2). In confessing their sins "to one another" (James 5.16) Christians are following the teachings of Christ:

> "Moreover if your brother sins against you, go and tell him his fault between you and him alone. If he hears you, you have gained your brother…" (Matthew 18.15)

The confession of sins "to one another" refers also to the intercessory prayers of Christians for one another:

> "Confess *your* trespasses to one another, and pray for one another, that you may be healed. The effective, fervent prayer of a righteous man avails much." (James 5.16)

The intercessory work of Christ as high priest is unique. However, it does not prevent Christians from praying for each other. In fact, prayer as anything else should be made "in the name of the Lord Jesus" (Colossians 3.17; John 14.13; 16.26).

The "name" of Jesus refers to who he is, the essence of his person. This is about faith in him as we pray. This is about a matter of the heart, like when we confess his name:

> **8** "But what does it say? 'The word is near you, in your mouth and in your heart' (that is, the word of faith which we preach): **9** that if you confess with your mouth the Lord Jesus and believe in your heart that God has raised Him from the dead, you will be saved. **10** For with the heart one believes unto righteousness, and with the mouth confession is made unto salvation." (Romans 10.8-10)

Prayer

We thank you, God, for all the blessings we enjoy and that come from you. We thank you especially for the salvation we have in Jesus your Son. We pray that our hearts can be purified daily by the knowledge of your salvation and the truth of your word. We want to serve you in spirit and in truth today. We pray this in Jesus' name. Amen.

Day 6

> **174** "I long for Your salvation, O Lord,
> And Your law *is* my delight.

175 Let my soul live, and it shall praise You;
And let Your judgments help me.
176 I have gone astray like a lost sheep;
Seek Your servant,
For I do not forget Your commandments."
   (Psalms 119.174-176)

Psalm 119, the longest Psalm of the Bible, ends with a reminder that even the writer has "gone astray like a lost sheep". At whatever point one is in his walk with Christ, the fact that "all have sinned" and that we can still sin should never be forgotten. This awareness of one's inclination to sin is what can help us remain on the path of holiness and faithfulness.

Throughout Psalm 119 the writer extols the wonders of the Word of God. He even ends his teaching with the words, "I do not forget Your commandments". But he knows how easily the sheep can wander away from the good shepherd. He never forgets how dependent he is upon the teachings and the salvation of the good shepherd.

When the writers of the New Testament address churches or individual believers, there is always an element of warning in their writings that goes along with the comfort that comes from enjoying a salvation that no one can take away from them. The assurance of salvation should be understood as an essential element to continued faithfulness, and not as a pretext to sin (Romans 6).

The prayer of the Pharisee was the prayer of one assured of his standing before God. The prayer of the tax collector was the prayer of one who knew his weaknesses and his need for daily help from God (Luke 18.9-14).

8 "Finally, brethren, whatever things are true, whatever things *are* noble, whatever things *are* just, whatever things *are* pure, whatever things *are* lovely, whatever things *are* of good report, if *there is* any virtue and if *there is* anything praiseworthy—meditate on these things. **9** The things which you learned and received and heard and saw in me, these do, and the God of peace will be with you."(Philippians 4.8.9)

Prayer

Father in heaven, we come before you today seeking your forgiveness and your strength. We want to live as grateful children of yours, as people who now belong to you. We want to fill our hearts and thoughts with only what is good and praiseworthy. Help us in this, Father. We pray in the name of Jesus, our Lord. Amen.

Day 7

> **70** "He also chose David His servant,
> And took him from the sheepfolds;
> **71** From following the ewes that had young He brought him,
> To shepherd Jacob His people,
> And Israel His inheritance.
> **72** So he shepherded them according to the integrity of his heart,
> And guided them by the skillfulness of his hands."
>   (Psalms 78.70-72)

David is a prophetical figure of the Messiah (anointed king) who was to come. David was not without his faults, but he maintained the worship of God against all the idolatrous practices surrounding Israel. After David, the worship of God deteriorated and was replaced by idolatry both in the northern kingdom and in the south, until the people was exiled and the temple destroyed. The speech of Stephen in Acts 7 is a summary of Israel's unfaithfulness to God.

This too was an illustration of how unique "David" was and through his prophetical figure how unique the Messiah "son of David" would be. The "integrity" of the heart is seen here as the source of David's faithfulness, and was also the source of Jesus' faithfulness.

The qualities of Jesus as Messiah are brought out in the Gospels and the New Testament teachings. Foremost, we learn that he was without sin:

> **29** "The Father has not left Me alone, for I always do those things that please Him." **30** As He spoke these words, many believed in Him." (John 8.29,30)

> "And you know that He was manifested to take away our sins, and in Him there is no sin." (1 John 3.5)

> **18** "...knowing that you were not redeemed with corruptible things, *like* silver or gold, from your aimless conduct *received* by tradition from your fathers, **19** but with the precious blood of Christ, as of a lamb without blemish and without spot. (1 Peter 1.18,19)

22 "For to this you were called because Christ also suffered for us, leaving us an example, that you should follow His steps: **23** "Who committed no sin, nor was deceit found in His mouth" (1 Peter 2.22,23)

"For He made Him who knew no sin *to be* sin for us, that we might become the righteousness of God in Him." (2 Corinthians 5.21)

14 "Seeing then that we have a great High Priest who has passed through the heavens, Jesus the Son of God, let us hold fast *our* confession. **15** For we do not have a High Priest who cannot sympathize with our weaknesses, but was in all *points* tempted as *we are, yet* without sin." (Hebrews 4.14,15)

Prayer

Father in heaven, thank you for Jesus the lamb of God. Thank you for your plan of salvation that we now enjoy. We pray that this day we can do all things to glorify the name of Jesus, our Lord. We pray also for our family members, our loved ones. May they act today in a way that will be pleasing to you. And if not, may you lead them to you, to your truth, to your salvation. This is our prayer in the name of Jesus, our Lord. Amen.

Week 27: Words of Grace

Day 1

> **1** "God be merciful to us and bless us,
> *And* cause His face to shine upon us, *Selah*
> **2** That Your way may be known on earth,
> Your salvation among all nations.
> **3** Let the peoples praise You, O God;
> Let all the peoples praise You.
> **4** Oh, let the nations be glad and sing for joy!
> For You shall judge the people righteously,
> And govern the nations on earth. *Selah*
> **5** Let the peoples praise You, O God;
> Let all the peoples praise You.
> **6** *Then* the earth shall yield her increase;
> God, our own God, shall bless us.
> **7** God shall bless us,
> And all the ends of the earth shall fear Him."
> (Psalms 67.1-7)

This Psalm is a prophecy of how God's grace and mercy will extend to all the gentiles, all the nations. The salvation of all nations, of gentiles, is brought out from the time that God makes a covenant with Abraham:

> **1** "Get out of your country,
> From your family
> And from your father's house,
> To a land that I will show you.
> **2** I will make you a great nation;
> I will bless you
> And make your name great;
> And you shall be a blessing.
> **3** I will bless those who bless you,
> And I will curse him who curses you;

And in you all the families of the earth shall be blessed." (Genesis 12.1-3)

The numerous prophecies concerning the Gentile nations to be saved confirm God's will to save all peoples:

> **1** "Therefore, I exhort first of all that supplications, prayers, intercessions, *and* giving of thanks be made for all men, **2** for kings and all who are in authority, that we may lead a quiet and peaceable life in all godliness and reverence. **3** For this *is* good and acceptable in the sight of God our Savior, **4** who desires all men to be saved and to come to the knowledge of the truth. **5** For *there is* one God and one Mediator between God and men, *the* Man Christ Jesus, **6** who gave Himself a ransom for all, to be testified in due time, **7** for which I was appointed a preacher and an apostle—I am speaking the truth in Christ *and* not lying—a teacher of the Gentiles in faith and truth." (1 Timothy 2.1-7)

> **8** "But, beloved, do not forget this one thing, that with the Lord one day *is* as a thousand years, and a thousand years as one day. **9** The Lord is not slack concerning *His* promise, as some count slackness, but is longsuffering toward us, not willing that any should perish but that all should come to repentance." (2 Peter 3.8,9)

All those whom God saves in the end — whether from Israel or all the nations (see Romans 11.25-27) — are "written in the book of life" (Daniel 12.1; Psalms 69.27,28; Luke 10.20; Hebrews 12.22,23; Philippians 4.3; Revelation 3.5; 13.8; 17.8; 21.27).

They are known by God from all eternity:

> **28** "And we know that all things work together for good to those who love God, to those who are the called according to *His* purpose. **29** For whom He foreknew, He also predestined *to be* conformed to the image of His Son, that He might be the firstborn among many brethren. **30** Moreover whom He predestined, these He also called; whom He called, these He also justified; and whom He justified, these He also glorified." (Romans 8.28-30)

Prayer

Father in heaven, we praise you today for your grace and salvation. We praise you for the work you have accomplished through Jesus your Son. Thank you, Lord, for the forgiveness of sins. Thank you for giving us many wonderful blessings found in the Kingdom of your Son, in the Church. We pray this in Jesus' name. Amen.

Day 2

> **1** "Praise the Lord!
> For *it is* good to sing praises to our God;
> For *it is* pleasant, *and* praise is beautiful.
> **2** The Lord builds up Jerusalem;
> He gathers together the outcasts of Israel.
> **3** He heals the brokenhearted
> And binds up their wounds.
> **4** He counts the number of the stars;
> He calls them all by name.
> **5** Great *is* our Lord, and mighty in power;
> His understanding *is* infinite.
> **6** The Lord lifts up the humble;
> He casts the wicked down to the ground."
> (Psalms 147.1-6)

These words of grace are expressed by those who have now been able to return from captivity and to rebuild Jerusalem (see also Psalms 148.1-14 and 149.1-9). When we read the New Testament, we find similar expressions of joy for the salvation found in Jesus and for the Church of the Lord (Galatians 5.22; Romans 14.17; 1 Peter 1.8).

The healing of the Gospel is a healing of the broken heart. Jesus brings healing to those who have been mistreated or abused in a world of sin:

> **27** "All things have been delivered to Me by My Father, and no one knows the Son except the Father. Nor does anyone know the Father except the Son, and *the one* to whom the Son wills to reveal *Him*. **28** Come to Me, all *you* who labor and are heavy laden, and I will give you rest. **29** Take My yoke upon you and learn from Me, for I am gentle and lowly in heart, and you will

find rest for your souls. **30** For My yoke *is* easy and My burden is light." (Matthew 11.27-30)

In order for us to find this healing, we need to "learn from Jesus". This learning is based on the entirety of his life and his teachings. However, at the heart of this "teaching" which heals is the Good News of his death and resurrection and the forgiveness of sins promised to those who put their trust in him:

> **3** "For I delivered to you first of all that which I also received: that Christ died for our sins according to the Scriptures, **4** and that He was buried, and that He rose again the third day according to the Scriptures, **5** and that He was seen by Cephas, then by the twelve. **6** After that He was seen by over five hundred brethren at once, of whom the greater part remain to the present, but some have fallen asleep. **7** After that He was seen by James, then by all the apostles. **8** Then last of all He was seen by me also, as by one born out of due time." (1 Corinthians 15.3-8)

Prayer

Lord in heaven, we praise you and thank you. We pray that today we will seek your kingdom and righteousness and trust fully in your promises. We confess to you our sins. We also pray for our loved ones and our close friends. May you keep them close to you and strengthen them. We pray this in the name of Jesus. Amen.

Day 3

> **11** "Teach me Your way, O Lord;
> I will walk in Your truth;
> Unite my heart to fear Your name.
> **12** I will praise You, O Lord my God, with all my heart,
> And I will glorify Your name forevermore.
> **13** For great *is* Your mercy toward me,
> And You have delivered my soul from the depths of Sheol."
>   (Psalms 86.11-13)

The Psalmist is confident his requests will be heard by God because of His mercy. The conviction that stands out of this Psalm as in so many others has to do with the character of God. The psalmist worships and seeks God on the basis of His goodness, His abundant mercy (v.5), His wondrous works (v.10).

A lack of trust in God or a lack of appreciation for God's goodness will inevitably harm the life of prayer and praise. The Lord's model prayer and the requests in this prayer are founded on the Father's holiness mentioned at the beginning of the prayer (Matthew 6.9). When we pray or praise God, we are praying to the God who is without any sin or blemish, the God who is perfect (Matthew 5.48).

It is a mistaken assumption to view God in the Old Testament as different in character from the God of the Gospels and the New Testament. The God of the books of Genesis or Exodus, of Kings or Isaiah is full of mercy and "ready to forgive".

The judgments of God on individuals or nations, including Israel, always follow the longsuffering and patience of God. However, His prophets are most of the time rejected, if not put to death. They are mocked. Noah was a preacher of righteousness during God's patience before the flood: "…who formerly were disobedient, when once the Divine longsuffering waited in the days of Noah, while *the* ark was being prepared, in which a few, that is, eight souls, were saved through water." (1 Peter 3.20).

God's wrath throughout the Bible is never an uncontrolled emotional reaction, as it is usually with human beings. It is the working out of His justice after a long period of waiting and trying to draw people back to Him.

> **16** "But they and our fathers acted proudly,
> Hardened their necks,
> And did not heed Your commandments.
> **17** They refused to obey,
> And they were not mindful of Your wonders
> That You did among them.
> But they hardened their necks,
> And in their rebellion
> They appointed a leader
> To return to their bondage.
> But You *are* God,
> Ready to pardon,
> Gracious and merciful,
> Slow to anger,
> Abundant in kindness,
> And did not forsake them. (Nehemiah 9:16, 17)

Prayer

We praise you Father for your holiness, your goodness and mercy. We believe the testimony of your Word, of your prophets and Jesus your Son. We praise you for another day to serve you on this earth. Give us today strength and wisdom through your Holy Spirit. We pray this in the name of Jesus our Lord, Amen.

Day 4

> **6** "*There are* many who say,
> 'Who will show us *any* good?'
> Lord, lift up the light of Your countenance upon us.
> **7** You have put gladness in my heart,
> More than in the season that their grain and wine increased.
> **8** I will both lie down in peace, and sleep;
> For You alone, O Lord, make me dwell in safety."
>   (Psalms 4.6-8)

This Psalm is a prayer of David to God during the rebellion of his son Absalom and others (2 Samuel 15). Those who opposed God's anointed "loved worthlessness and falsehood". We can see in this a prophetical picture of the opposition to God's Messiah as described in other Psalms (for example in Psalms 2 and 22; cf. John 12.6; 2 Peter 2.14).

The word for "countenance" literally means "face" in Hebrew. James Moffatt translated the verse by "smile upon us". The writer recognizes God as the source of the gladness in his heart. This stands in contrast with the unhappiness and dissatisfaction of so many around us. But what can the unbeliever expect? Without God's love and promises there is not much to expect from this world: "Man *who is* born of woman is few of days and full of trouble." (Job 14.1)

> **2** "Vanity of vanities says the Preacher;
> Vanity of vanities, all *is* vanity.
> **3** What profit has a man from all his labor
> In which he toils under the sun?" (Ecclesiastes 1.2,3)

"Therefore, my beloved brethren, be steadfast, immovable, always abounding in the work of the Lord, knowing that your labor is not in vain in the Lord." (1 Corinthians 15.58) Our hope is not in this earth or even a better environment. The earth is doomed to destruction, and we are waiting for God's manifestation of his glory at the coming of Christ. (2 Peter 3.10-13).

Prayer

Father in heaven, we praise you! We thank you for the Word you have given us through your prophets and apostles. May we always be willing to learn from you and grow in holiness. We praise you from the bottom of our hearts and ask you today for a clear mind and strength for all the work that lies ahead. This we pray in Jesus' name. Amen.

Day 5

> **1** "I will praise *You*, O Lord, with my whole heart;
> I will tell of all Your marvelous works.
> **2** I will be glad and rejoice in You;
> I will sing praise to Your name, O Most High."
> (Psalms 9.1,2)

Commentators have wondered about the historical circumstances of this Psalm and what victories of Israel are alluded to here when for example the writer says: "When my enemies turn back, they shall fall and perish at Your presence" (v.3); "The nations have sunk down in the pit *which* they made; In the net which they hid, their own foot is caught." (v.15)

The thought of God dealing with "enemies" or of even having enemies often troubles believers. But Jesus himself never said his followers would have only friends; he taught us to pray for our enemies (Matthew 5.43-48).

The apostle Paul taught us to live at peace with everyone:

> **17** "Repay no one evil for evil. Have regard for good things in the sight of all men. **18** If it is possible, as much as depends on you, live peaceably with all men. **19** Beloved do not avenge yourselves, but *rather* give place to wrath; for it is
> written, 'Vengeance *is* Mine, I will repay,' says the
> Lord. **20** Therefore 'If your enemy is hungry, feed him; If he is thirsty, give him a drink; For in so doing you will heap coals of fire on his head.' **21** Do not be overcome by evil, but overcome evil with good." (Romans 12.17-21)

The Hebrew writers used the present or past tense regarding the promise of future events. God's pronouncements for the future will happen, since his "foreknowledge" is perfect (see Romans 8.28-30). The faithful can face the present, past or future with assurance. They can praise God in the midst of affliction and in the midst of deliverance. They can remain faithful like Job even when life is very difficult for them (James 5.7-11).

16 "Rejoice always, **17** pray without ceasing, **18** in everything give thanks; for this is the will of God in Christ Jesus for you." (1 Thessalonians 5.16-18)

4 "Rejoice in the Lord always. Again, I will say, rejoice! **5** Let your gentleness be known to all men. The Lord *is* at hand. **6** Be anxious for nothing, but in everything by prayer and supplication, with thanksgiving, let your requests be made known to God; **7** and the peace of God, which surpasses all understanding, will guard your hearts and minds through Christ Jesus." (Philippians 4.4-7)

Prayer

Father in heaven, we come to you with praises knowing that you take care of us. Even when we face difficult situations or difficult people, we know you have the power to keep our hearts in peace and to give us wisdom to know how to act and speak. Be with us today in everything we do. May we act and speak to glorify you. We pray this in the name of Jesus. Amen.

Day 6

1 "Lord, who may abide in Your tabernacle?
Who may dwell in Your holy hill?
2 He who walks uprightly,
And works righteousness,
And speaks the truth in his heart;
3 He *who* does not backbite with his tongue,
Nor does evil to his neighbor,
Nor does he take up a reproach against his friend;
4 In whose eyes a vile person is despised,
But he honors those who fear the Lord;
He *who* swears to his own hurt and does not change;
5 He *who* does not put out his money at usury,
Nor does he take a bribe against the innocent.
He who does these *things* shall never be moved."
   (Psalms 15.1-5)

This Psalm mentions five negative traits of the unrighteous, versus six traits of the righteous man. Such lists are not "all-inclusive" but are typical where bribery, oppression of the poor and slander are widely prevalent. The person with the qualities described here would have been a great light shining in the midst of thick darkness.

The six positive traits are walking uprightly, working righteousness, speaking the truth, despising the vile, honoring those who fear the Lord, keeps his promises.

The five negative traits are "does not backbite with his tongue", "does no evil to his neighbor", "does not take up a reproach against a friend", "does not put his money at usury", "does not take a bribe against the innocent".

It is significant that the righteous person avoids evil actions and practices good. This idea is found throughout the Scriptures and is even consistent with the ten commandments (for example, he does not take God's name in vain and he honors his parents). Righteousness consists not only of doing what is right, but also in avoiding what is wrong.

> **1** "Therefore, laying aside all malice, all deceit, hypocrisy, envy, and all evil speaking, **2** as newborn babes, desire the pure milk of the word, that you may grow thereby, **3** if indeed you have tasted that the Lord *is* gracious." (1 Peter 2.1-3)

This confirms the teaching of giving up the "works of the flesh" while being led by the Spirit (Galatians 5.16-26).

This goes with the idea of putting off the "old man" and putting on the new man:

> **20** "But you have not so learned Christ, **21** if indeed you have heard Him and have been taught by Him, as the truth is in Jesus: **22** that you put off, concerning your former conduct, the old man which grows corrupt according to the deceitful lusts, **23** and be renewed in the spirit of your mind, **24** and that you put on the new man which was created according to God, in true righteousness and holiness." (Ephesians 4.20-24)

Prayer

Lord in heaven we thank you for the grace and salvation we enjoy in Christ. As we read this Psalm, we pray that we can practice the Christian virtues you have taught us in your word. We also pray we can be delivered of evil actions or thoughts. Please forgive our sins and give us a renewed heart and mind. In Jesus' name, we pray, Amen.

Day 7

> **1** "O Lord my God, in You I put my trust;
> Save me from all those who persecute me;
> And deliver me,
> **2** Lest they tear me like a lion,
> Rending *me* in pieces, while *there is* none to deliver."
>   (Psalms 7.1,2)

In the midst of persecution or having to deal with difficult people, we should put our trust in God and give ourselves to prayer. Yes, we need to pray for our "enemies" and even bless them (Matthew 5).

When persecuted and mistreated, we also have the legitimate right to ask deliverance from God, as the martyrs in the book of Revelation:

> **9** "When He opened the fifth seal, I saw under the altar the souls of those who had been slain for the word of God and for the testimony which they held. **10** And they cried with a loud voice, saying, "How long, O Lord, holy and true, until You judge and avenge our blood on those who dwell on the earth?" **11** Then a white robe was given to each of them; and it was said to them that they should rest a little while longer, until both *the number of* their fellow servants and their brethren, who would be killed as they *were,* was completed." (Revelation 6.9-11)

This is also why the saints along with John pray and say, "Come Lord Jesus" (Revelation 22.20)

In the vision given to him by Jesus, the apostle John sees the souls of those who have been martyred and who sing the song of victory:

> **1** "After these things I heard a loud voice of a great multitude in heaven, saying, 'Alleluia! Salvation and glory and honor and power *belong* to the Lord our God! **2** For true and righteous *are* His judgments, because He has judged the great harlot who corrupted the earth with her fornication; and He has avenged on her the blood of His servants *shed* by her.'" (Revelation 19.1,2)

Jesus' prayer for deliverance from evil certainly includes deliverance from those who persecute or mistreat the faithful:

"And do not lead us into temptation but deliver us from the evil one. For Yours is the kingdom and the power and the glory forever. Amen." (Matthew 6.13)

Prayer

Father in heaven, we pray for patience and love when we endure opposition. We also pray for greater trust in you day by day. May we always remember your promises of victory and perfect justice, despite the evils of this world. May we not fear to preach and teach the Good News to those we meet each day. We pray this in Jesus' name. Amen.

Week 28: Wisdom from Above

Day 1

> **30** "The mouth of the righteous speaks wisdom,
> And his tongue talks of justice.
> **31** The law of his God *is* in his heart;
> None of his steps shall slide."
>   (Psalms 37.30,31)

The Hebrew *hakam* (wisdom) and related terms, appear over 300 times in the Old Testament. Wisdom is first of all to be skillful, to make the right choices, to live life skillfully.

When faced with evil people and with injustice in this world, the righteous needs to "wait upon the Lord" (v.v.7, 39). A key theme in Psalm 37 is how to succeed in the midst of evil in the world without resorting to evil. These two verses show that this is first of all a matter of the heart: "The law of his God is in his heart".

Note that people cannot rely on their own hearts (Proverbs 3.5). God's law needs to be written on their heart:

> **23** "Keep your heart with all diligence,
> For out of it *spring* the issues of life.
> **24** Put away from you a deceitful mouth,
> And put perverse lips far from you." (Proverbs 4.23)

> "The mouth of the righteous *is* a well of life,
> But violence covers the mouth of the wicked." (Proverbs 10.11)

> **34** "Brood of vipers! How can you, being evil, speak good things? For out of the abundance of the heart the mouth speaks. **35** A good man out of the good treasure of his heart brings forth good things, and an evil man out of the evil treasure brings forth evil things. **36** But I say to you that for every idle word men may speak they will give account of it in the day

of judgment. **37** For by your words you will be justified, and by your words you will be condemned." (Matthew 12.34-37)

Prayer

Our Lord and Father in heaven, we pray for wisdom as we go about this day. Help us keep your will in our hearts. Help us wait on you for wisdom and how we speak. May we speak words of wisdom. May we speak words of justice. We pray this in Jesus' name. Amen.

Day 2

> **7** "The law of the Lord *is* perfect, converting the soul;
> The testimony of the Lord *is* sure, making wise the simple;
> **8** The statutes of the Lord *are* right, rejoicing the heart;
> The commandment of the Lord *is* pure, enlightening the eyes;
> **9** The fear of the Lord *is* clean, enduring forever;"
>   (Psalms 19.7-9)

The testimony of the Lord is sure and makes wise the simple. Verse 7 in this Psalm begins with the divine name Yahweh (LORD) in introducing the knowledge of God through the law, his testimony, statutes and commandment (the reference to creation from verses 1 to 6 is introduced by the name *El* for God which refers to His power as the creator).

The word law (*torah*) can also have the broad meaning of instruction, doctrine or teaching. It is used in the Old Testament of prophecy (Isaiah 1.10; 8.16) and even prophetically of the Gospel (Isaiah 2.3). In the "law" as throughout the Scriptures we find a testimony to the ministry and life of the Messiah (Luke 24.44; see John 5.39,40).

The law is "perfect" (*temimah*, without defect or blemish) which means here harmless, well-meaning, meant for the well-being of people. Jesus came not to "abolish" the law but to complete it, to allow us to live accordingly to the law (Matthew 5.17; Romans 7.7 and Romans 13.8-10).

The "simple" is the one who is easily led astray. The word "simple" (*peti*) is from the root word meaning "spread out, open" as one vulnerable to being led astray, to being misguided. Compare this to:

> **14** "But you must continue in the things which you have learned
> and been assured of, knowing from whom you have
> learned *them*, **15** and that from childhood you have known the
> Holy Scriptures, which are able to make you wise for salvation
> through faith which is in Christ Jesus." (2 Timothy 3.15).

24 "Therefore, whoever hears these sayings of Mine, and does them, I will liken him to a wise man who built his house on the rock: **25** and the rain descended, the floods came, and the winds blew and beat on that house; and it did not fall, for it was founded on the rock." (Matthew 7.24,25)

Prayer

Father, we thank you for this day. We thank you for Jesus and the forgiveness of sins. We pray today for a better understanding of your will and more wisdom. Help us today put into practice your will and seek your kingdom and righteousness. Keep our loved ones in your peace and in your grace. We pray this in the name of Jesus. Amen.

Day 3

1 "An oracle within my heart concerning the transgression of the wicked:
There is no fear of God before his eyes.
2 For he flatters himself in his own eyes,
When he finds out his iniquity *and* when he hates.
3 The words of his mouth *are* wickedness and deceit;
He has ceased to be wise *and* to do good.
4 He devises wickedness on his bed;
He sets himself in a way *that is* not good;
He does not abhor evil."
   (Psalms 36.1-4)

The wicked has ceased to be wise and to do good. This one who "has ceased to be wise" is described in these four verses:

1. He has no fear of God.

2. He flatters himself in his own eyes.

3. He has hatred.

4. His words are wickedness and deceit.

5. He devises wickedness on his bed.

6. He sets himself in a way that is not good.

7. He does not abhor evil.

The wicked is one who has ceased or "has given up" wisdom and doing good ("to give up" as in 1 Samuel 23.13). So here it seems to describe one who at some point had sought wisdom and doing good, but did not persist or persevere. It reminds us of the parable of the soils in Matthew 13, especially the "soil" full of thorns:

> **22** "Now he who received seed among the thorns is he who hears the word, and the cares of this world and the deceitfulness of riches choke the word, and he becomes unfruitful. **23** But he who received seed on the good ground is he who hears the word and understands *it*, who indeed bears fruit and produces: some a hundredfold, some sixty, some thirty." (Matthew 13.22,23)

This is not simply the description of one who is weak and sins and needs to repent (See Psalms 37.23,24 and 1 John 1.9,10) but of someone "entangled" and "overcome" by the pollutions of the world as in 2 Peter 2.20-22 which refers especially to "false teachers" who promise liberty when "they are themselves slaves of corruption." The language describes those snared or made captive by "sin" to the point they have no wish to overcome their sins or to live a more holy life.

When we read these verses of Psalms 36, we understand clearly this idea of a soil that has been exposed to the word of truth, but which does not produce good fruit since it is full of thorns. These verses also help us understand that one sin does not stand on one's own; that sinfulness is an overall condition of the mind and heart which can only be described as "death" (Ephesians 2.1-3).

Jesus came as the lamb that takes away "the sin" of the world — a condition of the human condition which touches all aspects of life and that has touched the entire world (John 1.29). The man who did not build his house on the rock and was foolish did not listen to Jesus' teachings and practice them:

> **26** "But everyone who hears these sayings of Mine, and does not do them, will be like a foolish man who built his house on the sand: **27** and the rain descended, the floods came, and the winds blew and beat on that house; and it fell. And great was its fall." (Matthew 7.26,27)

Prayer

Father in heaven, we come to you with a desire to do your will and become better disciples today. We pray for help and strength in our struggle with sin and our temptations in this world. Deliver us from evil and lead us not into temptation. Bless us through your Holy Spirit and your Word of truth. We pray this in Jesus' name. Amen.

Day 4

> **1** "Hear this, all peoples;
> Give ear, all inhabitants of the world,
> **2** Both low and high,
> Rich and poor together.
> **3** My mouth shall speak wisdom,
> And the meditation of my heart *shall give* understanding.
> **4** I will incline my ear to a proverb;
> I will disclose my dark saying on the harp."
> (Psalms 49.1-4)

The wisdom we find in this Psalm (v.3) is contrasted with the folly of those "who trust in their wealth and boast in the multitude of their riches". This Psalm reminds us of Jesus' teachings such as "A man's life consists not in the abundance of his possessions" or his encounter with the rich young ruler or the parable of the rich fool (Luke 12.15; Matthew 19.16-22; Luke 12.13-21).

In this Psalm, the Word of God is addressing both "rich and poor" for they both need to understand the folly of trusting in material riches. Wealth cannot "redeem" anyone (v.7). Both the wise and the fool die and "leave their wealth to others" (v.10). One should not be "afraid" or impressed by someone who becomes rich (v.16-19). His destiny is in sharp contrast with the one whose soul is redeemed from the power of the grave; that one shall be received by God (v.15, see Enoch and Elijah, Genesis 5.24; Psalms 73.24).

This assurance of victory over death and eternal life with God was brought to light by Jesus:

> **9** "who has saved us and called *us* with a holy calling, not according to our works, but according to His own purpose and grace which was given to us in Christ Jesus before time began, **10** but has now been revealed by the appearing of our Savior Jesus Christ, *who* has abolished death and brought life and immortality to light through the gospel" (1 Timothy 2.9.10)

Prayer

Our Lord, we thank you for this day and every opportunity to serve you and to do good. We need your wisdom and guidance in order to act wisely and put into practice the teachings of Jesus. So, we ask from you for wisdom and a renewed heart. Help us as we meet people during the day so that we can be faithful servants of yours. In Jesus' name, we pray. Amen.

Day 5

> **1** "*It is* good to give thanks to the Lord,
> And to sing praises to Your name, O Most High;
> **2** To declare Your lovingkindness in the morning,
> And Your faithfulness every night,
> **3** On an instrument of ten strings,
> On the lute,
> And on the harp,
> With harmonious sound.
> **4** For You, Lord, have made me glad through Your work;
> I will triumph in the works of Your hands.
> **5** O Lord, how great are Your works!
> Your thoughts are very deep.
> **6** A senseless man does not know,
> Nor does a fool understand this.
> **7** When the wicked spring up like grass,
> And when all the workers of iniquity flourish,
> *It is* that they may be destroyed forever."
> (Psalms 92.1-7)

The senseless man does not know God and his works, nor does the fool understand them either (v.6). This verse reminds us of Psalm 14:

> "The fool has said in his heart,
> '*There is* no God.'
> They are corrupt,
> They have done abominable works,
> There is none who does good." (Psalms 14.1,2)

Wisdom lies in knowing the LORD and understanding His works.

"But without faith *it is* impossible to please *Him*, for he who comes to God must believe that He is, and *that* He is a rewarder of those who diligently seek Him." (Hebrews 11.6)

The fool does not understand the "depths" of God's thoughts (v.5). Whenever he is faced with questions or issues that are difficult for him, he quickly abandons his faith or says in his heart, "there is no God". He does not realize that if God is who He claims to be and is presented in the Scriptures, there will be unanswered questions, there will be "mysteries" too deep for him to comprehend:

33 "Oh, the depth of the riches both of the wisdom and knowledge of God! How unsearchable *are* His judgments and His ways past finding out!
34 "For who has known the mind of the Lord?
Or who has become His counselor?"
35 "Or who has first given to Him
And it shall be repaid to him?" **36** For of Him and through Him and to Him *are* all things, to whom *be* glory forever. Amen."
(Romans 11.33-36)

When Jesus spoke of "eating his flesh and drinking his blood" many left him not understanding the spiritual meaning of his words. "Therefore, many of His disciples, when they heard *this*, said, 'This is a hard saying; who can understand it?'" (John 6.60)

Prayer

Father in heaven, we pray for understanding as we meditate and study your Word. We believe that you provide wisdom and understanding to all who ask of you. Thank you for a new day to serve you and to speak to you. Thank you for a new day to praise your name. In Jesus' name, we pray. Amen.

Day 6

8 "Understand, you senseless among the people
And *you* fools; when will you be wise?
9 He who planted the ear, shall He not hear?
He who formed the eye, shall He not see?
10 He who instructs the nations, shall He not correct,
He who teaches man knowledge?

11 The Lord knows the thoughts of man,
That they *are* futile."
(Psalms 94.8-11)

These words are addressed to those who say: "The Lord does not see, nor does the God of Jacob understand." (v.7). These "senseless" and "fools" are like the "foolish and ignorant" who are "like a beast" of Psalm 73.21,22.

These "fools" mentioned in this Psalm are first individuals among the Israelites, God's people. They break to pieces God's people, afflict His heritage and slay widows and strangers (vv.5,6. See Ezekiel ch.34 on the shepherds of Israel).

In verse 10 there is also mention of the "nations" who are also needing instruction and correction from God. The "thoughts of man" are futile: the reference to "man" would include both those of Israel and those among the nations.

So, then, who is wise? It is the one who understands that the one who made the ear is also able to hear. The one who made the eye is also able to see. The intelligent design demonstrated in God's creation and demonstrated by the eye and ear is proof of God's ability to hear and see.

We should note that the psalmist does not say "He that planteth the ear, hath he not an ear" but "He that planteth the ear, shall he not hear?". We should not attribute physical attributes to God who is "spirit". God is not like the "idols" represented as having physical bodies and attributes. He is not like Jupiter of Crete who was pictured without ears because he would not attend to the small matters of human beings.

Whether it is the ear or the eye, they manifest the wisdom of the Creator, the power and skill demonstrated through His amazing creation. The God who is the author of such an amazing creation is also the one who instructs and corrects the nations, who teaches them knowledge.

Let us also remember how the Lord Jesus — full of wisdom — is also described as the one who was there at the creation:

1 "In the beginning was the Word, and the Word was with God, and the Word was God. **2** He was in the beginning with God. **3** All things were made through Him, and without Him nothing was made that was made. **4** In Him was life, and the life was the light of men. **5** And the light shines in the darkness, and the darkness did not comprehend it." (John 1.1-5)

Prayer

Father in heaven, we thank you for a new day. We thank you for all your blessings. Give us today a heart full of thankfulness and gratefulness. We also pray for our loved ones, that you might keep them in your grace and peace. Bless every person we will meet today. May we be for them light and salt. This we pray in Jesus' name. Amen.

Day 7

> "The fear of the Lord *is* the beginning of wisdom;
> A good understanding have all those who do *His commandments*.
> His praise endures forever."
> (Psalms 111.10)

This text is similar to a statement found especially in the book of Proverbs: "The fear of the Lord *is* the beginning of wisdom, and the knowledge of the Holy One *is* understanding." (Proverbs 9.10 and Proverbs 1.7; 2.1-11; 8.12,13; 15.33; see Job 28.20-28). The "fear of the LORD" is mentioned about three hundred times in the Old Testament.

Both the love and fear of God are chief components of true wisdom. A person who has no love for God or fear of God remains a "fool", whatever his or her accomplishments or knowledge. Like the love of the LORD, the fear of the LORD is not some kind of emotional condition, but the active practice of faith. A good understanding means practicing His commandments.

The pharaoh brought disaster to himself and his people because he did not fear the LORD (Exodus 9.29-31). The leaders chosen by Moses to lead the nation "did not take bribes" because they feared the LORD (Exodus 18.20-22). Obedience to the commandments in the Old Testament was the result of true fear of the LORD (Leviticus 19.14,32).

Sinful individuals are described as having "no fear of the LORD":

> **16** "Destruction and misery *are* in their ways; **17** and the way of peace they have not known.**18** There is no fear of God before their eyes." (Romans 3.16-18)

> "Therefore, having these promises, beloved, let us cleanse ourselves from all filthiness of the flesh and spirit, perfecting holiness in the fear of God." (2 Corinthians 7.1)

28 "Therefore, since we are receiving a kingdom which cannot be shaken, let us have grace, by which we may serve God acceptably with reverence and godly fear. **29** For our God *is* a consuming fire." (Hebrews 12.27–28)

Prayer

We are grateful to you, Father, and want to honor you each day of our lives. So, we ask for wisdom and understanding today. We ask for a deep sense of respect for you and your commandments. Bless us today with grace and peace as we seek to serve you and every person we meet. We pray in Jesus' name. Amen.

Week 29: The Heart

Day 1

> **5** "But I have trusted in Your mercy;
> My heart shall rejoice in Your salvation.
> **6** I will sing to the Lord,
> Because He has dealt bountifully with me."
>   (Psalms 13.5,6)

There is a striking difference between these verses and the beginning of this Psalm:

> **1** "How long, O Lord? Will You forget me forever?
> How long will You hide Your face from me?
> **2** How long shall I take counsel in my soul,
> *Having* sorrow in my heart daily?" (vv.1,2)

The Psalm has three parts: Lament and sorrow (vv.1,2); Prayer and supplication (v.3-5a); Rejoicing (vv.5b,6). The life of the faithful is characterized by sorrow, supplication, but also rejoicing.

The rejoicing of the heart follows the prayer of faith: "Consider *and* hear me, O Lord my God; enlighten my eyes…" This is a reminder of what we find in other parts of Scripture, such as:

> **6** "Be anxious for nothing, but in everything by prayer and supplication, with thanksgiving, let your requests be made known to God; **7** and the peace of God, which surpasses all understanding, will guard your hearts and minds through Christ Jesus."
> (Philippians 4.6,7)

To "believe" or trust is to remain faithful in sorrow. To trust is also to pray when there is sorrow. To trust is also to be able to rejoice. What this means is that the essential element of the righteous or faithful life is this continued trust in the LORD.

In this Psalm the faithful trusts specifically in God's mercy. He continues to believe in the goodness and mercy of God even when life is difficult, and he is in pain. His joy is in God. His joy is not overcome by the sadness and sorrows brought by life.

Like Job we want to be steadfast, patient in tribulation, knowing that God is very compassionate and merciful (James 5.11).

Prayer

We pray to you Father for trust, for faithfulness. Give us strength and courage as we face sadness. We believe that all strength comes from you, the God of goodness and mercy. Keep our loved ones in your grace and peace. Renew their spirits in hope. We pray this in Jesus' name. Amen.

Day 2

7 "Purge me with hyssop, and I shall be clean;
Wash me, and I shall be whiter than snow.
8 Make me hear joy and gladness,
That the bones You have broken may rejoice.
9 Hide Your face from my sins,
And blot out all my iniquities.
10 Create in me a clean heart, O God,
And renew a steadfast spirit within me.
11 Do not cast me away from Your presence,
And do not take Your Holy Spirit from me." (Psalms 51.7-11)

The word heart is found over one thousand times in the Bible and is the most common term to refer to any part of the human nature. The heart is the center of moral, intellectual and emotional activity. It is in the heart that is found the "inward man" which is renewed day by day: "Therefore we do not lose heart. Even though our outward man is perishing, yet the inward *man* is being renewed day by day." (2 Corinthians 4.16)

"Create in me a clean heart, O God". This psalm written over three thousand years ago could have been written yesterday, as it describes what repentance means for the sinner.

The requests in these verses follow the statement found in verse 6: "Behold, You desire truth in the inward parts, and in the hidden *part* You will make me to know wisdom." Not only God desires this, but He has the power to do it if we humbly trust him and ask him (see also James 1.5).

David heard from Samuel since his youth that God looks at the heart: "But the Lord said to Samuel, 'Do not look at his appearance or at his physical stature, because I have refused him. For *the Lord does* not *see* as man sees; for man looks at the outward appearance, but the Lord looks at the heart.'" (1 Samuel 16.7).

"Keep your heart with all diligence, for out of it *spring* the issues of life." (Proverbs 4.23)

The first and greatest commandment first given to Israel and taught by Jesus has to do with the heart:

> **4** "Hear, O Israel: The Lord our God, the Lord *is* one! **5** You shall love the Lord your God with all your heart, with all your soul, and with all your strength." (Deuteronomy 6.4,5; Matthew 22.37-40).

It is from the heart that one confesses faith in the risen Christ:

> **8** But what does it say? 'The word is near you, in your mouth and in your heart' (that is, the word of faith which we preach): **9** that if you confess with your mouth the Lord Jesus and believe in your heart that God has raised Him from the dead, you will be saved. **10** For with the heart one believes unto righteousness, and with the mouth confession is made unto salvation. **11** For the Scripture says, 'Whoever believes on Him will not be put to shame.'" (Romans 10.8-11)

Prayer

Father in heaven, we pray as David for a clean heart that comes from your forgiveness and your Holy Spirit. We believe that you want us to have a clean heart and that you are able to change our hearts day by day. Keep us faithful to you, Lord, and help us to be faithful throughout a new day. We pray this in Jesus' name. Amen.

Day 3

> **23** "Oh, love the Lord, all you His saints!
> *For* the Lord preserves the faithful,
> And fully repays the proud person.
> **24** Be of good courage,
> And He shall strengthen your heart,
> All you who hope in the Lord."

(Psalms 31.23,24)

This Psalm was written as David was fleeing for his life before the jealousy of king Saul (1 Samuel chapters 18, 21-23). Verses 23 and 24 constitute a closing exhortation for all of God's saints to trust Him.

One cannot read this Psalm without recognizing a description of the Messiah similar to what we find in Isaiah 53, Psalms 16 and 22. Verse 5 has the same statement made by Jesus on the cross: "Into your hand I commit my spirit" (see Luke 23.46).

To love and trust the LORD is the foundation of our relationship with God. Those who "hope in the LORD" are those who "wait upon the LORD": those who are patient even in difficult circumstances (as Job in James 5.11). Those who live with love and trust in God are told to be of good courage and are promised that God will strengthen their heart.

The Hebrew word for "courage" in "Be of good courage" is from the root word *chazaq* which means "to be or grow strong, to strengthen". The idea of courage and strength are closely linked in the Scriptures.

See the exhortations to courage and strength in the following Scriptures:

"Be strong and of good courage, do not fear nor be afraid of them; for the Lord your God, He *is* the One who goes with you. He will not leave you nor forsake you." (Deuteronomy 31.6)

"Then Joshua said to them, 'Do not be afraid, nor be dismayed; be strong and of good courage, for thus the Lord will do to all your enemies against whom you fight.'" (Joshua 10.25)

> **3** "Strengthen the weak hands,
> And make firm the feeble knees.
> **4** Say to those *who are* fearful-hearted,
> Be strong, do not fear!
> Behold, your God will come *with* vengeance,
> *With* the recompense of God;
> He will come and save you." (Isaiah 35.3,4; cf. Hebrews 12.12)
>
> **13** Watch, stand fast in the faith, be brave, be strong. **14** Let all *that* you *do* be done with love." (1 Corinthians 16.13,14)

Prayer

Lord in heaven, we thank you for this day. Be with us and strengthen our hearts and minds so that we will stand up for truth and righteousness. Be with us and fill us with hope based on your Word and your work of salvation through Jesus.

We know you are faithful and will be with us this day. In Jesus' name, we pray. Amen.

Day 4

> **10** With my whole heart I have sought You;
> Oh, let me not wander from Your commandments!
> **11** Your word I have hidden in my heart,
> That I might not sin against You.
>   (Psalms 119.10,11)

In his discourse to the Athenians, the apostle Paul gave a definition of the goal of any human life:

> **26** "And He has made from one blood every nation of men to dwell on all the face of the earth, and has determined their pre appointed times and the boundaries of their dwellings, **27** so that they should seek the Lord, in the hope that they might grope for Him and find Him, though He is not far from each one of us." (Acts 17.26,27)

Seeking and finding the Lord is the ultimate reason for being born and existing on this earth. Without this, every life is "vanity" (smoke, wind):

> **2** "Vanity of vanities," says the Preacher;
> "Vanity of vanities, all *is* vanity."
> **3** What profit has a man from all his labor
> In which he toils under the sun? (Ecclesiastes 1.2,3)

> "Remember now your Creator in the days of your youth,
> Before the difficult days come,
> And the years draw near when you say,
> 'I have no pleasure in them'" (Ecclesiastes 12.1)

> **13** "Let us hear the conclusion of the whole matter:
> Fear God and keep His commandments,
> For this is man's all.
> **14** For God will bring every work into judgment,
> Including every secret thing,
> Whether good or evil." (Ecclesiastes 12.13,14)

Jesus is the "word" — the one who gives "meaning" to existence and in whom dwells the fulness of the godhead, the fulness of knowledge:

8 "Beware lest anyone cheat you through philosophy and empty deceit, according to the tradition of men, according to the basic principles of the world, and not according to Christ. **9** For in Him dwells all the fullness of the Godhead bodily; **10** and you are complete in Him, who is the head of all principality and power." (Colossians 2.8-10; John 1.1-4)

Prayer

Lord our God and Father, we thank you for making yourself known to us through Jesus your beloved Son. We thank you for the teachings He has given us and for the sacrifice he offered for our redemption and salvation. We know that you want to purify our hearts day by day, and pray that you will help us today to reach out to you and find strength in you. In Jesus' name, we pray. Amen.

Day 5

69 "The proud have forged a lie against me,
But I will keep Your precepts with *my* whole heart.
70 Their heart is as fat as grease,
But I delight in Your law."
    (Psalms 119.69,70)

As we read the Psalms, we continually see descriptions of the coming Messiah. Here we have a description of one who has kept God's precepts with his whole heart and has endured opposition from those who lie and are proud.

The heart of the proud is "as fat as grease". This is a figure of speech used to describe insensibility and an inability to be moved by God (Psalms 17.10; Psalms 73.7; Isaiah 6.10).

The Messiah is humble. His humility is a constant challenge to the proud. He did not come to be served but to serve:

2 "For He shall grow up before Him as a tender plant,
And as a root out of dry ground.
He has no form or comeliness;
And when we see Him,
There is no beauty that we should desire Him.
3 He is despised and rejected by men,
A Man of sorrows and acquainted with grief.
And we hid, as it were, *our* faces from Him;
He was despised, and we did not esteem Him." (Isaiah 53.2,3)

> **5** "Let this mind be in you, which was also in Christ Jesus, **6** who, being in the form of God, did not consider it robbery to be equal with God, **7** but made Himself of no reputation, taking the form of a bondservant, *and* coming in the likeness of men. **8** And being found in appearance as a man, He humbled Himself and became obedient to *the point of* death, even the death of the cross." (Philippians 2.5-8)

Prayer

Our Father in heaven, we glorify your name today. We want to serve you with a humble heart. Help us to have a humble heart and disposition. May your Holy Spirit produce the good fruit of humility and service in our lives today. This is our prayer in Jesus' name. Amen.

Day 6

> **111** "Your testimonies I have taken as a heritage forever,
> For they *are* the rejoicing of my heart.
> **112** I have inclined my heart to perform Your statutes
> Forever, to the very end."
>   (Psalms 119.111,112)

The one who writes this Psalm is threatened and his life is in danger (v.87). However, he does not depart from God's word. He has taken possession of God's testimonies forever (see v.98). He may lose everything, but God's testimonies are his heritage, for which he is willing to give up everything else.

This is similar to Jesus' teachings about the value of the Kingdom compared to what is most precious in the eyes of man:

> **44** "Again, the kingdom of heaven is like treasure hidden in a field, which a man found and hid; and for joy over it he goes and sells all that he has and buys that field. **45** "Again, the kingdom of heaven is like a merchant seeking beautiful pearls, **46** who, when he had found one pearl of great price, went and sold all that he had and bought it." (Matthew 13.44,45)

What will a man have gained is he loses his soul?

> **24** "Then Jesus said to His disciples, "If anyone desires to come after Me, let him deny himself, and take up his cross, and follow

Me. **25** For whoever desires to save his life will lose it, but whoever loses his life for My sake will find it. **26** For what profit is it to a man if he gains the whole world, and loses his own soul? Or what will a man give in exchange for his soul? **27** For the Son of Man will come in the glory of His Father with His angels, and then He will reward each according to his works." (Matthew 26.24-27)

Prayer

Lord in heaven, we want to remain attached to the heritage which comes from your Word. We know you are the source of life and all blessing. Help us today to seek first your kingdom and righteousness. Help us to love you more and more day by day and serve you with all our hearts. We pray in Jesus' name. Amen.

Day 7

> **10** "The days of our lives *are* seventy years;
> And if by reason of strength *they are* eighty years,
> Yet their boast *is* only labor and sorrow;
> For it is soon cut off, and we fly away.
> **11** Who knows the power of Your anger?
> For as the fear of You, *so is* Your wrath.
> **12** So teach *us* to number our days,
> That we may gain a heart of wisdom."
>   (Psalms 90.10-12)

This is a prayer of Moses, who lived to be 120. The "boast" of our years is only labor and sorrow. The "boast" or "pride" (*rohab*) of our years causes mainly trouble, labor or toil (*amal*) as in Job 3.10 or 4.8 and sorrow, distress, grief, vanity (*aven*) as in Deuteronomy 26.14 or Job 5.6.

One important way to understand the boast and pride of human life is to consider God's wrath and the need to fear Him. The implication of these verses is that in general men do not take seriously the wrath of God. He is not some over-indulgent grandfather who pays little attention to the terrible and ugly actions occurring on this earth. But on his day of judgment, "all the tribes of the earth shall mourn over him" (Revelation 1.7).

The "fear of the Lord" which is the basis of wisdom cannot be separated from a biblical understanding of sin. Gaining a heart of wisdom is connected to a serious consideration of God's judgment and righteous anger with sinfulness.

In Romans chapters 1 to 3 the apostle Paul establishes the seriousness and universality of sin. A recognition of sinfulness is required for true faith and repentance to lead one to salvation through Jesus. The preaching of the Gospel, which is the power of God to save (Romans 1.16) cannot be dissociated from a declaration of the gravity and consequences of sin:

> **18** "For the wrath of God is revealed from heaven against all ungodliness and unrighteousness of men, who suppress the truth in unrighteousness, **19** because what may be known of God is manifest in them, for God has shown *it* to them." (Romans 1.18,19)

> "Those who practice such things are deserving of death, not only do the same but also approve of those who practice them." (Romans 1.32)

> **4** "Or do you despise the riches of His goodness, forbearance, and longsuffering, not knowing that the goodness of God leads you to repentance? **5** But in accordance with your hardness and your impenitent heart you are treasuring up for yourself wrath in the day of wrath and revelation of the righteous judgment of God," (Romans 2.4,5)

> **23** for all have sinned and fall short of the glory of God, **24** being justified freely by His grace through the redemption that is in Christ Jesus, **25** whom God set forth *as* a propitiation by His blood," (Romans 3.23-25)

Prayer

Father in heaven, we praise you for the mercy you have shown to us day by day. We pray for our hearts to grow in thankfulness and humble service to you and our neighbor. We keep in our prayers our brothers and sisters in the Lord who are afflicted or discouraged. Bless them with your grace and peace, Lord. This we pray in Jesus' name. Amen.

Week 30: Death

Day 1

> **13** "As a father pities *his* children,
> *So* the Lord pities those who fear Him.
> **14** For He knows our frame;
> He remembers that we *are* dust.
> **15** *As for* man, his days *are* like grass;
> As a flower of the field, so he flourishes.
> **16** For the wind passes over it, and it is gone,
> And its place remembers it no more.
> **17** But the mercy of the Lord *is* from everlasting to everlasting
> On those who fear Him,
> And His righteousness to children's children,
> **18** To such as keep His covenant,
> And to those who remember His commandments to do them."
> (Psalms 103.13-18)

A number of biblical passages describe man's condition with basically the same words: 1 Peter 1.24; Isaiah 37.27; 40.6,7; 51.12; James 1.10. We should consider the reality of our death, but also the reality of God's everlasting love.

The fear of the LORD has nothing to do with the idea of God being some kind of angry tyrant acting arbitrarily. The fear mentioned here is a basic recognition of our physical and spiritual limitations; a recognition that we will die, that sin has already brought death to our souls (1 Peter 1.24; Ephesians 2.1-4).

To "fear" the LORD without an understanding of His grace and mercy, of His fatherly love for His children, is to misunderstand the fatherhood of God. The theme of the "father" who pities his children is present in the teachings of Jesus. For example:

> **11** If a son asks for bread from any father among you, will he
> give him a stone? Or if *he asks* for a fish, will he give him a ser-
> pent instead of a fish? **12** Or if he asks for an egg, will he offer
> him a scorpion? **13** If you then, being evil, know how to
> give good gifts to your children, how much more will *your* heav-

enly Father give the Holy Spirit to those who ask Him!'" (Luke 11.11-13).

20 "And he arose and came to his father. But when he was still a great way off, his father saw him and had compassion, and ran and fell on his neck and kissed him. **21** And the son said to him, 'Father, I have sinned against heaven and in your sight, and am no longer worthy to be called your son.'" (Luke 15.20,21)

God the Father is holy. His love and mercy are perfect, as well as His justice: "His mercy is from everlasting to everlasting".

He is the one we pray to as we come together, the one who provides for all our needs:

9 "Our Father in heaven,
Hallowed be Your name.
10 Your kingdom come.
Your will be done
On earth as *it is* in heaven.
11 Give us this day our daily bread." (Matthew 6.9–11)

Prayer

We come to you in prayer, Father in heaven. We join our voices and hearts in confessing your perfect holiness, your goodness and mercy. We are grateful for your Father's heart towards us and your pity as you look at our lives. Please Father forgive us and give us the wisdom and faith to forgive those who have sinned against us. This we pray in Jesus' name. Amen.

Day 2

1 "Lord You have been our dwelling place in all generations.
2 Before the mountains were brought forth,
Or ever You had formed the earth and the world,
Even from everlasting to everlasting, You *are* God.
3 You turn man to destruction,
And say, 'Return, O children of men.'
4 For a thousand years in Your sight
Are like yesterday when it is past,
And *like* a watch in the night.
5 You carry them away *like* a flood;
They are like a sleep.

In the morning they are like grass *which* grows up.
6 In the morning it flourishes and grows up;
In the evening it is cut down and withers."
   (Psalms 90.1-6)

God is the eternal and uncreated God:

> "Even from everlasting to everlasting, You are God." Verse 4 of Psalm 90 is quoted by Peter (2 Peter 3.8).

In contrast to God, "children of men" (human beings) are turned to "destruction" — in Hebrew *dakka,* which describes anything crushed as dust. The same word is used of the humble and contrite; they are those who basically do not forget their mortal condition (Psalms 34.18; Isaiah 57.15).

God is the dwelling place or habitation of God's people (Psalms 26.8). This "dwelling place" is not fragile and temporary as our human habitations. Death cannot touch this "habitation". Those who are "in Christ" are raised with Christ and their life is "hidden with Christ in God" (Colossians 3.1-3). They are members of God's household, the Church (1 Timothy 3.15).

God and the lamb are the temple of the holy city, which comes down from heaven:

> **22** "But I saw no temple in it, for the Lord God Almighty and the Lamb are its temple. **23** The city had no need of the sun or of the moon to shine in it, for the glory of God illuminated it."
> (Revelation 21.22,23)

Prayer

Our Father in heaven, you are our holy habitation, you are our hope. We want to dwell in your house forever, close to your kind and noble heart. We want to enjoy your loving presence forever. We ask you Father to guide our thoughts, actions and words today in a way that would honor you. We pray this in Jesus' name. Amen.

Day 3

1 The Lord *is* my shepherd;
I shall not want.
2 He makes me to lie down in green pastures;

He leads me beside the still waters.
3 He restores my soul;
"He leads me in the paths of righteousness
For His name's sake.
4 Yea, though I walk through the valley of the shadow of death,
I will fear no evil;
For You *are* with me;
Your rod and Your staff, they comfort me.

(Psalms 23.1-4)

These verses of Psalm 23 use the image of God as the Good shepherd who provides for His people. Later prophecies announce the visible coming of the Good shepherd to lead His sheep (Isaiah 40.11; Ezekiel 34.23). Jesus teaches Israel that he is the good shepherd that was to come to save his people (John 10).

"Green pastures" describe a resting place such as an oasis found in the desert. This place has "green pastures" because of the presence of water. Water is also a symbol of God's living presence and His Spirit (Psalms 1; Ezekiel 36. 25-27; John 7.37-39).

The paths that His people need to follow and where God leads them are "paths of righteousness" (Proverbs 2.20; 4.11; Isaiah 2.3).

The rod and staff of the Good shepherd are for guidance and protection (Micah 7.14; Numbers 21.18). Even in complete darkness, like in "the valley of the shadow of death" God's faithful are in safety, are guided and protected by God (Job 10.21; 28.3; Jeremiah 2.6).

The "evil" mentioned in verse 4 is the Hebrew word *ra'* which has a wide range of meanings and describes pains of life such as adversity, disease, unhappiness. The word can also be related to the Lord's prayer: "And do not lead us into temptation but deliver us from the evil one. For Yours is the kingdom and the power and the glory forever. Amen." (Matthew 6.13). All "evil" can be traced back to "the evil one" thus this prayer could refer to "evil" or "the evil one".

The presence of the Good shepherd takes away fear of adversity and pain or the fear of the evil one or even the evil he brings to the world. It is in this sense that perfect love takes away fear:

18 "There is no fear in love; but perfect love casts out fear, because fear involves torment. But he who fears has not been made perfect in love. **19** We love Him because He first loved us." (1 John 4.18,19).

Faith in Jesus takes away the fear of death:

> **13** "I will put My trust in Him. And again: 'Here am I and the children whom God has given Me.' **14** Inasmuch then as the children have partaken of flesh and blood, He Himself likewise shared in the same, that through death He might destroy him who had the power of death, that is, the devil, **15** and release those who through fear of death were all their lifetime subject to bondage." (Hebrews 2.13-15)

Prayer

Father in heaven, we praise you for your work of salvation. We thank you for our forgiveness and hope. We pray that you will help us today to live in a manner worthy of you. Please give us strength and understanding through your Holy Spirit. Be with our loved ones, our family members, that they might also receive strength from you. We pray this in Jesus' name. Amen.

Day 4

> **18** "You have ascended on high,
> You have led captivity captive;
> You have received gifts among men,
> Even *from* the rebellious,
> That the Lord God might dwell *there*.
> **19** Blessed *be* the Lord,
> *Who* daily loads us *with benefits*,
> The God of our salvation! *Selah*
> **20** Our God *is* the God of salvation;
> And to God the Lord *belong* escapes from death."
> (Psalms 68.18-20)

Commentators consider this Psalm as one of the most triumphant and descriptive of God's victories. It is significant that it is quoted by the apostle Paul in the context of teaching about the fact of Jesus' victory over death and the consequences of Jesus' resurrection.

The anointed (Messiah) of the LORD is described as one who "ascended on high" and "escapes death". As a consequence, he gave to the Church gifted individuals: apostles, prophets, evangelists, shepherds, teachers:

> **7** "But to each one of us grace was given according to the measure of Christ's gift. **8** Therefore He says:
> 'When He ascended on high,
> He led captivity captive,
> And gave gifts to men.'
>   (…)
> …for the equipping of the saints for the work of ministry, for the edifying of the body of Christ, **13** till we all come to the unity of the faith and of the knowledge of the Son of God, to a perfect man, to the measure of the stature of the fullness of Christ;" (Ephesians 4.7,8,12,13)

Psalms 68 is prophetical about Jesus' resurrection and ascension. It is also prophetical about the continuation of Jesus' work through apostles and other teachers. Foremost in the teaching given to the Church by the Lord is the witness and teaching of the apostles — through their witness and inspired teachings, they laid the foundation of the Church:

> **19** "Now, therefore, you are no longer strangers and foreigners, but fellow citizens with the saints and members of the household of God, **20** having been built on the foundation of the apostles and prophets, Jesus Christ Himself being the chief corner*stone,* **21** in whom the whole building, being fitted together, grows into a holy temple in the Lord, **22** in whom you also are being built together for a dwelling place of God in the Spirit." (Ephesians 2.19-22)

Some have taught that "apostles" and "prophets" (inspired with new revelations) must continue for the Church to be able to grow in the knowledge of God. However, there are not today inspired teachers in the Church, no new revelations given to the Church beyond what we can read in the New Testament which contains the perfect will of God for the Church:

> **3** "Beloved, while I was very diligent to write to you concerning our common salvation, I found it necessary to write to you exhorting you to contend earnestly for the faith which was once for all delivered to the saints. **4** For certain men have crept in unnoticed, who long ago were marked out for this condemnation, ungodly men, who turn the grace of our God into lewdness and deny the only Lord God and our Lord Jesus Christ." (Jude 1.3,4)

Prayer

We thank you, God and Father, for the eternal life you have given us through Jesus the Messiah. We thank you for his faithfulness and victory over death, and for the promise of life through Him. We also thank you for the teachings you have provided to the Church through inspired apostles and prophets and through evangelists and teachers. We pray for faithfulness to these teachings until you come for the judgment and the resurrection. This we pray in Jesus' name. Amen.

Day 5

> **1** "Bow down Your ear, O Lord, hear me;
> For I *am* poor and needy.
> **2** Preserve my life, for I *am* holy;
> You are my God;
> Save Your servant who trusts in You!
> **3** Be merciful to me, O Lord,
> For I cry to You all day long.
> **4** Rejoice the soul of Your servant,
> For to You, O Lord, I lift up my soul.
> **5** For You, Lord, *are* good, and ready to forgive,
> And abundant in mercy to all those who call upon You."
>   (Psalms 86.1-5)

Can the faithful really pray to God and say, "Preserve my life, for I am holy; You are my God"?

Is it not true that death looms over every human being?

This Psalm is also about the "mob of violent men" who want to kill God's anointed (v.14) and how God delivered his servant: "And you have delivered my soul from the depths of Sheol" (v.13 and Psalm 16.9-11 and Acts 2.25-32 see Hebrews 5.5-7).

The Lord Jesus himself taught his disciples that everything in the Old Testament Scriptures pointed to his life and work:

> **44** Then He said to them, 'These *are* the words which I spoke to you while I was still with you, that all things must be fulfilled which were written in the Law of Moses and *the* Prophets and *the* Psalms concerning Me.' **45** And He opened their understanding, that they might comprehend the Scriptures." (Luke 24.44,45)

Let Us Come Before His Presence

The victory over death and final resurrection are also promised to those who believe in Christ, who belong to the Christ and have been raised with Him:

4 "But God, who is rich in mercy, because of His great love with which He loved us, **5** even when we were dead in trespasses, made us alive together with Christ (by grace you have been saved), **6** and raised *us* up together, and made *us* sit together in the heavenly *places* in Christ Jesus, **7** that in the ages to come He might show the exceeding riches of His grace in *His* kindness toward us in Christ Jesus." (Ephesians 2.4-7)

11 "In Him also we have obtained an inheritance, being predestined according to the purpose of Him who works all things according to the counsel of His will, **12** that we who first trusted in Christ should be to the praise of His glory." (Ephesians 1.11,12)

Prayer

We praise you Father for the grace we have received in Christ. We praise you for the victory over death now and forever we have received in Christ. Give us today the wisdom we need to follow you will, to love you and to love our neighbor. Be Lord with our brethren throughout the world and in our own congregation. Bless them with your grace and peace. We pray this in Jesus' name. Amen.

Day 6

1 "I love the Lord, because He has heard
My voice *and* my supplications.
2 Because He has inclined His ear to me,
Therefore I will call *upon Him* as long as I live.
3 The pains of death surrounded me,
And the pangs of Sheol laid hold of me;
I found trouble and sorrow.
4 Then I called upon the name of the Lord:
'O Lord, I implore You, deliver my soul!'
5 Gracious *is* the Lord, and righteous;
Yes, our God *is* merciful.
6 The Lord preserves the simple;
I was brought low, and He saved me.

7 Return to your rest, O my soul,
For the Lord has dealt bountifully with you.
8 For You have delivered my soul from death,
My eyes from tears,
And my feet from falling."
   (Psalms 116.1-8)

This Psalm is about an individual; the words "I", "me" and "my" occur thirty-three times in the Psalm. This Psalm fits many of the messianic texts of the Psalms and the Old Testament, which describe the victory of the Messiah over death (Psalms 16 and 22; Isaiah 53). This Psalm is also a comfort for all who are facing illness or imminent death. However, this comfort cannot be dissociated from the work of God's anointed, the Messiah.

When death is imminent or has happened, this Psalm teaches an important truth about what death means for the faithful: "Precious in the sight of the Lord *is* the death of His saints." (v.15). The word precious used here (*yaqar*) can be translated "costly", "rare", "splendid" ; see Psalms 72.14; 1 Kings 5.17 and 7.9-11. Most commentators understand that God will not easily suffer his saints to perish; the cost of their death is too great.

It is not merely the death of His saints that are precious, it is the saints themselves who are precious in God's sight. He cherishes His saints and cares about them at all times:

"Fear not, for I *am* with you;
Be not dismayed, for I *am* your God.
I will strengthen you,
Yes, I will help you,
I will uphold you with My righteous right hand." (Isaiah 41.10)

"For I, the Lord your God, will hold your right hand,
Saying to you, 'Fear not, I will help you.'" (Isaiah 41.13)

"When you pass through the waters, I *will be* with you;
And through the rivers, they shall not overflow you.
When you walk through the fire, you shall not be burned,
Nor shall the flame scorch you." (Isaiah 43.2)

6 "Therefore, humble yourselves under the mighty hand of
God, that He may exalt you in due time, **7** casting all your care
upon Him, for He cares for you." (1 Peter 5.6,7)

Let Us Come Before His Presence

Prayer

Our Lord and Father, we know you are the living God, the God who created the world and raises the dead. We come to you trusting your Word of promise when it comes to death. You have given us life in Jesus your son and will keep us alive in him. We cast our cares upon you because we know you care for us. We pray this in Jesus' name. Amen.

Day 7

> **11** "In God I have put my trust;
> I will not be afraid.
> What can man do to me?
> **12** Vows *made* to You *are binding* upon me, O God;
> I will render praises to You,
> **13** For You have delivered my soul from death.
> *Have You* not *kept* my feet from falling,
> That I may walk before God
> In the light of the living?"
>   (Psalms 56.11-13)

In verse 8 of this Psalm the writer confesses that the LORD already knows the number of his tears, just as He knows the number of his days (see Psalms 139.6):

> "You number my wanderings;
> Put my tears into Your bottle;
> *Are they* not in Your book?" (v.8)

Jesus reminded us that God even numbers each hair on our head (Matthew 10.30)!

God, who heals the brokenhearted and binds their wounds, is the one who counts the number of the stars:

> **3** "He heals the brokenhearted
> And binds up their wounds.
> **4** He counts the number of the stars;
> He calls them all by name." (Psalms 147.3,4)

According to Psalms 139.1-12, the LORD is involved in the "details" of our lives. He never lets us out of his sight. His fatherly hand guides every one of our moves. He is never limited or surprised by our circumstances.

Such a knowledge of God's power — knowledge and care towards us — helps us confess, "I will not be afraid. What can man do to me?" (v.11).

Men tried to kill the Messiah because he told them the truth (John 8.40). But Jesus' message was about life even when his adversaries did not understand the truth he taught:

> **49** "Jesus answered, 'I do not have a demon; but I honor My Father and you dishonor Me. **50** And I do not seek My *own* glory; there is One who seeks and judges. **51** Most assuredly, I say to you, if anyone keeps My word, he shall never see death.' **52** Then the Jews said to Him, 'Now we know that You have a demon! Abraham is dead, and the prophets; and You say, 'If anyone keeps My word, he shall never taste death.' **53** Are You greater than our father Abraham, who is dead? And the prophets are dead. Who do You make Yourself out to be?'" (John 8.49-53)

It is to religious leaders that Jesus also said,

> **39** You search the Scriptures, for in them you think you have eternal life; and these are they which testify of Me. **40** But you are not willing to come to Me that you may have life." (John 5.39,40)

Prayer

Our Lord and Father, we praise you for your perfect goodness and holiness. We praise you for the plan you had to bring us forgiveness and salvation. We know we do not deserve your salvation, that it is a gift from you. Help us Lord to live grateful lives and to have thankful hearts today. Help us to be forgiving to those we encounter today. Bless us through your Holy Spirit. We pray this in Jesus' name. Amen.

Week 31: Anguish

Day 1

> **4** "One *thing* I have desired of the Lord,
> That will I seek:
> That I may dwell in the house of the Lord
> All the days of my life,
> To behold the beauty of the Lord,
> And to inquire in His temple.
> **5** For in the time of trouble
> He shall hide me in His pavilion;
> In the secret place of His tabernacle
> He shall hide me;
> He shall set me high upon a rock."
> (Psalms 27.1-5)

"In time of trouble" describes the outward forces that shake us, as well as the emotions that accompany this "shaking". The word trouble (*raah*) is used many times in the Old Testament, and found for the first time in Genesis 2.9 about the "tree of knowledge of good and evil". We often take the word evil in its moral sense as describing what is opposite to good. However, the word has also the broader meaning of what is adverse, unpleasant, painful. The "knowledge of good and evil" can also refer to the intimate and personal experience of adversity and pain (thus death) that will come through the eating of the tree.

In the Genesis 2 account the man and the woman are taken out of God's presence, away from the tree of life and will endure adversity, pain and death. In this Psalm, it is the return to the presence of God, to His house or tabernacle, that provides protection from "evil". We are here reminded of the Lord's prayer about deliverance from evil or "the evil one": "And do not lead us into temptation but deliver us from the evil one. For Yours is the kingdom and the power and the glory forever. Amen." (Matthew 6.13)

The LORD who is "our Father" takes care of those who take refuge in Him. When all seems lost, the LORD gives courage and promises to take care of the faithful (vv.10,14).

> **1** "Let not your heart be troubled; you believe in God, believe also in Me. **2** In My Father's house are many mansions; if *it were* not *so*, I would have told you. I go to prepare a place for you." (John 14.1,2)

There is no safety on earth that can be compared with the safety found "in the LORD". Obstacles and opposition may happen, as well as the threat of death, but Jesus's words are true in every trouble:

> **27** "Whatever I tell you in the dark, speak in the light; and what you hear in the ear, preach on the housetops. **28** And do not fear those who kill the body but cannot kill the soul. But rather fear Him who is able to destroy both soul and body in hell." (Matthew 10.27,28)

> **6** Be anxious for nothing, but in everything by prayer and supplication, with thanksgiving, let your requests be made known to God; **7** and the peace of God, which surpasses all understanding, will guard your hearts and minds through Christ Jesus." (Philippians 4.6,7)

We live in a broken and fallen world where we experience evil and adversity. However, the Scriptures always encourage us to come to the LORD, to seek Him and to take refuge in Him whatever our circumstances.

Prayer

Our Father in heaven, we proclaim your holiness and faithfulness. We believe that in your presence, in your House, we find perfect peace and protection. We know you are a good and loving Father. We bring to you all our troubles and pains. Give us your peace and wisdom as we go through the troubles of life. In Jesus' name, we pray. Amen.

Day 2

> **4** "I sought the Lord, and He heard me,
> And delivered me from all my fears.
> **5** They looked to Him and were radiant,
> And their faces were not ashamed.
> **6** This poor man cried out, and the Lord heard *him*,
> And saved him out of all his troubles.
> **7** The angel of the Lord encamps all around those who fear

Him,
And delivers them."
(Psalms 34.4-7)

The LORD saves the faithful from "all his troubles" (*sarowtaw*) from the root word *tsarah*. This is the word closest to the modern idea of "anguish" or "anxiety". It is most of the time translated by "distress" as in Genesis 35.3; Deuteronomy 31.21; 2 Samuel 4.9.

In the book of Job, his friend Eliphaz believes that Job's troubles must come from some unfaithfulness he has shown, some sin in his life. But Eliphaz is wrong in his judgment of Job. Eliphaz as well as his friends in their diatribes against Job use this word quite often, and it is usually translated "troubles" (as in the "six troubles" of verse 19):

17 "Behold, happy *is* the man whom God corrects;
Therefore do not despise the chastening of the Almighty.
18 For He bruises, but He binds up.
He wounds, but His hands make whole.
19 He shall deliver you in six troubles,
Yes, in seven no evil shall touch you." (Job 5.9)

The book of Job is important since it teaches us that the faithfulness of the LORD or the faithfulness of an individual should not be questioned in the case of one who is in great trouble or adversity. This is even more important when we realize that the Messiah himself would go through a lot of trouble and pain in order to obey God and become the Savior (Isaiah 53 and Psalm 22). We are reminded of the remarks of those who stand at the cross and seem to think that the crucified one is not favored by God:

42 "'He rescued others,' they said, 'but he can't rescue himself!
All right, so he's the King of Israel! — well, let him come down
from the cross right now, and then we'll really believe that he
is! **43** He trusted in God; let God deliver him now, if he's that
keen on him — after all, he did say he was God's son!'"
(Matthew 27.42,43)

Jesus taught his disciples not to let their hearts be troubled and to trust him (John 14.1,2). But he did not teach that they would never endure adversity and pain. In fact, he warned them of sufferings that would come through their witness and faithfulness:

22 "And you will be hated by all for My name's sake. But he who endures to the end will be saved. **23** When they persecute you in this city, flee to another. For assuredly, I say to you, you will not have gone through the cities of Israel before the Son of Man comes." (Matthew 10.22,23)

The words of this Psalm resemble greatly the words of Eliphaz and his friends in their judgment of Job. This is an example of people who quote biblical words out of context and that do not apply to the persons or situations they are dealing with.

Prayer

Father in heaven, we believe in your promises and protection. We also believe that we are called to serve you and to be faithful even when life is difficult, when pain and grief are heavy upon us. We trust you, Father, and we trust your Word throughout every trouble we endure. Give us faith and confidence today even as we go through troubles. We pray this in Jesus' name. Amen.

Day 3

1 "I waited patiently for the Lord;
And He inclined to me,
And heard my cry.
2 He also brought me up out of a horrible pit,
Out of the miry clay,
And set my feet upon a rock,
And established my steps.
3 He has put a new song in my mouth—
Praise to our God;
Many will see *it* and fear,
And will trust in the Lord."
   (Psalms 40.1-3)

Sometimes all the faithful can do is to "wait patiently for the LORD". Sometimes the faithful can only "cry" to the LORD.

The idea that the faithful will go through life without any trouble, with everything made easy for him or her, is contrary to so much we read about in God's Word. And more importantly, it is contrary to the best example we have of a faithful human being — the Messiah:

> **41** "And He was withdrawn from them about a stone's throw, and He knelt down and prayed, **42** saying, 'Father, if it is Your will, take this cup away from Me; nevertheless not My will, but Yours, be done.' **43** Then an angel appeared to Him from heaven, strengthening Him. **44** And being in agony, He prayed more earnestly. Then His sweat became like great drops of blood falling down to the ground." (Luke 22.41-44)

> **7** "Who, in the days of His flesh, when He had offered up prayers and supplications, with vehement cries and tears to Him who was able to save Him from death, and was heard because of His godly fear, **8** though He was a Son, *yet* He learned obedience by the things which He suffered." (Hebrews 5.7,8)

Jesus went through anguish, great pain and death. He went through this when he had the power to stop it. But he knew why he had come to earth and what his mission was:

> **17** "Therefore, My Father loves Me, because I lay down My life that I may take it again. **18** No one takes it from Me, but I lay it down of Myself. I have power to lay it down, and I have power to take it again. This command I have received from My Father." (John 10.17,18)

When Saul was chosen by the Lord to be his apostle, he was told how much he would suffer for his service:

> **13** "Then Ananias answered, 'Lord, I have heard from many about this man, how much harm he has done to Your saints in Jerusalem. **14** And here he has authority from the chief priests to bind all who call on Your name.' **15** But the Lord said to him, 'Go, for he is a chosen vessel of Mine to bear My name before Gentiles, kings, and the children of Israel. **16** For I will show him how many things he must suffer for My name's sake.'" (Acts 9.13-16)

The words of "blessing" pronounced by Jesus on those who are humble and faithful do not cancel his teachings on pain or persecutions that would occur in their service:

> **11** "Blessed *are* those who are persecuted for righteousness' sake, for theirs is the kingdom of heaven. Blessed are you when they

revile and persecute you and say all kinds of evil against you falsely for My sake. **12** Rejoice and be exceedingly glad, for great *is* your reward in heaven, for so they persecuted the prophets who were before you." (Matthew 5.11,12)

A lot of anxiety can be created by those who teach that the faithful will always have it easy, that they will always be "blessed", meaning "blessed with good health and wealth" or whatever else they ask of God.

But the "blessings" of God have oftentimes nothing to do with material or physical considerations, even if in Scripture they can be equated with what is material and physical. The life and teachings of Jesus help us understand the limitations of understanding God's blessings in such a materialistic way.

Prayer

Our Father, we praise you and want to serve you this day. We believe in all your promises. We trust you today and want to be faithful in all our ways. Give us grateful hearts and joy through your Holy Spirit. May be today a light and salt to the earth. May we be a blessing to others today with your help. This we pray in Jesus' name. Amen.

Day 4

> **8** "Trust in Him at all times, you people;
> Pour out your heart before Him;
> God *is* a refuge for us. *Selah*
> **9** Surely men of low degree *are* a vapor,
> Men of high degree *are* a lie;
> If they are weighed on the scales,
> They *are* altogether *lighter* than vapor.
> **10** Do not trust in oppression,
> Nor vainly hope in robbery;
> If riches increase,
> Do not set *your* heart *on them*."
>   (Psalm 62.8-10)

A lot of anxiety in life can come from the type of society we live in. We learn about how Noah or Lot suffered from the immoral environment they were living in:

> **4** For if God did not spare the angels who sinned, but cast *them* down to hell and delivered *them* into chains of darkness, to be reserved for judgment; **5** and did not spare the ancient world, but saved Noah, *one of* eight *people*, a preacher of righteousness, bringing in the flood on the world of the ungodly; **6** and turning the cities of Sodom and Gomorrah into ashes, condemned *them* to destruction, making *them* an example to those who afterward would live ungodly; **7** and delivered righteous Lot, *who was* oppressed by the filthy conduct of the wicked **8** (for that righteous man, dwelling among them, tormented *his* righteous soul from day to day by seeing and hearing *their* lawless deeds)" (2 Peter 2.4-8)

Although both Noah and Lot lived thousands of years before Peter wrote these words, they were an example of faithful individuals who endured anxiety while living among ungodly and wicked people.

It is easy to fall into discouragement or even to stop being faithful to God when one is in such an environment. It is easy to forget that we are called to pursue holiness in every way:

> **14** "Pursue peace with all *people,* and holiness, without which no one will see the Lord: **15** looking carefully lest anyone fall short of the grace of God; lest any root of bitterness springing up cause trouble, and by this many become defiled; **16** lest there *be* any fornicator or profane person like Esau, who for one morsel of food sold his birthright. **17** For you know that afterward, when he wanted to inherit the blessing, he was rejected, for he found no place for repentance, though he sought it diligently with tears." (Hebrews 12.14-17)

One important warning in this Psalm concerns wealth: "If riches increase, do not set *your* heart *on them*." Riches in themselves are not evil, but we can be entrapped by "the love of money" or wealth, as we can be entrapped by the love of anything else in this world. It is in such a context that Jesus warned us that one cannot serve two masters ("mammon" being from the Hebrew *mihamon*, a word that conveys the idea of accumulation or hoarding which is a form of idolatry):

"No one can serve two masters; for either he will hate the one and love the other, or else he will be loyal to the one and despise the other. You cannot serve God and mammon." (Matthew 6.24; see Luke 16.9-13)

6 "Now godliness with contentment is great gain. **7** For we brought nothing into *this* world, *and it is* certain we can carry nothing out. **8** And having food and clothing, with these we shall be content. **9** But those who desire to be rich fall into temptation and a snare, and *into* many foolish and harmful lusts which drown men in destruction and perdition. **10** For the love of money is a root of all *kinds of* evil, for which some have strayed from the faith in their greediness and pierced themselves through with many sorrows." (1 Timothy 6.6-10)

Prayer

Our Father in heaven, we praise you for your holiness and perfections. We thank you for every blessing you have showered on us. Give us wisdom to know how to live among the wicked or immoral, and to know how to live when wealth increases. Keep our hearts close to you, Lord. We pray in Jesus' name. Amen.

Day 5

1 I will lift up my eyes to the hills—
From whence comes my help?
2 My help *comes* from the Lord,
Who made heaven and earth.
3 He will not allow your foot to be moved;
He who keeps you will not slumber.
4 Behold, He who keeps Israel
Shall neither slumber nor sleep.
5 The Lord *is* your keeper;
The Lord *is* your shade at your right hand.
6 The sun shall not strike you by day,
Nor the moon by night.
7 The Lord shall preserve you from all evil;
He shall preserve your soul.
8 The Lord shall preserve your going out and your coming in
From this time forth, and even forevermore."
   (Psalms 121.1-8)

This is a beautiful Psalm expressing complete trust in God and His care for the faithful. The faith that saves and that God desires from us is rooted in the biblical truths found first in Genesis 1 and 2 and which have to do with the creation.

It is also with a reference to creation that the book of Hebrews defines true faith:

> **1** "Now faith is the substance of things hoped for,
> the evidence of things not seen. **2** For by it the elders obtained
> a *good* testimony. **3** By faith we understand that the worlds were
> framed by the word of God, so that the things which are seen
> were not made of things which are visible." (Hebrews 11.1-3)

God's Creation in six days is a fundamental biblical truth and there are numerous references to the creation account throughout the Scriptures: Exodus 20.11; 2 Kings 19.15; Nehemiah 9.6; Psalms 8.3; 134.3; Proverbs 3.19; Isaiah 37.16; John 1.1-14; Romans 8.21.

God does not sleep or slumber, is a comforting truth. God even works on our behalf while we sleep. We don't have to believe that all depends on us. We can rest, fully assured that God takes care of the world and of us:

> **26** "And He said, "The kingdom of God is as if a man
> should scatter seed on the ground, **27** and should sleep by night
> and rise by day, and the seed should sprout and grow, he himself
> does not know how." (Mark 4.26,27)

The prayer of faith of the faithful is that the LORD preserves him from evil. This fundamental trust in God's protection from evil should not lead us to neglect praying as Jesus taught us:

> "And do not lead us into temptation,
> But deliver us from the evil one.
> For Yours is the kingdom and the power and the glory forever.
> Amen." (Matthew 6.13)

The story of Job teaches us how Satan attacked the righteous Job. The story shows us how Job remained faithful throughout his ordeal. This story is important in order to understand the world we live in. It is a broken and fallen world, a world with evil and in which we can be tested and tempted. It is also a world in which we can trust God to take care of us. The question has always been to reconcile these two seemingly contradictory realities. However, we are called to live in the tension between these two truths: first, the truth that we live in a broken world, a world of sin; secondly, the truth that God is still the sovereign Lord whose will dominates all that happens and whose will ends up giving victory and life to those who trust in Him: "For Yours is the kingdom and the power and the glory forever."

The life of Job, but also the life of Jesus, demonstrate the reality of these two truths. The final victory of God is demonstrated in the resurrection of Jesus. If there is no resurrection, the Christian faith is in vain and there is no hope for the believer:

> **12** "Now if Christ is preached that He has been raised from the dead, how do some among you say that there is no resurrection of the dead? **13** But if there is no resurrection of the dead, then Christ is not risen. **14** And if Christ is not risen, then our preaching *is* empty and your faith *is* also empty." (1 Corinthians 15.12-14)

Prayer

Dear Lord, we come to you with faith, asking you to keep is today. We pray especially that you will keep our hearts faithful to you, faithful to your Word. Keep also our loved ones, keep and bless our co-workers and everyone we meet today. May you bless them all. We pray this in Jesus' name. Amen.

Day 6

> **14** "The Lord *is* my strength and song,
> And He has become my salvation.
> **15** The voice of rejoicing and salvation
> *Is* in the tents of the righteous;
> The right hand of the Lord does valiantly.
> **16** The right hand of the Lord is exalted;
> The right hand of the Lord does valiantly.
> **17** I shall not die, but live,
> And declare the works of the Lord.
> **18** The Lord has chastened me severely,
> But He has not given me over to death."
>   (Psalms 118.14-18)

This Psalm describes someone who has endured affliction and has been delivered by the LORD: "I called on the LORD in distress" (v.5); "All nations surrounded me" (v.10); "You pushed me violently" (v.10); "The stone which the builders rejected" (v.22).

Verse 22 of this Psalm is quoted in Matthew, Mark, Luke, Acts and by Peter which makes it one of the most often quoted Old Testament Scripture (Matthew 21.42; Mark 12.10; Luke 20.17; Acts 4.11; 1 Peter 2.7):

> **22** "The stone *which* the builders rejected
> Has become the chief cornerstone.
> **23** This was the Lord's doing;
> It *is* marvelous in our eyes." (Psalms 118.22,23)

As we read this Psalm, it becomes clear that it is prophetical about the Messiah, about Jesus.

> "Jesus said to them, 'Have you never read in the Scriptures: 'The stone which the builders rejected has become the chief cornerstone. This was the Lord's doing, and it is marvelous in our eyes'?" (Matthew 21.42)

The Gospel of Matthew teaches us that Jesus was talking about the chief priests and Pharisees :

> **45** "Now when the chief priests and Pharisees heard His parables, they perceived that He was speaking of them. **46** But when they sought to lay hands on Him, they feared the multitudes, because they took Him for a prophet." (Matthew 21.45,46)

In this Psalm, affliction and pain are the lot of the faithful because of "those who hate" him (v.7). The Psalm describes strong opposition to "the tents of the righteous". The rejection of the Messiah was the result of unrighteousness, disobedience to God, which always produce oppression.

A secular society, devoid of the biblical worldview and biblical principles, will always become oppressive. And this oppression can weigh heavily on the back of the righteous and all those who seek to please God.

The promise of God in this Psalm, demonstrated in the life of Christ, is mentioned in the first and last verses: "For his mercy endures forever" (vv.1,29).

Prayer

Father in heaven, we proclaim your mercy. We understand in your Word that to live for you faithfully is a struggle with sin and the evil one. We continue to ask you to deliver us from the evil one. We continue to come to you for guidance and strength in the midst of adversity. We thank you, Father, for your enduring mercy. Our prayer is in Jesus' name. Amen.

Day 7

> **1** "Hear my prayer, O Lord,
> And let my cry come to You.
> **2** Do not hide Your face from me in the day of my trouble;
> Incline Your ear to me;
> In the day that I call, answer me speedily.
> **3** For my days are consumed like smoke,
> And my bones are burned like a hearth.
> **4** My heart is stricken and withered like grass,
> So that I forget to eat my bread."
> (Psalms 102.1-4)

This Psalm describes the afflictions of the faithful (vv.1-11), faith in God who gives hope (vv.12-22) and faith in God who does not change (vv.23-28).

Out of all this pain, God intends to bring about "a people yet to be created" that will praise His name (v.18). As we read this Psalm we also discover that the "people yet to be created" is made up of "the peoples gathered together": "When the peoples are gathered together, And the kingdoms, to serve the Lord." (v.22)

The pains of the righteous are always for a holy and glorious purpose. It is often through those pains that people are brought closer to God and purified to serve Him:

> **6** "In this you greatly rejoice, though now for a little while, if need be, you have been grieved by various trials, **7** that the genuineness of your faith, *being* much more precious than gold that perishes, though it is tested by fire, may be found to praise, honor, and glory at the revelation of Jesus Christ," (1 Peter 1.6,7)

> **22** Since you have purified your souls in obeying the truth through the Spirit in sincere love of the brethren, love one another fervently with a pure heart, **23** having been born again, not of corruptible seed but incorruptible, through the word of God which lives and abides forever," (1 Peter 1.22,23)

> **9** "But you *are* a chosen generation, a royal priesthood, a holy nation, His own special people, that you may proclaim the prais-

es of Him who called you out of darkness into His marvelous light; **10** who once *were* not a people but *are* now the people of God, who had not obtained mercy but now have obtained mercy." (1 Peter 2.9,10)

The Psalm does not deny the reality of pain and oppression even for the righteous. But it affirms that there is a hope, and that God will be faithful to all his promises. This is the point of verse 26-28 of this Psalm, quoted in the book of Hebrews:

> **10** "You, Lord, in the beginning laid the foundation of the earth,
> And the heavens are the work of Your hands.
> **11** They will perish, but You remain;
> And they will all grow old like a garment;
> **12** Like a cloak You will fold them up,
> And they will be changed.
> But You are the same,
> And Your years will not fail." (Hebrews 1.10-12)

Prayer

Our Father in heaven, we praise your holiness and perfection. We believe that you are always true to your Word. We pray for ourselves and for our loved ones and brothers and sisters. Strengthen our faith today. Protect us and keep our hearts close to your will. We pray in Jesus' name. Amen.

Week 32: Repentance

Day 1

> **1** "Have mercy upon me, O God,
> According to Your lovingkindness;
> According to the multitude of Your tender mercies,
> Blot out my transgressions.
> **2** Wash me thoroughly from my iniquity,
> And cleanse me from my sin."
>   (Psalms 51,1,2)

As we see in this Psalm, confession of sins whether under the Old covenant or the New Covenant is always directed to God (Psalms 32.5; Mark 11.25; 1 John 1.9).

The prayer of David in Psalms 51 is astonishing when one understands the attitude and behavior of the great majority of kings or rulers at the time of David. The odds of such a prophet as Nathan of losing his head were about one to a million had he confronted any other king or ruler in charge.

Psalms 51 is not just a prayer of repentance; it is a bright light shining in a densely dark world of ancient monarchs. It is a prefiguration of the importance in God's sight of change of heart, true repentance, including from the influential and the powerful such as described by Mary in her song:

> **51** "He has shown strength with His arm;
> He has scattered *the* proud in the imagination of their hearts.
> **52** He has put down the mighty from *their* thrones,
> And exalted *the* lowly." (Luke 1.51,52)

There is this strange belief held by many that true humility and repentance are only for the ignorant, lowly, or poor of the earth. It is a mistake to think that just because Jesus taught humility and poverty of spirit these spiritual qualities are not for the powerful and influential of the world. Jesus' teachings in those areas are not just descriptive, they are prescriptive. In order to be a disciple of Jesus and to inherit eternal life every person, whatever his or her position on earth, needs to become humble like a child:

> **2** "Then Jesus called a little child to Him, set him in the midst of them, **3** and said, 'Assuredly, I say to you, unless you are converted and become as little children, you will by no means enter the kingdom of heaven. **4** Therefore whoever humbles himself as this little child is the greatest in the kingdom of heaven. **5** Whoever receives one little child like this in My name receives Me.'"
> (Matthew 18.2-5)

To think that the rulers of the world are not called to an attitude of service and graciousness by Jesus just because they are in high positions is a great mistake. It is often the consequence of not seeing Jesus in his present kingship and not understanding the royal authority of his teachings (Matthew 7.28,29; Hebrews 1.8; Matthew 28.18; Ephesians 1.22,23; Revelation 15.3).

So, let us pray daily for kings and rulers "that we may live a quiet and peaceful life in all godliness and reverence, for this is good and acceptable in the sight of God our savior, who desires all men to be saved and to come to the knowledge of the truth." (1 Timothy 2.2-4)

Prayer

We thank you, Lord, for the kingship of Jesus, his present and future rule over the world. We thank you that we have a righteous and perfect king over His kingdom. We pray for rulers of this world. We pray for our nation and every person in authority. May your Gospel touch the hearts of all men. This we pray in Jesus' name. Amen.

Day 2

> **3** For I acknowledge my transgressions,
> And my sin *is* always before me.
> **4** Against You, You only, have I sinned,
> And done *this* evil in Your sight—
> That You may be found just when You speak,
> *And* blameless when You judge.
>   (Psalms 51.3,4)

True repentance honors God and gives glory to Him and to His holiness. When we confess what is evil, we are also declaring what is righteous and holy.

The word "sin" is used five times in Psalms 51 along other words such as "transgression" or "evil". True repentance is to acknowledge the reality of "sin". God is a "judge" and also the supreme lawgiver.

We know right from wrong because of God's revelation of a moral order (Romans 7.7-9) David's confession of sin is not based on a human opinion or philosophy, or on his own feelings. They are based on God having revealed already in the ten commandments that one should not commit adultery and should not murder, the two sins of David (Exodus 20.1-17).

Rulers and kings were often lawgivers and judges. But what we learn from the Bible is that above these human "lawgivers" is the supreme lawgiver and judge who is himself above these human lawgivers. Rulers and kings also will give account to God: "And I saw the dead, small and great, standing before God, and books were opened. And another book was opened, which is *the Book* of Life. And the dead were judged according to their works, by the things which were written in the books." (Revelation 20.12).

All of human history tends towards the final judgment of God, the time when God manifests fully his truth and holiness. As God's judgments are executed the perfect law of God, his perfect judgment, stand out before all to be acknowledged.

> **9** "Therefore, God also has highly exalted Him and given Him the name which is above every name, **10** that at the name of Jesus every knee should bow, of those in heaven, and of those on earth, and of those under the earth, **11** and *that* every tongue should confess that Jesus Christ *is* Lord, to the glory of God the Father." (Philippians 2.9–11)

> "*As* I live, says the Lord,
> Every knee shall bow to Me,
> And every tongue shall confess to God." (Philippians 2.10)

> **12** "So then, each of us shall give account of himself to God. **13** Therefore let us not judge one another anymore, but rather resolve this, not to put a stumbling block or a cause to fall in *our* brother's way." (Romans 14.12,13)

Prayer

Father in heaven we praise you for your holiness and love. We praise you for the truth of your word and your law. We come to you confessing our sins and asking for your forgiveness through Jesus our High priest. Dear God, deliver us from evil and lead us not into temptation. We pray this in the name of our Lord Jesus. Amen.

Day 3

> **5** "Behold, I was brought forth in iniquity,
> And in sin my mother conceived me.
> **6** Behold, You desire truth in the inward parts,
> And in the hidden *part* You will make me to know wisdom.
> **7** Purge me with hyssop, and I shall be clean;
> Wash me, and I shall be whiter than snow.
> **8** Make me hear joy and gladness,
> *That* the bones You have broken may rejoice.
> **9** Hide Your face from my sins,
> And blot out all my iniquities.
> (Psalms 51.5-9)

The sinful condition of human beings cannot be separated from the sinful condition of parents and this goes all the way back to Adam. This is also the thought expressed by the apostle Paul in Romans:

> **12** "Therefore, just as through one man, sin entered the world, and death through sin, and thus death spread to all men, because all sinned— **13** For until the law sin was in the world, but sin is not imputed when there is no law. **14** Nevertheless death reigned from Adam to Moses, even over those who had not sinned according to the likeness of the transgression of Adam, who is a type of Him who was to come." (Romans 5.12-14)

Thus, by one's man offense death reigned over all mankind:

> "For if by the one man's offense death reigned through the one, much more those who receive abundance of grace and of the gift of righteousness will reign in life through the One, Jesus Christ." (Romans 5.17)

We should take note of the fact that "death spread to all men" "because all sinned". This is also taught in Ephesians:

> **1** "And you *He made alive,* who were dead in trespasses and sins, **2** in which you once walked according to the course of this world, according to the prince of the power of the air, the spirit who now works in the sons of disobedience, **3** among whom also we all once conducted ourselves in the lusts of our flesh, fulfilling the desires of the flesh and of the mind, and were by nature children of wrath, just as the others." (Ephesians 2.1-3)

Forgiveness of sins and reconciliation with God as described in Psalms 51 are provided by God through the Lord Jesus whose death and resurrection are the means of justification before God:

> **1** "Therefore, having been justified by faith, we have peace with God through our Lord Jesus Christ, **2** through whom also we have access by faith into this grace in which we stand, and rejoice in hope of the glory of God." (Romans 5.1,2).

The efficacy of Jesus' sacrificial death extends even to those like David who lived under the old covenant. Jesus is the "world's sin offering" (1 John 2.2) which is not limited by time and space. Thus, David was forgiven by God (2 Samuel 12.13; Psalm 25.13; 32). David wrote by inspiration, "As far as the east is from the west, so far has He removed our transgressions from us" (103:12).

The "washing of sins" is through the blood of Jesus and not through any other means. The water of baptism does not have the power to wash sins. There is no such thing as "holy water" or "consecrated water" that can purify one from sins. However, in baptism the repentant believer comes into contact with the death and resurrection of Jesus and with his blood as taught throughout the New Testament (Romans 6.1-6; Colossians 2.11-15).

Prayer

We thank you, Father, for the sacrifice of Jesus our Lord. We thank you for his blood given for the sins of the world and for our sins. We pray for those we love and cherish and who have not faith in you today, who have not come to the point of repentance. May you Lord touch their hearts, and may they come to faith and repentance and receive forgiveness. We pray this in the name of Jesus. Amen.

Day 4

> **10** Create in me a clean heart, O God,
> And renew a steadfast spirit within me.
> **11** Do not cast me away from Your presence,
> And do not take Your Holy Spirit from me.
> (Psalms 51.10,11)

We find here mention of the creative power of God in creating a clean heart. But we also find a request made by a human being. The creative power of God to create a new heart only becomes active when one is seeking God. And true faith, as well as true repentance, are the work of the Word of God received in the heart (as in the Genesis 1 account, creation occurs as the result of God's word).

God brings about a new birth and makes people "a new creation" (2 Corinthians 5.17) if they believe in Jesus (John 3.16) and are born "of water and the Spirit" (John 3.1-5). Whether in the Old Testament or the New Testament God requires faith and "faith comes from hearing" His word:

> **14** "How then shall they call on Him in whom they have not believed? And how shall they believe in Him of whom they have not heard? And how shall they hear without a preacher? **15** And how shall they preach unless they are sent? As it is written: 'How beautiful are the feet of those who preach the gospel of peace, who bring glad tidings of good things!'" (Romans 10.14-15)
>
> "So, then faith *comes* by hearing, and hearing by the word of God." (Romans 10.17)

Ultimately, it is God who opens the heart, it is God who brings about repentance (see Acts 16.14). But God has chosen to do this through the work of Jesus on the cross and through the preaching or proclamation of that work:

> **1** "Moreover, brethren, I declare to you the gospel which I preached to you, which also you received and in which you stand, **2** by which also you are saved, if you hold fast that word which I preached to you—unless you believed in vain." (1 Corinthians 15.1,2)

The "new birth" is brought about by the seed of the Gospel which is proclaimed:

22 "Since you have purified your souls in obeying the truth through the Spirit in sincere love of the brethren, love one another fervently with a pure heart, **23** having been born again, not of corruptible seed but incorruptible, through the word of God which lives and abides forever" (1 Peter 1.22,23)

The Gospel is the proclamation of "the kindness and the love of God our Savior toward man" (Titus 3.4) manifested in Jesus Christ and which produces a "rebirth" (regeneration; Titus 3.5-7). "Of His own will He brought us forth by the word of truth, that we might be a kind of first fruits of His creatures." (James 1.18)

Prayer

Father in heaven we thank you for the Gospel. We thank you for Jesus' life, death and resurrection. We believe your Son is the lamb of God that takes away the sin of the world. Bless our day and our service to you. Bless our loved ones, friends and neighbors. May we grow in faith, hope and love through your Holy Spirit. This we pray in the name of Jesus our Lord. Amen.

Day 5

12 "Restore to me the joy of Your salvation,
And uphold me *by Your* generous Spirit.
13 *Then* I will teach transgressors Your ways,
And sinners shall be converted to You."
    (Psalms 51.12,13)

Joy is the fruit of true faith and repentance. Joy was a characteristic of the early Church in the book of Acts (Acts 2.25-28; 8.39; 13.52).

Another fruit is that the sinner can become a teacher to others because he has been forgiven.

The ultimate point of forgiveness is not just to receive forgiveness and rejoice over it. It is to become a servant of God in proclaiming this good news to the world.

Quite often in the Scriptures the question is asked "What must I do" (Luke 18.18; Mark 10.17; Matthew 19.16; Acts 2.37; Acts 16.30). When such a question is asked God never answers saying "There is nothing you can do!" This is a strange answer which sometimes is given by some today, but it is not found in the Scriptures.

God provides instructions to those who out of a sincere heart ask the question "What must I do to be saved?" However, the question is always the result of a conviction of sin which itself comes through teaching or preaching.

John the Baptist and Jesus came "preaching repentance":

> **4** "John came baptizing in the wilderness and preaching a baptism of repentance for the remission of sins. **5** Then all the land of Judea, and those from Jerusalem, went out to him and were all baptized by him in the Jordan River, confessing their sins." (Mark 1.4,5)

> **14** "Now after John was put in prison, Jesus came to Galilee, preaching the gospel of the kingdom of God, **15** and saying, 'The time is fulfilled, and the kingdom of God is at hand. Repent, and believe in the gospel.'" (Mark 1.14,15)

> "I tell you, no; but unless you repent you will all likewise perish." (Luke 13.3)

In Acts the question "what must we do" is also the result of Peter's preaching of the Gospel:

> "Now when they heard *this,* they were cut to the heart, and said to Peter and the rest of the apostles, 'Men *and* brethren, what shall we do?'" (Acts 2.37)

In verse 13 of Psalm 51 the verb translated "shall be converted" is the Hebrew *shub* meaning to turn back or to return. To "convert" is not to change religion, to attend another Church or even to change a belief but is to turn back or return to God. It has to do with coming into a new and personal relationship with God.

> **6** "And you became followers of us and of the Lord, having received the word in much affliction, with joy of the Holy Spirit, **7** so that you became examples to all in Macedonia and Achaia who believe. **8** For from you the word of the Lord has sounded forth, not only in Macedonia and Achaia, but also in every place. Your faith toward God has gone out, so that we do not need to say anything. **9** For they themselves declare concerning us what manner of entry we had to you, and how you turned to God from idols to serve the living and true God, **10** and to wait for His Son from heaven, whom He raised from the dead, *even* Jesus who delivers us from the wrath to come." (1 Thessalonians 1.6-10)

Prayer

Father in heaven, we thank you for the joy of salvation. We pray that we can rejoice today in this salvation through your Holy Spirit. We pray that we can show this joy of salvation at all times and in all circumstances. Give us wisdom today as we serve you and our fellow human beings. In Jesus' name we pray. Amen.

Day 6

> **15** O Lord open my lips,
> And my mouth shall show forth Your praise.
> **16** For You do not desire sacrifice, or else I would give *it;*
> You do not delight in burnt offering.
> **17** The sacrifices of God *are* a broken spirit,
> A broken and a contrite heart—
> These, O God, You will not despise.
>   (Psalms 51.15-17)

Repentance and confession of sins result in God's forgiveness. This forgiveness of sins is foundational to the praises we offer the Lord. We praise God for his grace and love, not for our own goodness or our achievements.

The disciples of Jesus who had been sent on a mission returned rejoicing over the things they had accomplished. But Jesus taught them, saying:

> **17** "Then the seventy returned with joy, saying, 'Lord, even the demons are subject to us in Your name.' **18** And He said to them, 'I saw Satan fall like lightning from heaven. **19** Behold, I give you the authority to trample on serpents and scorpions, and over all the power of the enemy, and nothing shall by any means hurt you. **20** Nevertheless do not rejoice in this, that the spirits are subject to you, but rather rejoice because your names are written in heaven.'" (Luke 10.17-20)

> **9** "But you *are* a chosen generation, a royal priesthood, a holy nation, His own special people, that you may proclaim the praises of Him who called you out of darkness into His marvelous light; **10** who once *were* not a people but *are* now the people of God, who had not obtained mercy but now have obtained mercy." (1 Peter 2.9,10)

13 "Therefore, let us go forth to Him, outside the camp, bearing His reproach. **14** For here we have no continuing city, but we seek the one to come. **15** Therefore by Him let us continually offer the forget to do good and to share, for with such sacrifices God is well pleased." (Hebrews 13.13-16)

Prayer

Father in heaven we praise you for Jesus your Son. We praise you for your wonderful gift of the Holy Spirit. May we seek you today and grow in our gratefulness and appreciation for your salvation and the hope of eternal life. We pray for each person we meet that we might be able to demonstrate the joy of the Gospel to them through our words and actions. We pray this in the name of Jesus. Amen.

Day 7

18 Do good in Your good pleasure to Zion;
Build the walls of Jerusalem.
19 Then You shall be pleased with the sacrifices of righteousness,
With burnt offering and whole burnt offering;
Then they shall offer bulls on Your altar.
   (Psalms 51.18,19)

This Psalm applies to David who was then in the act of building the wall around Jerusalem which was in fact finished by Solomon (1 Kings 3.1).

Building or working for the Lord can only do good as we are in a reconciled relationship with God. We need first to walk in God's ways, to live a life of repentance and holiness. Working for God must flow from this renewed life which springs from a renewed heart.

Psalm 51 is personal and teaches us how we need to repent and confess our sins. But it is also about God's work of building up his people. Personal repentance looks beyond our personal lives to God's plan for his people and for the world.

The work of edification follows the fact of reconciliation. The work of sanctification follows the fact of justification.

8 "For by grace you have been saved through faith, and that not of yourselves; *it is* the gift of God, **9** not of works, lest anyone should boast. **10** For we are His workmanship, created in Christ Jesus for good works, which God prepared beforehand that we should walk in them." (Ephesians 2.8,9)

> **4** "Coming to Him *as to* a living stone, rejected indeed by men, but chosen by God *and* precious, **5** you also, as living stones, are being built up a spiritual house, a holy priesthood, to offer up spiritual sacrifices acceptable to God through Jesus Christ." (1 Peter 2.4,5)

> "This is a faithful saying, and these things I want you to affirm constantly, that those who have believed in God should be careful to maintain good works. These things are good and profitable to men." (Titus 3.8)

The sacrifices that we are to offer to the Lord have to do with holy living:

> **1** "I beseech you therefore, brethren, by the mercies of God, that you present your bodies a living sacrifice, holy, acceptable to God, *which is* your reasonable service. **2** And do not be conformed to this world, but be transformed by the renewing of your mind, that you may prove what *is* that good and acceptable and perfect will of God." (Romans 12.1,2)

Prayer

Our prayer Lord is that today we live offer you sacrifices that are pleasing to you. May we present our bodies as a living sacrifice to you. May we offer to you the renewing of our minds and hearts. May we seek with all our heart what is acceptable and pleasing to you. We pray in Jesus' name. Amen.

Week 33: Glorifying the LORD

Day 1

> **7** "Give to the Lord, O families of the peoples,
> Give to the Lord glory and strength.
> **8** Give to the Lord the glory *due* His name;
> Bring an offering, and come into His courts.
> **9** Oh, worship the Lord in the beauty of holiness!
> Tremble before Him, all the earth."
> (Psalms 96.7-9)

These verses mention the idea of giving glory to the LORD three times. In verse 7, the honor due to God is not only required of Israelites or the faithful but is required of all "the families of the peoples" — all the peoples of the earth (cf. Genesis 12.3; 22.18). This idea of all peoples over the earth giving glory to God is already mentioned in verse 3: "Declare His glory among the nations, his wonders among all peoples."

What is meant by God's "glory"? And what does it mean to "glorify" God?

In English Bibles the Hebrew word "glory" (*kavod*) is also translated by different English words such as "wealth", "splendor", "honor". The Hebrew comes from a root meaning "heavy" or "weight" very often used for those who are "honored" or who deserve honor (kings, rulers and judges). We see this for example in Exodus 14.18: "Then the Egyptians shall know that I *am* the Lord, when I have gained honor for Myself over Pharaoh, his chariots, and his horsemen."

A statement found in Psalms 95.3 concerning the rule or sovereignty of God is repeated, in fact, through Psalms 96.1-13: "For the Lord *is* the great God, and the great King above all gods."

A foundational belief concerning the LORD is that He is the creator:

> **4** "For the Lord *is* great and greatly to be praised;
> He *is* to be feared above all gods.

5 For all the gods of the peoples *are* idols,
But the Lord made the heavens." (Psalms 96.4,5)

Without a firm belief in God as the one and only creator, there is no foundation to honor God. This is the theme of Paul's first chapter to the Romans:

21 "Although they knew God, they did not glorify *Him* as God, nor were thankful, but became futile in their thoughts, and their foolish hearts were darkened. **22** Professing to be wise, they became fools, **23** and changed the glory of the incorruptible God into an image made like corruptible man—and birds and four-footed animals and creeping things." (Romans 1.21-23)

All the sins described after Romans 1.21 are the result of not glorifying God and being thankful to Him:

28 "And even as they did not like to retain God in *their* knowledge, God gave them over to a debased mind, to do those things which are not fitting; **29** being filled with all unrighteousness, sexual immorality, wickedness, covetousness, maliciousness; full of envy, murder, strife, deceit…" (Romans 1.28,29)

Thus, belief in God as the creator, honoring God and being thankful are foundational to a right relationship with God. And sinfulness is a result of this lack of honor being given to God. The LORD we must honor is also the one who will judge us:

"For He is coming, for He is coming to judge the earth.
He shall judge the world with righteousness,
And the peoples with His truth." (Psalms 96.13)

Prayer

Our Father in heaven, we praise you and glorify you for your perfect goodness and love. We pray that you continue to be with us and change our hearts today. We pray that you sanctify all our thoughts and ways this day. This we pray in the name of Jesus. Amen.

Day 2

1 "Give unto the Lord, O you mighty ones,
Give unto the Lord glory and strength.

2 Give unto the Lord the glory due to His name;
Worship the Lord in the beauty of holiness.
3 The voice of the Lord *is* over the waters;
The God of glory thunders;
The Lord *is* over many waters.
4 The voice of the Lord *is* powerful;
The voice of the Lord *is* full of majesty."
   (Psalms 29.1-4)

This Psalm has been called the "Psalm of the seven thunders". These powerful thunderstorms are here as a reminder of the power and majesty of God. It is interesting to note that the book of Revelation refers to "seven thunders" called out by a mighty angel from heaven and signifying an intensity in God's judgments on evil in the world and on persecutors of the saints (Revelation 10.1-7).

The New King James translation "O you mighty ones" does not follow the Hebrew, which actually mentions "sons of the mighty" (see Psalms 29.1). Quite often, interpreters have understood these verses as referring to angelic beings. This is unlikely. It is preferable to understand "sons of the mighty" or "mighty ones" as referring simply to rulers and kings who are told to honor God. Note that it is David here who is telling "mighty ones" to honor God. It is doubtful that this could refer to angelic beings. More likely, David is telling the rich and powerful to honor God the true King and Ruler (compare this with the song of Mary in Luke 1.46-55 and the entire book of Revelation). In fact, verses 1 and 2 are quoted in Psalms 96.7 and addressed to humanity at large, thus to human beings and not angelic beings.

The glory and power of God are not simply felt in His creation (such as thunderstorms) but are also evident in the "beauty of holiness". We know of God's power through the creation, and we know of his holiness through his Word, especially "The Word" which is Jesus. The holiness of God describes his separation from sin, his "moral" perfection, his lack of any kind of sinfulness or evil.

God is holy also means he is "separate" or different from anyone we have every met or known. He is radically different, unusually and completely different from anyone else. It is also in that sense that Jesus is "the holy one" and fully divine (Hebrews 7,26; 1 John 3.5; 2 Corinthians 5.21; Hebrews 4.15; 1 John 3.3).

While Yahweh is called "the holy one" in the Old Testament (Leviticus 11.43-45) it is Jesus who is called this way in the New Testament (Acts 3.14; 4.27; 4.30; Mark 1.24; Luke 4.34; 1John 2.20).

God's holiness is foundational to the reason we pray to Him and no other (Matthew 6.9). The living creatures around God's throne declare His glory without ceasing (Revelation 4.8-11; see Isaiah 6.1-8).

Prayer

Dear Father in heaven, we praise you. We praise your holiness and perfection. We thank you for Jesus, your only Son who was without sin and who gave his life for us. We praise you for his resurrection and his intercession. May we today have thankful hearts and serve you in ways pleasing to you. We pray in the name of Jesus. Amen.

Day 3

> **1** "Not unto us, O Lord, not unto us,
> But to Your name give glory,
> Because of Your mercy,
> Because of Your truth.
> **2** Why should the Gentiles say,
> "So where *is* their God?"
> **3** But our God *is* in heaven;
> He does whatever He pleases.
> **4** Their idols *are* silver and gold,
> The work of men's hands."
>   (Psalms 115.1-4)

These four verses teach us three truths about giving glory to the LORD or to His name: 1. This is not to honor or give glory to Israel. 2. His glory is manifested in His mercy and His truth. 3. His glory is not understood by idolaters and not seen by the Gentiles when Israel does not give glory to Him.

The prophet Ezekiel said these words while in captivity:

> "Therefore say to the house of Israel, Thus says the Lord God:
> 'I do not do *this* for your sake, O house of Israel, but for My
> holy name's sake, which you have profaned among the nations
> wherever you went.'" (Ezekiel 36.22)

The behavior of the leaders of Israel in the time of Ezekiel did not honor the LORD or His name. These Scriptures show that the profanation of God's "name" — the word "name" stands for His person, His character and holiness — was the result of immorality and disobedience and not simply using God's name in vain as in the ten commandments (Exodus 20.7). Those who teach today that God commands everyone, even Christians, to use the name "Yahweh" or "Jehovah" while addressing God are mistaken in this regard. In fact, in the New Testament, the name "Yahweh" does not appear even once! We are to be baptized "in the name of Jesus" or "in the name of the Father, the Son and the Holy Spirit" (Acts 2.38; Matthew 28.19). It is at the "name of Jesus" that every knee will bow (Philippians 2.10).

God will, however, act in Israel's favor, and it is by this that the Gentiles will know about the LORD:

> **23** "And I will sanctify My great name, which has been profaned among the nations, which you have profaned in their midst; and the nations shall know that I *am* the Lord," says the Lord God, "when I am hallowed in you before their eyes. **24** For I will take you from among the nations, gather you out of all countries, and bring you into your own land. **25** Then I will sprinkle clean water on you, and you shall be clean; I will cleanse you from all your filthiness and from all your idols. **26** I will give you a new heart and put a new spirit within you; I will take the heart of stone out of your flesh and give you a heart of flesh." (Ezekiel 36.23-26)

As in verse 1 of this Psalm, these words of the prophet Ezekiel demonstrate the mercy of God towards His people and also the truth of His word.

Prayer

Lord, we pray to you, our creator and savior. We pray that today we will honor you and glorify you. Renew our hearts, give us a spirit of humility and repentance. Forgive us of our sins and give us wisdom to live holy lives in this world. We also pray for our loved ones and brethren, that you might do the same today in their lives. We pray this in the name of Jesus. Amen.

Day 4

> **11** "Teach me Your way, O Lord;
> I will walk in Your truth;
> Unite my heart to fear Your name.
> **12** I will praise You, O Lord my God, with all my heart,
> And I will glorify Your name forevermore.

13 For great *is* Your mercy toward me,
And You have delivered my soul from the depths of Sheol."
(Psalms 86.11-13)

These verses show the importance of receiving teachings from the LORD and show us the importance of truth. David is asking specifically to be taught God's "way". This is not theoretical or intellectual: he wants to learn how to live for God on a daily basis.

In the early years of Christianity, the Christian faith was called "the way" for the same reason. "The Way" is mentioned several times in the book of Acts (Acts 9:2; 19:9, 23; 22:4; 24:14, 22) in connection with early followers of Christ.

Knowing truth comes before fearing the name of the LORD, glorifying Him or praising Him. It is only the truth from God that can help us understand our need to fear Him and to praise Him. This needs to be kept in parallel to the words of the prophet Hosea:

"My people are destroyed for lack of knowledge.
Because you have rejected knowledge,
I also will reject you from being priest for Me;
Because you have forgotten the law of your God,
I also will forget your children." (Hosea 4.6)

Seeking to grow in the knowledge of God and his will is not a one-time thing. This is something we need on a daily basis. We are taught to grow in knowledge (Hebrews 5.12-14). We must read and study the Bible on a regular basis. It is on a daily basis that "man" shall not live by bread alone (Matthew 4.4).

Disciples of Christ need to meet on a regular basis for exhortation and encouragement (Hebrews 10.25). Christians gathered on the first day of the week to break bread, to share in the Lord's Supper (Acts 20.7; 1 Corinthians 16.1,2).

Deliverance from the place of the dead (*sheol*) is part of God's promises for His people (Psalms 56.13 1 Corinthians 15). This is also a promise accomplished for God's Messiah, who would be delivered from death (Psalms 16.9,10; Acts 2.33). The resurrection from death is foreseen in the Old Testament by such Scriptures (Psalms 107.13,14; 23.4).

In this Psalm as in many others it is the "mercy" of God which is seen as a key element in God's actions towards us. The Hebrew word for mercy is *"chesed"*. It is often translated favor, goodness, kindness or lovingkindness (Exodus 20.6; Numbers 14.19). The word does not mainly describe feelings or emotions on the part of God, but God's actions expressed in tangible ways.

A lack of mercy is very common with human beings (Proverbs 5.9; 12.10; Isaiah 13.18; 47.6; Jeremiah 6.23; 50.42). The ability to be merciful is intrinsic to the nature of God. In fact, God's mercy cannot be exhausted (2 Samuel 24.14; Lamentations 3.22). The mercy of God does not mean he is blind to sinfulness and evil and cannot bring judgment on evil. God at some point can withdraw his mercy and bring judgment (Lamentations 2.2; 2,21; Zechariah 1.12).

Prayer

Our Father in heaven, we praise you for your great mercy. We want to serve you today in a way that will honor you and that will manifest your truth. We want to continue today to learn from you and from your word. Grant us wisdom in the way we talk and act today towards people we meet. Grant also this wisdom to our friends and loved ones, to our co-workers. We pray this in the name of Jesus. Amen.

Day 5

> **1** Oh, sing to the Lord a new song!
> Sing to the Lord, all the earth.
> **2** Sing to the Lord, bless His name;
> Proclaim the good news of His salvation from day to day.
> **3** Declare His glory among the nations,
> His wonders among all peoples.
> (Psalms 96.1-3)

This Psalm is a call to worship addressed to "all the earth", "among the nations" and "among all peoples". As in a great number of Old Testament Scriptures, the LORD is sovereign over all nations because He is the creator, "For all the gods of the peoples are idols, but the LORD made the heavens" (v.5). He is also the judge of all the earth, "For He is coming, for He is coming to judge the earth. He shall judge the world with righteousness, and the peoples with His truth" (v.13).

The creation itself participates in giving glory to the LORD:

> **11** "Let the heavens rejoice, and let the earth be glad;
> Let the sea roar, and all its fullness;
> **12** Let the field be joyful, and all that *is* in it.

> Then all the trees of the woods will rejoice
> **13** before the Lord." (vv.11-13)

"Salvation" is proclaimed as "good news" in this Psalm (v.2). Salvation was intended for all nations, not only for Israel. This is the truth, the "good news", that is proclaimed both throughout the Old Testament and in the New Testament (Isaiah 56; Psalms 45.17; Jonah 3; Matthew 15.21-28; Galatians 3.25-19).

The proclamation of God's salvation to the nations and peoples of the earth is also a declaration of the glory of the LORD "among the nations". We are here reminded of the first chapter and Gospel of John which develops the theme of the manifestation of God's glory in Jesus: "And the Word became flesh and dwelt among us, and we beheld His glory, the glory as of the only begotten of the Father, full of grace and truth." (John 1.14). See especially Isaiah in 42.10; 52.7; 60.6; 66.19.

> **9** "After these things I looked, and behold, a great multitude which no one could number, of all nations, tribes, peoples, and tongues, standing before the throne and before the
> Lamb, clothed with white robes, with palm branches in their hands, **10** and crying out with a loud voice, saying, 'Salvation *belongs* to our God who sits on the throne, and to the Lamb!' **11** All the angels stood around the throne and the elders and the four living creatures, and fell on their faces before the throne and worshiped God, **12** saying: 'Amen! Blessing and glory and wisdom, Thanksgiving and honor and power and might, *Be* to our God forever and ever.' Amen." (Revelation 7.9-12)

Prayer

Our Father in heaven, we praise you for your salvation. We praise you for the giving of your only begotten Son, Jesus, who came and manifested your glory for all nations and peoples. Salvation belongs to you O LORD and also glory and wisdom. We thank you for all your blessings found in Christ Jesus. Amen.

Day 6

> **7** "Give to the Lord, O families of the peoples,
> Give to the Lord glory and strength.
> **8** Give to the Lord the glory *due* His name;
> Bring an offering, and come into His courts.
> **9** Oh, worship the Lord in the beauty of holiness!

Tremble before Him, all the earth.
10 Say among the nations, 'The Lord reigns;
The world also is firmly established,
It shall not be moved;
He shall judge the peoples righteously.'"
   (Psalms 96.7-10)

In these verses, the "families of the peoples" of the earth come into God's courts, which is the inner part of the temple where only Israelites could enter. This is announcing how the salvation of the Gentiles will allow them to come before God, in His presence:

"For from the rising of the sun, even to its going down,
My name *shall be* great among the Gentiles;
In every place incense *shall be* offered to My name,
And a pure offering;
For My name shall be great among the nations,
Says the Lord of hosts." (Malachi 1.11)

"Bring an offering" (v.8). The word for offering (*min-hah*) refers to a bloodless offering, such as a thanksgiving offering. Prophetically, the Gentiles are invited to bring sacrifices that are not blood sacrifices, since Christ will offer a sacrifice that will cover all sins (Isaiah 53). Believers in the new covenant are called "a spiritual house" and offer spiritual sacrifices acceptable to God through Christ (1 Peter 2.5).

12"Therefore, Jesus also, that He might sanctify the people with His own blood, suffered outside the gate. **13** Therefore let us go forth to Him, outside the camp, bearing His reproach. **14** For here we have no continuing city, but we seek the one to come. **15** Therefore by Him let us continually offer the sacrifice of praise to God, that is, the fruit of *our* lips, giving thanks to His name. **16** But do not forget to do good and to share, for with such sacrifices God is well pleased." (Hebrews 13.12-16)

1 "I beseech you therefore, brethren, by the mercies of God, that you present your bodies a living sacrifice, holy, acceptable to God, *which is* your reasonable service. **2** And do not be conformed to this world, but be transformed by the renewing of your mind, that you may prove what *is* that good and acceptable and perfect will of God." (Romans 12.1,2)

Prayer

We are grateful Father in heaven for the sacrifice of Jesus, for his life given for our salvation. We thank you for the forgiveness of sins. We pray that today we will offer to you our bodies as a living and holy offering to you. We pray that you will continue to transform our minds, that we can learn from you today and better understand your will. We pray this in the name of Jesus, our Lord. Amen.

Day 7

> **7** "Lift up your heads, O you gates!
> And be lifted up, you everlasting doors!
> And the King of glory shall come in.
> **8** Who *is* this King of glory?
> The Lord strong and mighty,
> "The Lord mighty in battle.
> **9** Lift up your heads, O you gates!
> Lift up, you everlasting doors!
> And the King of glory shall come in.
> **10** Who is this King of glory?
> The Lord of hosts,
> He *is* the King of glory. *Selah*"
>   (Psalms 24.7-10)

These verses of Psalms 24 describe the Lord's coming to His holy place. The "gates" and "doors" are the entrance to the temple. But this temple is the "heavenly temple" of which the earthly temple was only a shadow. The "doors" being everlasting for the everlasting king of glory.

> **3** "For every high priest is appointed to offer both gifts and sacrifices. Therefore, *it is* necessary that this One also have something to offer. **4** For if He were on earth, He would not be a priest, since there are priests who offer the gifts according to the law; **5** who serve the copy and shadow of the heavenly things, as Moses was divinely instructed when he was about to make the tabernacle. For He said, 'See *that* you make all things according to the pattern shown you on the mountain.' **6** But now He has obtained a more excellent ministry, inasmuch as He is also Mediator of a better covenant, which was established on better promises. (Hebrews 8.3-6)

This is a prophecy of the ascension of Jesus into heaven. The ascension of Jesus corresponds to his coronation and sitting at the right hand of God.

> "But from now on the Son of Man shall be seated at the right hand of the power of God." (Luke 22.69)

> "Who is to condemn? Christ Jesus is the one who died—more than that, who was raised—who is at the right hand of God, who indeed is interceding for us." (Romans 8.34)

> **1** "If then you have been raised with Christ, seek the things that are above, where Christ is, seated at the right hand of God. **2** Set your minds on things that are above, not on things that are on earth." (Colossians 3.1,2)

At his second coming, Christ will come in glory:

> "For whoever is ashamed of Me and My words, of him the Son of Man will be ashamed when He comes in His *own* glory, and *in His* Father's, and of the holy angels." (Luke 9.26)

> **26** "For what profit is it to a man if he gains the whole world, and loses his own soul? Or what will a man give in exchange for his soul? **27** For the Son of Man will come in the glory of His Father with His angels, and then He will reward each according to his works. (Matthew 16.26,27)

> **62** "And the high priest arose and said to Him, 'Do You answer nothing? What *is it* these men testify against You?' **63** But Jesus kept silent. And the high priest answered and said to Him, 'I put You under oath by the living God: Tell us if You are the Christ, the Son of God!' **64** Jesus said to him, '*It is as* you said. Nevertheless, I say to you, hereafter you will see the Son of Man sitting at the right hand of the power and coming on the clouds of heaven.'" (Matthew 26.62-64)

Prayer

We are thankful Father in heaven for the victory and reign of Jesus. We know you have given him all authority in heaven and on earth. Our prayer today is that we can be faithful to you throughout this day. Keep our hearts near to your will and give us the wisdom we need to live in this world with faithfulness. We pray to you in the name of Jesus. Amen.

Week 34: Joy

Day 1

> **1** "Praise the Lord!
> Sing to the Lord a new song,
> *And* His praise in the assembly of saints.
> **2** Let Israel rejoice in their Maker;
> Let the children of Zion be joyful in their King.
> **3** Let them praise His name with the dance;
> Let them sing praises to Him with the timbrel and harp.
> **4** For the Lord takes pleasure in His people;
> He will beautify the humble with salvation."
> (Psalms 149.1-4)

What do these verses say about joy and rejoicing? First, we understand that believers do not rejoice for the sake of rejoicing, but as a consequence of understanding who the LORD is. He is our Maker. He is our King. He takes pleasure in His people. He cares for the humble to which He offers salvation. Thus, the faithful are joyful in their Maker and King.

The verses that follow (vv.5-9) have sometimes been the subject of criticism because of the mention of "vengeance", "punishment" and even "a two-edged sword". These words seem to be inconsistent with the rejoicing in the LORD.

> **5** "Let the saints be joyful in glory;
> Let them sing aloud on their beds.
> **6** *Let* the high praises of God *be* in their mouth,
> And a two-edged sword in their hand,
> **7** To execute vengeance on the nations,
> And punishments on the peoples;
> **8** To bind their kings with chains,
> And their nobles with fetters of iron;

9 To execute on them the written judgment—
This honor have all His saints." (Psalm 149.5-9)

These verses describe the battle of a holy and righteous God against nations or individuals at war with Him. They are contrasted to the "humble" described in verse 4 who rejoice in the LORD. They also emphasize God's judgments on "kings" and "nobles" who bring pain and suffering to their peoples.

When Jesus comes into the world, his life and teachings bring hope and joy, but they also constitute a "judgment" on those who hold power over others. This is described for example in Mary's song:

51 "He has shown strength with His arm;
He has scattered *the* proud in the imagination of their hearts.
52 He has put down the mighty from *their* thrones,
And exalted *the* lowly." (Luke 1.51,52)

The Scriptures teach us to consider the holiness of God and His justice exercised against those who do evil. The words used in these verses are descriptive of the spiritual and moral battle of God against the forces of evil, against Satan himself.

There is nothing arbitrary in how God brings about "vengeance" or "punishment" and is an example for us :

19 "Beloved, do not avenge yourselves, but *rather* give place to wrath; for it is written, 'Vengeance *is* Mine, I will repay,' says the Lord. **20** Therefore 'If your enemy is hungry, feed him; If he is thirsty, give him a drink; for in so doing, you will heap coals of fire on his head.'" **21** Do not be overcome by evil, but overcome evil with good." (Romans 12.19-21)

Prayer

Our Father in heaven, we thank you for the joy you offer us through the Gospel, through Jesus your Son. We thank you for your word of promise and for your righteous judgments. So today we pray that we can bless and do good to everyone we meet. This we pray in the name of Jesus. Amen.

Day 2

1 "When the Lord brought back the captivity of Zion,
We were like those who dream.

2 Then our mouth was filled with laughter,
And our tongue with singing.
Then they said among the nations,
"The Lord has done great things for them."
3 The Lord has done great things for us,
And we are glad.
4 Bring back our captivity, O Lord,
As the streams in the South.
5 Those who sow in tears
Shall reap in joy.
6 He who continually goes forth weeping,
Bearing seed for sowing,
Shall doubtless come again with rejoicing,
Bringing his sheaves *with him*."
  (Psalms 126.1-6)

This Psalm has four parts: 1. Return from captivity (vv.1,2). A song (v.3). A prayer (v.4). A promise (vv.5,6). Joy and rejoicing are themes at the heart of this Psalm. Psalm 126 is also connected to the significance of Zion for those who rejoice — Zion being the mountain of God's choosing for His city Jerusalem. The joy that would spring from Zion would be sung "among the nations" (v.2).

The city is at the heart of the history, worship and salvation of Israel. It would be from Jerusalem revived that God's saving work would reach to the uttermost parts of the earth:

3 "For out of Zion shall go forth the law,
And the word of the Lord from Jerusalem.
4 He shall judge between the nations,
And rebuke many people" (Isaiah 2.3,4)

The centrality of Jerusalem is seen in the life and death of Jesus. It is from Jerusalem that the Gospel would be preached to the entire world (Luke 24. 46-48; Acts 1).

The joy that permeates this Psalm is not one that easily dispels the "tears" of those who sow and "continually go forth weeping". There is a sowing and there is a harvesting. Thus, the "joy" the faithful enjoys on this earth remains a joy "in hope". Hope implies that there is a greater joy in the future, that God's plan is unfolding and will unfold, and has not been completed yet.

Psalm 126 reaches back into the deliverance God has accomplished but remains focused on the future when those who have sowed with tears "doubtless" come again with rejoicing (v.6). God's former blessings are a pledge of present and future blessings. Nevertheless, the sower needs to persist in sowing if he wants to reap in joy.

> **12** "And again, Isaiah says:
> "There shall be a root of Jesse;
> And He who shall rise to reign over the Gentiles,
> In Him the Gentiles shall hope.'
> **13** Now may the God of hope fill you with all joy and peace in believing, that you may abound in hope by the power of the Holy Spirit." (Romans 15.12,13)

Prayer

Our Father in heaven, we pray that you open our hearts today to your word of hope spoken by Jesus and his apostles. Give us strength and joy in the midst of difficult labor. May we understand that our work is that of sowers and that you give the increase. We wait for the harvest with hopeful hearts. Amen.

Day 3

> **11** "But let all those rejoice who put their trust in You;
> Let them ever shout for joy, because You defend them;
> Let those also who love Your name
> Be joyful in You.
> **12** For You, O Lord, will bless the righteous;
> With favor You will surround him as *with* a shield." (Psalms 5.11,12)

These verses are the conclusion of Psalm 5 which starts as a personal prayer to God in verses 1-3. Even though prayer needs to encompass those around us and the condition of the lost, it is also a personal outpouring of our hearts to God, who wants this intimate connection with each one.

> **1** "Give ear to my words, O Lord,
> Consider my meditation.
> **2** Give heed to the voice of my cry,
> My King and my God,
> For to You I will pray.
> **3** My voice You shall hear in the morning, O Lord;

In the morning I will direct *it* to You,
And I will look up."

The holiness of God and his abhorrence of sin are brought out in verses 4 to 6 and 9 and 10. Prayer is only acceptable to God if those who pray are turning away from evil and from sin. One who puts his trust in God must consider God's call to holiness and follow that call:

> **22** "Now may the God of peace Himself sanctify you completely; and may your whole spirit, soul, and body be preserved blameless at the coming of our Lord Jesus Christ. **24** He who calls you *is* faithful, who also will do *it*." (1 Thessalonians 5.23,24).

> **20** "Now may the God of peace who brought up our Lord Jesus from the dead, that great Shepherd of the sheep, through the blood of the everlasting covenant, **21** make you complete in every good work to do His will, working in you what is well pleasing in His sight, through Jesus Christ, to whom *be* glory forever and ever. Amen." (Hebrews 13.20,21)

Joy is the fruit of a life of trust and seeking God's will. It is also part of the fruit of the Spirit, which cannot be separated from how God works holiness in our lives:

> **22** "But the fruit of the Spirit is love, joy, peace, longsuffering, kindness, goodness, faithfulness, **23** gentleness, self-control. Against such there is no law. **24** And those *who are* Christ's have crucified the flesh with its passions and desires. **25** If we live in the Spirit, let us also walk in the Spirit. **26** Let us not become conceited, provoking one another, envying one another." (Galatians 5.22-26)

Prayer

Our Father and Lord in heaven, we seek you today. We seek to understand and to practice your will. We pray that through the Holy Spirit we can show the fruit of love and joy in our lives. We ask for an understanding heart towards those who are broken or in pain. We pray this in the name of Jesus, our Savior. Amen.

Day 4

> **4** "Sing to God, sing praises to His name;
> Extol Him who rides on the clouds,
> By His name Yah,
> And rejoice before Him.
> **5** A father of the fatherless, a defender of widows,
> *Is* God in His holy habitation.
> **6** God sets the solitary in families;
> He brings out those who are bound into prosperity;
> But the rebellious dwell in a dry *land.*"
> (Psalms 68.1-6)

The victories and rule of God are a constant source of joy and rejoicing in the Psalms and the Scriptures (Psalms 20.5; 118.15; James 1.2).

Psalm 68 is a Psalm of praise to the victorious God. It is quoted in verse 18 by the apostle Paul in his teaching about the ascension of Christ and the gifts of teaching and leading offered to the Church for the building up of the body of Christ.

> **9** Now this, "He ascended"—what does it mean but that He also first descended into the lower parts of the earth? **10** He who descended is also the One who ascended far above all the heavens, that He might fill all things. **11** And He Himself gave some *to be* apostles, some prophets, some evangelists, and some pastors and teachers, **12** for the equipping of the saints for the work of ministry, for the edifying of the body of Christ, **13** till we all come to the unity of the faith and of the knowledge of the Son of God, to a perfect man, to the measure of the stature of the fullness of Christ; **14** that we should no longer be children, tossed to and fro and carried about with every wind of doctrine, by the trickery of men, in the cunning craftiness of deceitful plotting, **15** but, speaking the truth in love, may grow up in all things into Him who is the head—Christ— **16** from whom the whole body, joined and knit together by what every joint supplies, according to the effective working by which every part does its share, causes growth of the body for the edifying of itself in love. (Ephesians 4.9-16)

There is a connection between the triumphant victories of God in the Psalm and the victory of Christ over death and his ascension. It is through the ascension of Jesus at the right hand of God and his blessing the body of Christ with truth that we now see the victories of God. The wars of God against His enemies described in Psalms 68 are in Ephesians spiritual wars against "principalities, against powers, against the rulers of the darkness of this age, against spiritual hosts of wickedness in the heavenly places" (Ephesians 6.12).

The truth — the sword of the spirit which is the word of God — preached in love is the only weapon to be used against these "powers" which are spiritual and destructive to human beings: "But speaking the truth in love, may grow up in all things into Him who is the head — Christ" (Ephesians 4.15).

The spiritual battle of the saints is part of God's victories today. The "wars" Israel is to expect in the "last days" in Ezekiel 38 against Gog and Magog are shown in the book of Revelation to be wars against Satan, who brings together "the nations" and rulers of nations to combat the saints (Revelation 20.7-10). The "wars" are to be understood in a spiritual sense. The Lord fights with his people, and he carries with him "a sharp sword" — his word — to strike the nations. (See Hebrews 4.12,13).

> **4** "For the weapons of our warfare *are* not carnal but mighty in God for pulling down strongholds, **5** casting down arguments and every high thing that exalts itself against the knowledge of God, bringing every thought into captivity to the obedience of Christ, **6** and being ready to punish all disobedience when your obedience is fulfilled." (2 Corinthians 10.3-6)

Prayer

Our Father and Lord in heaven, we seek you today. We seek to understand and to practice your will. We rejoice for your salvation. We want to be good listeners to everyone we meet and know to respond to each one. Give us the wisdom we need, Father. In Jesus' name we pray. Amen.

Day 5

> **21** "Oh, that *men* would give thanks to the Lord *for* His goodness,
> And *for* His wonderful works to the children of men!
> **22** Let them sacrifice the sacrifices of thanksgiving,
> And declare His works with rejoicing."
>   (Psalms 107.21,22)

This Psalm is the first of Book 5 of the Psalms (107 to 150). Deuteronomy, the fifth book of the Torah, was given at the time the people of Israel were ready to enter the promised land after their deliverance from Egypt. In Psalm 107 the people of Israel are described as having been delivered from Exile in Assyria and Babylonia; verses 21 and 22 point to this deliverance.

This Psalm does not only recall past history. It teaches us still today how God is willing to bless His people and deliver human beings when they turn to Him in humility. The history of mankind is not written ahead of time in such a way that they are prisoners of it. Past mistakes or sins are not the guarantee of condemnation for the present or the future, which remain open to God's willingness to bless and give life. The past is there to encourage us to act differently, to trust in the God who does not change and is willing to bless and deliver those who come to Him. And if we act differently, God will do His part and bless us abundantly.

It was because Israel forgot to "give thanks to the LORD for His goodness" that they found themselves in captivity. The idea is already in verse 8 of the Psalm and repeated in verse 15. A lack of thankfulness is presented to Paul in Romans as the source of all sinful behavior:

> **21** "…although they knew God, they did not glorify *Him* as God, nor were thankful, but became futile in their thoughts, and their foolish hearts were darkened. **22** Professing to be wise, they became fools, **23** and changed the glory of the incorruptible God into an image made like corruptible man—and birds and four-footed animals and creeping things. **24** Therefore God also gave them up to uncleanness, in the lusts of their hearts, to dishonor their bodies among themselves…" (Romans 1.21-24)

This is the point made by the apostle Paul concerning Israel and the rejection of Jesus the Messiah by religious leaders in Israel (see Matthew 16.21):

> **11** "I say then, have they stumbled that they should fall? Certainly not! But through their fall, to provoke them to jealousy, salvation *has come* to the Gentiles. **12** Now if their fall *is* riches for the world, and their failure riches for the Gentiles, how much more their fullness!" (Romans 11.11,12).

The same thought is repeated several times in Romans chapter 11. Warning his gentile readers, the apostle reminds them of both God's severity and goodness which can be active any time either towards Israel or towards the Gentiles,

> **22** "Therefore consider the goodness and severity of God: on those who fell, severity; but toward you, goodness, if you continue in *His* goodness. Otherwise, you also will be cut off. **23** And they also, if they do not continue in unbelief, will be grafted in, for God is able to graft them in again." (Romans 11.22,23).

God's mercy and goodness towards Israel (as well as towards Gentiles) are not to be relegated to the past, but to be understood in view of the present and the future. God will greatly bless Israel and the Gentiles when Israel turns to their Messiah in faith. The salvation of the Gentiles does not preclude the salvation of Israel, since it was to them that the promised Messiah was promised in Isaiah:

> **26** And so, all Israel will be saved, as it is written: "The Deliverer will come out of Zion, and He will turn away ungodliness from Jacob; **27** For this *is* My covenant with them, when I take away their sins.'" (Romans 11.26,27 and Isaiah 59.20,21)

Prayer

Father in heaven, we pray for Israel, for the descendants of Abraham. We pray that faith in Jesus would spring and grow in the land of Israel today and in the hearts of Israelites today. We thank you for Jesus, the Messiah, the son of David, who accomplished your good purposes for all of humanity. May we always trust in your goodness, and may this goodness touch our hearts and humble us. This we pray in Jesus' name. Amen.

Day 6

> **14** "The Lord *is* my strength and song,
> And He has become my salvation.
> **15** The voice of rejoicing and salvation
> *Is* in the tents of the righteous;
> The right hand of the Lord does valiantly.
> **16** The right hand of the Lord is exalted;
> The right hand of the Lord does valiantly."
>   (Psalms 118.14-16)

Verses 22-24 of this Psalm are quoted in the New Testament and applied to Jesus:

> **42** "Jesus said to them, 'Have you never read in the Scriptures:
> 'The stone which the builders rejected
> Has become the chief cornerstone.
> This was the Lord's doing,
> And it is marvelous in our eyes'?
> **43** "Therefore I say to you, the kingdom of God will be taken from you and given to a nation bearing the fruits of it. **44** And whoever falls on this stone will be broken; but on whomever it falls, it will grind him to powder." (Matthew 21.42-44)

The righteous in the Psalm is the Messiah, the "stone which the builders rejected" (the builders were the religious leaders, the chief priests and Pharisees according to Jesus in Matthew 21.45,46).

Verse 22 of this Psalm is dramatic. However, the entire Psalm is all about the mercy, the salvation and the victory of God. Righteousness and mercy have the last word because they "last forever":

> **27** "God *is* the Lord,
> And He has given us light;
> Bind the sacrifice with cords to the horns of the altar.
> **28** You *are* my God, and I will praise You;
> *You are* my God, I will exalt You.
> **29** Oh, give thanks to the Lord, for *He is* good!
> For His mercy *endures* forever." (vv.27-29)

Prayer

Father in heaven, we thank you for your mercy which endures forever. We thank you that you overcome all unrighteousness and, in the end, even death. Your mercy LORD endures. Your grace and goodness are offered to us every day if we will come to you. Father, we pray for a humble heart and the wisdom we need for a new day. We pray this in Jesus' name. Amen.

Day 7

> **1** "*It is* good to give thanks to the Lord,
> And to sing praises to Your name, O Most High;
> **2** To declare Your lovingkindness in the morning,

And Your faithfulness every night,
3 On an instrument of ten strings,
On the lute,
And on the harp,
With harmonious sound.
4 For You, Lord, have made me glad through Your work;
I will triumph in the works of Your hands."
 (Psalms 92.1-4)

Being able to rejoice over God's works is a gift from above. Gladness in this Psalm are given to those who "give thanks to the LORD", who are not like the "senseless man who does not know":

5 "O Lord, how great are Your works!
Your thoughts are very deep.
6 A senseless man does not know,
Nor does a fool understand this." (Psalm 92.5,6)

In verses 12 and 13, this Psalm is a reminder of the great truths of the 1st Psalm:

2 "But his delight *is* in the law of the Lord,
And in His law he meditates day and night.
3 He shall be like a tree
Planted by the rivers of water,
That brings forth its fruit in its season,
Whose leaf also shall not wither;
And whatever he does shall prosper." (Psalms 1.2-3)

12 "The righteous shall flourish like a palm tree,
He shall grow like a cedar in Lebanon.
13 Those who are planted in the house of the Lord
Shall flourish in the courts of our God.
14 They shall still bear fruit in old age;
They shall be fresh and flourishing,
15 To declare that the Lord is upright;
He is my rock, and *there is* no unrighteousness in Him." (Psalm 92.12-15)

"Rejoice in the Lord always. Again, I will say, rejoice!"
(Phil 4.4).

10 "For if when we were enemies we were reconciled to God through the death of His Son, much more, having been reconciled, we shall be saved by His life. **11** And not only *that,* but we also rejoice in God through our Lord Jesus Christ, through whom we have now received the reconciliation." (Romans 5.10,11)

16 "Rejoice always, **17** pray without ceasing, **18** in everything give thanks; for this is the will of God in Christ Jesus for you." (1 Thessalonians 5.16-18)

Prayer

We rejoice LORD for your great works. We rejoice for the salvation you brought to this world through Jesus Christ. We rejoice that we have been reconciled to you, our Father in heaven. May we rejoice in whatever we need to do today to serve you and our neighbor. Thank you for this day and for your Word that guides us at every step. In Jesus' name we pray. Amen.

Week 35: Singing to the Lord

Day 1

> **1** Rejoice in the Lord, O you righteous!
> *For* praise from the upright is beautiful.
> **2** Praise the Lord with the harp;
> Make melody to Him with an instrument of ten strings.
> **3** Sing to Him a new song;
> Play skillfully with a shout of joy.
> **4** For the word of the Lord *is* right,
> And all His work *is done* in truth.
> **5** He loves righteousness and justice;
> The earth is full of the goodness of the Lord."
> (Psalms 33.1-5)

Psalm 33 links singing and praises to God with being righteous and praises given "from the upright" since the LORD loves righteousness and justice. All of God's work is "done in truth" and those who praise Him must display this truth in their behavior. The earth is "full of His goodness" and those who praise Him must also acknowledge and reflect God's goodness in their lives. Songs and praises that come from people full of pride and sinfulness do not please the LORD (Malachi 1.6-14; Proverbs 28.9).

Those who are invited to sing and praise the Lord are "the righteous". The Hebrew text for "O you righteous!" is in the plural, meaning "all you who are righteous" (*tsadiquim*). This Psalm describes worship in an assembly or public worship as it existed at the time of David, who was influential in the structuring of worship at Zion, at the tabernacle, and especially of singing.

Skilled singers were organized as well as players of diverse instruments. When David brought back the ark of the covenant to Jerusalem, God gave him instructions on the place of instruments used in Zion worship (1 Chronicles 16).

The response of the righteous to the truth and goodness of God is personal, but usually takes place in the form of public worship. Singing "together" or as an assembly is implied also in the New Testament Scriptures that mention singing (Romans 15.6; Hebrews 13.15; Ephesians 5.18-21; Colossians 3.16).

"Make melody to Him with an instrument of ten strings" is parallel to Ephesians 5.19, "making melody in your heart to the Lord". "Making melody" for God is a matter of the heart rather than the musical quality of the voice or the sounds. Having "one mind" is also part of public praises to God (Romans 15.6; see Romans 12.1,2; 1 Corinthians 1.10). Meaningful words are essential to public expression of praise (1 Corinthians 14.6-9).

Prayer

We thank you, Father, for all the praises and songs we find in your word. We want to praise your name today and worship you with our hearts and minds. We pray for wisdom as we serve you today and serve others around us. Forgive us all our sins and purify our hearts today. We pray this in Jesus' name. Amen.

Day 2

> **1** "Oh, sing to the Lord a new song!
> Sing to the Lord, all the earth.
> **2** Sing to the Lord, bless His name;
> Proclaim the good news of His salvation from day to day.
> **3** Declare His glory among the nations,
> His wonders among all peoples.
> **4** For the Lord *is* great and greatly to be praised;
> He *is* to be feared above all gods.
> **5** For all the gods of the peoples *are* idols,
> But the Lord made the heavens.
> **6** Honor and majesty *are* before Him;
> Strength and beauty *are* in His sanctuary."
>   (Psalms 96.1-6)

This Psalm expresses one of the most challenging messages proclaimed by Israel to the nations: the greatness and uniqueness of God, who is to be praised not only by Israel but by all nations and peoples over the earth. The foundation of this belief in the uniqueness of God is the fact of Him being the creator of all things: "For all the gods of the peoples are idols, but the Lord made the heavens".

This appeal to creation as foundational to the faith of Israel and a biblical worldview is repeated throughout the Scriptures (Exodus 20; Deuteronomy 4; Nehemiah 9; Job 38; Psalms 8, 19, 24, 33, 50, 102, 104…; Proverbs 8; Isaiah 40; Jeremiah 10; 31, 32; Amos 5; Acts 14, 17; Romans 1, 8). This is why it is "all the earth" that sings and praises the LORD (v.1).

The superscription of the Psalm is from the Greek Septuagint and says: "A song of praise to God coming in judgment". The word "song" here is the Greek word *ode* also used in the New Testament for the singing of the Church (Ephesians 5.19; Colossians 3.16 "spiritual songs"). These "songs" need to be "spiritual" which means focused on the truths of the Bible and the realm of the Spirit — see John 4.24)

The word "song" (*ode*) is more often used in the book of Revelation (5.9; 14.3; 15.3):

> **2** "They sing the song of Moses, the servant of God, and the song of the Lamb, saying:
> **3** 'Great and marvelous *are* Your works,
> Lord God Almighty!
> Just and true *are* Your ways,
> O King of the saints!
> **4** Who shall not fear You, O Lord, and glorify Your name?
> For *You* alone *are* holy.
> For all nations shall come and worship before You,
> For Your judgments have been manifested.'"(Revelation 15.2–4)

The LORD is not only the creator of the world, but He is also the sustainer of the world (see Hebrews 1.1-3):

> "Say among the nations, 'The Lord reigns;
> The world also is firmly established,
> It shall not be moved;
> He shall judge the peoples righteously.'" (v.10)

The entire earth rejoices over the "coming" of the LORD and his coming judgment:

> **11** "Let the heavens rejoice, and let the earth be glad;
> Let the sea roar, and all its fullness;
> **12** Let the field be joyful, and all that *is* in it.

> Then all the trees of the woods will rejoice
> **13** before the Lord.
> For He is coming, for He is coming to judge the earth.
> He shall judge the world with righteousness,
> And the peoples with His truth."

(vv.11-13)

Prayer

We praise you Father in heaven for your splendid creation. We praise you for your righteous judgments. Give us a thankful and joyful hearts today as we meditate upon your word and your works. We come to you for forgiveness, strengthening and wisdom in order to serve you today. We pray in the name of Jesus. Amen.

Day 3

> **4** "Sing praise to the Lord, you saints of His,
> And give thanks at the remembrance of His holy name.
> **5** For His anger *is but for* a moment,
> His favor *is for* life;
> Weeping may endure for a night,
> But joy *comes* in the morning."
>   (Psalms 30.4,5)

In Psalms 30 thanksgiving is offered to God for His deliverance (vv.1-3) and the people are invited to join in the thanksgiving (vv.4,5).

The author was in grief and mourning, but was delivered by God (vv.6-12). The message of the Psalm is that LORD will change all mourning into rejoicing: "Weeping may endure for a night, but joy comes in the morning".

> "He will swallow up death forever,
> And the Lord God will wipe away tears from all faces;" (Isaiah 25.8)

This is also a central message of the Gospel and of salvation and life in Christ:

> **15** "And He who sits on the throne will dwell among them. **16** They shall neither hunger anymore nor thirst anymore; the sun shall not strike them, nor any heat; **17** for the

Lamb who is in the midst of the throne will shepherd them and lead them to living fountains of waters. And God will wipe away every tear from their eyes." (Revelation 7.15-17)

1 "Now I saw a new heaven and a new earth, for the first heaven and the first earth had passed away. Also, there was no more sea. **2** Then I, John, saw the holy city, New Jerusalem, coming down out of heaven from God, prepared as a bride adorned for her husband. **3** And I heard a loud voice from heaven saying, "Behold, the tabernacle of God *is* with men, and He will dwell with them, and they shall be His people. God Himself will be with them *and be* their God. **4** And God will wipe away every tear from their eyes; there shall be no more death, nor sorrow, nor crying. There shall be no more pain, for the former things have passed away." **5** Then He who sat on the throne said, "Behold, I make all things new." And He said to me, "Write, for these words are true and faithful." (Revelation 21.1-5)

5 "For as the sufferings of Christ abound in us, so our consolation also abounds through Christ. **6** Now if we are afflicted, *it is* for your consolation and salvation, which is effective for enduring the same sufferings which we also suffer. Or if we are comforted, *it is* for your consolation and salvation. **7** And our hope for you *is* steadfast, because we know that as you are partakers of the sufferings, so also *you will partake* of the consolation." (2 Corinthians 1.5-7)

Prayer

We thank you LORD in heaven for your salvation. We praise you for offering life in Jesus the Christ and for your beautiful promises. We know that you are faithful to all your promises and want to live faithful lives in your sight. Purify our hearts through your Word and Holy Spirit. We pray this in the name of Jesus. Amen.

Day 4

1 "Sing aloud to God our strength;
Make a joyful shout to the God of Jacob.
2 Raise a song and strike the timbrel,

The pleasant harp with the lute.
3 Blow the trumpet at the time of the New Moon,
At the full moon, on our solemn feast day.
4 For this *is* a statute for Israel,
A law of the God of Jacob."
(Psalms 81.1-4)

The singing aloud with a joyful shout describes the voices of the people or the entire congregation (vv.1,2). Verse 3 is addressed to the Levites, who were the appointed singers and musicians dedicated to the divine services (2 Chronicles 5.12). Verse 4 is addressed to the priests who were to blow the silver trumpets (see also 2 Chronicles 5.12).

Singing with the timbrel, harp and lute as well as music with the trumpet was part of the worship of Israel in the tabernacle and later in the temple from the time of David. This Psalm is the Psalm of the feast of Trumpets (Numbers 29.1). The trumpets were blown at the feasts of Tabernacles and Passover. Both Tabernacles and Passover began on the day of the full moon.

God instructed the King of Israel concerning the worship of the people to God:

> **25** "And he stationed the Levites in the house of the Lord with cymbals, with stringed instruments, and with harps, according to the commandment of David, of Gad the king's seer, and of Nathan the prophet; for thus *was* the commandment of the Lord by His prophets. **26** The Levites stood with the instruments of David, and the priests with the trumpets." (2 Chronicles 29.25,26)

The instruments mentioned here are called "the instruments of David, king of Israel":

> "Then Hezekiah commanded *them* to offer the burnt offering on the altar. And when the burnt offering began, the song of the Lord *also* began, with the trumpets and with the instruments of David king of Israel." (2 Chronicles 29.27)

Verses 6 to 16 of Psalms 81 are the words of God to His people. In these verses, God recalls the history of His people, including their disobedience and God's faithfulness. The words of God in these verses remind us that God was and is always open to the repentance and faith of His people if they would "listen to Me" and "walk in My ways" (v.13).

The joyful singing and music described in this Psalm are directed to God, who remains faithful to Israel if they are faithful to Him. It is a source of joy and praise that the LORD is unchanging and always calling His people to return to Him (see James 1.17,18):

> **12** "Then the Lord appeared to Solomon by night and said to him: "I have heard your prayer, and have chosen this place for Myself as a house of sacrifice. **13** When I shut up heaven and there is no rain, or command the locusts to devour the land, or send pestilence among My people, **14** if My people who are called by My name will humble themselves, and pray and seek My face, and turn from their wicked ways, then I will hear from heaven, and will forgive their sin and heal their land." (2 Chronicles 7.12-14)

Prayer

We thank you, Father, for your faithfulness. We praise you for your Word, which gives us assurance of your love and mercy towards us and all who turn to you. We pray that this day we can serve you in a way that honors your name and your truth. May your Holy Spirit produce in our hearts the good fruit that comes from you. We pray in the name of Jesus. Amen.

Day 5

> **1** "Oh come, let us sing to the Lord!
> Let us shout joyfully to the Rock of our salvation.
> **2** Let us come before His presence with thanksgiving;
> Let us shout joyfully to Him with psalms.
> **3** For the Lord *is* the great God,
> And the great King above all gods.
> **4** In His hand *are* the deep places of the earth;
> The heights of the hills *are* His also.
> **5** The sea *is* His, for He made it;
> And His hands formed the dry *land*."
> (Psalms 95.1-5)

These beautiful verses are encouraging the believer to remain joyful and thankful in the worship of the "great God" and "great King" who is our creator. However, the remaining verses of this Psalm (especially verses 8-11) are a warning to believers not to harden their hearts through sin; verses quoted in Hebrews chapter 3 warning Christians to "hold fast the confidence and rejoicing of the hope firm to the end" (Hebrews 3.6-14). God's work of creation and work of redemption are blended together in this Psalm, as in so many others (especially Psalms 95 to 100).

The contrast between these verses at the beginning of Psalm 95 and the verses that end the Psalm is striking:

> **7** "Today, if you will hear His voice:
> **8** "Do not harden your hearts, as in the rebellion,
> As *in* the day of trial in the wilderness,
> **9** When your fathers tested Me;
> They tried Me, though they saw My work.
> **10** For forty years I was grieved with *that* generation,
> And said, 'It *is* a people who go astray in their hearts,
> And they do not know My ways.'
> **11** So I swore in My wrath,
> 'They shall not enter My rest.'" (vv.7c-11)

A disposition of thankfulness and worship can preserve believers from falling into sin. This Psalm speaks to those who claim that they can isolate themselves from the assemblies and worship of the congregation without consequences in their lives. The connection between neglecting the worship of the congregation and falling into sin is clearly made in Hebrews (Hebrews 10.24-27).

The call to worship addressed to Israel in this Psalm is addressed in Psalms 96 to all the nations and even the entire creation:

> **1** "Oh, sing to the Lord a new song!
> Sing to the Lord, all the earth.
> **2** Sing to the Lord, bless His name;
> Proclaim the good news of His salvation from day to day.
> **3** Declare His glory among the nations,
> His wonders among all peoples." (Psalms 97.1-3)

In Romans 15 the apostle Paul shows how God had planned to save the Gentiles through the Messiah so that they might also praise His name and worship Him (Romans 15.7-13; See Psalms 18.49; 32.43; 117.1; Isaiah 11.10).

Prayer

Our Father in heaven, we praise your name for your beautiful creation and work of salvation. We are blessed to have faith in you and to serve you through our lives. Today we ask your forgiveness for our sins, for our shortcomings and disobedience. Give us through your Holy Spirit a humble and grateful disposition. In Jesus' name, we pray. Amen.

Day 6

> **1** "Oh, sing to the Lord a new song!
> For He has done marvelous things;
> His right hand and His holy arm have gained Him the victory.
> **2** The Lord has made known His salvation;
> His righteousness He has revealed in the sight of the nations.
> **3** He has remembered His mercy and His faithfulness to the house of Israel;
> All the ends of the earth have seen the salvation of our God."
> (Psalms 98.1-3)

This Psalm is similar in many ways to Psalms 95, 96 and 97. There is an insistence in these Psalms on the worship of the LORD on the part of all peoples and even of the entire creation. Israel remains at the heart of God's worship, but God's salvation and righteousness are also known "in the sight of all nations". This is a "new song" — the song that proclaims God's salvation and forgiveness — because nothing like this exists in the pagan world surrounding Israel.

Jesus says to the Samaritan woman: "You worship what you do not know; we know what we worship, for salvation is of the Jews" (John 4.22). It is a salvation "from the Jews" but destined also for this Samaritan woman to whom Jesus offers "living water" (John 4.10).

We see in this Psalm God's intention to have His salvation extend throughout the earth, to all the nations. This is central to the entire message of the Jewish Scriptures:

> **44** "Then He said to them, 'These *are* the words which I spoke to you while I was still with you, that all things must be fulfilled which were written in the Law of Moses and *the* Prophets and *the* Psalms concerning Me.' **45** And He opened their understanding, that they might comprehend the Scriptures. **46** Then He said to them, "Thus it is written, and thus it was necessary for the Christ to suffer and to rise from the dead the third day, **47** and that repentance and remission of sins should be preached in His name to all nations, beginning at Jerusalem."
> (Luke 24.44-47)

Prayer

Our Father in heaven, we praise your name for your marvelous plan of salvation for Israel and for all nations. We thank you for having made known to us your salvation through Jesus your son. Our prayer is that today we will be able to share this message of salvation through our words and actions. Give us our peace as we serve you today. We pray in the name of Jesus. Amen.

Day 7

> **4** "Shout joyfully to the Lord, all the earth;
> Break forth in song, rejoice, and sing praises.
> **5** Sing to the Lord with the harp,
> With the harp and the sound of a psalm,
> **6** With trumpets and the sound of a horn;
> Shout joyfully before the Lord, the King.
> **7** Let the sea roar, and all its fullness,
> The world and those who dwell in it;
> **8** Let the rivers clap *their* hands;
> Let the hills be joyful together
> **9** before the Lord,
> For He is coming to judge the earth.
> With righteousness He shall judge the world,
> And the peoples with equity."
>   (Psalms 98.4-9)

These verses are a reminder of the worship of the Tabernacle under David (and later the worship in the temple); in verse 5 the union of singing and music made on stringed instruments as of the Levites and in verse 6 the sound of wind instruments as of the priests consecrated to this task.

Followers of Christ who once were not a people but now are "the people of God" are today a "royal priesthood" who "proclaim the praises of Him" who called them out of darkness into His marvelous light (1 Peter 2.9,10). They offer "continually the sacrifice of praise to God, that is the fruit of our lips giving thanks to His name" (Hebrews 13.15).

The coming judgment of God is not in these verses a cause of fear or dismay. It is a theme that brings about joyful worship on the part of the faithful. The judgment which we wait for today is not a day when Christ begins to reign or govern on earth, but "the day when he will end his reign on earth" (1 Corinthians 15.20-28). The reign of Christ is going on at the present time for those who have followed him and have remained faithful to him (Matthew 28.18-20; 1 Corinthians 15. 25,26):

> **20** "He raised Him from the dead and seated *Him* at His right hand in the heavenly *places,* **21** far above all principality and power and might and dominion, and every name that is named, not only in this age but also in that which is to come.**22** And He put all *things* under His feet and gave Him *to be* head over all *things* to the church, **23** which is His body, the fullness of Him who fills all in all." (Ephesians 1.20-23)

> **8** "But to the Son *He says:* 'Your throne, O God, *is* forever and ever; A scepter of righteousness *is* the scepter of Your kingdom. **9** You have loved righteousness and hated lawlessness; Therefore God, Your God, has anointed You With the oil of gladness more than Your companions.'" (Hebrews 1.8,9)

Prayer

Our Father in heaven, we praise your name for your reign and the reign of Jesus your son, who is at your right hand. We pray that we will listen to the teachings of Jesus and obey his commandments. We ask for wisdom from you and for grace and peace as we serve you and people we encounter during this day. We thank you for your goodness and care. We pray this in the name of Jesus. Amen.

Week 36: The Suffering Messiah

Day 1

> **1** "Why do the nations rage,
> And the peoples plot a vain thing?
> **2** The kings of the earth set themselves,
> And the rulers take counsel together,
> Against the Lord and against His Anointed, *saying,*
> **3** 'Let us break Their bonds in pieces
> And cast away Their cords from us.'"
> (Psalms 2.1-3)

The Psalms often present a picture of a victorious and ruling Messiah as well as a picture of a suffering Messiah. It is not possible to separate the two ideas. In Luke's account of the Gospel, Jesus says to his disciples that his sufferings and glory were written already about him in the Psalms:

> **25** "Then He said to them, 'O foolish ones, and slow of heart to believe in all that the prophets have spoken! **26** Ought not the Christ to have suffered these things and to enter into His glory?' **27** And beginning at Moses and all the Prophets, He expounded to them in all the Scriptures the things concerning Himself." (Luke 24.25-27)

> **44** "Then He said to them, 'These *are* the words which I spoke to you while I was still with you, that all things must be fulfilled which were written in the Law of Moses and *the* Prophets and *the* Psalms concerning Me.' **45** And He opened their understanding, that they might comprehend the Scriptures." (Luke 24.44,45)

Psalm 2.2 is the first reference to the Messiah, the "anointed" (translated *Khristos* in the Greek New Testament) in the book of Psalms. In this

Psalm, the Messiah is called God's king and God's Son (vv.6,7,12). Thus "God's Son" is another title to designate the Messiah, the king of Israel. Of this Son God says, "Today I have begotten you". Jesus refers to this expression when speaking to Nicodemus: "For God so loved the world that He gave His only-begotten Son, that whoever believes in Him should not perish but have everlasting life." (John 3.16). The expression "begotten Son" is a title given by God to Jesus and quoted also in Hebrews 1.5; 5.5 and Acts 13.33. It should be noted that Hebrews 1.5 quoting Psalm 2 uses the text to show that Jesus is above and superior to any of the angels, confirming the statement in Hebrews 1.2,3 which describe the Son's authority and power. To none of the angels did God say, "You are my Son, today I have begotten You". The expression "I have begotten you" does not refer to biology, but to authority. The apostle Paul uses the same reference in Acts 13.33 as having to do with Jesus' authority.

This aspect of Psalm 2 showing the authority and power of the Son follows the statements about the rejection of the Son by "kings of the earth" and "rulers" who take counsel against the Son.

We see this in the condemnation of Jesus to death:

> **18** Behold, we are going up to Jerusalem, and the Son of Man will be betrayed to the chief priests and to the scribes; and they will condemn Him to death, **19** and deliver Him to the Gentiles to mock and to scourge and to crucify. And the third day He will rise again." (Matthew 20.18,19)

The disciples in Jerusalem quote Psalms 2 in their prayer to God after Peter and John had been threatened by the Sanhedrin.

> **25** "Why did the nations rage,
> And the people plot vain things?
> **26** The kings of the earth took their stand,
> And the rulers were gathered together
> Against the Lord and against His Christ.'
> **27** "For truly against Your holy Servant Jesus, whom You anointed, both Herod and Pontius Pilate, with the Gentiles and the people of Israel, were gathered together **28** to do whatever Your hand and Your purpose determined before to be done."
> (Acts 4.25-27; see Mark 3.6)

Prayer

Father in heaven, we thank you for the work of salvation you have accomplished through Jesus the Messiah. We thank you for the Scriptures which presents your plan of redemption and encourages our faith. We pray that we can today live as faithful disciples of the Christ and carry out his will, which is also your will. Keep us today in your grace and in your peace. We pray in the name of Jesus. Amen.

Day 2

> **1** "My God, My God, why have You forsaken Me?
> *Why are You so* far from helping Me,
> *And from* the words of My groaning?
> **2** O My God, I cry in the daytime, but You do not hear;
> And in the night season and am not silent.
> **3** But You *are* holy,
> Enthroned in the praises of Israel.
> **4** Our fathers trusted in You;
> They trusted, and You delivered them.
> **5** They cried to You, and were delivered;
> They trusted in You, and were not ashamed."
> (Psalms 22.1-5)

Psalm 22 is a vivid description of the sufferings of the Messiah, written about a thousand years before the crucifixion of Jesus.

In Psalm 22 the Messiah cries out "My God my God why have you forsaken me?" (Mark 15.34). He prays without ceasing before his death (Matthew 26.38-39). He is despised and rejected by his own (Luke 23.21-23). He is mocked (Psalms 109.25; Matthew 27.39; Luke 23.36). He is surrounded by wicked and lawless beings (Acts 2.23). From his body flows blood and water (John 19.34). He is crucified (Matthew 27.35). He thirsts (John 19.28). There are those who say, "He trusted in God, let Him now deliver him" (Matthew 27.41-43). He is abandoned by his disciples (Mark 14.50). His hands and feet are pierced (Matthew 27.38). His garments are parted among the soldiers through the casting of lots (John 19.23-24). He is accused of false witness (Matthew 26.59-61). He cries out to God, saying, "Into thy hand I commend my spirit" (Luke 23.46). There are many attempts to kill him (Matthew 27.1).

Psalm 22 begins with the words "My God, My God, why have You forsaken Me?" and ends with triumph and victory and the rule of the Messiah over the nations (Matthew 28.18-20):

27 "All the ends of the world
Shall remember and turn to the Lord,
And all the families of the nations
Shall worship before You.
28 For the kingdom *is* the Lord's,
And He rules over the nations." (Psalms 22.27,28)

6 "Therefore, when they had come together, they asked Him, saying, 'Lord, will You at this time restore the kingdom to Israel?' **7** And He said to them, 'It is not for you to know times or seasons which the Father has put in His own authority. **8** But you shall receive power when the Holy Spirit has come upon you; and you shall be witnesses to Me in Jerusalem, and in all Judea and Samaria, and to the end of the earth.'" (Acts 1.6-8)

Prayer

Lord in heaven, we thank you for this day. We pray today for strength and wisdom, as well as comfort from your Holy Spirit. We can do nothing without you, Lord. We trust fully in your promises and pray that we will live today a life of hope and goodness towards those we meet. Give us a good understanding of your will as we try and shine your light in this world. We pray in the name of Jesus. Amen.

Day 3

9 "Have mercy on me, O Lord, for I am in trouble;
My eye wastes away with grief,
"*Yes,* my soul and my body!
10 For my life is spent with grief,
And my years with sighing;
My strength fails because of my iniquity,
And my bones waste away.
11 I am a reproach among all my enemies,
But especially among my neighbors,
And *am* repulsive to my acquaintances;
Those who see me outside flee from me.
12 I am forgotten like a dead man, out of mind;
I am like a broken vessel.
13 For I hear the slander of many;
Fear *is* on every side;

> While they take counsel together against me,
> They scheme to take away my life."
> (Psalms 31.9-13)

Verse 5 of this Psalm is quoted by Jesus as his last words on the cross: "Into your hand I commit my spirit" (Luke 23.46). This Psalm also describes the sufferings of the Messiah, but also the fact that God heard him and his victory:

> **21** "Blessed *be* the Lord,
> For He has shown me His marvelous kindness in a strong city!
> **22** For I said in my haste,
> "I am cut off from before Your eyes";
> Nevertheless You heard the voice of my supplications
> When I cried out to You." (PSalms 31.21,22)

"They scheme to take away my life" is a constant reality throughout the life of Jesus, from the start of his ministry until his crucifixion.

> **28** "So all those in the synagogue, when they heard these things, were filled with wrath, **29** and rose up and thrust Him out of the city; and they led Him to the brow of the hill on which their city was built, that they might throw Him down over the cliff. **30** Then passing through the midst of them, He went His way." (Luke 4.28-30)

> **13** "Then He said to the man, 'Stretch out your hand.' And he stretched *it* out, and it was restored as whole as the other. **14** Then the Pharisees went out and plotted against Him, how they might destroy Him." (Matthew 12.13,14)

> "Therefore, the Jews sought all the more to kill Him, because He not only broke the Sabbath, but also said that God was His Father, making Himself equal with God." (John 5.18)

> **47** "Then the chief priests and the Pharisees gathered a council and said, 'What shall we do? For this Man works many signs. **48** If we let Him alone like this, everyone will believe in Him, and the Romans will come and take away both our place and nation.'" (John 11.47,48)

> **3** "Then the chief priests, the scribes, and the elders of the people assembled at the palace of the high priest, who was called

Caiaphas, **4** and plotted to take Jesus by trickery and kill *Him*. **5** But they said, "Not during the feast, lest there be an uproar among the people." (Matthew 26.3,4)

1 "When morning came, all the chief priests and elders of the people plotted against Jesus to put Him to death. **2** And when they had bound Him, they led Him away and delivered Him to Pontius Pilate the governor." (Matthew 27.1,2)

The many attempts to kill the Messiah came from the rulers, those in authority whose power and privileges were threatened by the teachings of Jesus. Even Pilate understood that the religious rulers wanted to kill Jesus out of envy, jealousy:

15 "Now at the feast the governor was accustomed to releasing to the multitude one prisoner whom they wished. **16** And at that time they had a notorious prisoner called Barabbas. **17** Therefore, when they had gathered together, Pilate said to them, 'Whom do you want me to release to you? Barabbas, or Jesus who is called Christ?' **18** For he knew that they had handed Him over because of envy." (Matthew 27.15-18)

Pilate's understanding of why the rulers wanted to kill Jesus is linked to the title "Christ" (Messiah) attributed to Jesus. This title indicated great authority and honor for Jesus, who in fact had been welcomed by the inhabitants of Jerusalem in a kingly fashion:

37 "Then, as He was now drawing near the descent of the Mount of Olives, the whole multitude of the disciples began to rejoice and praise God with a loud voice for all the mighty works they had seen, **38** saying: 'Blessed *is* the King who comes in the name of the Lord! Peace in heaven and glory in the highest!' **39** And some of the Pharisees called to Him from the crowd, 'Teacher, rebuke Your disciples.' **40** But He answered and said to them, 'I tell you that if these should keep silent, the stones would immediately cry out.'" (Luke 19.37-40)

Prayer

Our Father in heaven, we glorify you today. We thank you for the salvation we enjoy in Jesus your Son. Give us a heart full of faith, hope and love for this new day. We pray that your Holy Spirit will give us strength and produce needed change in our hearts. We praise you, Father. In Jesus, we pray. Amen.

Day 4

> **12** "Those also who seek my life lay snares *for me;*
> Those who seek my hurt speak of destruction,
> And plan deception all the day long.
> **13** But I, like a deaf *man,* do not hear;
> And *I am* like a mute *who* does not open his mouth.
> **14** Thus I am like a man who does not hear,
> And in whose mouth *is* no response.
> **15** For in You, O Lord, I hope;
> You will hear, O Lord my God."
>   (Psalms 38.12-15)

This corresponds to the description of the Messiah in Isaiah:

> "He was oppressed, and He was afflicted
> Yet He opened not His mouth;
> He was led as a lamb to the slaughter,
> And as a sheep before its shearers is silent,
> So He opened not His mouth." (Isaiah 53.7)

> **61** "But at last, two false witnesses came forward **61** and said, This *fellow* said, 'I am able to destroy the temple of God and to build it in three days.' **62** And the high priest arose and said to Him, 'Do You answer nothing? What *is it* these men testify against You?' **63** But Jesus kept silent. And the high priest answered and said to Him, 'I put You under oath by the living God: Tell us if You are the Christ, the Son of God!'" (Matthew 26.60-63)

> "A eunuch who served under Candace, queen of Ethiopia, was returning home after worshipping in Jerusalem. He was reading Isaiah 53.7, 8 and asked Philip: 'of whom does the prophet say this, of himself or of some other man?'" (Acts 8.34).

"Then Philip opened his mouth, and beginning at this Scripture, preached Jesus to him" (Acts 8.35). At this point, the eunuch believed the testimony of Philip and asked: "Here is water. What hinders me from being baptized?" To which Philip answered: "If you believe with all your heart, you may." And the man answered, saying, "I believe that Jesus Christ is the son of God" (Acts 8.36,37).

After he had been baptized, the eunuch "went on his way rejoicing" (Acts 8.39). We also have here an example of how joy is connected to faith in the message of the Gospel, with all of its cruel implications, and a changed perspective on life.

Prayer

We thank you, Father in heaven, for the life and work of salvation of Jesus your Son. We thank you for the Scriptures which bear testimony to Jesus, both in the Old and New Testaments. We pray that you can increase our knowledge and understanding of the wonderful work of salvation in your Son Jesus. Give us today wisdom and love as we share and teach your Gospel to others. We pray this in the name of Jesus. Amen.

Day 5

> **19** "You know my reproach, my shame, and my dishonor;
> My adversaries *are* all before You.
> **20** Reproach has broken my heart,
> And I am full of heaviness;
> I looked *for someone* to take pity, but *there was* none;
> And for comforters, but I found none.
> **21** They also gave me gall for my food,
> And for my thirst they gave me vinegar to drink."
> (Psalms 69.19-21)

The Messiah would endure shame and dishonor. His heart would be full of heaviness and would be given vinegar to drink in the midst of his pain.

Jesus who was chosen by God as the leader and prince of His people would go through the shame of pain and rejection.

He healed the blind and lepers and was cursed as one doing this through the power of Satan (Matthew 12.22-37). He was rejected in favor of Barabbas, a criminal (Mark 15.7-15). He was spat upon, beaten and mocked by the Roman soldiers (Matthew 27.27-31).

He was nailed to the cross like a criminal and mocked on the cross (Matthew 27.35; Mark 15.24; Luke 23.33; John 19.18). The word cross (Greek *stauros*) refers mainly to the cross-beam, or transverse beam, of a Roman cross (in Latin *patibulum*) placed at the top of the vertical member to form a capital "T". This was the beam carried by the criminal.

Jesus "became obedient" to the point of death, "even the death of the cross" (Philippians 2.8).

The "message of the cross" is central to the preaching of the Gospel: "For the message of the cross is foolishness to those who are perishing, but to us who are being saved it is the power of God." (1 Corinthians 1.18).

Paul writes "God forbid that I should boast except in the cross of our Lord Jesus Christ by whom the world has been crucified to me, and I to the world." (Galatians 6.14) The word "cross" is here used as a verb (crucified) as in Matthew 27.35: "Then they crucified him" (with the Greek verb *stauro*, to crucify). Jesus prophesied that he would be delivered "to the Gentiles to mock and to scourge and to crucify" (Matthew 20.19).

> **1** "Therefore, we also since we are surrounded by so great a cloud of witnesses, let us lay aside every weight, and the sin which so easily ensnares *us*, and let us run with endurance the race that is set before us, **2** looking unto Jesus, the author and finisher of *our* faith, who for the joy that was set before Him endured the cross, despising the shame, and has sat down at the right hand of the throne of God." (Hebrews 12.1,2)

Prayer

Father in heaven, we praise you for your love and gift of Jesus to the world. We thank you for the forgiveness of our sins through the cross of Jesus. We thank you for his blood, which reconciles us to you. Strengthen us today in our faith and repentance, that we might serve you and that we might be sanctified by your Holy Spirit. Bless every person we encounter today and lead them to you. In Jesus' name, we pray. Amen.

Day 6

> **1** "Do not keep silent,
> O God of my praise!
> **2** For the mouth of the wicked and the mouth of the deceitful
> Have opened against me;
> They have spoken against me with a lying tongue.
> **3** They have also surrounded me with words of hatred,
> And fought against me without a cause.
> **4** In return for my love they are my accusers,

But I *give myself to* prayer.
5 Thus they have rewarded me evil for good,
And hatred for my love."
   (Psalms 109.1-5)

Psalm 109 describes the pains of the one who is rendered evil in return for the good he did, who is rendered hatred for his love. It also describes the gravity of the sin of those who render evil for good; those who render hatred for love as the book of Proverbs also teaches: "Whoever rewards evil for good, evil will not depart from his house." (Proverbs 17.13).

This was also the message of the prophet Jeremiah, who was rejected by the leaders of his people:

19 "Give heed to me, O Lord,
And listen to the voice of those who contend with me!
20 Shall evil be repaid for good?
For they have dug a pit for my life.
Remember that I stood before You
To speak good for them,
To turn away Your wrath from them." (Jeremiah 18.19,20)

This Psalm along with Psalms 69.25 is quoted in the New Testament as applying to Judas who betrayed Jesus and would be replaced as an apostle of Christ:

6 "Set a wicked man over him,
And let an accuser stand at his right hand.
7 When he is judged, let him be found guilty,
And let his prayer become sin.
8 Let his days be few,
And let another take his office." (Psalms 109.6-8; see Acts 1.15-17, 20-26)

Prayer

Our Father, we praise you and want to serve you faithfully today. Give us wisdom as we face obstacles of difficult decisions. Forgive us for our sins. Help us, Lord, to never render evil for good, but to do good to all people. Help us pray for every person we encounter and hope the best for them. May your Holy Spirit change us again today. In the name of Jesus, we pray. Amen.

Day 7

> **21** "I will praise You,
> For You have answered me,
> And have become my salvation.
> **22** The stone *which* the builders rejected
> Has become the chief cornerstone.
> **23** This was the Lord's doing;
> It *is* marvelous in our eyes.
> **24** This *is* the day the Lord has made;
> We will rejoice and be glad in it."
> (Psalms 118.21-24)

Jesus applied the words of this Psalm to himself:

> **42** "Jesus said to them, 'Have you never read in the Scriptures: The stone which the builders rejected has become the chief cornerstone. This was the Lord's doing, and it is marvelous in our eyes'? **43** Therefore I say to you, the kingdom of God will be taken from you and given to a nation bearing the fruits of it. **44** And whoever falls on this stone will be broken; but on whomever it falls, it will grind him to powder.' **45** Now when the chief priests and Pharisees heard His parables, they perceived that He was speaking of them. **46** But when they sought to lay hands on Him, they feared the multitudes, because they took Him for a prophet" (Matthew 21.42-46)

We note in Matthew that Jesus was not talking about every Jew or the entire Jewish people, but about the religious leaders of his day, especially a number of the chief priests and Pharisees. This is also the case in prophecies Jesus made concerning his rejection and crucifixion (Mark 8.31; 10.33; 14.10, 43, 55; 15.10; Matthew 16.21; 20.18; 26.14, 47, 59; 27.3,12; 28.11; Luke 9.22; 22.4; John 7.32; 18.35; 19.6, 21; Luke 20.19; 24.20).

Not all of Israel and not all generations of Israelites are the subject of Jesus' words. The apostle Paul teaches that God has planned to show mercy towards Israel as He does towards Gentiles (Romans 11.28-36).

The picture of the cornerstone refers back to the construction of the temple. Jesus as the "chief corner stone" is mentioned in Ephesians 2.20; Acts 4.11; 1 Peter 2.4,7.

Jesus taught the religious leaders (called "the Jews" by John) that he would rebuild the temple, and this would be done through his resurrection:

> **18** "So, the Jews answered and said to Him, 'What sign do You show to us, since You do these things?' **19** Jesus answered and said to them, 'Destroy this temple, and in three days I will raise it up.' **20** Then the Jews said, 'It has taken forty-six years to build this temple, and will You raise it up in three days?' **21** But He was speaking of the temple of His body. **22** Therefore, when He had risen from the dead, His disciples remembered that He had said this to them; and they believed the Scripture and the word which Jesus had said." (John 2.18-22)

Prayer

Our Father in heaven, we praise you and want to serve you faithfully today. We pray that today we will keep your Word in our heart and that we will be obedient to your will. We thank for your many blessings. We pray that your peace will be with our loved ones. Forgive us our sins and strengthen our hearts to do good. In the name of Jesus, the Christ, we pray. Amen.

Week 37: Thankfulness

Day 1

> **1** "Make a joyful shout to the Lord, all you lands !
> **2** Serve the Lord with gladness;
> Come before His presence with singing.
> **3** Know that the Lord, He *is* God;
> *It is* He *who* has made us, and not we ourselves;
> *We are* His people and the sheep of His pasture.
> **4** Enter into His gates with thanksgiving,
> *And* into His courts with praise.
> Be thankful to Him *and* bless His name.
> **5** For the Lord *is* good;
> His mercy *is* everlasting,
> And His truth *endures* to all generations."
> (Psalms 100.1-5)

This Psalm has been given the title "Psalm of Thanksgiving". As in Psalms 107.22 and 116.17 thanksgiving is an offering, a "sacrifice", that pleases the Lord. Offerings of thankfulness were also part of the public worship of God, as in the days of king Hezekiah:

> **30** "Moreover, King Hezekiah and the leaders commanded the Levites to sing praise to the Lord with the words of David and of Asaph the seer. So, they sang praises with gladness, and they bowed their heads and worshiped. **31** Then Hezekiah answered and said, 'Now *that* you have consecrated yourselves to the Lord, come near, and bring sacrifices and thank offerings into the house of the Lord.' So, the assembly brought in sacrifices and thank offerings, and as many as were of a willing heart *brought* burnt offerings." (2 Chronicles 29.30,31).

The offerings of thanksgiving were also called "peace offerings" and were not based on a fixed calendar, except for the offering of the two firstling lambs at Pentecost (Leviticus 23.19). The thank or peace offerings were spontaneous and offered as an occasion should arise and as a "free will offering" coming from the personal feelings of the worshipper (Leviticus 19.5).

This Psalm shows that these offerings sprung from a conviction or recognition of God's goodness, mercy, truth and faithfulness. Those who are called to such worship are people from "all lands" as in Psalms 98.4 and which describes "all the earth" or all peoples and nations belonging to the earth's population.

Ezekiel prophesied of the time when God would assemble His people under His servant David:

> **23** "I will establish one shepherd over them, and he shall feed them—My servant David. He shall feed them and be their shepherd. **24** And I, the Lord, will be their God, and My servant David a prince among them; I, the Lord, have spoken.**25** "I will make a covenant of peace with them, and cause wild beasts to cease from the land; and they will dwell safely in the wilderness and sleep in the woods." (Ezekiel 34.23-25).

Jesus the Messiah and son of David announced his work as the good shepherd of God's people scattered over the earth:

> **14** "I am the good shepherd; and I know My sheep and am known by My own. **15** As the Father knows Me, even so I know the Father; and I lay down My life for the sheep. **16** And other sheep I have which are not of this fold; them also I must bring, and they will hear My voice; and there will be one flock *and* one shepherd. **17** Therefore My Father loves Me, because I lay down My life that I may take it again. **18** No one takes it from Me, but I lay it down of Myself. I have power to lay it down, and I have power to take it again. This command I have received from My Father." (John 10.14-18)

The redeemed by the blood of the lamb offer thanksgivings to God for His salvation:

> **17** "But God be thanked that *though* you were slaves of sin, yet you obeyed from the heart that form of doctrine to which you were delivered. **18** And having been set free from sin, you became slaves of righteousness." (Romans 6.17,18)

17 "Therefore, do not be unwise, but understand what the will of the Lord *is*. **18** And do not be drunk with wine, in which is dissipation; but be filled with the Spirit, **19** speaking to one another in psalms and hymns and spiritual songs, singing and making melody in your heart to the Lord, **20** giving thanks always for all things to God the Father in the name of our Lord Jesus Christ, **21** submitting to one another in the fear of God." (Ephesians 5.17-21)

9 "After these things I looked, and behold, a great multitude which no one could number, of all nations, tribes, peoples, and tongues, standing before the throne and before the Lamb, clothed with white robes, with palm branches in their hands, **10** and crying out with a loud voice, saying, 'Salvation *belongs* to our God who sits on the throne, and to the Lamb!'" (Revelation 7.9,10)

Prayer

We thank you, Lord, for your mercy and grace towards us in Christ Jesus. Our prayer is that today we will remain thankful to you in all that we do and say. Strengthen our resolve, Lord, to overcome any sin in our lives. Strengthen our communion with you through your Holy Spirit. We pray this in the name of Jesus. Amen.

Day 2

30 "I will praise the name of God with a song,
And will magnify Him with thanksgiving.
31 *This* also shall please the Lord better than an ox *or* bull,
Which has horns and hooves.
32 The humble shall see *this and* be glad;
And you who seek God, your hearts shall live.
33 For the Lord hears the poor,
And does not despise His prisoners."
 (Psalms 69.30-33)

This Psalm is messianic and is the most quoted in the New Testament with the exception of Psalm 22. (Psalm 69.4 in John 15.25; 69.9 in John 2.17; 69.9 in Romans 15.3; 69.21 in Matthew 27.34,48; Mark 15.36; Luke 23.36; John 19.28,29. 69.22,23 in Romans 11.9,10; 69.25 in Acts 1.20.)

In Romans 11.9 the apostle Paul recognized David as the author of Psalms 69. The sufferings of David and prophetically of the Messiah described in this Psalm do not prevent the author from praising God and offering his thanksgiving. In Psalms 69 God's judgment will come upon the wicked who mistreat and persecute the righteous.

This has sometimes been interpreted as rashness on the part of God, but this is misunderstanding the context of God's righteous judgment on evil people.

This Psalm is also prophetical in showing how when the Messiah comes, there will be no need of animal sacrifices (v.31). Salvation and redemption (vv.18, 35) will not depend on animal sacrifices which are unable to "save the conscience" (Hebrews 10.1-4; 9.13,14):

> **19** "Therefore, brethren, having boldness to enter the Holiest by the blood of Jesus, **20** by a new and living way which He consecrated for us, through the veil, that is, His flesh, **21** and *having* a High Priest over the house of God, **22** let us draw near with a true heart in full assurance of faith, having our hearts sprinkled from an evil conscience and our bodies washed with pure water." (Hebrews 10.19-22)

> **12** "Therefore, Jesus also, that He might sanctify the people with His own blood, suffered outside the gate. **13** Therefore let us go forth to Him, outside the camp, bearing His reproach. **14** For here we have no continuing city, but we seek the one to come. **15** Therefore by Him let us continually offer the sacrifice of praise to God, that is, the fruit of *our* lips, giving thanks to His name. **16** But do not forget to do good and to share, for with such sacrifices God is well pleased." (Hebrews 13.12-16)

Prayer

Lord in heaven, we thank you for the Gospel of Jesus Christ by which we are saved. We thank you for His death on the cross and his resurrection. We pray Lord that we will today remain steadfast in our faith and hope; that we will remember your goodness and mercy. We pray for a forgiving spirit towards all and the wisdom to speak with truth and love towards everyone. We pray in the name of Jesus, our Lord. Amen.

Day 3

> 1 "Oh come, let us sing to the Lord!
> Let us shout joyfully to the Rock of our salvation.
> 2 Let us come before His presence with thanksgiving;
> Let us shout joyfully to Him with psalms.
> 3 For the Lord *is* the great God,
> And the great King above all gods.
> 4 In His hand *are* the deep places of the earth;
> The heights of the hills *are* His also.
> 5 The sea *is* His, for He made it;
> And His hands formed the dry *land.*"
> (Psalms 95.1-5)

In these verses of Psalm 95 joy and thanksgiving are brought together. The joy that is expressed here and throughout Scripture is the fruit of a thankful heart. It is also rooted in an admiration for His creation: the deep places of the earth, the heights of the hills, the sea and the dry land.

The Psalm will also include in this joyful thanksgiving and worship those who "kneel before the Lord our Maker" (v.6) and the maker of His people (v.7).

This Psalm of praise contains warnings in verses 8 to 11 which are quoted in the New Testament: "Today, if you will hear his voice: Do not harden your hearts as in the rebellion" (v.8, see Hebrews 3.7-15).

The Psalm shows the contrast between the thankful and joyful who worship the LORD and those who harden their hearts. Hardening of heart and sinfulness are incompatible with a thankful heart and joyful praises and worship.

The hardening of the heart is towards the "voice of God" or the word of God. It is a hardening against God's will revealed in history (Hebrews 1.1-4). The message of the cross was a stumbling block for Jews and foolishness for Gentiles, but the power of God to save all humanity (1 Corinthians 1.23). The teaching of the scribes and Pharisees hindered people to enter into God's kingdom (Matthew 23.13; Luke 11.52).

Living in sin is also rebellion against the word of God, against his commandments:

> 7 "'For the lips of a priest should keep knowledge,
> And *people* should seek the law from his mouth;
> For he is the messenger of the Lord of hosts.
> 8 But you have departed from the way;

You have caused many to stumble at the law.
You have corrupted the covenant of Levi,'
Says the Lord of hosts." (Malachi 2.7,8)

14 "But I have a few things against you, because you have there those who hold the doctrine of Balaam, who taught Balak to put a stumbling block before the children of Israel, to eat things sacrificed to idols, and to commit sexual immorality. **15** Thus you also have those who hold the doctrine of the Nicolaitans, which thing I hate. **16** Repent, or else I will come to you quickly and will fight against them with the sword of My mouth." (Revelation 2.14-16)

5 "But I want to remind you, though you once knew this, that the Lord, having saved the people out of the land of Egypt, afterward destroyed those who did not believe. **6** And the angels who did not keep their proper domain, but left their own abode, He has reserved in everlasting chains under darkness for the judgment of the great day; **7** as Sodom and Gomorrah, and the cities around them in a similar manner to these, having given themselves over to sexual immorality and gone after strange flesh, are set forth as an example, suffering the [d]vengeance of eternal fire." (Jude 6,7)

Prayer

Father in heaven, we need to grow in faithfulness and purity of heart. We need to be closer to your will day by day. Help us, LORD, to grow today closer to your will and your perfection in holiness and righteousness. Give us the wisdom and strength we need as we meet the challenges of this day. We pray in the name of Jesus, our Lord. Amen.

Day 4

1 "Praise the Lord!
Oh, give thanks to the Lord, for *He is* good!
For His mercy *endures* forever.
2 Who can utter the mighty acts of the Lord?
Who can declare all His praise?
3 Blessed *are* those who keep justice,
And he who does righteousness at all times!"

(Psalms 106.1-3)

In this Psalm, as in 95, thankfulness is the expression of those who seek righteousness. This is the answer to the question "Who can declare all His praise?" There is a clear connection with the righteous and holy life and the life of thanksgiving and praise.

"The Lord *is* far from the wicked,
But He hears the prayer of the righteous." (Proverbs 15.29)

"One who turns away his ear from hearing the law,
Even his prayer *is* an abomination." (Proverbs 28.9)

"If I regard iniquity in my heart,
The Lord will not hear." (Psalms 66.18)

"Let the wicked forsake his way,
And the unrighteous man his thoughts;
Let him return to the Lord,
And He will have mercy on him;
And to our God,
For He will abundantly pardon." (Isaiah 55.7)

1 "Behold, the Lord's hand is not shortened,
That it cannot save;
Nor His ear heavy,
That it cannot hear.
2 But your iniquities have separated you from your God;
And your sins have hidden *His* face from you" (Isaiah 59.1,2)

11 "For I know the thoughts that I think toward you, says the Lord, thoughts of peace and not of evil, to give you a future and a hope. **12** Then you will call upon Me and go and pray to Me, and I will listen to you. **13** And you will seek Me and find *Me,* when you search for Me with all your heart." (Jeremiah 29.11-13)

13 "When I shut up heaven and there is no rain, or command the locusts to devour the land, or send pestilence among My people, **14** if My people who are called by My name will humble themselves, and pray and seek My face, and turn from their wicked ways, then I will hear from heaven, and will forgive their sin and heal their land." (2 Chronicles 7.13,14)

2 "You lust and do not have. You murder and covet and cannot obtain. You fight and war. Yet you do not have because you do not ask. **3** You ask and do not receive, because you ask amiss, that you may spend *it* on your pleasures." (James 4.2, 3)

21 "Beloved, if our heart does not condemn us, we have confidence toward God. **22** And whatever we ask we receive from Him, because we keep His commandments and do those things that are pleasing in His sight. **23** And this is His commandment: that we should believe on the name of His Son Jesus Christ and love one another, as He gave us commandment." (1 John 3.21,22)

Prayer

We are grateful to you our Father for salvation in Jesus Christ. We are thankful for the blood of the lamb which washes away our sins. We come to you for strength and wisdom in order to live holy lives. We ask for forgiveness of sinful ways, thoughts or words. Help us, Lord, and keep us in your will. In Jesus' name, we pray. Amen.

Day 5

21 "Then they cried out to the Lord in their trouble,
And He saved them out of their distresses.
20 He sent His word and healed them,
And delivered *them* from their destructions.
21 Oh, that *men* would give thanks to the Lord *for* His goodness,
And *for* His wonderful works to the children of men!
22 Let them sacrifice the sacrifices of thanksgiving,
And declare His works with rejoicing."
    (Psalms 107.19-22)

May we be always thankful when the LORD has answered our prayers. May we not forget his blessings and answered prayers.

The offerings and sacrifices which are pleasing to the LORD are those that come from a thankful heart. Psalms 107 reminds the readers of God's deliverances towards Israel and God's servants. This is extended to all "men" all peoples who should give thanks to the LORD for His goodness and wonderful works "to the children of men".

This applies especially today to those who have put their trust in Jesus' sacrifice and have turned to him for salvation. The "sacrifice of praise" by which we "give thanks to His name" follows our faith in Jesus, who sanctified us by his own blood. Being thankful for the salvation we receive in Christ is essential to the life of the saints.

It is often one of the first things mentioned in the New Testament writings:

> **12** "Therefore, Jesus also, that He might sanctify the people with His own blood, suffered outside the gate. **13** Therefore let us go forth to Him, outside the camp, bearing His reproach. **14** For here we have no continuing city, but we seek the one to come. **15** Therefore by Him let us continually offer the sacrifice of praise to God, that is, the fruit of *our* lips, giving thanks to His name. **16** But do not forget to do good and to share, for with such sacrifices God is well pleased." (Hebrews 13.12-16)

> **3** "We give thanks to the God and Father of our Lord Jesus Christ, praying always for you, **4** since we heard of your faith in Christ Jesus and of your love for all the saints; **5** because of the hope which is laid up for you in heaven, of which you heard before in the word of the truth of the gospel" (Colossians 1.3-5)

> **8** "First, I thank my God through Jesus Christ for you all, that your faith is spoken of throughout the whole world. **9** For God is my witness, whom I serve with my spirit in the gospel of His Son, that without ceasing I make mention of you always in my prayers" (Romans 1.8,9)

> **3** "We are bound to thank God always for you, brethren, as it is fitting, because your faith grows exceedingly, and the love of every one of you all abounds toward each other, **4** so that we ourselves boast of you among the churches of God for your patience and faith in all your persecutions and tribulations that you endure" (2 Thessalonians 1.3,4)

Prayer

We thank you, our God and savior, for the wonderful blessing of forgiveness through the blood of the lamb Jesus. We praise you for this gift we have received and continue to enjoy day by day. We pray that today we will live with grateful hearts and that our actions will show our gratefulness to you. It is our prayer in the name of Jesus, our Lord. Amen.

Day 6

>**1** "Oh, give thanks to the Lord, for *He is* good!
>For His mercy *endures* forever.
>**2** Let Israel now say,
>'His mercy *endures* forever.'
>**3** Let the house of Aaron now say,
>'His mercy *endures* forever.'
>**4** Let those who fear the Lord now say,
>'His mercy *endures* forever.'"
>(Psalms 118.1-4)

Thankfulness and rejoicing for God's mercy and salvation are echoed throughout this Psalm (vv.1,14,15,21,29).

No text in the Old Testament is quoted more in the New Testament. Jesus and the New Testament apply this Psalm to the role and rule of Christ, "the stone which the builders rejected" and which became the chief cornerstone (v.22). Quoted by Jesus in Matthew 21.42; Mark 12,10,11; Luke 20.17. Quoted by Peter in Acts 4.11 (note also 1 Peter 2.7,8) and alluded to in Ephesians 2.20.

The focus of the Psalm is on the LORD from whom goodness, mercy and salvation come. Reading this Psalm, one should realize it is impossible to be thankful to God without a deep-seated conviction of God's goodness and the reality of His salvation.

The Psalm is introduced and concludes with the same words of thanksgiving for God's goodness and mercy:

>"Oh, give thanks to the Lord, for *He is* good!
>For His mercy *endures* forever." (vv.1,29)

At the heart of what the LORD has done or will do is the "marvelous" work described in verses 22 and 23 and which concern the Messiah:

>**22** "The stone *which* the builders rejected
>Has become the chief cornerstone.
>**23** This was the Lord's doing;

It *is* marvelous in our eyes.
24 This *is* the day the Lord has made;
We will rejoice and be glad in it." (vv.22–24)

Just as David had been rejected and had become King, so the rejected Christ would be the king of God's kingdom. It is significant that the Psalm alludes to attempts on the life of the King from verses 5 to 18. Verse 18 concludes this thought with the word: "He has not given me over to death". David did die, but was preserved throughout his life, so he could reign as king of Israel. Jesus also died and rose from the dead, as he himself predicted:

> **31** "He taught His disciples and said to them, 'The Son of Man is being betrayed into the hands of men, and they will kill Him. And after He is killed, He will rise the third day.' **32** But they did not understand this saying and were afraid to ask Him." (Mark 9.30-32)

> **3** "For I delivered to you first of all that which I also received: that Christ died for our sins according to the Scriptures, **4** and that He was buried, and that He rose again the third day according to the Scriptures" (1 Corinthians 15.3,4)

Thankfulness for the goodness and mercy of the LORD is based on what He has done despite all the opposition against His king. Jesus' victory and the blessings that flow from this are also proclaimed in verse 26: "Blessed is he who comes in the name of the LORD" (this verse is also quoted by Jesus in Matthew 23.39).

Prayer

Father in heaven, we praise you for the life, death and resurrection of Jesus. We are thankful for the forgiveness and salvation we find in him. We pray that we can grow today in our appreciation of your goodness and mercy. May you guide us today in our actions and decisions. We pray in the name of Jesus. Amen.

Day 7

7 "Sing to the Lord with thanksgiving;
Sing praises on the harp to our God,
8 Who covers the heavens with clouds,
Who prepares rain for the earth,

Who makes grass to grow on the mountains.
9 He gives to the beast its food,
And to the young ravens that cry."
  (Psalms 147.7-9)

19 "He declares His word to Jacob,
His statutes and His judgments to Israel.
20 He has not dealt thus with any nation;
And *as for His* judgments, they have not known them.
Praise the Lord!"
  (Psalms 147.19,20)

This Psalm can be divided in three parts that start with words of praise (verses 1, 7 and 12). The LORD is praised for having brought back His people to their land and for the rebuilding of Jerusalem (verses 1-6).

The prophets like Isaiah prophesy of the coming captivity of God's people, but also of their gathering together and of the rebuilding of Jerusalem (Isaiah 11.12). After the return from captivity under Cyrus in 538 B.C., it took almost one hundred years to rebuild Jerusalem (completed in 445 B.C. with the completion of the walls and the gates of the city). The exiles returned gradually to the land under Zerubbabel, Ezra and Nehemiah.

The LORD'S actions towards His people Israel were the work of the one who "calls all the stars by name", whose "understanding is infinite" (vv.4,5). They were also the work of the one who "heals the brokenhearted" and "lifts up the humble" (vv.3, 6).

The LORD who knows everything and is all powerful is also caring for "the young ravens that cry" (v.9); He "gives to the beast its food" (v.9) and "takes pleasure in those who fear Him" (v.11).

In verses 15 to 20 the LORD is the one who orders snow and cold through His word; He is also the one who gave His word to Jacob, "His statutes and His judgments to Israel". The ending of this Psalm confirms God's unique and special revelation to Israel: "He has not dealt thus with any nation" (v.20).

These verses remind us of the words of the apostle Paul in his letter to the Romans:

1 "I tell the truth in Christ, I am not lying, my conscience also bearing me witness in the Holy Spirit, **2** that I have great sorrow and continual grief in my heart. **3** For I could wish that I myself were accursed from Christ for my brethren, my countrymen according to the flesh, **4** who are Israelites, to whom *pertain* the adoption, the glory, the covenants, the giving of the law, the service *of God*, and the promises; **5** of whom *are* the fathers and from whom, according to the flesh, Christ *came*, who is over all, *the* eternally blessed God. Amen." (Romans 9.1-5)

God's favor upon the humble, those who fear Him and who hope in His mercy, is seen throughout the history of Israel. It is a key in understanding His word given to Israel.

Prayer

Our Lord and Father in heaven, we praise you today. We are thankful for your mercy and patience towards us. We pray that today we can be humble in our ways and thankful for every blessing you have provided us with. We ask for your wisdom as we act and make decisions for our families or in our work. We pray this in the name of Jesus. Amen.

Week 38: The God of Salvation

Day 1

> **21** "Blessed *be* the Lord,
> *Who* daily loads us *with benefits*,
> The God of our salvation! *Selah*
> **20** Our God *is* the God of salvation;
> And to God the Lord *belong* escapes from death."
>   (Psalms 68.19,20)
>
> **34** "Ascribe strength to God;
> His excellence *is* over Israel,
> And His strength *is* in the clouds.
> **35** O God *You are* more awesome than Your holy places.
> The God of Israel *is* He who gives strength and power
> to *His* people."
>   (Psalms 68.34,35)

In a limited sense, God can and will preserve us from death. David's life was threatened many times, but God delivered him. But "salvation" in the final analysis is the final victory over death, the greatest and last enemy. Christ reigns today until he has "put all his enemies under his feet" (1 Corinthians 15.25,26).

The keys of the grave and of death have been put into the hands of the Lord Jesus: "I *am* He who lives, and was dead, and behold, I am alive forevermore. Amen. And I have the keys of Hades and of Death." (Revelation 1.18).

By a man came death, also by a man comes the resurrection of the dead:

> **20** "But now Christ is risen from the dead *and* has become the first fruits of those who have fallen asleep. **21** For since by man *came* death, by Man also *came* the resurrection of the

dead. **22** For as in Adam all die, even so in Christ all shall be made alive." (1 Corinthians 15.20-22)

This conviction is founded on the fact of Jesus' resurrection. If Jesus has not risen, our faith is futile and believers are still in their sins (1 Corinthians 15.17).

Israel is called to "ascribe power" to God, who "went before His people" and provided for His people in the desert (vv.7-10). The God who performed mighty signs through Jesus and brings back the dead to life has gone "before us" and we can trust Him for the present and the future, even in the face of death:

30 "And truly Jesus did many other signs in the presence of His disciples, which are not written in this book; **31** but these are written that you may believe that Jesus is the Christ, the Son of God, and that believing you may have life in His name." (John 19.30,31)

Prayer

We praise you Father for all the great works you have accomplished in the life of Israel your people and the life of Jesus the Messiah. We thank you for your salvation, your forgiveness in Jesus, our Lord and savior. We pray that today you can strengthen us with greater faith, hope and love. Give us Father wisdom in how we act and talk to every person we meet today. In Jesus' name, we pray. Amen.

Day 2

8 "Oh, do not remember former iniquities against us!
Let Your tender mercies come speedily to meet us,
For we have been brought very low.
9 Help us, O God of our salvation,
For the glory of Your name;
And deliver us, and provide atonement for our sins,
For Your name's sake!"
   (Psalms 79.8,9)

This is a Psalm addressed to "the God of our salvation". This Psalm shows an emphasis on the mistreatment of Israel by the gentile nations: "O God, the nations have come into your inheritance; your holy temple they have defiled; they have laid Jerusalem in heaps". This was an important part of God's warnings to Israel through prophets such as Jeremiah and Ezekiel, and refers to the coming of Babylon against Jerusalem and the temple and the destruction of the city in 586 B.C.

This work of destruction accomplished by these heathen nations was the result of the sins of Israel's leaders (kings and priests) as depicted by the prophets of this era:

> **9** "Then He said to me, 'The iniquity of the house of Israel and Judah *is* exceedingly great, and the land is full of bloodshed, and the city full of perversity; for they say, 'The Lord has forsaken the land, and the Lord does not see!' **10** And as for Me also, My eye will neither spare, nor will I have pity, *but* I will recompense their deeds on their own head.'" (Ezekiel 9.9,10)

Thus, the mention of the "former iniquities" of Israel and the need for "atonement": "Oh, do not remember former iniquities against us!"; "And deliver us, and provide atonement for our sins". This Psalm is a call for "salvation" based on the "tender mercies" of God (v.8). The salvation brought about by God is always to "the glory" of His name, as mentioned by the prophet Ezekiel:

"But I acted for My name's sake, that it should not be profaned before the Gentiles among whom they *were,* in whose sight I had made Myself known to them, to bring them out of the land of Egypt." (Ezekiel 20.9).

Those who are saved through their faith in Jesus are now called to live for Him:

> **14** "For the love of Christ compels us, because we judge thus: that if One died for all, then all died; **15** and He died for all, that those who live should live no longer for themselves, but for Him who died for them and rose again." (2 Corinthians 5.14,15).

The salvation of both Jews and Gentiles through Jesus brings honor to God and to His sovereign plan to save all men:

> **33** "Oh, the depth of the riches both of the wisdom and knowledge of God! How unsearchable *are* His judgments and His ways past finding out!
> **34** 'For who has known the mind of the Lord?
> Or who has become His counselor?'
> **35** 'Or who has first given to Him
> And it shall be repaid to him?'

36 For of Him and through Him and to Him *are* all things, to whom *be* glory forever. Amen." (Romans 11.33-36)

Prayer

We are grateful to you, our God and Father in heaven, for your tender mercies. We thank you for your salvation, for the forgiveness we enjoy in Jesus. We want to serve you today with a grateful heart. We ask you to teach us and to guide us in our actions and decisions. Bless those with whom we will be in touch. May we be a blessing for every person we meet. We pray in the name of Jesus, our Lord. Amen.

Day 3

> **1** "Lord, you have been favorable to Your land;
> You have brought back the captivity of Jacob.
> **2** You have forgiven the iniquity of Your people;
> You have covered all their sin. *Selah*
> **3** You have taken away all Your wrath;
> You have turned from the fierceness of Your anger.
> **4** Restore us, O God of our salvation,
> And cause Your anger toward us to cease.
> **5** Will You be angry with us forever?
> Will You prolong Your anger to all generations?
> **6** Will You not revive us again,
> That Your people may rejoice in You?
> **7** Show us Your mercy, Lord,
> And grant us Your salvation."
> (Psalms 85.1-7)

This Psalm points to after the exile of Israel and the return to the land after the decree of Cyrus (536 B.C.). The people rejoice that they have been able to return to their land. However, the Psalm seems to linger on the "anger" of the Lord and his judgments. The return to the land from exile needs to be followed by spiritual revival, by spiritual restoration and by rejoicing:

Those who have left the "father's house" as the prodigal son and who come back to the father are invited to live in harmony with the father and with His family (Luke 15.11-32). We see how repentance leads to restoration and restoration leads to peace and righteousness:

> **10** "Mercy and truth have met together;
> Righteousness and peace have kissed.
> **11** Truth shall spring out of the earth,
> And righteousness shall look down from heaven." (Psalms 85.10,11)

Those who have been offered forgiveness in Christ are now to walk in good works planned by God for them:

> **8** For by grace you have been saved through faith, and that not of yourselves; *it is* the gift of God, **9** not of works, lest anyone should boast. **10** For we are His workmanship, created in Christ Jesus for good works, which God prepared beforehand that we should walk in them." (Ephesians 2.8,9)

> "This is a faithful saying, and these things I want you to affirm constantly, that those who have believed in God should be careful to maintain good works. These things are good and profitable to men." (Titus 3.8)

In this Psalm, forgiveness and revival lead also to rejoicing (v.6). The Ethiopian man rejoiced following his baptism:

> **38** "So, he commanded the chariot to stand still. And both Philip and the eunuch went down into the water, and he baptized him. **39** Now when they came up out of the water, the Spirit of the Lord caught Philip away, so that the eunuch saw him no more; and he went on his way rejoicing." (Acts 8.38,39)

> **16** "Rejoice always, **17** pray without ceasing, **18** in everything give thanks; for this is the will of God in Christ Jesus for you." (1 Thessalonians 5.16-18)

Prayer

We rejoice, Father, for your grace and love. We rejoice for giving us hope and eternal life, for final victory in the face of difficulties and even death. Help us, Lord, to be thankful for your salvation. Help us to seek revival and restoration. We believe in all your promises and pray that you will give us strength and wisdom for every action of this day. We pray in the name of Jesus. Amen.

Day 4

> **1** "O Lord, God of my salvation,
> I have cried out day and night before You.
> **2** Let my prayer come before You;
> Incline Your ear to my cry.
> **3** For my soul is full of troubles,
> And my life draws near to the grave.
> **4** I am counted with those who go down to the pit;
> "I am like a man *who has* no strength,
> **5** Adrift among the dead,
> Like the slain who lie in the grave,
> Whom You remember no more,
> And who are cut off from Your hand."
> (Psalms 88.1-5)

When faced with death or the most difficult situations, there is no other savior we can go to except the "God of my salvation". While death is part of the reality we must face, the living God is a greater part of that reality.

The pains and sufferings of living on this earth can feel overwhelming. Our feelings cannot overcome the brutal realities we face each day. What overcomes these realities is our faith and our faith is founded on the living God who spoke through Moses, Elijah or Jeremiah but who spoke especially through Jesus who is also called "The Word".

Even when our souls are "full of troubles" we still know deep in our hearts that Jesus has spoken truth and that we can depend completely on that truth. Faith in the biblical sense is to depend, to rely on, to build on. It is not a feeling; it is action based on the Word of God.

Our feelings come and go. But action based on God's Word is the only true medicine that can heal our spiritual and moral diseases, and can heal the spiritual and moral diseases of this world.

Faith without action is dead (James 2.26). Faith that is active submits to God, resists the devil, draws us near to God, purifies our hearts, helps us be more humble, keeps us from judging our brothers and sisters and makes us pray these words: "If the Lord wills, we shall do this or that" (James chapter 4)

Prayer

Our Father in heaven, we come to you for help for this day you offer us. This is a day given to us to glorify you, to honor you and to serve you. This is a day to act upon your Word. Lord, strengthen us in faith and in action based on that faith. We are thankful for Jesus who intercedes for us. It is in His name that we pray. Amen.

Day 5

> **1** "Oh come, let us sing to the Lord!
> Let us shout joyfully to the Rock of our salvation.
> **2** Let us come before His presence with thanksgiving;
> Let us shout joyfully to Him with psalms.
> **3** For the Lord *is* the great God,
> And the great King above all gods."
> (Psalms 95.1,2)

Very early on in the Bible, God is called "the Rock". A "rock" describes safety and protection. God is a rock because He is unmovable, he is consistent and not shaken. We can take refuge in Him. We can also build on Him:

> **3** "For I proclaim the name of the Lord:
> Ascribe greatness to our God.
> **4** *He is* the Rock, His work *is* perfect;
> For all His ways *are* justice,
> A God of truth and without injustice;
> Righteous and upright *is* He." (Deuteronomy 32.3,4).

In most cases, the LORD is called "the Rock" and not just "a rock" for His people. God was not and is not one source of safety and protection; He is the only source of safety and protection.

Besides the LORD, the only one who is described as "rock" or "stone" for His people is the Messiah; the "rock" God has given to His people to lean on or build on in times of trouble:

> "Therefore, thus says the Lord God:
> 'Behold, I lay in Zion a stone for a foundation,
> A tried stone, a precious cornerstone, a sure foundation;
> Whoever believes will not act hastily.'" (Isaiah 28.16).

This prophecy of Isaiah is quoted in the New Testament as referring to the Messiah, to Jesus in 1 Peter 2 and in Romans 9.

The "Stone" laid by God for His people is also mentioned in Psalms 118.22, 23:

22 "The stone *which* the builders rejected
Has become the chief cornerstone.
23 This was the Lord's doing;
It *is* marvelous in our eyes."

This is referred to by Jesus in Luke 20.17,18; Mark 12.10; Matthieu 21.42, and by Peter in Acts 4.11,12. The stone or "rock" laid by God is the only foundation of God's people:

> **9** "For we are God's fellow workers; you are God's field, *you are* God's building. **10** According to the grace of God, which was given to me, as a wise master builder I have laid the foundation and another builds on it. But let each one take heed how he builds on it. **11** For no other foundation can anyone lay than that which is laid, which is Jesus Christ." (1 Corinthians 3.9-11)

Jesus as the foundation provided by God to His house which is Israel applies also to Gentiles who come to God through Jesus:

> **19** "Now, therefore, you are no longer strangers and foreigners, but fellow citizens with the saints and members of the household of God, **20** having been built on the foundation of the apostles and prophets, Jesus Christ Himself being the chief corner*stone*, **21** in whom the whole building, being fitted together, grows into a holy temple in the Lord, **22** in whom you also are being built together for a dwelling place of God in the Spirit." (Ephesians 2.19-22)

Prayer

We thank you, Father, for your Son, Jesus, who is the Rock of the Church. We thank you for His salvation and for being part of your people. We thank you for access to you through Jesus, our High Priest. We confess to you our sins and shortcomings. We pray for forgiveness and wisdom in order to live a sanctified life in your sight. In Jesus' name, we pray. Amen.

Day 6

1 "Truly my soul silently *waits* for God;
From Him *comes* my salvation.
2 He only *is* my rock and my salvation;

He is my defense;
I shall not be greatly moved."
   (Psalms 62.1,2)

11 "God has spoken once,
Twice I have heard this:
That power *belongs* to God.
12 Also to You, O Lord, *belongs* mercy;
For You render to each one according to his work."
   (Psalms 62.11,12)

The first two verses of Psalm 62 are written in the first person: "My soul…my salvation…my defense". There is a balance in the Bible between the sense of community and individual responsibility. Verse 12 concludes with the words: "For you render to each one according to his work". God speaking through the prophet Ezekiel addresses the entire nation while reminding each individual of his or her responsibility (see also chapter 18 of Ezekiel):

> **3** "Now the glory of the God of Israel had gone up from the cherub, where it had been, to the threshold of the temple. And He called to the man clothed with linen, who *had* the writer's inkhorn at his side; **4** and the Lord said to him, 'Go through the midst of the city, through the midst of Jerusalem, and put a mark on the foreheads of the men who sigh and cry over all the abominations that are done within it.'" (Ezekiel 9.4)

Salvation is an individual matter. The statement of Jesus in John 3.14-16 makes this clear:

> **14** "And as Moses lifted up the serpent in the wilderness, even so must the Son of Man be lifted up, **15** that whoever believes in Him should not perish but have eternal life. **16** For God so loved the world that He gave His only-begotten Son, that whoever believes in Him should not perish but have everlasting life. **17** For God did not send His Son into the world to condemn the world, but that the world through Him might be saved."

The communal or national aspects of salvation never cancel the individual's responsibility before God. We find this balance throughout the Bible. In discussing the question of "sin" and guilt at the level of Israel, the apostle Paul confirms what the prophets teach in his letter to the Romans. Note especially these verses:

> **25** "For circumcision is indeed profitable if you keep the law; but if you are a breaker of the law, your circumcision has become uncircumcision. **26** Therefore, if an uncircumcised man keeps the righteous requirements of the law, will not his uncircumcision be counted as circumcision? **27** And will not the physically uncircumcised, if he fulfills the law, judge you who, *even* with *your* written *code* and circumcision, *are* a transgressor of the law? **28** For he is not a Jew who *is one* outwardly, nor *is* circumcision that which *is* outward in the flesh; **29** but *he is* a Jew who *is one* inwardly; and circumcision *is that* of the heart, in the Spirit, not in the letter; whose praise *is* not from men but from God." (Romans 2.25-29)

These statements by the apostle are in line with what we find throughout the Old Testament concerning the status of Israel as God's people, and confirmed throughout the New Testament:

> **17** "But as God has distributed to each one, as the Lord has called each one, so let him walk. And so I ordain in all the churches. **18** Was anyone called while circumcised? Let him not become uncircumcised. Was anyone called while uncircumcised? Let him not be circumcised. **19** Circumcision is nothing and uncircumcision is nothing but keeping the commandments of God *is what matters.*" (1 Corinthians 9.17-19)

> **4** "You have become estranged from Christ, you who *attempt to* be justified by law; you have fallen from grace. **5** For we through the Spirit eagerly wait for the hope of righteousness by faith. **6** For in Christ Jesus neither circumcision nor uncircumcision avails anything, but faith working through love." (Galatians 5.6)

> **14** "But God forbid that I should boast except in the cross of our Lord Jesus Christ, by whom the world has been crucified to me, and I to the world. **15** For in Christ Jesus neither circumcision nor uncircumcision avails anything, but a new creation." (Galatians 6.15)

The "fulness" of the Gentiles as well as "all Israel" are saved by the "deliverer" who comes from Zion when they have faith in Jesus and repent:

> **26** "And in this way all Israel will be saved. As it is written:
> 'The deliverer will come from Zion;
>   he will turn godlessness away from Jacob.
> **27** And this is my covenant with them
>   when I take away their sins.'" (Romans 11.26 and Isaiah 59.20)

Speaking to those of "the house of Israel" the apostle Peter calls on each one present to repent and be baptized in the name of Jesus Christ for the remission of sins (Acts 2.38). The message is for "the house of Israel" but faith, repentance and immersion are an individual matter:

> **13** "With many other words he warned them; and he pleaded with them, 'Save yourselves from this corrupt generation.' **41** Those who accepted his message were baptized, and about three thousand were added to their number that day." (Acts 2.40,41)

Prayer

Father in heaven, we come to you for forgiveness, for strength and for wisdom. Without you we can do nothing. May we this day be close to you in thoughts and desires. May our hearts grow closer to you and more loving toward our neighbor. We are thankful for the new birth. We are grateful for your salvation and all the blessings we have from you. We pray in the name of Jesus, our Lord. Amen.

Day 7

> **4** "Show me Your ways, O Lord;
> Teach me Your paths.
> **5** Lead me in Your truth and teach me,
> For You *are* the God of my salvation;
> On You I wait all the day."
>   (Psalms 25.4,5)

> **16** "Turn Yourself to me, and have mercy on me,
> For I *am* desolate and afflicted.
> **17** The troubles of my heart have enlarged;
> Bring me out of my distresses!

> **18** Look on my affliction and my pain,
> And forgive all my sins."
> (Psalms 25.16,17)

In Psalm 25 the writer asks for forgiveness for his sins three times (vv.7,11,18). Prayer for forgiveness is sometimes "collective" in the Bible (as in Daniel 9). But most of the time it is individual and personal. The personal dimension of the Psalm does not preclude a national or collective concern (vv.8-15).

Forgiveness of past sins is not an end in itself. Having sins forgiven through Jesus is not the end of what God intends to do in our lives. The first verses of the Psalm are looking to the present and the future, when God is teaching and leading the servant of God that he might lead others.

This is also what we learn in Psalm 51:

> **12** "Restore to me the joy of Your salvation,
> And uphold me *by Your* generous Spirit.
> **13** *Then* I will teach transgressors Your ways,
> And sinners shall be converted to You." (Psalms 51.12,13)

The last verse of Psalm 25 shows the writer's concern for all of God's people: "Redeem Israel, O God, out of all their troubles" (v.22).

Coming into a right relationship with God is the beginning of a new life for the believer. This new life is to be one of service and doing good:

> **8** "For by grace you have been saved through faith, and that not of yourselves; *it is* the gift of God, **9** not of works, lest anyone should boast. **10** For we are His workmanship, created in Christ Jesus for good works, which God prepared beforehand that we should walk in them." (Ephesians 2.8-10)

> "This is a faithful saying, and these things I want you to affirm constantly, that those who have believed in God should be careful to maintain good works. These things are good and profitable to men." (Titus 3.8)

Those who believe in the Gospel in Acts 2 are taught to "continue steadfastly" in the apostle's teachings. They are also to continue steadfastly in the fellowship, the breaking of bread and in prayers (Acts 2.42). This verse is a brief description of "the church" as described later in the New Testament. The idea that the word "church" describes exclusively gentiles who have come to the faith is incorrect, as can be seen from

Acts chapter 2. In this chapter, those who constitute the early Church are believers from "Israel". In the writings of the apostle Paul, the "church" is simply the "assembly" or "congregation" of the faithful of Israel to whom believing Gentiles are added:

> **3** "By revelation He made known to me the mystery (as I have briefly written already, **4** by which, when you read, you may understand my knowledge in the mystery of Christ), **5** which in other ages was not made known to the sons of men, as it has now been revealed by the Spirit to His holy apostles and prophets: **6** that the Gentiles should be fellow heirs, of the same body, and partakers of His promise in Christ through the gospel, **7** of which I became a minister according to the gift of the grace of God given to me by the effective working of His power." (Ephesians 3.4-7)

Prayer

We praise you Father for your salvation. We praise you for the Good News about Jesus, who went to the cross for our forgiveness. We come to you with thankfulness. We pray that we will live today in a way that honors you and your will. We ask for strength through your Holy Spirit. In the name of Jesus our Lord, we pray. Amen.

Week 39: God's House

Day 1

> **6** "I will wash my hands in innocence;
> So I will go about Your altar, O Lord,
> **7** That I may proclaim with the voice of thanksgiving,
> And tell of all Your wondrous works.
> **8** Lord, I have loved the habitation of Your house,
> And the place where Your glory dwells."
> (Psalms 26.6-8)

Loving God is the greatest commandment. It is this love of God which drives one to examine his ways: "Examine me, O LORD, and prove me; try my mind and my heart…" (Ps. 26.2). The love of the LORD drives the faithful to proclaim Him, extol Him with "the voice of thanksgiving" and tell of His wondrous works. It is also this love of the LORD that makes one "love" the habitation of the LORD'S House.

God's "holy habitation" is foremost and primarily in heaven: "Look down from Your holy habitation, from heaven, and bless Your people Israel and the land which You have given us, just as You swore to our fathers, 'a land flowing with milk and honey.'" (Deuteronomy 26.15).

Under the reign of Hezekiah, king of Judah (715 to 686 BC), there was a return to the worship of God and to His law. There was rejoicing as the people kept the feast of unleavened bread: "Now many people, a very great assembly, gathered at Jerusalem to keep the Feast of Unleavened Bread in the second month." (2 Chronicles 30.13). During this feast, there was great joy and "the priests, the Levites, arose and blessed the people, and their voice was heard; and their prayer came *up* to His holy dwelling place, to heaven." (2 Chronicles 30.27).

The temple in Jerusalem was at the center of this worship of the LORD and the keeping of the feasts with the priests and Levites. However, the text mentions that "their prayer came up to His holy dwelling place to heaven.".

As we discover in the prophecies of Jeremiah and Ezekiel, despite this return to the worship of God under Hezekiah the leaders of God's people ended up turning away from God to idolatry and evil practices ; the "glory" of the LORD in the temple ended up leaving the temple which was destroyed as well as the city when king Nebuchadnezzar came against it (Ezekiel chapters 6-11)

Preaching in the early days of the Church, the deacon Stephen reminds the people of Jerusalem that God's glory and holiness is not tied to any temple or place:

> **48** "However, the Most High does not dwell in temples made with hands, as the prophet says: **49** 'Heaven *is* My throne,
> And earth *is* My footstool.
> What house will you build for Me? says the Lord,
> Or what *is* the place of My rest?
> **50** Has My hand not made all these things?'" (Acts 7.48-50; Amos 5.25-27)

Prayer

Lord, we praise your name and holiness. We believe that you dwell in glory in heaven. We pray that today our lives can honor you and show your goodness and righteousness. So, help us to be faithful to the commandments of our Lord Jesus. Help us grow in your sight and produce the good fruit of the Holy Spirit. This is our prayer in the name of Jesus. Amen.

Day 2

> **1** "Praise the Lord!
> Praise the name of the Lord;
> Praise *Him,* O you servants of the Lord!
> **2** You who stand in the house of the Lord,
> In the courts of the house of our God,
> **3** Praise the Lord, for the Lord *is* good;
> Sing praises to His name, for *it is* pleasant.
> **4** For the Lord has chosen Jacob for Himself,
> Israel for His special treasure."
>   (Psalms 135.1-4)

These verses of Psalm 135 are an invitation for God's people Israel to praise the LORD. The actual praise is found in verses 5 to 21 of the Psalm.

In these verses, Israel is exhorted to "praise God". Those who are admonished by these words are not only the Levites who were serving in the temple, but all the people who stood in the "courts of the house of the LORD" (v.2).

The choice of "Jacob for Himself, of Israel for His special treasure" was manifested in the events of the Exodus described in verses 8-12 from the last plague of the firstborn of Egypt to the entrance into the land as "heritage".

The Psalm is also a reminder that "the idols of the nations" are worthless and do not deserve any worship:

> **15** "The idols of the nations *are* silver and gold,
> The work of men's hands.
> **16** They have mouths, but they do not speak;
> Eyes they have, but they do not see;
> **17** They have ears, but they do not hear;
> Nor is there *any* breath in their mouths.
> **18** Those who make them are like them;
> *So is* everyone who trusts in them." (vv.15-18)

In the "house of the Lord" and the "courts of the house of our God" the people were to praise the LORD the creator of the world (vv.5-7), who delivered His people from Egypt and made them a nation (vv.8-12) and who judges His people (vv.13,14). Thus, from this place were to be proclaimed the great and central truths about God and revealed in His Word.

God's congregation (Hebrew *edah*) or "church" is His people. In the Hebrew language, the word congregation describes God's people and is found throughout the Old Testament:

> **1** "And the Lord spoke to Moses, saying, **2** 'Speak to all the congregation of the children of Israel, and say to them: You shall be holy, for I the Lord your God *am* holy.'" (Leviticus 19.2. See Exodus 12.3,6; 1 Kings 8.5; 12.20).

When Jesus talks about building His Church (Matthew 16.18) he is referring back to the same concept: God's congregation or people. Through the work of Jesus, the Messiah of Israel, God has entered into his promised new covenant with Israel (Hebrews 8.1-13). The New Testament teaching is that Gentiles who come to Christ can now enter into this new covenant with Israel, can now be part of God's "household", congregation (church), people:

19 "Now, therefore, you are no longer strangers and foreigners, but fellow citizens with the saints and members of the household of God, **20** having been built on the foundation of the apostles and prophets, Jesus Christ Himself being the chief corner*stone*, **21** in whom the whole building, being fitted together, grows into a holy temple in the Lord, **22** in whom you also are being built together for a dwelling place of God in the Spirit." (Ephesians 2.19-22)

1 "For this reason I, Paul, the prisoner of Christ Jesus for you Gentiles— **2** if indeed you have heard of the dispensation of the grace of God which was given to me for you, **3** how that by revelation He made known to me the mystery (as I have briefly written already, **4** by which, when you read, you may understand my knowledge in the mystery of Christ), **5** which in other ages was not made known to the sons of men, as it has now been revealed by the Spirit to His holy apostles and prophets: **6** that the Gentiles should be fellow heirs, of the same body, and partakers of His promise in Christ through the gospel, **7** of which I became a minister according to the gift of the grace of God given to me by the effective working of His power." (Ephesians 3.1-7)

26 "For you are all sons of God through faith in Christ Jesus. **27** For as many of you as were baptized into Christ have put on Christ. **28** There is neither Jew nor Greek, there is neither slave nor free, there is neither male nor female; for you are all one in Christ Jesus. **29** And if you *are* Christ's, then you are Abraham's seed, and heirs according to the promise." (Galatians 3.26-29)

Those who belong to Christ belong to Israel's Messiah. They are by the same token "Abraham's seed" and "heirs according to the promise". Using the picture of the "olive tree" the apostle Paul teaches that Gentiles who come to Christ are the "wild olive tree" grafted into Israel, the tree planted by God (Romans 11.11-25).

The apostle Paul warns the elders of the Church in Ephesus of their responsibility in maintaining the truth of the Gospel among God's people, the Church; of their responsibility to remain faithful to the teachings of Jesus and his apostles: "Therefore take heed to yourselves and to all the flock, among which the Holy Spirit has made you overseers, to shepherd the church of God which He purchased with His own blood." (Acts 20.28).

Prayer

Father in heaven, we praise you for the salvation of Israel through faith in the Messiah, Jesus our Lord and Savior. We praise you and thank you for adding those from the Gentiles to your people Israel, of grafting them into the olive tree you have planted. Give us today a spirit of obedience and of trust in your Word. Give us wisdom as we seek to do your will. This we pray in Jesus' name. Amen.

Day 3

> **1** "I was glad when they said to me,
> "Let us go into the house of the Lord."
> **2** Our feet have been standing
> Within your gates, O Jerusalem!"
>   (Psalms 122.1,2)

King David had made Jerusalem his capital. He had also fortified the city and finally brought the ark of the covenant to the site purchased by David (2 Samuel 2; 24.18-25). Finally, David and the people of Israel come to worship in the "house of the LORD" (the tabernacle).

In this Psalm, we find the exhortation to "pray for the peace of Jerusalem". The Psalm concludes with a prayer for peace:

> **8** "For the sake of my brethren and companions,
> I will now say, 'Peace *be* within you.'
> **9** Because of the house of the Lord our God
> I will seek your good.'"

The city of "peace" is where the king, God's anointed, rules. The city of David is central to the work of the Messiah throughout the Scripture. In the prayer called *Shemoneh Esrei* the Jewish people continue to pray for the coming of the Messiah which includes blessings over Jerusalem; a restoration of justice and end of wickedness; a restoration of the line of king David and restoration of the temple service.

Throughout the Scriptures, the importance of Jerusalem and of "God's House" are central to the fulfillment of God's work through the Messiah. The prophet Zechariah is a good example of this:

> **9** "Rejoice greatly, O daughter of Zion!
> Shout, O daughter of Jerusalem!
> Behold, your King is coming to you;
> He *is* just and having salvation,
> Lowly and riding on a donkey,
> A colt, the foal of a donkey.
> **10** I will cut off the chariot from Ephraim
> And the horse from Jerusalem;
> The battle bow shall be cut off.
> He shall speak peace to the nations;
> His dominion *shall be* 'from sea to sea,
> And from the River to the ends of the earth.'" (Zechariah 9.9,10; Matthew 21.5)

In Jewish literature the time when the Messiah comes is called *Olam Habah* which means "the world to come". This corresponds also to the biblical expression "the latter days" (Isaiah 2.1). During these "latter days" of the "world to come" God's promises through the Messiah are realized: all peoples live together in peace; war ceases to exist; no sins are committed (Zephaniah 3.13). The New Testament refers to this also as "the last days" (Hebrews 1.2) when God spoke through His son or "last times" (1 Peter 1.20) when the Messiah "shed his blood as a lamb without blemish and without spot". We are living in "the last days" ever since Jesus' birth and life until he returns visibly from glory.

After his resurrection, Jesus taught Scripture to his disciples so that they might understand how everything written in the Old Testament had to do with his life, death, resurrection and the proclamation of the Gospel to all the world (Luke 24. 24-29) — the message of repentance: "that repentance and remission of sins should be preached in His name to all nations, beginning at Jerusalem." (Luke 4.47).

We see the realization of this beginning in Acts chapter 2 when Jews from all over the world believe in Jesus as the Christ, come to repentance and baptism and enter into the new covenant of peace and forgiveness. They are the first to be added to the congregation (church) of the Messiah, giving themselves to his teachings and to a life of faithfulness to God:

> **40** "And with many other words he testified and exhorted them, saying, 'Be saved from this perverse generation.' **41** Then those who gladly received his word were baptized; and that day about three thousand souls were added *to them*. **42** And they continued

steadfastly in the apostles' doctrine and fellowship, in the breaking of bread, and in prayers." (Acts 2.40-42)

Prayer

We thank you, Father, for the wonderful promises of your word. We praise you for the salvation offered to all through Jesus and his sacrifice. We rejoice in the hope you offer to all in the Gospel. Help us today to live in a way that honors you and the truth of your word. May your Holy Spirit produce in our lives His fruit of love, joy and peace. We pray in Jesus' name. Amen.

Day 4

> **8** "O Lord God of hosts hear my prayer;
> Give ear, O God of Jacob! *Selah*
> **9** O God, behold our shield,
> And look upon the face of Your anointed.
> **10** For a day in Your courts *is* better than a thousand.
> I would rather be a doorkeeper in the house of my God
> Than dwell in the tents of wickedness.
> **11** For the Lord God *is* a sun and shield;
> The Lord will give grace and glory;
> No good *thing* will He withhold
> From those who walk uprightly.
> **12** O Lord of hosts,
> Blessed *is* the man who trusts in You!"
> (Psalms 84.8-12)

In these verses of Psalm 84 and throughout the Psalm we see the centrality of God as the source of joy, blessings and protection for the faithful: "My heart and my flesh cry out for the living God" (v.2). In the history of Israel described in the Old Testament, God remained the shield of the faithful, despite whatever happened: "For the LORD God is a sun and shield".

In the days of the prophet Ezekiel during the Babylonian captivity, the temple was corrupted by the sins of the corrupt priests; the glory of the Lord had left the temple (Ezekiel chapters 1 to 8). Even in the midst of those circumstances, the words of this Psalm would have still resounded with hope and joy because God himself does not change. He remains faithful to those who are faithful to him. The sinfulness of the world brings pain and grief, but the holiness of God brings comfort and hope.

In the letter of James, those who are faithful to God under trials of all sorts are encouraged by the thought of God, who does not change:

> **17** "Every good gift and every perfect gift is from above, and comes down from the Father of lights, with whom there is no variation or shadow of turning. **18** Of His own will He brought us forth by the word of truth, that we might be a kind of first fruits of His creatures." (James 1.17,18).

The "house of God" is, in fact, the presence of God himself rather than a building somewhere. God does not need temples and His presence is accessible to all through the High Priest Jesus, who went beyond the veil and opened the way for us into God's presence in the "most holy place" (Acts 7.44-50; Hebrews 9.1-15).

Prayer

We thank you, Father, for the forgiveness we have through the blood of the lamb. We come to you for forgiveness and for help to live faithfully today. Strengthen our hearts and minds in your will. We want to serve you and speak faithfully and with truth to all. We need your wisdom and the work of your Holy Spirit in our lives today. Bless every person we meet. We pray for those who do not know you, that they might be touched in their hearts and come to you. We pray in the name of Jesus. Amen.

Day 5

> **4** "One *thing* I have desired of the Lord,
> That will I seek:
> That I may dwell in the house of the Lord
> All the days of my life,
> To behold the beauty of the Lord,
> And to inquire in His temple.
> **5** For in the time of trouble
> He shall hide me in His pavilion;
> In the secret place of His tabernacle
> He shall hide me;
> He shall set me high upon a rock."
>   (Psalms 27.4,5)

In this Psalm, David describes the beauty and the stability of God's "tabernacle", "temple" or "house". The richness of the description is an indication that David is not thinking here of the tabernacle or the temple (which in his lifetime had not been built!).

The "house of the LORD" is God's very presence, God's heavenly abode and kingdom. We may think of the words of Paul when reading these words of David:

> "*He who is* the blessed and only Potentate, the King of kings and Lord of lords, who alone has immortality, dwelling in unapproachable light, whom no man has seen or can see, to whom *be honor* and everlasting power. Amen." (1 Timothy 6.15)

We may also think of the many references to the heavenly realm of God, where we find the "heavenly Jerusalem":

> **22** "But you have come to Mount Zion and to the city of the living God, the heavenly Jerusalem, to an innumerable company of angels, **23** to the general assembly and church of the firstborn *who are* registered in heaven, to God the Judge of all, to the spirits of just men made perfect, **24** to Jesus the Mediator of the new covenant, and to the blood of sprinkling that speaks better things than *that of* Abel." (Hebrews 12.22,23).

As believers endure opposition and trials they are taught about the glory and perfection of the heavenly world where God resides and which will break in and become visible to all at the return of Christ, the resurrection of the dead and the final judgment:

> **9** "For they themselves declare concerning us what manner of entry we had to you, and how you turned to God from idols to serve the living and true God, **10** and to wait for His Son from heaven, whom He raised from the dead, *even* Jesus who delivers us from the wrath to come." (1 Thessalonians 1.9)

> **19** "For what *is* our hope, or joy, or crown of rejoicing? *Is it* not even you in the presence of our Lord Jesus Christ at His coming? **20** For you are our glory and joy." (1 Thessalonians 2.19)

> **12** "And may the Lord make you increase and abound in love to one another and to all, just as we *do* to you, **13** so that He may establish your hearts blameless in holiness before our God and Father at the coming of our Lord Jesus Christ with all His saints." (1 Thessalonians 3.12,13)

16 "For the Lord Himself will descend from heaven with a shout, with the voice of an archangel, and with the trumpet of God. And the dead in Christ will rise first. **17** Then we who are alive *and* remain shall be caught up together with them in the clouds to meet the Lord in the air. And thus, we shall always be with the Lord. **18** Therefore comfort one another with these words." (1 Thessalonians 4.16-18)

Prayer

Father in heaven, we believe in your eternal and holy kingdom. We believe in your everlasting kingdom of love and peace. We pray that today you will guide our hearts towards your will and give us strength and wisdom to be faithful in every way to you. Our prayer is also for our loved ones, our friends. May you also bless them today with your presence. We pray in the name of Jesus. Amen.

Day 6

1 "Unless the Lord builds the house,
They labor in vain who build it;
Unless the Lord guards the city,
The watchman stays awake in vain.
2 *It is* vain for you to rise up early,
To sit up late,
To eat the bread of sorrows;
For so He gives His beloved sleep.
3 Behold, children *are* a heritage from the Lord,
The fruit of the womb *is* a reward.
4 Like arrows in the hand of a warrior,
So *are* the children of one's youth.
5 Happy *is* the man who has his quiver full of them;
They shall not be ashamed,
But shall speak with their enemies in the gate."
   (Psalms 127.1-5)

This Psalm teaches us that everything depends on God's blessing and intervention. Jesus taught that even the sun and rain are given by God to the evil and the good (Matthew 5.45). No blessing from God should be taken for granted. An entire society that believed or claims it is "self-sufficient" in the sense of not needing God is fooling itself. Not one single blessing provided by God to even one single individual is to be taken for granted or with ungratefulness.

The life of every individual is sustained by God, who knows even the number of days that an individual will live. This is true for every single human being, whether they believe or not:

> **15** "My frame was not hidden from You,
> When I was made in secret,
> *And* skillfully wrought in the lowest parts of the earth.
> **16** Your eyes saw my substance, being yet unformed.
> And in Your book they all were written,
> The days fashioned for me,
> When *as yet there were* none of them." (Psalms 139.16)

In every one of their activities, human beings depend on God for success:

1. In building a house (v.1)
2. In guarding a city (v.2)
3. In daily activities from the morning on (v.2)

If God is the one who allows us to build a physical "house" how much more a spiritual house, a congregation or church! Dependence on God — trusting Him and remaining in humility and prayer — is of the utmost importance as we seek to serve God in preaching the Gospel and bringing believers together to serve and worship Him.

God even has the power to provide all blessings to "his beloved" when they sleep, when they are doing nothing! He makes the seed of his Word and especially His kingdom "grow" while the farmer sleeps: "And He said, 'The kingdom of God is as if a man should scatter seed on the ground, and should sleep by night and rise by day, and the seed should sprout and grow, he himself does not know how.'" (Mark 4.26,27)

> **26** "And He said, 'The kingdom of God is as if a man should scatter seed on the ground, **27** and should sleep by night and rise by day, and the seed should sprout and grow, he himself does not know how.'" (Mark 4.26,27)

One of the greatest blessings human beings can enjoy in this life is that of having "children". They too should not be taken for granted. To be the father or mother of children is a blessing from God, a source of strength and comfort for the future. Those who would love to have children and are not able to understand this!

In the beginning, God presented Adam and Eve with this great blessing of having children (Genesis 1.27). This follows the statement that He created "man" in His own image: "In the image of God He created him; male and female He created them" (Genesis 1.27). A society that despises having children and raising children is doomed to self-destruction.

Children are like "arrows in the hand of a warrior". A society without children is without "heritage" and without any protection for what lies in the future.

Prayer

Father in heaven, we thank you for our children. We thank you for the children of our congregation, the children of the world. We pray that you will comfort those who are not able to have children. May their hearts be encouraged despite their grief. Lord, help us take good care of the children you have entrusted us. Help us do our best to help those who are orphans. This we pray in the name of Jesus. Amen.

Day 7

>**1** "As the deer pants for the water brooks,
>So pants my soul for You, O God.
>**2** My soul thirsts for God, for the living God.
>When shall I come and appear before God?
>**3** My tears have been my food day and night,
>While they continually say to me,
>"Where *is* your God?"
>**4** When I remember these *things,*
>I pour out my soul within me.
>For I used to go with the multitude;
>I went with them to the house of God,
>With the voice of joy and praise,
>With a multitude that kept a pilgrim feast."
>   (Psalms 42.1-4)

The "house of God" is here the temple where this worshipper used to go with others to praise God. This Psalm was written at a time of great distress. The superscription says: "Yearning for God in the midst of distresses" (also translated "Praising God in trouble and exile"). Thus, the writer has in mind the exile of the northern tribes (Israel) in Assyria (722 BC) followed by the exile of Judah into Babylon (586 BC). This exile lasted until the decree of Cyrus allowing the exiles to return to their land (538).

The "house" of God was the temple, and it had endured moral and religious corruption prior to the captivity of Judah (see Ezekiel chapters 1-8). The worshiper remembers the time he used to worship with the multitude at the temple, but his aspiration is for God himself and his presence. The Psalm in a significant way shows how coming into the presence of God is included in the idea of believers gathering together for worship. There is no contradiction between the two ideas. God himself teaches His people to gather together, to form a "congregation" (church) in order to worship him. This is the case both in the Old and New Testaments. The inability of this worshipper to gather with his brethren to worship God, to go to the "house of God" puts him in a state of grief: "My tears have been my food day and night.". He also says: "Why are you cast down my soul?" (v.5).

This worshipper despite his pain and grief maintains his faith in God. He is in grief, but has not lost hope:

> "The Lord will command His lovingkindness in the daytime,
> And in the night His song *shall be* with me—
> A prayer to the God of my life." (v.8)

> "Why are you cast down, O my soul?
> And why are you disquieted within me?
> Hope in God;
> For I shall yet praise Him,
> The help of my countenance and my God." (v.11)

Prayer

Father in heaven, we pray for strength and encouragement for those who feel alone, without fellowship. May you be with those who are on the mission field and whose message and way of life is rejected. Give them enduring trust and hope in their grief. Provide them the encouragement and help they need. Keep them in your peace. We pray this in the name of Jesus. Amen.

Week 40: God the King

Day 1

> **19** "The Lord has established His throne in heaven,
> And His kingdom rules over all.
> **20** Bless the Lord, you His angels,
> Who excel in strength, who do His word,
> Heeding the voice of His word.
> **21** Bless the Lord, all *you* His hosts,
> *You* ministers of His, who do His pleasure.
> **22** Bless the Lord, all His works,
> In all places of His dominion.
> Bless the Lord, O my soul!"
> (Psalms 103.19-22)

The LORD whose throne is in heaven and who rules over all never uses His power and rule in a way to hurt people. However, He remains a judge for those who would hurt others. This is the lesson we learn about God's kingship throughout the Scriptures.

In this Psalm, the LORD whose throne is in heaven is and perfect and righteous in every way:

He forgives iniquities (v.3)
He heals (v.3)
He redeems (v.4)
He is full of lovingkindness (v.4)
He is full of tender mercies (v.4)
He executes righteousness and justice (v.6)
He is merciful and gracious (v.8)
He abounds in mercy (v.8)
He is a father (v.13)

The LORD'S perfection and righteous ways is demonstrated in His covenants. From the time He created Adam and Eve, the LORD has offered good covenants to people of faith. Through these covenants, men and women have entered into a blessed and personal relationship with the King whose throne is in heaven. These covenants are the expression of His fatherly care, of His mercy and righteousness:

> **17** "But the mercy of the Lord *is* from everlasting to everlasting
> On those who fear Him,
> And His righteousness to children's children,
> **18** To such as keep His covenant,
> And to those who remember His commandments to do them."
> (Psalms 103.17,18)

This Psalm demonstrates how God rules. His rule is not a way for Him to crush people or to exploit them. His rule is demonstrated most clearly in the life of Jesus the Messiah, and is in fact a rule bent on loving and serving. Thus, those who follow Jesus are taught to serve rather than rule over others, as do the rulers of the world:

> **25** "But Jesus called them to *Himself* and said, 'You know that the rulers of the Gentiles lord it over them, and those who are great exercise authority over them. **26** Yet it shall not be so among you; but whoever desires to become great among you, let him be your servant. **27** And whoever desires to be first among you, let him be your slave— **28** just as the Son of Man did not come to be served, but to serve, and to give His life a ransom for many.'" (Matthew 20.25-28)

Prayer

LORD we love you and want to serve you. We love you for who you are. We love you and want to serve you because of your rule of goodness and care, which is displayed in your word and in the life of Jesus your Son. LORD, help us become more like you today and every day. Help us today and every day to understand how you want us to act and to speak. We pray this in the name of Jesus. Amen.

Day 2

> **1** "Give unto the Lord, O you mighty ones,
> Give unto the Lord glory and strength.
> **2** Give unto the Lord the glory due to His name;
> Worship the Lord in the beauty of holiness."
> **10** "The Lord sat *enthroned* at the Flood,
> And the Lord sits as King forever.

11 The Lord will give strength to His people;
The Lord will bless His people with peace."
(Psalms 29.1–2, 10–11)

We note that the name LORD (Yahweh) appears 18 times in these 11 verses. In the Old Testament, the name Yahweh distinguishes the difference between the God of Abraham and of the burning bush and all the other "gods". This comes out in the way God mentions this name to Moses at the burning bush as He calls him to go before Pharaoh, himself considered a "god" of Egypt. In the Exodus there is a battle between the LORD (Yahweh) and all the other "gods" of Egypt as demonstrated in the plagues and the words of Moses to the king of Egypt.

All the elements of nature described in this Psalm, such as many waters, fire or thunder (v.3), produced awe and fear in men and this was the root of their false beliefs and idolatry. The LORD was "enthroned" at the flood, which was no accident but the expression of God's righteous rule.

The LORD who brought the flood did not act with arbitrary rage, like the "gods" of the heathen did. At the time of the flood: "Then the Lord saw that the wickedness of man *was* great in the earth, and *that* every intent of the thoughts of his heart *was* only evil continually." (Genesis 6.5)

He is the LORD who exists in the "beauty of holiness", the LORD who is righteous in all His ways. This LORD who "sits as King forever" will give strength to His people, will bless His people with peace. His intentions are always good, even when He chastises His people or nations for their evil ways.

> **9** "So, I say to you, ask, and it will be given to you; seek, and you will find; knock, and it will be opened to you. **10** For everyone who asks receives, and he who seeks finds, and to him who knocks it will be opened. **11** If a son asks for bread from any father among you, will he give him a stone? Or if *he asks* for a fish, will he give him a serpent instead of a fish? **12** Or if he asks for an egg, will he offer him a scorpion? **13** If you then, being evil, know how to give good gifts to your children, how much more will *your* heavenly Father give the Holy Spirit to those who ask Him!" (Luke 11.9-13)

Even believers who have received the gift of the Holy Spirit (Acts 2.38,39) need to continually pray so that they will be "led by the Spirit" (Galatians 5.18).

14 "For as many as are led by the Spirit of God, these are sons of God. **15** For you did not receive the spirit of bondage again to fear, but you received the Spirit of adoption by whom we cry out, "Abba, Father." **16** The Spirit Himself bears witness with our spirit that we are children of God, **17** and if children, then heirs—heirs of God and joint heirs with Christ, if indeed we suffer with *Him,* that we may also be glorified together." (Romans 8.13,14)

Prayer

Father in heaven, we thank you for the new birth and for the gift of the Holy Spirit. We come to you in all our weakness for forgiveness and for strength. We want to be led by your Holy Spirit and the truth of your word. We also pray for every person we meet today. May you bless each one of them, and may we be a blessing to them. We pray in the name of Jesus your Son. Amen.

Day 3

5 "God has gone up with a shout,
The Lord with the sound of a trumpet.
6 Sing praises to God, sing praises!
Sing praises to our King, sing praises!
7 For God *is* the King of all the earth;
Sing praises with understanding.
8 God reigns over the nations;
God sits on His holy throne.
9 The princes of the people have gathered together,
The people of the God of Abraham.
For the shields of the earth *belong* to God;
He is greatly exalted." (Psalms 47.5-9)

Psalm 47 refers a number of times to God as king or on His throne:
He is a great King over all the earth (v.2)
Sing praises to our King (v.6)
For God is the King of the whole earth (v.7)
God reigns over the nations (v.8)
God sits on His holy throne (v.8)

Modern atheistic philosophy considers it preposterous to believe in the rule or sovereignty of God — especially a holy and loving God — since this world is full of injustice, pain and suffering. In this common criticism of the Bible and the Christian faith, we seem to hear an echo of words found in the book of Job: "Do you still hold fast to your integrity? Curse God and die!" (Job 2.9).

This is a curious reaction to the reality of suffering in this world. Does the reality of suffering change anything to what is right or wrong? Does the fact that Job is now suffering and has lost everything become a valid argument against the importance of maintaining "integrity"? Do Job's sufferings validate cursing God's name?

If yes, on what basis? How does the reality of suffering for example authorize one to lie, to cheat on his wife or to murder his neighbor? There does not seem to be a necessary or logical connection between the fact that Job is suffering and him abandoning his integrity or cursing God! Such a conclusion appears quite foolish, as Job maintains himself (Job 2.10).

The moral imperatives coming from God do not depend on whether we are happy or whether we are unhappy in this life. They certainly cannot be changed at will because of our human experience, whether positive or negative. This I believe is the meaning of Job's words when he says: "Shall we indeed accept good from God, and shall we not accept adversity?" (Job 2.10).

Shall we love God only when everything is going well in our lives?
Shall we listen to God only when everything is going well in our lives?
Shall we obey God only when everything is going well in our lives?

The whole point of Job's testing by the adversary of God is to get Job to curse God:

"But stretch out Your hand now, and touch his bone and his flesh, and he will surely curse You to Your face!" (Job 2.5). However, an important statement about Job is that "In all this Job did not sin with his lips" (Job 2.10).

We can also ask the question: Does the reality of suffering make it commendable to "sin with our lips"? Is suffering as part of this world or part of our lives a logical or valid reason to start cursing people or cursing God?

It is interesting to note how Jesus who though he was mistreated and rejected "did not sin with his mouth" and became in this way an example for his followers:

> 21 "For to this you were called, because Christ also suffered for us, leaving us an example, that you should follow His steps:
> 22 'Who committed no sin, nor was deceit found in His mouth';
> 23 who, when He was reviled, did not revile in return; when He

suffered, He did not threaten, but committed *Himself* to Him who judges righteously" (1 Peter 2.21-23)

It is a common misconception today that on the basis of the reality of suffering in this world, we are justified in rejecting God, his goodness and even his existence. However, the entire Bible describes to us a suffering world, full of pain and death, in which God is calling individuals like Abraham and Sarah or Moses and David to proclaim God's goodness, his mercy and especially his Kingship.

So, we come full circle to this Psalm and need to ask ourselves the question: Does the reality of pain and suffering in this world prevent us logically from proclaiming God's reign, that he "sits on his holy throne"? Jesus suffered and was reviled, he was condemned unjustly and nailed to the cross, but "committed himself to Him who judges righteously". The fact of pain, suffering and death should not become a reason for us to become the judges of God. And we cannot be the judges of God for the simple reason that we are sinful and not in a position to judge God.

This conviction of God's sovereignty and rule should not lead us to deny the reality of sin or pain, as some have thought wise to do. It should not lead us to lack compassion towards those who are in pain. It should not make us become judges of those who are undergoing great pain, as was the case with Job's friends who became his critics and judges instead of bringing him comfort and friendship and thus sinned before God. We can hold on to the biblical truth that God reigns and still be compassionate with those who like Job are suffering without having an explanation for why they are suffering:

> **15** "Rejoice with those who rejoice, and weep with those who weep. **16** Be of the same mind toward one another. Do not set your mind on high things but associate with the humble. Do not be wise in your own opinion." (Romans 12.15)

Prayer

Father in heaven, we come to you often in the midst of grief and loss of hope. We come to you with deep hurts. We know Father that you are a caring and loving Father. We believe that you have proven your love to us in so many ways, and especially through the life and death of Jesus Christ. Give us Father wisdom and perseverance as we through the storms of life. Give us hearts of compassion for those who suffer all around us. We pray this in the name of Jesus. Amen.

Day 4

> **1** "Oh come, let us sing to the Lord!
> Let us shout joyfully to the Rock of our salvation.
> **2** Let us come before His presence with thanksgiving;
> Let us shout joyfully to Him with psalms.
> **3** For the Lord *is* the great God,
> And the great King above all gods.
> **4** In His hand *are* the deep places of the earth;
> The heights of the hills *are* His also.
> **5** The sea *is* His, for He made it;
> And His hands formed the dry *land*."
> (Psalms 95.1-5)

The call to praise and worship the LORD is founded on the premise of His work as creator and sustainer of the earth and of life. This is confirmed again in verse 6: "Let us kneel before the LORD our maker".

The LORD, who is the "maker" of the world, is also the "maker" of His people:

> **11** "Thus says the Lord, the Holy One of Israel, and his Maker: 'Ask Me of things to come concerning My sons; And concerning the work of My hands, you command Me. **12** I have made the earth, and created man on it.'" (Isaiah 45.11,12). "For your Maker *is* your husband, the Lord of hosts *is* His name; and your Redeemer *is* the Holy One of Israel; he is called the God of the whole earth." (Isaiah 54.5)

The LORD who is the creator and the "maker" of Israel is "the great King above all gods" (v.3). The exclusiveness of Israel's worship is based on the fact of the God of Israel being the creator both of the world and of Israel.

For other nations and other religious practices surrounding Israel, the exclusiveness of God as the only LORD and King was offensive. The ancient world of middle eastern religions was pluralistic as far as religion was concerned. Each nation held on to its numerous gods, but they were often shared by other nations and often under other names. Thus, the god Tammuz worshiped in the temple of God in the days of Ezekiel (Ezekiel 8.14) was Mesopotamian but also known as the god Inanna or Ishtar or Adonis among the Greeks.

When Paul visits the city of Athens, Acts chapter 17 records the many gods worshipped by the Athenians, who also worshipped Athena, the

Olympian goddess of wisdom and war and the patroness of the city of Athens.

In this account, we read Paul's speech at the Aeropagus:

> **22** "Then Paul stood in the midst of the Areopagus and said, 'Men of Athens, I perceive that in all things you are very religious; **23** for as I was passing through and considering the objects of your worship, I even found an altar with this inscription: TO THE UNKNOWN GOD.
> Therefore, the One whom you worship without knowing, Him I proclaim to you: **24** God, who made the world and everything in it, since He is Lord of heaven and earth, does not dwell in temples made with hands.'" (Acts 17.22-24)

Here also God is "the God who made the world and everything in it". This faith in God as creator is exclusive and dispels any reason to worship God in a temple, as was the case with the heathen gods; He "does not dwell in temples made with hands".

In this amazing speech, the apostle Paul establishes the essential truths the Athenians need to understand about the God who "made the world". In the Western post-Christian world of today, there is a growing ignorance concerning the elementary truths about God found in Acts 17 as throughout the Bible. These truths need to be made known and need to be understood before people can understand the Gospel of salvation; before people can "repent" (change their minds and hearts), Acts 17.30.

Prayer

Our Father in heaven, we praise you and we thank you for the gift of life. We need to grow LORD in faith, hope and love and come to you for help and wisdom. We thank you for the blessings of family and friendship, shelter and food. Give us grateful and humble hearts through your Holy Spirit. In Jesus' name, we pray. Amen.

Day 5

> **1** "Oh, sing to the Lord a new song!
> Sing to the Lord, all the earth.
> **2** Sing to the Lord, bless His name;
> Proclaim the good news of His salvation from day to day.
> **3** Declare His glory among the nations,
> His wonders among all peoples.

4 For the Lord *is* great and greatly to be praised;
He *is* to be feared above all gods.
5 For all the gods of the peoples *are* idols,
But the Lord made the heavens.
6 Honor and majesty *are* before Him;
Strength and beauty *are* in His sanctuary."
   (Psalms 96.1-6)

Psalm 96 is very similar to Psalm 95. In fact, Psalms 95 through 100 extol God as creator and thus King over the world and over all the gods of the heathen peoples.

There is even a greater emphasis in Psalms 96 on the rule or kingship of God over all nations and all peoples. Israel is to "Declare His glory among the nations, his wonders among all peoples." (v.3). This Psalm looks forward to the day when peoples of all nations will join Israel in the worship of the one true God. This is in keeping with the emphasis on God's work on behalf of Gentiles found throughout the Old Testament.

This work of salvation and blessing for those who come to faith is accomplished through God's anointed or Messiah. In Psalms 2 this message is conveyed with force to the rulers and kings of the earth:

8 "Ask of Me, and I will give *You*
The nations *for* Your inheritance,
And the ends of the earth *for* Your possession.
9 You shall break them with a rod of iron;
You shall dash them to pieces like a potter's vessel.' "
10 Now therefore, be wise, O kings;
Be instructed, you judges of the earth.
11 Serve the Lord with fear,
And rejoice with trembling." (Psalms 2.8-11)

The book of Revelation echoes this promise of the Old Testament:

9 "After these things I looked, and behold, a great multitude
which no one could number, of all nations, tribes, peoples, and
tongues, standing before the throne and before the
Lamb, clothed with white robes, with palm branches in their
hands, **10** and crying out with a loud voice, saying, 'Salvation *belongs* to our God who sits on the throne, and to the Lamb!' **11** All
the angels stood around the throne and the elders and the four
living creatures, and fell on their faces before the throne

and worshiped God, **12** saying: 'Amen! Blessing and glory and wisdom, Thanksgiving and honor and power and might, *Be* to our God forever and ever. Amen.'" (Revelation 7.9-12)

Prayer

We praise and worship you, O LORD. We believe that you are the creator and author of our salvation. We believe in the reign of our Lord Jesus as we listen to his teachings. We come to you through him who is our high priest and who came to save us. Bless us today with a renewed sense of thanksgiving for your salvation. We pray this in the name of Jesus. Amen.

Day 6

> **1** The Lord reigns, He is clothed with majesty;
> The Lord is clothed,
> He has girded Himself with strength.
> Surely the world is established, so that it cannot be moved.
> **2** Your throne *is* established from of old;
> You *are* from everlasting."
>   (Psalms 93.1,2)

This Psalm describes the stability of the world established by God the creator. Just as the physical earth was firmly established by God, so is His reign: "Surely the world is established...Your throne is established from of old."

God's rule over the world is contingent on His everlasting rule: His throne "is established from everlasting". In the creation account there is a "beginning" to creation and the world while the everlasting God is the source of that creation (Genesis 1.1). The question "Who created God" can be asked *again and again,* but the created order always comes from some creative source. The creation is not eternal and has its source in an eternal source: The God who is from everlasting. Whether there be one known universe, or a multitude of universes, does not change the fact that all creation comes from a creative source, which is God.

Nature can be turbulent, but remains under the care and control of God. The stability of the world is still true despite "the floods" that occur and mentioned in verses 3-5 of this Psalm. The stability of the world created by God is connected in this Psalm to the stability of God's testimonies or words, revelations:

> "Your testimonies are very sure;
> Holiness adorns Your house,
> O Lord, forever." (Psalms 93.5)

The quality of endurance and stability found in the creation and which is characteristic of God, is also characteristic of the Gospel truth:

> **22** "Since you have purified your souls in obeying the truth through the Spirit in sincere love of the brethren, love one another fervently with a pure heart, **23** having been born again, not of corruptible seed but incorruptible, through the word of God which lives and abides forever, **24** because
> 'All flesh *is* as grass,
> And all the glory of man as the flower of the grass.
> The grass withers,
> And its flower falls away,
> **25** But the word of the Lord endures forever.'
> Now this is the word which by the gospel was preached to you."
> (1 Peter 1.22-25)

Prayer

We praise and worship you, O LORD. Guide our thoughts today. May we focus on what is good, true and in accordance to your will as we go about our activities. We ask you for wisdom in how we speak to others and how we respond. May we do so with the help of your Holy Spirit. Forgive us, Father, for our sins. Give us a renewed desire to serve you faithfully. In Jesus' name we pray. Amen.

Day 7

> **1** "The Lord reigns;
> Let the peoples tremble!
> He dwells *between* the cherubim;
> Let the earth be moved!
> **2** The Lord *is* great in Zion,
> And He *is* high above all the peoples.
> **3** Let them praise Your great and awesome name —
> He *is* holy."
> (Psalms 99.1-3)

The LORD reigns and is high above all the peoples because of His holiness. The cherubim are angelic creatures that protect the access to His presence and holiness since the fall: "So He drove out the man; and He placed cherubim at the east of the garden of Eden, and a flaming sword which turned every way, to guard the way to the tree of life." (Genesis 3.24)

Sinful man was to die. He could not access the "tree of life" and thus become immortal. Angels such as cherubim play an important role in God's rule. They are supernatural beings created by God to serve Him and carry out His plans in heaven and on earth. The first mention of the cherubim (plural of cherub) is in Genesis 3. They are described in Ezekiel chapters 1 and 10 as powerful supernatural beings and are mentioned about 90 times in the Old Testament. They guard and protect what belongs to God.

Angels play an important part in the life and ministry of Jesus. When arrested, Jesus tells Peter how he could have appealed to legions of angels to deliver him from the terrible death he would endure:

> **52**"But Jesus said to him, 'Put your sword in its place, for all who take the sword will perish by the sword. **53** Or do you think that I cannot now pray to My Father, and He will provide Me with more than twelve legions of angels? **54** How then could the Scriptures be fulfilled, that it must happen thus?'" (Matthew 26.52-54)

Angels also play an important role in the visions given to the apostle John on the Isle of Patmos:

- They worship the LORD (Revelation 5.11)

- They play a part in God's judgments brought upon earth (Revelation 7.1)

- They blow the trumpets announcing God's judgments (Revelation 8.2)

- They play a part in the spiritual battle in heaven (Revelation 12.7-10)

- They play a part in the proclamation of the Gospel throughout the world (Revelation 14.6)

- They announce the fall of the earthly powers opposed to God (Revelation 14.8)

- The wicked are judged in the presence of angels (Revelation 14.10)

- The angels are workers in God's separation and harvest of the good and the evil (Revelation 14.17-19)
- Angels pour out God's bowls of judgment on the earthly powers opposed to God (Revelation 15 and 16; 19.17)
- An angel binds Satan, who oppresses the saints (Revelation 20.1-3)

God's angels are "spirits" and "servants" a "flame of fire" (Hebrews 1.7). They minister to the saints (Hebrews 1.14). There is joy in the presence of God's angels when even one sinner repents (Luke 15.10).

Prayer

Our Father in heaven, we praise your name and majesty. We worship you for your holiness and perfect love. We see in Jesus your Son your majesty and holiness and are grateful that he has come to us and has lived his perfect life. We know that you watch over us with great care and that you call us to be like you, to majestic holiness. May we seek today to do your will in our lives as it is done in heaven. We pray this in the name of Jesus the Christ.

Week 41: The God of Hope

Week 1

> **12** "O God do not be far from me;
> O my God, make haste to help me!
> **13** Let them be confounded *and* consumed
> Who are adversaries of my life;
> Let them be covered *with* reproach and dishonor
> Who seek my hurt.
> **14** But I will hope continually,
> And will praise You yet more and more.
> **15** My mouth shall tell of Your righteousness
> *And* Your salvation all the day,
> For I do not know *their* limits.
> **16** I will go in the strength of the Lord God;
> I will make mention of Your righteousness, of Yours only."
> (Psalms 71.12-16)

In verses 5 and 14 of this Psalm, the Word of God mentions "hope":

> "For you are my hope, O Lord God;
> You are my trust from my youth"

The Hebrew "my hope" could be translated "the hope of mine" (*tiqwati*). In the Hebrew word, we find the root word *kavah*, which means to bind together. The root word also goes back to the Hebrew word for a woven "cord". In Joshua chapter 2 the scarlet "thread" (*tiqva*) represented the promise that Rahab and her family would be spared (Joshua 2.17,18, 21).

The woven cord is strong. We can hang on to it as we go through life. The "hope" in this Psalm and Scripture is founded on the person of God.

The difficult part of "hope" is waiting. Rahab did not see the deliverance of her family right away. She had to wait for it: "Wait on the Lord;

be of good courage, and He shall strengthen your heart; wait, I say, on the Lord!" (Psalm 27.14)

Job does not lose faith in God or in His integrity, but he asks questions about "hope" and how long he can endure his pain:

> **15** "Where then *is* my hope?
> As for my hope, who can see it?
> **16** *Will* they go down to the gates of Sheol?
> Shall *we have* rest together in the dust?" (Job 17.15,16)

> "He breaks me down on every side,
> And I am gone;
> My hope He has uprooted like a tree." (Job 19.10)

Job's grief is not alleviated by the judgments of his friends, who believe wrongly that this man's sufferings are sent by God for sins he has committed:

> **21** "Have pity on me, have pity on me, O you my friends,
> For the hand of God has struck me!
> **22** Why do you persecute me as God *does*,
> And are not satisfied with my flesh?" (Job 19,21,22)

In his profound solitude and despite his questions Job holds on to his hope in God as one would hold on to a "threaded cord" when nothing else could save him:

> **25** "For I know *that* my Redeemer lives,
> And He shall stand at last on the earth;
> **26** And after my skin is destroyed, this *I know*,
> That in my flesh I shall see God,
> **27** Whom I shall see for myself,
> And my eyes shall behold, and not another.
> *How* my heart yearns within me!" (Job 19.25-27)

> "But I will hope continually,
> And will praise You yet more and more." (Psalms 71.14)

Prayer

Our Father in heaven, we come to you in the midst of many questions and even pain. We know you are the rock of salvation and that you will always be faithful to your word. We pray for patience as we wait for the realization of your promis-

es, *not only for us but for this world. Our hope is in you, and in none else. In Jesus' name we pray. Amen.*

Day 2

> **4** "Lord, make me to know my end,
> And what *is* the measure of my days,
> *That* I may know how frail I *am*.
> **5** Indeed, You have made my days *as* handbreadths,
> And my age *is* as nothing before You;
> Certainly every man at his best state *is* but vapor. *Selah*
> **6** Surely every man walks about like a shadow;
> Surely, they busy themselves in vain;
> He heaps up *riches,*
> And does not know who will gather them.
> **7** And now, Lord, what do I wait for?
> My hope *is* in You.
> **8** Deliver me from all my transgressions."
> (Psalms 39.4-8)

This Psalm teaches us an important way to "guard" our ways and not sin with our tongues (vv.1). It is to remember the brevity and "vapor" condition of our lives. It is to realize that our human and earthly ambitions can lead us away from God and the true meaning of life.

It is tempting for human beings to set their hope on material things and riches. The believer needs to set his or her hope "on God" and not on "riches". The words of Jesus are an echo of what we read here:

> **19** "Do not lay up for yourselves treasures on earth, where moth and rust destroy and where thieves break in and steal; **20** but lay up for yourselves treasures in heaven, where neither moth nor rust destroys and where thieves do not break in and steal. **21** For where your treasure is, there your heart will be also." (Matthew 6.19-21)

> "No one can serve two masters; for either he will hate the one and love the other, or else he will be loyal to the one and despise the other. You cannot serve God and mammon." (Matthew 6.24)

James also offers an echo to this Psalm:

13 "Come now, you who say, "Today or tomorrow we will go to such and such a city, spend a year there, buy and sell, and make a profit"; **14** whereas you do not know what *will happen* tomorrow. For what *is* your life? It is even a vapor that appears for a little time and then vanishes away. **15** Instead you *ought* to say, "If the Lord wills, we shall live and do this or that." **16** But now you boast in your arrogance. All such boasting is evil." (James 4.13-16)

Prayer

Our Father, we come before you and ask you to strengthen our faith in you and our hope. We need to stay close to you every day. We need to speak to you from the depth of our hearts so that we will not be led astray by vain things. You are the source of beauty, joy, peace and life. Give us your peace today, we pray! In the name of Jesus. Amen.

Day 3

5 "My soul, wait silently for God alone,
For my expectation *is* from Him.
6 He only *is* my rock and my salvation;
He is my defense;
I shall not be moved.
7 In God *is* my salvation and my glory;
The rock of my strength,
And my refuge, *is* in God."
   (Psalms 62.5,6)

Waiting silently for God is the theme of this Psalm, introduced already in verse 1 and is the most difficult part of hope: "Truly my soul silently waits for God". The word translated "expectation" is the Hebrew word for "hope" (*tiqwati*). The root word is *kavah*, which means "to bind together". The root word also goes back to the Hebrew word for a woven "cord". In Joshua chapter 2 the scarlet "thread" (*tiqva*) represented the promise that Rahab and her family would be spared (Joshua 2.17,18, 21).

Our hope or expectation is in God who is here described as "my rock", "my defense", "my salvation", "my glory", "my strength" and "my refuge". The pronoun "my" used throughout this Psalm beginning in verse 1 with "my soul" shows how important it is to understand that the relationship with God needs to be personal, despite the fact that it is also to be lived out in community. There is not in the Bible the idea that individuality disappears for the sake of community.

This is the reason that the Scripture narrative is so often rooted in the life and faith of one or a few individuals. Genesis begins with Adam and also Eve. The call of Abraham begins the narrative that leads to the creation of Israel as a nation. Humanity after the flood begins with Noah and his family. The call to Moses introduces the narrative of the Exodus. The promises of God for His people and even the nations are closely linked to the work of the "servant" of the LORD — the Messiah — as described for example in Isaiah 53:

> **4** "Surely, He has borne our griefs
> And carried our sorrows;
> Yet we esteemed Him stricken,
> Smitten by God, and afflicted.
> **5** But He *was* wounded for our transgressions,
> *He was* bruised for our iniquities;
> The chastisement for our peace *was* upon Him,
> And by His stripes we are healed." (Isaiah 53.4,5)

Scriptural teachings and exhortations are to be adhered to by each believer even when an entire community is addressed, as in the letter addressed to "the saints who are in Ephesus":

> "See then that you walk circumspectly, not as fools but as
> wise, redeeming the time, because the days are evil." (Ephesians 5.15).

The words used to describe the LORD in this Psalm refer to what we can surely rely upon, refer to strength, salvation and victory! The letter to the Romans offers an echo to this:

> **31** "What then shall we say to these things? If God *is* for us,
> who *can be* against us? **32** He who did not spare His own Son,
> but delivered Him up for us all, how shall He not with Him also
> freely give us all things?" (Romans 8.31,32)

Prayer

We praise you, our God, for inviting us into your Kingdom, for offering us to live eternally with you. We thank you for Jesus the way, the truth and the life. May we remain strong today in our faith, in our hope and in our love. We pray that your Holy Spirit will guide us and produce in us his fruit. We pray in the name of Jesus. Amen.

Day 4

> **18** "Behold, the eye of the Lord *is* on those who fear Him,
> On those who hope in His mercy,
> **19** To deliver their soul from death,
> And to keep them alive in famine.
> **20** Our soul waits for the Lord;
> He *is* our help and our shield.
> **21** For our heart shall rejoice in Him,
> Because we have trusted in His holy name.
> **22** Let Your mercy, O Lord, be upon us,
> Just as we hope in You."
>   (Psalms 33.18-22)

Psalm 33 extols the Sovereignty of God as revealer of His Word (v.4), as a good and righteous judge (v.5), as creator of the world (vv.8,9), as Lord of nations, peoples and kings (vv.10-17). It is on this basis that the Psalm concludes with words about hope in verses 18 to 22. Thus, the hope of the faithful is well grounded.

The hope of Psalm 33 is also a hope that is focused on God's mercy: "Those who hope in his mercy" (v.18) and "Let your mercy, O LORD, be upon us, just as we hope in you" (v.22).

The eye of the Lord is on those who fear Him, on those who hope in His mercy. The fear of the LORD is also founded upon the revelation God has given of himself in His word, through His people and in history.

Fear of the LORD and hope in His mercy are closely linked. This "fear" is a fear brought about by the knowledge of God's creative power as well as His righteousness and holiness (Psalms 103.17). It is a deep reverence for His Word, His commands, His will (Ecclesiastes 12.13; Matthew 6.9,10).

To hope in this verse is to "wait expectantly" upon the LORD (Hebrew *yachal*). This "waiting" or "hoping" upon the LORD characterized the righteous Job, who was accused as a sinner by his friends despite the fact that he was righteous:

> **13** "Hold your peace with me, and let me speak,
> Then let come on me what *may!*

14 Why do I take my flesh in my teeth,
And put my life in my hands?
15 Though He slay me, yet will I trust Him.
Even so, I will defend my own ways before Him.
16 He also *shall* be my salvation,
For a hypocrite could not come before Him." (Job 13.13-16)

The "I will trust Him" in Job 13.15 is the Hebrew *yachal* usually translated "hope" but often translated by "trust" in the book of Job (Job 14.14; 29.21; 32.11; 31.24).

Righteous Job is "waiting" (rather than "hoping") upon God and His mercy, as one waits for a person who has promised to come; or has one waits for a deliverance that has been announced to him or her.

The "hope" or "waiting" in this Psalm is a waiting upon God's mercy (from the Hebrew word *chesed*, favor). The word "mercy" has also been rendered by "kindness" or "lovingkindness" (New American Standard): "In Your lovingkindness You have led the people whom You have redeemed; in Your strength You have guided *them* to Your holy habitation." (Exodus 15.13).

"I will mention the loving kindnesses of the Lord
And the praises of the Lord,
According to all that the Lord has bestowed on us,
And the great goodness toward the house of Israel,
Which He has bestowed on them according to His mercies,
According to the multitude of His lovingkindnesses." (Isaiah 63.7)

Mercy could also be translated by "unfailing love". The two words for "love" in Hebrew are *ahav* as in the commandment to "love God" and our neighbor (Deuteronomy 6.5 ; Leviticus 19,18) and *chesed* as in this Psalm and Isaiah 63.7 about "God's love".

One could define the love God has for us as a "completely undeserved kindness and generosity" granted by someone in high position as in Lamentations, where *chesed* is translated "mercies" but could be rendered "love" or "lovingkindness":

31 For the Lord will not cast off forever.
32 Though He causes grief,
Yet He will show compassion
According to the multitude of His mercies.

33 For He does not afflict willingly,
Nor grieve the children of men. (Lamentations 3.31,32).

The love of God came to the Hebrew people while they were not seeking Him. God was true to his covenant with Abraham even though they so often broke it. This love is different from the "love" of humans because it is constant, giving, stable, dependable. It is not fickle, self-serving or grabbing. It is a love that proves God to be always faithful, reliable, upright. **"We love Him because He first loved us."** (1 John 4.19)

Prayer

We praise you, our LORD and Father, for your lovingkindness, your undeserved mercy towards us. We are thankful that you have loved us first. We pray that today our love towards you can grow and become stronger. We pray that your Word will give us understanding of your will for our lives. We pray for our loved ones, our friends and colleagues. Bless them, LORD, and bring them closer to you. We pray in Jesus' name. Amen.

Day 5

21 "Blessed *be* the Lord,
For He has shown me His marvelous kindness in a strong city.
22 For I said in my haste,
'I am cut off from before Your eyes';
Nevertheless You heard the voice of my supplications
When I cried out to You.
23 Oh, love the Lord, all you His saints!
For the Lord preserves the faithful,
And fully repays the proud person.
24 Be of good courage,
And He shall strengthen your heart,
All you who hope in the Lord."
   (Psalms 31.21-24)

Psalm 31 concludes with a word of "hope" given by someone who has experienced great trouble (vv.7,9), grief (v.9) and persecution (v.15). The Psalm describes a man against whom many take counsel together: "They scheme to take away my life" (v.13); "Pull me out of the net which they have secretly laid for me" (v.4).

The Psalm is quoted by Jesus as he pronounces his last words on the cross: "Into Your hands I commit my spirit" (v.5 and Luke 23.46).

Psalm 31 describes the faithful one who is persecuted and who is characterized by his trust in God (v.14), his love for God (v.23) and his hope in the LORD (v.24) — three themes we find later in the apostle Paul's writings: "And now abide faith, hope, love, these three; but the greatest of these is love" (1Corinthians 13.13; Colossians 1.3-5).

Somehow this faithful one will be preserved, will be delivered and can safely say:

> **21** "Blessed *be* the Lord,
> For He has shown me His marvelous kindness in a strong city!
> **22** For I said in my haste,
> "I am cut off from before Your eyes";
> Nevertheless You heard the voice of my supplications
> When I cried out to You." (Psalms 31.21,22)

These words are echoed in the New Testament about Jesus:

> **7** "Who, in the days of His flesh, when He had offered up
> prayers and supplications, with vehement cries and tears to
> Him who was able to save Him from death, and was heard because of His godly fear, **8** though He was a Son, *yet* He
> learned obedience by the things which He suffered. **9** And having been perfected, He became the author of eternal salvation to
> all who obey Him" (Hebrews 5.7-9)

Prayer

We thank you, Father, for Jesus the Christ. We are grateful to you for his life, his death and resurrection. We believe you have chosen him to be our High Priest. We come to you with all our sins and shortcomings and ask for your forgiveness. We want to love you today the way you commanded us to. Guide us and protect us, Father. We pray in the name of Jesus. Amen.

Day 6

> **49** "Remember the word to Your servant,
> Upon which You have caused me to hope.
> **50** This *is* my comfort in my affliction,
> For Your word has given me life.
> **51** The proud have me in great derision,
> *Yet* I do not turn aside from Your law.

52 I remembered Your judgments of old, O Lord,
And have comforted myself."
(Psalms 119.49-52)

The word of the LORD gives life and is a source of hope. In the Scriptures, God is the one who takes the initiative to speak and reveal himself to people or to accomplish His will. Without God's word, there would be no life — not even physical life as we know it.

It is by "His word" that God created everything (Genesis 1). It was the word of God that called Noah to build and ark so he and his family could be saved:

13 "And God said to Noah, 'The end of all flesh has come before Me, for the earth is filled with violence through them; and behold, I will destroy them with the earth. **14** Make yourself an ark of gopherwood; make rooms in the ark and cover it inside and outside with pitch.'" (Genesis 6.13,14).

God called Abraham out of his country to the land He would show him (Genesis 12.1-3).

In the New Testament, the Gospel is the seed that is planted in the human heart and produces a "new birth":

22 "Since you have purified your souls in obeying the
truth [i]through the Spirit in sincere love of the brethren, love
one another fervently with a pure heart, **23** having been born
again, not of corruptible seed but incorruptible, through the
word of God which lives and abides forever, **24** because
"All flesh *is* as grass,
And all the glory of man as the flower of the grass.
The grass withers,
And its flower falls away,
25 But the word of the Lord endures forever."
Now this is the word which by the gospel was preached to you."
(1 Peter 1.22–25).

The power of the Gospel to produce new life comes from the work of the Holy Spirit, who convinces the sinner and brings a person to repentance (Romans 1.16; 16.8; Titus 3.5; Acts 2.36; 16.14; John 16.8-11).

The Gospel is a message of hope. The hope of the Gospel points to Jesus' return and the resurrection of the dead:

13 "But I do not want you to be ignorant, brethren, concerning those who have fallen asleep, lest you sorrow as others who have no hope. **14** For if we believe that Jesus died and rose again, even so God will bring with Him those who sleep in Jesus." (1 Thessalonians 4.13,14).

51 "Behold, I tell you a mystery: We shall not all sleep, but we shall all be changed — **52** in a moment, in the twinkling of an eye, at the last trumpet. For the trumpet will sound, and the dead will be raised incorruptible, and we shall be changed. **53** For this corruptible must put on incorruption, and this mortal *must* put on immortality. **54** So when this corruptible has put on incorruption, and this mortal has put on immortality, then shall be brought to pass the saying that is written: 'Death is swallowed up in victory.' **55** 'O Death, where *is* your sting? O Hades, where *is* your victory?' **56** The sting of death *is* sin, and the strength of sin *is* the law. **57** But thanks *be* to God, who gives us the victory through our Lord Jesus Christ." (1 Corinthians 15.51-56)

Prayer

We thank you, Father, for Jesus the Christ. We are grateful to you for his life, his death and resurrection. We know your word has power through your Holy Spirit. We are grateful that you opened our hearts to your truth, that you brought to us the hope of eternal life, the hope of the resurrection. We pray that today you will help us live in the light of that hope. In Jesus our Lord we pray. Amen.

Day 7

5 "I wait for the Lord, my soul waits,
And in His word I do hope.
6 My soul *waits* for the Lord
More than those who watch for the morning—
Yes, more than those who watch for the morning.
7 O Israel, hope in the Lord;
For with the Lord *there is* mercy,
And with Him *is* abundant redemption.
8 And He shall redeem Israel
From all his iniquities." (Psalms 130.5-8)

In the word hope is found the idea of "expectation" and hope implies "waiting". "My soul, wait silently for God alone, for my expectation *is* from Him." (Psalms 62.5).

This Psalm is the prayer of one who is fully aware he is a sinner and without hope unless the LORD brings him forgiveness and redemption: "If you, LORD, should mark iniquities, O LORD, who could stand?" (v.3). The plea for forgiveness found here is "personal" ("hear my voice") but is also a prayer for Israel, for all of God's people.

Forgiveness and redemption found here and throughout the Old Testament is a "hope". It is, however, based on the revelation of the LORD as merciful, loving towards His people and His creation. This hope of forgiveness and redemption finds its fulfillment in the person of Jesus the Messiah.

The promised Messiah of Isaiah 53 is wounded for the transgressions of God's people:

> 4 "Surely, He has borne our griefs
> And carried our sorrows;
> Yet we esteemed Him stricken,
> Smitten by God, and afflicted.
> 5 But He *was* wounded for our transgressions,
> He *was* bruised for our iniquities;
> The chastisement for our peace *was* upon Him,
> And by His stripes we are healed.
> 6 All we like sheep have gone astray;
> We have turned, every one to his own way;
> And the Lord has laid on Him the iniquity of us all.
> 7 He was oppressed and He was afflicted,
> Yet He opened not His mouth;
> He was led as a lamb to the slaughter,
> And as a sheep before its shearers is silent,
> So He opened not His mouth.
> 8 He was taken from prison and from judgment,
> And who will declare His generation?
> For He was cut off from the land of the living;
> For the transgressions of My people He was stricken.
> 9 And they made His grave with the wicked—
> But with the rich at His death,
> Because He had done no violence,
> Nor *was any* deceit in His mouth." (Isaiah 53.4-6)

Forgiveness and redemption for Israel and for the individual believer are now offered through Jesus the Messiah (Christ) who gave his life and accomplished the redemptive plan of God for all humanity:

> **29** "The next day John saw Jesus coming toward him, and said, 'Behold! The Lamb of God who takes away the sin of the world! **30** This is He of whom I said, 'After me comes a Man who is preferred before me, for He was before me.' **31** I did not know Him; but that He should be revealed to Israel, therefore I came baptizing with water.'" (John 1.29-31)

> **13** "He has delivered us from the power of darkness and conveyed *us* into the kingdom of the Son of His love, **14** in whom we have redemption through His blood, the forgiveness of sins." (Colossians 1.13,14)

> **7** "In Him we have redemption through His blood, the forgiveness of sins, according to the riches of His grace **8** which He made to abound toward us in all wisdom and prudence, **9** having made known to us the mystery of His will, according to His good pleasure which He purposed in Himself, **10** that in the dispensation of the fullness of the times He might gather together in one all things in Christ, both which are in heaven and which are on earth—in Him. **11** In Him also we have obtained an inheritance, being predestined according to the purpose of Him who works all things according to the counsel of His will, **12** that we who first trusted in Christ should be to the praise of His glory." (Ephesians 1.7-12)

Prayer

Father in heaven, we come to you for forgiveness. We come with deep sorrow for our sins. We pray that you will renew our hearts and our hope. May we live the life you called us to, a life of holiness and joy. Today, may we learn to be workers of peace, how to proclaim with love the Good News of salvation in Jesus the Christ. Our prayer is in the name of Jesus. Amen.

Let us Come Before his Presence in the Sermon on the Mount

Week 42: Blessed by God (Matt 4.25 -5.12)

Day 1

> **24** "Then His fame went throughout all Syria; and they brought to Him all sick people who were afflicted with various diseases and torments, and those who were demon-possessed, epileptics, and paralytics; and He healed them. **25** Great multitudes followed Him—from Galilee, and *from* Decapolis, Jerusalem, Judea, and beyond the Jordan. **5** And seeing the multitudes, He went up on a mountain, and when He was seated His disciples came to Him. **2** Then He opened His mouth and taught them, saying…"
> (Matthew 4.25 – 5.2)

In Matthew 5.3 to 7.27 Jesus teaches both the multitudes that follow him and his disciples:

"Great multitudes" came from all the regions in northern Israel. The Greek *ochloi poloi* emphasizes the massive dimension of the multitudes coming to Jesus, stretching even to Syria (the distance between Damas the capital of Syria and Capernaum is about 70 miles). The Greek word *ochloi* means crowd, but usually refers to the common people. The word *polloi* emphasizes great numbers. Thus, both words together indicate thousands of people. It should also be noted that on that occasion, Jesus healed great numbers from "various" diseases.

Witnessing this, who would not have thought about a great blessing sent by God to His people? What greater blessing can there be than healing of one's diseases? Who would not have remembered the words of the prophet Isaiah concerning the light radiating from the Messiah, even in the regions of Naphtali and Galilee "of the Gentiles":

> **1** "Nevertheless, the gloom *will* not *be* upon her who *is* distressed,
> As when at first, He lightly esteemed

> The land of Zebulun and the land of Naphtali,
> And afterward more heavily oppressed *her*,
> *By* the way of the sea, beyond the Jordan,
> In Galilee of the Gentiles.
> **2** The people who walked in darkness
> Have seen a great light;
> Those who dwelt in the land of the shadow of death,
> Upon them a light has shined." (Isaiah 9.1,2)

Back then as today, the diseases of all these people were a sign of the spiritual condition of humanity; a sign of the certainty of death for each one. The blessings brought by the Messiah — the light that shines from him — go beyond the healings of physical diseases. The Messiah is also a healer of the soul and offers the blessings of spiritual reconciliation with God and between human beings. His teachings affirm the dignity of the downtrodden and poor; the meek and humble; those who are persecuted for seeking righteousness. His teachings bring peace to a world bent on conflict and cruelty.

In Leviticus 26 and Deuteronomy 27-28, the LORD set before His people the blessings they could receive if they kept His commandments but also the curses they would endure if they turned away from these commandments. Once they entered the land, the people would need to go to two mountains, Mount Ebal and Mount Garizim. Six tribes would stand on Mount Ebal and pronounce curses on those who would turn away from God's law. Six other tribes would then stand on Mount Garizim to pronounce all the blessings on those who would be faithful to God's law:

> **1** "Now it shall come to pass, if you diligently obey the voice of the Lord your God, to observe carefully all His commandments which I command you today, that the Lord your God will set you high above all nations of the earth. **2** And all these blessings shall come upon you and overtake you, because you obey the voice of the Lord your God: **3** 'Blessed *shall* you *be* in the city and blessed *shall* you *be* in the country.' **4** 'Blessed *shall be* the fruit of your body, the produce of your ground and the increase of your herds, the increase of your cattle and the offspring of your flocks.'" (Deuteronomy 28.1-4)

In the blessings pronounced by Jesus in his sermon on the mount, we find an echo of the "blessings" pronounced yearly on Mount Garizim. This is confirmed throughout the sermon as Jesus teaches about God's law, God's will and how to obey this will of God — Jesus who came not to abolish the law but to confirm or fulfill it:

> **17** "Do not think that I came to destroy the Law or the Prophets. I did not come to destroy but to fulfill. **18** For assuredly, I say to you, till heaven and earth pass away, one jot or one tittle will by no means pass from the law till all is fulfilled. **19** Whoever therefore breaks one of the least of these commandments, and teaches men so, shall be called least in the kingdom of heaven; but whoever does and teaches *them*, he shall be called great in the kingdom of heaven. **20** For I say to you, that unless your righteousness exceeds *the righteousness* of the scribes and Pharisees, you will by no means enter the kingdom of heaven." (Matthew 5.17-20)

Prayer

Father, we pray that today we will let your Word touch our hearts and change our life. We want to know you and to enjoy your presence forever. We know we were made for this and that you are perfect and loving. So, Father, let us come to you in humility, with a spirit of obedience. Strengthen us through your Holy Spirit. This is our prayer in the name of Jesus. Amen.

Day 2

> **27** And so, it was when Jesus had ended these sayings, that the people were astonished at His teaching, **29** for He taught them as one having authority, and not as the scribes."
> (Matthew 7.27,28)

We should note this reaction of the people following his teaching. The word for "people" here is the same word translated "multitudes" in Matthew 4.25 and 5.1 (Greek *ochloi*).

This is not the only time the Gospels mention Jesus as teaching "with authority" (see Mark 1.22; Luke 4.32). Jesus teaching "with authority" is not contrasted with the "law and the prophets" but with the interpretations of the Law as evidenced in the oral traditions of the scribes and Pharisees. These oral traditions went beyond anything intended in the Law and often canceled the Law itself (for example, in John 5.10; Matthew 12.11; Mark 7.1-8).

Throughout the sermon, and in contrast to the way of teaching of the scribes, the personal authority of Jesus is displayed. This begins with the "blessing" declarations in Matthew 5.1-12 which are common in Torah or other parts of the Old Testament to describe teachings coming from God (as in the "blessings" in Deuteronomy which come directly from "the voice of the LORD"). The blessings are promised in the Torah and elsewhere by God for those who "observe carefully" all of God's commandments (Deuteronomy 28.1,2).

The personal authority of Jesus stands out, as did the authority of the "prophets" who were persecuted:

> **11** "Blessed are you when they revile and persecute you and say all kinds of evil against you falsely for My sake. **12** Rejoice and be exceedingly glad, for great *is* your reward in heaven, for so they persecuted the prophets who were before you." (Matthew 5.11,12).

Throughout the sermon, Jesus points to his own authority, which is not even something that was done by the Old Testament prophets who spoke "on behalf of God". We see this in the constant repetition of the expression "I say to you" (for example in 5.18,20,22,26). In his teaching, Jesus even contrasts his personal authority with the oral traditions or interpretations of his day (as in Matthew 5.43,44).

The most obvious reference to Jesus' personal authority is in presenting himself as the judge (Matthew 7.21-23) and the foundation of a faithful life: "Therefore whoever hears these saying of mine and does them..." (Matthew 7.24-27).

Prayer

We pray Father that you will open our hearts to the words of Jesus. We pray that these words can change us day by day and allow us to produce fruit to your glory. As we meditate on the Sermon on the Mount, we pray that we will grow in our understanding of your will. In the name of Jesus, we pray. Amen.

Day 3

> **3** "Blessed *are* the poor in spirit,
> For theirs is the kingdom of heaven.
> **4** Blessed *are* those who mourn,
> For they shall be comforted.
> **5** Blessed *are* the meek,
> For they shall inherit the earth.

> 6 Blessed *are* those who hunger and thirst for righteousness,
> For they shall be filled."
> (Matthew 5.3-6)

Jesus declares God's blessings on those who were often considered as outcasts by those in positions of authority: the humble and the meek. The meek are not "weak" or passive individuals. Moses was known to be very meek, but was full of strength and demonstrated authority. The Greek word for meek *praute* was, in fact, used of strength under control. The idea is that one does not use his strength or authority to hurt others, but to build them up and help them. This was Moses as seen in Numbers 12.1-3 or Exodus 18.13-23.

In Hebrew, the word for meek is *anaw* which also describes one who is afflicted. Moses endured scorn and even rejection despite his great ability and authority. He wore himself out to serve the people and encourage them. He used his strength and authority to serve them, not to be served. The best example of meekness is Jesus himself, who had all power and authority at his disposition and chose to serve and to suffer in order to bring salvation to the world ("meek" is translated "gentle" in the NKJV of Matthew 11.29).

God is the one who can bless the faithful with these great promises: the "kingdom of heaven", "the land" (or earth), "comfort" in grief, food for the hungry.

From the start of his ministry, Jesus preached "the gospel of the kingdom of God" and how to be part of that kingdom or inherit that kingdom:

> "From that time Jesus began to preach and to say, 'Repent, for the kingdom of heaven is at hand.'" (Matthew 4.17).

Mark says:

> 14 "Now after John was put in prison, Jesus came to
> Galilee, preaching the gospel of the kingdom of God, 15 and
> saying, 'The time is fulfilled, and the kingdom of God is at hand.
> Repent, and believe in the gospel.'" (Mark 1.14,15)

Poverty in spirit, meekness, hunger and thirst for righteousness describe essential aspects or dimensions of God's kingdom or reign where happiness is to be found. The humble condition of a human being does not define his or her status before God or in God's reign, as is the case in human kingdoms plagued by the sinful hunger for power.

The word servant describes best what is in harmony with God's reign. The Messiah of Isaiah 52 and 53 is not introduced as the King but is but as the "righteous servant" of God (Isaiah 53.11): "Behold my servant shall deal prudently; he shall be exalted and extolled and be very high" (Isaiah 52.13).

The blessing statements describe the King himself, the Messiah. The Messiah was often described in the Old Testament as an outcast, one who was humble and meek (Isaiah 53; Zechariah 9). It should be noted that Jesus himself would present himself among the poor, the meek and those who mourn. He was "the servant of the LORD" who came to suffer for his people (Isaiah 53):

> **28** "Come to Me, all *you* who labor and are heavy laden, and I will give you rest. **29** Take My yoke upon you and learn from Me, for I am gentle and lowly in heart, and you will find rest for your souls. **30** For My yoke *is* easy and My burden is light."
> (Matthew 11.28-30)

Jewish teachers would discuss the contrast between the glorious and powerful Messiah as in Daniel 7.13 and the Messiah who comes in a lowly fashion riding upon a donkey as in Zechariah 9.9. An interpretation concerning the Messiah was that he would come in power and glory if Israel would deserve it or humble and lowly if Israel would be unworthy (Talmud, b. Sanhedrin 98a). Thus, the Messiah could not be glorious and lowly at the same time.

The idea that wealth and power demonstrated God's special blessing was very commonly believed in Jesus' days and even before, when we consider the book of Job. The poor in spirit, the meek (those who are gentle in dealing with others) and those who mourn are already presented as examples even in the Old Testament:

> "But the meek shall inherit the earth,
> And shall delight themselves in the abundance of peace."
> (Psalms 37.11)

> **8** "You caused judgment to be heard from heaven;
> The earth feared and was still,
> **9** When God arose to judgment,
> To deliver all the oppressed of the earth. *Selah*" (Psalms 76.8,9)

> "The humble He guides in justice,
> And the humble He teaches His way." (Psalms 25.9)

"Seek the Lord, all you meek of the earth,
Who have upheld His justice.
Seek righteousness, seek humility.
It may be that you will be hidden
In the day of the Lord's anger." (Zephaniah 2.3)

In Zephaniah, seeking humility and seeking righteousness go hand in hand. There is no righteousness before God with arrogance and pride. Humility and true righteousness accomplish the demands of the law. This is a "righteousness" that exceeds the righteousness of the scribes and Pharisees: "For I say to you, that unless your righteousness exceeds *the righteousness* of the scribes and Pharisees, you will by no means enter the kingdom of heaven." (Matthew 5.20)

> **5** "Let this mind be in you, which was also in Christ Jesus, **6** who, being in the form of God, did not consider it robbery to be equal with God, **7** but made Himself of no reputation, taking the form of a bondservant, *and* coming in the likeness of men. **8** And being found in appearance as a man, He humbled Himself and became obedient to *the point of* death, even the death of the cross. **9** Therefore God also has highly exalted Him and given Him the name which is above every name, **10** that at the name of Jesus every knee should bow, of those in heaven, and of those on earth, and of those under the earth, **11** and *that* every tongue should confess that Jesus Christ *is* Lord, to the glory of God the Father." (Philippians 2.5-11)

Prayer

We thank you, Father, for Jesus and his teachings. We thank you for his life and example. Our prayer is that we will follow Jesus and listen to him throughout the day and in all our circumstances. May your Holy Spirit produce in us the fruit of humility and gentleness towards others. This is our prayer in Jesus' name. Amen.

Day 4

"Blessed *are* the merciful,
For they shall obtain mercy.
  (Matthew 5.7)

Mercy or compassion are expressions of genuine love for our "neighbor". They describe a sharing in the pain and suffering of others and being active in helping them. This is the example of the Samaritan given by Jesus as he answers the question "Who is my neighbor" in the discussion of God's commandment to love our neighbor:

> **33** "But a certain Samaritan, as he journeyed, came where he was. And when he saw him, he had compassion. **34** So he went to *him* and bandaged his wounds, pouring on oil and wine; and he set him on his own animal, brought him to an inn, and took care of him." (See Luke 10.25-37)

This is in keeping with God's teachings in the Old Testament:

> "He has shown you, O man, what *is* good;
> And what does the Lord require of you
> But to do justly,
> To love mercy,
> And to walk humbly with your God?" (Micah 6.8)

This was something neglected by many scribes and Pharisees during Jesus' ministry:

> **23** "Woe to you, scribes and Pharisees, hypocrites! For you pay tithe of mint and anise and cummin and have neglected the weightier *matters* of the law: justice and mercy and faith. These you ought to have done, without leaving the others undone. **24** Blind guides, who strain out a gnat and swallow a camel!" (Matthew 23.23,24)

Jesus is our greatest example of this teaching, as he took upon himself human nature and giving his life that me might open the way to salvation. He demonstrated the character of God in his mercy for us: "But You, O Lord, are a God full of compassion, and gracious, longsuffering and abundant in mercy and truth." (Psalms 86.15)

> **4** "But God, who is rich in mercy, because of His great love with which He loved us, **5** even when we were dead in trespasses, made us alive together with Christ (by grace you have been saved), **6** and raised *us* up together, and made *us* sit together in the heavenly *places* in Christ Jesus..." (Ephesians 2.4-6)

> 3 "Blessed *be* the God and Father of our Lord Jesus Christ, the Father of mercies and God of all comfort, 4 who comforts us in all our tribulation, that we may be able to comfort those who are in any trouble, with the comfort with which we ourselves are comforted by God. 5 For as the sufferings of Christ abound in us, so our consolation also abounds through Christ." (2 Corinthians 1.3-5)

We can compare this statement to what Jesus says later about forgiveness:

> "And forgive us our debts, as we forgive our debtors." (Matthew 6.12)

> **14** "For if you forgive men their trespasses, your heavenly Father will also forgive you. **15** But if you do not forgive men their trespasses, neither will your Father forgive your trespasses." (6.13).

Prayer

Our Father in heaven, we thank you for your mercy towards us. We thank you for salvation, which is your free gift in Jesus. We pray that we can practice mercy today towards those we meet and are in grief or pain. Give us love and wisdom through your Holy Spirit, so we can be an encouragement and be helpful to others. This is our prayer in Jesus' name. Amen.

Day 5

> "Blessed *are* the pure in heart,
> For they shall see God."
> (Matthew 5.8)

Being "pure in heart" is not restricted to seeking moral purity at the level of behavior. Holiness is a matter of the heart or "mind". The biblical word "heart" refers primarily to the "mind". It is the "heart" (mind) that imagines (Genesis 6.5), understands (Matthew 15.13), reasons (Mark 2.8), thinks (Luke 9.47), believes (Romans 10.9), loves (1 Peter 1.22).

Holiness in behavior has its root in what the apostle Paul describes as a "renewing of the "mind":

> **1** "I beseech you therefore, brethren, by the mercies of God, that you present your bodies a living sacrifice, holy, acceptable to

God, *which is* your reasonable service. **2** And do not be conformed to this world, but be transformed by the renewing of your mind, that you may prove what *is* that good and acceptable and perfect will of God." (Romans 12.1,2)

Faithfulness to God and being transformed in thoughts and behavior is a way to come closer to God to "see Him". Moses endured and was faithful "as seeing him who is invisible" (Hebrews 11.27). We can be transformed when we remain close to God, when we abide in Christ:

> **1** "I am the true vine, and My Father is the vinedresser. **2** Every branch in Me that does not bear fruit He takes away; and every *branch* that bears fruit He prunes, that it may bear more fruit. **3** You are already clean because of the word which I have spoken to you. **4** Abide in Me, and I in you. As the branch cannot bear fruit of itself, unless it abides in the vine, neither can you, unless you abide in Me." (John 15.1-4)

The coming of the Lord is the promise of "seeing him": "And now, little children, abide in Him, that when He appears, we may have confidence and not be ashamed before Him at His coming." (1 John 2.28).

His coming and being able to see Him are central to God's promises and the hope of the faithful:

> **1** "Behold what manner of love the Father has bestowed on us, that we should be called children of God! Therefore, the world does not know us, because it did not know Him. **2** Beloved, now we are children of God; and it has not yet been revealed what we shall be, but we know that when He is revealed, we shall be like Him, for we shall see Him as He is. **3** And everyone who has this hope in Him purifies himself, just as He is pure." (1 John 2.1-3)

> **3** And there shall be no more curse, but the throne of God and of the Lamb shall be in it, and His servants shall serve Him. **4** They shall see His face, and His name *shall be* on their foreheads. **5** There shall be no night there: They need no lamp nor light of the sun, for the Lord God gives them light. And they shall reign forever and ever." (Revelation 22.3-5)

Prayer

We thank you, Father, for a new day. We come to you for strength to grow in holiness. We pray that you will keep our thoughts close to your will and your promises. Forgive us, Lord, for our sins. Guide us, keep and guide our loved ones today. Be with those who are entangled in sin and bring them to change their hearts through your Holy Spirit. Strengthen our faith, love and hope in the Lord Jesus. We pray in his name. Amen.

Day 6

"Blessed *are* the peacemakers,
For they shall be called sons of God."
(Matthew 5.9)

The "peacemakers" describes action in view of peace — with the Greek *eirenopoioi* comprised of the word for peace (*eirene*) and the verb "to do" or "to make" (*poio*). Jesus was born under the "pax romana" which describes a period of Roman history which started under the reign of Augustus the first Roman emperor and lasted about 200 years until the rule of Marcus Aurelius. It is considered to be a period of relative peace and prosperity. However, it was this period that introduced the greatest time of persecution for early Christianity. Thus, it may not be a coincidence that Jesus mentions "peacemakers" right before warning the disciples of coming persecution. The "peace" established by the emperors was a brutal and forced peace; a peace that was founded on the worship of the emperor and of Rome. In Romans, the apostle Paul includes in his description of sinful behavior: "The way of peace they have not known. There is no fear of God before their eyes." (Romans 3.17,18) Disciples of Jesus must "walk properly" and "not in strife and envy" (Romans 13.13).

Jesus is the "peacemaker" per excellence. His teachings and life have to do with bringing peace between God and man and between human beings. Disciples become "peacemakers" when they follow in the footsteps of Jesus the peacemaker. They will be persecuted for Jesus' sake and for his teachings ; for the sake of the Gospel and the truth. The peace brought about by Jesus is the peace that lives in the heart and is exhibited in the life of those who are "children of God" rather than children of the world.

25 "These things I have spoken to you while being present with you. **26** But the Helper, the Holy Spirit, whom the Father will send in My name, He will teach you all things, and bring to your remembrance all things that I said to you. **27** Peace I leave with you, my peace I give to you; not as the world gives, do I give to you. Let not your heart be troubled, neither let it be afraid. **28** You have heard Me say to you, 'I am going away and coming *back* to you.' If you loved Me, you would rejoice because I said, 'I am going to the Father,' for My Father is greater than I." (John 14.25-28).

The Gospel of Christ is the good news of peace (Romans 10.15). The peace that lives in the heart of disciples of Jesus is a fruit of the Holy Spirit that touches and transforms the heart:

> **22** "But the fruit of the Spirit is love, joy, peace, longsuffering, kindness, goodness, faithfulness, **23** gentleness, self-control. Against such there is no law." (Galatians 5.22,23). This verse confirms that "peace" goes with Christ-like qualities that are described as "fruit" and bring goodness in human relationships. It is the "Spirit of God" that renews the human heart, so one can be born of God and thus be a child of God (Titus 3.4-6):

> **14** "For as many as are led by the Spirit of God, these are sons of God. **15** For you did not receive the spirit of bondage again to fear, but you received the Spirit of adoption by whom we cry out, "Abba, Father." **16** The Spirit Himself bears witness with our spirit that we are children of God, **17** and if children, then heirs—heirs of God and joint heirs with Christ, if indeed we suffer with *Him,* that we may also be glorified together." (Romans 8.14-16)

Jesus is teaching his disciples to refuse being drawn into hatred, hostility or violence. By their words and actions based on wisdom "from above" they are called to the task of bringing peace to a conflicting world:

> **17** "But the wisdom that is from above is first pure, then peaceable, gentle, willing to yield, full of mercy and good fruits, without partiality and without hypocrisy. **18** Now the fruit of righteousness is sown in peace by those who make peace." (James 3.17,18; see Romans 14.17).

Peace is a significant theme of the apostle Paul in his letter to the Romans: Romans 1.7; 2.10; 5.1; 10.15; 12.18; 14.17; 15.13; 16.20.

Prayer

Our Father in heaven, we praise you for your holiness and goodness. We pray that we can be peacemakers today in this present world. Through your Holy Spirit, give us the words that will bring peace; the actions that will bring reconciliation and mutual understanding. May we be at peace in our hearts and strive to serve you faithfully in every way. We pray in the name of Jesus. Amen.

Day 7

> **10** "Blessed *are* those who are persecuted for righteousness' sake, for theirs is the kingdom of heaven. **11** Blessed are you when they revile and persecute you and say all kinds of evil against you falsely for My sake. **12** Rejoice and be exceedingly glad, for great *is* your reward in heaven, for so they persecuted the prophets who were before you."
> (Matthew 5.10-12)

The first "you" in verse 11 is in the singular (Greek, *este*) while the second is in the plural form (*humas*). In verses 12 to 16 the Greek "you" is mostly in the plural (you = all of you). Being "light of the world" is spoken to the disciples as they form a community of faith, who are one and have unity of spirit (see John 13.34,35). This use of the plural "you" in the use of the Greek pronoun or in the plural form of the verb itself is very common throughout the New Testament (for example: Colossians 1.2, "Grace to you (plural)"; Ephesians 5.15, "See that you walk circumspectly" where the imperative is in the plural; the communal aspect of these injunctions is confirmed in the verses that follow).

The contrast is striking between the blessing on those who are peacemakers while under the threat of persecution. Being peacemakers for God's kingdom does not endear one with this world bent on conflict. The contrast is also striking between Jesus, the prince of peace and a world that hates his teachings (John 15.18-25).

This last blessing repeats the promise of the first: "For theirs is the kingdom of heaven". Jesus is teaching here about persecution and mistreatment for the sake of God's kingdom: "when they revile and persecute you and say all kinds of evil against you falsely for my sake". Note that Jesus considers "reviling" and speaking evil falsely against his disciples as part of "persecution". Just because believers are not being put to death for their faith does not mean they are not being persecuted. Lies and "reproaches" against believers are also a way of persecuting them and can have far-reaching consequences in their lives.

The apostle Peter reminds his readers about this important aspect of "persecution":

> **14** If you are reproached for the name of Christ, blessed *are you,* for the Spirit of glory and of God rests upon you. On their part He is blasphemed, but on your part, He is glorified. **15** But let none of you suffer as a murderer, a thief, an evildoer, or as a busybody in other people's matters. **16** Yet if *anyone suffers* as a Christian, let him not be ashamed, but let him glorify God in this matter." (1 Peter 4.14-16)

The mention of persecution of the "prophets" is important; it brings the focus on those who preach or teach the truth revealed by God. Jeremiah was scourged (Jeremiah 20.2). Zechariah was stoned (2 Chronicles 24.21). According to Jewish tradition, Isaiah was sawn asunder by Manasseh. See also Nehemiah 9.26; Matthew 21.35; 23.32ff; Acts 7.52 and 1 Thessalonians 2.15.

Persecution is often the result of what disciples of the Messiah teach or preach:

> **20** "Remember the word that I said to you, 'A servant is not greater than his master.' If they persecuted Me they will also persecute you. If they kept My word they will keep yours also. **21** But all these things they will do to you for My name's sake, because they do not know Him who sent Me. **22** If I had not come and spoken to them, they would have no sin, but now they have no excuse for their sin." (John 14.20-22)

"Rejoice and be exceedingly glad": see Acts 5.41; 1 Peter 4.13; Revelation 19.7.

Prayer

Father in heaven, we come to you for strength as we follow your teachings in this world. We pray for wisdom and for the working of the Holy Spirit in our hearts, in our will and understanding. We thank you for every blessing we have from you every day. May we honor you today by our words and actions. We pray this in the name of Jesus. Amen.

Week 43: Salt, Light and the Law (Matt 5.13-20)

Day 1

> "You are the salt of the earth; but if the salt loses its flavor, how shall it be seasoned? It is then good for nothing but to be thrown out and trampled underfoot by men."
> (Matthew 5.13)

It is no coincidence that this statement follows directly the statement about prophets who were persecuted and introduces Jesus' important statements about keeping and teaching God's law.

In the Old Testament sacrifices were sprinkled with salt before being offered to God: "And every offering of your grain offering you shall season with salt; you shall not allow the salt of the covenant of your God to be lacking from your grain offering. With all your offerings you shall offer salt." (Leviticus 2.13) Salt itself was a sign of closeness and friendship (Numbers 18.19; 2 Chronicles 13.5). Newborn babies were rubbed with salt (Ezekiel 16.4).

Sacrifices offered to God in Israel were signs of God's friendship covenant with His people.

The "salt" represents the faithful and friendly disposition towards God required of those who offer their lives to God as a living sacrifice (see Romans 12.1-3). God requires a "righteousness" that exceeds the righteousness of the scribes and pharisees (Matthew 5.20). The reference to "salt" and "light" is already an introduction to the righteousness taught by Jesus and which is the fulfilling of the law (Matthew 5.21-48).

The apostle Paul wrote that without "love" it is meaningless and useless for one to try to honor God or serve him (1 Corinthians 13.1-3). Those who teach others must do so "with love":

> **15** "but, speaking the truth in love, may grow up in all things into Him who is the head—Christ— **16** from whom the whole

body, joined and knit together by what every joint supplies, according to the effective working by which every part does its share, causes growth of the body for the edifying of itself in love." (Ephesians 4.15)

The Church in Ephesus accomplished many good things and even recognized false teachers, but was lacking in love:

1 "To the angel of the church of Ephesus write, 'These things, says He who holds the seven stars in His right hand, who walks in the midst of the seven golden lampstands: **2** 'I know your works, your labor, your patience, and that you cannot bear those who are evil. And you have tested those who say they are apostles and are not and have found them liars; **3** and you have persevered and have patience and have labored for My name's sake and have not become weary. **4** Nevertheless I have *this* against you, that you have left your first love. **5** Remember therefore from where you have fallen; repent and do the first works, or else I will come to you quickly and remove your lampstand from its place—unless you repent.'" (Revelation 2.1-5)

Prayer

Father in heaven, we pray that your Holy Spirit will continue to teach us and guide us today. We pray that we will grow in love as we strive to serve you. May we today offer ourselves as holy and living sacrifices and honor you through our words and actions. We thank you for all your blessings and for the opportunity to come to you for strength and wisdom. In Jesus' name, we pray. Amen.

Day 2

14 "You are the light of the world. A city that is set on a hill cannot be hidden. **15** Nor do they light a lamp and put it under a basket, but on a lampstand, and it gives light to all *who are* in the house. **16** Let your light so shine before men, that they may see your good works and glorify your Father in heaven."
(Matthew 5.14–16)

As noted before, the "you" in verse 14 is in the singular, while in verse 16 the form of the verb and the pronoun are in the plural. As we read the New Testament, it is important to understand how these teachings of Jesus are not merely about individual behavior; they are addressed to the disciples in their relationships and also in their relationship to people outside their community (as in Matthew 5.44, "But I say to *you*" with the plural form of *you*).

Just as the "salt" refers back to the Old Testament, so does the "light" as describing the worship in the tabernacle and also the calling of Israel and the Messiah to bring light to the Gentile world.

Salt on the sacrifice was a sign of friendship with God. Light in the tabernacle was a sign of God's presence among His people. The "light" is first of all "God's light": his holiness, goodness, lovingkindness. In the Bible, these qualities of God are to be lived out by Israel and seen by Gentiles (they will also be the "light" brought about by Israel's Messiah); lived out by the Church and seen by the world:

> **1** "And the Lord spoke to Moses, saying, **2** "Speak to all the congregation of the children of Israel, and say to them: 'You shall be holy, for I the Lord your God *am* holy." (Leviticus 19.1-2)

> **1** "Behold! My Servant whom I uphold,
> My Elect One *in whom* My soul delights!
> I have put My Spirit upon Him;
> He will bring forth justice to the Gentiles.
> **2** He will not cry out, nor raise *His voice,*
> Nor cause His voice to be heard in the street.
> **3** A bruised reed He will not break,
> And smoking flax He will not quench;
> He will bring forth justice for truth.
> **4** He will not fail nor be discouraged,
> Till He has established justice in the earth;
> And the coastlands shall wait for His law." (Isaiah 42.1-4; see Matthew 12.19).

> **13** "Therefore, gird up the loins of your mind, be sober, and rest *your* hope fully upon the grace that is to be brought to you at the revelation of Jesus Christ; **14** as obedient children, not conforming yourselves to the former lusts, *as* in your ignorance; **15** but as He who called you *is* holy, you also be holy in all *your* conduct, **16** because it is written, 'Be holy, for I am holy.'" (1 Peter 1.13-16)

9 "But you *are* a chosen generation, a royal priesthood, a holy nation, His own special people, that you may proclaim the praises of Him who called you out of darkness into His marvelous light; **10** who once *were* not a people but *are* now the people of God, who had not obtained mercy but now have obtained mercy." (1 Peter 2.9-10)

14 Do all things without complaining and disputing, **15** that you may become blameless and harmless, children of God without fault in the midst of a crooked and perverse generation, among whom you shine as lights in the world, **16** holding fast the word of life so that I may rejoice in the day of Christ that I have not run in vain or labored in vain." (1 Peter 2.14-16)

The Church in Ephesus mentioned in Revelation 2 will cease to "shine" unless she repents. Her lampstand will be removed unless she returns to her "first love" (see 1 Corinthians 13.1-13).

Prayer

Our Father in heaven, we are grateful for your love and faithfulness. We thank you for providing for our needs. We pray for our loved ones as well as our neighbors and co-workers. May you bless them today and guide them close to you. May your forgiveness extend to all of them. Forgive us our sins and strengthen us in holiness and faithfulness. We pray in Jesus' name. Amen.

Day 3

"Let your light so shine before men, that they may see your good works and glorify your Father in heaven."
    (Matthew 5.16)

The pronoun used in this verse ("your") is in the plural and means "all of you". The command to "let you light shine" describes his disciples "together". Jesus is talking about the light that shines before "men" which is a word that can be applied to all peoples and nations, as in Matthew 4.19:

"Then He said to them, 'Follow Me, and I will make you fishers of men.' **20** They immediately left *their* nets and followed Him." (Matthew 4.19).

It is in the context of "community" or "church" that each disciple is called to live out his or her faith and called to accomplish "good works" (Matthew 16.16-18). The word "church" (*ekklesia*) does not reflect exclusively a New Testament concept since God's people, Israel, are also called "assembly" or "congregation" (The Hebrew word *qahal* in Leviticus 8.3,4; Deuteronomy 5.22; Nehemiah 8.1-9; Psalms 22.22). The Septuagint (about 270 BC) the Greek translation of the Hebrew Bible, translated the Hebrew *qahal* by the Greek *ekklesia* (assembly, church).

The "church" exists in order to be a light that shines before men. Five of the seven Churches in Asia in the book of Revelation are to repent. These churches are described as holding golden lampstands: "To the angel of the church of Ephesus write, 'He who holds the seven stars in His right hand, who walks in the midst of the seven golden lampstands" (Revelation 2.3).

The church in Ephesus must repent or else the Lord will remove its golden lampstand; she will cease to be a light to the world:

> **4** "Nevertheless I have *this* against you, that you have left your first love. **5** Remember therefore from where you have fallen; repent and do the first works, or else I will come to you quickly and remove your lampstand from its place—unless you repent." (Revelation 3.4,5)

Those who have been washed of their sins and saved by God's grace are called by God to walk in good works prepared by God,

> **8** "For by grace you have been saved through faith, and that not of yourselves; *it is* the gift of God, **9** not of works, lest anyone should boast. **10** For we are His workmanship, created in Christ Jesus for good works, which God prepared beforehand that we should walk in them." (Ephesians 2.8-10)

> "This is a faithful saying, and these things I want you to affirm constantly, that those who have believed in God should be careful to maintain good works. These things are good and profitable to men." (Titus 3.8)

Prayer

Our Father, we thank you and praise you. Help us Lord today to understand your will and to do the good works you have prepared for us. May your Holy Spirit work in our hearts and lives in such a way as to produce good fruit. May we have a servant attitude towards all. Thank you for the opportunity to serve you today. We pray in Jesus' name. Amen.

Day 4

> "Do not think that I came to destroy the Law or the Prophets. I did not come to destroy but to fulfill."

By mentioning "the law and the prophets" Jesus is referring to most of the Old Testament Scriptures or Jewish Tanakh. The law is the first five books of the Old Testament (the Torah) and the "Prophets" are the second large portion of the Old Testament (the Neviim). A similar reference to the "law and the prophets" is found in Luke's Gospel: "

> **25** Then He said to them, 'O foolish ones, and slow of heart to believe in all that the prophets have spoken! **26** Ought not the Christ to have suffered these things and to enter into
> His glory?' **27** And beginning at Moses and all the Prophets, He expounded to them in all the Scriptures the things concerning Himself." (Luke 24.25-27, 44,45.).

Jesus' teachings are not contrasted with the "law and the prophets" but with the interpretations of the Law as found in the oral traditions of the scribes and Pharisees. These oral traditions went beyond anything intended in the Law and often canceled the Law itself (for example, in John 5.10; Matthew 12.11; Mark 7.1-8).

The scribes and Pharisees were seen as those in authority to rightly interpret and teach the Law and Prophets, the Scripture — thus to help the people accomplish or fulfill the law:

> **1** "Then Jesus spoke to the multitudes and to His
> disciples, **2** saying: "The scribes and the Pharisees sit in Moses' seat. **3** Therefore whatever they tell you to observe, *that* observe and do, but do not do according to their works; for they say, and do not do." (Matthew 23.1-3).

In These words of the Sermon on the mount (and throughout his ministry) Jesus is demonstrating his authority as an interpreter of the Law and Prophets; this is what is meant by "I did not come to destroy but to fulfill". The Greek for "to fulfill" (*plerosai*) is the same word used at the moment of Jesus' baptism:

13 "Then Jesus came from Galilee to John at the Jordan to be baptized by him. **14** And John *tried to* prevent Him, saying, 'I need to be baptized by You, and are You coming to me?' **15** But Jesus answered and said to him, 'Permit *it to be so* now, for thus it is fitting for us to fulfill all righteousness.' Then he allowed Him." (Matthew 3.13-15).

To fulfill is to accomplish, to act in a way that is in harmony with the teachings of the Law and Prophets. Thus, in his personal life, Jesus accomplished the Law and Prophets. And this was done to such a degree that Jesus lived a sinless life (1 Peter 1.22; 1 John 3.5; John 8.29; 1 Peter 1.18,19; see Isaiah 53. 9).

The verb "to fulfill" (*pleroo*) is also used in the New Testament to show how the events of the life of Jesus fulfilled the Old Testament prophets who spoke about the coming Messiah, especially in the Gospel according to Matthew (Matthew 1.22; 2.15; 2.17; 3.15; 4.14; 8.17 etc.).

As the Gospel spreads to the nations, beginning in the book of Acts, Gentiles are touched by the Good News about Jesus the Messiah and come to faith in him and to repentance. As this happens, the question of whether or not the Gentiles will need to keep the Law of Moses just as Jews were keeping this law was raised by those of the Pharisees who had been converted to the faith:

13 "So, being sent on their way by the church, they passed through Phoenicia and Samaria, describing the conversion of the Gentiles; and they caused great joy to all the brethren. **4** And when they had come to Jerusalem, they were received by the church and the apostles and the elders; and they reported all things that God had done with them. **5** But some of the sect of the Pharisees who believed rose up, saying, 'It is necessary to circumcise them, and to command *them* to keep the law of Moses.'" (Acts 15.1-5)

This question was finally resolved by the apostles and leaders of the Church in Jerusalem and the conclusion is found in the words of Saul and Barnabas conveyed to the Church in Antioch in Acts 15.22-29. It is important to note at this point that the decision not to put the Gentile converts under the burden of the Law was directed by the Holy Spirit (Acts 15.28). In his letters, Paul also deals with the question of whether or not the Gentiles were to come under the law of Moses, just as were proselytes to Judaism. And Paul's teachings are in agreement with the message communicated to the Church in Antioch in Acts 15.

Prayer

Father in heaven, we pray that you will help us understand your will and fulfill your will in our lives. We ask for your wisdom, so we can remain faithful to you. We pray that your Holy Spirit will guide us in being faithful to your Word. Guide us and protect us today as we serve you and our neighbors. We pray in Jesus' name. Amen.

Day 5

> "For assuredly, I say to you, till heaven and earth pass away, one jot or one tittle will by no means pass from the law till all is fulfilled."
> (Matthew 5.18)

One cannot be salt of the earth or light of the world without this being the result of "fulfilling the law". The righteousness required by the Lord cannot be lawlessness. It is, in fact, a righteousness that exceeds the righteousness of "the scribes and Pharisees" (v.20). How the law is, in fact, understood and applied is an important part of Jesus' teachings throughout his ministry. The scribes and Pharisees did insist on respecting the smallest "jot" of the law which is the Greek *iota* standing for the smallest letter of the Hebrew alphabet; they even considered the small "title" of the law which is the Greek *keraia* describing a little projecting point in some of the letters of the Hebrew alphabet. However, Jesus rebukes these teachers for neglecting the weightier matters of the law (Matthew 23.16-23).

It is also an important dimension of the New Testament writings which should not be understood as a breaking away from God's law but as a fulfilling of that law, whether the ten commandments or the entire body of rules found in the law of Moses:

> **18** "Owe no one anything except to love one another, for he who loves another has fulfilled the law. **9** For the commandments, "You shall not commit adultery," "You shall not murder," "You shall not steal," "You shall not bear false witness," "You shall not covet," and if *there is* any other commandment, are *all* summed up in this saying, namely, "You shall love your neighbor as yourself." **10** Love does no harm to a neighbor; therefore, love *is* the fulfillment of the law." (Romans 13.8-10)

The law is also to be fulfilled in its messianic dimension. In its promise for example that in Abraham's seed all the families of the earth would be blessed, Genesis 12.13; 22.18; 26.4; 28.14 (Genesis, we must remember, is part of the Torah!).

We can also mention the promise of a greater prophet than Moses:

> **17** "And the Lord said to me: 'What they have spoken is good. **18** I will raise up for them a Prophet like you from among their brethren, and will put My words in His mouth, and He shall speak to them all that I command Him. **19** And it shall be *that* whoever will not hear My words, which He speaks in My name, I will require *it* of him." (Deuteronomy 18.17-19)

The apostle Peter quotes Genesis as well as Deuteronomy and applies these texts from the Law to Jesus and to "these days":

> **27** "You are sons of the prophets, and of the covenant which God made with our fathers, saying to Abraham, 'And in your seed all the families of the earth shall be blessed.' **26** To you first, God, having raised up His Servant Jesus, sent Him to bless you, in turning away every one *of you* from your iniquities."

It is true that as we read the Gospels and the New Testament, the interpretations of the law by the scribes and Pharisees are neglected. And the Gentiles who come to faith in the Jewish Messiah are not required to be circumcised or to practice all the regulations found even in the Torah of Moses. The reason for this is that the Messiah introduces a new covenant, unlike the covenant made at Sinai, and which itself was prophesied (see for example Hebrews 8.6-13 and Jeremiah 31.31-34).

Prayer

Father in heaven, we pray that we can understand your will for us and practice your will in our daily lives. We pray that we can fulfill all the commandments in a way that will be pleasing to you and will bring honor to your name and to your will. We ask for wisdom and for more holiness in everything we do or say. This we pray in the name of Jesus. Amen.

Day 6

> "Whoever therefore breaks one of the least of these commandments, and teaches men so, shall be called least in the

kingdom of heaven; but whoever does and teaches *them*, he shall be called great in the kingdom of heaven."

Jesus taught Israel and his disciples, saying that he came not to destroy the law but to fulfill it. He is now pointing more specifically first to those who teach men to break God's commandments and who break these commandments themselves; secondly, he points to those who teach God's commandments to men and keep those commandments themselves. The following verse (20) shows that he is specifically pointing to the teachers of the law, the scribes and Pharisees. Later in the Gospel, Jesus again points to the teachers of the law:

> **1** "Then Jesus spoke to the multitudes and to His disciples, **2** saying: "The scribes and the Pharisees sit in Moses' seat. **3** Therefore whatever they tell you to observe, *that* observe and do, but do not do according to their works; for they say, and do not do." (Matthew 23.1,2)

Jesus teaches the multitudes as the prophets of Israel did, by pointing God's people to the law, to God's commandments, God's will. The prayer he taught expressed the importance of taking seriously God's will: "Your kingdom come. Your will be done as it is in heaven" (Matthew 6.10).

The prophets of Israel were inspired and spoke with authority even when teaching about God's law, the Torah, as it had been revealed to Moses. However, they did not simply quote the law. They pointed the people to how they were to understand and practice the law. There was as much authority in the LORD speaking to His people through Jeremiah, Isaiah or Elijah as there was recorded in the book of Deuteronomy or any other part of the Torah:

> **13** "Yet the Lord testified against Israel and against Judah, by all of His prophets, every seer, saying, 'Turn from your evil ways, and keep My commandments *and* My statutes, according to all the law which I commanded your fathers, and which I sent to you by My servants the prophets.' **14** Nevertheless they would not hear, but stiffened their necks, like the necks of their fathers, who did not believe in the Lord their God." (2 Kings 17.13-14)

The prophet Malachi proclaimed a severe judgment on the nation of Israel and its leaders because of hypocritical worship (Malachi 1.7-14), injustice (2.10), heathen religious practices (2.11), abuse of divorce (2.16), withholding tithes and offerings from God (3.8-10)

There was no contradiction between the teaching of the Old Testament prophets such as Malachi and the teachings of Moses. God's prophets spoke with divine authority and taught what was in harmony and in keeping with God's commands.

According to Malachi, God would first send a prophet who would be a forerunner, to prepare the way for Him (Malachi 3:1). The forerunner would come in the likeness of an Old Testament prophet; he will stand in the tradition of the fiery man of God named Elijah (Malachi 4:5).

John the Baptist was that forerunner, that "Elijah". Jesus taught, saying:

> **11** "'Indeed, Elijah is coming first and will restore all things. **12** But I say to you that Elijah has come already, and they did not know him but did to him whatever they wished. Likewise, the Son of Man is also about to suffer at their hands.'" **13** Then the disciples understood that He spoke to them of John the Baptist." (Matthew 17.11-13)

When the Messiah would come to Israel, he would also teach God's people, as did the prophets of old. He would be the prophet even greater than Moses. The people would need to listen to him:

> "I will raise up for them a Prophet like you from among their brethren, and will put My words in His mouth, and He shall speak to them all that I command Him." (Deuteronomy 18.18)

In keeping with the Old Testament prophecies about the Messiah, Jesus in this sermon and throughout the Gospels speaks with the authority of a great prophet who calls God's people to fulfill God's laws. Jesus provides two examples of this keeping of God's law by first teaching on murder and adultery (Matthew 5.21-28).

Prayer

Father in heaven, we thank you for the teachings of our Lord Jesus. We pray for understanding and wisdom as we listen to these teachings and apply them to our lives. We pray that your will can be accomplished in our lives today. We also pray for forgiveness and for the help of your Holy Spirit. This we pray in the name of Jesus. Amen.

Day 7

> "For I say to you, that unless your righteousness exceeds *the righteousness* of the scribes and Pharisees, you will by no means enter the kingdom of heaven."
> (Matthew 5.20)

In the verses that follow, Jesus will show six different examples of keeping the law in a way that "exceeds" the righteousness of the scribes and the Pharisees. In his teaching, Jesus refers mostly to the oral interpretation of the law by the scribes and Pharisees: "You have heard that it was said...". These oral interpretations or traditions often led people to break the law: "For laying aside the commandment of God, you hold the tradition of men"; "Making the word of God of no effect through your tradition which you have handed down." (Mark 7.8,13).

The laws given by God through Moses have not disappeared with the coming of the Messiah. They have been emphasized even to a greater degree. The laws concerning murder, adultery, divorce, swearing, an eye for an eye, love your neighbor are to be understood by God's people in a way that their righteousness will exceed the oral interpretations and traditions handed down by the scribes and Pharisees (Matthew 5.21-48). The Greek word "exceed" (*pleion*) means greater, more excellent. Through these words, Jesus is also affirming the greater authority of his teachings over the teachings of the scribes and Pharisees: "For he taught has one having authority, and not as the scribes" (Matthew 7.29).

The New Testament shows us that an important question was raised in the early years of the Church. The question was whether or not the converts to the Messiah should be considered proselytes of Judaism, as was the custom at the time (see for example Matthew 23.15). Should the Gentiles who had put their faith in Jesus and repented be required to be circumcised and to follow the Torah, just as Jewish believers did?

This question was answered by the negative, as for example in Acts 15:

> **6** "Now the apostles and elders came together to consider this matter. **7** And when there had been much dispute, Peter rose up *and* said to them: 'Men *and* brethren, you know that a good while ago God chose among us, that by my mouth the Gentiles should hear the word of the gospel and believe. **8** So God, who knows the heart, acknowledged them by giving them the Holy Spirit, just as *He did* to us, **9** and made no distinction between us and them, purifying their hearts by faith. **10** Now therefore, why

> do you test God by putting a yoke on the neck of the disciples which neither our fathers nor we were able to bear? **11** But we believe that through the grace of the Lord Jesus Christ we shall be saved in the same manner as they.'" (Acts 15.6-11)

The New Testament teachings reiterate the importance of God's laws, as found for example in the Torah. However, Gentiles who come to faith are introduced into a new covenant, which is not the covenant of Sinai. God through the Messiah brought about a new covenant, as the prophets themselves had announced (Jeremiah 31.31-34; Hebrews 8.7-13). This covenant does not mean that Gentiles can live lawless lives in direct opposition to the requirements of the Torah. It means that when they follow the teachings of Jesus and his apostles, they are fulfilling the requirements of the law:

> **28** "Him we preach, warning every man and teaching every man in all wisdom, that we may present every man perfect in Christ Jesus. **29** To this *end* I also labor, striving according to His working which works in me mightily." (Colossians 1.28; see Romans 12.1,2; 13.8-10).

Prayer

Our Father, we come to you for help as we seek to do your will. Give us wisdom and willingness, strength from your Holy Spirit that we may each day seek you, talk to you and praise you. We are weak but with your strength, we can overcome our weakness and grow in strength. We also pray for our loved ones, our neighbors and our brothers and sisters in Christ that they may also grow in every way before you. In Jesus' name we pray. Amen.

Week 44: But I say to you (Matt 5.21-37)

Day 1

> "You have heard that it was said to those of old, 'You shall not murder, and whoever murders will be in danger of the judgment.'"
> (Matthew 5.21)

The people knew the Torah because they were used to "hearing" the law read in the Synagogue. To "murder" is the Hebrew verb *retsach* applies only to illegal killing such as premeditated murder or manslaughter. It is not used in the administration of justice or for killing at war. The translation "thou shalt not kill" as in the KJV is too broad.

The murderer is the "manslayer" for whom the law provided cities of refuge (Numbers 35) since the killing of someone could also be the result of an accident: "Then you shall appoint cities to be cities of refuge for you, that the manslayer who kills any person accidentally may flee there" (Numbers 35.11). In this verse, the Hebrew for "to kill" is *nakah*, used, for example, in war situations or even for punishment of a murderer (Genesis 14.15; often translated "defeat" or "smite"). The law of Moses required that "murder" should be punished by the forfeiture of life (Exodus 21.12,14; Leviticus 24.17,21) with a special emphasis on those who sacrificed their children to the gods, a common practice among pagans (Leviticus 20.1-5).

Jesus begins his teaching on the kind of "righteousness" God requires (5.19,20) by a reference to the 6th of the ten commandments concerning murder (Exodus 20.13): "You shall not murder". After the fall of Adam and Eve in the Genesis account, the first sinful act we find described in the Bible is the murder of Abel by his brother Cain (Genesis 4.1-8). There is a clear contrast between this violent death of Abel at the hands of his brother and the reference to the driving away of man and woman from "the tree of life". Thus, death is literally the consequence of God's warning to Adam even before God formed Eve:

> **15** "Then the Lord God took the man and put him in the garden of Eden to tend and keep it. **16** And the Lord God commanded the man, saying, 'Of every tree of the garden you may freely eat; **17** but of the tree of the knowledge of good and evil you shall not eat, for in the day that you eat of it you shall surely die.'" (Genesis 2.15-17)

Separation from "life" of which God is the source brings about "death" in many ways (Ephesians 2.1-3; Romans 5.12-15). One of these ways is that men show no respect for the lives of their brothers. James teaches how "murder" is the result of "friendship with the world":

> **1** "Where do wars and fights *come* from among you? Do *they* not *come* from your *desires for* pleasure that war in your members? **2** You lust and do not have. You murder and covet and cannot obtain. You fight and war. Yet you do not have because you do not ask. **3** You ask and do not receive, because you ask amiss, that you may spend *it* on your pleasures. **4** Adulterers and adulteresses! Do you not know that friendship with the world is enmity with God? Whoever therefore wants to be a friend of the world makes himself an enemy of God." (James 4.1-4).

Prayer

Father in heaven, we thank you for the commandments found in your Word. We thank you that you protect is from evil by giving us commandments that lead to life. We pray for all the wars we find in this world; that we might, in small ways, contribute to peace and reconciliation. We pray today that we can fully understand the meaning of your commandments and apply this to our lives. We pray this in the name of Jesus. Amen.

Day 2

> **21** "You have heard that it was said to those of old, 'You shall not murder, and whoever murders will be in danger of the judgment.' **22** But I say to you that whoever is angry with his brother without a cause shall be in danger of the judgment. And whoever says to his brother, 'Raca!' shall be in danger of the

council. But whoever says, 'You fool!' shall be in danger of hell fire." (Matthew 5.21-22).

This is a warning about "anger". See Ephesians 4.26,27,31. In these verses, we have apparently two conflicting instructions. In verse 26 we are taught that we can be angry but should not sin out of anger. In verse 31 we are taught to put away anger with bitterness and wrath. There is an anger which can be a manifestation of God's righteousness, as when Jesus cleaned the temple (Matthew 21.12-17). God can himself have anger without every sinning. He was angered or indignant by men turning to the worship of idols (Exodus 32.10; Deuteronomy 6.14,15); by the grumbling of the people (Numbers 11.1,10).

The words "raca" and "fool" are used here to describe contempt towards others. It is this contempt for others springing from the heart which is in view here. The fact is that it is very difficult for people to control the "tongue" and insults against others can have long-lasting consequences; like a "fire" set up by the tongue (James 3.5,6).

God our judge does call unfaithful or sinful people "fools" or lacking wisdom, as Jesus does himself in Matthew 7.26,27. Thus, the words of Jesus here in Matthew 5 should not be understood as a statement that nobody is "foolish" or "unwise" but as a warning against contempt and insults which only breed conflict, hatred and can even lead to murder: "He who answers a matter before he hears *it*, it *is* folly and shame to him." (Proverbs 18,13). "A wise *man* fears and departs from evil, but a fool rages and is self-confident." (Proverbs 14.16).

The 6th commandment not to murder was itself insufficient to bring about true "righteousness". Jesus was not saying something necessarily new. Similar statements are found in *Pirkei Avot* (a section of the Mishnah, itself a part of the Talmud) concerning, for example, the evil tongue through gossip or slander which are forms of "murder" (see James 3.5-8,10; 4.11,12).

All murder comes from the heart, as Jesus taught about every other sin:

> **21** "And He said, 'What comes out of a man, that defiles a man. **21** For from within, out of the heart of men, proceed evil thoughts, adulteries, fornications, **murders**, **22** thefts, covetousness, wickedness, deceit, lewdness, an evil eye, blasphemy, pride, foolishness. **23** All these evil things come from within and defile a man.'" (Mark 7.21-23).

And from the mouth comes what is in the heart:

33 "Either make the tree good and its fruit good, or else make the tree bad and its fruit bad; for a tree is known by *its* fruit. **34** Brood of vipers! How can you, being evil, speak good things? For out of the abundance of the heart the mouth speaks. **35** A good man out of the good treasure of his heart brings forth good things, and an evil man out of the evil treasure brings forth evil things. **36** But I say to you that for every idle word men may speak, they will give account of it in the day of judgment. **37** For by your words you will be justified, and by your words you will be condemned." (Matthew 12.33-37)

The same teaching is found in the letter of James:

33 "Either make the tree good and its fruit good, or else make the tree bad and its fruit bad; for a tree is known by *its* fruit. **34** Brood of vipers! How can you, being evil, speak good things? For out of the abundance of the heart the mouth speaks. **35** A good man out of the good treasure [g]of his heart brings forth good things, and an evil man out of the evil treasure brings forth evil things. **36** But I say to you that for every idle word men may speak they will give account of it in the day of judgment. **37** For by your words you will be justified, and by your words you will be condemned." (James 3.33-37)

Prayer

Our Father in heaven, we pray for wisdom as we speak today. We pray that you can purify our hearts of all bitterness and anger. Help us to speak with truth and confidence and maintain love and goodness for all. Help us, Lord, to teach the truth in love. May your Holy Spirit produce in our hearts and lives the fruit of peace. This is our prayer in Jesus' name. Amen.

Day 3

23 Therefore, if you bring your gift to the altar, and there remember that your brother has something against you, **24** leave your gift there before the altar, and go your way. First be reconciled to your brother, and then come and offer your gift."
(Matthew 5.23,24)

For the disciple, "righteousness" requires more than refusing to murder or even refusing to insult or despise another or fall into anger and bitterness. The follower of Jesus takes the initiative to bring reconciliation; to be a peacemaker. The religious act of bringing a gift to the "altar" cannot take the place of being a peacemaker, of acting on behalf of reconciliation. Our relationships matter a lot to God, just as much as our acts of worship. Without this work of reconciliation which Christ brings to the world, there is no end to the cycle of violence and retaliation.

The teachings of Jesus do not mean everyone will understand an initiative for reconciliation or everyone you act peacefully towards will like you or love you. In fact, some might even hate you despite your peaceful ways (see Matthew 5.42-48). Note the words of the apostle Paul:

> **17** "Repay no one evil for evil. Have regard for good things in the sight of all men. **18** If it is possible, as much as depends on you, live peaceably with all men.**19** Beloved, do not avenge yourselves, but *rather* give place to wrath; for it is written, 'Vengeance *is* Mine, I will repay,' says the Lord. **20** Therefore 'If your enemy is hungry, feed him; if he is thirsty, give him a drink; for in so doing you will heap coals of fire on his head.' **21** Do not be overcome by evil, but overcome evil with good." (Romans 12.17-21)

> **21** "Let no corrupt word proceed out of your mouth, but what is good for necessary edification, that it may impart grace to the hearers. **30** And do not grieve the Holy Spirit of God, by whom you were sealed for the day of redemption. **31** Let all bitterness, wrath, anger, clamor, and evil speaking be put away from you, with all malice. **32** And be kind to one another, tenderhearted, forgiving one another, even as God in Christ forgave you." (Ephesians 4.29-32)

> **5** "Walk in wisdom toward those *who are* outside, redeeming the time. **6** *Let* your speech always *be* with grace, seasoned with salt, that you may know how you ought to answer each one." (Colossians 4.5,6)

Prayer

Our Lord and God, we praise you for the truth of your Word. We praise you for our savior Jesus, who brought your heavenly peace to this earth. Give us Father a grateful heart and wisdom to know to answer to each one. Teach us to take the initiative in bringing about peace and reconciliation. May your Spirit continue to teach us your truth. In Jesus' name, we pray. Amen.

Day 4

> **25** "Agree with your adversary quickly, while you are on the way with him, lest your adversary deliver you to the judge, the judge hand you over to the officer, and you be thrown into prison. **26** Assuredly, I say to you, you will by no means get out of there till you have paid the last penny."
> (Matthew 5.25,26)

Even today in conflict management it is better to seek a peaceful resolution. Going before the judge or going into lawsuits will usually be more harmful and costly than taking the initiative for a reconciliation or a compromise. The words of Jesus here stand out as words of wisdom in a world plagued with litigation, which so often does not help any of the parties involved and ends up being extremely costly. The "judge" and even less the "officer" (in Greek, servant) are only following through the rules of the law and have no real concern for the parties involved, or the pains involved in a condemnation. The apostle Paul warns of the consequences and implications of litigation between Christians in 1 Corinthians 6.1-11. He is not encouraging Christians to give up or to go against the authorities, whose task is to maintain social order (Romans 13). But he is encouraging brethren to have enough wisdom not to have to fall into litigation with one another.

In his discussion, the apostle explains that lawsuits have to do with "small matters" when seen in the broad picture of God's judgments. Christians should choose their battles wisely. They are not wrestling "against flesh and blood" but "against principalities, against powers, against the rulers of the darkness of this age, against spiritual hosts of wickedness in the heavenly places" (Ephesians 6.12). These are the bigger matters believers are dealing with and need to focus on.

If disciples are called to be participants in the spiritual battle going on in the world, can they not become wise in order to deal with "the smallest matters" (1 Corinthians 6.2)? The judging of the world and of angels is connected to the spiritual nature of God's judgments, as described in Ephesians 6.

The apostle describes what we might call today the work of "mediation" between two parties in conflict: "one who will be able to judge between his brethren" (1 Corinthians 6.4,5). Wise mediation can help parties see the light and understand how they can come to be reconciled or at least come to a compromise. The wise Christian mediator can point out how the larger "interests" of the parties in conflict outweigh the "issues" that have brought about the conflict. We should note, in fact, that in 1 Corinthians the apostle is bringing wisdom to a divided church by pointing out the larger issues at stake, such as the questions of love and unity (1 Corinthians 13).

The servant of God who labors in teaching and preaching should especially act in a way that does not hurt the peace and unity of the body of Christ, the Church:

> **24** "And a servant of the Lord must not quarrel but be gentle to all, able to teach, patient, **25** in humility correcting those who are in opposition, if God perhaps will grant them repentance so that they may know the truth, **26** and *that* they may come to their senses *and escape* the snare of the devil, having been taken captive by him to *do* his will." (2 Timothy 2.24-26)

Prayer

Father in heaven, we are thankful to you for Jesus. We thank you for his life and teachings, and for his death on the cross and his resurrection. Help us today to live a peaceful and righteous life in this world often torn apart by conflict. Help us have the wisdom to mediate between those who should live at peace with each other. May your Spirit strengthen us to be peacemakers. We pray this in Jesus' name. Amen.

Day 5

> **27** "You have heard that it was said to those of old, 'You shall not commit adultery.' **28** But I say to you that whoever looks at a woman to lust for her has already committed adultery with her in his heart. **29** If your right eye causes you to sin, pluck it out and cast *it* from you; for it is more profitable for you that one of your members perish, than for your whole body to be cast into hell. **30** And if your right hand causes you to sin, cut it off and cast *it* from you; for it is more profitable for you that one of your members perish, than for your whole body to be cast into hell."
>
> (Matthew 5.27-30)

Jesus continues to teach about the righteousness that should exceed the righteousness of scribes and Pharisees. His teaching touches the 7th commandment of the decalogue concerning adultery (Exodus 20.14). Adultery is only the final step to lust, which in fact originates in the heart (see the sin of David in 2 Samuel 11). It is the heart of man which needs to radically change in order to reach the righteousness Jesus mentions in this sermon:

> **21** "For from within, out of the heart of men, proceed evil thoughts, adulteries, fornications, murders, **22** thefts, covetousness, wickedness, deceit, lewdness, an evil eye, blasphemy, pride, foolishness. **23** All these evil things come from within and defile a man." (Mark 7.21-23)

One promise in the Old Testament connected to the coming of the Messiah is that God would give people a new heart, would write his laws in their hearts (Ezekiel 11.19; 36.26; Jeremiah 31.33). The Gospel of Jesus-Christ is "the power" that brings about this transformation of the human heart (Romans 1.16). It was already the prayer of David for God to create in him a clean heart, to renew his spirit within him (Psalms 51.10). The Holy Spirit of God has the power to change or "circumcise" the heart :

> **28** "For he is not a Jew who *is one* outwardly, nor *is* circumcision that which *is* outward in the flesh; **29** but *he is* a Jew who *is one* inwardly; and circumcision *is that* of the heart, in the Spirit, not in the letter; whose praise *is* not from men but from God." (Romans 2.28,29)

Writing to the Corinthians, the apostle Paul reminds them how through the preaching of the Gospel and their faith in Christ, the Spirit of God had written His will on their "hearts" :

> **2** "You are our epistle written in our hearts, known and read by all men; **3** clearly you are an epistle of Christ, ministered by us, written not with ink but by the Spirit of the living God, not on tablets of stone but on tablets of flesh, *that is,* of the heart." (2 Corinthians 3.2,3).

The commandment is not sufficient to bring about the righteousness God is looking for. There needs to be a radical change in the human behavior which comes from a radical change in the heart. The hyperbolic language found in Jesus' words illustrates this principle. Jesus is not teaching here that one should pluck his eye or cut his arm. Even if someone were to pluck his right eye, would this mean he could not sin with his left eye? These words illustrate a principle found even for the health and life of the body. Even back in antiquity, people knew that sometimes a part of the body needed to be amputated in order to save the entire body.

These words also illustrate the fact that Jesus is appealing to the will, to a choice or decision on the part of those listening to him. This is found throughout the ministry of Jesus when he points out the radical choices that are implied in following him, as in Luke 9.56-62. The word "follow" is a key word in verses 57,59 and 61. Being a disciple of Jesus is more than just learning about him or from him; it means following him even when it might cost our life: "And whoever does not bear his cross and come after Me cannot be My disciple." (Luke 14.27).

> **66** "From that *time* many of his disciples went back and walked with Him no more. **67** Then Jesus said to the twelve, 'Do you also want to go away?' **68** But Simon Peter answered Him, 'Lord, to whom shall we go? You have the words of eternal life. **69** Also we have come to believe and know that You are the Christ, the Son of the living God.'" (John 6.66-68)

Prayer

We pray to you, our Father in heaven, with thanksgiving for your Son Jesus. We thank you for his teachings and the life he gave for us and for all mankind. Give us today the peace and joy that come from your Spirit. Strengthen our hearts in a resolve to live according to your will. May we offer our lives today to your service and your truth. We pray in the name of our Lord Jesus. Amen.

Day 6

> **31** Furthermore, it has been said, 'Whoever divorces his wife, let him give her a certificate of divorce.' **32** But I say to you that whoever divorces his wife for any reason except sexual immorality causes her to commit adultery; and whoever marries a woman who is divorced commits adultery.'"
> (Matthew 5.31,32)

The law of Moses in Deuteronomy allowed for divorce and required a certificate or letter of divorce (Deuteronomy 24.1-4). This also is alluded to in the discussion of Jesus with the Pharisees concerning divorce

(Matthew 19.1-10). Jesus teaches both in Matthew 5 and 19 that divorce is not permissible unless there is "sexual immorality" on the part of one of the partners. This is a direct response to the question they asked Jesus: "Is it lawful for a man to divorce his wife for just any reason?" (Matthew 19,3).

There was disagreement among the teachers of the law concerning the grounds of divorce. Rabbi Hillel (110 BC to 10 AD) interpreted the law of Moses as the option to divorce "for any reason", even for a "spoiled dish" (meal). However, Rabbi Shammai (50 BC to 30 AD) taught that Moses' law allowed divorce only for a "matter of indecency." This debate about divorce was well known when Jesus was teaching. In Matthew 19 Jesus goes further than Hillel or Shammai by pointing out God's original intent for marriage. It seems also that Christ through his teachings abolished the death penalty for adultery (John 8.11).

The emphasis of Jesus in this text is also on the responsibility of a man who initiates a divorce with his wife. Deciding to go through a divorce often implies multiple consequences, often unforeseen by divorcees. It had become the custom for too many men to put away their wives on the most whimsical ground. The law of Moses in Deuteronomy 24 was intended to mitigate an existing practice in the woman's interest. The discussions of the scribes or legal experts did nothing to restrain the capriciousness of husbands, their tendency to license. Jesus is here defending the rights of women by not allowing men to put away their wives for whimsical reasons. Jesus was reiterating the prophetic claim of God through the prophet Malachi: "I hate putting away". Note the words of Jesus recorded in Luke: "Whoever divorces his wife and marries another commits adultery; and whoever marries her who is divorced from *her* husband commits adultery." (Luke 16.18)

Both in Matthew 5 and 19 the point of Jesus' teachings is not to establish an original or new legislation. It is to show a high moral standard and emphasize a sense of responsibility on the part of married men in their behavior towards their wives. When people seek to draw precise legislation from these teachings of Jesus, they miss the focus of seeking the higher good, the higher goal of faithfulness and dedication to one another in the marriage covenant: the righteousness that exceeds the righteousness of scribes and Pharisees; the righteousness that is fulfilled in the commandment of love:

> 4 "Love suffers long *and* is kind; love does not envy; love does not parade itself, is not puffed up; **5** does not behave rudely, does not seek its own, is not provoked, thinks no

evil; **6** does not rejoice in iniquity, but rejoices in the truth; **7** bears all things, believes all things, hopes all things, endures all things." (1 Corinthians 13.4-7)

"Husbands, likewise, dwell with *them* with understanding, giving honor to the wife, as to the weaker vessel, and as *being* heirs together of the grace of life, that your prayers may not be hindered." (1 Peter 3.7)

> **25** "Husbands love your wives, just as Christ also loved the church and gave Himself for her, **26** that He might sanctify and cleanse her with the washing of water by the word, **27** that He might present her to Himself a glorious church, not having spot or wrinkle or any such thing, but that she should be holy and without blemish. **28** So, husbands ought to love their own wives as their own bodies; he who loves his wife loves himself. **29** For no one ever hated his own flesh, but nourishes and cherishes it, just as the Lord *does* the church. **30** For we are members of His body, of His flesh and of His bones. **31** 'For this reason a man shall leave his father and mother and be joined to his wife, and the two shall become one flesh.'" (Ephesians 5.25-31)

Prayer

Father, we pray today for our couples and families. We ask you to keep and strengthen our loved ones in their marriages and families. Give us love and wisdom in the way we act towards our loved ones, our family members. Forgive our sins and help us practice the teachings of Jesus towards our loved ones. We pray this in the name of Jesus. Amen.

Day 7

> **33** "Again, you have heard that it was said to those of old, 'You shall not swear falsely, but shall perform your oaths to the Lord.' **34** But I say to you, do not swear at all: neither by heaven, for it is God's throne; **35** nor by the earth, for it is His footstool; nor by Jerusalem, for it is the city of the great King. **36** Nor shall you swear by your head, because you cannot make one hair white or black. **37** But let your 'Yes' be 'Yes,' and your 'No,' 'No.' For whatever is more than these is from the evil one.'"
> (Matthew 5.33-37)

These words of Jesus are basically quoted by James:

> "But above all, my brethren, do not swear, either by heaven or by earth or with any other oath. But let your 'Yes' be 'Yes,' and *your* 'No,' 'No,' lest you fall into judgment." (James 5.12)

This teaching of Jesus is a reminder of what the law already states in Deuteronomy 23.21-23. In the law, "abstaining from vowing" is presented as an alternative to making vows; the principle in the law being "That which has gone from your lips you shall keep and perform…" The Pharisees used multiple types of vows described by Jesus and often connected to God himself: "by heaven"; "God's throne"; "the earth"; "Jerusalem"; "your head". The idea was that depending on the "vow" some could be kept, others not: "Woe to you, blind guides, who say, 'Whosoever swears by the temple, it is nothing; but whoever swears by the gold of the temple, he is obliged to perform it.'" (Matthew 23.16-23) These types of practices are part of Jesus' warning about "idle words" (Matthew 12.35-37).

Jesus is teaching here about integrity in the heart and in speech, which are an essential part of building up a righteousness that is pleasing to God (see 5.20). Lack of integrity is "from the evil one" who is also described in the Bible and by Jesus as the "father of lies" (Genesis 3.1-5; John 8.43-47). Integrity of speech is an important part of the New Testament teachings about life in the Church (Acts 5.3; Ephesians 4.29; Colossians 3.9).

Lying is easy and tempting for human beings, as the misuse and lack of control of the tongue James writes about (James 3.1-12). "Cheating" practiced in business, political activity or even by students can be categorized in this type of sinfulness. *Time* magazine almost thirty years ago published a cover article with the title "Lying: Everybody's Doing it." (*Time*, October 1992). The article pointed out how lying and dishonesty had become common in American public life.

Integrity of the heart and speech is incompatible with swearing. Jesus is not talking about the legal idea of "swearing" or taking an oath in court. Jesus was put under oath by the high priest with the question, "Tell us if you are the Christ, the Son of God". Jesus was required to respond in truth to the High priest when put under oath (Matthew 26.63,64; Leviticus 5.1). Thus, Jesus answered, "It is as you said" confirming his identity as the Son of God.

Prayer

Father in heaven, we pray for integrity of the heart and integrity of speech. Bless us today with a growth in integrity. May the Holy Spirit strengthen our resolve and progress in this area. May you give us the wisdom to know when to speak and how to speak. May we speak with integrity in our family, with our friends and in our workplace. We pray this in Jesus' name. Amen.

Week 45: The Second Mile and Enemies (Matt 5.38-48)

Day 1

> **38** "You have heard that it was said, 'An eye for an eye and a tooth for a tooth.' **39** But I tell you not to resist an evil person. But whoever slaps you on your right cheek, turn the other to him also."
> (Matthew 5.38,39)

The "eye for an eye and tooth for a tooth" principle found in the law of Moses should not be understood as a statement allowing the individual Israelite within the community to practice personal retaliation against someone who had committed a crime or an act of violence. This was a principle to be applied in a court of law, before judges, in the judgment of the crime or act of violence (see Exodus 21.24; Leviticus 24.20; Deuteronomy 19.21). The principle is located in the sections of the law that instruct judges how to punish criminals. It is strictly an instruction for courts of law, not for personal revenge. It was also meant to prevent arbitrary vigilante justice that could end up in a cycle of retaliation.

Beyond the legal aspects of the law, Leviticus 19.18 provides a warning against personal revenge as an expression of the commandment of love: "You shall not take vengeance, nor bear any grudge against the children of your people, but you shall love your neighbor as yourself: I *am* the Lord." Throughout the Gospels, Jesus is teaching his disciples to go beyond the simple legal elements of the law and to consider the "greatest commandment" (Matthew 12.30,31). This is what is meant by turning "the other cheek". Jesus is turning us away from the discussions and casuistry of "compensation" that preoccupied the teachers of the law and pointing into the direction of the greatest commandment.

The translation of the Greek *antistenai* by "resist not" is comparable to the King James version and gives the impression that Jesus is simply teaching docility. However, the word means to resist violently, to revolt, to engage in insurrection. A more accurate translation would be "Don't react violently against someone who is evil." (Scholars Version).

The "other cheek" is also a discussion by Jesus connected to the shame and honor aspect of ancient civilizations.

Striking someone on the right cheek was bad enough. But one presenting the left cheek would then be stricken with the left hand, which represented complete dishonoring, the reason being that the left hand was used for unclean tasks (this is mentioned in the Dead Sea Scrolls). The point that is being taught here is the intention to humiliate, to dishonor someone. And even a backhand slap with the right hand on the left cheek was the way inferiors such as slaves or children were admonished in order to be humiliated.

Jesus is teaching that being dishonored is not the worst thing that can happen to a person, despite the prevalence of the idea in the ancient world. The salvation of the world was made possible because the savior who came in the flesh "turned the other cheek", accepted to be dishonored by those who sought "honor" above righteousness :

> **48** "Then the Jews answered and said to Him, 'Do we not say rightly that You are a Samaritan and have a demon?' **49** Jesus answered, 'I do not have a demon; but I honor My Father, and you dishonor Me. **50** And I do not seek My *own* glory; there is One who seeks and judges. **51** Most assuredly, I say to you, if anyone keeps My word, he shall never see death.'" (John 8.48-51).

> **27** "Then the soldiers of the governor took Jesus into the Praetorium and gathered the whole garrison around Him. **28** And they stripped Him and put a scarlet robe on Him. **29** When they had twisted a crown of thorns, they put *it* on His head, and a reed in His right hand. And they bowed the knee before Him and mocked Him, saying, 'Hail, King of the Jews!' **30** Then they spat on Him, and took the reed and struck Him on the head. **31** And when they had mocked Him, they took the robe off Him, put His *own* clothes on Him, and led Him away to be crucified."(Matthew 27.29-31; See Luke 22.63; 23.11, 35).

Prayer

Father, we thank you for your creation and all the good people around us. We thank you for the Good News which has touched our hearts and lives. May we today keep your precious word in our hearts, in our thoughts. Help us, Lord, to seek you in everything we do and say, hope and wish. We pray this in the name of Jesus. Amen.

Day 2

> "If anyone wants to sue you and take away your tunic, let him have *your* cloak also."
> (Matthew 5.40)

Note the following statement found in James:

> **6** "But you have dishonored the poor man. Do not the rich oppress you and drag you into the courts? **7** Do they not blaspheme that noble name by which you are called?" (James 2.6,7)

We should notice in this statement by Jesus the reference to "suing" someone. The Greek verb used here (*kristhenai*) is the same used by the apostle Paul in 1 Corinthians 6.1: "Dare any of you, having a matter against another, go to law before the unrighteous, and not before the saints?" ("Go to law" is the Greek *krinesthai*). This Greek verb is used in the Septuagint and translated "contend" (Job 9.3; Ecclesiastes 6.10).

The tunic was the undergarment. The cloak was the outer garment and of greater monetary value. Most people had only one outer garment to wear because of its cost. This outer garment was often used as a bed cover at night; thus, the law of Moses limited the use of the outer garment to be retained as a pledge for indebtedness. Only the very poor would have nothing except their outer garment to be retained as a collateral for a loan. The law required that the outer garment be returned to the individual every evening at sunset (Exodus 22.26). Jesus is mainly speaking to the "poor" and teaching about the poor. They would often be stripped of their bare necessities because of indebtedness. It is thus surprising that Jesus would teach them to be willing to even give their outer garment (cloak) once their inner garment had been taken away (tunic). This would, in fact, bring them to utter nakedness as they would appear in court. We can imagine the creditor at court holding in his hands both the tunic and cloak of the poor man who now stands naked in court.

The creditor now looks ridiculous and mediocre in his "lawsuit" against the poor man. Thus, this teaching of Jesus touches also the concept of honor and shame that was so prevalent in the ancient world. Now, who is to be more ashamed? The creditor or the poor man in debt?

The question is not difficult to answer. It is the creditor who is to be ashamed, not the poor man.

And we might remember that Jesus himself was stripped of all his cloths at the crucifixion:

> **22** "And they brought Him to the place Golgotha, which is translated, Place of a Skull. **23** Then they gave Him wine mingled with myrrh to drink, but He did not take *it*. **24** And when they crucified Him, they divided His garments, casting lots for them *to determine* what every man should take." (Mark 15.22-24)

> **23** "Then the soldiers, when they had crucified Jesus, took His garments and made four parts, to each soldier a part, and also the tunic. Now the tunic was without seam, woven from the top in one piece. **24** They said therefore among themselves, 'Let us not tear it, but cast lots for it, whose it shall be,' that the Scripture might be fulfilled which says: 'They divided My garments among them, and for My clothing they cast lots.' Therefore, the soldiers did these things. (John 19.23,24)

Shame was the most terrible thing a person could experience in the world of Jesus. Even the Scriptures suggest this:

> **1** "To You, O Lord, I lift up my soul.
> **2** O my God, I trust in You;
> Let me not be ashamed;
> Let not my enemies triumph over me.
> **3** Indeed, let no one who waits on You be ashamed;
> Let those be ashamed who deal treacherously without cause."
> (Psalms 25.1-3)

Considering this Psalm and the background of honor and shame in Jesus' time, how do we understand the "cross" and all Jesus went through? Is this something that could turn people away from the Messiah? Was the "cross" itself a stumbling-block for this very reason (Luke 9.26; 1 Corinthians 1.1.23)?

Jesus was shamed during his trial and crucifixion. Seemingly, all "honor" was stripped from him. How could he then be a real king? A true teacher from God, as recognized by Nicodemus (John 3)? But who was more to be ashamed, he who hung naked on the cross or those who condemned and crucified him? Once again, the question is not difficult to answer.

"He is despised and rejected by men,
A Man of sorrows and acquainted with grief.
And we hid, as it were, *our* faces from Him;
He was despised, and we did not esteem Him." (Isaiah 53.3)

Prayer

Father in heaven, we thank you for all the pain you have born through Jesus in order to save us from our sins and lostness. We pray that we will always recognize how much you have given for our salvation, for giving us a living hope. May we never be ashamed of Jesus and His words. We pray in the name of Jesus, our Lord. Amen.

Day 3

"And whoever compels you to go one mile, go with him two." (Matthew 5.41)

These words of Jesus refer to the practice in the Roman Empire to force the inhabitants of a conquered country to transport military baggage as troops were passing through. We have an example of this practice when Simon is compelled to carry Christ's cross, which would otherwise have been done by the Romans soldiers (Matthew 27.32; Mark 15.21). Clearly Jesus refers to the Roman oppression and how the Jews would have reacted violently to it, as was the case for the zealots, a rebellious movement which sought to incite the people to rebel against the Roman Empire and expel it from the Holy Land by force of arms.

The Lord does not go along with thoughts of revolt. Jesus' teachings would have been rejected by the zealots, and would still be rejected by modern revolutionaries. However, the Lord is not simply teaching submission to the power of Rome. He is teaching to serve cheerfully, even beyond what is asked. We find similar teachings in the New Testament addressed to Christian slaves or "bond servants":

> **22** "Bond servants, obey in all things your masters according to the flesh, not with eye-service, as men-pleasers, but in sincerity of heart, fearing God. **23** And whatever you do, do it heartily, as to the Lord and not to men, **24** knowing that from the Lord you will receive the reward of the inheritance; for you serve the Lord Christ." (Colossians 3.22-24)

By adopting the attitude of willing service, of love even towards their "enemy", those who choose to follow Jesus do not lose their dignity or honor. There is complete dignity for the one who serves God and refuses to render evil with evil. This is the true calling of the disciple. This is how society can be utterly transformed through the teachings of Jesus. The laws of Cesar had no power over the loving disciple, the servant-heart. How would a Roman soldier react? What would he learn from this? What did the Roman soldier learn when observing the scene of the crucifixion, the ultimate act of shaming and dishonoring?

> "So, when the centurion saw what had happened, he glorified God, saying, 'Certainly this was a righteous Man!'" Luke 23.47

> **18** "For the message of the cross is foolishness to those who are perishing, but to us who are being saved it is the power of God. **19** For it is written: 'I will destroy the wisdom of the wise and bring to nothing the understanding of the prudent.'" (1 Corinthians 1.18,19)

> **22** "For Jews request a sign, and Greeks seek after wisdom; **23** but we preach Christ crucified, to the Jews a stumbling block and to the Greeks foolishness, **24** but to those who are called, both Jews and Greeks, Christ the power of God and the wisdom of God. **25** Because the foolishness of God is wiser than men, and the weakness of God is stronger than men." (1 Corinthians 1.22-25)

Prayer

Father in heaven, we thank you, Jesus your beloved Son. We pray that we can be faithful disciples of Jesus, who teaches us in your Word. Give us wisdom and strength to follow the teachings of Jesus, our lord and master. Help us today to practice what we have learned in the Sermon on the Mount. We pray in Jesus' name. Amen.

Day 4

> "Give to him who asks you, and from him who wants to borrow from you do not turn away."
> (Matthew 5.42).

The same teaching appears in Luke, with a statement that illuminates further its importance. We should take note that the statement in verse 31 begins with "and" which connects it to verse 30.

> **30** "Give to everyone who asks of you. And from him who takes away your goods do not ask *them* back. **31** And just as you want men to do to you, you also do to them likewise." (Luke 6.30,31)

By these words, Jesus confirms what God required of his people in the law:

> **35** "If one of your brethren becomes poor, and falls into poverty among you, then you shall help him, like a stranger or a sojourner, that he may live with you. **36** Take no usury or interest from him; but fear your God, that your brother may live with you. **37** You shall not lend him your money for usury, nor lend him your food at a profit. **38** I *am* the Lord your God, who brought you out of the land of Egypt, to give you the land of Canaan *and* to be your God." (Leviticus 25.35-38). See Deuteronomy 15.7,8.

This exhortation should be read along Jesus' teachings about laying up "treasures in heaven" (Matthew 6.19-21). This is also why the apostle Paul teaches the rich to be generous towards those in need:

> **17** "Command those who are rich in this present age not to be haughty, nor to trust in uncertain riches but in the living God, who gives us richly all things to enjoy. **18** *Let them* do good, that they be rich in good works, ready to give, willing to share, **19** storing up for themselves a good foundation for the time to come, that they may lay hold on eternal life." (1 Timothy 6.17-19)

Is this teaching about reckless giving or lending without any thought about who is asking or how the money will be used? Does the Christian need wisdom in how he exercises generosity (see James 1.5)? Let us not note for example what Paul says concerning those who refuse to work:

> **10** "For even when we were with you, we commanded you this: If anyone will not work, neither shall he eat. **11** For we hear that there are some who walk among you in a disorderly manner, not working at all, but are busybodies. **12** Now those who are such

we command and exhort through our Lord Jesus Christ that they work in quietness and eat their own bread." (2 Thessalonians 3.10-12)

Jesus is teaching a fundamental truth, which is that it is better to invest in people rather than hoarding treasures for oneself. This is especially true when we compare this to what Jesus says later about the scribes and Pharisees who "devour widows houses" (Matthew 23.14).

The statement in Luke 6.31 following Jesus' teachings on giving is important and often separated from its immediate context: "And just as you want men to do to you, you also do to them likewise." We need to be able to put ourselves in the shoes of one who is in real need, who has no one to turn to for help. This may be the widow, the orphan or the stranger who in the Bible are especially lonely (devoid of family or connections) and thus vulnerable and in need of help:

> **21** "You shall neither mistreat a stranger nor oppress him, for you were strangers in the land of Egypt. **22** You shall not afflict any widow or fatherless child. **23** If you afflict them in any way, *and* they cry at all to Me, I will surely hear their cry" (Exodus 22.21-23)

> "Cursed *is* the one who perverts the justice due the stranger, the fatherless, and widow." (Deuteronomy 27.19)

> "Pure and undefiled religion before God and the Father is this: to visit orphans and widows in their trouble, *and* to keep oneself unspotted from the world." (James 1.27)

Prayer

Our Lord and Father in heaven, we want to praise you for this day. We want to honor you and your will. Teach us about generosity and help us through your Holy Spirit to practice the will of Jesus to give to those who ask from us. We are grateful for the blessing of being able to give and bless others. May our hearts be rich in mercy and goodness towards those in need. We pray in Jesus' name. Amen.

Day 5

> **43** "You have heard that it was said, 'You shall love your neighbor and hate your enemy.' **44** But I say to you, love your ene-

mies, bless those who curse you, do good to those who hate you, and pray for those who spitefully use you and persecute you, **45** that you may be sons of your Father in heaven; for He makes His sun rise on the evil and on the good, and sends rain on the just and on the unjust. **46** For if you love those who love you, what reward have you? Do not even the tax collectors do the same?" (Matthew 5.42-46)

We don't find a statement in the Bible that joins the command to "love your neighbor" with the statement "hate your enemy". "You shall love your neighbor" comes from the law in Leviticus 19,18. Doing good to an "enemy" is implied by the law in the book of Exodus:

> **4** "If you meet your enemy's ox or his donkey going astray, you shall surely bring it back to him again. **5** If you see the donkey of one who hates you lying under its burden, and you would refrain from helping it, you shall surely help him with it." (Exodus 23.4,5)

Jesus' teachings on how to treat enemies is not new and is even presented as a trait of wisdom in the book of Proverbs:

> **21** "If your enemy is hungry, give him bread to eat;
> And if he is thirsty, give him water to drink;
> **22** For *so* you will heap coals of fire on his head,
> And the Lord will reward you." (Proverbs 25.21; Romans 12.19,20)

When Jesus mentions the "love" of enemies he is not talking about an emotion or feeling but about how we act towards enemies. This is shown in the actions that describe this "love". Instead of "hate" we have "love" expressed by verbs of action such as bless, do good, pray. We should also note that "hate" is mentioned as coming from "enemies" and how the disciple is to react by doing good when facing the hatred of others.

Beyond "hatred" on the part of enemies, Jesus is specific and teaches about those "who spitefully use you and persecute you." This teaching picks up on Jesus' statement already mentioned in Matthew 5.10,11 concerning those who "persecute you".

Jesus is not pointing mostly to national pride or a sense of privileged status on the part of the Israelites. It is not difficult to find religious aversion towards Gentiles expressed in the rabbinical teaching, but Jesus' words here have broader application and touch universal truths that would apply to any human society. Human beings tend to love those who love them, do good to them who do good to them, bless those who bless them. This broader meaning of Jesus' teachings is clear when he mentions the sun and the rain, the evil and the good, the just and the unjust. This is about being a "son [child] of the Father" in heaven, not simply being a good Israelite. This idea is strongly reiterated in verse 48: "Therefore you shall be perfect, just as your Father in heaven in perfect." The name "Father" given to God is prominent in the sermon, being used sixteen times.

Here, Jesus' teachings break the false idea that we find retributive justice from God on this earth. An idea that was clearly shown to be mistaken in the book of Job. In this life, God acts as Father towards all men. He is good even to the evil and the unjust. There is no exact correspondence between one's lot in life and character or personal righteousness. This is an important breach from an idea that was universally accepted in Jesus' days. A breach that would have far-reaching and positive consequences for human society up to the present day.

The tax collectors were unpopular as representing the yoke of Rome and rich rulers. They would often be guilty of acts of injustice (compare with Zacheus in Luke 19.1-10) but would act kindly among themselves, "loving those that loved them." The love taught by Jesus goes far beyond this "love" among friends or peers. Disciples of Jesus are called to a love that is "divine" in its nature; the only "love" that can radically transform the world and bring it peace.

Writing to the Christians in Rome, the apostle Paul teaches them how to obey the Lord's teachings in the Sermon on the mount in their social context. This is what would transform the ancient world and bring about divine righteousness to the entire world:

> **27** "Repay no one evil for evil. Have regard for good things in the sight of all men. **18** If it is possible, as much as depends on you, live peaceably with all men. **19** Beloved, do not avenge yourselves, but *rather* give place to wrath; for it is written, 'Vengeance *is* Mine, I will repay,' says the Lord. **20** Therefore 'If your enemy is hungry, feed him; if he is thirsty, give him a drink; for in so doing you will heap coals of fire on his head.' **21** Do not be overcome by evil, but overcome evil with good." (Romans 12.17-21)

Prayer

Our Father in heaven, we want to praise you for this day. Prepare our hearts and minds to know how to love our enemies and do good to them. Strengthen us by your Holy Spirit to accomplish the most difficult part of our Lord's teachings. We need your help and your wisdom in order to be faithful to your will. Thank you, Lord, for answering our prayers. In Jesus' name, we pray. Amen.

Day 6

"And if you greet your brethren only, what do you do more *than others?* Do not even the tax collectors do so?"
(Matthew 5.47)

The scribes and Pharisees had much to say about merit and rewards. They often thought themselves as better than the tax collectors but, in his ministry, Jesus points out how this is not true (see Luke 18.9-14). In order to be "better" than tax collectors, they need to listen and practice Jesus' teachings.

To "greet" in the ancient world of Judaism was part of maintaining friendly relations. It meant to act in a friendly manner. Jesus calls his disciples to greater goals than just being friendly to friends. Disciples are to seek spiritual and moral excellence, in order to reach a righteousness that exceeds the righteousness of scribes and Pharisees (Matthew 5.20). In fact, they are to seek "perfection" as exhibited by the Father in heaven (Matthew 5.48).

The biblical teaching about "love" is that God loved us before we loved him (1 John 4.8-10). Thus, we are called to love sinners unconditionally. We are called to love them even if they persist in sin or even persecute us. All people should be treated with respect and dignity because they are made in God's image: "Honor all people" (1 Peter 2.17).

8 "But no man can tame the tongue. *It is* an unruly evil, full of deadly poison. **9** With it we bless our God and Father, and with it we curse men, who have been made in the similitude of God. **10** Out of the same mouth proceed blessing and cursing. My brethren, these things ought not to be so. **11** Does a spring send forth fresh *water* and bitter from the same opening? **12** Can a fig tree, my brethren, bear olives, or a grapevine bear figs? Thus, no spring yields both salt, water and fresh." (James 3.8-12).

"See that no one renders evil for evil to anyone, but always pursue what is good both for yourselves and for all." (1 Thessalonians 5.15). See Romans 12.17-21.

Acting with kindness and love towards all people, including sinners, is not an encouragement to deny biblical teaching about sin and holiness. God himself who is good to the evil and the unjust calls sinners to repent, to turn back to Him. The "unconditional" love of God should not be understood as a love that is morally or spiritually neutral, as if the concept of "sin" itself were contrary to God's will. The truth of sin and the need to repent needs to be preached with love (Ephesians 4.15; see 2 Timothy 2.24-26). God loves the sinner while calling him or her to repentance (Psalms 5; 11; Malachi 1.3; Revelation 2.6; 2 Peter 3.9; James 1.27; Jude 1.22,23). The disciples are called throughout the New Testament to grow in every spiritual and moral area, to grow in holiness, in sanctification.

> **23** "Now may the God of peace Himself sanctify you completely; and may your whole spirit, soul, and body be preserved blameless at the coming of our Lord Jesus Christ. **24** He who calls you *is* faithful, who also will do *it*." (1 Thessalonians 5.23,24)

The life of a disciple is compared to a race, and one can never be content with the stage he or she has reached:

> **12** "Not that I have already attained, or am already perfected; but I press on, that I may lay hold of that for which Christ Jesus has also laid hold of me. **13** Brethren, I do not count myself to have apprehended; but one thing *I do*, forgetting those things which are behind and reaching forward to those things which are ahead, **14** I press toward the goal for the prize of the upward call of God in Christ Jesus." (Philippians 3.12-14)

Prayer

Our Father, we pray that we will know and understand what it means to love all people. As we share the good news of Jesus with all, help us to speak the truth in love. Help us through your Holy Spirit to be kind and loving to those who need to repent and return to you. May we also continually pray for all men that they might come to salvation. We pray in Jesus' name. Amen.

Day 7

> "Therefore, you shall be perfect, just as your Father in heaven is perfect."
> (Matthew 5.48)

This concluding statement of Matthew chapter 5 begins with the word "therefore" so that we can connect it to what Jesus has been teaching in the preceding verses. Taking this one verse out of its context could lead one to misunderstand this commandment of Jesus to seek "perfection" — as if one could for example claim to live a completely sinless life (see 1 John 1.8,9).

Concerning this "perfection" Jesus has given the example of the heavenly Father who "makes the sun rise on the evil and the good and sends rain on the just and the unjust." (5.45). This is the example we should follow in how we treat people around us.

The Greek adjective *teleios* does not mean "sinless" but mature, complete, of an adult age, disposition or understanding. This word is used throughout the New Testament:

> "Jesus said to him, 'If you want to be perfect [*teleios*], go, sell what you have and give to the poor, and you will have treasure in heaven; and come, follow Me.'" (Matthew 19.21)

> "However, we speak wisdom among those who are mature [*teleios*], yet not the wisdom of this age, nor of the rulers of this age, who are coming to nothing." (1 Corinthians 2.6)

> "Brethren, do not be children in understanding; however, in malice be babes, but in understanding be mature [*teleios*]." (1 Corinthians 14.20)

> "And do not be conformed to this world, but be transformed by the renewing of your mind, that you may prove what *is* that good and acceptable and perfect [*teleios*] will of God." (Romans 12.2)

> "Till we all come to the unity of the faith and of the knowledge of the Son of God, to a perfect [*teleios*] man, to the measure of the stature of the fullness of Christ" (Ephesians 4.13)

The emphasis on "perfection" is about imitation of God, becoming more like God, especially in the way we treat other people. It is "to love as I have loved you" (John 13.34; 1 John 4.10). We were reconciled to God while we were still enemies of God (Romans 5.9,10). This is also what is taught by the apostle Paul:

> **1** "Therefore, be imitators of God as dear children. **2** And walk in love, as Christ also has loved us and given Himself for us, an offering and a sacrifice to God for a sweet-smelling aroma." (Ephesians 5.1-2)

Prayer

Our Father in heaven, we come to you for wisdom and for strength through your Holy Spirit. We need your help every day to grow in faith, in hope and in love. So, Father, we pray that today we will learn and practice your will in a way that we will be able to love our neighbor as ourself, that we will be able to love the way you love us. We pray this in Jesus' name. Amen.

Week 46: Doing Good Deeds

Day 1

> **1** "Take heed that you do not do your charitable deeds before men, to be seen by them. Otherwise, you have no reward from your Father in heaven. **2** Therefore, when you do a charitable deed, do not sound a trumpet before you as the hypocrites do in the synagogues and in the streets, that they may have glory from men. Assuredly, I say to you, they have their reward. **3** But when you do a charitable deed, do not let your left hand know what your right hand is doing, **4** that your charitable deed may be in secret; and your Father who sees in secret will Himself reward you openly."
> (Matthew 6.1-4)

Matthew 6.1-18 deals basically with the question of religious hypocrisy (See verses 5 and 6). Jesus' teachings here are about doing good deeds "before men, to be seen by them", praying "standing in the synagogues," fasting to "appear to men".

Jesus deals with alms, prayer, and fasting, considered essential manifestations of a pious life by the religious leaders, Pharisees and the people. This topic of being "genuine" as opposed to hypocritical is taught throughout the Bible. Thus, during this week of Bible study and meditation, we will look at some other teachings found in the Bible outside of the Sermon on the Mount and concerning this question.

It has been said that character is who you are when no one is watching. In the three areas of giving or generosity, of prayer and fasting, Jesus is teaching us to do what we do as a way to reach out to God and learn from Him instead of as a way to be seen and receive praises from men.

In Jesus' day this was a prevalent issue, especially among those considered most religious such as the teachers of the law, the scribes and Pharisees. Of course, today, showing off our religiosity in a secular world is not necessarily going to bring praises. However, "moral outrage" can still today remain a way for people to be admired by others and thought as good. Showing off religiosity and moral outrage can be — just as in Jesus' days — a way to cover up sinful behavior that people try to hide, which is the definition of hypocrisy. This is what sometimes people today call "virtue signaling". This would be true especially in the area of "alms" or "giving". Prayer and fasting do not produce a lot of admiration in the secular and non-believing world. However, giving to the poor and being generous has remained a virtue in our secular world and often does bring praise. It is fashionable today to be seen as caring for the poor or underprivileged. Thus, it is tempting for people to become hypocritical in this area. It can also be part of political ideologies which base their case on "social justice" as expressed in giving to the poor and needy. Such political systems or ideologies may claim to be concerned with the poor and often appeal to the Bible in their political appeal. However, history has taught us that ruthless political ideologies can hide behind claims of social justice while seeking mainly to exercise control over people at any cost. In fact, Jesus never taught — and the New Testament never teaches — that giving must be legislated and forced on people. This is one lesson we learn from Acts 5 in the story of Ananias and Saphira, as we shall see on day 7 of this week.

In Matthew 5.1-4, giving, prayer, and fasting are three important ways of pleasing and serving God. They are not done in view of pleasing men or in order to receive praise from men. Our Father in heaven is the one we must seek to please and is the only one who can truly reward us for doing good: "That your charitable deed may be in secret; and your Father who sees in secret will Himself reward you openly." (Matthew 6.4; Hebrews 11.6).

Some Bible teachers or preachers also give the impression that a promise like the one we have in Matthew 5.4 means God is promising to give us back much more, especially whenever we give money. A Scripture that has been used for this erroneous teaching is:

> **6** "But this *I say:* He who sows sparingly will also reap sparingly, and he who sows bountifully will also reap bountifully. **7** *So let* each one *give* as he purposes in his heart, not grudgingly or of necessity; for God loves a cheerful giver." (2 Corinthians 9.6,7)

The Scripture does not tell us what God's reward will be when we give. It is an assumption made by these preachers that the reward will be monetary. There are many "rewards" we can receive from God that are far superior to money — such as grace and peace, lasting friendships, a united family, a profession we enjoy... All rewards that cannot be acquired with money and which are truly gifts from God. Also, the apostle Paul reminded Christians of the dangers of seeking to be rich (even with God's help!) and of the importance of contentment (1 Timothy 6.6-10).

Prayer

Father in heaven, we praise you for your generosity. We thank you for every blessing, for our daily bread. We want to give and to pray to please you and not to be praised by men. Help us always give generously and give "in the secret" and not to be seen. May you give us grace and peace today as we serve people we meet or work with. In Jesus' name. Amen.

Day 2

> **1** "Then Jesus spoke to the multitudes and to His disciples, **2** saying: 'The scribes and the Pharisees sit in Moses' seat. **3** Therefore whatever they tell you to observe, *that* observe and do, but do not do according to their works; for they say, and do not do. **4** For they bind heavy burdens, hard to bear, and lay *them* on men's shoulders; but they *themselves* will not move them with one of their fingers. **5** But all their works they do to be seen by men. They make their phylacteries broad and enlarge the borders of their garments.'"
> (Matthew 23.1-5)

The statement "all their works they do to be seen by men" is in keeping with Jesus' teachings in the sermon on the mount (Matthew 6.1-8). In Matthew 6 Jesus deals especially with the way the teachers of the law and Pharisees practice alms (giving), prayer and fasting. But in Matthew 23 Jesus shows a wider range of practices on the part of religious leaders in Israel. Jesus also makes it clear that he is not talking about the role of these teachers as they "sit in Moses' seat", in other words, as they teach Moses' law.

The word "phylacteries" used by Jesus comes from the Hebrew word *tefillin* ; the word "phylacteries" comes from the Greek *phylakterion*, meaning amulet. The "phylacteries" or *tefillin* were two small leather made cases containing quotations from the Law written on parchment. One small box was set in the middle of the forehead. The second box was set on the right or left arm. These were considered reminders of the obligation to keep the commandments of the law. The four passages written on these parchments were Exodus 13.2-10; Exodus 13.11-17; Deuteronomy

6.4-9 and Deuteronomy 11.13-22. The bigger the phylacteries, the more attention they would attract for people seeing them. Thus, Jesus' mention of the broadness of the phylacteries.

As teachers of the law, the scribes and Pharisees would have taught people to bound God's commandments as "a sign on your hand and as frontlets between your eyes" (Exodus 13.16; Deuteronomy 6.8; 11.18). The law did not mean by these words that the Israelites should literally have parchments with portions of Scripture written on them and attached between their eyes in the middle of the forehead. Originally and for centuries, the teachers of the law understood as figurative language the statements mentioning the commandments needing to be "a sign on your hand" and "frontlets between your eyes". However, in time, a literal understanding of these statements led to the practice of "phylacteries" mentioned in Matthew 23.

The phylacteries mentioned by Jesus are a perfect example of this tendency of the religious leaders to want to show off their religiosity and piety. A reading of the entire chapter of Matthew 23 also shows pride as the root of such practices, of wanting to be seen of men as pious. Thus, the real issue with the religious leaders was one of the heart:

> **6** "He answered and said to them, Well did Isaiah prophesy of you hypocrites, as it is written: 'This people honors me with *their* lips, but their heart is far from Me. **7** And in vain they worship me, Teaching *as* doctrines the commandments of men.'" (Mark 7.6,7)

Prayer

We come to you Father seeking your help and wisdom for this day. May all our ways, our thoughts and actions, be in accordance with your will. We pray that we can live with thankfulness and knowing that you are giving us a living and eternal hope through Jesus. We pray that in our encounters today, we will be an encouragement to others in their walk with you. This we pray in the name of Jesus, our Lord. Amen.

Day 3

> **25** "Woe to you, scribes and Pharisees, hypocrites! For you cleanse the outside of the cup and dish, but inside they are full of extortion and self-indulgence. **26** Blind Pharisee first cleanse the inside of the cup and dish, that the outside of them may be

clean also. **27** "Woe to you, scribes and Pharisees, hypocrites! For you are like whitewashed tombs which indeed appear beautiful outwardly, but inside are full of dead *men's* bones and all uncleanness. **28** Even so you also outwardly appear righteous to men, but inside you are full of hypocrisy and lawlessness." (Matthew 23.25-28)

It is helpful to read Matthew 6 along with Matthew 23 which illustrates a group of people (the scribes and Pharisees, 23.1) who are often the subject of what Jesus is teaching in the Sermon. The word "pharisee" means "separated". The Pharisees arose in Israel as a well-defined group shortly after the Maccabean revolt (165-160 B.C.), at a time of great religious and political strife. This group of teachers focused on the interpretation and application of the Torah, the Law of Moses (first 5 books of the Bible). Progressively, their interpretations became religiously binding and developed as a set of burdensome rules or traditions required for religious purity (Matthew 23.4). The Pharisees developed a harsh view of religious faithfulness to the point of neglecting "the weightier matters of the law" such as justice, mercy and faith (Matthew 23.23).

This teaching by Jesus concerning "weightier matters of the law" is not new since it is often brought out in the Old Testament in the law of Moses and by the prophets of Israel: Exodus 23.6; Leviticus 19.15; Deuteronomy 16.20; Psalms 37.30; Isaiah 1.17; Micah 6.8; Amos 5.21-24.

In their desire to obey and respect the law, the Pharisees often became "full of extortion and self-indulgence". To them also apply the words of Jesus in Matthew 7 about judging others and not applying to themselves that judgment. This is similar to the teachings found in James:

> **11** "For He who said, 'Do not commit adultery,' also said, 'Do not murder.' Now if you do not commit adultery, but you do murder, you have become a transgressor of the law. **12** So speak and so do as those who will be judged by the law of liberty. **13** For judgment is without mercy to the one who has shown no mercy. Mercy triumphs over judgment." (James 2.11-13)

God is righteous and wants us to be attentive to His will. But He is also merciful and gracious. Thus, Jesus is not teaching that one should neglect the "law" but that part of the requirements of the law is to show mercy and kindness. The New Testament writings are constantly reminding Christians of this important aspect of God's will:

30 "And do not grieve the Holy Spirit of God, by whom you were sealed for the day of redemption. **31** Let all bitterness, wrath, anger, clamor, and evil speaking be put away from you, with all malice. **32** And be kind to one another, tenderhearted, forgiving one another, even as God in Christ forgave you." (Ephesians 4.31,32)

The "hypocrisy" denounced by Jesus can be seen as the result of an imbalance. The Pharisees emphasized for example the importance of the ceremonial washings of dishes in order to avoid legal defilement. But they neglected the purifying of the heart and the mind. The consequence was that they grew in greediness and sinfulness despite their outward appearance of righteousness. They robbed widows and orphans and defrauded people through money changing.

Christians are warned against this kind of "hypocrisy" (from a word which means "actor" or "comedian"): Romans 2.1-5; 12.9; 2 Timothy 3.1-5; James 1.21-26; 2.14-26.

Prayer

Our Father in heaven, we thank you for your graciousness and mercy. We thank you for the salvation we have found in the Lord Jesus. Today, we want to praise you and serve you. We pray for wisdom and the work of your Holy Spirit within our hearts. Thank you for every blessing, for every person we meet today. May we serve you with sincerity and truth. We pray this in the name of Jesus, our Lord. Amen.

Day 4

1 "Then the scribes and Pharisees who were from Jerusalem came to Jesus, saying, **2** 'Why do Your disciples transgress the tradition of the elders? For they do not wash their hands when they eat bread.' **3** He answered and said to them, 'Why do you also transgress the commandment of God because of your tradition? **4** For God commanded, saying, 'Honor your father and your mother'; and, 'He who curses father or mother, let him be put to death.' **5** But you say, 'Whoever says to his father or mother, "Whatever profit you might have received from me *is* a gift *to God*'— **6** then he need not honor his father or mother.' Thus, you have made the commandment of God of no effect by your tradition. **7** Hypocrites! Well did Isaiah prophesy about

you, saying:
8 'These people draw near to Me with their mouth,
And honor Me with *their* lips,
But their heart is far from Me.
9 And in vain they worship Me,
Teaching *as* doctrines the commandments of men.'"
10 When He had called the multitude to *Himself*, He said to them, 'Hear and understand: **11** Not what goes into the mouth defiles a man; but what comes out of the mouth, this defiles a man.'"
(Matthew 15.1-10)

This text in Matthew 15 is part of a series of responses from various religious groups to the teachings of Jesus found in Matthew 13.54 to 16.20. The washing of hands in this text (see also Mark 7.1-23) is a washing concerned with ceremonial procedure or religious purification and is not about hygiene in the modern sense. The "washing of hands" as taught by the Pharisees and described as a "tradition of the elders" was considered as most sacred and binding, even ranking higher than the word of God itself. The word "tradition" describes an oral teaching handed down through the generations from older generations (the elders).

While insisting on these "traditions" the scribes and Pharisees were transgressing the commandments of God in many areas and found in the Scripture. Jesus gives the example of their transgression of the 5th of the ten commandments concerning honoring father and mother (Exodus 20.12). The "honoring" of father and mother in the 10 commandments has to do with respect, but also with financial or material support in case parents were needy. This principle is found also in the teachings of the apostle Paul: "But if anyone does not provide for his own, and especially for those of his household, he has denied the faith and is worse than an unbeliever." (1 Timothy 5.8).

The "tradition of the elders" made it possible for someone to disobey the 5th commandment by giving to the temple (this giving or offering was called *corban*). With such religious contributions and gifts, some would deny aid or support for needy parents, thus transgressing God's command. In the Gospel of Mark we see that Jesus points out that this was a general practice of the Pharisees and extended to many areas: "For laying aside the commandment of God, you hold the tradition of men— the washing of pitchers and cups, and many other such things you do." (Mark 7.8)

The word "hypocrite" is again used here by Jesus — a word we find applied to the scribes and Pharisees from the Sermon on the mount

(Matthew 6.5, 16). Jesus applies the words of the prophet Isaiah to the behavior of the scribes and Pharisees (Isaiah 29.13). They taught "doctrines and commandments of men" and gave no importance to what God was teaching them in His word (see Matthew 21.25).

The scribes and Pharisees were condemning Jesus' disciples for not respecting the ceremonial rules of handwashing. But Jesus points out to them that it is them and not his disciples who are transgressing the will of God.

Following these words, Jesus shows how the Pharisees commit greater sins in the way they speak, in their words:

> **10** "When He had called the multitude to *Himself,* He said to them, 'Hear and understand: **11** Not what goes into the mouth defiles a man; but what comes out of the mouth, this defiles a man.'" (Matthew 15.10,11)
>
> **33** "Either make the tree good and its fruit good, or else make the tree bad and its fruit bad; for a tree is known by *its* fruit. **34** Brood of vipers! How can you, being evil, speak good things? For out of the abundance of the heart the mouth speaks. **35** A good man out of the good treasure of his heart brings forth good things, and an evil man out of the evil treasure brings forth evil things. **36** But I say to you that for every idle word men may speak, they will give account of it in the day of judgment. **37** For by your words you will be justified, and by your words you will be condemned." (Matthew 12.33-37)

Prayer

Our Father in heaven, we want to be faithful to you in our hearts, in our words and actions. We pray for wisdom and the work of your Holy Spirit today in our lives. We thank you for the great love you have for every person, and we pray that we can also show that love to others. Forgive our sins and purify our hearts today. We pray in the name of Jesus. Amen.

Day 5

> **14** "Now the Pharisees, who were lovers of money, also heard all these things, and they derided Him. **15** And He said to them, 'You are those who justify yourselves before men,

but God knows your hearts. For what is highly esteemed among men is an abomination in the sight of God.'"
(Luke 16.14,15)

The sermon on the mount has also a lot to say about money and the love of money. In Matthew 6.19-21, Jesus' teaching on this subject follows immediately his warnings about religious hypocrisy. Luke 16 shows how the "love of money" is connected to "what is highly esteemed among men". It is a real error to look up to people on account of their wealth. God has no special consideration towards those who are rich (In the Bible, "poverty" in itself is not considered a virtue and possessing wealth is not a sin in itself). For example, the Bible teaches about the precious value of the heart in God's sight:

3 "Do not let your adornment be *merely* outward—arranging the hair, wearing gold, or putting on *fine* apparel— **4** rather *let it be* the hidden person of the heart, with
the incorruptible *beauty* of a gentle and quiet spirit, which is very precious in the sight of God." (1 Peter 3.3,4)

The expression "love of money" is also applied by Paul in his teachings and seen as "the root of all kinds of evil":

9 "But those who desire to be rich fall into temptation and a snare, and *into* many foolish and harmful lusts which drown men in destruction and perdition. **10** For the love of money is a root of all *kinds of* evil, for which some have strayed from the faith in their greediness and pierced themselves through with many sorrows." (1 Timothy 6.9,10)

In Luke 16.14 the verb "derided" is contrasted to the verb "esteemed" in verse 15. These Pharisees "derided" Jesus (*exemykterizon*) literally means "turned up the nose in contempt" at Jesus. It is the same verb used of the rulers who "sneered" at Jesus on the cross in Luke 23.35. What is "esteemed" (*hupselon*) is what is literally "high", lofty or exalted. The word is used to describe Jesus' majesty (Hebrews 1.3). The word is also used in Romans 11.20 for "haughty" and in Romans 12.16 for "high things": "Do not set your mind on high things but associate with the humble. Do not be wise in your own opinion."

The contempt of the religious leaders came from their sense of worth due to their wealth and social status, as contrasted to Jesus, who was poor and ministering to the poor among the people. "For you know the grace of our Lord Jesus Christ, that though He was rich, yet for your sakes He became poor, that you through His poverty might become rich." (2 Corinthians 8.9).

The book of James warns Christians against contempt towards the poor on the part of the wealthy:

> **1** "My brethren do not hold the faith of our Lord Jesus Christ, *the Lord* of glory, with partiality. **2** For if there should come into your assembly a man with gold rings, in fine apparel, and there should also come in a poor man in filthy clothes, **3** and you pay attention to the one wearing the fine clothes and say to him, 'You sit here in a good place,' and say to the poor man, 'You stand there,' or, 'Sit here at my footstool,' **4** have you not shown partiality among yourselves, and become judges with evil thoughts? **5** Listen, my beloved brethren: Has God not chosen the poor of this world *to be* rich in faith and heirs of the kingdom which He promised to those who love Him? **6** But you have dishonored the poor man. Do not the rich oppress you and drag you into the courts? **7** Do they not blaspheme that noble name by which you are called?" (James 2.1-7)

Prayer

We thank you, Father in heaven, for every blessing you have showered on us. We especially thank you for forgiveness of sins, for your grace towards us through Jesus. Give us a gracious heart towards every person we meet and towards those in poverty and dire need. May we know how to encourage and help those who lack the basic necessities of life. We pray this in the name of Jesus. Amen.

Day 6

> **9** "He who says he is in the light, and hates his brother, is in darkness until now. **10** He who loves his brother abides in the light, and there is no cause for stumbling in him. **11** But he who hates his brother is in darkness and walks in darkness, and does not know where he is going, because the darkness has blinded his eyes."
> (1 John 2.9)

> **20** "If someone says, 'I love God,' and hates his brother, he is a liar; for he who does not love his brother whom he has seen, how can he love God whom he has not seen? **21** And this com-

mandment we have from Him: that he who loves God *must* love his brother also."
(1 John 4.20)

These two Scriptures show the gravity of "hatred" towards people we are taught to "love". Hatred is clearly against the most important commandment as taught through the Scriptures and in a very unique way in the Sermon on the Mount (Matthew 5-7). These verses also help us understand the warnings of Jesus about hypocrisy. John writes about someone who says, "I love God" but who in his heart hates his brother or sister. He also writes about someone who claims to be in the light, but at the same time hates his brother or sister. Making Christian statements is not a proof of one's true state of heart and true relationship with God. We can apply this even to entire groups of believers.

A group of Christians or a church can claim faithfulness to the Bible or to God, but lack love towards other people or other groups or churches. Worse than lacking love, a group can actually encourage hatred towards others while claiming in other areas to remain faithful to God's teachings. It is important to understand that faithfulness to biblical teaching in certain areas does not preclude faithfulness in other areas. Loving people and treating them well is just as important as correct teaching about God, Jesus or the way of salvation.

Thus, we have in the New Testament numerous teachings given to the Church concerning the importance of love and respect towards all people. We may compare this to the teachings of Jesus concerning those who greet only their brethren:

> **47** "And if you greet your brethren only, what do you do more *than others?* Do not even the tax collectors do so? **48** Therefore you shall be perfect, just as your Father in heaven is perfect." (Matthew 5.47,48)

Here are some of these teachings:

> **8** "But no man can tame the tongue. *It is* an unruly evil, full of deadly poison. **9** With it we bless our God and Father, and with it we curse men, who have been made in the similitude of God. **10** Out of the same mouth proceed blessing and cursing. My brethren, these things ought not to be so." (James 3.8-10)

> "Let love *be* without hypocrisy. Abhor what is evil. Cling to what is good." (Romans 12.9)

Let Us Come Before His Presence

14 "Bless those who persecute you; bless and do not curse. **15** Rejoice with those who rejoice, and weep with those who weep." (Romans 12.14,15)

"Render therefore to all their due: taxes to whom taxes *are due,* customs to whom customs, fear to whom fear, honor to whom honor." (Romans 13.7)

17 "Repay no one evil for evil. Have regard for good things in the sight of all men. **18** If it is possible, as much as depends on you, live peaceably with all men." (Romans 12.17,18)

14 "Pursue peace with all *people,* and holiness, without which no one will see the Lord: **15** looking carefully lest anyone fall short of the grace of God; lest any root of bitterness springing up cause trouble, and by this many become defiled;" (Hebrews 12.14,15)

15 "But sanctify the Lord God in your hearts, and always *be* ready to *give* a defense to everyone who asks you a reason for the hope that is in you, with meekness and fear; **16** having a good conscience, that when they defame you as evildoers, those who revile your good conduct in Christ may be ashamed. **17** For *it is* better, if it is the will of God, to suffer for doing good than for doing evil." (1 Peter 3.15-17)

5 "Walk in wisdom toward those *who are* outside, redeeming the time. **6** *Let* your speech always *be* with grace, seasoned with salt, that you may know how you ought to answer each one." (Colossians 4.5,6)

13 "Watch, stand fast in the faith, be brave, be strong. **14** Let all *that* you *do* be done with love." (1 Corinthians 16.13,14)

Prayer

Father in heaven, we thank you for your Word, and we thank you for all your blessings and gifts. We pray today that we will grow in true love and respect for every person we meet. We pray that our love will be genuine and from the heart. May your Holy Spirit help us in acting like Jesus towards all people. We pray this in His holy name. Amen.

Day 7

> **1** "But a certain man named Ananias, with Sapphira his wife, sold a possession. **2** And he kept back *part* of the proceeds, his wife also being aware *of it*, and brought a certain part and laid *it* at the apostles' feet. **3** But Peter said, 'Ananias, why has Satan filled your heart to lie to the Holy Spirit and keep back *part* of the price of the land for yourself? **4** While it remained, was it not your own? And after it was sold, was it not in your own control? Why have you conceived this thing in your heart? You have not lied to men, but to God.'"
> (Acts 5.1-4)

This account in Acts is an example of hypocrisy in the early church. Hypocrisy exists where we find human beings. It should not be however a pretext to quit church or to isolate ourselves from other believers. This is not how the early Church and apostles dealt with the problem of hypocrisy among believers. Foremost, they pointed out the danger of hypocrisy in their teachings, as we have seen in the quotations of the preceding day. They also did not favor Christians or Church members when those members acted wrongly or with hypocrisy. Brothers and sisters are not to be treated with special favors when they sin. The Lord taught his disciples to exercise discipline when facing sinfulness among themselves:

> **15** "Moreover, if your brother sins against you, go and tell him his fault between you and him alone. If he hears you, you have gained your brother. **16** But if he will not hear, take with you one or two more, that 'by the mouth of two or three witnesses every word may be established.' **17** And if he refuses to hear them, tell *it* to the church. But if he refuses even to hear the church, let him be to you like a heathen and a tax collector." (Matthew 18.15-17)

The lesson in this account of Acts deals with a similar situation as described by Jesus in Matthew 6.1-4 about those who do their charitable deeds to be seen by men or who sound the trumpet. The account also shows how Christians should give or contribute financially: not out of drudgery, but as they have decided in their hearts and voluntarily (2 Corinthians 9.7). It was not really the intention of Ananias and Saphira to give to the Church the entire product of the sale of their land, but they wanted to give the impression that this is what they intended to do.

This is clear from the question Peter asks Saphira: "Tell me whether you sold the land for so much?" She said, "Yes, for so much."

This account does not teach that Christians are obligated to give a certain amount of what they possess or even a certain percentage of it. This is clear from Peter's following statements: "While it remained, was it not your own? And after it was sold, was it not in your own control?" There was no pressure on the part of the apostles, and there is no pressure in the New Testament teachings for Christians to be obligated in giving any amount of money to the Church or for charitable causes. There is freedom in this area because God "loves a cheerful giver". The disposition of the heart is more important to God than any amount of money anyone could give. Anything else, any other practice of giving, will only encourage hypocrisy and sinfulness.

Prayer

God in heaven and Lord of all things we come to you with thanksgiving in our hearts for all your blessings and especially for the salvation you give us in our Lord Jesus. We thank you for forgiveness, for the gift of your Holy Spirit, for caring every day for us. Today help us to be cheerful and sincere givers not only of any money but of our time, of our love towards others. We pray this in Jesus' name. Amen.

Week 47: Our Father (Matt 6.5-15; Luke 11.1-13)

Day 1

> "And when you pray, you shall not be like the hypocrites. For they love to pray standing in the synagogues and on the corners of the streets, that they may be seen by men. Assuredly, I say to you, they have their reward. But you, when you pray, go into your room, and when you have shut your door, pray to your Father who *is* in the secret *place;* and your Father who sees in secret will reward you openly."
> (Matthew 6.5,6)

In chapter 6 of Matthew, Jesus teaches about how to practice godly religion through charitable deeds (alms) as well as prayer and fasting in a way that is pleasing to God and according to His will. Thus, the theme of prayer is not introduced in Matthew simply by the question asked by one of the disciples as in Luke's account: "Now it came to pass, as He was praying in a certain place, when He ceased, *that* one of His disciples said to Him, 'Lord, teach us to pray, as John also taught his disciples.'"

However, the fact that Luke introduces this prayer as being taught in a different context shows the importance of this prayer as recalled by the disciples. One difference in Luke is the statement in Luke 11.4 following the request for God's forgiveness:

> "And forgive us our sins,
> For we also forgive everyone who is indebted to us."

The prayer in Luke is found in the context of a segment of Luke's Gospel that is focused on a number of Jesus' teachings starting with the parable of the good Samaritan and ending with the parable of the Pharisee and tax collector which also deals with prayer (Luke 9.51 to 18.14).

The Lord's prayer in Luke is followed by specific teachings about perseverance in prayer (Luke 11.5-13) not found in Matthew.

Luke's prayer is briefer and thus somewhat different, which shows that this was not meant to be a prayer that would be repeated word for word by Jesus' disciples on every occasion of prayer.

We should note that Luke 11.13 mentions the Holy Spirit as one of the things disciples of Jesus need to ask and seek, but which is not mentioned in Matthew. The context of the prayer in Matthew is a warning not to be like the hypocrites in their way of praying; the context of the prayer in Luke is the importance of prayer as an essential element of Jesus' teachings on many other matters and also how prayer needs to be done with perseverance and not just something occasional. This idea is found throughout the New Testament (Romans 12.12; 1 Thessalonians 5.16-18; Philippians 4.6; Ephesians 6.18; Colossians 4.2).

> **9** "*Let* love *be* without hypocrisy. Abhor what is evil. Cling to what is good. **10** *Be* kindly affectionate to one another with brotherly love, in honor giving preference to one another; **11** not lagging in diligence, fervent in spirit, serving the Lord; **12** rejoicing in hope, patient in tribulation, continuing steadfastly in prayer; **13** distributing to the needs of the saints, given to hospitality." (Romans 12.12)

The hypocrites love to pray in a way to be seen by men. They are not seeking to please God or to be rewarded by God, but to please men. In the three examples of charitable deeds, praye, and fasting, Jesus mentions the importance of going to the "Father who is in the secret place". In the three acts of piety, Jesus mentions the Father who rewards openly. Thus, there is a reward promised and "open" (a reward that will be obvious for all) for those who pray not to be seen of men but to please the Father in heaven.

Prayer in public is not to be rejected, but to be practiced with caution. And the value of public prayer is directly connected to the private prayer life of the disciple of Jesus. One who does not have this intimate connection with God through a life or prayer cannot do much good at praying publicly, even if he is not praying in order to be seen by men.

There may be another reason for caution in public prayer (such as restaurants) in the statement found in Matthew 7.6: "Do not give what is holy to the dogs; nor cast your pearls before swine, lest they trample them under their feet, and turn and tear you in pieces." Is it required that disciples express their faith in the public forum, in situations they know very well will bring scorn and mockery? Is it always a good idea to offer prayers before meals when in a restaurant or a public gathering? This has to be decided with wisdom because there are times and places when public prayer will invite scorn and ridicule or even violent reactions, which would not necessarily advance the truths of the Kingdom of God. Prayer is holy and as precious as "pearls". Like many other Kingdom realities such as fellowship, the Lord's Supper or praising God with singing, prayer should not be exposed to desecration. We should not treat all people as being all alike and expose the pearls of the Kingdom to all indiscriminately. There is a time for the disciple to be reserved when facing those who are compared here to "dogs and swine" which in Jewish thought represent shameless and unclean individuals. There are such people, and it is a mistake to ignore that fact:

> **22** "And on some have compassion, making a
> distinction; **23** but others save with fear, pulling *them* out of
> the fire, hating even the garment defiled by the flesh." (Jude
> v.22,23)

What is meant by the "secret place"? This could be an allusion to the Old Testament "Holies of Holies" of the tabernacle and temple, where none could enter except the High priest at the day of atonement. The disciple of Jesus has access to God's throne through the mediation of the high priest, Jesus. The veil has been opened, and the disciple can enter into the presence of God "with full assurance":

> **19** "Therefore, brethren, having boldness to enter the Holiest by
> the blood of Jesus, **20** by a new and living way which He consecrated for us, through the veil, that is, His flesh, **21** and *having* a
> High Priest over the house of God, **22** let us draw near with a
> true heart in full assurance of faith, having our hearts sprinkled
> from an evil conscience and our bodies washed with pure
> water." (Hebrews 10.19-22)

> "Praying always with all prayer and supplication in the Spirit, being watchful to this end with all perseverance and supplication
> for all the saints." (Ephesians 6.18)

> **26** "Likewise, the Spirit also helps in our weaknesses. For we do
> not know what we should pray for as we ought, but the Spirit
> Himself makes intercession for us with groaning which cannot
> be uttered. **27** Now He who searches the hearts knows what the

mind of the Spirit *is because* He makes intercession for the saints according to *the will of* God." (Romans 8.26,27)

Prayer

Father in heaven, we praise you, and we thank you for a new day. We ask for deeper faith, deeper love and deeper hope today and for the days ahead. We pray that our words and actions will honor you and the truth of your word. Help us to speak and act in a way that will bring glory to your name and to your truth. We pray in the name of Jesus, our Lord. Amen.

Day 2

7 And when you pray, do not use vain repetitions as the heathen *do*. For they think that they will be heard for their many words. **8** "Therefore do not be like them. For your Father knows the things you have need of before you ask Him." (Matthew 6.7,8)

In the Greek, the word translated repetitions comes from the name of a man called Battus who was the founder of the ancient Greek colony of Cyrene and its first king and who stammered when he spoke. The repetition of words by Battus was due to a lisp in his speech. Thus, he had a difficult time conveying what he needed to say. In a case like this, one needs much more time to communicate a message which could have been said in fewer words. Quite often, fewer words are more powerful than long discourses.

The "heathen" are the Gentiles or non-Jews. Jesus is pointing out a characteristic of pagan worship and of the pagan gods, which was to repeat long prayers using the same words and same phrases over and over again in order to obtain a response from the pagan gods. The repetition of phrases and rote prayers were very common in the worship of the gods in Greece or Persia and beyond. The fact that they worshipped so many gods also meant that the same prayers had to be repeated over and over when addressed to these different gods. With constant repetition of prayers, pagan religions practiced endless chanting of prescribed words, and this way of chanting has continued down the centuries until today.

The way the pagan practiced would not be acceptable to the true and living God who is our Father and whose knowledge is complete. We should ask our Father for daily bread and other things we need, but not thinking that we are informing Him of our needs as if He did not know about them. Believers should not think that we can get our Father to act based on the great many words we use. The Father is looking for a true and loving relationship coming from the heart, not a contrived relationship or one based on some kind of "business negotiation". Moreover, the repetition of words and mantras would get the pagans in a state of trance; they would be subject to doing things they would otherwise not do. The Father in heaven is not like that. He cannot be pushed around, manipulated or bought with money.

The teaching of Jesus at this point is closely linked to his teachings in Matthew 7.7-12 about asking, seeking and knocking. The prayer Jesus teaches as well as these teachings in the sermon on the mount are descriptive of a trusting and loving relationship with God; one that could exist between a father and a son. In the pagan world, the idols and "gods" are feared but can be pushed around on occasion. In pagan worship there was no thought of sincere love as the grounds of this relationship, of complete goodness on the part of God or of complete trust on the part of the worshipper.

Jesus' teachings address an important aspect of the religious life of the heathen and apply today in many parts of the world. One needs to remember that this teaching was not to be confined to Israel but would be later on taught as disciples would go to all the nations teaching all of Jesus' will, including the meaning and best practices of prayer:

> **18** And Jesus came and spoke to them, saying, 'All authority has been given to Me in heaven and on earth. **19** Go therefore and make disciples of all the nations, baptizing them in the name of the Father and of the Son and of the Holy Spirit, **20** teaching them to observe all things that I have commanded you; and lo, I am with you always, *even* to the end of the age. Amen.'" (Matthew 28.18-20)

The prayer taught by Jesus in Matthew 6 contains not one repetition. It is brief and to the point. It is not a mind-control technic. Thus, it is not done in "vain". This word "vain" is not in the original Greek but is added to the word "repetitions" in the translation to help us understand that the problem with prayer is not so much about "repetition" but about "vain repetitions". This idea of "vain" repetition is contained itself in the word "repetition" thus the translators needed to emphasize this thought in the translation. When we pray regularly to God, it is not a mistake to bring the same needs to Him, to mention the same people we are praying for.

The apostle Paul recommends that we "make supplications, prayers, intercessions and giving of thanks be made for all men". He is not saying that this needs to be done once for all. The verb "making" in 1 Timothy 2.1 is in the present infinitive (middle/passive) and describes something to be done on a regular basis and not once for all (this form of the verb "to do, to make" is used also in 2 Peter 1.10, 15).

We may connect this to the teachings of Jesus about prayer found in Luke 11.5-13 with the example of the friend insisting on receiving help from the friend he goes to and also the teachings of Jesus about the necessity to keep asking, seeking and knocking. We find here the idea of "repetition" but not of "vain repetition". Thus, there is a difference between the two ideas.

We find more teachings from Jesus concerning this aspect of prayer in Matthew 7.7-12. In Luke, it is found immediately following the prayer of Jesus. We see when comparing Matthew and Luke the different aspects of Jesus' teachings on prayer. In fact, Jesus' teachings about prayer are not limited to what we find in the sermon on the mount, whether in Matthew or Luke. We find teachings on prayer throughout all the Gospels.

Prayer is a central theme of Jesus' teachings. For example, the parable of the persistent widow in Luke 18.1-8 teaches the central lesson that the disciples should "always pray and not give up".

> **16** "Rejoice always, **17** pray without ceasing, **18** in everything give thanks; for this is the will of God in Christ Jesus for you." (1 Thessalonians 5.16-18)

> **12** rejoicing in hope, patient in tribulation, continuing steadfastly in prayer; **13** distributing to the needs of the saints, given to hospitality." (Romans 12.12)

> **6** "Be anxious for nothing, but in everything by prayer and supplication, with thanksgiving, let your requests be made known to God; **7** and the peace of God, which surpasses all understanding, will guard your hearts and minds through Christ Jesus." (Philippians 4.6,7)

Prayer

We pray today Father with thanksgiving. We are grateful for your love, for the gift of your Son, for forgiveness and salvation. Bless our loved ones with a heart that seeks you. Bless our neighbors also the same way. We pray for the leaders of our city, of our nation. For all those who are in position of leadership. May we live in peace, being able to freely worship and to proclaim your Word. We pray in the name of Jesus. Amen.

Day 3

> "In this manner, therefore, pray: Our Father in heaven,
> Hallowed be Your name."
> (Matthew 6.9)

Jesus taught us how to pray by first showing us the central and foremost place of God in our prayer life. He also taught how prayer is a collective or communal expression of faith in God and of praise to Him. Does this mean this prayer can only be pronounced on certain occasions when a community of believers has gathered? Not necessarily since so many prayers in the Bible are from one single individual, but are spoken as "we". Jesus taught the importance of one praying to God alone "in the secret place" but this does not mean that one who is alone in the secret place isolates himself from his family, his brethren, his church or his nation.

David in the Psalms often prays to God expressing his personal praises and concerns but also the praises and concerns of his brethren, his people. "Truly my soul silently waits for God, from Him comes my salvation. He only is my rock and my salvation; He is my defense; I shall not greatly be moved." (Psalms 62.1,2). "O God, you have cast us off; you have broken us down; you have been displeased; Oh, restore us again!" (Psalms 60.1).

All alone in his room, Daniel prays to God as if surrounded by the presence of his people:

> **3** "Then I set my face toward the Lord God to make request by prayer and supplications, with fasting, sackcloth, and
> ashes. **4** And I prayed to the Lord my God, and made confession, and said, 'O Lord, great and awesome God, who keeps His covenant and mercy with those who love Him, and with those who keep His commandments, **5** we have sinned and committed iniquity, we have done wickedly and rebelled, even by departing from Your precepts and Your judgments.'" (Daniel 9.3-5)

This prayer in the Sermon on the Mount is in the plural (Our Father who is in heaven) just as all the teachings of the Sermon are addressed to the community, the *ekklesia* (church) the Christ has come to save and shape. The essential aspects of our prayer life found here should be the focus of "the church" in its heavenly and spiritual dimension and in its earthly and localized life. It directs us to a "way of life" that leads us to the Father, to heaven. It is the prayer that is illustrated by teachings such as the following statement from the apostle Paul:

> **1** "If then you were raised with Christ, seek those things which are above, where Christ is, sitting at the right hand of God. **2** Set your mind on things above, not on things on the earth. **3** For you died, and your life is hidden with Christ in God. **4** When Christ *who is* our life appears, then you also will appear with Him in glory." (Colossians 3.1-3)

The idea that God is "our Father" is not a revelation reserved to the New Testament, it is rooted in the Old Testament and expresses the unique relationship enjoyed between Israel and the God of Abraham, Isaac and Jacob (Deuteronomy 32:6; Isaiah 63:16; 64:8; Jeremiah 3:4,19; 31:9; Malachi 1:6; 2:10).

Knowing the Father is crucial for inheriting eternal life. And this knowledge of the Father is closely linked to the knowledge of Jesus the Christ, the Son (the Messiah):

> **1** "Jesus spoke these words, lifted up His eyes to heaven, and said: 'Father, the hour has come. Glorify Your Son, that Your Son also may glorify You, **2** as You have given Him authority over all flesh, that He should give eternal life to as many as You have given Him. **3** And this is eternal life, that they may know You, the only true God, and Jesus Christ whom You have sent. **4** I have glorified You on the earth. I have finished the work which You have given Me to do. **5** And now, O Father, glorify Me together with Yourself, with the glory which I had with You before the world was.'" (John 17.1-5)

Prayer

Our Father, we praise you for your creation and your work of salvation throughout the ages. We thank you that you have revealed to us your Fatherly love, your care and holiness. We come to you for greater holiness and righteousness, for becoming better servants today. May your Holy Spirit produce in us the fruit of holiness and righteousness. We pray in the name of Jesus, our Lord. Amen.

Day 4

> "Your kingdom come,
> Your will be done
> On earth as *it is* in heaven."
> (Matthew 6.10)

Our prayers should first of all be confessional: they should express our deep appreciation for God and love for God — The God who cares and loves like a father; the God who is holy, whose Kingdom is the everlasting kingdom and whose will we should seek every day of our lives. These expressions of faith in God and appreciation for who He is should form the basis of any other aspect of coming to Him in prayer, whether it is for our daily material needs such as food or whether it is for our daily spiritual needs such as forgiveness or help in times of temptations or trials.

From the start of his ministry, Jesus had preached that the Kingdom is near. He was referring to the messianic kingdom of God; the kingdom that would be established as a consequence of the work of the Messiah:

> **14** "Now after John was put in prison, Jesus came to
> Galilee, preaching the gospel of the kingdom of God, **15** and
> saying, 'The time is fulfilled, and the kingdom of God is at hand.
> Repent, and believe in the gospel.'" (Mark 1.14).

There is a sense in which the kingdom of God has come to earth in the person of Jesus. There is also a sense in which people have been invited into the kingdom of God. People respond to this invitation by faith and repentance. The present rule of Jesus as Messiah at the right hand of God is also part of that reality of the messianic kingdom.

> **55** "But he, being full of the Holy Spirit, gazed into heaven and
> saw the glory of God, and Jesus standing at the right hand of
> God, **56** and said, 'Look! I see the heavens opened and the Son
> of Man standing at the right hand of God!'" (Acts 7.55,56)

> "Who *is* he who condemns? *It is* Christ who died, and furthermore is also risen, who is even at the right hand of God, who also makes intercession for us." (Romans 8.34)

Jesus has come to rule as Messiah (king). Jesus being that ruler today, how does the prayer "Your kingdom come" apply?

The word "kingdom" is also about the rule of God, the rule of His Christ in the life of men and women who are associated with that kingdom by their new birth of water and Spirit (John 3.1-8). The concept of "kingdom" is directly connected to the doing of God's will. God's rule in our lives is a reality when His will is accomplished in our lives. This is similar to the idea that disciples of Jesus are called "saints" and still need to pursue sanctification. We should pray that the reign of God comes into this world through our lives, our teaching and the preaching of the Gospel. This is the thought expressed in Paul's letter to the Colossians: "If then you were raised with Christ, seek those things which are above, where Christ is, sitting at the right hand of God.

> **2** Set your mind on things above, not on things on the earth. **3** For you died, and your life is hidden with Christ in God. **4** When Christ *who is* our life appears, then you also will appear with Him in glory." (Colossians 3.1-4).

Prayer

Our Father in heaven, we pray that today we can accomplish your will in our lives. We need your help and strength and also the work of your Holy Spirit, so that, Father, we can accomplish your will in our lives. So, we come to you with gratitude and seeking your wisdom for this to be true in our lives today. In the name of Jesus, we pray. Amen.

Day 5

> "Give us this day our daily bread."
> (Matthew 6.11)

The Lord's prayer for "daily bread" is not about "my daily bread" but about "our daily bread". We can easily be hardened by the fact of having everything we need for our physical lives, forgetting the need and plight of others. This is especially grievous when we think of the *ekklesia* (church) which Jesus came to build (Matthew 16.18). Those who share in the bread and cup on the Lord's day must not forget to share their care and love for their brethren in all their needs with just as much seriousness. In fact, in every aspect of our lives, we should be caring and loving towards brothers and sisters in need:

3 *"Let* nothing *be done* through selfish ambition or conceit, but in lowliness of mind let each esteem others better than himself. **4** Let each of you look out not only for his own interests, but also for the interests of others." (Philippians 2.3)

"See that no one renders evil for evil to anyone, but always pursue what is good both for yourselves and for all." (1 Thessalonians 5.15)

19 "So then, my beloved brethren, let every man be swift to hear, slow to speak, slow to wrath; **20** for the wrath of man does not produce the righteousness of God." (James 1.19)

8 "And above all things have fervent love for one another, for "love will cover a multitude of sins." **9** *Be* hospitable to one another without grumbling." (1 Peter 4.8,9)

14 "What *does it* profit, my brethren, if someone says he has faith but does not have works? Can faith save him? **15** If a brother or sister is naked and destitute of daily food, **16** and one of you says to them, "Depart in peace, be warmed and filled," but you do not give them the things which are needed for the body, what *does it* profit? **17** Thus also faith by itself, if it does not have works, is dead." (James 2.14-16)

Prayer

Father in heaven, we pray that our loves will grow in understanding your will. We pray that our prayer today can help us come closer to you in love, in faith and in hope. Give us your wisdom and through your Holy Spirit change our hearts, our ways and our understanding. We want to do you will today in our lives. Help us, God, do this. We pray in the name of Jesus. Amen.

Day 6

"And forgive us our debts,
As we forgive our debtors."
(Matthew 6.12)

14 "For if you forgive men their trespasses, your heavenly Father will also forgive you. **15** But if you do not forgive men their trespasses, neither will your Father forgive your trespasses."
(Matthew 6.14,15)

"And forgive us our sins,
For we also forgive everyone who is indebted to us."
(Luke 11.4)

The fact that Jesus mentions forgiveness in this short prayer underlines its importance. There are many things we can pray for such as wisdom or health but are not mentioned here. We should, however, consider forgiveness as a priority in the life of a disciple.

To be forgiven has the very basic meaning of being indebted to someone and being graciously relieved of that debt. This primary meaning of forgiveness should not be forgotten, and is illustrated for example in the parable of the unforgiving servant (Matthew 18.23-35). The story illustrates the contrast between how much the servant of the king owed — an impressive amount, ten thousand talents (about 15 years of salary for a typical worker) — and how much the servant is owed one hundred denarii by a fellow servant, which was a negligible amount compared to ten thousand talents (one hundred denarii would have been the equivalent of 100 days of wages for the average worker).

The verb "to forgive" in the Greek language (*aphiemi*) had the basic meaning of "to send away, to leave alone, to permit, to release". The forgiveness of God through the work of the Messiah is the relieving of a debt or a moral and spiritual debt incurred because of sin. This was an important aspect of Jesus' revelation about himself as one who has the power as the Son of man (a messianic title) to forgive sins, which only God has:

4 "But Jesus, knowing their thoughts, said, 'Why do you think evil in your hearts? **5** For which is easier, to say, '*Your* sins are forgiven you,' or to say, 'Arise and walk'? **6** But that you may know that the Son of Man has power on earth to forgive sins" —then He said to the paralytic, "Arise, take up your bed, and go to your house." **7** And he arose and departed to his house."
(Matthew 9.4-7)

To forgive sins is to relieve one of the debts incurred by sin. This idea is found for example in the institution of the Lord's supper:

27 "Then He took the cup, and gave thanks, and gave *it* to them, saying, "Drink from it, all of you. **28** For this is My blood of the new covenant, which is shed for many for the remission of sins." (Matthew 26.27,28).

The same idea is found in John's first letter:

"If we say that we have no sin, we deceive ourselves, and the truth is not in us. **9** If we confess our sins, He is faithful and just to forgive us *our* sins and to cleanse us from all unrighteousness. **10** If we say that we have not sinned, we make Him a liar, and His word is not in us." (1 John 1.8-10).

This remitting of the debt of sinfulness is already promised in the Old Testament as the heart of the New Covenant promised to Israel (Jeremiah 31.31-34), "For I will forgive their iniquity, and their sin I will remember no more." God's forgiveness for our sins is the relief of a debt we must pay: "And I testify again to every man who becomes circumcised that he is a debtor [Greek *opheiletes,* as in Matthew 18.24] to keep the whole law" (Galatians 5.3).

We should note that forgiveness has to do with "sin", with what people do, and not with who people are. If someone is dishonest or lazy, we can't say that we need to forgive that person for being lazy or dishonest. But if someone has acted dishonestly towards us, we can forgive that action, that dishonest deed. But as far as that person "being" dishonest, that is not something we can actually forgive. Thus, we can tell a person "I forgive you for what you have done but work on this sin in your life, give up being dishonest". It is absurd and non-biblical for someone to say to us "forgive me for being dishonest" because this is not a "debt" the person has incurred towards us. If a person is dishonest and has an issue with that particular sin, it is to God they need to turn for forgiveness in order to make things right with God, which includes repentance, a change of life and attitude (2 Corinthians 7. 8-12). Our forgiving people who have sinned against us does in no way relieve them from the necessity for them to mourn for their sinfulness, to repent, and to come to God for forgiveness.

In Matthew 6.14,15, forgiveness has to do with trespasses others have done against us. It has nothing to do with the spiritual status before God. But it is important for us to be forgiving of what others have done against us, just as God has forgiven us of what we have done against him. We should also take note that even when God forgives us, it does not mean we should continue in the same sins against God; it does not mean that there is no need for us to change our ways (See Romans 6.1-14).

31 "Let all bitterness, wrath, anger, clamor, and evil speaking be put away from you, with all malice. **32** And be kind to one another, tenderhearted, forgiving one another, even as God in Christ forgave you." (Ephesians 4.31,32)

12 "Therefore, as *the* elect of God, holy and beloved, put on tender mercies, kindness, humility, meekness, longsuffering; **13** bearing with one another, and forgiving one another, if anyone has a complaint against another; even as Christ forgave you, so you also *must do*. **14** But above all these things put on love, which is the bond of perfection." (Colossians 3.12-14)

Prayer

Father in heaven, we come to you and pray for those who have sinned against us, spoken evil against us. We pray that we will forgive their sins towards us. We pray that they will come to you with repentant hearts to seek your forgiveness and that their lives will be turned around. We pray that they may find peace in your forgiveness and find the joy of your salvation. We pray in the name of Jesus, our lord and savior. Amen.

Day 7

"And do not lead us into temptation,
But deliver us from the evil one.
For Yours is the kingdom and the power and the glory forever.
Amen."
   (Matthew 6.13)

The two words "temptation" and "evil one" have led to different understandings of what Jesus means here. In cases like this, we do not need to be "dogmatic" about what is meant. The word "temptation" is the Greek *peirasmon,* which has the basic meaning of trial or testing, even calamity or affliction. However, depending on the context the word can refer to a testing of our faith (such as for example Job went through) or a "temptation" a test that is meant to lead us to sin. In that sense, God never tempts people:

> **12** "Blessed *is* the man who endures temptation; for when he has been approved, he will receive the crown of life which the Lord has promised to those who love Him. **13** Let no one say when he is tempted, 'I am tempted by God'; for God cannot be tempted by evil, nor does He Himself tempt anyone. **14** But each one is tempted when he is drawn away by his own desires and enticed. **15** Then, when desire has conceived, it gives birth to sin; and sin, when it is full-grown, brings forth death." (James 1.12-15).

When Jesus was led into the desert by the Holy Spirit, he was then tempted by Satan, the evil one. It was not the Spirit or God who tempted Jesus, but Satan.

> **1** "Then Jesus was led up by the Spirit into the wilderness to be tempted by the devil. **2** And when He had fasted forty days and forty nights, afterward He was hungry. **3** Now when the tempter came to Him, he said, 'If You are the Son of God, command that these stones become bread.'" (Matthew 4.1-3)

The second part of verse 13 — "But deliver us from the evil one" — seems to indicate that this is talking about Satan, who tempts us to make us fall and drive us away from God. The word translated "the evil one" is the Greek "*tou ponerou*" with the genitive could either be neuter or masculine. If neuter the translation would be "evil" and if masculine the translation would be "the evil one" and refer to Satan. Trials exist, they come and go. But they are not what is worse in our lives. What is worse in our lives is what comes through the work of the "evil one" who wants to turn us away from God; the one who is a dangerous "lion":

> **8** "Be sober, be vigilant because your adversary the devil walks about like a roaring lion, seeking whom he may devour. **9** Resist him, steadfast in the faith, knowing that the same sufferings are experienced by your brotherhood in the world." (1 Peter 5.8,9).

Of course, Satan can use trials and pains to lure us away from God, as demonstrated in the book of Job. Thus, the distinction between trial and temptation is not always that clear. Satan can very well use our pains to tempt us to sin our turn away from God.

The third part of verse 13 is introduced by the conjunction "for" which indicates that we have here a key statement that clarifies the meaning of the entire verse. The sovereignty of God is what should always be kept in mind, and which is foundational to the biblical teaching and to our faith.

We should never equate the power or influence of the evil one with the power of God. The evil one can hurt us and will try to hurt us, but he is extremely limited in what he can do when compared to God, who possesses all power and glory. The evil one is also limited in what he knows (only God has omniscience). We pray more out of complete trust in God (and might say "fear of God") instead of a fear of Satan. We can actually resist Satan, and he will flee far away from us:

> **7** "Therefore submit to God. Resist the devil and he will flee from you. **8** Draw near to God and He will draw near to you. Cleanse *your* hands, *you* sinners; and purify *your* hearts, *you* double-minded." (James 4.7,8)

> **8** "Finally, brethren, whatever things are true, whatever things *are* noble, whatever things *are* just, whatever things *are* pure, whatever things *are* lovely, whatever things *are* of good report, if *there is* any virtue and if *there is* anything praiseworthy—meditate on these things. **9** The things which you learned and received and heard and saw in me, these do, and the God of peace will be with you." (Philippians 4.8,9)

Prayer

Our Father in heaven, we are safe in your hands. You watch over us at all times. We pray that we will stay close to you today, that our thoughts will always be directed to what is good and pure, what is praiseworthy. Keep our hearts close to you, help us through your Holy Spirit to walk according to the Spirit and not the flesh. Forgive us any sin and give us your wisdom. We pray this in the name of Jesus. Amen.

Week 48: Fasting, Treasures and Worry (Matt 6.16-34; Luke 12.13-34)

Day 1

> **16** "Moreover, when you fast, do not be like the hypocrites, with a sad countenance. For they disfigure their faces that they may appear to men to be fasting. Assuredly, I say to you, they have their reward. **17** But you, when you fast, anoint your head and wash your face, **18** so that you do not appear to men to be fasting, but to your Father who *is* in the secret *place;* and your Father who sees in secret will reward you openly."
> (Matthew 6.16-18)

Fasting, like prayer and giving, can easily lead to religious hypocrisy. The sad countenance of those who fast has to do with grief or mourning, which often in the Scripture leads to fasting and praying (1 Samuel 1.7,8; 20.34; Psalms 69.10). But there is another reason for fasting which is an expression of true repentance (2 Corinthians 7.8,9), of consecration to God:

> **12** "Now, therefore, says the Lord,
> 'Turn to Me with all your heart,
> With fasting, with weeping, and with mourning.
> **13** So rend your heart, and not your garments;
> Return to the Lord your God,
> For He *is* gracious and merciful,
> Slow to anger, and of great kindness;
> And He relents from doing harm.
> **14** Who knows *if* He will turn and relent,
> And leave a blessing behind Him—
> A grain offering and a drink offering
> For the Lord your God?'" (Joel 2.12-14)

This fasting is important since it comes from the "heart" and has to do with our personal relationship with God who "sees in the secret". This fasting is not an expression of mourning, but rather an expression of joy to come. Consecration and repentance lead to authentic joy and peace. This is a fasting that brings us closer to God: "Who knows *if* He will turn and relent and leave a blessing behind Him."

On the day of Pentecost, those who heard the preaching of the Good News "were cut to the heart". Told by the apostle Peter to repent, they "gladly received his word" and were baptized. Later, they "continued with one accord...with gladness and simplicity of heart" (Acts 2.37-46).

The repentance God is calling us to does not just involve grief and mourning, but leads to joy and hope. This is a "fasting" that allows us to get closer to God, closer to His will. It is the fasting preached by the prophets which opens the door to God's comfort and salvation. It is the "fasting" of giving up wickedness, of letting the oppressed go free, of breaking every yoke, of sharing our bread with the hungry and which leads to healing and joy.

> **8** "Then your light shall break forth like the morning,
> Your healing shall spring forth speedily,
> And your righteousness shall go before you;
> The glory of the Lord shall be your rear guard.
> **9** Then you shall call, and the Lord will answer;
> You shall cry, and He will say, 'Here I *am*.'" (Isaiah 58.8,9)

Prayer

Our Father in heaven, our hearts are broken when we sin. We want to serve you today in ways that will please you. We want to fast from sin, from evil. Purify our hearts through your word, through prayer today and through your Holy Spirit. We also pray that you will lead those of our friends, our loved ones, who have not come to you yet or who need to return to you. Our prayer is in the name of Jesus, our Lord. Amen.

Day 2

> **19** "Do not lay up for yourselves treasures on earth, where moth and rust destroy and where thieves break in and steal; **20** but lay up for yourselves treasures in heaven, where neither moth nor rust destroys and where thieves do not break in and steal. **21** For

where your treasure is, there your heart will be also." (Matthew 6.19-21)

The teachings of Jesus in Luke 12 are very similar to this part of the Sermon on the mount in Matthew. Luke also adds the parable of the rich fool (Luke 12.13-21). In this parable two important aspects stand out which are:

1. The foolishness of not taking care of one's soul (Luke 12.20)

2. The importance of being rich toward God (Luke 12.21)

This is not just about becoming wealthy through work or business acumen. These teachings have to do with the specific pursuit of "laying up for ourselves" wealth. There are two options presented here: 1) Laying up treasures for ourselves on this earth, or 2) Laying up treasures for ourselves in heaven. In both cases, we find exactly the same idea of laying up treasures and this for ourselves.

To "lay up treasures" is to store up, to accumulate, to amass, to lay aside or put away. The verb is used by James and translated "heaped up" (NKJV):

> **1** "Come now, *you* rich, weep and howl for your miseries that are coming upon *you!* **2** Your riches are corrupted, and your garments are moth-eaten. **3** Your gold and silver are corroded, and their corrosion will be a witness against you and will eat your flesh like fire. You have heaped up treasure in the last days."
> (James 5.1-3)

In Matthew 6 and Luke 12 this "amassing" of earthly treasures is the result of worrying about the basic needs of life such as food or clothing (Luke 12.22-34). It seems that in this passage we have worry which produces amassing of wealth, which in turn produces a turning of the heart away from God and his will towards the amassed wealth: "For where your treasure is, there your heart will be also."

This teaching is not telling disciples of Christ that it is wrong to be wealthy or to become wealthy. The apostle Paul does not teach this when addressing those who are wealthy and who are Christians. We should note the statement, "God who gives us richly all things to enjoy" which goes against the idea of considering poverty as a religious or spiritual virtue.

Paul's teachings to Timothy concerning wealth can be understood as a commentary on Jesus' statement in Luke 12.21 about being rich towards God:

> **17** "Command those who are rich in this present age not to be haughty, nor to trust in uncertain riches but in the living God, who gives us richly all things to enjoy. **18** *Let them* do good, that they be rich in good works, ready to give, willing to share, **19** storing up for themselves a good foundation for the time to come, that they may lay hold on eternal life." (1 Timothy 6.17,19)

Prayer

Father in heaven, we are grateful for the ability to work, to provide for our families and those in need. Help us to always consider this as an expression of your grace and goodness. Help us today to be rich in good works, to be ready to give and willing to share. We pray this in the name of Jesus, our Lord. Amen.

Day 3

> **22** "The lamp of the body is the eye. If therefore your eye is good, your whole body will be full of light. **23** But if your eye is bad, your whole body will be full of darkness. If therefore the light that is in you is darkness, how great *is* that darkness!"
> (Matthew 6.22,23)

Luke's Gospel also quotes a similar statement, but introduces it similarly to what we read in Matthew 5.15:

> **15** "Nor do they light a lamp and put it under a basket, but on a lampstand, and it gives light to all *who are* in the house. **16** Let your light so shine before men, that they may see your good works and glorify your Father in heaven."

Thus, these verses which begin with the statement "The lamp of the body is the eye" have to do with the call of Jesus to shine in a way that others might "see your good works and glorify your Father in heaven".

The statement in Matthew 6.22,23 is an illustration of what Jesus started teaching about those who do "their charitable deeds", who pray or who fast in order to be "seen by men". Generosity towards the needy, prayer and fasting in order to be seen by men and receive praise by men is what Jesus teaches against.

This seems almost contradictory to the statement in Matthew 5.14,15 about the light of the disciples, which needs to shine and be seen by all so that the Father will be glorified. However, acting upon Jesus' teachings in this entire section — with an emphasis on generosity, prayer and fasting — is actually bringing light to the world, not hiding it. Hypocrisy sheds no light in the world, while worship that is authentic and from the heart actually brings light to the world. This light that Jesus is talking about is a "light that is in you"; thus it has it source in the heart (Matthew 6.21).

In the words of Jesus about not doing good deeds "to be seen by men" he is not minimizing the importance of action, of good deeds which are constantly emphasized in the New Testament (see for example Galatians 6.9; Colossians 3.17; James 2.26; 4.17; Hebrews 10.24; Titus 2.7-9; 2 Timothy 3.17); he is not contradicting the statement of Matthew 5.16 about letting our "light shine before men". He is talking about the heart, about authentic love for God. We may conclude that there is a bad way to be seen by men as we live our Christian lives and a good way to be seen by men.

To talk about the importance of the heart — "For where your treasure is, there your heart will be also" — Jesus uses a comparison to explain how the light that is from inside — from the eye — is so significant for the entire body. The body needs the eye in order to receive light and move around. The light that comes through the eye is what the body needs. But if the eye is bad and not functioning, if there is no light inside the human heart, all the light from outside is useless. The entire body will still be moving around in darkness.

Prayer

Our Father in heaven, we praise you for the Word of truth that you have given us, that we can listen to and understand. We thank you for Jesus, for His teachings and His life. Help us today to listen from the heart to your truth and to practice your truth. Help us to shine as we grow closer to you in love and obedience. We pray this in the name of Jesus. Amen.

Day 4

> "No one can serve two masters; for either he will hate the one and love the other, or else he will be loyal to the one and despise the other. You cannot serve God and mammon."
> (Matthew 6.24)

Jesus presents a clear choice of life and lifestyle by presenting the consequence of trying to serve two masters at the same time. This verse follows directly the teachings of 6.19-21 about laying up treasures for ourselves on earth. God and mammon are two masters, and we cannot serve both at the same time. This is a comment on what it means to love God and to be loyal to God. It means being undivided in our commitment to God, in our service to him. It is a warning about the risk of having "mammon" as an idol, a god we love and serve or worship (to serve is a key concept that describes worship). We can note that in James 1.1 James writes about being "a servant of God and of the Lord Jesus Christ" which in itself demonstrates that the Lord Jesus is God. James was not serving "two masters" but by serving the Lord Jesus he was serving God.

The word "mammon" is an Aramaic word for "riches" also used in Luke 16.9,11,13. In the parable of Luke 16 the emphasis is about a servant who is capable and wise ("shrewdly" in Luke 16.8) in serving his master in the use of money and wealth. One who is not wise in the use of earthly treasures will not be entrusted with heavenly treasures. Luke 16.9 in particular can be misunderstood as teaching that we should be friends of mammon, of wealth. But the parable illustrates that disciples must be faithful in how they handle heavenly treasures, just as they would be faithful in handing earthly treasures. Parables are comparisons, illustrations of moral and spiritual truths, and should not be understood as conveying moral imperatives in themselves. Luke 16.13 concludes the parable about the faithful servant with the same words as Matthew 6.24.

The statement in Matthew 6.24 also has to do with practical wisdom in dealing with riches that belong to God. This is in harmony with the conclusion of the sermon in Matthew 7.24-27 and its emphasis on being wise. Too often the concept of "wisdom" has not been emphasized in how to serve God and has been replaced with an exclusively moral imperative outlook. In other words, the teachings of Jesus and even of the entire Bible have been seen as "imperatives" unrelated to the actual realities of life and daily decisions that we make as servants of God. In this way, the practicality of the Christian life as described in the Bible has too often been overlooked. See for example 2 Timothy 3.16; James 2.20; Ephesians 4.15; Philippians 4.8; Colossians 1.9-11.

The text that follows about "worry" in Matthew 6.25-34 begins with the word "therefore" showing the connection of these teachings with what Jesus has just been talking about. The teachings in the New Testament are not about whether or not a disciple of Christ should be poor or rich, or how much wealth one he or she should have or not have. Those who are wealthy and end up serving wealth as their master could very well be those who are worried about food and drink. Worry is not about how much one has or does not have, but about trusting or not God in providing what we need. A very wealthy man can actually be worried over his basic needs, and a poor man can actually be fully trusting God despite his poverty (see James 2.5).

This confirms the statement of the apostle Paul about the importance of contentment:

> **10** "But I rejoiced in the Lord greatly that now at last your care for me has flourished again; though you surely did care, but you lacked opportunity. **11** Not that I speak in regard to need, for I have learned in whatever state I am, to be content: **12** I know how to be abased, and I know how to abound. Everywhere and in all things, I have learned both to be full and to be hungry, both to abound and to suffer need. **13** I can do all things through Christ who strengthens me. **14** Nevertheless you have done well that you shared in my distress." (Philippians 4.10-14)

Prayer

Dear Father in heaven, we offer you our hearts and lives with complete trust in you. Help us today to understand your will in every aspect of our lives. Help us to find the strength and wisdom to practice your will. We need your help, your Holy Spirit, for this new day. Father, thank you for your amazing promises and amazing goodness. We are thankful to you in the name of Jesus.

Day 5

> **25** "Therefore, I say to you, do not worry about your life, what you will eat or what you will drink; nor about your body, what you will put on. Is not life more than food and the body more than clothing? **26** Look at the birds of the air, for they neither

sow nor reap nor gather into barns; yet your heavenly Father feeds them. Are you not of more value than they? **27** Which of you by worrying can add one cubit to his stature? **28** "So why do you worry about clothing? Consider the lilies of the field, how they grow: they neither toil nor spin; **29** and yet I say to you that even Solomon in all his glory was not arrayed like one of these. **30** Now if God so clothes the grass of the field, which today is, and tomorrow is thrown into the oven, *will He* not much more *clothe* you, O you of little faith? **31** "Therefore do not worry, saying, 'What shall we eat?' or 'What shall we drink?' or 'What shall we wear?' **32** For after all these things the Gentiles seek. For your heavenly Father knows that you need all these things. **33** But seek first the kingdom of God and His righteousness, and all these things shall be added to you. **34** Therefore do not worry about tomorrow, for tomorrow will worry about its own things. Sufficient for the day *is* its own trouble." (Matthew 6.25-34)

While it is not possible to "serve to masters" it is possible to serve one master and still worry. It is possible to be a follower of Christ, a believer, a servant of the Lord and still worry. Thus, the encouragement not to be anxious, not to worry, is taught throughout the Bible (Proverbs 12.25; Isaiah 41.10; Philippians 4.6,7; 1 Peter 5.7).

Worrying is not like trying to serve two masters, but it produces a distraction, a division of the mind. The Greek verb for "to worry" (*merimnao*) describes being concerned about a part instead of the whole, to be divided into pieces or pulled apart in different directions. It basically describes someone who is divided and distracted. It is used in 1 Corinthians 7.34 to describe one who is married and is more concerned for the things of the world. According to Philippians 4.6 we should strive not to be divided in any area. This idea of being divided or concerned about different things is opposed to the teaching of 6.33, "But seek first the Kingdom of God and His righteousness".

Jesus mentions the example of the "birds" and there are cynics who are critical of this example by stating for example that the birds can sometimes feed themselves at the farmer's expense, or than birds can also perish in the winter months. Do they think Jesus does not know this, he who is, in fact, the Creator? The point of the teaching in 6.26 is not about birds but is a comparison destined for Jesus' disciples, "And are you are not of more value than they?"

This teaching is a call to understand our priorities and is a call to faith or trust in God. This is how we should live. And by saying this, Jesus is not saying his disciples will never encounter difficult times like all other human beings; he is not promising a life without troubles, without ups and downs. Has he not already mentioned that those who follow him will be persecuted? And we know that the faithful can find themselves under persecution and even lose their livelihood and even their lives. However, the biblical teaching to remain faithful and to love God under all circumstances is constant:

> "Fear not, for I *am* with you;
> Be not dismayed, for I *am* your God.
> I will strengthen you,
> Yes, I will help you,
> I will uphold you with My righteous right hand." (Isaiah 41.10)

12 "I know how to be abased, and I know how to abound. Everywhere and in all things, I have learned both to be full and to be hungry, both to abound and to suffer need. **13** I can do all things through Christ who strengthens me." (Philippians 4.12,13)

Prayer

Father in heaven, we pray for greater faith and greater understanding of what it means to seek first your kingdom. We pray for wisdom when we are faced with difficult people or difficult situations. When we are faced with questions to which we have no answers. May you keep us joyful and faithful this day. We pray in the name of Jesus. Amen.

Day 6

13 Then one from the crowd said to Him, "Teacher, tell my brother to divide the inheritance with me." **14** But He said to him, 'Man, who made Me a judge or an arbitrator over you?' **15** And He said to them, 'Take heed and beware of covetousness, for one's life does not consist in the abundance of the things he possesses.' **16** Then He spoke a parable to them, saying: 'The ground of a certain rich man yielded plentifully. **17** And he thought within himself, saying, 'What shall I do, since I have no room to store my crops?' **18** So he said, 'I will do this: I will pull down my barns and build greater, and there I will store all my crops and my goods. **19** And I will say to

my soul, "Soul, you have many goods laid up for many years; take your ease; eat, drink, *and* be merry." **20** But God said to him, 'Fool! This night your soul will be required of you; then whose will those things be which you have provided?'
21 "So *is* he who lays up treasure for himself and is not rich toward God."
(Luke 12.13-21)

Jesus responds this way to the request of a brother to divide his inheritance, despite the fact that He knew how it should have been divided. According to the law, one-third to the younger, two-thirds to the elder (Deuteronomy 21.17). This request from the crowd could have been made to Jesus because he just mentioned those who on his account would be brought before magistrates and authorities (Luke 12.11). The request could also come from the fact of Jesus having mentioned their value as compared to the value of sparrows.

Despite the fact that Jesus was the supreme judge and knew the answer, he responds, "Who made me a judge over you?" Better than reminding these brothers of the rules of the law and better than acting as a judge or an arbitrator, Jesus goes to the root of what is man's sin by teaching them on the sin of "covetousness". Instead of the teaching of Deuteronomy 21 Jesus turns their attention to the tenth commandment: "You shall not covet your neighbor's house; you shall not covet your neighbor's wife, nor his male servant, nor his female servant, nor his ox, nor his donkey, nor anything that *is* your neighbor's." (Exodus 20.17)

"To covet (Hebrew, *tahmod*) means to desire or take pleasure in, to take delight in. It is first used as an adverb (*pleasant* in the NKJV) in Genesis 2.9, "And out of the ground the Lord God made every tree grow that is pleasant to the sight and good for food." The same word is used again in Genesis 3.6 in the context of the temptation (*pleasant* in the NKJV) "So when the woman saw that the tree *was* good for food, that it *was* pleasant to the eyes, and a tree desirable to make *one* wise..."

Considering this, we can understand that the 10th commandment is a clear commandment on the right to private property. The problem in the commandment is not that something is pleasant and desirable; the problem is that it rightfully belongs to another.

Jesus in his teaching goes beyond simply a desire for things or the right of property. Through the parable of the wealthy farmer, he points his disciples to something more significant which comes at the conclusion of his words, "So *is* he who lays up treasure for himself and is not rich toward God." Note the contrast between laying up treasure "for himself" and being rich toward God. The man in the parable was all about himself, pointing to his utter selfishness. There was no thought for anybody else but himself in this story ("my crops", "my goods") not realizing these were "his" only temporarily. Why then did he live as if what he had belonged forever to him?

As in the words of Jesus, we should note that the apostle Paul does not teach the rich to become poor but to "do good, willing to give, willing to share" which would be a way for them to store "for the time to come" (1 Timothy 6.19). This was also the point of Jesus' exhortation to the rich young ruler. The point was not for the young ruler to be poor instead of rich but to be generous and thoughtful of the poor and needy, "Then Jesus, looking at him, loved him, and said to him, 'One thing you lack: Go your way, sell whatever you have and give to the poor, and you will have treasure in heaven; and come, take up the cross, and follow Me.'" (Mark 10.21)

The early Christians shared willingly so that the poor and needy would receive help. However, this was always a voluntary and a personal decision. The apostles or church leaders in Acts never acted as "judges" or "arbitrators" but taught and encouraged the followers of Jesus to practice generosity and reject covetousness (See Acts 5.1-11; Romans 1.29; Mark 7.22; Ephesians 5.3; Hebrews 13.5; Colossians 3.5).

Prayer

Our Lord and Father in heaven, we thank you for every blessing we have from you. We want to glorify you name today and also do your will. Please give us the wisdom we need to understand your word and to practice it today. We pray that we can learn to be generous and thoughtful for those in need or pain. We pray in the name of Jesus. Amen.

Day 7

32 "Do not fear, little flock, for it is your Father's good pleasure to give you the kingdom. **33** Sell what you have and give alms; provide yourselves money bags which do not grow old, a treasure in the heavens that does not fail, where no thief approaches nor moth destroys. **34** For where your treasure is, there your heart will be also." (Luke 12.32-34)

For their service to God and the Gospel, the apostles will be greatly challenged. Not that they needed to make any kind of "vow of poverty" but that they would need to be willing to put the mission of God first in their lives. Those who are sent out by God for the mission of proclaiming the Good News and bringing the message of reconciliation to a dying world will be greatly challenged and thus must be like the soldier who cannot fight if he is caring for the things of the world, like the athlete who must exercise and have discipline, like the hard-working farmer:

> **1** "You, therefore, my son, be strong in the grace that is in Christ Jesus. **2** And the things that you have heard from me among many witnesses, commit these to faithful men who will be able to teach others also. **3** You therefore must endure hardship as a good soldier of Jesus Christ. **4** No one engaged in warfare entangles himself with the affairs of *this* life, that he may please him who enlisted him as a soldier. **5** And also if anyone competes in athletics, he is not crowned unless he competes according to the rules. **6** The hard-working farmer must be first to partake of the crops. **7** Consider what I say, and may the Lord give you understanding in all things. (2 Timothy 2.1-7)

The principle taught by Jesus here concerning challenges facing the preaching of the Gospel should not be made into a binding rule. There were times when Paul lived in hardship and times when he had everything in abundance. This shows that to use the teachings of Jesus to create rules for everyone is to misunderstand the purpose of these teachings.

Jesus did teach a young ruler who was healthy to sell all he had and follow him. But he did not teach this to all the rich individuals he encountered, such as Zacchaeus. This shows that we are not to understand this as some kind of rule to be applied to everybody who wishes to serve God. This does not mean for example that churches who have the means to support financially preachers and teachers should keep them in poverty and needy since they are serving God. There is no vow of poverty or celibacy for preachers or evangelists in the Word of God. In fact, bishops also called "elders" and "pastors" should be married men who take good care of their families (1 Timothy ch. 3 ; Titus ch. 1). The apostle Paul teaches that it is the responsibility of those who are taught to support their teachers and leaders and even uses the strong word "right" to explain the legitimacy of supporting of evangelists, so they can refrain from other type of work that would occupy all their time and energy (even though Paul often did not request any support for himself and "presented the Gospel without charge"):

3 "My defense to those who examine me is this: **4** Do we have no right to eat and drink? **5** Do we have no right to take along a believing wife, as *do* also the other apostles, the brothers of the Lord, and Cephas? **6** Or *is it* only Barnabas and I *who* have no right to refrain from working? **7** Whoever goes to war at his own expense? Who plants a vineyard and does not eat of its fruit? Or who tends a flock and does not drink of the milk of the flock? **8** Do I say these things as a *mere* man? Or does not the law say the same also? **9** For it is written in the law of Moses, "You shall not muzzle an ox while it treads out the grain." Is it oxen God is concerned about? **10** Or does He say *it* altogether for our sakes? For our sakes, no doubt, *this* is written, that he who plows should plow in hope, and he who threshes in hope should be partaker of his hope. **11** If we have sown spiritual things for you, *is it* a great thing if we reap your material things? **12** If others are partakers of *this* right over you, *are* we not even more?" (1 Corinthians 9.3-12)

17 "Let the elders who rule well be counted worthy of double honor, especially those who labor in the word and doctrine. **18** For the Scripture says, 'You shall not muzzle an ox while it treads out the grain,' and, 'The laborer *is* worthy of his wages.'" (1 Timothy 5.17,18)

Prayer

Father in heaven, we thank you for this day and for your every blessing. We pray that we can have grateful dispositions today, that we can learn to say thank you in our hearts. We ask for wisdom in sharing of our blessings with those in greater need. We pray for those who serve you in preaching and teaching, that they may be provided for and encouraged in their labors. We pray this in the name of the Lord Jesus. Amen.

Week 49: Do not Judge, Ask, Seek and Knock (Matt 7.1-12; Luke 7.37-40)

Day 1

> **1** "Judge not, that you be not judged. **2** For with what judgment you judge, you will be judged; and with the measure you use, it will be measured back to you."
> (Matthew 7.1,2)

As we read these verses dealing with judgment (1-5) we notice that the idea of "judging" is only mentioned in the first verse which starts with the imperative "Judge not". Some have taken this command by Jesus as a statement meaning that there is no moral or spiritual truth we can refer to; that there is no way to know if someone is sinning. In that case, the one with the plank in his eyes could not even know his sins; he could not take out the plank in his eye if there is no way for him to know the difference between good and evil, right and wrong.

The idea of "judging" is not mentioned by Jesus afterwards because the Lord is then teaching his auditors a better way to help their "brother" who has sinned or needs to be corrected. Judging the brother is of no use. What is helpful to the brother with the "speck" in his eye is for the other brother to be able to "remove" his plank (to work on his own sins) and in this way to be in a position to help his brother remove the "speck" in his eye. Thus, it is about how to be able to help our brother who is dealing with sin (because sin is always an issue and brings pain it needs to be dealt with in our lives and the life of others).

Verses 1 and 2 are best understood in the light of the statement made by Jesus in verse 12: "Therefore, whatever you want men to do to you, do also to them, for this is the Law and the Prophets." Would we want others to judge us as we judge them? How would we want others to help us with our sin?

By contrast with reading verse 1 as a blank statement, we could quote Jesus' words to religious leaders about "judgment":

> **23** "If a man receives circumcision on the Sabbath, so that the law of Moses should not be broken, are you angry with Me because I made a man completely well on the Sabbath? **24** Do not judge according to appearance, but judge with righteous judgment." (John 7.24)

Many of the religious leaders who heard Jesus saw themselves not only as judges, but as righteous judges. They had lost the ability to look at their own sins and failures (see Matthew 23.26,27; John 8.1-12). Moreover, these "judges" were unable to have any mercy or compassion on others (see Matthew 23.23). This theme is developed in the first twelves verses of Matthew 7. The theme is also found in Luke's Gospel:

> **37** "Judge not, and you shall not be judged. Condemn not, and you shall not be condemned. Forgive, and you will be forgiven. **38** Give, and it will be given to you: good measure, pressed down, shaken together, and running over will be put into your bosom. For with the same measure that you use, it will be measured back to you." (Luke 6.37,38)

Note also this other statement in the context of the Pharisees condemning Jesus' disciples for plucking and eating heads of grains on the Sabbath: "But if you had known what this means, 'I desire mercy and not sacrifice,' you would not have condemned the guiltless. 8 For the Son of Man is Lord even of the Sabbath." (Matthew 12.7,8)

The same theme is also picked up by James when writing about the sin of partiality towards the poor:

> **8** "If you really fulfill *the* royal law according to the Scripture, 'You shall love your neighbor as yourself,' you do well; **9** but if you show partiality, you commit sin, and are convicted by the law as transgressors. **10** For whoever shall keep the whole law, and yet stumble in one *point,* he is guilty of all. **11** For He who said, 'Do not commit adultery,' also said, 'Do not murder.' Now if you do not commit adultery, but you do murder, you have become a transgressor of the law. **12** So speak and so do as those who will be judged by the law of liberty. **13** For judgment is without mercy to the one who has

shown no mercy. Mercy triumphs over judgment." (James 2.8-13; cf. Leviticus 19.15)

James again discusses "judgment" in chapter 4. There we see how, by judging others, we can easily fall into committing the sin of speaking evil of others:

> **1** "Do not speak evil of one another, brethren. He who speaks evil of a brother and judges his brother, speaks evil of the law and judges the law. But if you judge the law, you are not a doer of the law but a judge. **12** There is one Lawgiver, who is able to save and to destroy. Who are you to judge another?" (James 4.11,12)

This theme of "judges" who risk being judged themselves is also found in Paul's letter to the Romans:

> **1** "Therefore you are inexcusable, O man, whoever you are who judge, for in whatever you judge another you condemn yourself; for you who judge practice the same things. **2** But we know that the judgment of God is according to truth against those who practice such things. **3** And do you think this, O man, you who judge those practicing such things, and doing the same, that you will escape the judgment of God?" (Romans 2.1-3)

Prayer

Father in heaven, we praise your name and come to you for strength and wisdom for a new day. We need you at every moment and know you are near and loving. We pray we can show mercy to others as you have shown mercy to us. We thank you for every blessing. Be with us today in the way we act towards others, that we might bring a blessing to them. We pray in the name of Jesus. Amen.

Day 2

> **3** "And why do you look at the speck in your brother's eye, but do not consider the plank in your own eye? **4** Or how can you say to your brother, 'Let me remove the speck from your eye'; and look, a plank *is* in your own eye? **5** Hypocrite! First remove the plank from your own eye, and then you will see clearly to remove the speck from your brother's eye."

(Matthew 7.3-5)

The speck (*karphos*) is a minute dry particle of chaff or wood. The plank (*dokos*) is a wooden beam. The comparison between these two is interesting coming from one who worked as a carpenter and must have experienced particles of wood coming into the eye. Even a speck would bring a lot of pain in the eye and the person who would actually need the help of another to take it out.

The beam coming into the eye is an impossibility, just like the camel going through the eye of the needle (Matthew 19.24). The point of the contrast is to shock the listeners and also help them remember the teaching itself. The comparison also brings out the absurdity or foolishness of the one condemning his brother while himself having a beam in his eye (note the idea of "foolishness" at the conclusion of the sermon in Matthew 7.26,27).

Three important teachings follow this comparison: 1) The one with the beam in his eyes is not in a position to help his brother, who has a speck in his eye. It should be noted that the brother with the "speck" does need someone to help him. 2) The one with the beam should first remove the beam from his eye. 3) One who is able to remove the beam from his eye can see clearly and is then able to help his brother remove the speck from his eye.

As we read this verse, we should not just understand the first point. The point of the teaching is to show how we can help a brother with a speck in his eye. Or we could say that the point of the teaching is to grow in wisdom instead of remaining "foolish" which is also part of the conclusion of the sermon (Matthew 7.24,25).

In fact, a lot of teaching in the Bible has to do with helping people improve morally and spiritually. Jesus is not saying that we should give up on the idea of helping our brethren. What Jesus is doing is showing us the wise way of doing this. We could compare this for example to the following statement:

> **1** "Brethren, if a man is overtaken in any trespass, you who *are* spiritual restore such a one in a spirit of gentleness, considering yourself lest you also be tempted. **2** Bear one another's burdens, and so fulfill the law of Christ. **3** For if anyone thinks himself to be something, when he is nothing, he deceives himself. **4** But let each one examine his own work, and then he will have rejoicing in himself alone, and not in another. **5** For each one shall bear his own load." (Galatians 6.1-5)

Ignoring sin or trying to relativize it does not help us or anyone else. What help us is to be able to confess our sin and grow in holiness and faithfulness. Jesus does not teach such moral relativism, but teaches a way of wisdom, a way to deal with sin in ourselves and in our world. It is hard to imagine for example someone telling John the Baptist preaching repentance "Why don't you take out the plank from your eye". If John was living today, there probably would be individuals using Jesus' words this way.

> **13** "Therefore, gird up the loins of your mind, be sober, and rest *your* hopefully upon the grace that is to be brought to you at the revelation of Jesus Christ; **14** as obedient children, not conforming yourselves to the former lusts, *as* in your ignorance; **15** but as He who called you *is* holy, you also be holy in all *your* conduct, **16** because it is written, 'Be holy, for I am holy.'" (1 Peter 1.14-16)

> **1** "Therefore, laying aside all malice, all deceit, hypocrisy, envy, and all evil speaking, **2** as newborn babes, desire the pure milk of the word, that you may grow thereby, **3** if indeed you have tasted that the Lord *is* gracious." (1 Peter 2.1-3)

> **9** "Do you not know that the unrighteous will not inherit the kingdom of God? Do not be deceived. Neither fornicators, nor idolaters, nor adulterers, nor homosexuals, nor sodomites, **10** nor thieves, nor covetous, nor drunkards, nor revilers, nor extortioners will inherit the kingdom of God. **11** And such were some of you. But you were washed, but you were sanctified, but you were justified in the name of the Lord Jesus and by the Spirit of our God." (1 Corinthians 6.9-11)

Prayer

Father, we come to you today, humbled by your holiness and goodness and by our sin. We want to confess to you any thought, word or action that goes against your will and that hurts others. We also come for help to grow in your likeness, to grow in love and righteousness. May your Holy Spirit produce your holiness in our hearts today. We pray this in the name of Jesus. Amen.

Day 3

> "Do not give what is holy to the dogs; nor cast your pearls before swine, lest they trample them under their feet, and turn and tear you in pieces."
> (Matthew 7.6)

It is not difficult to see in this statement a warning against misunderstanding Jesus' teachings as being "amoral", a point of view so prevalent today (to be "amoral" is to be devoid of a standard of morality — different from "immoral" which means opposed to a known standard of morality).

Jesus taught "Judge not" and gave us the best way to deal with sin. But right away the Lord warns us that we must know people; the statement "judge not" is meant to lead us to wisdom not to naiveté, which is precisely a lack of wisdom or ability to judge. We are in danger whenever we are not able to discern those who are not able to receive nor understand the teachings of the Lord, and especially when we are unable to distinguish between what is holy and what is unholy. Moral criticism is inevitable, and Jesus himself practiced it. Jesus judged the proud, pretentious and cruel Pharisees on behalf of the weak and despised. So, there is no room for moral relativism in Jesus' teachings or the New Testament. It is always about moral wisdom, which is what our world needs the most.

The danger of not being able to have moral judgment is brought out by the verb "they tear you to pieces" (*rhexosin*). The dogs and swine represent shameless and unclean individuals. They are dangerous individuals who can harm us and will harm society at large. The Greek verb *rhegnumi* means to break apart, to throw down and is used of an evil spirit that mistreated an individual: "And wherever it seizes him, it throws him down; he foams at the mouth, gnashes his teeth, and becomes rigid." (Mark 9.18).

Preachers and evangelists in the Church should also be attentive to the principle that "a little leaven leavens the whole lump? 7 Therefore purge out the old leaven, that you may be a new lump, since you truly are unleavened." (1 Corinthians 5.6,7).

> 7 "You ran well. Who hindered you from obeying the truth? 8 This persuasion does not *come* from Him who calls you. 9 A little leaven leavens the whole lump. 10 I have confidence in you, in the Lord, that you will have no other mind; but

he who troubles you shall bear his judgment, whoever he is." (Galatians 5.7-10).

This is also the reason Church leaders such as elders and deacons must be chosen with great care and must demonstrate moral and spiritual qualities (1 Timothy 3 ; Titus 1).

> **21** "I charge *you* before God and the Lord Jesus Christ and the elect angels that you observe these things without prejudice, doing nothing with partiality. **22** Do not lay hands on anyone hastily, nor share in other people's sins; keep yourself pure." (1 Timothy 5.21,22).

Christians and churches need to grow in their relationship to God and in knowledge in order to maintain the high moral standards of God among God's people (see Hebrews 5.12-14; 1 Timothy 3.14,15):

> "But now I have written to you not to keep company with anyone named a brother, who is sexually immoral, or covetous, or an idolater, or a reviler, or a drunkard, or an extortioner—not even to eat with such a person." (1 Corinthians 5.11)

> **33** "Do not be deceived: 'Evil company corrupts good habits.' **34** Awake to righteousness, and do not sin; for some do not have the knowledge of God. I speak *this* to your shame." (1 Corinthians 15.33-34)

> **10** "But these speak evil of whatever they do not know; and whatever they know naturally, like brute beasts, in these things they corrupt themselves. **11** Woe to them! For they have gone in the way of Cain, have run greedily in the error of Balaam for profit, and perished in the rebellion of Korah." (Jude 10,11)

> **22** "And on some have compassion, making a distinction; **23** but others save with fear, pulling *them* out of the fire, hating even the garment defiled by the flesh." (Jude 22,23)

Prayer

Lord, we come to you confessing from our hearts our daily need to grow and learn from your Word. Help us today in our walk with you. Help us to grow in knowledge, love and wisdom. We need the help of your Holy Spirit to carry good fruit. May your Spirit shape our walk. We are thankful for your patience and goodness towards us. We intercede for the leaders of the country and for leaders everywhere. May they trust in you and turn to you. In the name of Jesus, we pray. Amen.

Day 4

> **7** "Ask, and it will be given to you; seek, and you will find; knock, and it will be opened to you. **8** For everyone who asks receives, and he who seeks finds, and to him who knocks it will be opened."
> (Matthew 7.7,8)

The encouragement to ask, seek and knock taught by Jesus should not stand on its own. Its meaning must be understood in a way that is compatible with Jesus' teachings throughout the sermon and his ministry. For example, we cannot dissociate this asking and seeking from the prayer taught by Jesus in Matthew 6.9-13 where we learn essential truths for example about "asking" — asking for our daily bread, for forgiveness and for deliverance from evil (or the evil one). It is only when we are willing to seek the Father's will and His kingdom first (6.33) or that we cease being worried that our asking can have any impact. We cannot assume that we always know what is good for us (verse 11) or that we are asking with the right spirit.

James warns Christians about this:

> **1** "Where do wars and fights *come* from among you?
> Do *they* not *come* from your *desires for* pleasure that war in your members? **2** You lust and do not have. You murder and covet and cannot obtain. You fight and war. Yet you do not have because you do not ask. **3** You ask and do not receive, because you ask amiss, that you may spend *it* on your pleasures. **4** Adulterers and adulteresses! Do you not know that friendship with the world is enmity with God? Whoever therefore wants to be a friend of the world makes himself an enemy of God. **5** Or do you think that the Scripture says in vain, 'The Spirit who dwells in us yearns jealously'? **6** But He gives more grace. Therefore, he says: 'God resists the proud, but gives grace to the humble.'"
> (James 4.1-6)

The word "adulterer" is very strong and shows a spiritual unfaithfulness to God; a divided love and a divided mind, as also mentioned in the following texts:

> **5** "If any of you lacks wisdom, let him ask of God, who gives to all liberally and without reproach, and it will be given to him. **6** But let him ask in faith, with no doubting, for he who doubts is like a wave of the sea driven and tossed by the wind. **7** For let not that man suppose that he will receive anything from the Lord; **8** *he is* a double-minded man, unstable in all his ways." (James 1.5-8)

> **7** "Therefore, submit to God. Resist the devil, and he will flee from you. **8** Draw near to God, and He will draw near to you. Cleanse *your* hands, *you* sinners; and purify *your* hearts, *you* double-minded. **9** Lament and mourn and weep! Let your laughter be turned to mourning and *your* joy to gloom. **10** Humble yourselves in the sight of the Lord, and He will lift you up." (James 4.7-10)

Luke gives us an important hint about the spiritual dimension of "asking" when he mentions the "Holy Spirit":

> "If you then, being evil, know how to give good gifts to your children, how much more will *your* heavenly Father give the Holy Spirit to those who ask Him!" (Luke 11.13).

We know that the Holy Spirit is a gift from God, but it is only those who seek it and desire it who receive it. The book of Acts says:

> "And we are His witnesses to these things, and *so* also *is* the Holy Spirit whom God has given to those who obey Him." (Acts 5.32)

Those who are promised the Holy Spirit in Acts 2 are those who ask the question — thus showing they are seekers — "Now when they heard *this*, they were cut to the heart, and said to Peter and the rest of the apostles, "Men *and* brethren, what shall we do?" (Acts 2.37).

Those who seek God's kingdom, who seek to love and obey God, who seek God's salvation and wisdom are those who when they "ask", "knock" or "ask", receive Good things from the Father. They are those who ask "according to His will":

> **14** "Now this is the confidence that we have in Him, that if we ask anything according to His will, He hears us. **15** And if we know that He hears us, whatever we ask, we know that we have the petitions that we have asked of Him." (1 John 5.14,15)

Prayer

Our Father in heaven, we ask you for wisdom and a loving heart. We pray for a spirit of gratefulness. Give us the words to speak to others about the salvation in Jesus. Give us of your Holy Spirit that we might be filled with the holiness that comes from your Spirit. Give us today to grow in your sight and to have a better understanding of your will. Bless the work of our hands and minds. We pray this in Jesus' name. Amen.

Day 5

> **9** "Or what man is there among you who, if his son asks for bread, will give him a stone? **10** Or if he asks for a fish, will he give him a serpent? **11** If you then, being evil, know how to give good gifts to your children, how much more will your Father who is in heaven give good things to those who ask Him!" (Matthew 7.9,10)

Our Father's goodness was already underlined in chapter 5 and applied to the "evil" and "unjust":

> **43** "You have heard that it was said, 'You shall love your neighbor and hate your enemy.' **44** But I say to you, love your enemies, bless those who curse you, do good to those who hate you, and pray for those who spitefully use you and persecute you, **45** that you may be sons of your Father in heaven; for He makes His sun rise on the evil and on the good, and sends rain on the just and on the unjust." (Matthew 5.43-45)

There is no indication in these words of Jesus that a father will give anything or everything a child asks. We must take note that a father may refuse a child's request, but he will not mock him; he will not give the child a serpent when he asks for bread. The word for "serpent" (Greek *ophin*) could refer to a scale-less fish or serpent-like fish that was caught in the sea of Galilee and was thrown away because it could not be eaten (See Leviticus 11.12).

Sometimes the following questions are asked, "What do I need to pray for?" or "How can I be certain I am asking according to God's will?" One good way to answer these questions is to go to the Bible and see what God is encouraging us to pray for:

- Pray for our enemies (Matthew 5.44)

- Pray for harvesters — evangelists, missionaries (Luke 10.2)
- Pray on behalf of ministers of the Gospel (Colossians 4.3; 2 Thessalonians 3.1)
- Pray for those in authority and for peace (1 Timothy 2.1-3)
- Pray for relief from pain and affliction and healing of the sick (James 5.13,16)

Prayer

Father in heaven, we pray for all the above. We ask that you encourage those who are teaching us from your Word on a regular basis. We pray for the shepherds of the flock and the deacons who are serving in the church. We pray to the Lord for the missionaries we know or even support. May you encourage them and provide all they need. We pray this in the name of Jesus Christ. Amen.

Day 6

> "If you then, being evil, know how to give good gifts to your children, how much more will your Father who is in heaven give good things to those who ask Him!"
> (Matthew 7.11)

Jesus makes two interesting remarks concerning "men": 1. They are evil and 2. They know how to give good gifts to their children. The Bible does not teach a doctrine of complete depravity of all men and women.

It is when compared to God and not so much when compared with each other that men and women really fall short: "How much more will your Father who is in heaven give good things to those who ask Him.". Men and women are made "in God's image" and thus deserve to be seen in that light and treated with love and respect:

> **9** "With it we bless our God and Father, and with it we curse men, who have been made in the similitude of God. **10** Out of the same mouth proceed blessing and cursing. My brethren, these things ought not to be so. **11** Does a spring send forth fresh *water* and bitter from the same opening? **12** Can a fig tree, my brethren, bear olives, or a grapevine bear figs ? Thus, no spring yields both salt water and fresh." (James 3.9-12)

We see here that sinfulness of men or the evil done by men should not be pushed to an extreme that completely erases the good they do. This would not be in harmony with a biblical view of man, which is never extreme. Additionally, the Bible declares that "all have sinned" (Romans 3.23) but does not say that sinners are never able to do any good, to have any faith, to obey anything from God. Through multiple examples, the Bible give us men and women to emulate (for example, in Hebrews chapter 11).

In his teachings, Jesus gives us assurance of the goodness of the Father. This goes against the modern tendency of bringing "judgment" on God as explained in C.S. Lewis' books such as "God in the Dock" or "The Problem of Pain".

> **6** "For when we were still without strength, in due time Christ died for the ungodly. **7** For scarcely for a righteous man will one die; yet perhaps for a good man someone would even dare to die. **8** But God demonstrates His own love toward us, in that while we were still sinners, Christ died for us." (Romans 5.6-8)

Prayer

Our Father in heaven, we thank you for this day. We thank you for Jesus and his life of love and sacrifice. We thank you for his death and resurrection. Forgive our sins and renew our spirit and resolve. We want to serve you today with faithfulness and truth. Help us love our neighbors and those we labor with today. Give us the words we need to say in order to help others come closer to you. This we pray in the name of Jesus, our Lord. Amen.

Day 7

> "Therefore, whatever you want men to do to you, do also to them, for this is the Law and the Prophets." (Matthew 7.12).

This statement has been called "the golden rule". In everything he did and said, Jesus lived and ministered by this "rule". By doing this, he has also shown us the love of God, who only wants what is good for his children (compare with verse 11 immediately preceding).

The expression "the law and the prophets" is referred to by Jesus in 5.17: "I did not come to destroy the law and the prophets. I did not come to destroy, but to fulfill". This can be considered as a reference to most of Scripture (compare with Luke 24.44). A similar statement is made by Jesus concerning the two greatest commandments of "love" in

Matthew 22.36-40 and Mark 12.28-34. Thus, we can understand the "golden rule" as another way of stating the greatest commandment, focused on love of God and love of neighbor. See also Romans 13 8-10, especially "Love does no harm to a neighbor; therefore, love is the fulfillment of the law".

The word "therefore" at the beginning of this statement indicates a transition with a connection to what we read in the previous verses. Especially in "judgment" — as we saw in 7.1-5 — it is important to first look at ourselves and also to always treat people with kindness and respect (see Galatians 6.1-3).

In James 2.8-13, James gives us an application which reminds us of this verse. These verses emphasize a number of points in how we should treat (and judge) others. They may be compared to teachings of Paul in his letter to the Romans:

1. Without partiality. **8** "If you really fulfill *the* royal law according to the Scripture, 'You shall love your neighbor as yourself,' you do well; **9** but if you show partiality, you commit sin, and are convicted by the law as transgressors." (See also Romans 2.11)

2. With full righteousness and respect of God's law. **11** "For He who said, 'Do not commit adultery,' also said, 'Do not murder.' Now if you do not commit adultery, but you do murder, you have become a transgressor of the law." (See also Romans 2.1,2)

3. With mercy. **12** "So speak and so do as those who will be judged by the law of liberty. **13** For judgment is without mercy to the one who has shown no mercy. Mercy triumphs over judgment." (See also Romans 2.4)

By being careful in these three areas, we will be accomplishing more closely the injunction of Matthew 7.12

Prayer

Our Father in heaven, we thank you today for the life you have given us. We pray that our hearts will be full of your will and full of wisdom. Grant us Father a better understanding of your will and greater wisdom for the day. We pray for every person we will meet today, that you will allow us to love each one the way you want us to. We pray for our loved ones. Keep them today under your protection and bless them. We pray this in the name of Jesus, our Lord. Amen.

Week 50: The Narrow Way and False Prophets (Matt 7.13-20)

Day 1

> **13** "Enter by the narrow gate; for wide *is* the gate and broad *is* the way that leads to destruction, and there are many who go in by it. **14** Because narrow *is* the gate and difficult *is* the way which leads to life, and there are few who find it."
> (Matthew 7.13,14)

We need to connect this statement about the gate and way to the entire sermon. The gate and way represent a prior commitment and a continuous way of life for disciples of Jesus. Verse 14 states with more force and explains what verse 13 is already saying.

In this explanation, we learn that the "gate" is narrow. This indicates that there are not many ways to enter "life" — compare this with John 10 about the "door" being Jesus and the abundant life found in him. The idea of "entering" is important because it brings us back to the discussion of Jesus and Nicodemus about "entering" into the Kingdom of God through the new birth by the water and Spirit, "Most assuredly I say to you, unless one is born of water and the Spirit, he cannot enter the kingdom of God" (John 3.5).

Jesus points out that the way to enter the kingdom of God is "narrow": that there is no other way to enter or see God's Kingdom except by the new birth. Jesus talks about himself as "the way":

> **4** "Thomas said to Him, **5** 'Lord, we do not know where You are going, and how can we know the way?' **6** Jesus said to him, 'I am the way, the truth, and the life. No one comes to the Father except through Me.'" (John 14.4–6)

The life of the disciple in God's kingdom is not an easy life. Literally, the way of life, the way in the Kingdom is "compressed" (from the Greek *thlibo*, to press or to afflict). The verb form describes the ministry of the

Gospel and the life of believers in Jesus (2 Corinthians 4.8; 7.5; 1 Thessalonians 3.4; 2 Thessalonians 1.6,7; 1 Timothy 5.10; Hebrews 11.7).

Jesus talks of himself as "the door":

> **7** "Then Jesus said to them again, 'Most assuredly, I say to you, I am the door of the sheep. **8** All who *ever* came before Me are thieves and robbers, but the sheep did not hear them. **9** I am the door. If anyone enters by Me, he will be saved, and will go in and out and find pasture. **10** The thief does not come except to steal, and to kill, and to destroy. I have come that they may have life, and that they may have *it* more abundantly.'" (John 10.7-10)

We should not separate the teachings of Jesus and his work of salvation as if they were not connected to one another. The Christ who came to give his life for our sins is also the one who taught us to listen to his teachings and follow them:

> **1** "I am the true vine, and My Father is the vinedresser. **2** Every branch in Me that does not bear fruit He takes away; and every *branch* that bears fruit He prunes, that it may bear more fruit. **3** You are already clean because of the word which I have spoken to you." (John 15.1–3)

> **7** "If you abide in Me, and My words abide in you, you will ask what you desire, and it shall be done for you. **8** By this My Father is glorified, that you bear much fruit; so you will be My disciples." (John 15.7,8)

> **9** "As the Father loved Me, I also have loved you; abide in My love. **10** If you keep My commandments, you will abide in My love, just as I have kept My Father's commandments and abide in His love." (John 15.9,10)

> "No longer do I call you servants, for a servant does not know what his master is doing; but I have called you friends, for all things that I heard from My Father I have made known to you." (John 15.15)

> "These things I command you, that you love one another." (John 15.17)

Prayer

Our Father, we are thankful to you for your love and mercy. Thank you, Father, for the forgiveness in the Lord Jesus. Thank you for the promise of his return and the promise of eternal life. May we listen to you today and obey your Word. We pray for help from the Holy Spirit. We pray for wisdom in everything we do and say today. This we pray in the name of Jesus. Amen.

Day 2

> "Beware of false prophets, who come to you in sheep's clothing, but inwardly they are ravenous wolves."
> (Matthew 7.15)

This verse is similar to 7.6 where Jesus mentions the danger of "dogs" and "swine" — individuals who have no interest or hunger for holiness in "what is holy". Thus, their lives show an obvious unholiness of behavior or conduct. What they are "inwardly" can be seen in their actions. A "ravenous" wolf is a wolf (person) that is characterized by "greed" by seeking personal gain. The Greek *harpax* means "rapacious". The King James Version translates the word (*harpages*) as "extortioners" (Luke 18.11; 1 Corinthians 6.10). See Isaiah 56.11; Ezekiel 34.1-10.

False prophets in the Scriptures fall into several categories: those who encourage the worship of other gods (Deuteronomy 13.1-5; see 1 Kings 18-19); the prophets who seek personal gain (Micah 4.11; Amos 7.12); the prophets who take their own thinking or feelings for a revelation from God despite the fact that God has not spoken to them (Jeremiah 23.16; 26.2,3). Note that false prophets are part of those who are judged severely by the Lord in 7.22 "Lord, have we not prophesied in your name?"

The word "prophet" has the basic meaning of one who speaks on behalf of God. Thus, one who speaks on behalf of God must not be a "false" prophet (Greek *pseudopropheton*). We note that in the New Testament we also have "false apostles" (2 Corinthians 11.13); "false doctors or teachers" (2 Peter 2.1); "false christs" (Matthew 24.24). In 7.23 we see that false prophets even have the power to perform "wonders" in the name of Christ. But by their words they turn people away from the will of God ("you who practice lawlessness").

These false prophets come "in sheep's clothing". They appear harmless. They appear gentle and innocent; they speak with "unction" and are able to deceive even the elect:

24 "False christs and false prophets will rise and show great signs and wonders to deceive, if possible, even the elect. **25** See, I have told you beforehand." (Matthew 24.24-25).

In Revelation 13 the beast that comes out of the earth resembles a lamb but speaks like a dragon (Satan). He has certain "powers" which he uses to deceive people and bring them into submission (Revelation 13.11-18).

The New Testament church is constantly warned about false prophets and false teachings: Acts 20.29-31; 2 Corinthians 11.1-3; 2 Thessalonians 2.1-12; 1 Timothy 4.1-5; 2 Timothy 3.1-8; 4.1-5; 2 Peter 2.1-3; 3.-17; Jude vs.3,4; Revelation 2.18-29.

Prayer

We praise you Father and ask for a renewed heart and mind as we begin our day. We pray that you will be with our nation and its leaders. We pray for all who are in authority. Father allow us to live in peace. We pray for the missionaries throughout the world and all the churches everywhere on all continents. Bless your children, Father. Bless those who teach and lead, elders and evangelists. Bless your churches. We pray this in the name of Jesus. Amen.

Day 3

"You will know them by their fruits. Do men gather grapes from thorn bushes or figs from thistles?"
(Matthew 7.16)

False prophets are disguised, but their works are clearly distinguishable. A wolf in "sheep's clothing" remains a wolf, and the wolf seeks to "devour" and hurt the "sheep". This teaching of Jesus resembles what he taught in John 10. The teaching in John 10 describes those who attempt to enter into the sheepfold by some other way besides the one door which is Jesus himself (John 10.1-7).

The central issue in John 10 is about Jesus being the "door" and the "good shepherd". The wolf is also mentioned:

9 "I am the door. If anyone enters by Me, he will be saved, and will go in and out and find pasture. **10** The thief does not come except to steal, and to kill, and to destroy. I have come that they may have life, and that they may have *it* more abundantly. **11** "I am the good shepherd. The good shepherd gives His life for the sheep. **12** But a hireling, *he who is* not the shepherd, one who does not own the sheep, sees the wolf coming and leaves the sheep and flees; and the wolf catches the sheep and scatters them." (John 10.9-12)

The "hireling" in John 10.12 who does not care about the sheep reminds us of the "ravenous" wolves (see Matthew 7.15)— both are characterized by greed and seeking personal gain. Judas sought personal gain and betrayed Jesus (see Matthew 26.14-16; John 12.6). Jesus made it clear in that the disciples are not to focus on laying up treasures on earth and that one cannot serve God and mammon (Matthew 6.19-21, 24). The bad fruit of "ravenous wolves" or "false prophets" is thus connected to their greed and love of money, which is a clear sign of their apostasy. This was the case with the Pharisees rebuked by Jesus (Luke 16.14; Matthew 23.14).

Those who were sent by the apostle Paul to carry a large collection to Jerusalem had to be "approved", 1 Corinthians 16.3 (Greek *dokimazo*): "to accredit, examine, test, approve, scrutinize". The verb was used for those who check if something is fake or genuine, such as gold or silver. It is translated "approve" in the NKJV, "And when I come, whomever you *approve* by your letters, I will send to bear your gift to Jerusalem". The apostle Paul was not naïve when it came to fraudulent claims and thieves. This is also what Jesus taught as in Matthew 7.6 "Do not give dogs what is holy and do not throw pearls before pigs, lest they trample them underfoot and turn to attack you."

Both the Old and New Testaments teach about the evil of greed and love of money (Proverbs 11.28; 13.11; 15.27; 22.1; Ecclesiastes 5.10; Luke 12.15; Acts 5; Hebrews 13.5; 2 Corinthians 9.5; 11.14,15; 1 Peter 5.2,3; James 5.1-6; 1 Timothy 6. 6-10,17-19).

Prayer

We praise you, Father! We praise your glorious holiness and goodness. Our prayer today is that you will keep us from all greed or love of money. May we also grow in generosity, in kindness and concern for all those in need. Thank you for blessing us for daily food, for clothing and shelter. We pray that your Holy Spirit will give us wisdom daily to know how to deal with material things and finances. This we pray in the name of Jesus, our Lord. Amen.

Day 4

"Even so, every good tree bears good fruit, but a bad tree bears bad fruit."

(Matthew 7.17)

31 "When the Son of Man comes in His glory, and all the holy angels with Him, then He will sit on the throne of His glory. **32** All the nations will be gathered before Him, and He will separate them one from another, as a shepherd divides *his* sheep from the goats. **33** And He will set the sheep on His right hand, but the goats on the left. **34** Then the King will say to those on His right hand, 'Come, you blessed of My Father, inherit the kingdom prepared for you from the foundation of the world: **35** for I was hungry and you gave Me food; I was thirsty and you gave Me drink; I was a stranger and you took Me in; **36** I *was* naked and you clothed Me; I was sick and you visited Me; I was in prison and you came to Me.'"
(Matthew 25.31-36)

When the Lord speaks of "himself" he is referring to his disciples, to the body of Christ. Thus, when the Church in Acts was persecuted Jesus said to Saul, "Then he fell to the ground, and heard a voice saying to him, 'Saul, Saul, why are you persecuting Me?'" (Acts 9.4). The disciples of Jesus will be persecuted, rejected, put in prison and even put to death. In Matthew 25 the Lord pronounces a blessing on those who have come to the help of these disciples, have given them water, offered them hospitality, visited them in prison. This principle was already taught by Jesus when he sent out the twelve,

9 "Provide neither gold, nor silver nor copper in your money belts, **10** nor bag for *your* journey, nor two tunics, nor sandals, nor staffs; for a worker is worthy of his food. **11** 'Now whatever city or town you enter, inquire who in it is worthy, and stay there till you go out. **12** And when you go into a household, greet it. **13** If the household is worthy, let your peace come upon it. But if it is not worthy, let your peace return to you.'"
(Matthew 10.9-13).

Jesus also points out that evil speech is also a sign of an evil heart,

33 "Either make the tree good and its fruit good, or else make the tree bad and its fruit bad; for a tree is known by *its* fruit. **34** Brood of vipers! How can you, being evil, speak good things? For out of the abundance of the heart the mouth speaks. **35** A good man out of the good treasure of his heart brings forth good things, and an evil man out of the evil treasure brings forth evil things. **36** But I say to you that for every idle word men may speak, they will give account of it in the day of judgment. **37** For by your words you will be justified, and by your words you will be condemned." (Matthew 12.33-37; See James 1.26; 3.5,6; 7-12).

Prayer

Our Father in heaven, we praise you today! We want to serve you by bringing good fruit into the world. Help us, Lord of heaven and earth to produce good fruit this very day. Help us through your Holy Spirit to grow the fruit of love, peace and joy. We also pray this for our loved ones and for our brothers and sisters in Christ. This we pray in the name of Jesus. Amen.

Day 5

"A good tree cannot bear bad fruit, nor *can* a bad tree bear good fruit."
(Matthew 7.18).

22 "But the fruit of the Spirit is love, joy, peace, longsuffering, kindness, goodness, faithfulness **23** gentleness, self-control. Against such there is no law. **24** And those *who are* Christ's have crucified the flesh with its passions and desires. **25** If we live in the Spirit, let us also walk in the Spirit. **26** Let us not become conceited, provoking one another, envying one another." (Galatians 5.22-26)

James teaches a similar principle about the "impossibility" of a good tree to bear bad fruit or of a bad tree to bear good fruit, especially in the area of "speech":

8 "But no man can tame the tongue. *It is* an unruly evil, full of deadly poison. **9** With it we bless our God and Father, and with it we curse men, who have been made in the similitude of God. **10** Out of the same mouth proceed blessing and cursing. My brethren, these things ought not to be so. **11** Does a spring send forth fresh *water* and bitter from the same opening? **12** Can a fig tree, my brethren, bear olives or a grapevine bear figs? Thus, no spring yields both salt water and fresh." (James 3.8-12)

The apostle Paul writes about the Holy Spirit which produces good fruit in the believer, while James writes about the believer who needs to "be a doer" of the word and not just a hearer of the word (James 1.23). It is not necessary to consider these two aspects of "fruit" bearing as opposed to one another. Rather, they are complimentary or two sides of the same coin. The one who looks into the "word" can see like in a mirror what he or she needs to be doing. And this word or mirror is itself given to us through the Holy Spirit. In the word, we can see and understand what good fruit is as opposed to bad fruit. This understanding and discernment coming from the teachings of the Word is necessary (see Philippians 1.8-11). We should not separate the truth revealed by the Holy Spirit in the Word and the work of the Holy Spirit in our hearts.

Thus, the Scripture is "profitable for doctrine, for reproof, for correction, for instruction in righteousness, that the man of God may be complete, thoroughly equipped for every good work" (2 Timothy 3.16,17). There is no contradiction here between what the Scripture can accomplish in our lives when we study it and put it into practice and what the Holy Spirit accomplishes into our lives. The "perfect law of liberty" is the "law" of Christ that frees us from sin and enables us to "fulfill the law of Christ" (James 1.25; Galatians 6.2).

Prayer

We pray Lord that today we can keep the commands given to us by Jesus in your word. We pray also that you forgive our sins and give us a renewed desire to grow in faithfulness and love towards you. May your Spirit guide and strengthen us. May we be attached to your teachings as found in your word and not stray away from them. Thank you, Lord, for every blessing and for a new day. We pray in the name of Jesus. Amen.

Day 6

> "Every tree that does not bear good fruit is cut down and thrown into the fire."
> (Matthew 7.19)

8 "Therefore, bear fruits worthy of repentance, 9 and do not think to say to yourselves, 'We have Abraham as *our* father.' For I say to you that God is able to raise up children to Abraham from these stones. 10 And even now the ax is laid to the root of the

trees. Therefore, every tree which does not bear good fruit is cut down and thrown into the fire." (Matthew 3.10)

> **1** "I am the true vine, and My Father is the vinedresser. **2** Every branch in Me that does not bear fruit He takes away; and every *branch* that bears fruit He prunes, that it may bear more fruit." (John 15.1,2). Note that in John, Jesus speaks of himself not as "the vine" but as "the true vine". It is from Him that each branch can bear good fruit.

The need for God's people to bear good fruit is a constant theme in the entire Bible (Psalms 80.8,9; Hosea 10.1; Isaiah 5; Jeremiah 2; Ezekiel 15.1). Jesus used the symbol of the vine and vineyard for the fruit God expects of His people (Mark 12.1-12).

In Romans chapter 11 the apostle Paul writes about the "olive tree" as a symbol of God's people. The Gentiles are described as a "wild olive tree" that was grafted into the "natural" or "cultivated" olive tree which is Israel and enjoyed the "root and fatness of the olive tree" which are the patriarchs, especially Abraham (Romans 11.17, 24). Branches of the cultivated olive tree had been cut off because of unbelief; God did not spare the "natural olive tree". This should teach Gentiles about "the goodness and severity of God" (Romans 11.22).

The apostle's desire and prayer to God is that Israel "may be saved" and produce good fruit (Romans 10.1). This salvation and production of fruit happens through faith in Jesus the Messiah (Romans 10.2-13). Thus, any individual from Israel can be "grafted" back into the natural olive tree and thus produce good fruit for God:

> **23** "And they also, if they do not continue in unbelief, will be grafted in, for God is able to graft them in again. **24** For if you were cut out of the olive tree which is wild by nature, and were grafted contrary to nature into a cultivated olive tree, how much more will these, who *are* natural *branches,* be grafted into their own olive tree?" (Romans 11.23,24)

In this way, God has shown mercy to the Gentiles and to Israel. Through his amazing plan, God has made available salvation both to Israel and to the Gentiles if they believe in the Messiah and produce good fruit. The salvation of both Gentiles and Israel is through the "deliverer" who has come to Zion and has introduced the new covenant, a covenant of forgiveness (Romans 11.26 and Isaiah 59.20,21. See also Jeremiah 31.31-34; Hebrews 8.7-13).

The teaching of Jesus in Matthew 7.19; 3.10 and John 15 echoes the teachings of the Old Testament prophets and of John the Baptist concerning the fruit God expects from His people. In each case, there is a "judgment of God" upon His people in order to bring them to repent and thus bear fruit.

Prayer

Father in heaven, we thank you for your son Jesus, who came into the world to teach us and save us. Help us to understand his teachings and help us to practice them today. We pray that we will always return to repentance whenever we fall into sin or disobedience. Bless our loved ones and our brothers and sisters today. May they be encouraged and comforted in their pains. We pray in the name of Jesus, our Lord. Amen.

Day 7

"Therefore, by their fruits you will know them."
(Matthew 7.20)

The word translated "therefore" is formed of two words (*ara* and *ge*) which mean "then certainly" or "then surely". The meaning is thus an expression of certainty.

These words of Jesus continue his teachings about false prophets (v.15). This verse is important as a conclusion of verses 15 to 19 but also as an introduction to the scene of judgment in 7.21-23. In these verses, Jesus will mention those who "practice lawlessness" who do not live according to the "law" or teachings of Christ. Understood in the context of the entire sermon (Matthew 5 to 7) the teachings of Christ are what He demands of his disciples, of those who want to please God. And these "demands" or "commands" of Jesus do not include things done in his name such as prophesying, casting out demons or doing many wonders.

Thus, the "fruits" Jesus is talking about are those "fruits" God has always required from His people and which constitute a fulfillment of His law. The fruits are the realization of the will of God on earth as it is in heaven. These fruits include such behaviors as loving enemies or doing good to them who hate us, blessing those who curse us.

This is confirmed by the conclusion of the sermon, where Jesus mentions those who hear His teachings and "does them" (7.24). This teaching of Jesus is not only a warning about "false prophets" but a warning to everyone claiming to follow him but not practicing what he has taught us.

The importance of bearing good fruit is found throughout the New Testament epistles:

> "That you may walk worthy of the Lord, fully pleasing *Him,* being fruitful in every good work and increasing in the knowledge of God" (Colossians 1.10)

> **22** "But the fruit of the Spirit is love, joy, peace, longsuffering, kindness, goodness, faithfulness, **23** gentleness, self-control. Against such there is no law." (Galatians 5.22, 23)

> **21** "Therefore, by Him let us continually offer the sacrifice of praise to God, that is, the fruit of *our* lips, giving thanks to His name. **16** But do not forget to do good and to share, for with such sacrifices God is well pleased." (Hebrews 13.15,16)

> **9** "And this I pray, that your love may abound still more and more in knowledge and all discernment, **10** that you may approve the things that are excellent, that you may be sincere and without offense till the day of Christ, **11** being filled with the fruits of righteousness which *are* by Jesus Christ, to the glory and praise of God." (Philippians 1.9-11)

> **16** "For even in Thessalonica you sent *aid* once and again for my necessities. **17** Not that I seek the gift, but I seek the fruit that abounds to your account." (Philippians 4.16,17)

> "Therefore, my brethren, you also have become dead to the law through the body of Christ, that you may be married to another—to Him who was raised from the dead, that we should bear fruit to God." (Romans 7.4)

> "For as the body without the spirit is dead, so faith without works is dead also." (James 2.26)

> "Can a fig tree, my brethren, bear olives, or a grapevine bear figs? Thus, no spring yields both salt water and fresh." (James 3.12)

Let Us Come Before His Presence

Prayer

Our Father in heaven, we come to you with grateful hearts. We thank you because you are perfectly holy and righteous. Help us today to understand and to practice your will. We pray that today we will produce good fruit in your honor and to your glory. Give us wisdom in everything we do and speak. Keep us safely in your will. We pray in the name of Jesus. Amen.

Week 51: Judgment Day (Matt 7.21-23; 3.7-12; 10.12-15; 11.20-24; 25.37-43)

Day 1

> "Not everyone who says to Me, 'Lord, Lord,' shall enter the kingdom of heaven, but he who does the will of My Father in heaven."
> (Matthew 7.21)

> **46** "But why do you call Me 'Lord, Lord,' and not do the things which I say? **47** Whoever comes to Me, and hears My sayings and does them, I will show you whom he is like…" (Luke 6.46-47)

The tense of the two words for "says" (*legon*) and "does" (*poion*) shows a constant activity of "saying" and of "doing" and a contrast between these two activities. The two verbs are made into nouns by adding the "*ho*" (the) to the form of the verb; it could be translated by "the sayers" and "the doers". In the verse, the "not all the sayers" is contrasted to "but the doers". The Greek word for "everyone" (*pas*) indicates that many people on the day of judgment will be saying "Lord, Lord". This brings us back to the statement of Jesus that "wide is the gate and broad is the way that leads to destruction, and there are many who go in by it." (Matthew 7.13).

The word "Lord" (*kurios*) applied by Jesus to himself is a strong word, denoting authority and rule. It is a word used most often for God, and is also applied to the Messiah. We find the word in confessions of faith found throughout the New Testament. The word "Lord" is used for the first time in this verse and then used consistently in the Gospel of Matthew (8.6; 9.28; 11.25). The word is used repeatedly in Matthew 25 about the Lord on the day of judgment. In this chapter, we see the same severity of Jesus towards those who come to him thinking they should be accepted into the presence of the Lord and into his kingdom.

The word "Lord" is an important word in confessions of faith and worship of Jesus as Messiah found throughout the New Testament:

> **35** "Jesus heard that they had cast him out; and when He had found him, He said to him, "Do you believe in the Son of God?" **36** He answered and said, "Who is He, Lord, that I may believe in Him?" **37** And Jesus said to him, "You have both seen Him, and it is He who is talking with you." **38** Then he said, "Lord, I believe!" And he worshiped Him." (John 9.35-38)

> "She said to Him, 'Yes, Lord, I believe that You are the Christ, the Son of God, who is to come into the world.'" (John 11.27)

> **28** "And Thomas answered and said to Him, 'My Lord and my God!' **29** Jesus said to him, 'Thomas, because you have seen Me, you have believed. Blessed *are* those who have not seen and *yet* have believed.'" (John 20.28,29)

> **4** *"There is* one body and one Spirit, just as you were called in one hope of your calling; **5** one Lord, one faith, one baptism; **6** one God and Father of all, who *is* above all, and through all, and in you all." (Ephesians 4.4-6)

> **9** "Therefore, God also has highly exalted Him and given Him the name which is above every name, **10** that at the name of Jesus every knee should bow, of those in heaven, and of those on earth, and of those under the earth, **11** and *that* every tongue should confess that Jesus Christ *is* Lord, to the glory of God the Father." (Philippians 2.9-11)

Prayer

Our Father in heaven, we praise you for all your blessings and especially for Jesus, your only Son. Give us wisdom and strength today to seek you through prayer, in word and in our hearts. We can do nothing without you. May you help us as we face difficult challenges that we can do so with complete trust in you and with an obedient heart. We pray in the name of Jesus. Amen.

Day 2

> "Many will say to Me in that day, 'Lord, Lord, have we not prophesied in Your name, cast out demons in Your name, and done many wonders in Your name?'"
> (Matthew 7.22)

"That day" is the day of judgment also called "The great day of the Lord" by the OT prophets (Isaiah 2.20; 25.9). Continuing from verse 21 the text repeats the idea of those who merely "say" Lord contrasted with those who do the will of the Father in heaven. The repetition of the word "Lord" applied to Jesus gives emphasis to the divine nature of Jesus, his full deity as affirmed by the apostles in the New Testament (Colossians 2.9,10; Philippians 2.5-11; 1 John 5.20,21; 1 Timothy 3.16).

A further contrast is made between those who do the Father's will with those who prophesy in Jesus' name, who cast out demons in his name and perform many wonders in his name. An important question in connection with this is, "How is it possible that those who perform miracles and wonders" in the name of Jesus could be rejected by him? Is there something vital to the will of the Father and the will of His Christ that devout and religious people can forget? Was it not the case that the Corinthians are warned to focus on the "more excellent way" while prophecies and tongues would pass away (1 Corinthians 13)?

Jesus had taught that there is a "greater commandment" — loving God and loving our neighbor — and thus it is the fulfillment of that commandment which should carry the greatest weight in our lives (Matthew 22.36-40). Disciples of Jesus are to be known by the love they have for each other (John 13.34,35).

There also are those who will prophesy in Jesus' name without his sanction. This is in keeping with the context of Jesus' warnings concerning "false prophets" (verse 15). The verb to prophecy does not always indicate the foretelling of future events. It is mostly equivalent to "preach". See 1 Corinthians 12.10 and 14.3 "He who prophecies speaks edification and exhortation and comfort to men". Are these words of Jesus addressing the issue of religious authority, which some preachers take upon themselves without Jesus' sanction? Those who do this are falling into the error exposed by Jesus in His ministry:

> **5** "Then the Pharisees and scribes asked Him, "Why do Your disciples not walk according to the tradition of the elders, but eat bread with unwashed hands?" **6** He answered and said to

them, "Well did Isaiah prophesy of you hypocrites, as it is written, 'This people honors Me with *their* lips, But their heart is far from Me. **7** And in vain they worship Me, teaching *as* doctrines the commandments of men.' **8** For laying aside the commandment of God, you hold the tradition of men— the washing of pitchers and cups, and many other such things you do." (Mark 7.5-8)

Prayer

Our heavenly Father, we praise you for the salvation offered in Jesus. We pray that we will today follow Jesus in every way and in every teaching. We pray that whenever we think we have done something great for Jesus, we can reflect upon the danger of relying on this rather than on your word of promise and your commandments. Help us God to be faithful in times of great accomplishments for you. We pray this in the name of Jesus. Amen.

Day 3

And then I will declare to them, 'I never knew you; depart from Me, you who practice lawlessness!'
(Matthew 7.23)

The declaration "I never knew you; depart from Me" would be shocking coming from any other than the Christ. It is a declaration of Jesus' authority. The contrast between this statement and the first verse of chapter 7 is striking! It also helps us understand the reaction to his teaching mentioned in verses 28 and 29,

28 "the people were astonished at His teaching, **29** for He taught them as one having authority, and not as the scribes."

"False prophets" who claim to speak in Jesus' name and perform wonders in his name are known by their "bad fruit" (v.17) which Jesus describes here as "lawlessness". They are sinful and unholy, and teach others to act the same way. They are "ravenous" (greedy for financial gain) wolves (v.15) as described in other teachings of the apostles,

11 "Woe to them! For they have gone in the way of Cain, have run greedily in the error of Balaam for profit, and perished in the rebellion of Korah (…) **16** These are grumblers, complainers, walking according to their own lusts; and they mouth great swelling *words*, flattering people to gain advantage." (Jude 11,16).

Like the cities of Sodom and Gomorrah, they give themselves to sexual immorality (Jude 7).

We should not think that Jesus is unconcerned about his disciples growing in holiness and overcoming sin. This would be contrary to the entire New Testament teaching, which confirms what was already required by God of Israel,

> **13** "Therefore gird up the loins of your mind, be sober, and rest *your* hopefully upon the grace that is to be brought to you at the revelation of Jesus Christ; **14** as obedient children, not conforming yourselves to the former lusts, *as* in your ignorance; **15** but as He who called you *is* holy, you also be holy in all *your* conduct, **16** because it is written, "Be holy, for I am holy." (1 Peter 1.13-16; Leviticus 19.2).

Jesus will declare to those who treat sin lightly and do not seek holiness "I never knew you" (*oudepote egnon humas*), "I was never acquainted with you". This does not describe theoretical knowledge, but personal and experimental knowledge. There was never a connection between these individuals and Jesus.

Prayer

Our Father in heaven, we come to you today in a silent place in order to live this day close to you and your will. We want to take seriously the call to holy living. Help us through your Holy Spirit to live a life that honors you and your holiness. Help us to think and act through each moment of the day in a way that would be pleasing to you. We pray this in Jesus' name. Amen.

Day 4

> **7** "But when he saw many of the Pharisees and Sadducees coming to his baptism, he said to them, "Brood of vipers! Who warned you to flee from the wrath to come? **8** Therefore bear fruits worthy of repentance, **9** and do not think to say to yourselves, 'We have Abraham as *our* father.' For I say to you that God is able to raise up children to Abraham from these stones. **10** And even now the ax is laid to the root of the trees. Therefore, every tree which does not bear good fruit is cut

down and thrown into the fire. **11** I indeed baptize you with water unto repentance, but He who is coming after me is mightier than I, whose sandals I am not worthy to carry. He will baptize you with the Holy Spirit and fire. **12** His winnowing fan *is* in His hand, and He will thoroughly clean out His threshing floor, and gather His wheat into the barn; but He will burn up the chaff with unquenchable fire."
(Matthew 3.7-12)

The message of the sermon on the mount in Matthew chapter 7 agrees with the preaching of John the Baptist: with the coming of the Messiah comes salvation, but also judgment (see also John 3.10-21). The need to "repent" — to turn away from sin and an unholy life — goes along with the message of salvation: "I tell you, no; but unless you repent, you will all likewise perish." (Luke 13.3).

The preaching of John in Matthew 3 gives emphasis to the coming judgment: "even now the ax is laid to the root of the trees"; "every tree which does not bear good fruit is cut down and thrown into the fire"; "He will baptize you with the Holy Spirit and fire"; "He will burn up the chaff with unquenchable fire". The Messiah baptizes (immerses) in the Holy Spirit — the great gift of the new covenant (Acts 2.38,39 see 1 Corinthians 12.13; Titus 3.4,5). He also baptizes in fire, which describes His coming judgment. It is only through him and in him that condemnation does not fall upon sinners (Romans 8.1).

The Gospel is "the power of God to salvation" (Romans 1.16). This statement can be taken as a summary of the entire epistle to the Romans. That power is manifested in the forgiveness granted as a free gift (Romans 3.21-24). It is also manifested in the transformed lives of the forgiven "who do not walk according to the flesh but according to the Spirit" (Romans 8.4). It will be manifested at the resurrection (Romans 8.23-26).

Prayer

Father in heaven, we come to you with gratefulness for your salvation and the gift of the Holy Spirit. We want to walk not according to our flesh, but according to your Spirit. We come to you today for help during this day. May each moment be seen as an opportunity to better serve and love you. We pray this in Jesus' name. Amen.

Day 5

> **11** "Now whatever city or town you enter, inquire who in it is worthy, and stay there till you go out. **12** And when you go into a household, greet it. **13** If the household is worthy, let your peace come upon it. But if it is not worthy, let your peace return to you. **14** And whoever will not receive you nor hear your words when you depart from that house or city, shake off the dust from your feet. **15** Assuredly, I say to you, it will be more tolerable for the land of Sodom and Gomorrah in the day of judgment than for that city!"
> (Matthew 10.12-15)

In this passage, Jesus refers to the "day of judgment". He is sending the twelves "to the lost sheep of Israel" (Matthew 10.6). They are to preach that "the kingdom of God is at hand". Jesus is the "Ruler who will shepherd" God's people (Matthew 2.6). His presence introduces God's Kingdom or the messianic rule to the people of Israel. The signs that accompany the preaching of the twelve will bear testimony to the rule of Christ (Matthew 10.8). The message from the ruler of Israel, the Messiah, is to be received honorably through the apostles he is sending, "for a worker is worthy of his food" (Matthew 10.10).

To reject or dishonor the message of the Christ puts one in spiritual jeopardy and certainty of the coming judgment. This rejection is further described by Jesus:

> **16** "Behold, I send you out as sheep in the midst of wolves. Therefore, be wise as serpents and harmless as doves. **17** But beware of men, for they will deliver you up to councils and scourge you in their synagogues. **18** You will be brought before governors and kings for My sake, as a testimony to them and to the Gentiles." (Matthew 10.16-18).

This has been clearly taught by Jesus in his sermon on the mount:

> **10** "Blessed *are* those who are persecuted for righteousness' sake, for theirs is the kingdom of heaven. **11** Blessed are you when they revile and persecute you and say all kinds of evil against you falsely for My sake. **12** Rejoice and be exceedingly glad, for great *is* your reward in heaven, for so they persecuted the prophets who were before you." (Matthew 5.10-12)

The rejection of the Messiah is an expression of unbelief and leads to condemnation,

> **18** "He who believes in Him is not condemned; but he who does not believe is condemned already, because he has not believed in the name of the only-begotten Son of God. **19** And this is the condemnation, that the light has come into the world, and men loved darkness rather than light, because their deeds were evil. **20** For everyone practicing evil hates the light and does not come to the light, lest his deeds should be exposed. **21** But he who does the truth comes to the light, that his deeds may be clearly seen, that they have been done in God." (John 3.18-21)

Prayer

Lord, we come before your throne today because we love the light, we are seeking the light. We pray you will enlighten our hearts and our lives. We pray that today's challenges and challenging people will not lead us astray from you and your will. May your Holy Spirit guide our thoughts, actions and words. We pray this in the name of Jesus, our Lord. Amen.

Day 6

> **20** Then He began to rebuke the cities in which most of His mighty works had been done, because they did not repent: **21** 'Woe to you, Chorazin! Woe to you, Bethsaida! For if the mighty works which were done in you had been done in Tyre and Sidon, they would have repented long ago in sackcloth and ashes. **22** But I say to you, it will be more tolerable for Tyre and Sidon in the day of judgment than for you. **23** And you, Capernaum, who are exalted to heaven, will be brought down to Hades; for if the mighty works which were done in you had been done in Sodom, it would have remained until this day. **24** But I say to you that it shall be more tolerable for the land of Sodom in the day of judgment than for you.'"
> (Matthew 11.20-24)

Chapter 11 of Matthew contains large portions of text alluding to the judgment on "this generation" (v.16) and the cities of Chorazin and Bethsaida. Chorazin, Bethsaida and Capernaum were situated close to each other by only a few miles. At the time of Jesus, these were prosperous and populated cities. Andrew and Peter, as well as Philip, came from

Bethsaida (John 1.44) and Capernaum is called Jesus' "own city" (Matthew 9.1).

The contrast of these towns with Tyre and Sidon and even Sodom is striking. The lack of repentance in those towns despite the "mighty works" Jesus performed is considered a greater sin than the sins of the pagan towns of Tyre and Sidon and ancient Sodom. Those who are given greater opportunity to know God bear a greater responsibility as compared to others who do not have these opportunities. This is also the message of the apostle Paul in Romans 2.1-24. It seems that in the concept of divine judgment there are degrees of punishments and even rewards.

Degrees of punishments and rewards appear to be a biblical concept in the following Scriptures: Rewards: Mark 9:41; Matt. 5:12,46; 6:1-4,5-6,6-18; 10:41-42; 16:27; 25:14-23; Luke 6:23,35; 19:11-19,25-26. Punishments: Mark 12:38-40; Luke 10:12; 12:47-48; 19:20-24; 20:47; Matthew 5:22,29,30; 7:19; 10:15,28; 11:22-24; 13:49-50; 18:6; 25:14-30; James 3:1. Hebrews 10.29; Revelation 20.12,13; 22.12.

An important truth about the Lord's judgments is that they did not come as some kind of necessity on the part of God, but because of sin and a lack of repentance. When Nineveh repented, the city was spared (book of Jonah).

Prayer

We thank you, our God and Father, for your perfect righteousness in your judgments. We know your love for us is beyond anything we can conceive or understand fully, but we believe in your love through your word and the life of Jesus. We want to have today a humble and repentant disposition so that we might enjoy a perfect communion with you. Help us with your Holy Spirit to overcome sin and to grow in holiness. We pray this in the name of Jesus.

Day 7

37 "Then the righteous will answer Him, saying, 'Lord, when did we see You hungry and feed *You*, or thirsty and
give *You* drink? **38** When did we see You a stranger and take *You* in, or naked and clothe *You*? **39** Or when did we see You sick, or in prison, and come to You?' **40** And the King will answer and say to them, 'Assuredly, I say to you, inasmuch as you did *it* to one of the least of these My brethren, you did *it* to Me.' **41** "Then He will also say to those on the left hand, 'Depart

from Me, you cursed, into the everlasting fire prepared for the devil and his angels: **42** for I was hungry and you gave Me no food; I was thirsty and you gave Me no drink; **43** I was a stranger and you did not take Me in, naked and you did not clothe Me, sick and in prison and you did not visit Me.'
(Matthew 25.37-43)

The true followers of Jesus throughout the centuries and even today have often endured opposition. They have gone hungry and have been thrown in prison. In Matthew 25 there is an emphasis on how people have treated Jesus' brethren and it will play a role in the final judgment.

> **29** Jesus answered and said, "Assuredly, I say to you, there is no one who has left house or brothers or sisters or father or mother or wife or children or lands, for My sake and the gospel's, **30** who shall not receive a hundredfold now in this time —houses and brothers and sisters and mothers and children and lands, with persecutions—and in the age to come, eternal life. **31** But many *who are* first will be last, and the last first."
> (Mark 10.29,30)

> **18** "If the world hates you, you know that it hated Me before *it hated* you. **19** If you were of the world, the world would love its own. Yet because you are not of the world, but I chose you out of the world, therefore the world hates you. **20** Remember the word that I said to you, 'A servant is not greater than his master.' If they persecuted Me, they will also persecute you. If they kept My word, they will keep yours also." (John 15.18-20)

> **10** "But you have carefully followed my doctrine, manner of life, purpose, faith, longsuffering, love, perseverance, **11** persecutions, afflictions, which happened to me at Antioch, at Iconium, at Lystra—what persecutions I endured. And out of *them* all the Lord delivered me. **12** Yes, and all who desire to live godly in Christ Jesus will suffer persecution. **13** But evil men and impostors will grow worse and worse, deceiving and being deceived."
> (2 Timothy 3.10-12)

Those who demonstrated compassion towards even to one of Jesus' brethren (followers) are described by Jesus as righteous and will be ushered into eternal life (25.46). This is striking in many ways. It shows the deep and intimate connection between Jesus and his brethren (his followers). It shows also how the world has treated Jesus' followers plays an important part in the final judgment. Moreover, those who demonstrated compassion to any of the needy of this earth "to the least of these" have acted this way towards Jesus himself. Here Jesus identifies himself with the needy and poor of the earth.

James addresses both the care of the needy within the body of Christ and the care for the poor in general:

> **1** "My brethren do not hold the faith of our Lord Jesus Christ, *the Lord* of glory, with partiality. **2** For if there should come into your assembly a man with gold rings, in fine apparel, and there should also come in a poor man in filthy clothes, **3** and you pay attention to the one wearing the fine clothes and say to him, 'You sit here in a good place,' and say to the poor man, 'You stand there,' or, 'Sit here at my footstool,' **4** have you not shown partiality among yourselves, and become judges with evil thoughts?" (James 2.1-4)

> **5** "Listen, my beloved brethren: Has God not chosen the poor of this world *to be* rich in faith and heirs of the kingdom which He promised to those who love Him? **6** But you have dishonored the poor man. Do not the rich oppress you and drag you into the courts? **7** Do they not blaspheme that noble name by which you are called?" (James 2.5-7)

Prayer

Dear Father, we come today into your presence with a heart full of gratefulness. We are grateful for the forgiveness of sins and the call to a holy life. We are grateful for the gift of your Holy Spirit, who encourages us and guides us. We pray that today our lives will reflect our gratefulness towards you in the way we think, the way we act and speak. In Jesus' name, we pray. Amen.

Week 52: Wisdom, foolishness and Jesus' supreme authority (Matt 7.24–27; Luke 6.46–49); Matt 28.18; Rev 1.12–18)

Day 1

> "All authority has been given to Me in heaven and on earth. Go therefore and make disciples of all the nations"
> (Matthew 28.18)

The authority of Jesus comes out in these concluding words of the sermon on the mount and is confirmed by the reaction of the people (vs 28,29). He is claiming that his words are the source of wisdom and solidity. In this Sermon, Jesus is also demanding obedience to His teachings (Matthew 7.22; Luke 6.46). There is also a great sense of authority in the title "Lord" used by Jesus about himself.

One cannot at the same time exalt the wisdom and goodness of Jesus and reject his claims about himself. Jesus' claims are so significant that either he is telling the truth and one should trust him, or he is lying, and one should not trust him. As far as accepting or rejecting Jesus, one cannot stand in the middle. We find this authority as the foundation of Jesus' sending his apostles on the great mission of evangelizing the nations:

> **18** "And Jesus came and spoke to them, saying, 'All authority has been given to Me in heaven and on earth. **19** Go therefore and make disciples of all the nations'" (Matthew 28.18,19)

Jesus also declared that the words he taught would judge men at the last day (John 12.48). Jesus also taught, saying, "Heaven and earth shall pass away, but my words shall not pass away" (Matthew 24.35) The Holy

Spirit guided and inspired the apostles and apostolic witness so that their teachings would reflect the will of Christ,

> **12** "I still have many things to say to you, but you cannot bear *them* now. **13** However, when He, the Spirit of truth, has come, He will guide you into all truth; for He will not speak on His own *authority,* but whatever He hears He will speak; and He will tell you things to come. **14** He will glorify Me, for He will take of what is Mine and declare *it* to you. **15** All things that the Father has are Mine. Therefore, I said that He will take of Mine and declare *it* to you." (John 16.12-15)

In this comparison, or similitude, we do not need to seek a meaning to every detail, as would be the case in an allegory. The reference to the rock in Scripture is primarily to God himself. As in all of his teachings, Jesus points to himself in an authoritative manner (see verses 28,29). As the Messiah, Jesus is also "rock" as God is throughout Scripture: Isaiah 28.16; 1 Peter 2.6-8. See 2 Samuel 22.2 (Psalms 18.2); Psalms 18.32; 18.47; 23.3; 28.1; 31.2. Psalms 61.2; Isaiah 32.2; 44.8; 1 Corinthians 10.4 (see 1 Corinthians 3.10,11).

The wise man is the person who takes seriously the claims and will of Jesus and lives according to these claims. These words of Jesus provide the entire framework to understand the purpose of the teachings of Jesus on the mount. The purpose is to call people to wisdom and a life built on what is enduring and indestructible, the practice of Jesus' teachings. The importance of practicing the teachings of Jesus and the promise of blessing in this are underlined by James in his epistle:

> **22**"But be doers of the word, and not hearers only, deceiving yourselves. **23** For if anyone is a hearer of the word and not a doer, he is like a man observing his natural face in a mirror; **24** for he observes himself, goes away, and immediately forgets what kind of man he was. **25** But he who looks into the perfect law of liberty and continues *in it* and is not a forgetful hearer but a doer of the work, this one will be blessed in what he does." (James 1.22-25)

It is sometimes claimed that these teachings of Jesus are too difficult to keep, that we should not teach them as required by Jesus for faithful living. But these words of Jesus are very clear when it comes to the necessity of keeping his teachings (see also Matthew 28.18). The fact that we keep these teachings imperfectly is no excuse to pretend that Jesus does not require his disciples to do their best to practice his teachings. This reminds us of the words of G.K. Chesterton about the Sermon on the Mount: "The Christian ideal has not been tried and found wanting; it has been found difficult and left untried." The question we must ask ourselves is, "I am willing to try?"

Prayer

Father in heaven, we thank for your forgiveness, for your love towards us. Today, we want to serve you through our actions and words. Help us to remember the teachings of your Son during his earthly ministry. Help us to believe that we are called to try and do our best to keep his teachings, which are your teachings. And give us help in this through your Holy Spirit. We pray in the name of Jesus.

Day 2

> **26** "But everyone who hears these sayings of Mine, and does not do them, will be like a foolish man who built his house on the sand: **27** and the rain descended, the floods came, and the winds blew and beat on that house; and it fell. And great was its fall."
> (Matthew 7.26,27)

As is often the case in the book of Proverbs, the choice presented to us by God is either being wise or being foolish. Many are those who think of themselves very intelligent and wise, and because of this reject the idea of following the teachings of Jesus. These teachings are destined to those who are humble and willing to learn. Wisdom is found in humility and a willingness to learn, not in the pride of thinking we already know and have no need of teaching:

> **32** "He who disdains instruction despises his own soul, but he who heeds rebuke gets understanding. **33** The fear of the Lord *is* the instruction of wisdom, and before honor *is* humility." (Proverbs 1.32-33)

> "When pride comes, then comes shame; but with the humble *is* wisdom." (Proverbs 11.2)

> **32** "He who disdains instruction despises his own soul, but he who heeds rebuke gets understanding. **33** The fear of

the Lord *is* the instruction of wisdom, and before honor *is* humility." (Proverbs 15.32,33)

"By humility *and* the fear of the Lord *are* riches and honor and life." (Proverbs 22.4)

"He who trusts in his own heart is a fool, but whoever walks wisely will be delivered." (Proverbs 28.26)

"The fool has said in his heart, '*There is* no God.'" (Psalms 14.1)

"For My people *are* foolish,
They have not known Me.
They *are* silly children,
And they have no understanding.
They *are* wise to do evil,
But to do good they have no knowledge." (Jeremiah 4.22)

20 "Where *is* the wise? Where *is* the scribe? Where *is* the disputer of this age? Has not God made foolish the wisdom of this world? **21** For since, in the wisdom of God, the world through wisdom did not know God, it pleased God through the foolishness of the message preached to save those who believe." (1 Corinthians 1.20,21)

21 "Although they knew God, they did not glorify *Him* as God, nor were thankful, but became futile in their thoughts, and their foolish hearts were darkened. **22** Professing to be wise, they became fools, **23** and changed the glory of the incorruptible God into an image made like corruptible man—and birds and four-footed animals and creeping things." (Romans 1.21-23)

"God resists the proud but gives grace to the humble." (James 4.6)

Prayer

Our Lord and Father in heaven, we want to thank you for a new day to serve and learn. Open our hearts to those we meet and to understand how we can serve each one. Give us wisdom in each encounter and with each person. We confess our sings and weaknesses and ask you for strength and growth in your wisdom. May you change us every day into the likeness of Jesus. We pray this in his name. Amen.

Day 3

> **28** "And so it was, when Jesus had ended these sayings, that the people were astonished at His teaching, **29** for He taught them as one having authority, and not as the scribes."
> (Matthew 7.28,29)

The authority of Jesus stands out in the Sermon on the Mount. His teachings surpass in authority the teachings of the scribes, of the decalogue, Moses and every human authority. By authority is meant the right to control and govern. The crowds were amazed or astonished at this. This idea of astonishment is used in Acts 13 when a man was struck after opposing the preaching of the Gospel:

> **11** "And immediately a dark mist fell on him, and he went around seeking someone to lead him by the hand. **12** Then the proconsul believed, when he saw what had been done, being astonished at the teaching of the Lord."

The expression "Truly I say to you" is repeated throughout the sermon (5.18; 6.2,5,16,25,29). The expression "But I say to you" carries also a sense of personal authority on the part of Jesus (5.22,28,32,34,39,42). By saying "But I say to you" Jesus clarifies the meaning of the law and teaches the heart of the law.

Jesus' authority stands out as he applies truth in fresh and new ways, different from many of the arbitrary teachings of the scribes. The Sermon in its entirety seeks to give priority to the weightier matters, such as mercy. This is true throughout Matthew (for example, in 12.1-4). The authority of Jesus as a teacher is brought out throughout Matthew (see day 6). The authority of Jesus' teachings come out also from the purity of Jesus' life and the signs and miracles that accompanied his teachings (see Matthew 4.23-25).

This conclusion of the sermon reminds us of the power and perfection of truth as found in God's word. It is significant that the words of the Lord are purified "seven times", the number of completeness and perfection (there are seven seals to the scroll of Revelation, Rev. 5.1).

> **6** "The words of the Lord *are* pure words,
> *Like* silver tried in a furnace of earth,

Purified seven times.
7 You shall keep them, O Lord,
You shall preserve them from this generation forever." (Psalms 12.6,7)

Prayer

We thank you, Father in heaven, for the teachings of Jesus and for your Word. We pray today for wisdom and faithfulness in applying these teachings to our lives. We need your truth at every moment and with every encounter. Bless us with an understanding of your will through the Holy Spirit. We pray this in the name of Jesus, our Lord. Amen.

Day 4

46 "But why do you call Me 'Lord, Lord,' and not do the things which I say? **47** Whoever comes to Me, and hears My sayings and does them, I will show you whom he is like: **48** He is like a man building a house, who dug deep and laid the foundation on the rock. And when the flood arose, the stream beat vehemently against that house, and could not shake it, for it was founded on the rock. **49** But he who heard and did nothing is like a man who built a house on the earth without a foundation, against which the stream beat vehemently; and immediately it fell. And the ruin of that house was great."
(Luke 6.46-48)

Luke records Jesus' sermon on the mount with differences. This should not be surprising. None of the Gospel accounts about Jesus' teachings or actions purport to be reporting fully every word or action of Jesus (see John 20.30; 21.25). The sermon itself could have been longer than what is reported. It is also believed by some that Luke's sermon was preached at some other time, possibly later, even if close to the timing of Matthew's Gospel.

What is significant in Luke's account here is the connection of Jesus' statement both in Luke 6.46 similar to Matthew 7.22, "But why do you call me 'Lord, Lord' and not do the things which I say"; "Many will say to me in that day, 'Lord, Lord'..."

Both in Matthew and Luke, wisdom is not in simply listening to the teachings of Jesus or even comprehending them, but in doing them. This can be paralleled to the teachings of James in his epistle and also to those who would be reading the book of Revelation:

> **21** "Therefore, lay aside all filthiness and overflow of wickedness, and receive with meekness the implanted word, which can save your souls. **22** But be doers of the word, and not hearers only, deceiving yourselves. **23** For if anyone is a hearer of the word and not a doer, he is like a man observing his natural face in a mirror; **24** for he observes himself, goes away, and immediately forgets what kind of man he was." (James 1.21-24)

> "Here is the patience of the saints; here are those who keep the commandments of God and the faith of Jesus." (Revelation 14.12)

Prayer

We praise you, our Father, for your holiness and perfection. We worship and love you. We pray that you will comfort our hearts and also strengthen them in doing always what is in keeping with your will. Help us resist temptation and come to you for help and for wisdom. Bless those we will meet today, and may we be able to help them come closer to you and seek you. This we pray in the name of Jesus. Amen.

Day 5

> "And Jesus came and spoke to them, saying, 'All authority has been given to Me in heaven and on earth.'"
> (Matthew 28.18)

The emphasis on Jesus's authority is stressed throughout the Gospel of Matthew until the last words of the Lord, recorded in chapter 28.

In Matthew 8 Jesus authority is referenced in both his exchange with the centurion and his rebuke of the storm. Even the wind and the waves obeyed him (Matthew 8.27).

The crowds are amazed that such authority was given to men (9.8)

Matthew shows the authority of Jesus through the expression "something greater": Christ is greater than David (12.3,4). Christ is greater than the Temple (12.5,6). Matthew says that Something greater than Jonah is here (12.42). Something greater than Solomon is here (12.43)

The question of authority continues to be central in the Gospel of Matthew (21.33)

And when he entered the temple, the chief priests and the elders of the people came up to him as he was teaching, and said, "By what *authority* are you doing these things, and who gave you this *authority*?"'

Jesus' authority is the source and foundation of evangelism (Matthew 28.18-20)

Prayer

Our Father in heaven, we are grateful to you for your perfect holiness and love. We want to learn from you every day and ask for your wisdom. Help us to bear the fruit of the Holy Spirit. Help us to pray, to intercede for everyone. Thank you, Father, for the new life we have received in Jesus and help us to live the true life of a disciple of Jesus.

Day 6

> **18** "And Jesus came and spoke to them, saying, 'All authority has been given to Me in heaven and on earth. **19** Go therefore and make disciples of all the nations, baptizing them in the name of the Father and of the Son and of the Holy Spirit, **20** teaching them to observe all things that I have commanded you; and lo, I am with you always, *even* to the end of the age. Amen.'"
> (Matthew 28.18-20)

The conclusion of the sermon on the mount emphasizes the need to not only listen to Jesus' teachings, but to put them in practice. The last words of Jesus recorded in Matthew are clear as to the necessity for disciples of the Lord to observe all things Jesus has commanded. This is in harmony, especially with Jesus' teachings during the last supper:

> **15** "If you love Me, keep My commandments. **16** And I will pray the Father, and He will give you another Helper, that He may abide with you forever." (John 14.15,16)

> "He who has My commandments and keeps them, it is he who loves Me. And he who loves Me will be loved by My Father, and I will love him and manifest Myself to him." (John 14.21)

> **23** "Jesus answered and said to him, 'If anyone loves Me, he will keep My word; and My Father will love him, and We will come to him and make Our home with him. **24** He who does not love

Me does not keep My words; and the word which you hear is not Mine but the Father's who sent Me.'" (John 14.23,24)

9 "As the Father loved Me, I also have loved you; abide in My love. **10** If you keep My commandments, you will abide in My love, just as I have kept My Father's commandments and abide in His love." (John 15.9,10)

When this aspect of the Gospel is mentioned, people and even believers often react by saying that it is too difficult to keep the commandments of Jesus; the thinking is that Jesus did not really mean for us to take this seriously since we are weak human beings and know from the Bible that we cannot be sinless.

This teaching of Jesus to instruct new converts — baptized in the name of the Father, of the Son and of the Holy Spirit — is in harmony with the totality of Scripture and even the New Testament. Everything that is recorded for us in Scripture is from God, is important for "every good work".

14 "But you must continue in the things which you have learned and been assured of, knowing from whom you have learned *them*, **15** and that from childhood you have known the Holy Scriptures, which can make you wise for salvation through faith which is in Christ Jesus. **16** All Scripture *is* given by inspiration of God, and *is* profitable for doctrine, for reproof, for correction, for instruction in righteousness, **17** that the man of God may be complete, thoroughly equipped for every good work." (2 Timothy 3.14-17)

The process of salvation and becoming holy is described in Ephesians chapter 2.1-10. These verses recapitulate God's plan of salvation by stating key truths about the human condition and salvation:

1. We are dead in our trespasses and sin in which we walk (Ephesians 2.1-3)

2. But God through his great love made us alive with Christ, raised us with Christ into the heavenly places — an action only God could perform outside any human effort or works (Ephesians 2.4-9)

3. Those who have been raised with Christ are God's workmanship, created in Christ Jesus in order to perform good works (Ephesians 2.10,11)

The Gospel is the good news about Jesus' death and resurrection for our forgiveness and reconciliation with God (1 Corinthians 15.1-4). But the good news does not limit itself to this work of forgiveness, it calls us to a new life in Christ, a holy and dedicated life. This is described throughout the New Testament (for example, Romans 6; Colossians 3; Philippians 3).

Prayer

We praise you, our Father for your holiness and perfection. We worship and love you. We want to keep our hearts in your will today. We want to grow today and use every moment to serve you in every way. With your Holy Spirit, we believe we will be able to do this and be useful to your kingdom. May you bless everyone we meet today. We pray this in Jesus' name. Amen.

Day 7

> **12** "Then I turned to see the voice that spoke with me. And having turned I saw seven golden lampstands, **13** and in the midst of the seven lampstands *One* like the Son of Man, clothed with a garment down to the feet and girded about the chest with a golden band. **14** His head and hair *were* white like wool, as white as snow, and His eyes like a flame of fire; **15** His feet *were* like fine brass, as if refined in a furnace, and His voice as the sound of many waters; **16** He had in His right hand seven stars, out of His mouth went a sharp two-edged sword, and His countenance *was* like the sun shining in its strength. **17** And when I saw Him, I fell at His feet as dead. But He laid His right hand on me, saying to me, "Do not be afraid; I am the First and the Last. **18** I *am* He who lives, and was dead, and behold, I am alive forevermore. Amen. And I have the keys of hades and of death."
> (Revelation 1.12-18)

Jesus the teacher is also Jesus the savior, the ruler and judge. His authority and power is not only in his words, in the truth of his teachings, but in his actions. He was dead and he lives. He is the first and the last. He holds the keys of hades and death, which means he has power and authority over hades and death.

The sight of the glory and power of Jesus made John fall as dead. But this sight was not meant to bring fear, but to bring comfort and reassurance. Revelation, the last book of the Bible, is not meant to bring fear, but to bring comfort. As the Lord testifies to the seven churches in Revelation chapters 2 and 3 the words of Jesus to these churches is a word of encouragement so that they will repent when needed and will finally overcome the difficulties and obstacles they are facing. The teachings of the Sermon of the Mount and of the entire Bible are there to help the believer "overcome", obtain victory.

We can conclude from the sermon that there is no lasting foundation, no lasting hope, no final victory for humanity outside listening to the teachings of Jesus the Christ and abiding by these teachings. This is also the conclusion of the last book of the Bible.

> "Blessed *are* those who do His commandments, that they may have the right to the tree of life and may enter through the gates into the city." (Revelation 22.12)

As Peter preached on the day of Pentecost in Acts chapter 2, he proclaimed the victory Jesus obtained through his faithful life, his death, his resurrection and his ascension at the right hand of God.

On that day, many heard this good news and the call of Peter, "Be saved from this perverse generation" (Acts 2.40). Those who gladly received his words were baptized for the remission of their sins as ordered by the Lord himself and the apostle Peter and were added to the body of believers: "Then those who gladly received his word were baptized; and that day about three thousand souls were added *to them*." (Acts 2.41; 2.38).

Prayer

My prayer today is that the Gospel will be preached throughout the world, in your country, your town or village and that many will gladly receive the Gospel with faith and repentance and be joined to the Lord Jesus in baptism and be added by the Lord himself to his Church: "And the Lord added to the church daily those who were being saved." (Acts 2.47)

About the Author

Yann Opsitch is an author, minister, teacher, and evangelist to the nations. He is the director of l'Ecole du Maître (School of the Master), an online Bible training program for Christian leaders living in the French-speaking world. Yann studied at the North Ireland Bible School, University of Geneva (Switzerland), Abilene Christian University, University of North Texas. If you enjoyed this book, please consider leaving an online review. The author would appreciate reading your thoughts.

Visit the author's website at: https://yannopsitchauthor.com

You can also follow the author on social media at:

Instagram: @yannopsitch
Twitter: @opsitch
FaceBook: https://www.facebook.com/yannopsitch/
Linkedin: www.linkedin.com/in/yannopsitch

About the Publisher

Sulis International Press publishes select fiction and nonfiction in a variety of genres under four imprints: Riversong Books, Sulis Academic Press, Sulis Press, and Keledei Publications.

For more, visit the website at
https://sulisinternational.com
Subscribe to the newsletter at
https://sulisinternational.com/subscribe/

Follow on social media
https://www.facebook.com/SulisInternational
https://twitter.com/Sulis_Intl
https://www.pinterest.com/Sulis_Intl/
https://www.instagram.com/sulis_international/